Library of
Davidson College

Handbook of Scales for Research in Crime and Delinquency

Perspectives in Law & Psychology

Series Editor: **BRUCE DENNIS SALES**, *University of Arizona, Tucson*

Volume 1   **THE CRIMINAL JUSTICE SYSTEM**
Edited by Bruce Dennis Sales

Volume 2   **THE TRIAL PROCESS**
Edited by Bruce Dennis Sales

Volume 3   **JUVENILES' WAIVER OF RIGHTS**
Legal and Psychological Competence
Thomas Grisso

Volume 4   **MENTAL HEALTH LAW: Major Issues**
David B. Wexler

Volume 5   **HANDBOOK OF SCALES FOR RESEARCH IN CRIME AND DELINQUENCY**
Stanley L. Brodsky and H. O'Neal Smitherman

Volume 6   **MENTALLY DISORDERED OFFENDERS**
Perspectives from Law and Social Science
Edited by John Monahan and Henry J. Steadman

Handbook of Scales for Research in Crime and Delinquency

Stanley L. Brodsky
University of Alabama
Tuscaloosa, Alabama

and

H. O'Neal Smitherman
Partlow State School
Tuscaloosa, Alabama

PLENUM PRESS · NEW YORK AND LONDON

Library of Congress Cataloging in Publication Data

Brodsky, Stanley L., 1939-
　Handbook of scales for research in crime and delinquency.

　(Perspectives in law & psychology; v. 5)
　Bibliography: p.
　Includes index.
　1. Prisoners—Attitudes—Research—Statistical methods—Handbooks, manuals, etc. 2. Juvenile delinquents—Attitudes—Research—Statistical methods—Handbooks, manuals, etc. 3. Criminal behavior, Prediction of—Research—Statistical Methods, Handbooks, manuals, etc. 4. Scaling (Social sciences)—Handbooks, manuals, etc. I. Smitherman, H. O'Neal, 1949-
II. Title. III. Series: Perspectives in law and psychology; v. 5.
HV9274.B76　1982　　　　　　364'.072　　　　　　82-18142
ISBN 0-306-40792-2

© 1983 Plenum Press, New York
A Division of Plenum Publishing Corporation
233 Spring Street, New York, N.Y. 10013

All rights reserved

No part of this book may be reproduced, stored in a retrieval system, or transmitted in any form or by any means, electronic, mechanical, photocopying, microfilming, recording, or otherwise, without written permission from the Publisher

Printed in the United States of America

To the memory of my father, Harry Brodsky
S.L.B.

To my wife and family
H.O.S.

Acknowledgments

There are many colleagues and friends who have offered constructive suggestions in the preparation of this handbook. Don Gottfredson, Michael Hindelang, and Marvin Shaw served as an advisory committee and their ideas appear in many ways throughout this handbook. We are grateful for their assistance and collaboration.

Bruce Sales has been extraordinarily helpful; as editor of the Plenum *Perspective in Law and Psychology* series, he has worked with us, adding consistency, sense, and style to the text.

Ten years ago, in the very early stages of this effort, Linda Jacobson and Jon Baughman joined in some of the early scale reviews. Since then, Glenda Williamson invested heavily of her time and effort and performed the yeoperson's work in searching out materials. Robin Ingall aided in the MMPI and CPI literature review.

The Department of Psychology at the University of Alabama graciously extended much support during development of this project. In particular, we appreciate the secretarial and collegial help of Gwendolyn Thomas, Leona Johnson, and Marjie Hall.

We also would like to extend our appreciation to Saleem Shah, Thomas Lalley, and their colleagues at the Center for Studies in Crime and Delinquency in the National Institute of Mental Health. The Center provided the financial support necessary for the implementation of this project and the staff helped shape early drafts of our ideas in many positive ways. For their scholarly perspectives and kind assistance, we are much indebted.

We are most grateful to the individuals and organizations that are referenced below, who have granted us permission to use their scales in this volume.

Accessibility Scale by Irving Jacks. Reprinted from the *Journal of Criminal Law and Criminology*, 1964, 55, 100–106, with permission of the author and the Journal of Criminal Law and Criminology.

Aggression-Altruism Scale by K. S. Larsen. Reprinted from the *Journal of Personality Assessment*, 1971, 35, 275–281, with permission of the Journal of Personality Assessment.

Aggression in Youth by R. Dembo. Reprinted from the *British Journal of Criminology*, 1973, *13*, 246, with permission of the Institute for the Study and Treatment of Delinquency.

Anger Disposition Scale by Donald L. Loy is reprinted with permission of the author.

Attitude toward Any Institution by I. V. Kelley. Reprinted from the *Purdue University Studies in Higher Education*, 1934, *35*, 18–36, with permission of the University of Chicago Press.

Attitude toward Capital Punishment by L. L. Thurstone. Reprinted from *Motion Pictures and Attitudes of Children*, University of Chicago Press, 1932, with permission of the University of Chicago Press.

Attitudes toward Government Workers by P. B. Weston. Reprinted from *Criminology*, 1965, *6*, 83–96, with permission of the author and Sage Publications.

Attitudes toward Juvenile Delinquency by Nicholas A. Reuterman is reprinted with permission of the author.

Attitudes toward Juvenile Detention by Don M. Gottfredson is reprinted with permission of the author.

Attitude toward Law and Justice Scale by C. L. Hulin and B. A. Maher is reprinted with permission of the authors.

Attitudes towards Offenders and Mental Patients by R. E. Lamy. Reprinted from the *Journal of Consulting Psychology*, 1966, *30*, 450–455, with permission of the author and the American Psychological Association.

Attitude toward Police by Jerri Linn Phillips and Robert Coates is reprinted with permission of the authors.

Attitudes toward Police (Competency/Hostility) by Mary Love is reprinted with permission of the author.

Attitude toward Police Questionnaire by D. Bouma. Reprinted from *Kids and Cops*, 1969, with permission of the author and the William B. Eerdsmans Publishing Company.

Attitude toward the Law by J. P. Martin and J. P. McConnell. Reprinted from *Criminology*, 1972, *13*, 111–116, with permission of the authors and Sage Publications.

Attitude toward the Law Scale by Katz Timkovich. Reprinted from *Scales for the Measurement of Social Attitudes*, L. L. Thurstone (Ed.), the University of Chicago Press, 1931, with permission of the University of Chicago Press.

Attitudes toward the Prevalence of Stealing by J. Ball. Reprinted from the *Journal of Criminal Law and Criminology*, 1957, *48*, 259–274, with permission of the author and the Journal of Criminal Law and Criminology.

Attitude toward Prisoners Scale by Kenneth Melvin is reprinted with permission of the author.

Awareness of Limited Opportunity Scale by Judson R. Landis is reprinted with permission of the author.

Behavior Cards by R. M. Stogdill. Reprinted from *The Stogdill Behavior Cards: A Test-Interview for Delinquent Children*, Stoelting Company, 1941, with permission of the Stoelting Company.

Behavior Prediction Scale by S. Rettig. Reprinted from the *British Journal of Criminology*, 1964, *5*, 582–590, with permission of the author and the Institute for the Study and Treatment of Delinquency.

Beverly-Grant Opinion Schedule by Robert S. Beverly is reprinted with permission of the author.

Capital Punishment Attitude Questionnaire by G. L. Jurow. Reprinted from the *Harvard Law Review*, 1971, *84*, 567–611, with permission of the author and the Harvard Law Review.

Children's Perceptions of the Police by R. L. Derbyshire. Reprinted from the *Journal of Criminal Law, Criminology, and Police Science*, 1968, *59*, 183–190, with permission of the author and the Journal of Criminal Law, Criminology, and Police Science.

Citizen Perceptions of Police Scale by R. I. Klyman and J. Kruckenberg. Reprinted from the *Journal of Criminal Justice*, 1974, *2*, 219–233, with permission of the authors and Permamon Press, Inc.

Clues Test by Robert B. Mills is reprinted with permission of the author.

ACKNOWLEDGMENTS

Competency Screening Test by L. D. Lipsitt, D. Lelos, and L. McGarry. Reprinted from *The American Journal of Psychiatry*, 1971, *128*, 137-141, with permission of the author and The American Psychiatric Association.

Comprehensive Miranda Rights Scale by J. Thomas Grisso is reprinted with permission of the author.

Compulsive Masculinity Scale by Ira J. Silverman is reprinted with permission of the author.

Correctional Institutions Environment Scale by Rudolf Moos, sample items reprinted with permission of the author.

Correctional Staff Evaluation Scale by A. D. Cheatwood. Reprinted from the *Journal of Research in Crime and Delinquency*, July, 1974, *11*, 173-179, with permission of the National Council on Crime and Delinquency.

Criminal Attitude Scale by A. J. W. Taylor. Reprinted from *Journal of Criminal Law, Criminology, and Police Science*, 1968, *59*, 37-40, with permission of the author and the Journal of Criminal Law, Criminology, and Police Science.

Criminal Profile by J. Gunn and G. Robertson. Reprinted from the *British Journal of Criminology*, 1976, *16*, 156-160, with permission of the author and the Institute for the Study and Treatment of Delinquency.

Criminality Level Index by W. Reckless. Reprinted from *Criminology*, 1966, *6*, 71-82, with permission of the author and Sage Publications.

Criminally Insane Attitude Scale by Jaswant L. Khanna is reprinted with permission of the author.

Cynicism Questionnaire by Arthur Niederhoffer is reprinted with permission of the author.

Delinquency Checklist by J. A. Kulik, K. B. Stein, and T. R. Sarbin. Reprinted from the *Journal of Counseling and Clinical Psychology*, 1968, *32*, 375-382, with permission of the authors and the American Psychological Association.

Delinquency Potential Scale by E. K. E. Gunderson is reprinted with permission of the author.

Delinquency Proneness Scale by T. F. Marshall. Reprinted from the *British Journal of Criminology*, 1973, *13*, 227-236, with permission of the Institute for the Study and Treatment of Delinquency.

Delinquency Questionnaire by M. L. Erickson. Reprinted from the *Journal of Criminal Law, Criminology, and Police Science*, 1972, *63*, 388-395, with permission of the author and the Journal of Criminal Law, Criminology, and Police Science.

Delinquency Scale (PN Version) by D. R. Peterson, H. D. Quay, and G. R. Cameron. Reprinted from the *Journal of Consulting Psychology*, 1959, *23*, 395-399, with permission of the author and the American Psychological Association.

Delinquent Attitudes and Self-Esteem Scale by S. A. Rathus and L. J. Siegel. Reprinted from *Adolescence*, 1973, *8*, 265-276, with permission of Libra Publishers, Inc.

Differential Behavioral Classification System by Herbert C. Quay is reprinted with permission of the author.

Ethics Inventory by C. G. Watson is reprinted with permission of the author.

Family-Change Scale by D. P. Schneller. Reprinted from *The American Journal of Correction*, 1975, *37*, 29-33, with permission of the author and the American Correctional Association.

Family Information Test by P. S. Venezia. Reprinted from the *Journal of Research in Crime and Delinquency*, 1968, *5*, 148-173, with permission of the National Council in Crime and Delinquency and the Journal of Research in Crime and Delinquency.

Future Events Test by Kenneth B. Stein is reprinted with permission of the author.

Hopelessness Scale by A. T. Beck, A. Weissman, D. Lester, and L. Trexler. Reprinted from *Consulting Psychology*, 1974, *42*, 861-865, with permission of the authors and the American Psychological Association.

Hostility and Aggression Scale by R. T. Green and G. Santori. Reprinted from *Peace Research*, 1969, *1*, 13-22, with permission of the Canadian Peace Research Institute.

Hostility and Aggression Scales by R. Blackburn is reprinted with permission of the author.

Index of Conformity to Staff Expectations by Stanton Wheeler. Reprinted from *American Sociological Review*, 1961, *26*, 699–712, with permission of the author and the American Sociological Association.

The Inmate Perception on Impact by T. G. Eynon, H. E. Allen, and W. C. Reckless. Reprinted from *Journal of Research in Crime and Delinquency*, 1971, *8*, 93–107, with permission of the authors and National Council on Crime and Delinquency.

Inmates' Perception of Significant Others by D. H. Chang, C. H. Zastro, and D. L. Blazicek. Reprinted from *International Journal of Criminology and Penology*, 1975, *3*, 85–96, with permission of the authors and Academic Press.

Inmate Personality Survey by Kenneth A. Carlson is reprinted with permission of the author.

Institutional Life Questionnaire by D. Marcus. Reprinted from *British Journal of Criminology*, 1969, *9*, 272–281, with permission of the Institute for the Study and Treatment of Delinquency.

Integrative Delinquency Scale by C. Davis and J. H. Panton. Reprinted from *Clinical Psychology*, 1974, *30*, 186–189, with permission of the authors and the Journal of Clinical Psychology.

Intentionality in Criminal Situations Scale by Charles Blake Keasey is reprinted with permission of the author.

Interpersonal Personality Inventory by K. B. Ballard, R. H. Foren, J. Neiswonger, R. Fowler, J. Belasco, and R. Taylor. Reprinted from *Interpersonal Personality Inventory Manual*, September, 1963, 1966, with permission of the authors and the American Justice Institute.

Jesness Inventory by C. F. Jesness. Sample items reprinted from *The Jesness Inventory: Development and Validation*, California Youth Authority Research Report No. 29, March 1972, with permission of the author.

Judicial Role Perception Scale by T. D. Ungs and L. R. Baas. Reprinted from *Law and Society Review*, 1972, *6*, 343–366, with permission of the authors and the Law and Society Association.

Juvenile Court Volunteer Effectiveness Interview Scale by Charles R. Horejsi is reprinted by permission of the author.

Law Encounter Severity Scale by A. D. Witherspoon, D. K. deValera, W. O. Jenkins. Reprinted from *The Law Encounter Severity Scale (LESS): A Criterion for Criminal Behavior and Recidivism*, Experimental Manpower Laboratory for Corrections, 1973, with permission of the author and the Rehabilitation Research Foundation.

Law Enforcement Perception Questionnaire by F. Lee. Reprinted from *Manual for the Law Perception Questionnaire*, Psychometric Affiliates, 1970, with permisison of the author and the Center for the Study of Crime, Law Enforcement, and Corrections.

Legal Attitudes Questionnaire by V. R. Boehm. Reprinted from *Wisconsin Law Review*, 1968, *1968*, 734–750, with permission of the author and the Wisconsin Law Review.

Legal Dangerousness Scale by Joseph J. Cocozza is reprinted with permission of the author.

Maladaptive Behavior Record by W. O. Jenkins is reprinted with permission of the author.

Means-Ends Problem-Solving Procedure by Jerome J. Platt is reprinted with permission of the author.

Miniature Situations Test by S. Santostefono is reprinted with permission of the author.

Organizational Structure and Prisonization Scale by Charles W. Thomas is reprinted by permission of the author.

Parental Punitiveness Scale by R. Epstein, S. S. Komorita. Reprinted from *Journal of Child Development*, 1965, *36*, 129–142, with permission of the Society for Research in Child Development.

Perceptions of Police Scales by I. Hadar and J. R. Snortum. Reprinted from *Criminal Justice and Behavior*, 1975, *2*, 37–54, with permission of the author and Sage Publications.

Police–Citizen Interaction Rating Scales by D. Cruse and J. Rubin. Reprinted from *Journal of Psychiatry and Law*, 1973, *1*, 167–222, with permission of Federal Legal Publications, Inc.

ACKNOWLEDGMENTS

Police-Citizen Interaction Rating Scales by David Martin and Jon McConnell. Reprinted from *Criminology*, 1972, *10*, 111–116 with permission of Sage Publications.

Police Task Preference Questionnaire by R. Olson. Reprinted from *Personnel Journal*, December, 1970, *49*, 1015–1020, with permission of the Personnel Journal.

The Prison Adjustment Index by Marvin E. Wolfgang is reprinted with permission of the author.

Prison Fantasy Questionnaire by Benjamin Beit-Halahni is reprinted with permission of the author.

Prison Profile Inventory by Hans Toch is reprinted from *Living in Prison: The Ecology of Human Survival*, New York: Free Press, 1977, with permission of the author and Free Press.

Prisoners' Attitude Scales by G. P. Alpert and D. A. Hicks. Reprinted from *Criminology*, 1977, *14*, 461–482, with permission of the authors and Sage Publications.

Probation Officer–Client Relationship Valence Scale by Romine R. Deming is reprinted with permission of the author.

Problem Checklist by Frances H. Simon. Reprinted from *Prediction Methods in Criminology*, Her Majesty's Stationery Office, 1971, with permission of the author and Her Majesty's Stationery Office.

Public Offender Counseling Inventory by R. C. Page and R. Myrick. Reprinted from *Criminal Justice and Behavior*, 1978, *5*, 141–150, with permission of the authors and Sage Publications.

Reaction Inventory: Anger by David R. Evans is reprinted with permission of the author.

Recidivism Outcome Index by D. O. Moberg and R. C. Ericson. Reprinted from *Federal Probation*, 1972, *36*, 50–57, with permission of the authors and Federal Probation Quarterly.

Rehabilitation in Correctional Settings Attitude Scale by Ronald Rice is reprinted with permission of the author.

Risk Perception Questionnaire by Daniel S. Claster is reprinted with permission of the author.

Self-Attitude Inventory by L. A. Bennett, D. E. Sorensen, and H. Forshay. Reprinted from *Research in Crime and Delinquency*, 1971, with permission of the authors and National Council on Crime and Delinquency.

Self-Reported Delinquency Scales by W. R. Arnold. Reprinted from *Social Problems*, 1965, *15*, 59–66, with permission of Social Problems.

Self-Reported Delinquency Scale by D. T. Farrington. Reprinted from the *Journal of Criminal Law and Criminology*, 1973, *64*, 99–110, with permission of the Journal of Criminal Law and Criminology.

Self-Reported Delinquency Scales by F. I. Nye and J. F. Short. Reprinted from *American Sociological Review*, 1957, *22*, 326–331, with permission of the authors and American Sociological Association.

Seriousness of Delinquency Scale by D. H. Kelly and R. W. Winslow. Reprinted from *British Journal of Criminology*, 1970, *10*, 124–135, with permission of the Institute for the Study of Crime and Delinquency.

Teenage Slang Test by Kulik, Sarbin, and Stein is reprinted with permission of the authors.

Traits Indicating Attitude Scale by G. Russon. Reprinted from *Corrective Psychiatry and Social Therapy*, 1969, *15*, 38–48, with permission of Corrective and Social Psychiatry.

Value Orientation Scale by Judson R. Landis is reprinted with permission of the author.

Violence Scale by J. M. Andrew. Reprinted from *Criminal Justice and Behavior*, 1974, *1*, 123–130, with permission of the author and Sage Publications.

The Way It Looks to Me—Self-Concept Inventory by Walter C. Reckless is reprinted by permission of the author.

Weekly Activity Record by W. O. Jenkins is reprinted by permission of the author.

What Teenagers Think by Kenneth V. Stein is reprinted by permission of the author.

Finally, we are grateful to the authors and publishers listed below for allowing us to reprint the following tables in this book:

Table 6. From "Two Scales for Measuring Attitudes toward Police" by J. L. Philips and R. Coates, *Wisconsin Sociologist,* 1971, *8,* 3–19, Table 2.

Table 12. From "Prisoners' Attitudes toward Components of the Legal and Judicial System" by G. P. Alpert and D. A. Hicks, *Criminology* 1977, *14,* 461–482, Table 5.

Table 14. From "Children's Perceptions of the Police" by R. L. Derbyshire, *Journal of Criminal Law and Criminology,* 1968, *59,* 183–190, Table 3.

Table 15. From "Black Militant Ideology and the Law" by J. D. McConnell and J. D. Martin, *Criminology,* 1972, *10,* 111–116, Table 1.

Tables 16 and 17. From "Changes in Attitudes towards Law Concomitant with Imprisonment" by C. L. Hulin and B. A. Maher, *Journal of Criminal Law and Criminology,* 1959, *50,* 245–248, Tables 1 and 2.

Table 18. From "Competency for Trial: A Screening Instrument" by P. D. Lipsitt, D. Lelos, and L. McGarry, *American Journal of Psychiatry,* 1971, *128,* 137–141, Table 2.

Table 21. From "Social Climates in Prison: An Attempt to Conceptualize and Measure Environmental Factors in Total Institutions" by E. A. Wenk and R. H. Moos, *Journal of Research in Crime and Delinquency,* 1972, *9,* 134–148, Table 1.

Tables 22 and 23. From *Living in Prisons: The Ecology of Prison Survival* by H. Toch, Tables 12-4 and 12-5. Copyright 1977 by the Free Press, New York, New York.

Table 25. From "Dimensions and Patterns of Adolescent, Anti-Social Behavior" by J. A. Kulik, K. B. Stein, and T. R. Sarbin, *Journal of Consulting and Clinical Psychology,* 1968, *32,* 375–382, Table 2.

Tables 26 and 27. From "The Changing Relationship between Official and Self-Reported Measures of Delinquency: An Exploratory Predictive Study" by M. L. Erickson, *Journal of Criminal Law, Criminology, and Police Science,* 1972, *63,* 388–395, Tables 1 and 2.

Table 28. From "Scaling Delinquent Behavior" by F. I. Nye and J. F. Short, *American Sociological Review,* 1957, *22,* 326–331, Table 1.

Table 29. From "Basic Attitude in Delinquency" by G. Russon, *Corrective Psychiatry and Journal of Social Therapy,* 1969, *15,* 38–48, Table p. 45.

Tables 36 and 37. From "Delinquency as a Function of Intrafamily Relationships" by P. Venezia, *Journal of Research in Crime and Delinquency,* 1968, *5,* 147–173, Tables 1 and F.

Table 38. From "Future Time Perspectives: Its Relation to the Socialization Process and the Delinquent Role" by K. B. Stein, T. R. Sarbin, and J. A. Kulik, *Journal of Consulting and Clinical Psychology,* 1968, *32,* 257–264, Table 2.

Table 40. From "Construct Validity of the Miniature Situations Test. II. The Performance of Institutional Delinquents and High School Adolescents" by S. Santostefano and G. Wilson, *Journal of Clinical Psychology,* 1968, *24,* 355–358, Table 1.

Tables 42 and 43. "From Self-Concept Measure of Potential Delinquency" by S. Dinitz and W. C. Reckless, *American Journal of Orthopsychiatry,* 1962, *32,* 159–168.

Tables 44 and 45. From "Adolescent Morality: Its Differentiated Structure and Relation to Delinquent Conduct" by D. B. Stein, T. R. Sarbin, C. L. Chu, and J. A. Kulik, *Multivariate Behavioral Research,* 1967, *2,* 199–210, Tables 3 and 5.

Tables 47 and 48. From *The Stodgill Behavior Cards: A Test-Interview for Delinquent Children* by R. M. Stodgill, p. 6, Table 1; p. 8, Table 4. Copyright 1941 by the Stoelting Company, Chicago, Illinois.

Table 49. From *Comprehension of Miranda Rights: Manual for Administration and Scoring* by J. T. Grisso and S. Manoogian. Copyright 1977 by J. T. Grisso, St. Louis, Missouri.

ACKNOWLEDGMENTS

Table 50. From "Prisoners' Perceptions of the Impact of Institutional Stay" by K. L. Sindwani and W. C. Reckless, *Criminology,* 1973, *11,* 461–471, Table 1.

Tables 52 and 53. From "Language, Socialization, and Delinquency" by J. A. Kulik. T. R. Sarbin, and K. B. Stein, *Developmental Psychology,* 1971, *4,* 434–439, Tables 3 and 4.

Table 60. From "Inmates' Perceptions of Significant Others and the Implications for the Rehabilitation Process" by D. H. Chang, C. H. Zastro, and D. L. Blazicek, *International Journal of Criminology and Penology,* 1975, *3,* 85–96, Table 3.

Table 69. From *The Development and Validation of Scales to Measure Hostility and Aggression* by R. Blackburn, p. 7, Table 3. Copyright 1974 by the Special Hospitals Research Unit, London, England.

Table 71. From "A Comparison of the Ethical Self-Presentations of Schizophrenics, Prisoners and Normals" by C. G. Watson, *Journal of Clinical Psychology,* 1972, *28,* 479–483, Table 2.

Table 72. From "The Attitudes of Offenders toward Occupations in the Administration of Justice" by P. B. Watson, *Criminology,* 1965, *6,* 83–96, Table 1.

Table 73. From "Delinquent Attitudes and Self-Esteem" by A. Rathus and J. Siegel, *Adolescence,* 1973, *8,* 265–276, Table 2.

Table 74. From *EITS Manual: Bristol Social Adjustment Guides,* pp. 14–15, Table C. Copyright 1972 Education and Industrial Testing Service, San Diego, California.

Table 79. From "The Measurement of Pessimism: The Hopelessness Scale" by A. T. Beck, A. Weissman, D. Lester, and L. Trexler, *Journal of Consulting Psychology,* 1974, *42,* 861–865, Table 3.

Tables 80 and 81. From *Means-Ends Problem-Solving Procedure; Manual and Tentative Norms* by J. Platt, G. Spivack, and M. Bloom, pp. 27–29, Tables 1 and 2. Copyright 1971 by the Department of Mental Health Sciences, Hahnemann Medical College and Hospital, Philadelphia, Pennsylvania.

Tables 82 and 83. From "The Application of Self-Esteem in a Correctional Setting: I. Reliability of the Scale and Relationship to Other Measures" by L. A. Bennett, D. E. Sorenson, and H. Forshay, *Journal of Research in Crime and Delinquency,* 1971, *8,* 1–9, Tables 1 and 2.

Contents

CHAPTER 1
Scale Needs and Utilization 1

CHAPTER 2
Search and Selection of Scales for Review 9

CHAPTER 3
Using This Handbook 21

CHAPTER 4
Ethical Issues and the Protection of Human Subjects 25

CHAPTER 5
MMPI and CPI Special Scales 31

CHAPTER 6
Law Enforcement and Police 43

Law Enforcement Attitude Scales: Reviews 44
    Attitudes toward Police (Competence–Hostility) 44
    Attitude toward Police (Semantic Differential and Likert Formats) 47
    Attitude toward Police Questionnaire 50
    Law Enforcement Perception Questionnaire 55

Perceptions of Police Scales	59
Prisoners' Attitude Scales	65
Law Enforcement Attitude Scales: Listings	69
Attitudes toward the Criminal Justice System	69
Attitudes toward Law Enforcement	69
Attitudes toward Police	69
Attitudes toward Police	69
Attitude toward the Police	70
Attitudes toward the Police	70
Police Community-Relations Interview	70
Police Opinion of Work Questionnaire	70
Police Perspectives and Behaviors in a Campus Disturbance	71
Portune Attitude-toward-Police Scale	71
Law Enforcement Behavior Ratings: Reviews	71
Police-Citizen Interaction Rating Scales	71
Law Enforcement Behavior Ratings: Listings	74
Client Telephone Questionnaire	74
Cop Personality Questionnaire	74
Performance Rating Systems for Police (Performance Rating Scales)	75
Police Peer Evaluation Scale	75
Police Task Performance Scale	75
Law Enforcement Personality Measures: Reviews	75
Cynicism Questionnaire	75
Law Enforcement Personality Measures: Listings	80
Police Flexibility Measurement	80
Police Job Stress Interview	80
Law Enforcement Milieu Ratings: Listings	81
Professionalization Assessment for Police Organizations	81
Law Enforcement Prediction: Reviews	81
Clues Test	81
Law Enforcement Prediction: Listings	83
Public Personnel Association Test (PPA)	83
Law Enforcement Description: Reviews	83
Children's Perceptions of the Police	83
Citizen's Perception of Police Scale	86
Foot Patrolman Observation Test	90
Police Task Preference Questionnaire	92
Law Enforcement Description: Listings	95
Abbreviated Police Identification Scale	95
ADAPT Scale (*Arrest Decisions As Preludes To*)	95
Information Handling in Police Decision Making	95
Job Analysis and Interest Measurements	95
Perceptions of Justice Interview	96

Police Image Questionnaire	96
Police Isolation Questionnaire	96
Police Prediction of Public Attitudes Questionnaire	96

CHAPTER 7
Courts and the Law 97

Courts and the Law Attitude Scales: Reviews	97
Attitude toward Capital Punishment	97
Attitude toward the Law (Martin and McConnell)	100
Attitude toward the Law Scale (Katz)	104
Attitude toward Law and Justice Scale: A Sentence-Completion Test	107
Capital Punishment Attitude Questionnaire	111
Juvenile Court Volunteer Effectiveness Interview Scale	114
Legal Attitudes Questionnaire	117
Courts and the Law Attitude Scales: Listings	121
Attitudes toward the Law	121
Attitudes toward Legal Agencies	122
Attitudes toward the Legal System (Thomas, Petersen, and Zingraff)	122
Attitudes toward the Legal System (Torney)	122
Attitudes toward Due Process and the Juvenile Court	122
Attitude toward Probation Officers	123
Ideological and Law-Abidingness Scales	123
Juvenile Justice—What Do You Think?	123
Knowledge of Student Rights Scale, Cynicism about the Law and Legal System Scale, Knowledge of the Law in General Scale	123
Law Scale	124
Courts and the Law Personality Assessment: Reviews	124
Competency Screening Test	124
Competency to Stand Trial Assessment Instrument	128
Courts and the Law Milieu Ratings: Listings	133
Pre-trial Intervention Program Questionnaire	133
Courts and the Law Prediction: Listings	133
Pre-trial Release Decisions	133
Courts and the Law Description: Reviews	133
Judicial Role Perception Scale	133
Probation Officer–Client Relationship Valence Scale	139
Problem Checklist	142
Courts and the Law Description: Listings	146
Goal Attainment Scale	146
Judicial Roles Questionnaire	146
Juvenile Court Role Expectations Questionnaire	147

Perception of Stigma Interview Procedure 147
Probationer and Volunteer Evaluation Questionnaires 147

CHAPTER 8
Corrections ... 149

Corrections Attitude Scales: Reviews 150
   Attitudes toward Juvenile Detention 150
   Institutional Life Questionnaire 160
   Rehabilitation in Correctional Settings Attitude Scale 164
Corrections Attitude Scales: Listings 171
   Attitude toward the Death Penalty 171
   Attitudes toward Enforced Group Psychotherapy 171
   Attitude to Psychiatry Scale 171
   Attitude toward Punishment of Criminals 172
   Parole Officer Punishment and Reintegrative Orientation
      Questionnaire 172
   Rehabilitative Value Perception Scale 172
Corrections Behavior Ratings: Reviews 172
   The Prison Adjustment Index 172
   Recidivism Outcome Index 175
Corrections Behavior Ratings: Listings 178
   Probation Program Ratings 178
   Work–Release Staff Role Questionnaire 179
Corrections Personality Assessment: Reviews 179
   Prison Projective Test 179
Corrections Personality Assessment: Listings 181
   Alienation Measure 181
   Prisoner–Therapist Q-Sort 181
Corrections Milieu Ratings: Reviews 182
   Correctional Institutions Environment Scale 182
   Prison Profile Inventory 186
Corrections Milieu Ratings: Listings 193
   Child Care Work Questionnaire 193
   Classification for Placement in Training Schools 193
   Group Evaluation Criterion Card Sort 193
   Index of Perspectives on Institution and Staff.................... 193
   Institutional Living and Inmate Code Scales 194
   Response to Incarceration Questionnaire 194
   Training in Differential Treatment Assessment Instruments 194
Corrections Prediction: Reviews 194
   Hunch Parolability Scale 194
   Parolability Questionnaire 198

CONTENTS

Corrections Prediction: Listings 206
   Institutional Adjustment Inventory 206
   Parole Adjustment Scale 206
   Parole Prediction Procedure with Women Offenders 206
   Parole Prediction Scale 207
   Parole Prediction through Variable Interactions 207
   Parole Success Attributes 207
   Postprison Success Prediction 207
   Recidivism Base Expectancy Scale 208
   Recidivism Prediction Scale 208
Corrections Description: Reviews 208
   Index of Conformity to Staff Expectations 208
   Organizational Structure and Prisonization Scale 211
   Public Offender Counseling Inventory 215
Corrections Description: Listings 218
   Alternatives to Incarceration Client Questionnaire 218
   Assessment of *I*-Level Knowledge 218
   CJC Questionnaire 219
   Correctional Officers' Interest Blank 219
   Critical Incident Test 219
   Differential Treatment Pretraining Questionnaires—Trainees'
      Supervisor 219
   Inmate Questionnaire 220
   Inmates' Recreation Activities Checklist 220
   Inmate Social Role Adaptation Scale 220
   Institutional Impact Questionnaires 220
   Interview Rating Questionnaire 221
   Long-Term Prisoners Interview Schedule 221
   Parole Decision Instruments 221
   Parole Decision Making Scale 221
   Parole Officer Evaluation of Vocational Rehabilitation Services ... 222
   Prerelease Furlough Questionnaire 222
   Pretraining Questionnaire—Trainee 222
   Prison Guard Job Perceptions Questionnaire 222
   Treatment–Custody Conflict Questionnaire 223
   Values and Sociometric Choices Questionnaire 223

CHAPTER 9
Delinquency 225

Delinquency Attitude Scales: Reviews 225
   Attitudes toward Juvenile Delinquency 225

Delinquency Attitude Scales: Listings	234
Juvenile Delinquency Attitude Scale	234
Delinquency Behavior Ratings: Reviews	234
Delinquency Checklist	234
Delinquency Questionnaire	237
Self-Reported Delinquency Scales (Arnold)	241
Self-Reported Delinquency Scale (Gibson)	246
Self-Reported Delinquency Scales (Nye and Short)	249
Traits Indicating Attitude Scale	253
Violence Scale	256
Delinquency Behavior Ratings: Listings	260
Delinquent Behavior Interview Schedule	260
Group Data Schedule	260
Inmate Management Scale	261
Institutional Adjustment Index	261
Peer Rating Instrument	261
Self-Report Delinquency Questionnaire	261
Self-Reported Delinquency Scale	261
Self-Reported Delinquent Behavior Questionnaire	262
Youngster Behavior Inventory	262
Delinquency Personality Assessment: Reviews	262
Beverly-Grant Opinion Schedule	262
Correctional Staff Evaluation Scale	264
Delinquency Scale (PN Version)	267
Differential Behavioral Classification System	273
Family Information Test	284
Future Events Test	289
Jesness Inventory	292
Miniature Situations Test	298
Way It Looks to Me—Self-Concept Inventory	301
What Teenagers Think	306
Delinquency Personality Assessment: Listings	317
Behavioral Syndromes	317
Delinquency Differential Classification System	317
Delinquency Scale	317
Delinquency Self-Concept Scale	317
Delinquency Self-Concept Items	318
Foster Parent Preference Survey	318
Group Home Parents Interview Schedules	318
How the Future Looks to Me Scale	318
Kohlberg Interview	319
Parental Attitude Research Instrument	319
Psychiatric Data Schedule	319

Sentence Completion Test	319
Treatment Personnel Inventory	320
Value Consensus Scale	320
Delinquency Milieu Rating: Listings	320
Attitudes toward School Questionnaire	320
Life Functioning Assessment	320
Social Climate Questionnaire	321
Delinquency Prediction: Reviews	321
Integrative Delinquency Scale	321
Delinquency Proneness Scale	324
Delinquency Prediction: Listings	327
Individual Child Fact Sheet and Rating Form	327
KD Checklist	328
KD Proneness Scale	328
School Interest Inventory	328
Student Opinion Survey and Parent Interview Schedule	328
Delinquency Description: Reviews	329
Behavior Cards	329
Comprehensive Miranda Rights Scale	336
Inmate Perception of Impact	344
Seriousness of Delinquency Scale	352
Teenage Slang Test	356
Delinquency Description: Listings	367
Approval of Illegal Behaviors Questionnaire	367
Characteristics of Youngsters Questionnaire	368
Delinquency and Popularity Scale	368
Differential Association Questionnaire	368
Evaluation of Delinquency Preventative Measure	368
Exposure to Deviance Index	368
Family Background and Urban Delinquency Questionnaire	369
Family and Peer Group Valuation Scales	369
Female Juvenile Recidivism Descriptive Checklist	369
Goal Orientations Inventory	369
Importance Questionnaire	370
Interest and Activities Inventory	370
Juvenile Probation Administrative Action Scale	370
Marion County Youth Study Questionnaires	370
Potential Cost Scales	371
Probation Counselors' Success Rating Scale	371
Sellin-Wolfgang Delinquency Index	371
Severity of Offense Scale	371
Social Data Schedule	372
Social Work Data Schedule	372

CHAPTER 10
Offenders 373

Offenders Attitude Scales: Reviews............................... 374
   Attitudes toward Offenders and Mental Patients.................. 374
   Attitude toward Prisoners Scale 377
   Criminally Insane Attitude Scale 381
Offenders Behavior Ratings: Reviews 387
   Criminal Profile... 387
   Law Encounter Severity Scale 391
Offenders Behavior Ratings: Listings 395
   Index of Social Contacts....................................... 395
   Personal Characteristics Rating Report 395
Offenders Personality Assessment: Reviews 396
   Accessibility Scale 396
   Inmate Personality Survey 401
   Interpersonal Personality Inventory 412
   Prison Fantasy Questionnaire 418
Offenders Personality Assessment: Listings 425
   Criminal Self-Conceptions Assessment 425
   I-Level Classification 425
   Inmate Dependency Scale...................................... 425
   Multimethod Assessment System 425
   Porteus Maze Test... 426
   Powerless Scale 426
   Postprison Expectation Scale 426
   Stereoscopic Resolution Procedure.............................. 426
   Stratton Identification with Criminal Others and Orientation to
      Criminal Means Scales 427
Offender Description: Reviews.................................... 427
   Inmates' Perception of Significant Others 427
   Ohio Penal Classification Test 436
Offenders Description: Listings 438
   Community Follow-up Interview................................ 438
   Criminality Scales 438
   Criminal Attitudes and Values Scales 438
   Involvement Questionnaire 439
   Images of Criminality Questionnaire 439
   Perception of Addicts and Addiction Scale 439
   Prisoner Attribute Typology 439
   Recidivism Seriousness Classification 440
   Social Organization of Burglary Questionnaire 440

CHAPTER 11
Crime and Criminality 441

Crime and Criminality Attitude Scales: Reviews 442
    Aggression-Altruism Scale 442
    Attitude toward the Prevalence of Stealing 445
    Criminal Attitude Scale 450
    Criminality Level Index 453
Crime and Criminality Attitude Scales: Listings 456
    Attitudes toward Violence Scales 456
    Public Attitudes toward Crime and Corrections Survey 457
    Public Opinion about Crime Questionnaire 457
Crime and Criminality Behavior Ratings: Reviews 457
    Aggression in Youth 457
    Maladaptive Behavior Record 460
Crime and Criminality Personality Assessment: Reviews 466
    Giannell Index of Criminality 466
    Intentionality in Criminal Situations Scale 469
Crime and Criminality Personality Assessment: Listings 472
    Hostility and Direction of Hostility Questionnaire 472
    Scrambled Sentence Test 472
    Stereoscopic Perception of Violence 472
Crime and Criminality Prediction: Reviews 473
    Anger Disposition Scale 473
    Delinquency Potential Scale 482
    Hostility Scale–Aggression Scale 487
    Legal Dangerousness Scale 493
Crime and Criminality Description: Reviews 496
    Ethics Inventory 496
    Parental Punitiveness Scale 504
    Risk Perception Questionnaire 512
Crime and Criminality Description: Listings 519
    African View of Crime Interview Schedule 519
    Attitudes toward Crime and Punishment 519
    Crime Control Orientation Scale 519
    Crime Seriousness Ratings 519
    Criminal Justice Attitudes and Knowledge Scale 520
    Exposure to Family and Peer Deviance Indices 520
    Fear of Crime and Fear of the Police Interviews 520
    Offense Perception Assessment 520
    Perception of Crime Scale 521
    Perception of Deviancy Schema 521

Public Surveys of Crime and Criminal Justice 521
Treatment of Violent Patients Questionnaire 521

CHAPTER 12
General Scales 523

General Attitude Scales: Reviews 524
   Attitude toward Any Institution 524
   Attitudes toward Government Workers 529
   Delinquent Attitudes and Self-Esteem Scale 532
General Attitude Scales: Listings 536
   Attitudes toward Deviant Behavior 536
   Attitude toward Disabled Persons 536
   Child–Parent Relationship Scale 536
   Itkin Attitudes toward Parents and Children Scales 536
   Policeman's View of Citizens' Support Scales 537
   Stanford Parent Attitude Questionnaire 537
General Behavior Ratings: Reviews 537
   Bristol Social Adjustment Guides 537
   Weekly Activity Record 542
General Behavior Ratings: Listings 546
   Behavioral Coding System 546
General Personality Assessment: Reviews 546
   Compulsive Masculinity Scale 546
   Hopelessness Scale 550
   Hostility and Aggression Scale 554
   Means-Ends Problem-Solving Procedure 558
   Reaction Inventory: ANGER 563
   Self-Attitude Inventory 569
General Personality Assessment: Listings 574
   The Adjective Checklist 574
   Authoritarianism Scale (A Scale) 574
   Balanced Dogmatism Scales 574
   Barratt Impulsiveness Scale 574
   Buss-Durkee Hostility Scale 575
   Cartoon Aggression Test 575
   Community Adaptation Schedule 575
   Edwards' Personal Preference Schedule 575
   Eyesenck Personality Inventory 575
   F Scale and F Scale Revisions 576
   Hand Test 576
   Hogan Moral Conduct Scales 576

Interpersonal Checklist 576
Jourard Self-Disclosure Questionnaire 577
Just World Scale 577
Kahn Test of Symbol Arrangement 577
Maudsley Personality Inventory 578
Miale-Holsopple Sentence Completion Test 578
Mosher Incomplete Sentence Test (MIST) 578
Offer Self-Image Questionnaire 579
Personal Orientation Inventory 579
The Rokeach Dogmatism Scale 579
Rokeach Value Survey 579
Rotter I-E Scale 580
Shapiro Adjective Checklist 580
Tennessee Self-Concept Scale (TSCS) 580
Twenty Statements Test 580
Values Inventory for Children 581
Zimmer Sentence Completion Test (ZSCT) 581
General Scales—Description: Reviews 581
Awareness of Limited Opportunity Scale 581
Behavior Prediction Scale 584
Family-Change Scale 591
Value Orientation Scale 594
General Scales—Description: Listings 597
Deviance Control Scale 597
Role Behavior Test 597
Semantic Differential Technique 597

Bibliography 599

Index 603

CHAPTER 1

Scale Needs and Utilization

In reviewing the evaluations of crime and delinquency research, it is far easier to find negative, critical, and discouraging statements than to find positive ones. As Hirschi and Selvin (1967) point out in the delinquency area, "the critic . . . does not have a difficult time justifying his existence . . . theorists, practitioners, and laymen are virtually unanimous in condemning . . . this research as inconclusive and inconsistent" (p. 15). In fact, virtually every area within these two topics has been strongly criticized. The present work addresses itself to an important set of these criticisms—that of availability, reliability, and validity of research instruments and scales. Improvement in this area may well have a dual effect. First, it will allow better questions to be asked, since scientists often formulate problems to study by using existing techniques and instruments. As these tools improve, so too should the resulting questions and issues studied. Second, it will increase the probability that these scales, questionnaires, and other instruments will yield objective, reliable, and valid answers.

But what is the best approach for obtaining instruments that have desirable characteristics? The National Advisory Commission on Criminal Justice Standards and Goals (1973), in its report on the criminal justice system, recommended the development of new, useful measures. Yet, our operating assumption is that it is wasteful and repetitive for individuals to develop new instruments for each study in which they are engaged. Rather a major need exists for assessing and having access to currently available research instruments and scales.

Is this genuinely a problem? Do individuals actually seek to develop new instruments or is there widespread and informed use of existing instruments for criminal justice research? In order to test for this kind of investigatory provincialism—that is, believing that nobody else has investigated the same topic area or developed a measuring device for the same purposes—a brief survey was conducted of the criminality articles in 39 recent issues of the journals: *Crime and Delinquency*; *Criminology*; *Journal of Research in Crime and Delinquency*; and *Journal of Consulting and Clinical Psychology*. There were 224 relevant articles in these issues; 77 of them, or 34.1% utilized a total of 184 rating scales or questionnaires. The kinds of instruments used are shown in Table 1.

TABLE 1. Use of Existing and Newly Constructed Scales in Criminolgical Research

Journal	Years and volumes	Articles Total	With scales	New scales (N = 84) Rating	Questionnaire	Modification of existing scales	Existing scales (N = 100) Rating	Questionnaire	Miscellaneous
Crime and Delinquency	1970–1972 Vol. 16–18	108	23	2	24	0	7	—	—
Criminology	1971–1973 Vol. 9–11	73	25	23[a]	9	1	29	—	1[b]
Journal of Research in Crime and Delinquency	1971–1972 Vol. 8–9	27	13	10	2	3	14[c]	—	2[d]
Journal of Consulting & Clinical Psychology	1970–1972	16	16	3	3	4[e]	46	—	1[b]
Subtotals		224	77	38	38	8	96	0	4

[a] A variety of scales were used in one study, but not specified.
[b] Measurement of personal space.
[c] Four of these were batteries.
[d] Case histories.
[e] These were modifications of the MMPI Mf scale.

Of the 184 instruments used, 84 (45.6%) were developed for the study being conducted, 8 were modifications of existing scales, and 76 were fully new. One hundred existing instruments were used, or 54.5% of the total, and 96 of these were rating scales. Based on this sample, it appears that almost as many researchers develop their own measures as use existing ones. A spot check of the same journals in 1976–1978 yielded essentially the same results.

Given the repeated and often unnecessary development of new instruments, as well as the use of instruments that are unreliable or insufficiently valid, what does this mean for the state of research into criminality? First, it suggests that many potentially useful studies will have no value because the instruments do not accurately measure what they are intended to measure. Secondly, it means that there will be considerable effort directed toward the development of new instruments that could be better directed toward design and implementation of the research studies themselves. Finally, it means that results are not comparable.

Although, as Table 1 indicates, there are a number of people who draw on existing scales and literature as they prepare their research plans, they face an additional problem—finding existing material. Descriptions of these instruments are usually only found in journal articles where they are most commonly discussed within the purposes of the study itself. Evidence for psychometric soundness or the value of the instrument is often not presented with the first publication of the scale, and there may be no description whatever of its development. It is also rare for information about norms, or an acknowledgement of the instrument's weaknesses, to be available in published reports. Thus, the information that is published is highly biased so the author will look good in the eyes of his or her readers and colleagues; pertinent information from which the reader could make decisions on future choices of instruments is usually not at hand. Mahoney (1976) has reported a series of experiments demonstrating just this process. His conclusions are that "a large percentage of contemporary scientists engage in conventional research methods which are blatantly illogical" (p. 153), as well as use tools and reasoning that confirm their preexisting scholarly biases.

A fundamental need then is to gather critical, evaluative information about crime and delinquency research instruments in ways that meet five criteria: that the review be comparative, relevant, objective, comprehensive, and centrally available.

1. *Comparative:* To provide information so that the choice of the instrument may be dictated by its greater and more apt forms of reliability and validity when compared to other measures.
2. *Relevant:* To allow investigators to choose instruments to match the specific goals and anticipated achievements of the research.
3. *Objective:* To allow investigators to choose instruments based on their scientific merits.
4. *Comprehensive:* To review a broad range of available instruments in crime and delinquency research.

5. *Centrally available:* To make available these instruments and their assessments in a single source document. This availability should facilitate their appropriate use in research.

THE CASE FOR VINTAGE AND QUALITY

The process of developing criminological scales can be compared to that of making quality wine. A good grape must have fertile soil and the right climate in which to grow. It needs the opportunity to flourish and develop. Indeed, wine, until it has met the test of time and the test of the consumer, may be tentative and unproven. Thus, many wines, fresh out of the cask without the opportunity to age, may be distasteful. The consumer may find them unpalatable and, once tried, they may be discarded. This kind of wine may appear in one form or another again and again, but it passes by with no lasting audience.

Let us pursue this metaphor further. The very best wine is one in which the individual can count on the exceptional quality in it. Within a given year, there will be great reliability or consistency within its taste. If the wine does what is anticipated, that is, it tastes the way it is supposed to and, if it has been produced right, aged appropriately, and stored correctly, it will be a source of great satisfaction to the consumer.

Research scales work much the same way. Many individuals will develop research scales like a knee jerk, reflexively in response to a need for assessment. These scales have no breeding whatever. Clipped off the vine of the developer's scientific thought, they have no heritage. What they lack in taste, they make up for in pretentiousness.

The basic parallel in this analogy is that most newly developed scales, like most new wines, are of uncertain quality. The new scales are of unknown value, and while they may be developed cheaply and quickly, they typically do not achieve the purposes of providing consistent, valid information about the topic they examine. Important and useful scales are like old wines. They have been bred carefully, developers know what they are doing, the quality is consistent, and there is a heritage on which they are based. The heritage in criminological research scales is that of repeated studies that have ascertained, through reliability and validity studies, that the scales are of known qualities, that their parameters of measurement are accessible and have been evaluated, and that, like a fine wine served with a gourmet meal, they enhance the appreciation of the context in which they are set.

Yet not all old wines are necessarily good. Some are base, as are some old scales. There continue to be consumers who will use existing, poorly validated scales, and taste what Milton has called "the sweet poison of misused wine." Part of our purpose is to take the old wines of criminological research and to present a vintage chart so that the quality scales may be used and appreciated and so that the bitter scales, those without substantial validity or worth, may be poured down the drain and discarded from our research storehouses and cellars.

Some wines are for use as aperitifs and others are for use only as sweet dessert wines. Still others have developed a special place, a special setting so that in one kind of serving they are excellent and in another they are misfits. So it is with scales. There are some uses with limited goals or particular needs where some instruments fit well and appropriately; yet put to other uses, they are dissonant misfits, disflavoring the worth of the entire research effort. Our present work seeks to sort the quality of scales, suggesting not only their worth but their worth in some context. We examine here the particular applications, the whens, wheres, and hows as well as the "how goods."

In one aspect of scale usage, the wine analogy begins to break down. If a wine drinker needs only to convince himself or herself that a wine is good, then the scale user must convince readers by research that the scale is useful. In this respect the publishing researcher becomes like the wine producer, and the readers of research reports become consumers who make their own decision as to the merits of the scale.

Although we see our purpose as the fit of scale characteristics and consumer needs, it is difficult for any consumer to learn about wines or scales only by reading. It is impossible to become a connoisseur of good wine by reading about how it should taste. No one can develop the notion of a nutty or dry or a full bouquet wine entirely in his or her mind unless that person has an extraordinarily developed sense of gustatory imagery. In the same sense, one cannot read about instruments and learn immediately their every use and application. Thus, this work is offered with no sense of it being an absolute solution to the path to meaningful research. We suggest, instead, that it be used by readers as one of many maps or guides that indicate the nature of the path and the terrain. Where they are going and how they get there is still an issue for the researcher and is not decided by the compass he or she carries.

THE GATHERING OF RESEARCH INSTRUMENTS: OTHER EFFORTS

Research instruments in other fields have been gathered in compilations that include evaluative information. Although most instruments may be traced historically to German nineteenth-century comprehensive handbooks of sciences, the modern patriarch of research instrument handbooks is the series of *Mental Measurement Yearbooks* (MMY) produced by Oscar Buros. The MMYs describe 2,802 paper-and-pencil educational and personality tests, present comprehensive bibliographies on each, and include critical reviews by one or more experts for many of the tests. Three drawbacks exist in the MMYs. First, there are different reviewers, potentially yielding inconsistent standards, although the quality of the reviews is very high. Second, many tests that are not commercially published

TABLE 2. Handbooks of Behavior Measures

	Number of scales	Content	Includes reliability reports	Includes validity reports	Includes norms	Includes items on the measures
Comrey, Baker, & Glaser (1973)	1100 abstracts of measures	One paragraph abstracts of lesser known instruments not included in ISR project	Yes	Yes	No	No
Goldman & Saunders (1974)	339 measures	Experimental test instruments in 22 categories of mental measurement	Yes correlation coefficients only	Yes correlation coefficients only	No	No
Johnson (1976)	Almost 900 measures	Child development tests and measures	Yes	Yes	Yes	Examples of items
Lake, Miles, & Earle (1973)	84 measures and 20 compendia	Measures of social functioning based on conceptual schema	Yes	Yes	Reviewed but not reported	No
Lyerly (1973)	36 measures	Scales for rating behavior and symptomatology	Yes	Yes	No	Yes for unpublished scales

Miller (1970)	35 measures	Sociometric scales that show promise of high validity and utility	Yes	Yes	No	Yes
Price (1972)	22 measures	Measures of organizations using published instruments	Yes	Yes	No	Yes
Robinson & Shaver (1971)	106 measures	Social psychological attitude scales	Yes	Yes	Sometimes	Yes
Shaw & Wright (1967)	176 measures	Attitude scales	Yes	Yes	No	Yes
Simon & Boyer (1974)	99 observation systems	Observation instruments which describe verbal and nonverbal behavior	No	No	No	Yes
Straus (1969)	319 measures	Techniques to measure family behavior	Yes	Yes	Yes	No
Brodsky & Smitherman (1983)	118 measures plus 301 other listings	Crime and delinquency research instruments	Yes	Yes	Sometimes	Yes

are omitted. Third, the potential user still has to take additional steps to obtain the instruments.

The MMYs have spawned a number of parallel handbooks (Comrey, Baker, & Glaser, 1973; Goldman & Saunders,1974; Johnson, 1976; Lake, Miles, & Earle, 1973; Lyerly, 1973; Miller, 1970; Price, 1972; Robinson & Shaver, 1971; Shaw & Wright, 1967; Simon & Boyer, 1974; Straus, 1969) usually characterized by the following traits:

1. They include information on development and scoring of the instrument.
2. They contain assessments of several instruments by one evaluator.
3. The reliability, validity, and utilization limitations are presented.
4. The instruments are organized in specific behavioral science measurement or social problem areas.

The contents of these handbooks are reported in Table 2, which allows them to be compared to our effort. As will be noted from an inspection of that table, the Shaw and Wright (1967) collection of 176 scales is the model for our work. In their effort, large numbers of measures are collected, assessed, and organized according to likely application. More space and time is given to the assessment than to the simple process of gathering and making accessible. The key studies on each scale, and often all studies, are cited and utilized in the evaluation. While the criteria for selection of measures to be reviewed in our effort are discussed in the next chapter, the major differences between Shaw and Wright and this volume are in our attention to crime and delinquency instruments and in our presentation of norms.

Finally, it should be remembered that many research studies in crime and delinquency do not call for criminological measures. Those investigators will find extensive collections of scales listed in Buros, *Tests in Print,* as well as in the Johnson (1976), Shaw and Wright (1967), and other listed sources.

CHAPTER 2

Search and Selection of Scales for Review

This chapter discusses our search for crime and delinquency scales and the decisions for their inclusion. We began with a search for relevant scales and research studies conducted on them *(identification)*, then sought to obtain copies of the scale items *(acquisition)*, to select those of greatest use or promise *(selection)*, and finally to write concise evaluations *(review)*. Each of these steps required a number of procedures and produced several decision points.

IDENTIFICATION

First, all psychological, sociological, and criminological journals currently published were searched covering the period of the last 15 years for scales used in criminal justice research. When relevant scales were found, the reference information was placed on file.

Next, psychological, sociological, and criminological abstracts were searched for scales using these key terms: Adjudication, Aggression, Corrections, Crime, Criminals, Delinquency, Female Criminals, Female Juvenile Delinquents, Hostility, Juries, Juvenile Delinquency, Law, Law Enforcement Personnel, Male Criminals, Male Juvenile Delinquents, Measurement, Parole, Police, Prisoners, Prison, Probation, Scales, Testing, and Violence. Abstracts indexed by these words were reviewed, those which contained scales relevant to criminal justice were noted, and the information gathered from each was placed on file.

The third avenue for the search was a mail survey. Originally, 12 researchers in the area of criminal justice were nominated by a project advisory committee as knowledgeable scholars and practitioners. Letters were written to each of these persons requesting their help in finding scales that they had used in their work and other researchers who should be contacted for further information. When these responses were returned, a second set of letters was mailed. All of the

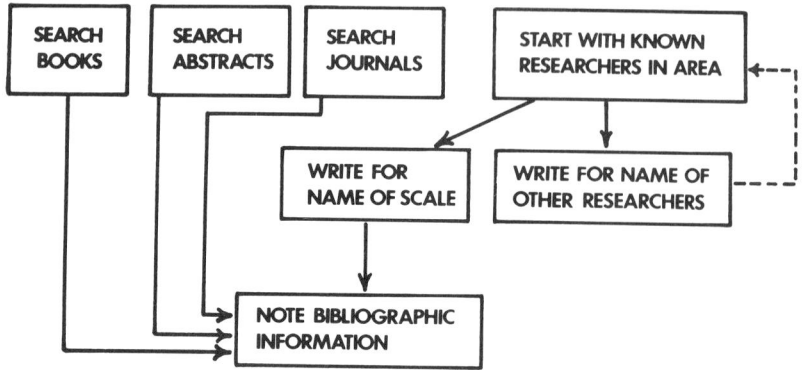

FIGURE 1. Identification.

nominees of the first group were contacted and, in addition, letters were sent to approximately 200 other researchers who were actively using or developing crime and delinquency scales. Some names for the latter group were obtained from the abstract and journal search previously noted, while the rest came from personal knowledge. Each letter asked for the nomination of scales used for crime and delinquency research and the names of any other researchers active in such scale development and use. Not all of the researchers responded to the request, and some were not available at the address to which the letter was mailed. However, of those to whom the letter was assumed to be delivered, almost 50% responded. This "chain-letter" methodology yielded not only a listing of scales and active researchers, but also a check on which scales were used most frequently and which researchers were referred to most often.

Figure 1 shows the two routes used for the identification of relevant scales.

ACQUISITION

Once a scale was identified, we attempted to find the scale itself and copies of the research reports in which it appeared. If the article could be located and the scale was reproduced within it, they were copied and placed on file. If the article was not available or the scale items not included, a letter was sent to the first author requesting the needed information. If no response was received, we wrote to the second author. Figure 2 illustrates this sequence of events.

This approach was hampered by some difficulties and constraints. First, some crime and delinquency journals have had very brief lives and some scale developers have had very brief careers, disappearing from possible contact. The publishing houses sometimes were able to provide copies of articles in defunct journals. However, the difficulties in locating some authors were more serious.

SEARCH AND SELECTION OF SCALES FOR REVIEW

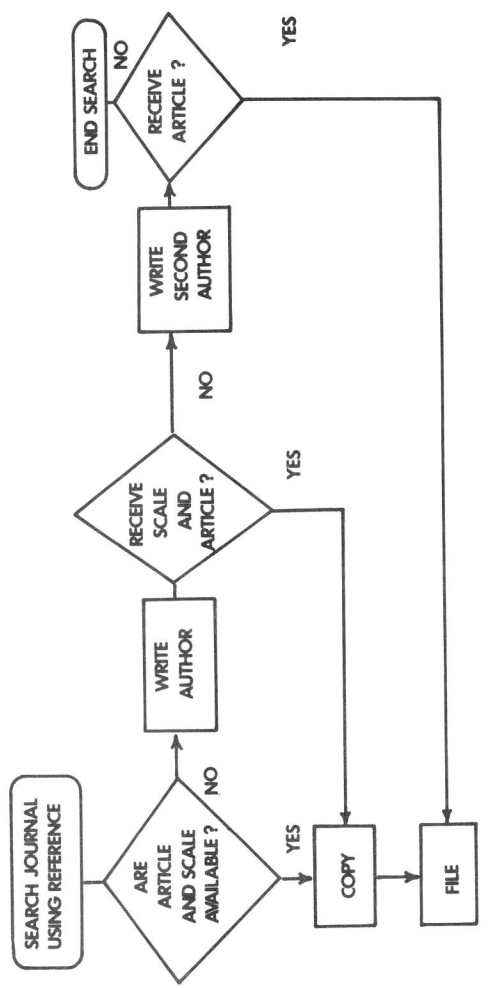

FIGURE 2. Acquisition.

For a surprisingly large number of authors—perhaps 40—all mail was returned stamped "forwarding address unknown" and secretaries and colleagues neither remembered them nor knew where they were located.

The commercially published scales also presented occasional dilemmas. Widely used instruments, such as the *California Psychological Inventory,* and its scales relevant to this project, presented no problems. The instrument was already in the public domain and widely available. At the most, a review and presentation of sample items would be in order. The scale was accessible. Several scales, however, had been commercially published by small companies especially formed for this purpose, usually owned by the scale developer. These scales typically were not widely circulated. Yet, if the scale was available and if it met our selection criteria, permission was requested, and often received, to reproduce the scale in this book. The *Law Enforcement Perception Questionnaire* and the *Bimodal Personality Inventory* fit into this category.

A final problem we faced concerned the fact that some scales would evolve over a period of years, with as many as a half-dozen versions being created and used. In this circumstance, our practice was to select the most recent version for inclusion, unless an earlier version appeared to be both more widely used and more valid for its stated purposes.

SELECTION

The selection process refers to the review of each scale for the purpose of deciding whether it should be evaluated and included. Figure 3 presents this decision tree.

Each article was read and it was noted whether direct or indirect estimates of reliability were within the minimally acceptable range of .60 or greater. If reliability was low, the next decision was whether the scale was relevant to an area which is in special need of research tools, since even modest scale contributions were sometimes considered valuable as a starting point. If the area was not in exceptional need of work, the decision issue changed to whether the scale had been used frequently. In those cases of frequent use, the scale was reviewed to show potential users the strong and weak points in the scale's administration and interpretation. Scales that received little attention, were not in a needed area, and reported reliability estimates less than .60 were excluded from the evaluation section. However, all scales that were located were listed, and a reference or a source was given.

A pervasive issue was the judgment about scale validity. Generally, except in the case of a needed area or frequent use, those scales were excluded that did not show a minimally adequate level of content validity. Content validity was defined as systematic evaluation of the items and their relationships to concepts being tested. If evidence for validity was available, an effort to locate relevant

SEARCH AND SELECTION OF SCALES FOR REVIEW

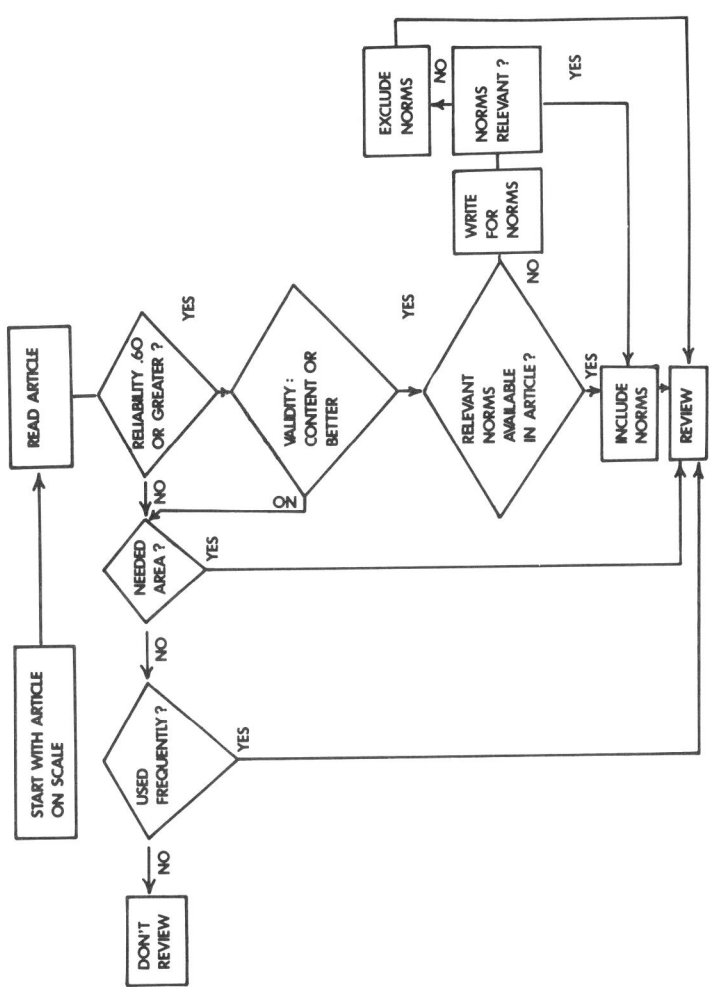

FIGURE 3. Scale selections.

norms was conducted. When norms were not presented in articles describing the scale, the authors were contacted for this information. The availability of norms was positively weighted in the decision to review the scale.

REVIEW

In 1974, the American Psychological Association (APA) published the revised *Standards for Educational and Psychological Tests*. These *Standards* are intended to apply to any assessment procedure, device, or aid that leads to the making of inferences about the characteristics of persons, and are among the most thoughtful and well-developed criteria for such tests. In this section we will examine the *Standards,* identify the major issues in our gathering of scales as related to them, and note the points of departure of the present scales from them. Some minor criticisms will be included with analyses of major deficits, but an effort has been made to keep some perspective. George Bernard Shaw's derogation of newspaper reporting—as seemingly unable to discriminate between a bicycle accident and the collapse of civilization—is a potential hazard here as well. Thus,

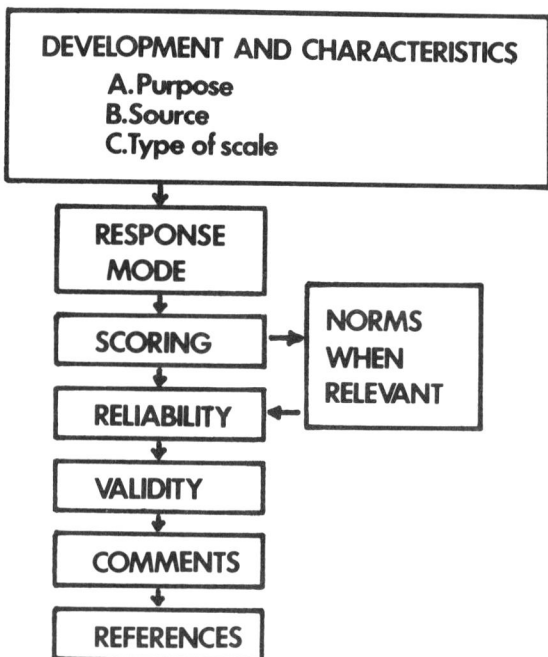

FIGURE 4. Organization of scale reviews.

our critiques will attend more to the major shortcomings of a scale. Figure 4 presents the sections that are covered in each review.

Development and Characteristics

The *Standards* call for tests to be accompanied by manuals that describe the development of the test, its rationale, revisions, references, common misuses, purposes, applications, and all necessary information for administration and interpretation. The manual should similarly describe the theory underlying the test's development, and who is qualified to administer and interpret the results. The *Standards* state: "A test manual should describe fully the development of the test: The rationale, specifications followed in writing items or selecting observations, and procedures and results of item analysis or other research" (p. 11). Yet in the process of locating and examining more than 400 scales, we rarely found accompanying manuals. In no case was the manual sufficiently developed and adequate to meet the stringent *Standards*.

In view of the lack of well-developed manuals, our scale reviews follow a format designed to provide the reader with pertinent information (which might otherwise be available in a manual) that is needed to appropriately select, use, and interpret criminal justice scales. Six sections were included in each review. The introductory section is concerned with the scale's *development and characteristics* and includes a statement of the scale's purpose, a description of the method and procedures used in its construction, and a general characterization of its final version.

Response Mode and Scoring

Some of the standards are to assure administration under standardized conditions and scoring under controlled circumstances. For example, "The directions for administration should be present in the test manual with sufficient clarity and emphasis so that the test user can duplicate, . . . the administrative conditions under which the norms and the data on reliability and validity were obtained" (APA, p. 18). The *Standards* also require that the examinee be sufficiently prepared for the examination through sample material or instructions, that the procedures for scoring be presented with a maximum of detail and clarity, and that means of taking into account interrater variability of scoring be noted. Some of the scales reviewed here meet these conditions. Often they are group administered tests with brief instructions and objective, explicit scoring procedures.

The administration and scoring procedures are described in separate sections within each of the scale reviews. The first section is the *response mode* description of the behaviors expected of the respondent. This information should be valuable, since the research may be limited by the types of responses that can be requested from different groups of respondents because of their age, reading levels, and manual dexterity. The second section is a presentation of *scoring* procedures that indicates the format used for attaining scale values and whether individual, group, or machine scoring procedures are utilized.

Norms

The *Standards* require, at the time the test is released for operational use, that norms be presented that refer to "defined and clearly described populations," which are comparable to the populations being tested. In our examination of crime and delinquency scales, this standard was rarely followed. Local norms were typically not available, means and standard deviations were only sometimes reported, and transformations of raw scores to standardized scores were infrequently present. In fact, for the overwhelming majority of tests studied, little or no normative information was presented.

Reliability

Reliability refers to the consistency within the scales (internal consistency), over time (temporal stability), or between different forms of the scales (parallel forms). Reliability defines the extent to which "the results of testing are attributable to systematic sources of error." All the unsystematic errors that affect the results are sources of unreliable information. The *Standards* require evidence of reliability, including estimates of the standard error of measurement, since this is important for assessing whether a scale is reliable enough for intended uses and subjects. It is essential that the stability of the test scores over time be reported along with identification of the time intervals and the characteristics of the different subjects. The *Standards* also require that parallel form reliability information be presented.

Reliability information may take several forms. Standard estimates of internal consistency, such as item-to-total and item-to-item correlations may be used, and may include coefficient alpha and other variations of the Kuder–Richardson correction formula. Also, factor loads from factor analyses (when present) are reported as evidence of internal consistency. Measures of temporal stability, such as test–retest procedures, are also important data when considering the value of a scale. If an instrument does not yield consistent results from one testing to the next, one must question whether the variable purportedly being measured is likely to fluctuate over time. If the variable is known to be relatively stable and scores change from test to retest, there is reason to believe that the scale is not measuring the appropriate concept. This type of reliability estimate can be made by readministering the same scale or by administering another version of the same scale (parallel form). Another type of reliability measure frequently presented is a measure of interrater reliability. This estimate is used predominantly with rating scales. It may be presented as a Pearson correlation coefficient or as some type of difference estimate.

Our reviews report these data as well as other information that reflect on the reliability of the instrument. Occasionally, intuitive statements by the developer are included when they add to the ability to evaluate the usefulness of a scale.

Validity

The *Standards* state that the purposes of a scale and its applications must be explicit and that the test should help users to make correct interpretations. Frequently, however, the articles in which scales are presented only loosely or casually relate to scale interpretation. This practice increases the difficulty of discovering the appropriate uses of an instrument. Most of the scales presented here, therefore, do not have rigidly defined boundaries and are in need of further exploration of their usefulness. Thus, it is not surprising that there is little hint of validity in most of the tests we reviewed. Large numbers of tests were developed on a one-time basis on unspecified samples with ill-defined criteria and with the results reported in skimpy terms. Furthermore, mail inquiries to scale developers often provided no further information about the development features of these scales. Even when investigators did respond, it was not unusual for them to present negative views of the scales, including, occasionally, that its development was futile. Thus, of the review components, the *validity* section was the most difficult to synthesize.

Where information that testifies to the ability of the instrument to carry out its purpose was available, it has been presented. A developer's attempts to demonstrate the validity of a scale sometimes took the form of correlating the scale with other measures of similar concepts or with measures of concepts that are believed to be related theoretically (concurrent and/or construct validity). Predictive (or criterion) validity may be estimated by a correlation between the test score and a predictive criterion. Results of factor analytic work are considered factorial validity. Even positive results from hypothesized relationships between the variable supposedly measured by the scale and other variables are considered supportive. Finally, those scales that have no evidence or questionable evidence of validity are subjected to a systematic and careful review of the items as a check for content validity.

Comment

The *comment* portion of our reviews departs from the objective nature of the preceding sections and consists of evaluative and summary evaluations. We hoped that our judgments in this section would promote a critical perspective and provide evaluative information not available from other sources.

There was a great temptation, when writing the comment, to end each review with the phrase "Further research is indicated." Instead, we note here that essentially all the scales offered in this book need further research. By presenting the work and pointing to the strong and weak areas, we believe researchers in the future can be aided in avoiding previous problems and in remedying mistakes of other investigators.

References

The *references* section presents a list of the publications that were cited in the text of the review. This section is not always inclusive of all studies on a scale; however, it does include the important studies cited within the review.

THE SCALES AND THE STANDARDS: MEASURING UP

Measured against the *Standards,* the number of adequate crime and delinquency scales is very small indeed; meaningful validity, reliability, normative, and manual information are rarely present. Thus, if the reader is seeking tests on which to make individual decisions about persons with whom they are concerned, we strongly urge caution and selective choices. For the most part these scales do not lend themselves to immediate predictive use or for distinctions between persons. They are not instruments that yield a reliable diagnosis. They do not allow decision making about delinquents, criminals, prisoners, probationers, police officers, and, indeed, college professors. Nor do they apply to agency decision making; that is, a policy-making decision should not be based solely on these scales and techniques.

At this point, the discerning reader should ask, "What value is this work if so little of it allows for individual or agency decision making? If the characteristic state of knowledge is amorphous, how can one justify investing time in these scales?" These are questions that we have seriously considered. After all, one possible conclusion of our efforts was that the best one could do would be to vigorously discourage the use of all the valueless tests. In the same sense, William Stern, the German psychologist who coined the terms *intelligence quotient* and *mental quotient* saw the great misuse in the 1920s of intelligence testing and was reported to have sent one of his disciples to the United States with explicit instructions to "Kill the IQ." Not only has the IQ survived, but intelligence testing has also survived and flourished and developed over time into one of the more reliable and valid psychometric procedures.

Our work reflects belief in the worth of assessment and in the important role that valid and reliable tests can have in understanding the nature of crime and criminal justice phenomena. Our commitment then in preparing this book is to make knowledge accessible, to share information, and to allow researchers and practitioners to have the most current and full perspective of potentially relevant instruments. If, as a result of this work, some instruments that have previously been misused or ill-used suffer a quick, professional, and scientific death, their demise will not be premature. H. L. Mencken, in *Prejudices: Sixth Series,* observed that one of the crying needs of the time is for a suitable Burial Service for the admittedly damned. But we are not optimistic that this compendium will stop the use of inappropriate instruments in research and practices. Many such instruments have a life of their own and through fads or bad judgment such devices continue to appear in scientific literature. Rather we are hopeful that our reviews will promote further development and refinement of the promising scales and greater accountability in their use. In fact, there are many scales that deserved greater attention and development. The questions we asked were, "Why didn't the author do a reliability study on this test?" or "Why didn't the individual take the next logical step in the development of this scale?" or "If only this developer had cross-validated his/her scale, this would be a useful and important research device."

So how can further research be mobilized toward gathering needed information for the scales? Well, we issue a clarion call to all students searching for masters theses or doctoral dissertation topics and to all crime and delinquency researchers and practitioners. Read the scale reviews, look at the suggestions, pick up the challenge, and pursue these needs in crime and delinquency research.

When we have encountered scales that have been carefully developed, and present reliability and validity information, we have responded with enthusiasm. Indeed, if there is an overly positive set in an evaluation, it reflects the context in which scales are viewed. In the midst of hundreds of scales that are minimally useful or totally useless, there are many that are developed hastily and not presented or published in fully descriptive forms. It is no wonder then that we do tend to treat the small virtues in crime and delinquency scales as grand accomplishments. Our source for this perspective is that of W. S. Gilbert, who presents the definitive position of molehill-to-mountain transformation:

> King Borria Bungalee Boo
>   Was a man-eating African swell;
> His sigh was a hullabaloo,
>   His whisper a horrible yell—
>   A horrible, horrible yell.
>
> W. S. Gilbert,
> *Pirates of Penzance, Pinafore, Mikado, and Bab Ballads,*
> "King Boria Bungalee Boo"

The reader, therefore, is implored to temper our enthusiastic huzzahs and yells with kindness, as our amplified whispers of praise contrast with the clatter and roars of criticism and condemnation.

CHAPTER 3
Using This Handbook

No single conceptual or disciplinary framework exists for research dealing with crime and delinquency psychometrics. In addition, the diversity of the research literature, as found in criminological, psychological, sociological, political science, anthropological, or law journals, tends to make researchers (including us), conceptually limited by discipline and by the looking glass of their experiences and journals. Nevertheless, we have tried to cut across scholarly fields and periodicals to create a conceptualization for one effort that would be most useful to the researcher and practitioner.

We have organized this volume in the following ways. We categorized scales by their *targets*. By this term we refer to the object of the assessment, which may be a phenomenon, such as a crime, a group, such as law enforcement officers, or an institution, such as criminal courts. We then distinguished targets from *respondents*, which refer to the subject of the assessment. For example, in the scale called *Inmates Perception of Significant Others*, the inmates (respondents), rate 13 target groups, including people in general, physicians, police, and themselves. Obviously, it is possible for individuals who serve as respondents to be identical with targets in some scales. We also distinguished targets from scale *purpose*, which refers to the type of assessment devices utilized, including attitude measurement (Likert, Guttman, Thurstone scaling, etc.), behavior ratings, personality assessments, milieu ratings, prediction techniques, and description procedures. The purposes of a scale affect its targets and respondents. For example, when the purpose of the scale has been personality assessment, the targets and respondents are identical. When the purposes are to describe behavior and measure attitudes, it is not unusual to see targets and respondents differ. Many attitudes toward crime scales have this particular discrepancy, and can be seen in its attitude of the general public when they rate specific deviant behaviors or groups.

The targets are divided into seven groups, each of which is presented and described in separate chapters.

1. *Law enforcement and the police:* The process of law enforcement, and officers and/or agencies responsible for policing.

2. *Courts and the law:* The judiciary as an institution and as a process; includes probationary personnel and others who participate in judicial activities.
3. *Corrections:* Institutions, processes, and policies relating to confinement and other social control after conviction. Included are prisoners, guards, parole officers, and prisoner treatment staff.
4. *Delinquency:* Juvenile crime and offenders, including persons in need of supervision. Includes social processes associated with juvenile violations.
5. *Offenders:* Adults who have acquired the formal status of criminal offenders but who are not necessarily currently involved as prisoners or parolees in the corrections process.
6. *Crime and criminality:* The phenomena of law violation and law violators.
7. *General scales:* Citizens in general, as well as specific groups of noncriminals.

In each chapter, following the target presentations, each set of scale purposes is listed.

1. *Attitude measurement:* Scales that attempt to assess relatively enduring evaluative judgments about and emotional reactions to the targets. Typically, these instruments are Likert scales, Guttman scales, or the Thurstone method of equally appearing intervals.
2. *Behavior ratings:* Instruments that rely on the observation and recording of past or present behavior, including self-ratings as well as ratings by others of observable behaviors.
3. *Personality assessment:* Scales that attempt to measure typical or consistent psychological and internal components of targets.
4. *Milieu ratings:* Instruments used to describe a social, structural, or organizational climate or environment.
5. *Prediction:* Scales used to identify future components of the target's behaviors. These components may include adjustment, skills, observable behaviors, or test results.
6. *Description:* Any systematic procedure used to catalog or compile other behaviors, components, or aspects of the target, including case histories, perceptual measures, and peer judgments.

These six purposes reflect common groupings and do not always indicate neat or easy divisions. Some predictive instruments, for instance, were made up of behavior ratings. In the cases when two such clear purposes emerged, the scale is presented or listed in the first to appear, and cross-referenced later. When we did not know how to place a scale, it was put under "description," a general enough heading to cover both our thinking deficits and miscellaneous scales.

By their nature, some purposes have been little valued or investigated in the literature. Few milieu ratings relevant to crime and delinquency have been undertaken, for example. And since milieu ratings are directed toward places and not people, the category of "milieu ratings-offenders" has no entries. In contrast, several target-by-purpose units show especially extensive research and the development of many scales. The category of "prediction-corrections" shows the large number of investigations and many efforts to predict parole success and prison adjustment.

This handbook faces the problem of serving two audiences. One consists of persons who use scales because of the requirements of a project, because funding agencies dictate assessment components, because they want to see the results of a new training or treatment technique appear in a journal, or because their graduate instructors argue convincingly that research calls for measurement, and measurement calls for formal observation, ratings, or scales. The other audience consists of researchers who are much more familiar with scales as tools. These persons are more aware of the intricacies of scale development, reliability, and validity issues. The two types of users might see different things in the scale reviews. The former may find too much technical detail in each report whereas the latter may lament a lack of more technical detail. We hope that both users will realize the need for a middle ground and be able to select the material that they need or wish to take from the text.

CHAPTER 4

Ethical Issues and the Protection of Human Subjects

Ethical concerns about research are usually presented in books and reports specifically written on such topics. They are not considered in most scales and scale collections. Yet, these concerns do apply sufficiently to the use of research scales that special attention seems necessary. This chapter will present ethical problems that arise in the development and use of these scales and will indicate the ways in which these issues might be addressed. The points of departure are the contemporary history and standards for human subjects research.

The last two decades of behavioral and biomedical research in the United States have seen an increasing awareness of the need for the protection of the rights of human subjects. Traumatic exposés and violations of the rights of subjects have come to the public attention. For example, human subjects research in prisons today has been compared to the mistreatment of prisoners in the concentration camp experiments during World War II (Palmer, 1976). Certainly, the revelations of the injection of live cancer cells into nonconsenting patients at a nursing home and the discovery of the research with untreated syphilis patients in Tuskegee, Alabama, represent two cases that have made human subjects protection a matter of public and professional concern.

These same issues apply to justice system research. In her book, *Kind and Usual Punishment* (1973), Jessica Mitford has identified the kinds of medical experiments that frequently occur in justice settings. For example, Mitford reported experiments that were performed on the efficacy of Vitamin C medication and treatment for scurvy, long after the nature and cure of this disorder had been known to medical researchers and practitioners. In this and many other cases, prisoners have been submitted to noxious, unjustified research conditions.

At the case level, a series of federal court decisions continue to define the boundary between individual rights and society's right to coerce. At the policy level, there have been ethical statements by justice agencies, federal departments, and scholarly associations concerned with offender research. Many of these statements have been directed at drug and medical research but have encompassed social-science studies as well. The American Correctional Association (1976) issued a statement on human experimentation with prisoners essentially condemning such investigations in part because "the assessment of risks attached to human experiments is ordinarily beyond the competence of those who bear the ultimate responsibility for approving human research projects" (p. 14).

Other agencies and associations have developed standards for research that echo the theme of caution and consideration. Thus, the American Psychological Association task force on the role of psychology in the criminal justice system states that correctional psychologists sometimes feel:

> They are damned if they do and damned if they don't: condemned as "having something to hide" if they fail to pursue vigorously the evaluation of their services and vilified as turning prisoners into "guinea pigs" as soon as they ask people to fill out a form. (Monahan, 1980, p. 10)

The task force concluded that research into psychological services in criminal justice actually is both necessary and possible. For individuals to participate in research under the 1974 APA ethical standards, a high degree of informed consent, confidentiality, and minimum of harm without deception is required. In 1976, the National Commission for the Protection of Human Subjects in Biomedical and Behavioral Research issued a comprehensive report and a set of recommendations. The recommendations were subsequently implemented (Office of the Secretary, HEW, 1978) for all HEW supported research and encompassed federal, adult, and juvenile prisoners, persons in jails and in diversion programs, and mentally disordered offenders in security hospitals. Following a review by an institutional review board, permitted research was limited to:

(a) Study of the possible causes, effects, and processes of incarceration, provided that the study represents minimal or no risk and no more than inconvenience to the subjects;
(b) Study of prisons as institutional structures or of prisoners as incarcerated persons, provided that the study presents minimal or no risk and no more than inconvenience to the subjects; or
(c) Research on practices, both innovative and accepted, which have the intent and reasonable probability of improving the health and well-being of the subject. (p. 1053)

In addition, such organizations as the Fraternal Order of Police and the unions of correctional officers have developed the case for the necessity of protecting the rights of justice agency employees. In any setting, either formal or informal, approval by these employee organizations is required before full participation in research by the employees will be allowed. Indeed, the requirement that individuals take questionnaires for promotion, for internal research, or any other intra-agency purpose has emerged as one bargaining issue between unions and administrators of such public agencies.

CRIME AND DELINQUENCY SCALES AND THE PROTECTION OF HUMAN SUBJECTS

The protection of subjects in research using these scales is an important issue. Every research procedure has the potential to intrude on the privacy or the well-being of those who have taken the scales. This is true for research scales as well as scales used for deciding a person's fate. Although the scales that are used exclusively for research have much less potential for such harm and such intrusion, the line between scales used for research and scales used in decision making lies within the hands of the investigators and the agency. More than one research study has found itself transformed immediately into policy decisions and indeed some researchers see the particular value of their own work as just such a theoretical-to-applied metamorphosis.

In the use of crime and delinquency research scales, two kinds of ethical issues relating to human subjects may be identified. The first set of ethical issues relate to the scales themselves: their construction, psychometric characteristics, methodology, publication, and descriptions. The second set of ethical issues lies within the application of the scales. For each instrument and assessment procedure chosen by a researcher, the dimensions of potential intrusiveness, harm, and safeguards of the procedure should be assessed. Both sets of issues suggest the following questions as guides in evaluating human subject protection.

1. *Is there significant harmfulness in the outcome or content of the assessment procedure itself?* The harmfulness question may be posed in several ways: Is a pejorative label required as a result of the assessment? Will terms like "future delinquent," "possible troublemaker," or "violence-prone" be used? Would any research-acquired assessment or label become known to the subjects, to peers, or to program supervisors? Could the procedure or its content bring background or borderline problems of behavior into the foreground? Could it exacerbate existing adjustmental difficulties, especially in vulnerable individuals?

Arguments have been stated both for and against any labeling in prediction research. On the one hand, it has been suggested that only through careful longitudinal investigations and *a priori* predictions can delinquency (or any other behavioral phenomenon) be understood. Careful controls can and do protect the identity and welfare of research subjects. On the other hand, it has been suggested that *a priori* labeling and predictions, when accessible to virtually anyone, even researchers in the laboratory, have ways of influencing individuals' behaviors and future lives.

These labeling consequences may properly be considered secondary harmfulness and certain minimum preventive precautions are in order. The data should be kept separate from agency records and research information should not be used in administrative decisions. Confidentiality should be maintained and the identifying information should be destroyed or coded and locked.

If labeling effects represent secondary harmfulness, then the negative impact of the scales or questions in the assessment should be viewed as primary harmfulness. If harm were to occur, it most likely would be immediate and usually visible. Thus, for the vulnerable subjects, careful observation and ready referral for treatment would be necessary. Yet, there may be some nonobvious continuing harm. For example, over the course of 10 years of police training, we have received a repetitive request from at least two dozen officers. In each case, the officer reluctantly approached, asked about the meaning of personality tests, and then derogated the value of figure drawings. The officer then slowly revealed how he had taken such a test in the seventh or eighth grade and had been told by his teacher that he had hidden homosexual tendencies. With the confession and the subsequent discussion, it always became apparent that some concern still existed and that nonobvious anxiety about the diagnostic process had been maintained. The presence or absence of such tendencies was not at issue.

2. *Is there routine use of informed consent for subjects?* Although the term *informed consent* arose out of medical settings, where it is used to describe knowledge about and voluntary agreement for surgical procedures, informed consent now applies to behavioral research in all settings. It means that the person knows the nature and likely consequences of the research or actions in which he or she is to be involved. In our review of crime and delinquency research scales, informed consent forms were rarely used or their use was omitted from the published reports. This may be because there is little knowledge relating to the potential harm from the group-administered, pencil-and-paper tests that constitute most of these research instruments. In addition, it is generally assumed that these tests are minimally harmful because of the attitudinal nature of so many scales and the brief, low-level intrusion with which the research usually is conducted. Unfortunately, however, the assumption may not always be supported in the particular setting or with the particular research being conducted. Informed consent should routinely be obtained in writing, even with juvenile and prison subjects who may not be able to consent fully and freely. The basic principle is:

> Ethical research practice requires the investigator to respect the individual's freedom to decline to participate in research or to discontinue participation at any time. The obligation to protect this freedom requires special vigilance when the investigator is in a position of power over the participant. (American Psychological Association, 1973, p. 42)

Indeed, in four prisons in which consent forms were used, it was reported that 98% of the subjects felt that they had been given correct and accurate information (Tannenbaum & Cooke, 1976) and favorably viewed their paid participation in these studies.

3. *To what extent is deceit used in the procedure?* By deceit we mean that subjects believe one procedure (or none) is undertaken while the major concern is another aspect not known to them. Many of the scales reported here are straightforward opinion or behavior rating scales in which no deceit whatever is

used in their application. In the cases of ratings of subjects by peers or supervisors, gathering of case history information, among other procedures, a secondary level of deceit may be inferred. That is, the manipulations or evaluations may be conducted in ways that are not known to the subjects. One of the authors (Brodsky) visited a penal institution that was having a major debate about making available to the inmates the rules that govern the institution. When he asked why the administrators would not make written rules available, he was informed that if the inmates knew the rules and had them written down, they would find dozens of ways of getting around them and manipulating the staff for their own purposes. Thus, the written rules were withheld. In a related sense, a withholding of information that individuals are serving as subjects in research may be considered a level of deceit that occurs with some moderate frequency in crime and delinquency scales. Such deceits should be undertaken only after outside evaluators assess the risk–benefits ratio of the research.

4. *What are the particular human subject sensitivities in the settings in which the assessment procedure is used?* Research in justice agencies and into justice processes calls for especially aware ethical judgments. The potential for self-fulfilling prophecies and for cumulative labeling impact is great. This need for sensitivity contrasts with the often stated reports of prisoners that they have no objections whatsoever to research participation. Indeed many prisoners welcome the break from an otherwise monotonous and sometimes noxious routine. The fact that they participate in such a rigid, dull, daily life means that the attraction to participate even in uneventful as well as intrusive research procedures, is strong. Thus, the investigator must be sensitive to the context in which the individual subject is living and for that reason should view the protection of the rights of the subjects with special care.

5. *Are subjects debriefed?* Debriefings are procedures in which the participating subjects are told, after the experiment or data collection, the nature of the data collected, what is going to be done with it, and why the research was undertaken. Subjects have the right to such information. Debriefings take place in a number of settings. Few debriefings, however, have been noted in the research reports examined and presented here. In the utilization of these scales, it is recommended that a debriefing be routinely undertaken and that it be recorded in the article or document summarizing the nature of the research.

6. *Are claims of the value of findings overstated?* Researchers who are working at preliminary stages of scale development often become enthusiastic about the potential for their research. It is not unusual for a modest, preliminary study or scale to be touted as a grand discovery, divinely inspired, which will resolve most criminological and human dilemmas. This behavior usually represents bad professional judgment, but it is often not harmful. While overstatements are grouped in the general category of ethical issues here, this is a judgment issue; some exaggerations of scale virtues can simply be considered questions of taste, expansiveness, and reporting style. Such braggadocio is unethical, however,

when it leads to premature or excessive reliance on inadequately developed scales, either in research or practice.

7. *Are race, sex, and setting limitations noted?* When scales are standardized and developed on one racial group, or on male or female subjects only, or in one setting, the generalizability of the scale is limited. Yet, developers often fail to indicate the limits of applying even preliminary results to other settings and samples. Thus, an important ethical and judgmental procedure for scale users is to note carefully the fundamental characteristics of the standardization group, including the racial and sexual composition, the age, and the setting, and to use that information when drawing conclusions about the utility of the scale.

8. *Is the identity of subject confidential?* It is of primary importance that subjects be protected from the repercussions of the research. It is also important that a subject's responses not be used in individual diagnosis or treatment. It is therefore, imperative that confidentiality be maintained.

CONCLUSION

> It is not necessarily a zero sum game in which every gain for prisoners' rights and integrity represents a loss for research rigor and scholarly methodology. Rather the potential for cooperative improvement in which prisoners and institutions alike are allied with the goals of the research may yield more productive and meaningful and humane findings that serve the interests of the human subjects and scientific pursuits alike. (Brodsky, 1980, p. 87)

And so it is for scale development and usage. The ethical concerns and precautions may contribute to a more empathic alliance between researchers and subjects, in which mutual understanding and progress may result. It is with this perspective that we now turn to a review of crime and delinquency research scales.

CHAPTER 5
MMPI and CPI Special Scales

The special scales developed from the *Minnesota Multiphasic Personality Inventory* (MMPI) and the *California Psychological Inventory* (CPI) merit attention apart from the other scales that will be reviewed. These scales have a number of characteristics in common. To begin with, the scales are embedded in MMPI and CPI general administration and scoring; that is, the entire MMPI or CPI is administered, almost always in groups, to the target population, and then these special scales are scored. The embeddedness is an important factor since it is possible that scales administered separately out of the context of the whole instrument are not comparable to original embedded administrations. Dahlstrom, Welsh, and Dahlstrom (1972) note that "the effects of administering the items of a single scale out of the context of the rest of the item pool have not been established or studied systematically" (p. 18). They do go on to observe that some preliminary research on separate scale administration has been reassuring.

Using items from the MMPI or CPI, one can develop new scales, as, for example, special scales that did not appear in the parent instrument. The MMPI or CPI items may be administered first to large groups of subjects who presumably include many persons high and low on the characteristic under study. Scale development then is empirical. Items are chosen that successfully differentiate contrasting groups on the key variable. An item analysis is employed that selects items appearing with sufficient frequency on either the control or the experimental group and not on the other (using a D statistic). Most frequently, the chosen items are then cross-validated on an independent sample.

The cross-validation often eliminates from research reports many scales that otherwise would be utilized. Thus, Mills (personal communication) has described the development of a police personality scale. Using new police officers in training, he found 55 MMPI items that differentiated between high- and low-promising officers. In a cross-validation, only five items successfully differentiated between two new samples, and the scale was discarded.

The development of new scales does not always employ the empirical procedure of a study of contrasting groups. A typical alternate methodology was employed by McLachlan (1976) in the development of his MMPI Hostility Scale. He began by combining existing content validity scales relating to hostility. Then he performed a content analysis of the combined items and used the surviving items to make up his hostility scale.

Developing subscales within existing MMPI or CPI scales is a second area of scale development. In this instance, the overall concept that is measured is perceived as insufficiently specific for the purposes at hand. Thus, subscales are developed to allow particular research or applications. The subscale constructions follow a number of methods. Cluster analysis is the procedure employed by Stein, Gough, and Sarbin (1966) in their development of three subscales within the socialization scale of the CPI.

Using a similar method, Harris and Lingoes (1955) performed a five-part content analysis of the MMPI Psychopathic Deviate *(Pd)* Scale. These subscales can be used in clinical as well as in research applications.

The content analysis procedure and the few items that are produced are weaknesses in the subscale development. The quality of the content analysis is dependent on the instructions and the perspective of the judges, and content analyses sometimes have suspect reproducibility. Further, the comparatively few items in subscales have a potential for leading to low reliability of subscales.

Some of the CPI and MMPI scales have assumed a special prominence in criminal justice research. These scales have had several validation studies and have come to represent particularly important applications to crime and delinquency. The remainder of this chapter identifies and describes those scales. For the CPI, the *Socialization, Delinquency Proneness, CPI-Z,* and *Law and School Difficulty* scales are reviewed. For the MMPI, The Megargee offender classification system and a list of criminal justice relevant scales are presented, and the *Sociopathy* and *Overcontrolled Hostility* scales are reviewed.

CALIFORNIA PSYCHOLOGICAL INVENTORY

The *California Psychological Inventory* is a group-administered, paper-and-pencil test of personality that contains 480 items, 12 of which are repeated. The CPI is one of the most carefully developed of all objective personality instruments. Megargee's (1972) handbook for the CPI reviews thoroughly the development, philosophy, and nature of the CPI scales, discusses interpretation and conceptualization of the scales, and describes research and evaluation applications. The CPI user is referred to this handbook for comprehensive information on this test instrument.

Of the 18 usually scored CPI scales, three have particular relevance to crime and delinquency research. These scales are Socialization *(So)*, Responsibility *(Re)*, and Self Control *(Sc)*. Of these, by far the most important is the *So* scale, which is designed to measure delinquency and the dimension of asocial to social behaviors. The *So* scale has been consistently successful in assessing socialization and differentiating delinquent from nondelinquent groups. In his review, Megargee (1972) concludes "an impressive array of data have accumulated, demonstrating the concurrent, predictive, and construct validity of the CPI Socialization Scale in the United States and elsewhere. There seems to be little doubt that the *So* scale is one of the best-validated and most powerful personality scales available" (p. 65). Stein, Gough, and Sarbin (1966) conducted a cluster analysis of the CPI *So* scale on 318 males, both delinquent and nondelinquent. Three clusters emerged, which were called *stability* (stable home and school adjustment), *optimism* (optimism and trust in others), and *control* (observation of convention versus asocial roles and attitudes). The items for the *stability* cluster are, scored positively—396, 336, 214, 420, 302, 431, 164, 428; and scored negatively—168, 212, 367, 223. The items for the *optimism* cluster are all scored positively except number 245, which is scored negatively. These items are 398, 416, 94, 156, 345, 184, 457, 327, 435, 385. The *control* cluster consists of the following three items scored positively: 393, 36 and 339, and the following five items scored negatively: 323, 373, 389, 409, 198. Scoring consists of a simple sum method based on the keyed items answered in the indicated direction.

In an independent sample, a cross validation yielded the means shown in Table 3, with significant differences by t test between paired means.

This method is of considerable importance because it is one of the few very carefully developed attempts to subdivide or prepare subscales for the *So* scale of the CPI. Again, because of the careful development, extensive validity results and wide use of the *So* scale, these clusters and subscales would appear to be valuable to criminological and delinquency research.

The *Sc* and *Re* scales have been much less successfully validated than the *So* scale. As indicated by its title, the *Sc* scale is intended to assess the adequacy of self-control and self-regulation. The *Re* scale is intended to assess traits of felt conscientiousness, responsibility, and dependability. Inconsistent results have emerged from the validation research on both scales.

Our attention here will be directed to one example each of a special CPI scale, a special scoring, and a moderator variable that relate to crime, delinquency, and criminal justice research with the CPI.

TABLE 3. Delinquents and Nondelinquents Compared on Three *So* Clusters

	Delinquents ($N = 121$)		Nondelinquents ($N = 121$)	
	$\bar{X}$	SD	$\bar{X}$	SD
Stability	2.43	1.69	6.64	2.63
Optimism	6.27	2.22	7.75	1.99
Control	4.06	1.58	5.69	1.35

Delinquency Proneness Scale

The *Delinquency Proneness Scale* (DPSL) of the CPI was developed by Lovegrove to distinguish between samples of delinquent and nondelinquent adolescent male youth. The rationale for developing this scale in addition to the *So* scale of the CPI was that the *So* scale sample consisted largely of institutionalized individuals, whereas the DPSL was developed primarily on boys on probation. Thus, the plan was to create a more sensitive instrument for discriminating delinquency proneness.

A sample of 78 delinquent boys was drawn from 68 Melbourne, Australia youths on probation and 10 in an institution for delinquent offenders. They were compared with 116 nondelinquent youth, all nonoffenders matched for age. The 12 repeated items of the CPI were deleted for this analysis as were 18 other randomly selected items. After conducting a first item analysis, 69 items remained; after a second level of item analysis, 40 items finally were present.

Scoring consists of assigning a value of 1 for each true or "scored" response, a value of 2 for each "false" response, and then adding 10 to this score. The delinquent subjects had a mean delinquency proneness score of 42.1 and a standard deviation of 5.5; the nondelinquent subjects had a mean of 51.2 and a standard deviation of 4.9.

The scale construction sample was used in all the validation information, thus seriously limiting the potential utility of such research. Using a cutoff score of 48 in the construction sample, the DPSL identified as "delinquent-prone" 68 delinquents and 28 nondelinquents. It identified as "not delinquent prone" 10 delinquents and 72 nondelinquents. Furthermore, in comparing the DPSL to 6 scales identified in a prior factor analysis of the CPI, the range of correlations ran from $-.01$ to $+.74$ with a modal correlation of .26. Lovegrove (1973) observed that the factor structure of the DPSL was very similar to that of the *So* scale, but that the *So* scale is more important in assessing lack of feelings of adequacy and well being.

The DPSL has many of the same purposes of the CPI *So* scale. The validity information is incomplete, but promising. The scale developers' assertion that the *So* scale and the DPSL are not psychologically equivalent still remains to be supported. The DPSL remains decidedly inferior to the *So* scale in delinquency research, but, nevertheless, the DPSL is more carefully developed and shows greater promise than most general test scales used in delinquency research.

The CPI-Z: Interpersonal Maturity Measurement

A method of measuring interpersonal maturity using five scales of the *California Psychological Inventory* (CPI) was developed by Gottfredson and Ballard (1963), in conjunction with the Social Agency Effectiveness Study, which produced the *Interpersonal Personality Inventory* (IPI). The theory of interpersonal maturity of Sullivan, Grant, and Grant (1957) postulates that the maturity classification of an offender will allow an appropriate treatment classification and a subsequent productive change in a group-living situation.

Over a period of several years, beginning in 1958, all adult male felons entering California reception–guidance centers were routinely administered the CPI and the IPI along with other tests. With the goal in mind of a possible method of "after-the-fact" maturity classification, 156 men appearing for parole consideration were randomly selected and tested with the CPI and the IPI. An additional 141 men served as a cross-validation sample. The data indicated that the Dominance *(Do)*, Responsibility *(Re)*, Tolerance *(To)*, Good Impression *(Gi)*, and Self Control *(Sc)* scales of the CPI accounted for most of the variance in IPI scores. Weights were assigned by multiple-linear regression (yielding CPI-Y scores) and discriminant analysis (CPI-Z scores) function to give the best separation of "high" and "low" IPI maturity groups.

The following formula was used to derive the CPI-Y score from the raw scores of the five CPI scales:

$$\text{CPI-Y} = .30 + .26\, Do + .24\, Re + .89\, To - .12\, Gi - .24\, Sc$$

The formula for the CPI-Z score was:

$$\text{CPI-Z} = .5\, Do + 1.2\, Re + 1.5\, To + .1\, Gi - 1.0\, Sc$$

Since CPI-Y and CPI-Z scores correlated .96, only the CPI-Z score was reported in detail. Suggested CPI-Z score cutoff points for maximum discrimination with minimum misclassification were: 41 or less, low maturity; 42–46, unclassified; 47 or above, high maturity. In the validation sample, this scheme yielded nearly 16% unclassified and about 30% misclassified.

CPI-Y and CPI-Z scores can be calculated with any groups for whom the scores on these five CPI subtests are known. The manual presents mean CPI-Z scores for 19 male groups and 11 female. Frequency and percentage distributions and standard scores for each CPI-Z score are given for the validation and construction samples. The mean CPI-Z score for the validation sample ($N = 302$) was 42.29.

Reliability data for the CPI scales employed were taken from test–retest administrations of the full CPI by Gough (1960) for 200 California prison males. The test–retest sessions were separated by 7 to 21 days. Test–retest correlations for the individual scales were: *Do,* .80; *Re,* .85; *Sc,* .86; *To,* .87; *Gi,* .81.

Two indices of validity were presented in the manual. The first used the combined construction and validation groups ($N = 302$) reported by Ballard *et al.* (1963) in developing the IPI. All subjects had been classified as high- or low-maturity level by independent interview. The biserial correlation coefficient between CPI-Z scores and interview-rated maturity level was .51.

The second indication of validity of CPI-Z scores was based on the mean

CPI scores of the 30 occupational, educational, patient, and inmate samples (Gough, 1960). Nine correctional staff ranked the average social-maturity level of the various samples. The rank order correlations between the median judges' rankings and the mean CPI-Z score rankings were .85 for males and .88 for females.

The careful, empirical development, extensive norms and large amount of inmate data make the CPI-Z score useful for assessment of inmate maturity levels. The CPI-Z score has adequate reliability, and offers substantial concurrent validity support with the IPI and promising construct validation, as well. The utilization of the CPI-Z has been restricted by the limited professional access to the research, and little further work has been pursued. This derived score appears to have considerable potential for use in the context of interpersonal maturity theory.

The Law and School Difficulty Scale

The *Law and School Difficulty Scale* (LS) was developed by Stein, Vadum, and Sarbin (1970) to serve as a moderator variable in dealing with problems of false negatives and false positives on the CPI *So* scale. From a sample of 996 boys of high-school age, including institutionalized delinquents, noninstitutionalized delinquents, and non-delinquents, 30 matched pairs of true and false negative delinquents and 27 matched pairs of true-and-false positives were selected, using an *So* cutoff score of 30. The LS scale is a series of items developed by Kulik (1966) for rating deviant behavior on a five-point scale ranging in frequency from "never" to "four or more times." When the *So* scale was used with this sample alone, with a cutting score of 29.5, the results showed 72.5% accurate prediction to the legal criterion. When the *So* cutting score was employed together with a cutting score of 14.5 on the LS, the accuracy became 87.5%—a significant increase.

THE MMPI

The *Minnesota Multiphasic Personality Inventory* is a 566 item, true-false test that may be administered to groups or to individuals in booklet or card form. Since the original MMPI scales were developed over 40 years ago (Hathaway Monachesi, 1938), hundreds of special scales and thousands of research studies have been conducted with this instrument. Once source reported 5028 published MMPI articles through 1978 (Buros, 1978), and the MMPI has been described as ". . . the most extensively researched instrument in personality assessment" (Alker, 1978). In one review of MMPI developments, King (1978) has asserted that the MMPI is matchless for the objective assessment of psychopathology and ". . . still holds the place as the *sine qua non* in the psychologist's armamentarium of psychometric aids" (p. 938).

The MMPI has had the widest applications to criminal justice and crime of any psychological test. Of equal significance in understanding crime and delinquency applications is the intent of the test developers. Dahlstrom, Welsh, and Dahlstrom (1975) point out that "integral to the development of the basic set of MMPI scales was a concern for the kinds of decisions required in effectively administering a criminal justice system" (p. 60), and especially for coping with problems of delinquents. In the original scales, the primary vehicle for achieving these objectives was through the Psychopathic Deviate *(Pd)* Scale, a 50-item scale developed by item analyses of psychiatrically examined young offenders compared to mostly older, married, rural Minnesota normals and to college control subjects.

In their review of psychological test research with criminals, Waldo and Dinitz (1967) reported that the CPI and the MMPI and particularly the *Pd* scale, differentiated between offenders and nonoffenders more often and better than any other measure. In 28 of 29 MMPI studies, significant differences were found. The *Pd* scale has been especially productive when evaluated in combination with other scales. A description of these combinations and patterns is available elsewhere (Dahlstrom *et al.*, 1975, pp. 60–74).

Fourteen scales are routinely scored and interpreted on the MMPI. Because the plethora of existing literature addresses these issues so thoroughly (e.g., Butcher, 1969; Marks, Seeman, & Haller, 1974), present attention is directed toward specially developed scales and procedures relevant to offenders and criminal justice.

Megargee Classification System

Early in the study of MMPI results with offenders, it became clear that a key, meaningful task was distinguishing among offenders, who are themselves a heterogeneous group. The most far-reaching and comprehensive such effort has been undertaken by Megargee (1977), working with young prison inmates confined at the Federal Correctional Institution in Tallahassee, Florida. Using hierarchical profile analyses, Megargee identified and then cross-validated the existence of 10 discrete MMPI types among offenders. The criteria were behavior ratings, case histories, institutional actions, interviews, and other psychological data gathered over a three-year period.

This new classification transforms MMPI elevation and profile patterns into offender-specific types. The Megargee research has triggered a series of other studies with the typology, both assessing its applications to varying correctional populations and searching anew for types, using the same methodology and new populations.

The Megargee method is of considerable importance because it offers an extensive taxonomic data base, a reliable and cross-validated MMPI-based typology, and a system that allows for economical and logical ways of distinguishing among offenders for both research and programmatic reasons.

Computer Systems

Working within a state prison department, Panton has developed several scales to assess corrections-specific behaviors and potential. The scales include the *Parole Violator Scale,* the *Adjustment to Prison Scale,* and the *Assaultive Sexual Offender Scale.* Panton (1970) has developed a computerized system for scoring the MMPI on the special scales, issuing a prisoner classification profile, and suggesting anticipated prisoner adjustment problems.

Fowler (1974), in contrast, has used the standard MMPI profile and scales, in limited combination with separate correctional scales. His system is also used for prisoner classification and produces a narrative statement of personality interpretation, drawn from a computer library of interpretive sentences for different MMPI patterns.

Separate Scales

Beyond the primary 14 MMPI scales, over 500 additional scales have been developed. These separate scales are listed with item scoring instruction in Dahlstrom, Welsh, and Dahlstrom (1972) and Dahlstrom *et al.* (1975). The most frequent method of scale development was item analysis using contrasting samples, one group containing and one group without the variable under consideration. Often cross-validations have been undertaken.

Many of these scales are at preliminary stages of development with few investigations available to the potential user. Two studies have addressed the validity of the separate scales relating to hostility and antisocial behavior. Megargee and Mendelsohn (1962) attempted to cross-validate 12 MMPI scales of hostility and control. Johnson (1975) performed a cross-validation of 17 MMPI measures of antisocial behavior. Both studies reported that the separate scales failed to be validated or produced significant results in the direction not predicted.

Nevertheless, these scales are of interest for a historical perspective as well as for their specificity. Furthermore, some scales have shown impressive discerning abilities in limited studies. Some examples of the research scales will be reviewed shortly. A count of the separate scales shows that over three dozen crime and delinquency related scales have been constructed. Table 4 contains a listing of scales that are abstracted primarily from the Dahlstrom *et al.* (1972, 1975) handbooks.

Sociopathy Scale

Beginning with the observation that the "psychopathic" profile occurs as a combination of scale elevations, O'Hagan (1972) developed the Sociopathy *(Spy)* Scale as a single measure of "the degree to which an individual possesses those basic personality components which underlie the constellation of characteristics and behaviors described by Cleckly as defining the psychopathic personality" (p.

TABLE 4. Separate MMPI Scales Relevant to Crime and Delinquency Research

Name of scale		Reference	Number of items
Adjustment to prison	Ap-r	Beall & Panton, 1959	36
Acting-out hostility	AH	Foulds, Caine, & Creasy, 1960	13
Authority problems	Pd2	Harris & Lingoes, 1968	11
Delinquency	De	Gough & Peterson, 1952	12
Delinquency	Dq	Hathaway & Monachesi, 1957	33
Delinquency (females)		Kanun & Monachesi, 1960	91
Delinquency (males)		Kanun & Monachesi, 1960	59
Escapism	Ec	Beall & Panton, 1957	41
Factor scale IV (Acting out)		Eichman, 1962	20
Familial discord	Pdl	Harris & Lingoes, 1955/1968	11
Habitual criminalism	Hc	Panton, 1962	77
Hostility	Ho	Cook & Medley, 1954	50
Impulsivity	Im	Gough, 1957	27
Inhibition of aggression	Hy5	Harris & Lingoes, 1955/1968	7
Judged manifest hostility	Jn	Siegel, 1956	47
Neurotic overcontrol	No	Block, 1953	18
Neurotic undercontrol	Nu	Block, 1953	33
Nonoverlapping purified	Pd	Adams & Horn, 1965	20
Obvious psychopathic deviate	Pd-O	Weiner & Harmon, 1946	28
Parole violation	PaV	Panton, 1962	26
Pedophile	Pe	Toobert, Bartleme, & Jones, 1959	24
Psychopathic deviate	Pd	McKinley & Hathaway, 1944	50
Psychopathic manipulation		Finney, 1965	22
Pure psychopathic deviate		Welsh, 1952	18
Recidivism	Rc	Clark, 1948	24
Self alienation	Pd4B	Harris & Lingoes, 1955/1968	15
Social alienation	Pd4A	Harris & Lingoes, 1955/1968	18
Social imperturbility	Pd3	Harris & Lingoes, 1955/1968	12
Social responsibility	Re	Gough & McClosky, 1951	32
Social responsibility (revised)	Re-r	Gough & McClosky, 1951	20
Socialized delinquency	SD	Tsubouchi & Jenkins, 1969	47
Subtle psychopathic deviate	Pd-s	Weiner & Harmon, 1946	22
Suppression and outbursts of hostility		Finney, 1965	24
Unconscious acting out of hostility		Finney, 1965	14

6). Three successive item analyses yielded 20 items that discriminated psychopaths from normals. The subjects in a validation study were 30 inmates scoring in the upper 20% on the *Spy* scale and 30 inmates scoring in the lowest 20%. The high *Spy* subjects were rated as showing more psychopathic traits by the researcher, and scoring higher as predicted in one of three Quay behavioral classification measures. The high *Spy* subjects also scored lower on the CPI *So* scale and on prison adjustment ratings.

The Sociopathy Scale

True:	21	91	181	280	412
	28	99	250	391	533
False:	96	148	172	201	378
	138	171	183	332	509

Overcontrolled Hostility Scale (O-H)

When Megargee and Mendelsohn (1962) observed that existing separate MMPI scales intended for this purpose failed to discriminate assaultive from nonassaultive individuals, the construct of overcontrolled hostility was developed. Assaultive persons were seen as two types: those with few inhibitions against expression of aggression—the chronically undercontrolled—and those with massive inhibitions against the expression of any anger or aggression—the chronically overcontrolled. The assaultive actions of the overcontrolled occur with extreme intensity, the potential having accumulated from repeated, undischarged instigations to aggression. Thus Megargee, Cook, and Mendelsohn (1967) developed a 31-item scale to discriminate the overcontrolled assaultive criminal from undercontrolled assaultive subjects, nonviolent criminals, and normals.

The O-H scale in use emerged as the most successful of six provisional scales in detecting all 39 extremely and moderately assaultive criminals, while minimally misclassifying the nonviolent subjects. The O-H distribution among extremely assaultive criminals shows a bimodal pattern; very high among the overcontrolled subjects and average among the undercontrolled subjects. The items are passive and nonaggressive. Several cross-validations by Megargee, his students, and other investigators have generally affirmed the construct validity of the O-H scale.

The O-H Scale

False:	1	90	129	165	290	395	475
	30	102	130	181	329	439	501
	81	109	141	183	382	466	534
True:	73	229	333	394	488		
	91	319	373	425	559		

SUMMARY

In contrast to the great diversity of other crime and delinquency research measures, those drawn from the CPI and the MMPI have much in common. They are taken from standardized instruments administered under controlled conditions, with known stimulus properties and validity indicators. The CPI and MMPI measures will frequently be instruments of choice in research on personality and psychodynamics of offenders.

CHAPTER 6

Law Enforcement and Police

This chapter encompasses a variety of scales that refer to law enforcement or police agencies. Unfortunately, in the case of many scales, these terms are used simply with the assumption that the respondents understand the concepts and use them in the same way as researchers. In other cases, however, specific policing functions are identified and described.

As noted in Chapter 3, a standard order of scale presentation is followed. First the *attitudes* scales are presented, followed by the *behavior ratings, personality measures, milieu ratings, prediction measures* and finally the very broad category of *description*. After the reviews are completed within each subcategory, other scales in that category are listed. (See Chapter 2 for a description of the criteria that were used in deciding upon whether a scale would be reviewed or simply listed.) Listed scales are presented by title and bibliographic reference, followed by a very brief description. The listing typically reports the number of items, the format (true-false, Likert-type, or other format), and the scale objectives. If a current review is available to the scholarly public, this is noted as well.

In this chapter, by far the largest numbers of reviews and listings are for attitude scales. Nine are reviewed and ten are listed. This heavy weighting reflects the attention that attitudes toward police have had in criminological research. While most of the attitude scales are concerned with the public's views of the police, the description scales in this chapter focus much more on views and experiences of police officers, and ratings performed by police officers. Thus, the *Foot Patrolman Observation Test* and *Police Task Preference Questionnaire* are reviewed as measures of needed skills and activity choices, respectively. Finally, most of the scales reported here have been developed in the 1970s. Assessment and measurement related to law enforcement is a fairly recent phenomenon and one that seems to be accelerating in both production and use—a most welcome trend.

LAW ENFORCEMENT ATTITUDE SCALES: REVIEWS

Attitudes toward Police (Competence–Hostility)

Development and Characteristics

The *Attitudes toward Police Scale* (ATPS) developed by Love (1973) was designed to measure two dimensions of attitudes toward police: (1) the perceived competency of police; and (2) the perceived hostility of the police for others. The ATPS began with a set of 29 items that were believed to measure hostility and 25 items designed to measure competency. After these were administered to 52 junior and senior high school students, 13 items from the competency scale and 16 items from the hostility scale were eliminated as poor discriminators or because they produced low item-to-total correlations. This left a total of 12 competency items and 13 hostility items.

Response Mode

The test items are short statements about the police followed by two columns of blanks designated "yes" and "no." Subjects are instructed to read the statements and check the "yes" blank if they agree and the "no" blank if they disagree.

Scoring

Two scores are obtained: one for the perceived competency of the police and one for the perceived hostility of police. A procompetent response and a prohostility response each receives a score of 1. Then each scale score is summed so that the higher the score, the more competence the subject is assumed to assign to the police, and the more hostile the subject feels that police are to him or her.

Norms

No standardized norms are presently available, but for a group of 14 black activists and 11 small-town police officers, the data in Table 5 were obtained.

TABLE 5. Attitudes toward Police of Black Activists and Police Officers

	Competency mean	Competency SD	Hostility mean	Hostility SD
Black activists	3.50	3.00	11.00	2.10
Police officers	9.00	2.01	2.00	1.39

Reliability

Test–retest correlations (product–moment) for 42 high school social studies students over a three-month period are .76 for the competency dimension and .68 for the hostility dimension. Intraclass correlations, which measure more precisely the agreement between the two administrations, were .62 and .73, for competency and hostility, respectively. Coefficient alphas were .79 and .85 for competency and hostility and the homogeneity ratios were .19 and .29, respectively.

Validity

Criterion groups were compared as a check for validity; when the scores of the 14 black student activists were compared to those of 11 small-town police officers (see Table 5), the police officers scored significantly higher on the competency scale and the black student activists scored significantly higher on the hostility scale ($p < .001$).

Comments

This test shows adequate reliability and validity which indicates that it may be a useful tool. Improvements, however, might be sought concerning a number of issues. First, the sample used to validate the instrument is sufficiently small to question the replicability of the results. For this reason, cross-validation attempts would be highly desirable. Another issue of concern is the fact that the questions in the scale contain the word "cop"—this may tend to bias responses. Finally, there is some question as to the general conceptualization of the test. Both scales are simple, evaluative instruments, and there may be a strong interrelationship between the two scales which should be investigated.

REFERENCES

Love, N. J. *Juvenile attitudes of hostility-competency toward the police as a function of progression through the juvenile justice system.* Unpublished master's thesis, Southern Illinois University at Edwardsville, 1973.

ATTITUDES TOWARD POLICE
(COMPETENCE-HOSTILITY)

Put a check (✓) if you agree with statement.
Put a cross (x) if you disagree with the statement.

Competency Items

Item
2. A lot of cops are awfully dumb.
5. Most cops are smart enough to do a good job.
8. A lot of cops are not very good at their work.
9. Most cops are good at protecting people.
10. Cops often make some pretty dumb mistakes.
11. Most cops are pretty good at their job.
13. Cops try to help all they can.
15. Cops do the best job they can.
17. Cops are good at keeping law and order.
18. Most cops are very dedicated to their work.
23. Cops do a good job in most cities.
25. A lot of cops don't really care about enforcing the law.

Hostility Items

Item
1. Cops are usually fair with kids.
3. Cops usually provide good protection for kids like me.
4. Cops never believe you even when you're telling the truth.
6. Cops usually don't give you a chance to explain.
7. Cops usually treat kids right.
12. Most cops think they're big shots.
14. Cops get smart with you when you ask a question.
16. Cops always blame kids when things go wrong.
19. Cops are usually not respectful toward kids like me.
20. Cops are usually pretty nice guys.
21. Cops are okay for grownups, but watch out if you are a kid.
22. A lot of cops think they're really smart.
24. A lot of cops carry grudges against kids like me.

Attitude toward Police (Semantic Differential and Likert Formats)

Development and Characteristics

The *Attitude toward Police Scale* designed by Phillips and Coates (1971) is really two scales. One is a 19-item Semantic Differential using "police" while the other is an 11-item Likert-type scale. The development of the scales began with an original pool of 35 adjectives for use in the Semantic Differential and 27 Likert items (14 positively worded and 13 negatively worded), which were administered to: (1) members of a campus chapter of CORE (undergraduate blacks) ($N = 33$); (2) a class of police instructors with approximately four years of police service ($N = 20$); (3) a group of college graduates ($N = 24$); and (4) a group of upper level sociology and education students ($N = 40$). These groups produced a total sample of 117 males from whom responses to the 62 items were requested. Items which yielded an item-to-item correlation coefficient of .6 or greater within each of the two scales were retained.

Response Mode

For the Semantic Differential, the respondent is asked to make a checkmark to evaluate the target (police) along a 7-point continuum between an adjective pair such as violent . . . peaceful. The Likert-type uses a standard 5-point scale in which the respondent reads a statement and then marks (1) "Strongly Agree," (2) "Agree," (3) "Neutral," (4) "Disagree," or (5) "Strongly Disagree."

Scoring

Each item is coded in the directions of positive valence for police. Then a summation of item scores yields the degree of positive evaluation of police for each of the two scales. Therefore, the higher the scores on both scales, the more positive one's attitude toward police.

Norms

Table 6 shows the mean responses for each of the groups tested.

Reliability

Because of the method of scale construction, all items have item-to-total correlations of .6 or greater. In addition, split half-correlations reported were .92 for the semantic differential and .84 for the Likert scale.

TABLE 6. Distribution of Response Means by Criterion Groups[a]

Criterion group	Semantic differential scale Scale positions							
	1	2	3	4	5	6	7	N
CORE	0	2	9	18	4	0	0	33
Sociology	0	0	4	5	10	6	0	25
Graduates	0	2	5	7	8	2	0	24
Education	0	0	0	5	6	4	0	15
Police	0	0	0	0	6	11	3	20
	0	4	18	35	34	23	3	117
	gamma = .58							

	Likert scale Scale positions					
	1	2	3	4	5	N
CORE	0	9	21	3	0	33
Sociology	0	4	6	15	0	25
Graduates	0	7	10	7	0	24
Education	0	0	5	9	1	15
Police	0	0	0	10	10	20
	0	20	42	44	11	117
	gamma = .62					

[a] A summated score was computed for each respondent on each scale (with a possible range of 19–133 for the Semantic Differential scale and 11–55 for the Likert scale). For clarity of presentation, these scores were divided by the total number of items on each scale (19 and 11), and respondents were assigned to categories by rounding the resulting figure to the nearest integer.

Validity

A systematic review of the items indicates content validity. Further, support for validity by criterion groups can be seen in the tables in the Norms subsection. The CORE and police groups showed the extreme positions (negative to positive, respectively) and other groups ordered themselves in between.

In addition to the two scales, respondents were asked to "indicate whether they considered their feelings toward the police were Strongly Positive, Mildly Positive, Mildly Negative, or Strongly Negative." When the responses to this question were compared to the scale scores, much agreement was found. The gamma values obtained for the Semantic Differential scale and the Likert scale were .89 and .97, respectively.

Comments

These two scales seem to be useful in research. They discriminate well between extreme positions, but the use of the highly contrasted comparison groups does not offer information about more subtle differences in attitude. Thus, there is a need for testing more criterion groups, and for cross validation with independent samples.

REFERENCES

Phillips, J. L., & Coates, R. Two scales for measuring attitudes toward police. *Wisconsin Sociologist,* 1971, *8,* 3–19.

ATTITUDE TOWARD POLICE

Instructions. The following pairs of adjectives might be used to describe the police. Rate the police according to each adjective pair by placing a check (√) at the point between the two words which best describes the police.

1. violent ___:___:___:___:___:___:___ peaceful
2. lazy ___:___:___:___:___:___:___ industrious
3. intelligent ___:___:___:___:___:___:___ unintelligent
4. just ___:___:___:___:___:___:___ unjust
5. irresponsible ___:___:___:___:___:___:___ responsible
6. illegal ___:___:___:___:___:___:___ legal
7. nice ___:___:___:___:___:___:___ awful
8. rude ___:___:___:___:___:___:___ polite
9. clean ___:___:___:___:___:___:___ dirty
10. important ___:___:___:___:___:___:___ unimportant
11. honest ___:___:___:___:___:___:___ dishonest
12. unfair ___:___:___:___:___:___:___ fair
13. foolish ___:___:___:___:___:___:___ wise
14. cruel ___:___:___:___:___:___:___ kind
15. cowardly ___:___:___:___:___:___:___ brave
16. unlikeable ___:___:___:___:___:___:___ likeable
17. discourteous ___:___:___:___:___:___:___ courteous
18. valuable ___:___:___:___:___:___:___ worthless
19. pleasant ___:___:___:___:___:___:___ unpleasant

Instructions. Following are some statements with which you may agree or disagree. Beside each statement write the symbol which best represents your position on that statement.

Symbol	Feeling
SA	Strongly Agree
A	Agree
N	Neutral
D	Disagree
SD	Strongly Disagree

1. Policemen try to protect things which belong to you.
2. Police often overstep their legal authority.
3. On the whole, policemen are honest.
4. Policemen are pretty nice guys.
5. Things would be better off if there were fewer policemen.
6. Policemen don't care what happens to you after they pick you up.
7. Police enjoy kicking people around.
8. Policemen are a great help to folks.
9. The police are unresponsive to the lower-class community.
10. Policemen are just as crooked as the people they arrest.
11. Police do an excellent job of enforcing the law.

Attitude toward Police Questionnaire

Development and Characteristics

The *Attitude toward Police Questionnaire* was designed to measure a variety of feelings held by young people toward the police (Bouma, 1969). This questionnaire was originally developed in a study of the relationship between young people and police in which the major emphasis was the degree of mutual hostility. The first use of the questionnaire involved approximately 10,000 students whose individual item responses were analyzed separately. Even though the purpose of the scale was to measure general attitudes toward police, items were included that also measured attitudes toward school teachers, willingness to cooperate with police, and respondents' perceptions of attitudes toward police held by their friends and parents.

The final version of the questionnaire contained 57 items that deal directly with attitudes toward the police and other authority figures.

Response Mode

The test is a paper-and-pencil type containing 57 questions to which the respondent is asked to answer either "yes," "no," or "not sure," by placing a checkmark in the appropriate space.

Scoring

This instrument is not a formal scale. That is, no cumulative score was tabulated to represent the entire set of items.

Norms

Because scores have not been calculated, the major analysis of this questionnaire has been in the form of cross-tabulation and percentages of "yes," "no," or "not sure" responses to individual questions. The normative data in Bouma (1969) consists of tables contrasting student–group responses by race and other characteristics.

Reliability

No efforts to estimate the reliability of this questionnaire were reported. However, Bouma and Williams (1972) used the questionnaire to measure attitude changes over one year toward the police within school systems that had police counselor programs as compared with school systems that had none. Their findings indicated significantly more posttest negative attitudes in the control school that had no counselor programs. Thus in the no treatment condition, temporal stability was not found.

Validity

No efforts to validate the entire questionnaire were reported. However, systematic inspection of the items indicates high content validity. It is questionable whether the 57 items of the questionnaire represent one dimension that can be labeled "attitudes toward police." Some of the questions refer to attitudes toward police; some to perceived parents' or friends' attitudes toward police; some to perceptions of police treatment of others; some to the degree to which one might assist a police officer in his or her duty; some to attitudes towards teachers and principals and other authority figures in general; some to an individual's direct experience with the police. The degree to which many independent attitudes are assessed in not established and this impairs the test's value.

Comments

The validity of the test has not been established. It is intended as a measure of attitudes toward police, but only individual item responses are useful. As a unidimensional scale, scores would be uninterpretable. It appears likely that several factors are operative in the responses to this questionnaire and a test for homogeneity of variance could resolve some of these issues. Further, tests for reliability are of little value until scoring and validity questions have been resolved.

This set of items is still a loose set of questions, rather than a scale. The concepts that were used in developing the items and the items themselves, however, appear to have potential as a measure of attitudes toward police.

REFERENCES

Bouma, D. *Kids and cops: A study of mutual hostility.* Grand Rapids, Michigan: William B. Eerdmans Publishing Co., 1969.

Bouma, D., & Williams, D. G. Police school liaison: An evaluation of programs. *Intellect,* 1972, 119–122.

ATTITUDE TOWARD POLICE QUESTIONNAIRE

1. Do you think that policemen are pretty nice guys?
   Yes_____ No_____ Not sure_____
2. Do you think that the city would be better off if there were more policemen?
   Yes_____ No_____ Not sure_____
3. Do you think that the police try not to arrest innocent people?
   Yes_____ No_____ Not sure_____
4. Do you feel that police are always picking on Negroes?
   Yes_____ No_____ Not sure_____
5. Do you think that police don't even give you chance to explain?
   Yes_____ No_____ Not sure_____
6. Do you feel that policemen treat rich boys the same as poor boys?
   Yes_____ No_____ Not sure_____
7. Would you like to be a policeman as a future job?
   Yes_____ No_____ Not sure_____
8. Do you think that the police have it in for, or pick on, young people?
   Yes_____ No_____ Not sure_____
9. Do you feel that most policemen would let you buy your way out of trouble?
   Yes_____ No_____ Not sure_____
10. Do you think that the police think they are "big shots" because they wear a badge?
    Yes_____ No_____ Not sure_____
11. Do you think that police are always picking on the guy who has been in trouble before?
    Yes_____ No_____ Not sure_____
12. Do you think that being a policeman is a good job for an intelligent guy?
    Yes_____ No_____ Not sure_____

LAW ENFORCEMENT AND POLICE

13. Do you feel that policemen treat all people alike?
    Yes_____ No_____ Not sure_____

14. Do you think that the police are mean?
    Yes_____ No_____ Not sure_____

15. Do you think that the police can steal and get away with it?
    Yes_____ No_____ Not sure_____

16. If you needed help, would you go to the policemen?
    Yes_____ No_____ Not sure_____

17. Do you think that the police treat blacks and whites alike?
    Yes_____ No_____ Not sure_____

18. Do you think criminals usually get caught?
    Yes_____ No_____ Not sure_____

19. Do you think police accuse you of things you didn't even do?
    Yes_____ No_____ Not sure_____

20. Would you tell the police if you saw a friend break into a store?
    Yes_____ No_____ Not sure_____

21. Would you call the police if you saw a friend stealing a car?
    Yes_____ No_____ Not sure_____

22. Would you tell the clerk if you saw a friend take some small items from a store without paying for them?   Yes_____ No_____ Not sure_____

23. Would you tell the police if you saw a friend commit a murder?
    Yes_____ No_____ Not sure_____

24. Do you think police treat members of all churches alike?
    Yes_____ No_____ Not sure_____

25. Do you think police treat all nationalities alike?
    Yes_____ No_____ Not sure_____

26. Do you think the police get criticized too often?
    Yes_____ No_____ Not sure_____

27. Do you think the police are strict in one district and not in another?
    Yes_____ No_____ Not sure_____

28. Do you think people would be better off without the police?
    Yes_____ No_____ Not sure_____

29. Do you think teachers and principals treat all pupils alike?
    Yes_____ No_____ Not sure_____

30. Do you think that teachers and principals treat Negro and white students alike?
    Yes_____ No_____ Not sure_____

31. Do you feel that teachers and principals treat rich students the same as poor students?   Yes_____ No_____ Not sure_____

32. Do you think that teachers and principals are pretty nice guys?
    Yes_____ No_____ Not sure_____

33. Do you think that being a teacher is a good job for an intelligent guy?
    Yes_____ No_____ Not sure_____

34. Do you think that teachers and principals are always picking on the guy who has been in trouble before? Yes_____ No_____ Not sure_____
35. Do you think that teachers and principals are mean? Yes_____ No_____ Not sure_____
36. Do your friends think that the police treat Negro and white people alike? Yes_____ No_____ Not sure_____
37. Do your friends feel that policemen treat rich boys and poor boys alike? Yes_____ No_____ Not sure_____
38. Do your friends think that policemen are pretty nice guys? Yes_____ No_____ Not sure_____
39. Do your friends think that police are "big shots" because they wear a badge? Yes_____ No_____ Not sure_____
40. Do your friends think that police are always picking on the guy who has been in trouble before? Yes_____ No_____ Not sure_____
41. Do your friends think people would be better off without the police? Yes_____ No_____ Not sure_____
42. Do your friends think that the police are mean? Yes_____ No_____ Not sure_____
43. Do your friends think that the police can steal and get away with it? Yes_____ No_____ Not sure_____
44. Do your friends think that the police accuse you of things you didn't even do? Yes_____ No_____ Not sure_____
45. Would your friends call the police if they saw another friend break into a store? Yes_____ No_____ Not sure_____
46. Would your friends call the police if they saw another friend steal a car? Yes_____ No_____ Not sure_____
47. Would your friends tell the clerk if they saw another friend take some small items from a store without paying for them? Yes_____ No_____ Not sure_____
48. Would your friends tell the police if they saw another friend commit a murder? Yes_____ No_____ Not sure_____
49. Do your parents think people would be better off without the police? Yes_____ No_____ Not sure_____
50. Do your parents think that policemen are pretty nice guys? Yes_____ No_____ Not sure_____
51. Do your parents feel that the police treat Negro and white people alike? Yes_____ No_____ Not sure_____
52. Do your parents think that the police are "big shots" because they wear a badge? Yes_____ No_____ Not sure_____
53. Do your parents think that police are always picking on the guy who has been in trouble before? Yes_____ No_____ Not sure_____
54. Do your parents think that the police treat rich people and poor people alike? Yes_____ No_____ Not sure_____

55. Do your parents think that the police are mean?
    Yes____ No____ Not sure____
56. Do your parents think that the police can steal and get away with it?
    Yes____ No____ Not sure____
57. Do your parents think the police accuse you of things you didn't even do?
    Yes____ No____ Not sure____

Law Enforcement Perception Questionnaire

Development and Characteristics

The *Law Enforcement Perception Questionnaire* (LEPQ) was developed by Lee (1970) over a 12-year period while serving as a law enforcement officer and interacting with law enforcement officials. The LEPQ consists of 30 items all having the words "law enforcement" in them. The manual reports that the items were selected from those that survived empirical tests, although no information about the nature of the tests is provided.

The 30 items are divided into 3 subtests of 10 items. The first subtest, Items 1–10, is designed to tap attitudes toward the job (difficulty, pay, danger, opportunity), the second subtest, Items 11–20, is designed to tap attitudes toward the value of the job (satisfaction, respect, standards) and the third, Items 21–30, assesses attitudes toward characteristics of people in law enforcement work (intelligence, dedication, loyalty).

Response Mode

Respondents are requested to rate agreement or disagreement with a statement contained in each item by checking one of six scale points from +3 (I agree very much) to −3 (I disagree very much) on the first 20 items, and by circling "more," "just as," or "less" on the remaining 10.

Scoring

Scores are computed by assigning the values 6 to each "+3" that was circled, 5 to each "+2," 4 to each "+1," and so on. Values of 2, 4 and 6 are assigned to "more," "just as," and "less," respectively. Of the items 12 of 30 are reversed for scoring (see scale items, p. 57). Higher scores are associated with positive attitudes toward law enforcement jobs and personnel on Subtests A and B (Higgins, 1975), and with negative attitudes on Subtest C.

TABLE 7. LEPQ Norms

Subject groups	Subtest A Attitude toward jobs		Subtest B Value of law enforcement		Subtest C Characteristics of people in law enforcement	
	$\bar{X}$	SD	$\bar{X}$	SD	$\bar{X}$	SD
Basic trooper school (N = 51)	40.5	4.7	22.4	3.9	28.9	4.5
First basic police school (N = 49)	39.4	5.2	24.0	4.8	29.8	4.4
Second basic police school (N = 47)	40.9	4.7	24.2	5.4	20.2	5.1
Experienced policemen (N = 13)	36.4	5.1	21.4	3.5	30.6	4.5
College students (N = 48)	40.7	4.3	26.2	5.0	38.4	5.4
Hard-core unemployed (N = 33)	36.2	4.5	33.4	7.1	39.0	6.3
Convicted felons (No information reported)	36.4	7.1	34.1	7.3	39.8	8.5
Delinquent girls on parole (N = 23)	36.5	4.8	31.7	6.2	36.6	6.8
Delinquent girls on probation (N = 23)	36.9	5.3	31.5	5.7	38.2	4.5

Norms

Unfortunately, the method of computing norms across the three subscales is not explained. Subtest means are presented in Table 7 for seven samples, including the subject groups already noted (Higgins, 1975).

Reliability

Three temporal reliability coefficients have been reported: test–retest reliabilities for the two police school groups were +.408 and +.707 while the test–retest reliability in the correctional psychology class used for the norms was +.646.

Validity

Validity information is presented in the form of the differences in means between the normative groups. Partial item analyses indicate that some items discriminate among the four groups; the items in Subtest A do not appear to discriminate among them, while those in Subtests B and C do. There is no additional supporting validity information.

Comments

This test presents a short, easily understood, and simple set of items for use in determining perceptions of law enforcement work and officers. The scoring system is unnecessarily complicated, with high scores indicating positive attitudes on Subtests A and B, and negative attitudes on Subtest C. Sparse validity data limits its utility. The subtests were developed on an a *priori* basis, no reliability information is available for the subtests, and rather low reliability for the full scale. The overt nature of the items probably makes any use questionable with populations motivated to fake good or bad answers. The scale, however, does offer the potential user normative information that distinguishes well in the expected directions on Subtests B and C.

REFERENCES

Higgins, G. M. *The law enforcement perceptions questionnaire: Revised manual.* Munster, Indiana: Psychometric Affiliates, 1975.

Lee, J. F. *Manual for the law enforcement perception questionnaire.* Brookport, Illinois: Psychometric Affiliates, 1970.

LAW ENFORCEMENT PERCEPTION QUESTIONNAIRE

Rate your agreement or disagreement with each statement according to the following values:

+ 3 "I agree very much"
+ 2 "I agree on the whole"
+ 1 "I agree a little"
-1 "I disagree a little"
-2 "I disagree on the whole"
-3 "I disagree very much"

1. Law enforcement work is rather difficult compared to other kinds of jobs.
2. Law enforcement work is generally a lonely job.

*3. Law enforcement work is well-paid compared to other jobs.

*4. Law enforcement work is more challenging than other jobs.

5. Law enforcement work makes less demands on an officer's time than other jobs.

6. Law enforcement jobs in general do not call for a great deal of formal education.

*7. Law enforcement jobs in general do not require a great deal of physical labor.

8. In general, law enforcement work is more dangerous than other types of work.

9. Law enforcement work is boring compared to other kinds of jobs.

*10. Law enforcement work offers more opportunity for advancement than other kinds of jobs.

11. Law enforcement work is more personally satisfying to the individual than other kinds of jobs.

12. Law enforcement is an absolutely necessary function in our society.

*13. The average person does not realize how his own life and property are protected by law enforcement.

14. Law enforcement is as essential to our society as medical services.

15. A competent law enforcement officer makes as much of a contribution to a society as a competent teacher.

16. The standard for becoming a law enforcement officer should be very high.

*17. In general, society gives law enforcement the support that it deserves.

*18. Any average person, given the proper training, can become a good law enforcement officer.

19. The law enforcement officer should receive as much respect from the community as the businessman.

20. I would be pleased for my child to go into law enforcement work as a lifetime career.

Circle One: (More — Just As — Less)

21. People in law enforcement work tend to be (more — just as — less) honest than the average person.

22. People in law enforcement work tend to be (more — just as — less) intelligent than the average person.

23. People in law enforcement work tend to be (more — just as — less) loyal to each other than persons in other groups.

24. People in law enforcement work tend to be (more — just as — less) mature than the average person.

25. People in law enforcement work tend to be (more — just as — less) patriotic than the average person.

*26. People in law enforcement work tend to be (more — just as — less) racially prejudiced than the average person.

*27. People in law enforcement work tend to loaf on the job (more than — just as much as — less than) the average person.

*28. People in law enforcement work tend to take advantage of their position (more than — just as much as — less than) other persons.

*29. Most people in law enforcement work could do (better — about the same — not as well) economically in another kind of job.

*30. Most people in law enforcement work tend to be (more — just as — less) dedicated to their job than (as) persons in other occupational groups.

* Scoring is reversed on these items.

Perceptions of Police Scales

Development and Characteristics

The *Perceptions of Police Test* was employed to "identify particular features of police behavior which are differentially perceived by the police and the people they serve" (Hadar & Snortum, 1975). This test is a composite of six distinct scales. The first is a Semantic Differential scale, which uses as targets "the typical and ideal policeman," and which evaluates these targets using a total of 12 bipolar adjectives—therefore yielding 24 pairs of adjectives. These adjectives are classified into the Semantic Differential's three conceptual dimensions. The activity dimension is measured by the adjectives ambitious-lazy, fast-slow, active-passive. The potency dimension is measured by brave-cowardly, hard-soft, and strong-weak. Finally, the evaluation dimension is measured by the adjectives friendly-unfriendly, smart-dumb, kind-cruel, good-bad, fair-unfair, and honest-dishonest.

The remaining five scales contain a total of 25 Likert-type items. Two of these scales, the *Anomic Authoritarianism Scale* and the *Police Violence Scale*, are minor revisions of scales resulting from a factor analysis of items from a questionnaire developed by Louis Harris and Associates (Kirkham, Levy, & Crotty, 1970). Kirkham *et al.* (1970) factor analyzed the responses of 1,176 adults to form a 25-item test. These items, which came from various sources, formed five basic factors: (1) anomic authoritarianism, (2) political vengence, (3) the acceptance of political violence, (4) police violence, and (5) military violence. Only the 5-item anomic authoritarianism and the 5-item police violence subscales were used as components for the *Perception of Police Test*.

The *Anomic Authoritarianism Scale* attempts to measure the degree to which the respondent values an authoritarian system and authoritarian leadership. The *Police Violence Scale* attempts to measure the perceived use of violence on the part of police. Five items also were present in each of the remaining three scales. *Punitive Morality, Racial Discrimination* and *Youth Discrimination* were constructed from unreported item sources. Items from the *Punitive Morality Scale* deal with questions of severity of punishment for "moral crimes" such as homosexuality, abortion, sex crimes, and so forth. The *Racial Discrimination Scale* consists of items that refer to police interaction with racial minorities. Finally, the *Youth Discrimination Scale* deals with police interaction with youth and youth groups.

Response Mode

This is a paper–pencil type procedure that requires two types of responses. For the Semantic Differential scale, the respondent is asked to concentrate on the target and make an evaluation at some point along the 7-point scale between two extreme adjectives as to her/his judgment about the target. The other five scales are basic Likert-type items consisting of statements about which the respondent is asked to strongly agree, agree, record a neutral response, disagree or strongly disagree.

Scoring

Scores are obtained for each of the three dimensions of the Semantic Differential scale, for a typical and for an ideal police officer. The highest score, 7, represents the least perceived activity possible, the least potency, and the lowest evaluation.

The items for the remaining five scales are arranged so that strong agreement with a positively worded item or strong disagreement with a negatively coded item, counts five points. Strong disagreement with a positively worded item or strong agreement with a negatively worded item counts one point, etc. Thus a *high anomic authoritarianism* score represents a strong feeling in favor of authoritarianism; a high *punitive morality* score indicates a feeling for a strong need to punish moral crimes; a high *police violence* score indicates a belief that the police are not overly brutal in the conduct of their duties; a high *racial discrimination* score represents a belief that police officers do discriminate against racial minorities; and a high *youth discrimination* score indicates the belief that policemen discriminate against youth.

Norms

Table 8 indicates the average score on each of the scales for a total of 202 residents of suburban communities east of Los Angeles and 53 Los Angeles police officers. The residents are divided into three groups: white ($N = 139$), Mexican-American ($N = 17$), and black ($N = 46$).

Caution should be exercised in using these scores as normative data. The fact they were all drawn from communities around Los Angeles indicates possible regional biasing. Although the community residents were initially drawn by random selection from a residential grid map of the adjacent communities, other

TABLE 8. Mean Scores among Police and Ethnic Groups on the Semantic Differential and Attitude Measures

	Mean item scores			
Scale	Police ($N = 53$)	White ($N = 39$)	Mexican-American ($N = 17$)	Black ($N = 46$)
Typical policeman				
Activity	2.53	2.94	3.98	3.38
Evaluation	2.34	2.88	3.73	4.07
Ideal policeman				
Activity	2.01	2.15	2.37	2.43
Evaluation	1.81	1.57	1.83	2.02
Anomic authoritarianism	2.78	2.72	2.73	2.80
Punitive morality	2.66	2.56	2.67	2.21
Police violence	3.00	2.95	2.59	2.44
Racial discrimination	1.90	2.31	2.58	3.15
Youth discrimination	2.68	2.78	3.06	3.26

respondents were included because of lack of availability of the original total sample.

Reliability

Hadar and Snortum (1975) report, in Table 9, item intercorrelation coefficients when corrected for scale size using the Spearman-Brown formula. All the reliability coefficients except *Potency* were within acceptable limits. Because of the low level of homogeneity of response within the potency scale, it was excluded from analyses of the test's validity.

TABLE 9. Perceptions of Police Test:Item Intercorrelations

Scale	r
Activity	.64
Potency	.39
Evaluation	.97
Anomic authoritarianism	.58
Punitive morality	.64
Police violence	.68
Racial discrimination	.71
Youth discrimination	.55

TABLE 10. Police versus Ethnic Groups

	t_{P-W}	t_{P-MA}	t_{P-B}
Typical policeman			
Activity	2.68[b]	2.00[a]	4.32[b]
Evaluation	3.25[b]	5.54[b]	8.21[b]
Ideal policeman			
Activity	.87	1.50	1.83
Evaluation	2.23[a]	.12	1.18
Anomic authoritarianism	.62	.29	.10
Punitive morality	.93	.06	3.50[b]
Police violence	1.38	3.29[b]	5.40[b]
Racial discrimination	4.45[b]	5.04[b]	10.61[b]
Youth discrimination	1.26	2.55[a]	5.21[b]

[a] $p < .05$.
[b] $p < .01$.

Validity

Content validity is good for each subscale. The Likert-type items appear to directly deal with scale content. The Semantic Differential scale has been established in other sources, as has the use of these particular pairs of adjectives.

Factorial validity for the *Anomic Authoritarianism Scale* and the *Police Violence Scale* was established using a sample of 1,176 adults (Kirkham et al., 1970). Those results were obtained from a 25-point scale with other items intermingled and the effects of these item-sets as separate scales is not known.

Multiple t tests were calculated comparing the mean scores on each scale between the groups police (P), white (W), Mexican-American (MA), and black (B). Table 10 indicates the results of those comparisons. Activity and evaluation scores differentiated between police and citizen groups when typical police officer was the target; however, when ideal police officer was the target, only the evaluation score differentiated between police and the white community.

It is difficult to assess validity of each of these scales based on the information presented. The Semantic Differential seems to indicate that there is a difference in police and residents' views of the typical police officer, but not of the ideal police officer. The fact that the *Anomic Authoritarianism Scale* did not differentiate between the groups, indicates that if the scale is measuring authoritarian attitudes the police are no different from the resident groups. The *Police Violence, Racial Discrimination,* and *Youth Discrimination Scales* all appear to be reflecting appropriate directions as hypothesized by the developers.

Comments

This test seems to be a useful instrument for measurement of individuals' perceptions of police officers. Internal consistency measures of reliability are adequate, while content validity is good. The group comparisons, however, do not conclusively support the validity of all scales, especially the *Anomic Authoritarianism Scale*. Indicators of concurrent validity, such as comparison of these scale results with other established scales, would be helpful. In general, this set of scales seems to be useful as a composite test.

REFERENCES

Hadar, I., & Snortum, J. R. The eye of the beholder: Differential perceptions of police by the police and the public. *Criminal Justice and Behavior,* 1975 2(1), 37–54.

Kirkham, J. F., Levy, S. G., & Crotty, W. J. *Assassination and political violence.* New York: Bantam, 1970.

PERCEPTIONS OF POLICE SCALES

Instructions: The following pairs of adjectives might be used to describe a policeman. For the first set imagine you are rating the "typical policeman," indicate your rating according to each adjective pair by placing a check mark (✓) at the point between the two words which best describes the "typical policeman." Then follow the same procedure for rating the "ideal policeman."

Typical Policeman

Ambitious	__:__:__:__:__:__:__	Lazy
Fast	__:__:__:__:__:__:__	Slow
Active	__:__:__:__:__:__:__	Passive
Brave	__:__:__:__:__:__:__	Cowardly
Hard	__:__:__:__:__:__:__	Soft
Strong	__:__:__:__:__:__:__	Weak
Friendly	__:__:__:__:__:__:__	Unfriendly
Smart	__:__:__:__:__:__:__	Dumb
Kind	__:__:__:__:__:__:__	Cruel
Good	__:__:__:__:__:__:__	Bad
Fair	__:__:__:__:__:__:__	Unfair
Honest	__:__:__:__:__:__:__	Dishonest

Ideal Policeman

Ambitious	__:__:__:__:__:__:__	Lazy
Fast	__:__:__:__:__:__:__	Slow
Active	__:__:__:__:__:__:__	Passive
Brave	__:__:__:__:__:__:__	Cowardly
Hard	__:__:__:__:__:__:__	Soft
Strong	__:__:__:__:__:__:__	Weak
Friendly	__:__:__:__:__:__:__	Unfriendly

Smart	___:___:___:___:___:___:___	Dumb
Kind	___:___:___:___:___:___:___	Cruel
Good	___:___:___:___:___:___:___	Bad
Fair	___:___:___:___:___:___:___	Unfair
Honest	___:___:___:___:___:___:___	Dishonest

PERCEPTIONS OF POLICE

Instructions: Following are some statements with which you may agree or disagree. Beside each statement write the symbol which best represents your position on that statement.

Symbol	Feeling
SA	Strongly Agree
A	Agree
N	Neutral
D	Disagree
SD	Strongly Disagree

A   1. People were better off in the old days when everyone knew just how they were expected to act. (+)

E   2. The responsibility for the improvement of police-youth relations lies mainly with the police. (+)

A   3. Everything changes so quickly these days that I often have trouble deciding which are the right rules to follow. (+)

C   4. People blow police brutality way out of proportion. (+)

B   5. Homosexuals are criminals and should be punished. (+)

D   6. Policemen are more rough with black people than with any other minority. (+)

B   7. Gambling should be legalized. (-)

A   8. A few strong leaders could make this country better than all the laws and talk. (+)

D   9. Any black person who becomes a policeman is sold out and should not be trusted. (+)

B   10. Sex criminals should be sent to prison for life for the protection of society. (+)

B   11. Marijuana should be legalized. (-)

C   12. Some people don't understand anything but force. (+)

D   13. Most policemen are out to get race minorities. (+)

D   14. Chicanos are treated better than blacks by the police. (+)

B   15. Any woman who consents to abortion should be arrested. (+)

C   16. Any man who insults a policeman has no complaint if he gets roughed up in return.

D   17. There is substantial racial discrimination on the part of the police. (+)

C	18.	The police frequently use more force than they need to when carrying out their duties. (-)
E	19.	There will always be a gap between the police and youth. (+)
A	20.	What young people need most of all is strong discipline by their parents. (+)
C	21.	The police are wrong to beat up unarmed protesters, even when these people are rude and call them names.
A	22.	Justice may have been a little rough and ready in the days of the Old West, but things worked better than they do today with all the legal red tape. (+)
E	23.	Young people give the police a hard time. (-)
E	24.	Most policemen are out to get young people. (+)
E	25.	There is no discrimination against young people by the police. (-)

Prisoners' Attitude Scales

Development and Characteristics

The *Prisoners' Attitude Scales* (PAS) were designed to measure prisoners' attitudes toward three different targets, the police, law and the judicial system, and lawyers (Alpert & Hicks, 1977). Items for the PAS were drawn from five law scales which were developed by Katz (1931), Rundquist and Sletto (1936), Cleaver, Mylonas, and Reckless (1968), Watt and Maher (1958), and Alpert and Alpert (1977). In an attempt to clarify the constructs being measured and to reduce the number of items, the original item pool was administered to 241 male prisoners in the Washington State Prison System and the responses were factor analyzed. The results were rotated using varimax rotation, and an item factor load of .50 was needed for inclusion in a scale. These criteria produced three factors which contained five Likert-type items each. The factors were defined as attitudes toward the police, attitudes toward law and the judicial system, and attitudes toward lawyers.

Response Mode

The respondents are requested to read each item and indicate whether they (1) "strongly agree," (2) "agree," (3) "are neutral," (4) "disagree," or (5) "strongly disagree."

Scoring

Each item receives a score ranging from 1–5. A total score for each of the three scales, then, is obtained by adding the item scores within each scale. The statements are worded and tabulated so that a high score indicates a negative attitude and a low score indicates a positive attitude. Scores for each scale range from 5–25.

Norms

Table 11 gives the means and standard deviations on each of the scales for 241 male prisoners in Washington State Prisons.

Reliability

No measures of temporal stability are presently available, but the factor analysis used in the construction of the scales indicates acceptable internal consistency.

Validity

In addition to the factor analysis, the responses of the 241 male inmates were analyzed with reference to other variables. First, scale scores were compared across the variables of race, marital status, education, prior employment, type of offense, prior criminality, and whether the respondent chose his own defense attorney. Table 12 shows the strength of relationship (as measured by Cramer's *V*) between the three PAS scales and these variables.

Inspection of the table indicates that all three scales are positively related to the variable "defense attorney." This means that inmates who had hired their own attorney held more positive attitudes toward all three target groups than inmates for whom attorneys were appointed. Whether or not the offense was characterized by violence (character of offense) appears to be related to attitudes toward police officers and lawyers. The more violent the crime, the more negative the offender's attitude. Unfortunately, no tests of significance were performed on these modest correlations.

Comments

While the PAS presents little evidence for validity, the use of factor analysis in the development supports the internal consistency of the scales. Another major

TABLE 11. Attitude Scale Score Means and Standard Deviations

Scale	Mean	SD
Attitudes toward police	3.76	.86
Attitudes toward law and the justice system	2.92	1.01
Attitudes toward lawyers	2.88	.92

TABLE 12. A Comparison of Status Factors across Attitude Domains

	Strength of relationship		
Factor	Police	Law and the judicial system	Lawyers
Race	.27	.31	.10
Marital status	.24	.09	.23
Education	.12	.24	.15
Prior employment	.14	.19	.13
Character of offense	.27	.17	.33
Prior criminality	.22	.28	.12
Defense attorney	.38	.35	.30

problem with this instrument is the lack of cross-validation. Scale development and testing was apparently performed on the same sample. Despite these deficiencies, the PAS's promise arises from its careful development and the utilization of items from established scales.

REFERENCES

Alpert, G. P., & Hicks, D. A. Prisoners' attitudes toward components of the legal and judicial system. *Criminology,* 1977, *14,* 461–482.

Alpert, G. P., & Alpert, S. W. Personal communication, 1977.

Cleaver, P. T., Mylonas, A. D., & Reckless, W. C. Gradients in attitudes toward law, courts and police. *Sociological Focus,* 1968, *2,* 29–48.

Katz, D. R. Attitude toward the law scale. In L. L. Thurstone (Ed.), *The measurements of social attitudes.* Chicago: University of Chicago Press, 1931.

Rundquist, H. C., & Sletto, R. F. *Personality in the depression.* Minneapolis: University of Minnesota Press, 1936.

Watt, W., & Maher, B. Prisoners' attitudes toward home and the judicial system. *Journal of Criminal Law, Criminology, and Police Science,* 1958, *49,* 327–330.

PRISONERS' ATTITUDE SCALES

Instructions: Following are some statements with which you may agree or disagree. Beside each statement write the symbol which best represents your position on that statement.

Symbol	Feeling
SA	Strongly Agree
A	Agree
N	Neutral
D	Disagree
SD	Strongly Disagree

Attitudes Toward Police

Policemen are more loyal to the police than to the citizens.*

Cops often carry a grudge against men who get in trouble with the law and treat them cruelly.*

Police hound ex-convicts.*

Policemen are just as crooked as the people they arrest.*

Police put on a show by arresting people.*

Attitudes Toward Law and the Judicial System

I believe in the use of force to overthrow the law.*

Law is the enemy of freedom.*

Many of the people in prison are actually innocent of the crimes they were convicted of.*

Laws are so often made for the benefit of small selfish groups that a man cannot respect the laws.*

On the whole, judges are honest.

Attitudes Toward Lawyers

You can generally trust a lawyer.

Most of the lawyers who have worked for me have done good jobs.

Lawyers have made things worse for me.*

When a lawyer is appointed by the court, he is generally on your side.

Lawyers are basically honest.

*Scored negatively.

LAW ENFORCEMENT ATTITUDE SCALES: LISTINGS

Attitudes toward the Criminal Justice System

Waldo, G. P., & Hall, N. E. Delinquency potential and attitudes toward the criminal justice system. *Social Forces,* 1970, *49,* 291–298.

This scale is a composite of nine Guttman-type scales that were designed to measure several dimensions of attitudes toward the criminal justice system. The scales were administered to seventh-grade boys who were enrolled in schools in lower class areas of a large midwestern city. The scales were believed to measure "policemen relationships with kids, policemen legitimacy, policemen characteristics, probation officer relationship with kids, probation officer legitimacy, juvenile courts relationship with kids, juvenile courts legitimacy, law relationship with kids, and law legitimacy" (p. 293).

Attitudes toward Law Enforcement

Khan, Z. R., & Spragens, W. C. American and Pakastani policemen's attitudes toward law enforcement. *Western Political Quarterly,* 1968, *23,* 579–588.

This instrument was designed to measure the differences between attitudes of Americans and Pakastanis toward the police of their country.

Attitudes toward Police

Diamond, M. J., & Lobitz, W. C. When familiarity breeds respect: The effects of an experimental depolarization program on police and student attitudes toward each other. *Journal of Social Issues,* 1973, *29,* 95–109.

This 53-item, Likert-type questionnaire was designed to tap students' cognitive and affective reactions to police, as well as their knowledge of police officers' attitudes and behavior.

Attitudes toward Police

Larsen, K. S. Authoritarianism and attitudes toward police. *Psychological Reports,* 1968, *23,* 349–350.

This 24-item, Likert-type scale was designed to assess college students' favorability of attitudes toward police and law enforcement.

Attitude toward the Police

Chapman, A. W. Attitudes toward legal agencies of authority for juveniles: A comparative study of one hundred thirty-three delinquent and one hundred thirty-three non-delinquent boys in Dayton, Ohio. *Dissertation Abstracts,* 1960, *20,* No. 7.

Shaw, M. E., & Wright, J. M. *Scales for the measurement of attitudes.* New York: McGraw-Hill, 1967.

This 26-item Likert scale has been used for assessing teenage boys' attitudes toward police. Shaw and Wright (1967) review it as having adequate reliability and validity.

Attitudes toward the Police

Williams, D. G. *Youth attitudes toward the police and law enforcement: A contextual analysis* (Western Michigan University, 1969, Sociology). Ann Arbor, Michigan: Xerox University Microfilms, 70-12936, 1970.

This 32-item, "Yes/No" scale has been used to investigate youth attitudes toward police. A typical item is "Do you think the police have it in for, or pick on, young people?"

Police Community-Relations Interview

Bordua, D. J., & Tifft, L. L. Citizens interviews, organizational feedback, and police-community relations decisions. *Law and Society Review,* 1971, *6,* 155–182.

This structured interview measured attitudes and gathered information from persons who had encountered patrol or tactical force officers.

Police Opinion of Work Questionnaire

Olson, B. T. Public opinions of work: An exploratory study. *Police Chief,* 1971, *38,* 23–38.

The *Police Opinion of Work Questionnaire* consists of 145 statements that respondents are asked to rate according to the degree they perceive each to be a problem; four additional attitude questions concern an individual's perception of his work. The questionnaire is designed to measure what police officers perceive as crucial job-related problems and their magnitude.

Police Perspectives and Behaviors in a Campus Disturbance

Dynes, R. R., Quarantelli, E. L., & Ross, J. L. Police perspectives and behavior in a campus disturbance. *Journal of Police Science and Administration,* 1974, *2,* 344–351.

This questionnaire was designed to measure attitudes and perceptions of police about themselves, their work, and their various clienteles.

Portune Attitude-toward-Police Scale

The Cincinnati police juvenile attitude project: A demonstration in police-teacher curriculum development (Project report). The Law Enforcement Assistance Association, 1968, Grant No. 0521965.

This 20-item, Likert-type scale is designed to measure attitudes toward the police of white and black teenage boys and girls.

LAW ENFORCEMENT BEHAVIOR RATINGS: REVIEWS

Police-Citizen Interaction Rating Scales

Development and Characteristics

The *Police-Citizen Interaction Rating Scales* (PCIRS) were designed "to select out and highlight those aspects of police and citizen behavior which [seem] most important to observe and study" and to "record a great deal of information in a small amount of time" (Cruse & Rubin, 1973, p. 177). The set is composed of three separate scales, the *Police Behavior Scale* (PBS), the *Citizen Behavior Scale* (CBS), and the *Pre-Call Observations Scale* (PCOS). All were developed and tested by systematic observation of the same 12 police officers whose experience ranged from two years or less to six years or more. Therefore, they will be described together.

These behavior rating scales require some training, but raters should have little difficulty learning the procedures. The PBS contains seven categories of behavior that are rated on 5-point scales indicating the degree to which the characteristic is present. These behaviors are: (1) controlling behavior; (2) educate-counsel; (3) assisting; (4) sympathizing; (5) suspicious; (6) threatens; and (7) humorous. In addition, the PBS contains three multiple-alternative items that relate to physical contact, weapon, and arrest.

The CBS contains 11 items, 5 of which are descriptive and 6 of which use a 5-point rating scale. These include: (1) subject role; (2) sex; (3) race; (4) dress;

(5) age; (6) size; (7) cooperate; (8) verbal aggression; (9) physical aggression; (10) complain; and (11) ask for assistance.

The PCOS indicates observations of significant changes in behavior of the police officers that occur between the time the call comes over the radio and the actual police–citizen encounter. These include: (1) change in speed of driving; (2) change in frequency of speech; (3) whether traffic signals are obeyed; and (4) evidence of muscle tension.

Response Mode

Because these are behavior rating scales, no responses are required of the individuals under observation. The rater is responsible for observing behavior and indicating on the rating form his or her judgments about the characteristics of the encounter.

Scoring

Items may be scored and evaluated individually or total scores may be obtained. A total PBS score is calculated by adding the rating scores for the first seven items (controlling behavior, etc.) then dividing by seven to yield an average of officer activity. Thus, the higher the value, the more active the officer was judged to be.

The CBS summary score is composed of the algebraic sum of the *Cooperation and Asking for Assistance Scales* (added as positive numbers) and the *Verbal Aggression, Physical Aggression,* and *Complaining Scales* (added as negative numbers). This sum is divided by five and represents an average of how the citizen responded to the police officer.

The PCOS score is obtained by adding scores from the four item-categories and dividing by four to yield an average of observable stress-related activities.

Reliability

Cruse and Rubin (1973) report an interrater reliability of .91 for four police officer-observers who had undergone observation training.

Validity

The items are systematic representations of major concerns related to police–citizen interaction, and therefore have content validity. Further, when results of the rating scales were compared to subjective judgments, there was general agreement.

Comments

Each of these scales appears to have content validity and reasonable reliability if the rater is trained in observation techniques. The items represent major concerns about police–citizen interaction and the form of the rating checklists is easily amenable to qualitative and quantitative analysis. The question of whether this set of rating scales is valuable for any particular research situation depends on the circumstances. This procedure does seem to be useful as an indicator of (1) characteristics the police officer takes into the interaction (PBS), (2) the citizens behavior in the interaction (CBS), and (3) overt stress behaviors of the officer preceding the anticipated interaction.

REFERENCES

Cruse, D., & Rubin, J. Police behavior (Part I). *Journal of Psychiatry and Law,* 1973, *1,* 167–222.

POLICE-CITIZEN INTERACTION RATING SCALES

Police Behavior Scale

Rate the behavior of the policeman along the following dimensions.

	Low				High
1. Controlling Behavior	1	2	3	4	5
2. Educate-counsel	1	2	3	4	5
3. Assisting	1	2	3	4	5
4. Sympathizing	1	2	3	4	5
5. Suspicious	1	2	3	4	5
6. Threatens	1	2	3	4	5
7. Humorous	1	2	3	4	5

8. Physical contact: No_____ Aggressive_____ Friendly_____
9. Weapon: Yes_____ No_____ Kind_____ Officer Subject(s)
   Against persons_____ Against property_____
10. Arrest: Yes_____ No_____

Citizen Behavior Scale

Rate the behavior of the citizen along the following dimensions.
1. Subject role   Victim_____   Complainant_____   Witness_____
                  Witness_____   Offender_____   Other_____

2. Sex   Male_____   Female_____
3. Race   Black____   White____   Spanish____   Other____
4. Dress
5. Age_____   1   2   3   4   5
6. Size   Small_____   Medium_____   Large_____
7. Cooperate   1   2   3   4   5
8. Verbal aggression   1   2   3   4   5
9. Physical aggression   1   2   3   4   5
10. Complain   1   2   3   4   5
11. Ask for assistance   1   2   3   4   5

Pre-Call Observation Scale

1. Changes in driving speeds   1   2   3   4   5
2. Changes in frequency of speech   1   2   3   4   5
3. Traffic signals ignored   1   2   3   4   5
4. Muscle tension   1   2   3   4   5

LAW ENFORCEMENT BEHAVIOR RATINGS: LISTINGS

Client Telephone Questionnaire

Driscoll, J. M., Meyer, R. G., & Schanie, C. F. Training police in family crisis intervention. *Journal of Applied Behavioral Science,* 1973, *9,* 62–82.

This 6-item scale is designed to measure six separate dimensions of police performance during a crisis intervention. Household residents are telephoned after intervention and asked about officer rapport, involvement, and perceived success, and client satisfaction, regard, and acceptance.

Cop Personality Questionnaire

Tifft, L. L. The "cop personality" reconsidered. *Journal of Police Science and Administration* 1974, *2,* 266–278.

The cop personality ratings were designed to measure observers' judgments of police officers attitudes toward citizens. Ratings were made on dimensions of *friendly, distant, cynical distrust, condescending,* and *dislike.*

Performance Rating Systems for Police (Performance Rating Scales)

Balch, D. E. Performance rating systems—suggestions for the police. *Journal of Police Science and Administration,* 1974, *2,* 40–49.

This instrument is a set of six different types of rating procedures (graphic rating scales, forced-choice system, forced-distribution technique, ranking of order, paired-choice method, peer rating) which is designed to assess the performance of police officers.

Police Peer Evaluation Scale

Hess, L. R. *Police entry tests and their predictability of scores in police academy and subsequent job performance.* Unpublished doctoral dissertation, Marquette University, 1972.

This 60-item rating uses a 6-point Likert scale for evaluating a police officer's personal qualities and performance of duties.

Police Task Performance Scale

Robinson, D. D. Predicting police effectiveness from self reports of relative time spent in task performance. *Personnel Psychology,* 1970, *23,* 327–345.

This 76-item questionnaire was designed to measure law enforcement officers' tasks and effectiveness. Factor analysis yielded six homogeneous and rational factors.

LAW ENFORCEMENT PERSONALITY MEASURES: REVIEWS

Cynicism Questionnaire

Development and Characteristics

The *Cynicism Questionnaire* (CQ) was based on the law enforcement experience of the developer and was designed to measure police cynicism in relation to their work (Niederhoffer, 1967). *Cynicism* is defined as "diffuse feelings of hate and envy; . . . a sense of powerlessness to express these feelings actively against the person or social stratum evoking them; and . . . a sour grapes pattern which asserts merely that desired but unattainable objectives do not actually embody the prized values" (P. 93). Cynicism is presented as both a typical adaptation to police organization anomie and as a developmental antecedent of anomie in police careers.

The CQ consists of 20 incomplete sentences followed by three possible completions. The first completion always represents the professional police view, the second is a common sense, middle-of-the-road approach, while the third is the cynical response.

Response Mode

Respondents are requested to read each sentence stem and indicate the alternative ending most appropriate for them.

Scoring

A choice of the first completion is scored as 1, a second completion is scored 3 and a choice of the third completion is scored 5. Items left blank are scored 3. The range of scores is 20 to 100, high scores indicating cynicism.

Norms

Two hundred and twenty New York City police officers made up the normative sample. Thirty-four newly appointed officers who had not yet entered training were considered as control subjects. They were compared to five other police groups of varying experience and status on each item, as well as the full questionnaire. Table 13 shows the frequency distribution of responses, the means and standard deviations, and the percentage of cynics (defined as those with

TABLE 13. Norms for the Cynicism Questionnaire[a]

Group	N	Percentage of choices			Mean	SD	Percentage of cynics
		A	B	C			
Total sample	220	31	39	30	59.2	12.9	43
All but control	186	26	41	33	62.2	11.7	50
Control	34	57	30	13	42.6[b]	8.5	3
Recruits	60	31	37	32	60.1	11.0	45
Patrolmen 2–12 years	42	22	40	38	66.5[b]	11.3	56
Patrolmen 13–19 years	42	23	45	32	62.7	11.8	64
Detectives	15	34	39	27	58.0	10.0	46
Superior officers	27	26	45	29	61.5	11.4	40

[a] Adapted from Tables 16 and 17, Niederhoffer (1967).
[b] Significantly different from the group mean.

scores higher than the sample mean, excluding control subjects, of 62.2%). Further norms by content clusters are available for 84 New York City Police patrolmen and 212 patrolmen from an unidentified, northeastern industrial city (Fafky, 1975).

Reliability

The CQ was found to have a split-half reliability of .62 and mean item–scale correlations of .48 for 396 officers (Rafky 1975).

Validity

The questionnaire items have content validity; they seem to tap many important areas of police officer functioning and concern. Niederhoffer (1967) reports agreement by experienced officers that the questionnaire taps police cynicism.

Rafky (1975) replicated the Neiderhoffer work using multivariate techniques. Anomie and selected measures of frustration (such as rank and education) were unrelated to cynicism, and extreme cynicism was not present in Rafky's population of an entire police department. Two major modes of cynicism were found: cynicism about police work itself and cynicism with regard to the public. Years of service as an officer was the only variable that predicted cynicism vis-à-vis the public.

Comments

The CQ was developed to measure the construct of police cynicism. It is unrelated to anomie and frustration among officers, both central issues in construct validity. However, the Rafky study has defined well the parameters of the CQ and it does offer satisfactory reliability. The validity data in support of the CQ are limited. Still, the construct of police cynicism is important and continues to stimulate measurement efforts (Poole & Regoli, 1979).

REFERENCES

Niederhoffer, A. *Behind the shield: The police in urban society*. Garden City, N.Y.: Doubleday, 1967.

Poole, E. D., & Regoli, R. M. Police professionalism and cynicism: An empirical assessment. *Criminal Justice Behavior,* 1979, *6,* 201–206.

Rafky, D. M. Police cynicism reconsidered: An application of smallest space analysis. *Criminology,* 1975, *13,* 168–192.

THE CYNICISM QUESTIONNAIRE

In each of the following items, please circle the letter of the statement which, in your opinion, is most nearly correct.

1. The average police superior is _____
   a. very interested in the welfare of his subordinates.
   b. somewhat concerned about the welfare of his subordinates.
   c. mostly concerned with his own problems.

2. The average departmental complaint is a result of _____
   a. the superior's dedication to proper standards of efficiency.
   b. some personal friction between superior and subordinate.
   c. the pressure on superiors from higher authority to give out complaints.

3. The average arrest is made because _____
   a. the patrolman is dedicated to perform his duty properly.
   b. a complainant insisted on it.
   c. the officer could not avoid it without getting into trouble.

4. The best arrests are made _____
   a. as a result of hard work and intelligent dedication to duty.
   b. as a result of good information from an informer.
   c. coming from the "coop."

5. A college degree as a requirement for appointment to the police department _____
   a. would result in a much more efficient police department.
   b. would cause friction and possibly do more harm than good.
   c. would let into the department men who are probably ill suited for police work.

6. When you get to know the department from the inside, you begin to feel that _____
   a. it is a very efficient, smoothly operating organization.
   b. it is hardly any different from other civil service organizations.
   c. it is a wonder that it does one-half as well as it does.

7. Police Academy training of recruits _____
   a. does a very fine job of preparing the recruit for life in the precinct.
   b. cannot overcome the contradictions between theory and practice.
   c. might as well be cut in half. The recruit has to learn all over when he is assigned to a precinct.

8. Professionalization of police work _____
   a. is already here for many groups of patrolmen.
   b. may come in the future.
   c. is a dream. It will not come in the forseeable future.

LAW ENFORCEMENT AND POLICE

9. When a patrolman appears at the police department Trial Room _____
   a. he knows that he is getting a fair and impartial trial by the legal safeguards.
   b. the outcome depends as much on the personal impression he leaves with the trial commissioner as it does on the merits of the case.
   c. he will probably be found guilty even when he has a good defense.

10. The average policeman is _____
    a. dedicated to high ideals of police service and would not hesitate to perform police duty even though he may have to work overtime.
    b. trying to perform eight hours of duty without getting into trouble.
    c. just as interested in promoting private contacts as he is in performing police work.

11. The rules and regulations of police work _____
    a. are fair and sensible in regulating conduct off and on duty.
    b. create a problem in that it is very difficult to perform an active tour of duty without violating some rules and regulations.
    c. are so restrictive and contradictory that the average policeman just uses common sense on the job, and does not worry about rules and regulations.

12. The youth problem is best handled by police who are _____
    a. trained in a social service approach.
    b. the average patrolman on post.
    c. by mobile, strong-arm Youth Squads who are ready to take strong action.

13. The majority of special assignments in the police department _____
    a. are a result of careful consideration of the man's background and qualifications, and depend on merit.
    b. are being handled as capably as you could expect in a large civil service organization.
    c. depend on whom you know, not on merit.

14. _____ average detective _____
    a. has special qualifications and is superior to a patrolman in intelligence and dedication to duty.
    b. is just about the same as the average patrolman.
    c. is a little chesty and thinks he is a little better than a patrolman.

15. Police department summonses are issued by policemen _____
    a. as part of a sensible pattern of enforcement.
    b. on the basis of their own ideas of right and wrong driving.
    c. because a patrolman knows he must meet his quota even if this is not official.

16. The public _____
    a. shows a lot of respect for policemen.
    b. considers policemen average civil service workers.
    c. considers policemen very low as far as prestige goes.

17. The public _____
    a. is eager to cooperate with policemen to help them perform their duty better.
    b. usually has to be forced to cooperate with policemen.
    c. is more apt to obstruct police work if it can, than cooperate.

18. Policeman _____
    a. understand human behavior as well as psychologists and sociologists because they get so much experience in real life.
    b. have no more talent in understanding human behavior than any average person.
    c. have a peculiar view of human nature because of the misery and cruelty of life which they see every day.

19. The newspapers in general _____
    a. try to help police departments by giving prominent coverage to items favorable to police.
    b. just report the news impartially whether or not it concerns the police.
    c. seem to enjoy giving an unfavorable slant to news concerning the police and prominently play up police misdeeds rather than virtues.

20. Testifying in court_____
    a. policemen receive real cooperation and are treated fairly by court personnel.
    b. police witnesses are treated no differently from civilian witnesses.
    c. too often the policemen are treated as criminals when they take the witness stand.

LAW ENFORCEMENT PERSONALITY MEASURES: LISTINGS

Police Flexibility Measurement

Knowles, P., & Peterson, R. Measurement of flexibility in state police officers. *Journal of Police Science and Administration,* 1973, *1,* 219–223.

The *Police Flexibility Questionnaire* combines police officers' age, introversion/extroversion, political liberalism, political conservatism, educational level, level of school achievement, and social distance, to yield an estimate of personal and professional flexibility.

Police Job Stress Interview

Kroes, W. H., Margolis, B. L., & Hurrell, Jr., J. J. Job stress in policemen. *Journal of Police Science and Administration,* 1974, *2,* 145–155.

The *Police Job Stress Interview* is a semistructured interview schedule which was designed to gather information concerning the stress that police officers perceive they experience in their jobs.

LAW ENFORCEMENT MILIEU RATINGS: LISTINGS

Professionalization Assessment for Police Organizations

Oppenheim, P. J. *An organizational analysis of professionalization in police departments* (The National Institute of Law Enforcement and Criminal Justice). Washington, D.C., June, 1975.

This instrument was designed to measure organizational characteristics of police departments on the dimensions of professionalization, interorganizational field linkage, organizational size, organizational wealth, organizational complexity, organizational desensitization, and environmental context.

LAW ENFORCEMENT PREDICTION: REVIEWS

Clues Test

Development and Characteristics

The *Clues Test* is a situational test designed to measure the ability of an individual to make inferences about a hypothetical person based on the clues left in his or her office (Mills, McDevitt, & Tonkin, 1966). This instrument was adapted from the "Belongings" test (Murray, 1948) to assess police investigation skills. The present version of the test requires that a portion of a room be roped off and contain such office equipment as a desk, a chair, calendars, and other equipment that might be found in the office of a city employee. A set of carefully selected "clues" are left behind that suggest inferences about the personality, habits, whereabouts, and possible plight of the office employee who was supposed to have worked at the desk. The clues include race track sheets, Scotch bottles, tranquilizers and aspirins, dunning letters from local jewelry stores, perfumed love letters, a pay voucher, a passport application, and a memo from the city manager requiring an audit of accounts.

Response Mode

The respondents are asked to investigate the mysterious disappearance of this hypothetical person. They are given 10 minutes and an opportunity to take notes. Then they are asked to fill in the blank spaces in a questionnaire that requests information about the situation. These questions range from simple, factual data to hypotheses or guesses as to where the city employee might be, why he or she might have left the job, what his or her probable mental state was, and whether there were any bases for prosecution.

Scoring

During the respondent's investigation of the situation, a staff member who is working quietly in another part of the room unobtrusively observes the respondent's approach to the task. The staff member encourages inquiries and expressions of attitudes about the test and makes evaluations as to the performance of the respondent. The exact criterion used for grading one's performance is not available. However, it was reported that a total of 60 possible points could be obtained through a combination of answering the factual questions correctly, making appropriate hypotheses and approaching the problem in a desirable fashion.

Norms

No norms are presently available.

Reliability

No reliability information is presently available.

Validity

The *Clues Test* has face validity as a measure of an individual's ability to apply available information and make inferences based on that information.

Attempts to demonstrate predictive validity have been made for two groups of subjects. The first attempt included a group of 62 Cincinnati police candidates enrolled in a police training academy. Forty-two of these candidates eventually completed the training course at the academy. These were called the "success" group; 20 others unable to complete the training course were labeled the "failure" group. The *Clues Test*, along with several other instruments, was administered to the entire group at the beginning of their training. When the mean score of the success group (31.2) was compared to that of the failure group (26.2), the difference was in an appropriate direction, but did not reach statistical significance ($p < .05$). However, when the scores of the 62 recruits were rank ordered for the *Clues Test* and compared to their rank ordered standing in the police academy, a correlation coefficient of .375 ($p < .05$) resulted. This outcome indicates that the *Clues Test* possesses modest predictive ability.

When these results were cross-validated with a group of 25 other recruits at the police academy training center, results were similar. In the group of 25 recruits, 15 successfully completed the training, while 10 were unable to finish. The mean scores for the two groups showed no significant difference. However, the rank ordered correlation between the *Clues Test* and police academy standing was .725, and statistically significant ($p < .05$).

Comments

The *Clues Test* does not purport to be a measure of an individual's overall ability as a police officer. It does, however, have support for its ability to measure an individual's capacity to assimilate information and draw inferences. There is modest evidence for predictive ability.

REFERENCES

Mills, R. V., McDevitt, R. J., & Tonkin, S. Situational tests in metropolitan police recruit selection. *Journal of Criminal Law, Criminology, and Police Science,* 1966, *57,* 99–106.

Murray, H. *Assessment of men: Selection of personnel for the office of strategic services.* New York: Rinehart and Co., 1948.

LAW ENFORCEMENT PREDICTION: LISTINGS

Public Personnel Association Test (PPA)

Flynn, J. T., & Peterson, M. The use of regression analysis in police patrolman selection. *The Journal of Criminal Law, Criminology and Police Science,* 1972, *63,* 564–569.

This test was designed to assess the extent to which a person possesses the skill necessary for successful performance as a police officer. Flynn and Peterson report the use of the PPA and other indices as criteria for the selection of police officers.

LAW ENFORCEMENT DESCRIPTION: REVIEWS

Children's Perceptions of the Police

Development and Characteristics

The Children's Perceptions of the Police Scale (CPPS) was designed to measure the general attitudes of children toward policemen (Derbyshire, 1968). This scale was developed on the assumption that children's image of policemen or their attitudes toward policemen can be measured by evaluating their drawings of policemen "doing their job." Derbyshire initially suggested that the CPPS drawings be evaluated according to content as it relates to (1) aggressiveness,

(2) authoritarianism, (3) hostility, (4) kindness, (5) goodness, (6) strength, and (7) anger. It was also suggested that a general measure of negative attitudes or "antipathy" should be evaluated in each of the drawings.

After performing a content analysis of data obtained from 90 third-grade youngsters, the developer suggested four major categories rather than the seven originally proposed. These categories are: (1) Aggressive police behavior: fighting, chasing, shooting; (2) assistance with negative overtones: unloading a paddywagon, searching a building, in a car with prisoners, giving traffic tickets; (3) neutral behavior: walking, riding in a car, directing traffic; or (4) assistance with a positive connotation: talking with children, giving directions. In addition, the general antipathy score was maintained.

Response Mode

The respondents are provided with a set of crayons and a sheet of 12" × 16" manila paper and asked to "draw a picture of a policeman at work." They are given as much time as needed to complete the picture and if any questions are raised as to how or what to draw, they are reminded that they should draw a picture of "a policeman at work, doing his job or performing his tasks."

Scoring

Two types of scores are used. First, a general antipathy score can be obtained through a subjective evaluation of children's feelings as presented in the drawings of police tasks. This judgment should include affective implications of color, movement, and line variation as well as the content indicated in the drawing. A 7-point scale is used ranging from (1) no antipathy to (7) highest antipathy.

The second scoring scheme utilizes the four content categories: (1) police behavior; (2) assistance with negative overtones; (3) neutral behavior; and (4) assistance with positive connotations. This procedure involves noting which of the four categories best describes each picture. This technique is typically used when comparing the responses of one group of children to those of another group of children. The comparisons might include a percent of aggressive responses, percent of assistance with negative overtones and so forth.

Norms

All of the available normative information is for the antipathy rating. In Table 14, means, standard deviations, and ranges were estimated for third-graders from three different schools in the Los Angeles area: 30 children were from the Watts school district (a mostly disadvantaged black area), 32 from Westchester (a predominantly white, higher socioeconomic status (SES school district) and 30 from El Soreno (a school somewhat between Westchester and Watts in SES).

TABLE 14. Mean Antipathy Scores across Seven Scales

	Watts	Westchester	El Soreno
Mean	4.33	4.03	4.47
SD	.695	.794	.793
Range	5.58–2.28	5.50–2.83	5.53–2.95
N	30	32	30

Reliability

Derbyshire (1968) presented interrater reliability for four independent raters of antipathy scores. Three of the four raters were third or fourth year resident psychiatrists in a social psychiatry training program. The fourth (the scale developer) was an Associate Professor of Sociology in the Department of Psychiatry. Derbyshire (1968) reports statistically significant correlations ranging from +.60 to +.90 between three of the four raters for two sets of drawings.

Validity

The developer has suggested that children from lower socioeconomic backgrounds would be more likely than children from higher SES backgrounds to have had contact with police officers and to have experienced them as aggressive, cruel, bad, authoritarian, etc. The differential contact should be evident in the drawings of children from different school districts, and, it was hypothesized that children from low SES school districts (i.e., Watts or El Soreno) would have higher antipathy scores than those children from Westchester. There were no statistically significant differences between Watts and Westchester or between Watts and El Soreno. There were, however, statistically significant differences between El Soreno and Westchester, lending only partial support to the validity of antipathy scores as a measure of negative attitudes toward police.

Evidence of validity was found in another study. A group of 26 youngsters was given the CPPS which was scored according to the four content areas. They were then exposed to the "Policemen Bill Program" (PBP) in which a police officer came to the classroom and talked to the children about himself and his duties. Then the children were asked again to draw pictures of police officers at work. There was a significant increase in the number of positive drawings from 11 to 21 and a decrease in the number of negative drawings from 13 to 5 ($\chi^2 = 8.33, p < .002$).

Comments

The CPPS is in an early stage of development. More specific criteria need to be designated for rater evaluation of antipathy and for the assignment of pictures to one of the four categories outlined. Designation of these criteria would help to standardize the scoring procedure and make this scale more useful to a wider range of researchers. Nevertheless the interrater reliability evidence indicates that consistent judgments can be made.

The evidence of validity is promising. There is reason to believe that the drawings of children will reflect their antipathy about the police. Furthermore, the influence of the PBP on the drawings of the children lends validity support. There is a question, however, of whether the PBP actually changed attitudes or simply changed the number and types of tasks in which the children were able to conceive of policemen engaging.

Finally, the CPPS offers an opportunity to measure attitudes of children in a way which is nonverbal and relatively unobtrusive. Most elementary school children are requested to draw many objects or situations; therefore, the CPPS would not be seen as some different kind of task.

REFERENCES

Derbyshire, R. L. Children's perceptions of the police: A comparative study of attitudes and attitude change. *Criminal Law, Criminology, and Police Science,* 1968, *59,* 183–190.

Citizens' Perception of Police Scale

Development and Characteristics

The *Citizens' Perception of Police Scale* (CIPS) was designed to "measure citizen perceptions of police based on the following: (1) extent of racial prejudice demonstrated by the police, (2) extent of police abuse of citizens, (3) extent of unethical police behavior, (4) extent of police indirect harassment of citizens, and (5) extent to which police man power is adequately extended" (Klyman & Kruckenberg, 1974, p. 222–223). A total of nine Likert-type items were written to measure these specific components.

Response Mode

The respondent is requested to read each statement and decide according to a 7-point continuum the degree to which he agrees or disagrees with the statement.

Scoring

Each item is stated in such a way that it represents a negative feeling toward the police. Therefore, a response of agree very much (7) indicates a highly negative feeling. Conversely, a score of disagree very much (1) indicates positive feelings toward police. Individual item scores can be added together to form a single score representing an individuals' perception of the police. A high score represents a negative perception and a low score represents a positive perception.

Norms

No norms are available.

Reliability

Klyman and Kruckenberg (1974) report a split-half reliability calculated from the Spearman-Brown formula of .73 for the responses of 1,000 citizens on the CIPS.

Validity

Content validity of the CIPS must be based upon the types of perceptual information desired by the researcher. Scale developers suggest that the methodology and type of scale construction are more important as models than are the particular items themselves. They note that areas of interest may differ from one community to another and that a restatement of particular items may be necessary under varying conditions.

The CIPS has been presented to a stratified random sample of 1,000 individuals living within the Los Angeles area. Stratification was based upon race, sex, income and age. Results indicated that white respondents held more positive attitudes toward the police than non-white respondents. No statistically significant differences were found between the respondents' level of dogmatism and the CIPS or between the CIPS and any of the other tested variables.

Comments

The CIPS has adequate internal consistency and has received some support for its validity as a measure of attitudes toward police. The casual references to the specific content and wording of items, however, indicates that the CIPS is not sufficiently developed as a measure of perception of police officers. The scale developers suggest that the methodology involved in the construction and usage of this scale represent an improvement of previous techniques. However, the developmental procedures seem to be of less value than that of the standard Likert type scale construction.

REFERENCES

Klyman, F. I., & Kruckenberg, J. A methodology for assessing citizens' perceptions of police. *Journal of Criminal Justice,* 1974, *2,* 219–233.

CITIZENS' PERCEPTION OF POLICE SCALE

Instructions: Following are some statements with which you may agree or disagree. Place a check (✓) beside the alternative following each item which best represents your feeling about the statement.

1. Regardless of the reason, police response time is slower in neighborhoods other than white neighborhoods.

    Disagree very much
    Disagree on the whole
    Disagree a little
    Neutral
    Agree a little
    Agree on the whole
    Agree very much

2. Policemen give the impression of feeling superior to people who are not white.

    Disagree very much
    Disagree on the whole
    Disagree a little
    Neutral
    Agree a little
    Agree on the whole
    Agree very much

3. Police officers are more careful when arresting nonwhites because nonwhites are more likely to commit crimes of violence against police officers than whites.

    Disagree very much
    Disagree on the whole
    Disagree a little
    Neutral
    Agree a little
    Agree on the whole
    Agree very much

4. There is pressure exerted on policemen by other policemen to make fun of nonwhite people.

    Disagree very much
    Disagree on the whole

LAW ENFORCEMENT AND POLICE

   Disagree a little
   Neutral
   Agree a little
   Agree on the whole
   Agree very much

5. The likelihood of a citizen being abused by a policeman in this city is high.

   Disagree very much
   Disagree on the whole
   Disagree a little
   Neutral
   Agree a little
   Agree on the whole
   Agree very much

6. Policemen are often unethical (they sponge off merchants and even other people).

   Disagree very much
   Disagree on the whole
   Disagree a little
   Neutral
   Agree a little
   Agree on the whole
   Agree very much

7. Police spend too much time and energy on too many unimportant things.

   Disagree very much
   Disagree on the whole
   Disagree a little
   Neutral
   Agree a little
   Agree on the whole
   Agree very much

8. The use of helicopters by police in my neighborhood is disturbing.

   Disagree very much
   Disagree on the whole
   Disagree a little
   Neutral
   Agree a little
   Agree on the whole
   Agree very much

9. In many situations in which the police respond to civil disorder, they are either "damned" if they do or "damned" if they do not.

   Disagree very much
   Disagree on the whole
   Disagree a little
   Neutral
   Agree a little
   Agree on the whole
   Agree very much

Foot Patrolman Observation Test

Development and Characteristics

The *Foot Patrolman Observation Test* (FPOT) is a situational test designed to measure observational abilities, motivation for police career, and latent attitudes of police trainees toward law enforcement and minority groups (Mills, McDevitt, & Tonkin, 1966). The FPOT was developed on the assumption that situational tests make possible the observation of characteristics that might appear only infrequently in normal activities. No information is given as to the process by which this instrument was developed. It appears, however, to be based on the belief that the characteristics for a good foot patrolman can be measured by observing recruits participating in activities similar to those encountered daily by the police officer.

Two aspects of individual trainees are measured by this instrument. The first part of the FPOT addresses itself to the ability of trainees to remember details of the environment through which they patrol. This is measured by their ability to choose correctly the answers to 25 multiple-choice questions of fact concerning such things as the number of intersections transversed, location of key stores, type of street lights, color of fire plugs, type of paving in street, and similar observations.

The second part of the FPOT is an open-ended essay that assesses attitudes about aspects of trainees' roles as police officers. This section taps attitudes toward law enforcement in general, attitudes toward minority groups, and motivation for becoming a police officer.

Response Mode

The trainees are given a specific set of instructions that direct them to proceed on foot, unaccompanied, to a specific part of a city. They are advised to observe closely everything along the route, and bear in mind that questions might be asked about anything that they may have observed along the way. The prescribed route is marked with chalk arrows on the sidewalk at every intersection.

Each respondent, on completion of the walk, is asked to respond to 25 multiple choice questions. The following example is typical of the questions:

> The flag pole before Police Headquarters bears the inscription:
> a. Commemorating those who have given their lives in the performance of their sacred duty
> b. Cincinnati Police
> c. Police Division Headquarters, City of Cincinnati
> d. The flag pole bears no inscription at all.

The second part asked the individuals to write a short essay addressing such topics as (1) their impressions of the persons living in the neighborhood through which they passed, and (2) feelings about "keeping the peace" in this section of town.

Scoring

A score for the first part of the test is obtained by adding the number of total correct responses. The second part is evaluated qualitatively by police academy members and notes are made when strengths and weaknesses are encountered.

Norms

No normative information is available.

Reliability

No reliability information is available.

Validity

Efforts have been made to investigate the predictive validity of the FPOT. Along with other situational, personality, and intelligence tests, this instrument was administered to 62 Cincinnati police candidates. Forty-two candidates eventually completed their recruit training in the police academy. These were referred to as the "success" group, while 20 candidates who did not complete the training course were termed "failure" candidates. When the Part 1 responses of the success group to the FPOT were compared to those of the failure group, the success group showed a higher score (14.7) than the failure group (14.0). The difference, however, was not large enough to be statistically significant for this sample size. In addition, when the FPOT scores were rank ordered and compared to police academy standing during the training period, a nonsignificant correlation coefficient of .137 resulted.

A second group of 25 police academy candidates was tested under the same conditions. Of these, 15 completed the police academy training, while 10 did not. Again, the success group scored slightly but not significantly higher on the FPOT (15.1) as compared to the failure group (14.8). Also, when FPOT scores were correlated with police academy standing for this group, the correlation coefficient of .159 failed to reach statistical significance (.05).

Comments

The FPOT represents an interesting approach to measuring the ability of police officer candidates to carry out some of the objectives of the foot patrolman. It appears to have face validity, but efforts to show its predictive validity for class standing within the police academy have been disappointing. At least two explanations are possible. First, the criterion variable, "standing within the police academy" may be inappropriate. It is conceivable that those traits being measured by the FPOT are more like on-the-job activities than those of the police academy. The second explanation is that a score assessing the number of correct guesses about details of an area may not be an effective predictor of other police abilities.

REFERENCES

Mills, R. B., McDevitt, R. J., & Tonkin, S. Situational tests in metropolitan police recruit selection. *Journal Criminal Law, Criminology, and Police Science*, 1966, 57, 99–106.

Police Task Preference Questionnaire

Development and Characteristics

The *Police Task Preference Questionnaire* (PTPQ) was designed "to explore (1) whether distinct task preferences do exist for policemen and if so, (2) whether there are large or minor differences in such preferences" (Olson, 1970, p. 1016). Items for the PTPQ were developed to measure activities under four major categories. These are criminal apprehension, traffic, crime prevention, and public service. A total of four items were written for each category with the stipulation that each item should be a simple statement of a potential police activity and that the entire test should take no more than five minutes to complete.

The 16 items that made up the final version of the questionnaire were chosen from a large item pool representing activities in which most police officers would engage in annually. After each item was categorized and edited, it was reviewed by police officers who were asked to judge the authenticity of the task.

Response Mode

The respondents are asked to read each task description and choose the response which most closely represents their feelings about the task: (1) "dislike very much," (2) "dislike," (3) "neither like nor dislike," (4) "like," or (5) "like very much."

Scoring

Item scores are determined by the degree to which the respondents indicate their likes for each task. A score of 1 represents dislike very much and 5 represents like very much. Subscale scores for each major category have a possible range of 4–20 with a high score indicating liking for the type of task.

Norms

No norms are available.

Reliability

Conventional reliability estimates are not available. However, Olson (1970) reports Leik scores for each of the 16 items, which range from .33 to .88 for a group of 131 law enforcement officers who had served for one year or more on the force. The Leik score is a measure of interrater agreement calculated such that a low score indicates considerable inconsistency in item ratings and a high score indicates considerable consistency (Leik, 1960).

Validity

The PTPQ has content validity arising from the manner of scale construction. Items listed under each task type describe particular behaviors involved in that kind of police activity.

No further evidence of validity is available.

Comments

The PTPQ is not an empirically established scale. Indeed, it represents an early stage in the development of an instrument designed to measure activity preference of police officers. On the positive side, it is one of the few efforts in this area and offers an alternative to behavior rating techniques. On the other hand, however, it lacks validation and reliability testing and one might question whether the examples given for each preference category are comprehensive. The lack of comprehensiveness may limit the applicability of findings.

REFERENCES

Leik, R. K. A measure of ordinal consensus. *Pacific Sociological Review,* 1966, *9,* 85–90.

Olson, B. An exploratory study of task preferences. *Personnel Journal,* 1970, *49,* 1015–1020.

POLICE TASK PREFERENCE QUESTIONNAIRE

Instructions: Please read each of the following items and indicate whether you 1: Dislike It Very much; 2: Dislike It; 3: Are Neutral to It; 4: Like It; or 5: Like It Very Much.

A. Criminal Apprehension

1. Catching a burglar at work
   1 2 3 4 5

2. Identifying and apprehending someone who has criminally assaulted another person
   1 2 3 4 5

3. Breaking up a ring of car thieves
   1 2 3 4 5

4. Identify drug pushers and users
   1 2 3 4 5

B. Traffic

1. Investigating and writing up a traffic accident
   1 2 3 4 5

2. Speaking to groups about traffic enforcement and safety
   1 2 3 4 5

3. Directing traffic at a hazardous intersection if a traffic light has stopped working
   1 2 3 4 5

4. Issuing a traffic ticket to a driver who has violated a traffic law
   1 2 3 4 5

C. Crime Prevention

1. Talking to groups of school children about the importance of observing the law
   1 2 3 4 5

2. Visiting bars and other public places to see who's around and what's going on
   1 2 3 4 5

3. Advising a home owner how to protect his property from burglars
   1 2 3 4 5

4. Checking the houses of persons who are away on vacation
   1 2 3 4 5

D. Public Service

1. Helping a citizen who has lost his keys get back into his house
   1 2 3 4 5

2. Observing and reporting hazardous streets, curbs, and sidewalks to higher authority
   1 2 3 4 5

3. Going to a domestic call to cool things down
   1   2   3   4   5
4. Responding to a call from a citizen who complains a neighbor boy broke a window
   1   2   3   4   5

LAW ENFORCEMENT DESCRIPTION: LISTINGS

Abbreviated Police Identification Scale

Ford, R. E., Meeker, J., & Zeller, R. Police, students, and racial hostilities. *Journal of Police Science and Administration,* 1975, *3,* 9–14.

The *Abbreviated Police Identification Scale* is a 6-item, Likert-type instrument that measures the degree to which an individual identifies with police officers.

ADAPT Scale (*Arrest Decisions As Preludes To*)

Neithercutt, M. G., & Moseley, W. H. *Arrest decisions as preludes to? An evaluation of police related research.* Davis, California: National Council on Crime and Delinquency, 1974.

This 48-item interview schedule covers four areas relating to arrest decisions: (1) Efforts to avoid making arrests; (2) effects of decisions not to arrest; (3) factors influencing the decision to arrest; and (4) effects of being arrested.

Information Handling in Police Decision Making

Sullivan, D. C., & Seigel, L. J. How police use information to make decisions: An application of decision games. *Journal of Crime and Delinquency,* 1972, *9,* 253–262.

The *Police Prediction of Public Attitudes Questionnaire* is a 5-item interview schedule and questionnaire that was designed to elicit public attitudes toward police officers and police perceptions of those attitudes.

Job Analysis and Interest Measurements

Trojanowicz, R. C. The contrasting behavioral styles of policemen and social workers. *Public Personnel Review,* 1971, *32,* 246–251.

This self report instrument contains 34 scales and is designed to measure an individual's perception of his or her job and his or her degree of interest in it. Trojanowicz reports the responses of a sample of 100 social workers and 100 police officers.

Perceptions of Justice Interview

Jacob, H. Black and white perceptions of justice in the city. *Law and Society Review,* 1971, *6,* 69–89.

This instrument consists of an extensive interview in which respondents are asked about their satisfaction in contact with police, courts, and other legal agencies.

Police Image Questionnaire

Gurevitch, M., Danet, B., & Schwartz, G. The image of the police in Israel. *Law and Society Review,* 1971, *5,* 367–388.

This 23-question interview was designed to measure the public's expectations of police behavior, the public's evaluation of personal qualities of police officers' work, and the willingness of citizens to become involved in situations that do not directly concern them.

Police Isolation Questionnaire

Clark, J. P. Isolation of the police: A comparison of the British and American situations. *The Journal of Criminal Law, Criminology, and Police Science,* 1965, *56,* 307–319.

This questionnaire was designed to measure "(1) the social isolation of police officers and their families, (2) the quality and quantity of police interaction with other agencies and social control, (3) the consensus among the police, public, and other social control agency personnel on certain moral attitudes, and (4) the consensus among the public, police, and other social control agency personnel on the conception of proper police action in 'police situations.' "

Police Prediction of Public Attitudes Questionnaire

Crawford, T. J. Police overperception of ghetto hostility. *Journal of Police Science and Administration,* 1973, *1,* 168–174.

The *Police Prediction of Public Attitudes Questionnaire* is a 5-item interview schedule and questionnaire that was designed to elicit public attitudes toward police officers and police perceptions of those attitudes.

CHAPTER 7
Courts and the Law

This chapter contains scales and listings that are concerned with courts and the law. Three groupings of scales are included: (1) Those dealing with courtroom personnel, roles, processes, and events; (2) those relating to probation and parole officers, judges and sentencing, court volunteers, and diversion; and (3) those relating to the law—attitudes toward justice, law, and capital punishment. The scope of coverage ranges further to juvenile courts, pretrial programs and participants, and due process and citizen rights. To our knowledge, researchers have not developed instruments to measure personality traits or behavior ratings related to court processes; thus these categories have no entries in this chapter, aside from two competency assessment measures. As in Chapter 6, the largest number of entries is in the category of attitude scales.

COURTS AND THE LAW ATTITUDE SCALES: REVIEWS

Attitude toward Capital Punishment

Development and Characteristics

The *Attitude toward Capital Punishment Scale* (ATCPS) was designed to measure attitudes toward capital punishment for the crime of murder (Balogh & Mueller, 1960). An original item pool of 100 statements believed to be relevant to capital punishment was collected from magazine articles and books and were presented to 15 criminology students who were requested to place each item in one of seven files indicating the degree of favorability toward capital punishment. An item was placed in file one if it indicated a very favorable attitude toward capital punishment. It was placed in file four if the item was neutral with respect to capital punishment, and in file seven if it was least favorable to capital punishment.

A total of 20 items produced acceptable Q values. An item analysis of these

20 items was performed and each item was evaluated according to its ability to discriminate between high and low scores. Five items that were poor discriminators were dropped and a total of 15 items were left in the final version of the ATCPS.

Response Mode

Respondents are requested to read each item and place a check mark beside those with which they agree and a cross mark next to those with which they disagree. Only the check marks are scored.

Scoring

A total score is obtained by adding the scale value of all items that received a check mark. High scores indicate negative attitudes toward capital punishment.

Norms

No normative data are available.

Reliability

No reliability estimates are available.

Validity

The ATCPS has been shown to discriminate between 25 police officers and 25 individuals in the general population (Balogh & Mueller, 1960). Further, Shaw and Wright (1967) suggest that content validity for the question whether murderers should face capital punishment is good, but that the question of capital punishment in general does not seem to be addressed by the items.

Comments

The ATCPS appears to measure attitudes concerning capital punishment of convicted murderers. Although no reliability estimates have been reported, the use of item analysis in the scale development suggests that internal consistency should be acceptable. The scoring system is flawed by the lowered scores of "question mark" or undecided responses, which functionally weight ATCPS scores toward positive attitudes toward capital punishment.

REFERENCES

Balogh, J., & Mueller, M. A. A scaling technique for measuring social attitudes toward capital punishment. *Sociology and Social Research,* 1960, *45,* 24–26.

Shaw, M. E., & Wright, J. M. *Scales for the measurement of attitudes.* New York: McGraw-Hill, 1967.

ATTITUDE TOWARD CAPITAL PUNISHMENT

Put a check mark (✓) if you agree with the statement. Put a cross mark (X) if you disagree with the statement. If you simply cannot decide about a statement, you may mark it with a question mark.

Scale value		
4.0	1.	Capital punishment is not morally right or wrong; it is merely just one method of punishment.
1.1	2.	A murderer deserves to die.
1.3	3.	Murderers are social misfits and are useless to society; therefore it is best to execute them.
6.7	4.	Society does not have the right to take a human life no matter what the circumstances.
2.6	5.	The public would feel less secure if capital punishment were abolished.
6.7	6.	When a murderer is sentenced to death, society is just as bad as the condemned.
5.1	7.	Since capital punishment has not prevented murders, society should abolish it.
1.2	8.	Murder is a sin and should be punished by death.
5.6	9.	Statistics show that a person will only kill once; therefore, the murderer should be allowed to live and prove himself.
6.1	10.	Since murderers can be rehabilitated, they deserve the chance to become useful citizens.
3.4	11.	Capital punishment will do until something better is found.
5.5	12.	Society should make murderers work for the state rather than execute them.
2.9	13.	Capital punishment seems to have proven to be a fairly effective deterrent to murder.
6.8	14.	When society sentences a murderer to death, we ourselves become murderers.
6.0	15.	Rather than execute a murderer, society should try to help him through treatment.

Attitude toward the Law (Martin and McConnell)

Development and Characteristics

This *Attitude toward the Law Scale* was designed specifically to indicate "the image of the law contained in the ideology of black militants" (Martin & McConnell, 1972, p. 111). The scale contains 24 Likert-type items developed to measure six types of attitudes: (1) legitimacy of the law (three items); (2) necessity of the law (five items); (3) corruption or lack of it among legal decisions (three items); (4) good faith of legal decision makers (five items); (5) accuracy of decision making (five items); and (6) discrimination against the disadvantaged (three items).

Response Mode

The respondent is asked to read each item, then note on a 5-point scale whether he or she: (1) "Strongly Agrees," (2) "Agrees," (3) "is Neutral," (4) "Disagrees," or (5) "Strongly Disagrees."

Scoring

Scoring can be based on a 5-point maximum for each item or simply by noting the number of agree or disagree responses. The latter format was used for the original study.

Norms

Table 15 represents the proportion of responses within each category that indicated a positive attitude for the law. The black group data were obtained in a predominately black community that had been experiencing conflict with the police. One police officer had been shot and the interviewer (a young black male) was a close friend of the man accused of the shooting. For this reason, the developers felt that the black subjects would respond in ways consistent with the militant black ideology.

The students were selected from Washington State University. The mail-poll group was selected randomly from the telephone directory of Spokane, Washington (population approximately 25,000). The Kiwanis Club sample was also chosen from members in the Spokane area. Finally, the surveyed judges were members of the Superior Court of the State of Washington.

Of course, because of the sampling procedures, these scores are not intended to represent general norms.

The table shows that the black subjects indicated an overall mean of 10%

TABLE 15. Attitudes toward the Law in Five Samples[a]

Summary by category	Black		Student		Mail-poll	
	$\bar{X}$	Range	$\bar{X}$	Range	$\bar{X}$	Range
I. Legitimacy of the law	18	0–29	91	85–97	92	89–96
II. Necessity of the law	36	3–18	90	71–95	91	83–98
III. Corruption or lack of it among legal decision makers	4	0–8	51	20–80	83	60–91
IV. Good faith of law enforcement machinery	8	2–17	58	20–76	70	47–85
V. Accuracy of decision making	2	0–8	61	22–97	68	32–89
VI. Discrimination against the disadvantaged	1	0–2	34	10–78	54	28–77

	Kiwanis		Judges		Overall mean
I. Legitimacy of the law	97	97–97	100	100–100	80
II. Necessity of the law	95	90–100	96	88–100	79
III. Corruption or lack of it among legal decision makers	90	80–97	97	94–100	64
IV. Good faith of law enforcement machinery	77	51–90	95	82–100	61
V. Accuracy of decision making	72	32–95	76	39–100	56
VI. Discrimination against the disadvantaged	58	19–90	71	42–97	44

[a] All means are rounded percentages of endorsement by group.

approving aspects of the law, whereas all other groups rarely showed less than 50% approval and usually responded at the 80% approval level, or higher.

Reliability

No reliability measures were reported.

Validity

One source of support for validity is by comparison groups. This scale differentiated between groups in the general direction that might be expected. In general, blacks (the militant ideology) showed lowest positive regard, students showed much more, but less than the mail-poll, which in turn scored less than the Kiwanis. Finally, the most approval came from judges. Also of interest is the trend of decreasing approval, through all groups, as the measure moved from theoretical statements (i.e., necessity of law) to more conventional and applied statements (i.e., discrimination against the disadvantaged).

There is some question, however, whether the categories are really different aspects of attitudes toward the legal system or just different questions about the same kinds of attitudes. For example, question one (under legitimacy of the law) may be measuring the same attitude as question 12 (under good faith of legal decision makers).

Comments

Development of this scale showed little attention to formal construction procedures or efforts to demonstrate reliability and validity. In spite of this, it seems to have face validity and some validity support through differences between comparison groups. There is a need for reliability measures, some test of heterogeneity for the categories, and cross-validation work. In general, the scale is in an early stage of development, but it seems to be reasonably on-target as a general measure of attitudes toward the American legal system and its use of law.

REFERENCES

Martin, J. D., & McConnell, J. P. Black militant ideology and the law. *Criminology,* 1972, *10,* 111–116.

McConnell, J. P., & Martin, J. D. Judicial attitudes and public morals. *American Bar Association Journal,* 1969, *55,* 1129–1133.

ATTITUDE TOWARD THE LAW

Instructions: Following are some statements with which you may agree or disagree. Beside each statement write the symbol which best represents your position on that statement.

Symbol	Feeling
SA	Strongly Agree
A	Agree
N	Neutral
D	Disagree
SD	Strongly Disagree

I. Legitimacy of the Law

1. The judges and juries are more guilty than those appearing before them. (Disagree)
2. There is no reason for people like me to obey the law. (Disagree)
3. I don't blame a guy for breaking the law if he can get away with it. (Disagree)

II. Necessity of the Law

4. For the protection of the individual, fairly extensive laws do seem to be necessary. (Agree)
5. Every civilized society needs some means of settling disputes. (Disagree)
6. Mankind is basically good, and if the authorities would just let people alone, crime would be no problem. (Disagree)
7. Compliance with the law would probably be greater if we fired all the police and made it voluntary. (Disagree)
8. We would be better off without laws or law enforcement. (Disagree)

III. Corruption or Lack of It among Legal Decision-Makers

9. The main purpose of traffic law enforcement is to provide revenue from the fines. (Disagree)
10. When a man is charged with a traffic offense, what happens depends more on who he knows than on what he did. (Disagree)
11. Judges, juries, and witnesses are bribed pretty regularly. (Disagree)

IV. Good Faith of Legal Decision-Makers

12. Judges and juries generally do the best job they can. (Agree)
13. Most policemen do their jobs as well as they can. (Agree)
14. When a crime is committed, you may be sure that they will find someone, guilty or not, to stand trial for it. (Disagree)
15. Our courts are essentially arbitrary in determining guilt or innocence. (Disagree)
16. Laws ought to take a great deal more account of the circumstances involved before holding a party guilty. (Disagree)

V. Accuracy of Decision-Making

17. Innocent people are seldom convicted of any sort of crime. (Agree)
18. Not very many innocent people are convicted of major crimes such as murder, robbery, and arson. (Agree)
19. A guilty person has a good chance of getting away with his crime. (Disagree)
20. Little crooks are more likely to go to jail than big crooks. (Disagree)
21. Verdicts of guilt and innocence are largely a matter of chance. (Disagree)

VI. Discrimination against the Disadvantaged

22. Law is a means by which the rich and powerful exploit the poor and weak. (Disagree)
23. A Negro or Mexican is much more likely to be found guilty of crime, even though innocent. (Disagree)
24. Men of substance and property usually get better treatment from the law. (Disagree)

Attitude toward the Law Scale (Katz)

Development and Characteristics

The *Attitude toward the Law Scale* (ATLS) was designed to measure an individual's attitude toward the law or laws under which he or she lives (Katz, in Thurstone, 1931). The scale was developed using a Thurstone procedure in which a group of judges rated the favorability of each item in the original pool. An item was retained for inclusion in the final version if there was sufficient agreement among the judges as to that item. Forty items met the Thurstone criterion for inclusion and were then divided to form two scales, each of which included items with a wide range of scale values (favorability scores). The result is a pair of 20 item equivalent form versions of the ATLS.

Response Mode

The respondent is requested to read each item carefully and agree (checking the statement) or disagree (making a cross by the statement).

Scoring

A scale value has been determined for each item, based on the median score obtained during development of the ATLS. A total score is obtained by adding the scale values for all the items with which the respondent has agreed. Therefore, a high score reflects a favorable attitude toward the law.

Norms

No norms are available.

Reliability

Reliability coefficients ranging from .47 to .64 have been reported for this scale (Ferguson, 1944). Equivalent forms reliability, however, appears to be much lower; it was reported to be .33 by Goodstein (1953). Shaw and Wright (1967) note that despite the statistical significance of this value, such a correlation coefficient is quite low for equivalent forms estimates.

Validity

Kimbrough (1956) analyzed the ATLS using a depthness scalogram procedure. He discovered that 14 of the 20 items in form A were appropriate for inclusion. This finding offers partial support for the unidimensionality of the scale. Further, the ATLS appears to have face validity.

Correlations of .30 and .50 have been reported between the ATLS and Thurstone's *Attitude toward the Treatment of Criminals Scale,* in the responses of 75 men and 103 women (Diggory, 1953). Further, the ATLS has been found to correlate highly with Thurstone's *Attitude toward Patriotism Scale* (Goodstein, 1953).

Comments

The ATLS appears to have some validity support. Reliability estimates, however, range from fairly acceptable to unacceptable. Estimates of equivalent forms reliability are especially discouraging.

Despite low reliability estimates, this scale has been much used in scholarly studies. The revised Guttman form (Kimbrough & Cofer, 1958) seems to be slightly more acceptable. Shaw and Wright (1967) report that the Guttman version has predictive validity as indicated by the comparison of scale scores with free associations to verbal stimuli.

REFERENCES

Diggory, J. C. Sex differences in the organization of attitudes. *Journal of Personality,* 1953, *22,* 89–200.

Ferguson, L. W. A revision of the primary social attitude scales. *Journal of Psychology,* 1944, *17,* 229–241.

Goodstein, L. W. Intellectual rigidity in social attitudes. *Journal of Abnormal and Social Psychology,* 1953, *48,* 345–353.

Kimbrough, W. W., Jr. A study of certain implications of a conception or attitudes as implicit verbal responses. *Dissertation Abstracts,* 1956, *16,* 1183–1184.

Kimbrough, W. W., Jr., & Cofer, C. N. Attitudes and stimuli as determiners of response. *Psychological Reports,* 1958, *4,* 61.

Shaw, M. E., & Wright, J. M. *Scales for the measurement of attitudes.* New York: McGraw-Hill, 1967.

Thurstone, L. L. *Scales for the measurement of social attitudes.* Chicago: University of Chicago Press, 1931.

ATTITUDE TOWARD THE LAW

Put a check mark (✓) if you agree with the statement. Put a cross (X) if you disagree with the statement.

Form A

Scale
value

4.1	1.	We have too many laws.
10.1	2.	Law is the greatest of our institutions.
0.8	3.	The law is just another name for tyranny.
7.4	4.	Individual laws are frequently harmful but the law as a whole is sound.
8.8	5.	In the long run law and justice are synonymous.
0.2	6.	I believe in the use of force to overthrow the law.
4.6	7.	We should have complete freedom of speech even for those who criticize the law.
5.7	8.	Between a society completely bound by law and a state of anarchy there is a happy medium.
10.5	9.	The law is more than the enactments of Congress; it is a sacred institution.
9.7	10.	The law represents the wisdom of the ages.
3.4	11.	Men are not all equal before the law.
6.7	12.	We should obey the law even though we criticize it.
5.2	13.	After all, the law is merely what people do.
9.1	14.	The sanctity of the law should be taught in all schools.
2.9	15.	The law is made in response to the pressure of lobbies in Washington.
6.1	16.	Some laws command our respect while others are mere regulations.
2.2	17.	The law is often the refuge of the scoundrel.
7.9	18.	It is not judges who punish criminals, it is the law.
1.5	19.	Law is the enemy of freedom.
8.3	20.	The law prevents wholesale crime and murder.

Form B

3.7	1.	Individual laws are frequently unjust.
9.0	2.	The law should take its course no matter how individuals may suffer.
4.4	3.	Some parts of the law are bad.
8.1	4.	The law is fundamentally sound in spite of mistakes by Congress and courts.

6.3	5.	Though it is our duty to obey all laws, we can try to have them changed.
9.3	6.	The individual who refuses to obey the law is a menace to civilization.
2.4	7.	The law is for the poor to obey, and for the rich to ignore.
8.5	8.	Disobedience of the law leads to anarchy.
0.0	9.	All law should be overthrown.
1.9	10.	The law is a means of enslaving the mass of humanity for the benefit of a small minority.
5.5	11.	Since law is made by man, it may be either good or bad.
5.9	12.	Individual liberty and legal restrictions are equally important factors in society.
7.8	13.	The law is superior to individual codes of conduct.
9.9	14.	No man can violate the law and be my friend.
3.3	15.	The law does not benefit the common man.
4.9	16.	Though we obey the law, we can still criticize it.
1.1	17.	We would be better off without any laws at all.
10.4	18.	The law is the true embodiment of eternal justice.
0.3	19.	The law is rotten to the core.
7.0	20.	The less one tampers with the law, the better.

Attitude toward Law and Justice Scale: A Sentence-Completion Test

Development and Characteristics

The *Attitude toward Law and Justice Scale* (ATLJS), a modification of the *Rotter Incomplete Sentences Blank Scale* (Rotter & Rafferty, 1950), was designed to "investigate the effects of incarceration upon the attitudes of prisoners" (Hulin & Maher, 1959, p. 245). The original form of the ATLJS contained 60 items that were designed to elicit opinions of the respondents. A pilot study of 20 prisoners showed that 20 items produced very low variability between the inmates. The remaining 40 items were used alone in the first testing of the scale. Originally, only a general attitude toward law and justice was measured which resulted in more than one dimension or factor being involved in the responses to the sentence stems. Many of the test results showed an apparent inconsistency: Approving of the law in general, yet having negative feelings toward aspects of the justice process due to personal experience.

This concern triggered an effort to begin testing for concrete experience as well as general attitude toward law and justice that necessitated a change in some of the stems. For example, "A judge" in the first form of the test was modified to read "My judge" in order to test specific experience with law and justice. Thirty items remained the same in the scale revision. Nine others were either modified or replaced. The resulting scale contained 39 items that can measure attitudes pertinent to abstract justice as well as concrete experience with the law.

Response Mode

This scale can be administered individually or in groups. The respondents are asked to read each sentence stem and write in their own feelings or opinions to complete the sentence.

Scoring

Scores are obtained by initially making a judgment as to the relevance of each response either to the general concept of law and justice or a concrete experience with the law and justice process. (A response that is not relevant to either of these is not scored.) If it is considered relevant to either, a 5-point scale is applied. A score of 1 is assigned to a response which represents extreme disapproval, nonconformity or a very negative response. For example, "justice stinks." A score of 2 represents mild disapproval, medium rejection or criticism, such as "My trial did not bring out all the truth." A score of 3 represents a neutral feeling, a definition, or a description. For example, "Witnesses are found in court." A score of 4 indicates approval or medium conformity, such as "A judge is a good man." A score of 5 indicates approval, conformity, or an extremely positive response. For example, "A cop is our friend."

The item scores of responses relevant to abstract justice and concrete experiences are added up separately with a mean computed for each.

Norms

Table 16 presents the response means of 126 prisoners, divided by offense categories. No significant differences existed between means of each of the crime categories.

TABLE 16. Intelligence, Length of Sentence, and Attitude Scores of Prisoner Groups

Factors	Murderers	Violent offenders	Sex offenders	Intellectuals
N	35.0	26.0	33.0	32.0
Age (years)	35.5	30.1	35.9	33.6
Months served	26.1	31.7	24.5	19.8
Abstract score	2.6	2.7	2.7	2.7
Concrete score	2.6	2.6	2.5	2.8

TABLE 17. Correlations between Attitudes toward Abstract and Concrete Age, Time Served in a Prison Population, Intelligence, and Justice

	Age	Time served	Army alpha	Justice
N	126	126	98	126
Abstract	.115	−.504[b]	.214[a]	.541[b]
Concrete	.103	−.644[b]	.212[a]	—

[a] .05 level of significance.
[b] .01 level of significance.

Reliability

Hulin and Maher (1959) reported an interscorer reliability coefficient of .93, when comparing the mean attitude scores from 30 protocols using two scorers.

Validity

Neither the abstract nor the concrete score was able to differentiate significantly between categories of offenders. Table 17, however, shows significant relationships between abstract and concrete scores as related to time served and the *Army Alpha Intelligence Test* (Hulin & Maher, 1959, p. 247). A partial correlation coefficient between the abstract and concrete scores was computed, first holding time served constant, and secondly holding intelligence constant. The results, .32 and .52 respectively, seem to indicate that time served and to a small degree, the scores on the *Army Alpha Intelligence Test,* are associated with the relationship between the abstract and concrete scores.

Content validity is difficult to establish using this type of scale, even though the word stems appear to stimulate thinking along the lines desired. If the raters' decisions are appropriate in actual use, however, the validity of the scale should be high.

Comments

In general, the ATLJS offers an opportunity for open-ended response from the subjects, but introduces possible error on the part of the raters. The high interscore reliability reported is evidence for consistency of evaluation.

Sentence-completion tests used in justice settings have been constructed on a predominantly intuitive and informal basis. Items typically are drawn from existing tests and from the clinician's experience. The ATLJS has utilized a multidimensional, replicable scoring procedure and a systematic development of items. While its psychometric limitations have been noted, the ATLJS appears to be among the sounder of such sentence-completion tests.

REFERENCES

Hulin, C. L., & Maher, B. A., Changes in attitudes towards law concomitant with imprisonment. *Journal of Criminal Law and Criminology,* 1959, *50,* 245–248.

Rotter, J. B., & Rafferty, J. E. *The Rotter incomplete sentences manual.* The Psychological Corp.: New York, 1950.

Watt, N. & Maher, B. A. Prisoners' attitudes towards home and the judicial system. *Journal of Criminal Law and Criminology,* 1958, *49,* 327–330.

ATTITUDE TOWARD LAW AND JUSTICE SCALE

Complete these sentences to express your real feelings. Try to do every one. Be sure to make a complete sentence.

1. With women I am _____.
2. Back home _____.
3. Parents _____.
4. My intelligence _____.
5. Marriage _____.
6. Justice _____.
7. Childhood _____.
8. The state's witness _____.
9. My greatest fear _____.
10. Most cops _____.
11. My personality _____.
12. A man's wife _____.
13. The law I broke _____.
14. When I was a child _____.
15. People treat me _____.
16. My lawyers _____.
17. A prisoner should be _____.
18. All my life _____.
19. My religion _____.
20. Our laws _____.
21. I regret _____.

22. Other people_____.
23. My father _____.
24. Only a sucker _____.
25. My sentence_____.
26. I trust _____.
27. My judge _____.
28. A mother _____.
29. The legal profession _____.
30. I pray _____.
31. The officer who arrested me _____.
32. Punishment _____.
33. I feel sad _____.
34. If I could be someone else _____.
35. Witnesses _____.
36. I _____.
37. Strict discipline for a child _____.
38. Under certain circumstances crime _____.
39. The happiest time _____.

Capital Punishment Attitude Questionnaire

Development and Characteristics

The *Capital Punishment Attitude Questionnaire* (CPAQ) was designed to measure two aspects of attitudes toward capital punishment (Jurow, 1971). Section A purports to "measure general attitude toward capital punishment." Section B "is more specific: it asks a potential juror how he would consider the death penalty if he were serving on a jury" (Jurow, 1971, p. 577). The distinction between these two attitudes toward capital punishment was made because the developer felt that "jurors may be able to distinguish between a personal, more private use, and what they regard as their legal duty." With this distinction in mind, the two attitude-items which make up the CPAQ were constructed.

Response Mode

The scale consists of two attitude-choices which are requested of the respondent. The first statement asks that the respondent check one of five statements that best summarizes his/her "general views" about capital punishment in criminal cases. The second statement asks that the respondent assume he/she is on a jury and is asked to determine the sentence for a defendant who has already been convicted of a very serious crime. The respondent then must choose the death penalty, life imprisonment, or some other penalty. Five alternatives are available. In both situations the respondent is asked to read the alternatives and place a check mark beside the statement that best describes his/her feelings.

Scoring

The five alternatives for each item are arranged so that the lowest number, 1, represents absolute opposition to capital punishment. The middle number, 3, indicates a neutral response and the highest number, 5, suggests a strong preference for capital punishment. The other numbers are degrees along this continuum. Therefore, the higher the number of the alternative chosen, the more favorable the attitude toward capital punishment (Section A), or the more likely a juror would be to vote in favor of the death penalty (Section B).

Norms

No relevant norms are available.

Reliability

No reliability estimates are available.

Validity

The developer hypothesized that an individual who favors capital punishment is more likely to convict a defendant than one who is not in favor of capital punishment. To test this hypothesis, he designed two simulations of court trials and enlisted the aid of 211 employees of the Sperry-Rand Corporation to serve as juror–subjects. In one case with evidence against the defendant, the B section was able to discriminate at the .01 level, while the A section proved to be significant only at the .10 level. In the other trial simulation with evidence favorable to the defendant, neither of the components of the CPAQ differentiated at a statistically significant level.

The CPAQ has been compared to the *Thurstone Capital Punishment Attitude Scale,* the *Rokeach Conservatism–Liberalism Scale* (a measure of conservative versus liberal political attitudes), the *California F Scale* (a measure of the complex authoritarian traits that characterize the right-wing, fascist individual), and the *Legal Attitudes Questionnaire* (LAQ) (which classifies subjects as having "authoritarian, antiauthoritarian, and egalitarian" legal attitudes). For the 211 respondents mentioned earlier, Sections A and B scores are significantly related to each of these tests (with the exception of the LAQ antiauthoritarian subscale, and the CPAQ Section B), indicating that "the more a subject is in favor of capital punishment, the more likely he is to be politically conservative, authoritarian and punitive in assigning penalties upon conviction" (Jurow, 1971, p. 588).

Comments

The developer notes that selecting jurors on the basis of their attitude toward capital punishment can have important implications for the courtroom system of justice. If a juror who favors capital punishment is more politically conservative, authoritarian, and punitive in assigning penalties, then conviction rates may be inflated by selecting out those individuals who are not in favor of capital punishment.

The CPAQ has the advantage of offering two types of attitudes toward capital punishment: One's professed attitude and the attitude one might take to be a legal duty as a juror. There is some support for the validity of this instrument. However, only two items make up the scale and these are divided into two subscales, indicating that scale scores can be erroneous with respect to the respondent's true attitude. An expansion of the number of items could help minimize this reliability issue.

REFERENCES

Goldberg, F. Toward expansion of Witherspoon: Capital scruples, jury bias, and the use of psychological data to raise legal perceptions. *Harvard Civil Rights-Civil Liberties Law Review,* 1970, *5,* 53.

Jurow, G. L. New data on the effect of "death qualified" jury on the guilt determination process. *Harvard Law Review,* 1971, *84,* 567–611.

CAPITAL PUNISHMENT ATTITUDE QUESTIONNAIRE

Directions: Check the <u>one</u> statement which <u>best</u> summarizes your <u>general</u> views about capital punishment (the death penalty) in criminal cases:

1. I am opposed to capital punishment under any circumstances.

2. I am opposed to capital punishment except in a few cases where it may be appropriate.

3. I am neither generally opposed nor generally in favor of capital punishment.

4. I am in favor of capital punishment except in a few cases where it may not be appropriate.

5. I am strongly in favor of capital punishment as an appropriate penalty.

Directions: Assume <u>you are on a jury</u> to determine the sentence for a defendant who has <u>already</u> been convicted of a very serious crime. If the law gives you a <u>choice</u> of death, or life imprisonment, or some other penalty: (check <u>one</u> only)

1. I could not vote for the death penalty regardless of the facts and circumstances of the case.
2. There are some kinds of cases in which I know I could not vote for the death penalty even if the law allowed me to, but others in which I would be willing to consider voting for it.
3. I would consider all of the penalties provided by the law and the facts and circumstances of the particular case.
4. I would usually vote for the death penalty in a case where the law allows me to.
5. I would always vote for the death penalty in a case where the law allows me to.

Juvenile Court Volunteer Effectiveness Interview Scale

Characteristics and Development

The *Juvenile Court Volunteer Effectiveness Interview Schedule* (JCVEIS) was developed by Horejsi (1971) to assess parental opinions about "the attitude or behavioral changes (in probationers), which might be attributed to volunteer intervention." The JCVEIS is administered to parents or parent-surrogates in less than one hour and is said to be nonthreatening and easily understood.

There are four parts to the schedule: 3 orientation items to insure that the parents know of the probationer's relationship with the volunteer; 10 items about parent characteristics; 37 items about the probationer's attitudes and behaviors; and 1 open-ended question about "any other way that the volunteer has been either helpful or harmful to (the probationer) you or to your family."

The schedule was constructed to focus on common life problems and attitudes that are to be given without the interviewer having specific or confidential knowledge about the probationer and his or her family. The major part of the JCVEIS used for research is the 37-item part about attitude and behavior change. The one open-ended question has been used to report on the subjective and unhappy experiences of the parents with the volunteers (Horejsi, 1972a,b).

Response Mode

Parents of probationers are interviewed. For each item they are asked to indicate whether the probationer had "improved," "remained the same," or "gotten worse" with respect to the behavior or attitude discussed. If the response was "remained the same," the researcher goes to the next item; otherwise, he or she asks the parents to indicate to what extent they believe the change was due to the volunteer who worked with the probationer (great deal, quite a bit, only a little, and nothing).

Scoring

A value of +2 was assigned to the response "improved," 0 to "remained the same," and −2 to "gotten worse." Then values of 5, 3, 1, and 0 were given to "great deal," "quite a bit," "only a little," and "nothing" respectively. An item score is the product of the two responses and the total score is the sum of the item scores. Therefore, a high positive score indicates that the parent feels much improvement was due to the volunteer, a low positive score shows little improvement was due to the volunteer, and a negative score results when the parent feels that the probationer "got worse" because of the volunteer.

Norms

No norms are available.

Reliability

Split-half reliability was estimated by calculating the Spearman rank order correlation coefficient *(rho)* between sums of odd and even numbered items. The resultant *rho* value for 45 parents was .877 (Horejsi, 1971).

Validity

The scale appears to have face validity. The items cover comprehensively the areas of probationer functioning about which parents and courts would be concerned.

Comments

This scale has acceptable reliability and face validity, and has the attraction of being a relatively direct method for assessing the impact of volunteer intervention on probationers. The central concern is the fact that the source of the information is the parents. It is possible that tbe probationer, probation officer, and the volunteer have different perceptions of the situation.

REFERENCES

Horejsi, C. R. *Parents' perceptions of the effect of volunteers on juvenile probationers.* Unpublished doctoral dissertation, University of Denver, 1971.

Horejsi, C. R. Unhappy experiences with court volunteers: Source of learning. *Volunteer Administration,* 1972, *7* (2), 18–22. (a)

Horejsi, C. R. Attitude of parents toward juvenile court volunteers. *Federal Probation,* 1972, *36,* 13–18. (b)

JUVENILE COURT VOLUNTEER EFFECTIVENESS INTERVIEW SCALE

Instructions to Interviewer: Indicate whether probationer has "improved," "remained the same," or "gotten worse" for each item. If the response is "improved" or "gotten worse," indicate the degree to which the change was due to the volunteer worker (a great deal, quite a bit, only a little, and nothing).

1. Probationer's ability to stay out of trouble.
2. How well the probationer and the parent are able to discuss things and talk things over without arguing.
3. How often the probationer seems to be in a happy or cheerful mood.
4. Amount of trust the parent has in the probationer.
5. How the probationer used (his) (her) spare time.
6. The amount of respect the probationer shows for the rights and feelings of other people.
7. How often the probationer causes the parent to become upset or angry.
8. Probationer's willingness to accept responsibility for (his) (her) own actions.
9. How well the probationer can accept correction.
10. How often the probationer attends school.
11. How often the probationer gets into arguments or fights with other kids.
12. Amount of self-confidence and self-respect the probationer seems to have.
13. Kind of grades the probationer receives in school.
14. Probationer's ability to be honest and truthful with the parent.
15. Probationer's general attitude toward school.
16. Probationer's ability to accept restrictions.
17. Probationer's willingness to obey or do what the parent thinks is best.
18. Probationer's willingness to come home when he is supposed to.
19. Probationer's self-control.
20. How well the parent is able to understand how the probationer thinks and feels.
21. Probationer's self-control.
22. Amount of respect the probationer has for authority.

COURTS AND THE LAW

23. Type or number of clubs or organizations the probationer belongs to.
24. Probationer's attitude toward doing homework.
25. How well the probationer takes care of (his) (her) clothing and other personal belongings.
26. How often probationer asks parent for advice or opinions.
27. Frequency with which the parent and the probationer have disagreements.
28. Probationer's grooming and dress.
29. How well the probationer gets along with boys (his) (her) own age.
30. Type of language the probationer uses.
31. Probationer's ability to accept ordinary disappointments.
32. How well everyone gets along in the probationer's family.
33. Probationer's ability to handle money in a responsible manner.
34. Probationer's willingness to pitch in and do necessary work around home.
35. The sort of plans the probationer is making for the future.
36. How well the probationer gets along with girls (his) (her) own age.
37. Probationer's general physical health.

Legal Attitudes Questionnaire

Development and Characteristics

The *Legal Attitudes Questionnaire* (LAQ) was designed to "measure attitudes that take legal issues as a framework" (Boehm, 1968, p. 739). It is based on the assumption that a scale that accurately measures legal attitudes should also be correlated with authoritarian and dogmatism scales, and should predict behavior in a quasi-jury situation. Further, it is assumed that three attitudinal dimensions would be necessary to accurately depict legal attitudes. These are authoritarianism, antiauthoritarianism and egalitarianism (lack of bias). For the purposes of the LAQ, *authoritarianism* is defined as a right-wing philosophy that indiscriminately endorses the acts of constituted authority and represents an essentially punitive nature. *Antiauthoritarianism* is represented by left-wing sentiments, the implication that antisocial acts are a result of societal structure, and an indiscriminant rejection of constituted authority. *Egalitarianism* is defined by a lack of bias with regard to constituted authority and is represented by traditional liberal, but nonextreme positions on legal questions.

Items pertaining to these dimensions were elicited from sources that included civil liberties advocates, newspapers, the United States Constitution, United States Supreme Court decisions, and conversations with knowledgeable persons. When these responses were analyzed and assembled into item form, a total of 54 items

(18 representing each attitude) resulted. These were arranged into nine sets of six items each, in which two items containing each of the three dimensions were contained. This first version of the LAQ was administered to graduate students in social psychology who were asked to indicate their degree of agreement with each statement. When their responses were submitted to an item analysis, items that best predicted high and low scores for each dimension were chosen.

The 10 best items for each attitude dimension were chosen to constitute a revised form of the LAQ. This version was constructed so that 10 sets of three items each were grouped together. Each set contained one authoritarian, one antiauthoritarian and one egalitarian item. The individual's ranking of agreement to the statements within each set are used as a measure of his or her attitudes along the three dimensions.

Response Mode

The respondents are requested to read the items in each of the 10 sets, make judgments as to which of the three items in a set they agree with the most, and place a plus beside that item. Then they are requested to place a minus mark beside the item with which they agree the least.

Scoring

The item within each set of three that receives a plus response is given a score of 3. Each item that receives a minus mark is scored a 1 and a score of 2 is given to each unmarked item in the triad. By adding all of the item scores for each dimension (authoritarianism, antiauthoritarianism, and egalitarianism) three separate scores with ranges from 10–30 are possible. In each of the three subscales, a high score represents high agreement for that attitude dimension.

Norms

No norms are available.

Reliability

No numerical estimates of reliability are available. However, the use of item analysis in scale construction indicates some degree of internal consistency for each of the three dimensions.

Validity

The LAQ was administered to 50 civil rights workers, who were northern college students. When their responses to the LAQ were compared to the F scale, the authoritarian subscale of the LAQ was found to relate positively and the antiauthoritarian and egalitarian subscales related negatively. Dogmatism scores were found to relate positively to both the authoritarian and antiauthoritarian subscales of the LAQ, but related negatively with the egalitarian subscales. These results indicate some support for the construct validity of the three subscales of the LAQ.

Next, the LAQ was tested in a quasi-jury experiment. Two versions of a court case were presented to a group of 151 psychology students at the University of California. In one version, the evidence indicated guilt; in the other the evidence was slanted toward innocence. A manipulation check indicated that the two versions were indeed perceived differently by the respondents and they appropriately predicted actual verdicts.

The results of this experiment indicated that individuals who scored higher on authoritarianism were more likely to render a "guilty" verdict in both instances. Conversely, those scoring high on antiauthoritarianism were more likely to acquit the hypothetical defendant in both cases.

Comments

The LAQ has received support for its validity and its internal consistency, although, in the latter case, the evidence is indirect. There is some question, however, as to its multidimensionality. Although the developer discusses "the dimensions" of attitudes being measured by the LAQ, these should not be interpreted as orthogonal, distinct factors. Indeed, the LAQ was constructed so that the subscales, of necessity, would be correlated; the ipsative response and scoring procedures insure it.

This apparent lack of distinct, uncorrelated subscales, however, is not a shortcoming, but a consideration for interpretation. In general, the LAQ appears to be a useful instrument that has been carefully developed and partially validated.

REFERENCES

Boehm, V. R. Mr. Prejudice, Miss Sympathy, and the authoritarian personality; an application of psychological measuring techniques to the problem of jury bias. *Wisconsin Law Review,* 1968, 734–750.

LEGAL ATTITUDES QUESTIONNAIRE

On the following pages are ten groups of statements, each expressing a commonly held opinion about law enforcement, legal procedures, and other things connected with the judicial system. There are three statements in each group.

Put a plus (+) on the line next to the statement in a group that you agree with most, and a minus (-) next to the statement you agree with the least.

An example of a set of statements might be:

  _+_ A. The failure of a defendant to testify in his own behalf should not be taken as an indication of guilt.
  ____ B. The majority of persons arrested are innocent of any crime.
  _-_ C. Giving an obviously guilty criminal a long, drawn-out trial is a waste of the taxpayer's money.

In this example, the person answering has agreed most with statement A and least with statement C.

Work carefully, choosing the item you agree with most and the one you agree with least in each set of statements. There is no time limit on this questionnaire, but do not spend too much time on any set of statements. Some sets are more difficult than others, but please do not omit any set of statements.

Set I

____A. Unfair treatment of underprivileged groups and classes is the chief cause of crime.   AA
____B. Too many obviously guilty persons escape punishment because of legal technicalities.   A
____C. The Supreme Court is, by and large, an effective guardian of the Constitution.   E

Set II

____A. Evidence illegally obtained should be admissible in court if such evidence is the only way of obtaining a conviction.   A
____B. Most prosecuting attorneys have a strong sadistic streak.   AA
____C. Search warrants should clearly specify the person or things to be seized.   E

Set III

____A. No one should be convicted of a crime on the basis of circumstantial evidence, no matter how strong such evidence is.   AA
____B. There is no need in a criminal case for the accused to prove his innocence beyond a reasonable doubt.   E
____C. Any person who resists arrest commits a crime   A

Set IV

____A. When determining a person's guilt or innocence, the existence of a prior arrest record should not be considered.   E
____B. Wiretapping by anyone and for any reason should be completely illegal.   AA
____C. A lot of recent Supreme Court decisions sound suspiciously communistic.   A

Set V

____A. Treachery and deceit are common tools of prosecutors.   AA
____B. Defendants in a criminal case should be required to take the witness
stand.   A
____C. All too often, minority group members do not get fair trials.   E

Set VI

____A. Because of the oppression and persecution minority group members
suffer, they deserve leniency and special treatment in the courts.   AA
____B. Citizens need to be protected against excess police power as well as
against criminals.   E
____C. Persons who testify in court against underworld characters should be
allowed to do so anonymously to protect themselves from retaliation.   A

Set VII

____A. It is better for society that several guilty men be freed than one innocent
one wrongfully imprisoned.   E
____B. Accused persons should be required to take lie-detector tests.   A
____C. When there is a "hung" jury in a criminal case, the defendant should always be freed and the indictment be dismissed.   AA

Set XI

____A. A society with true freedom and equality for all would have very little
crime.   AA
____B. It is moral and ethical for a lawyer to represent a defendant in a criminal
case even when he believes his client is guilty.   E
____C. Police should be allowed to arrest and question suspicious-looking
persons to determine whether they have been up to something illegal.   A

Set IX

____A. The law coddles criminals to the detriment of society.   A
____B. A lot of judges have connections with the underworld.   AA
____C. The freedom of society is endangered as much by overzealous law
enforcement as by the acts of individual criminals.   E

Set X

____A. There is just about no such thing as an honest cop.   AA
____B. In the long run, liberty is more important than order.   E
____C. Upstanding citizens have nothing to fear from the police.   A

COURTS AND THE LAW ATTITUDE SCALES: LISTINGS

Attitudes toward the Law

Thomas, C. W., & Williams, J. S. *The construction of Likert-type attitude scales: An examination of alternative techniques of item selection.* Paper presented to the Rural Sociological Society Convention, Montreal, Canada, August 1974.

This 11-item,Likert-type scale was developed in a methodological exercise in measurement of attitudes. It is intended to assess attitudes toward the justness of laws and obedience to laws.

Attitudes toward Legal Agencies

Chapman, A. W. Attitudes toward legal agencies of authority for juveniles. A comparative study of 133 delinquent and 133 nondelinquent boys in Dayton, Ohio. *Dissertation Abstracts International,* 1960, *20,* No. 7.

Shaw, M. E., & Wright, J. M. *Scales for the measurement of attitudes.* New York: McGraw-Hill, 1967.

This 49-item,Likert-type scale was designed to measure juvenile offender attitudes toward juvenile court, detention, and boys' industrial schools.

Attitudes toward the Legal System

Thomas, C. W., Petersen, D. M., & Zingraff, M. T. Student drug use: A reexamination of the "hang-loose ethic" hypothesis. *Journal of Health and Social Behavior,* 1975, *16,* 63–73.

This scale is an 11-item,Likert-type instrument designed to measure students' attitudes toward law and the legal system.

Attitudes toward the Legal System

Torney, J. V. Socialization of attitudes toward the legal system. *Journal of Social Issues,* 1971, *27,* 137–154.

This 8-item interview schedule measures socialization effects on childrens' attitudes toward the legal system, law, and police officers. Three items concern law and five items concern evaluation judgments of police.

Attitudes toward Due Process and the Juvenile Court

Franklin, J., & Gibbons, D. C. Directions for juvenile courts: Probation officers' views. *Crime and Delinquency,* 1973, *19,* 508–518.

This 26-item,forced-choice questionnaire was designed to measure probation officers', social workers', and other counselors' attitudes toward due process for juveniles and limitations on the scope and powers of juvenile courts.

Attitude toward Probation Officers

Chapman, A. W. Attitudes toward legal agencies of authority for juveniles. A comparative study of 133 nondelinquent boys in Dayton, Ohio. *Dissertation Abstracts International*, 1960, *20*, No. 7.

Shaw, M. E., & Wright, J. M. *Scales for the measurement of attitudes*. New York: McGraw-Hill, 1967.

This 22-item,Likert-type scale was designed to measure the attitudes of male youthful probationers toward their probation officers.

Ideological and Law-Abidingness Scales

Gregory, W. S. Ideology and affect regarding "law" and their relation to law-abidingness. Part 1. *Character and Personality*, 1939, *7*, 265–284.

Shaw, M. E., & Wright, J. M. *Scales for the measurement of attitudes*. New York: McGraw-Hill, 1967.

The Ideological scale consists of six subscales totaling 67 items, relating to the nature of law. The *Law-Abidingness Scale* contains 14 items relating to the extent of conformity to laws, especially traffic laws. Both are Thurstone-type scales that yield multiple scores.

Juvenile Justice—What Do You Think?

Sarri, R., & Hasenfeld, Y. (Eds.). *Brought to justice? Juveniles, the courts and the law*. Washington, D.C.: U. S. Department of Justice, 1976.

The scales are designed to measure the attitudes of individuals involved in the criminal justice system. There are six different scales in this group. The respondents are judges (102 items), court administrators (84 items), probation/intake workers (79 items), detention administrators (116 items), staff in juvenile corrections (107 items), and delinquent youth (115 items). Considerable item overlap exists. Full questionnaires may be obtained directly from Dr. Rosmary Sarri, School of Social Work, University of Michigan, Ann Arbor, Michigan 48109.

Knowledge of Student Rights Scale, Cynicism about the Law and Legal System Scale, Knowledge of the Law in General Scale

Rafky, D. M., & Sealey, R. W. The adolescent and the law: A survey. *Crime and Delinquency*, 1975, *21*, 131–138.

These three scales are designed to measure the feelings of high school students concerning contact with the law, attitude toward the law and knowledge of the law. The *Knowledge of Student Rights* is a 7-item, yes-no scale dealing with rights to use different methods of protest, to privacy and to due process. The *Cynicism About the Law and Legal System Scale* is a 9-item, agree-disagree scale drawn from the *Rundquist-Sletto Law Scale*. The *Knowledge of the Law in General Scale* is a 10-item, yes-no questionnaire asking "Is it a crime" to commit 10 listed acts.

Law Scale

Rundquist, E. A., & Sletto, R. F. *Personality in the depression.* Minneapolis: University of Minnesota Press, 1936.

Shaw, M. E., & Wright, J. M. *Scales for the measurement of attitudes.* New York: McGraw-Hill, 1967.

This 22-item, Likert-type scale has been widely used as a measure of attitudes toward multiple aspects of the law and legal processes.

COURTS AND THE LAW PERSONALITY ASSESSMENT: REVIEWS

Competency Screening Test

Development and Characteristics

The *Competency Screening Test* (CST) is a sentence-completion type test that was designed to distinguish the competency issue from other legal and mental health issues, and individuals not competent to stand trial from other client populations administered by mental health services (Lipsett, Lelos, & McGarry, 1971). The first version of the test contained 50 items or sentence stems that the respondent was asked to complete. These items focused on the three areas used for competency evaluations: (1) The potential for a constructive relationship between client and lawyer, (2) the client's understanding of the court process, and (3) the client's ability to deal emotionally with the criminal process.

These 50 items were administered to a group of people who had been designated as competent or incompetent to stand trial; 22 items were useful in discriminating between the two groups.

Response Mode

The CST can be administered in two different ways. The subject may be asked to read the items or sentence stems and then write down his or her completing remarks, or the sentence may be read to the subject, in which case he or she would be asked to respond verbally.

Scoring

The CST score is based on a 3-point scale. A score of 2 is assigned for a normal, appropriate response. A score of 1 is given to a response that is below the standard, but not clearly inappropriate and a score of 0 is given to a clearly poor response. The scoring handbook provides specific instructions for each item sample responses. For example, the following excerpt was given for Item 1.

1. The lawyer told Bill that
   (a) Legal criteria: ability to cooperate in own defense, communicate, relate
   (b) Psychological criteria: ability to relate or trust

   SCORE 2: includes obtaining and/or accepting advice or guidance
   examples: "he should plead not guilty"
   "he was free"
   "he should plead nolo"
   "he should plead guilty"
   "he would take his case"
   "he would need to know all the facts concerning the case"
   "he should turn himself in"
   "the outlook was good"
   "he will try to help him"

   SCORE 1:
   examples: "he is innocent"
   "everything is all right"
   "be truthful"
   "he will be going to court soon"
   "he is competent to stand trial"
   "it will be filed"

   SCORE 0: includes regarding lawyer as accusing or judgmental
   examples: "he was wrong in doing what he did"
   "he is guilty"
   "he is going to be put away"
   "no comment"

Norms

Table 18 shows the results of CST scores for six groups of respondents. The student group is composed of 13 undergraduate students who were enrolled in a course in juvenile delinquency. The Bridgewater control group was a group of 47 men at the Bridgewater, Massachusetts mental hospital who had been deemed relatively undisturbed. The men's club was a group of noninstitutionalized men who belonged to a church-affiliated breakfast club. The state hospital, civilly committed subjects were patients from Boston State Hospital. The accused non-hospitalized group was a sample of people who had been accused of crimes, but

TABLE 18. Means and Standard Deviations for
Competency Screening Test Scores

Group	N	Mean	SD
Student	13	25.92[a]	7.20
Bridgewater control	47	24.64[b]	7.79
Men's club	28	24.36[a]	7.00
State hospital, civilly committed	19	23.84[a]	6.82
Accused, nonhospitalized	11	23.09[c]	6.58
Bridgewater experimental	43	18.45	8.17

[a] $p < .01$, in comparison with the Bridgewater experimental group.
[b] $p < .001$, in comparison with the Bridgewater experimental group.
[c] No significant difference in comparison with the Bridgewater experimental group.

who were sent directly to trial without questioning their competency. Finally, the Bridgewater experimental group was a sample of 43 men who were diagnosed as most disturbed from the state mental hospital. Their median age was 30, they scored an average IQ of 92 on the WAIS, and their average educational level was ninth grade.

As can be seen from the table, the experimental group, those considered most emotionally disturbed, scored the lowest mean score and differed significantly from all groups except the accused nonhospitalized group.

Reliability

Lipsitt, Lelos, and McGarry (1971) report an interrater reliability of .93, when the raters were bachelor's degree level testers who had had a brief period of training.

Validity

The fact that the CST differentiates between those "disturbed patients" at Bridgewater and all other "nondisturbed" groups (except "accused, nonhospitalized" subjects) is evidence of its validity. Lipsitt et. al. (1971) also compared CST scores to actual pretrial dispositions of 43 respondents. Of the subjects, 16 who scored low were actually committed for treatment (a correct prediction), 17 who scored high on the CST were deemed competent to stand trial (a correct prediction), 7 of the low scorers were tried (an incorrect prediction), and 3 of the high scorers were committed to hospitals (another incorrect prediction).

The test developers suggest that the errors encountered were explainable. For example, the three subjects who scored high on the competency screening test, but were eventually committed to a mental institution had committed crimes that may be considered extremely repugnant to the community. One patient had murdered a child, another had sexually assaulted a child, and a third, although charged only with disturbing the peace, had threatened to kill a police officer during a disruption. The developers suggested that community feelings were so strong that an influence was exerted in the direction of removal of these individuals from society. In the case of those individuals who scored low on the CST, but who were returned for trial, there is evidence that they were mentally deficient and, according to psychological criteria, unable to defend themselves in court.

A third attempt at validation was factor analysis. However, this analysis was unable to give consistent results when separate samples were analyzed.

Comments

The developers proposed the CST to be used as a substitute for hospitalization and interviewing for decisions of competency to stand trial. The lack of factorial validity support, however, and the lack of sensitivity of the instrument to discriminate between nonextreme cases, suggests that the test is not sufficiently established as a clinical instrument. In addition, the use of a poorly defined cutoff point (estimated to be 20) indicates the need for more research on the CST.

The entire task of competency assessment has been characterized by subjective procedures, vaguely specified criteria, and confusion of severity of disorder with incompetence. This sentence-completion test holds promise, however, as an adjunct to clinical assessment and formal checklists in competency evaluations.

REFERENCES

Lipsitt, P. D., Lelos, D., & McGarry, L. Competency for trial: A screening instrument. *American Journal of Psychiatry,* 1971, *128,* 137–141.

COMPETENCY SCREENING TEST

Complete these sentences to express your real feelings. Try to do every one. Be sure to make a complete sentence.

1. The lawyer told Bill that
2. When I go to court the lawyer will
3. Jack felt that the judge
4. When Phil was accused of the crime, he
5. When I prepare to go to court with my lawyer

6. If the jury finds me guilty, I
7. The way a court trial is decided
8. When the evidence in George's case was presented to the jury
9. When the lawyer questioned his client in court, the client said
10. If Jack has to try his own case, he
11. Each time the D.A. asked me a question, I
12. While listening to the witnesses testify against me, I
13. When the witness testifying against Harry gave incorrect evidence, he
14. When Bob disagreed with his lawyer on his defense, he
15. When I was formally accused of the crime, I thought to myself
16. If Ed's lawyer suggests that he plead guilty, he
17. What concerns Fred most about his lawyer
18. When they say a man is innocent until proven guilty
19. When I think of being sent to prison, I
20. When Phil thinks of what he is accused of, he
21. When the jury hears my case, they will
22. If I had a chance to speak to the judge, I

Competency to Stand Trial Assessment Instrument

Development and Characteristics

The *Competency to Stand Trial Assessment Instrument* (CTSTAI) was "designed to improve communication between the behavioral science disciplines (particularly psychiatry) and the law in an area of mutual responsibilities—the determination of competency to stand trial" (McGarry, 1973, p. 99). The items were written based on their relevance to the criteria used by professional clinicians making judgments concerning the competency of an individual to stand trial.

The CTSTAI consists of a set of 13 considerations that may be important in the assessment of individuals' abilities to cope with the trial process and to adequately protect themselves. The items represent a systematic search through appellate court cases, legal literature, and clinical and legal courtroom experience for criteria that are used to judge an individual's competency to stand trial.

The developers suggest that the weighting of individual items from one case to another and from one courtroom situation to another may vary. The CTSTAI, however, may provide objective data upon which the court can draw and use as it deems important.

Response Mode

The CTSTAI is a rating form that is completed by a clinical professional. Information used in rating an individual according to each of the items must be obtained through an interview. The individual being rated is asked to participate by responding to the questions of the interviewer.

Scoring

Each of the 13 items is scored along a 6-point continuum that is rated as follows:

> A score of 1 on the instrument indicates that, for the individual scored, a close to or total lack of capacity to function exists on the order of a mute, incoherent person, or a severe retardate.
> A score of 2 indicates that, for the item scored there is severely impaired functioning and substantial question of adequacy for a particular function.
> A score of 3 indicates that there is moderately impaired functioning and a question of adequacy for the particular function in question.
> A score of 4 indicates that, for the items scored, there is mildly impaired functioning and little question of adequacy for a particular function. An individual can be mildly impaired on the basis of lack of experience in the legal process or a sociocultural deprivation, with or without attendant psychic pathology. A score of 5 indicates that, for the items scored, there is no impairment and no question that the defendant can function adequately.
> A score of 6 indicates that the available data do not permit a rating that is within reasonable clinical certainty. (McGarry, 1973, p. 101)

No total score is obtained. The developers suggest that for screening purposes "a majority or a substantial accumulation of scores of three or lower in the 13 items could be regarded as grounds for a period of inpatient observation and more intensive work" (McGarry, 1973, p. 100).

Norms

No norms are available.

Reliability

McGarry (1973) reports an intraclass r reliability coefficient of .92 for the ratings of project staff members in the assessment of 18 patient–defendants. Further, when ratings by 216 clinicians (psychiatrists, psychologists, social workers, and nurses) who had studied the handbook were compared and averaged, a reliability coefficient of .84 was obtained. These results were based on ratings for 13 different patient–defendants in eight sessions at state hospitals. The reliability coefficients for this entire group ranged from .72 for those clinicians who had no prior opportunity to study the administration guidelines from the handbook, to .84 for observers who had an opportunity to study the handbook prior to examination.

Validity

The scale developers suggest that the validity of the CTSTAI will be determined by its acceptance and utilization in the courtroom. In a set of 15 cases presided over by one judge, the assessments made according to the CTSTAI were upheld by the judge in 14 cases. Thus, in this situation the assessment procedure was acceptable.

Comments

Competency-to-stand-trial assessments have traditionally been performed in subjective ways against uncertain criteria. While the stated goals are court–psychiatrist communication and court acceptance, the more important objective is specification of the operational clinical evaluation issues in competency assessments. That objective is achieved well. The good reliability, the content validity, and the preliminary predictive validity suggest that the CTSTAI has much promise as a research instrument.

REFERENCES

McGarry, A. L. *Competency to stand trial and mental assessment* (DHEW Publication No. ADM 74-103). Washington, D.C.: U.S. Government Printing Office, 1973.

COMPETENCY TO STAND TRIAL ASSESSMENT INSTRUMENT

Note: No instructions were provided for this scale because the author obtained his data through an interview procedure. Any instructions which require the subject to choose one of the alternatives provided and to answer every question will probably suffice.

		Degree of Incapacity				
	Total	Severe	Moderate	Mild	None	Unratable
1. Appraisal of available legal defenses	1	2	3	4	5	6

(This calls for an assessment of the accused's awareness of his possible legal defense and how consistent these are with the reality of his particular circumstances.)

2. Unmanageable behavior   1   2   3   4   5   6

(This item calls for an assessment of the appropriateness of the current motor and verbal behavior of the defendant and the degree to which this behavior would disrupt the conduct of a trial. Inappropriate or disruptive behavior must arise from a substantial degree of mental illness or mental retardation.)

3. Quality of relating to attorney   1   2   3   4   5   6

(This item calls for an assessment of the interpersonal capacity of the accused to relate to the average attorney. Involved are the ability to trust and to communicate relevantly.)

4. Planning of legal strategy, including guilty plea to lesser charges where pertinent   1   2   3   4   5   6

(This item calls for an assessment of the degree to which the accused can understand, participate, and cooperate with his counsel in planning a strategy for the defense which is consistent with the reality of his circumstances.)

5. Appraisal of role of:

a. Defense counsel	1	2	3	4	5	6
b. Prosecuting attorney	1	2	3	4	5	6
c. Judge	1	2	3	4	5	6
d. Jury	1	2	3	4	5	6
e. Defendant	1	2	3	4	5	6
f. Witnesses	1	2	3	4	5	6

(This set of items calls for a minimal understanding of the adversary process by the accused. The accused should be able to identify prosecuting attorney and prosecution witnesses as foe, defense counsel as friend, the judge as neutral, and the jury as the determiners of guilt or innocence.)

6. Understanding of court procedure   1   2   3   4   5   6

(This item calls for an assessment of the degree to which the defendant understands the basic sequence of events in a trial and their import for him; e.g., the different purposes of direct and cross examination.)

7. Appreciation of charges   1   2   3   4   5   6

(This item calls for an assessment of the accused's understanding of the charges against him and, to a lesser extent, the seriousness of the charges.)

8. Appreciation of range and nature of possible penalties   1   2   3   4   5   6

(This item calls for an assessment of the accused's concrete understanding and appreciation of the conditions and restrictions which could be imposed on him and their possible duration.)

9. Appraisal of likely
   outcome   1   2   3   4   5   6

(This item calls for an assessment of how realistically the accused perceives the likely outcome and the degree to which impaired understanding contributes to a less adequate or inadequate participation in his defense. Without adequate information on the part of the examiner regarding the facts and circumstances of the alleged offense, this item would be unratable.)

10. Capacity to disclose
    to attorney available
    pertinent facts sur-
    rounding the offense
    including the defendant's
    movements, timing, mental
    state, and actions at the
    time of the offense   1   2   3   4   5   6

(This item calls for an assessment of the accused's capacity to give a basically consistent, rational, and relevant account of the motivational and external facts. Complex factors can enter into this determination These include intelligence, memory, and honesty. The difficult area of the validity of an amnesia may be involved and may prove unresolvable for the examining clinician. It is important to be aware that there may be a disparity between what an accused is willing to share with a clinician as opposed to what he will share with his attorney, the latter being the more important.)

11. Capacity to real-
    istically challenge
    prosecution witnesses   1   2   3   4   5   6

(This item calls for an assessment of the accused's capacity to recognize distortions in prosecution testimony. Relevant factors include attentiveness and memory. In addition, there is an element of initiative in that if false testimony is given, the degree of activism with which the defendant will appraise his attorney of inaccuracies is of importance.)

12. Capacity to testify
    relevantly   1   2   3   4   5   6

(This item calls for an assessment of the accused's ability to testify with coherence, relevance, and independence of judgment.)

13. Self-defeating versus
    self serving motivation
    (legal sense)   1   2   3   4   5   6

(This item calls for an assessment of the accused's motivation to adequately protect himself and appropriately utilize legal safeguards to this end. It is recognized that accused persons may appropriately be motivated to seek expiation and appropriate punishment in their trials. At issue here is the pathological seeking of punishment and the deliberate failure by the accused to avail himself of appropriate legal protections. Passivity or indifference do not justify low scores on this item. Actively self-destructive manipulation of the legislative process arising from mental pathology does justify low scores.)

COURTS AND THE LAW MILIEU RATINGS: LISTINGS

Pre-trial Intervention Program Questionnaire

Rovner-Pieczenik, R. *Pre-trial intervention strategies: An evaluation of policy-related research and policy-maker perceptions.* Washington, D.C.: American Bar Association, Commission on Correctional Facilities and Services, 1974.

This 18 item, 3-point scale was designed to assess the utility of pretrial intervention programs as judged by criminal justice policy makers.

COURTS AND THE LAW PREDICTION: LISTINGS

Pre-trial Release Decisions

Gottfredson, M. R. An empirical analysis of pre-trial release decisions. *Journal of Criminal Justice,* 1974, *2,* 287–304.

A prediction of who can reasonably be expected to appear for trial and who cannot is derived from the use of background factors and the Vera Institute *Pretrial Release Decisions Scale.*

COURTS AND THE LAW DESCRIPTION: REVIEWS

Judicial Role Perception Scale

Development and Characteristics

The *Judicial Role Perception Scale* (JRPS) was designed in an effort to study a typology of orientations of court judges (Ungs & Baas, 1972). JRPS is based on the assumption that judges see their roles in four distinctly different ways. Some judges see themselves as a law interpreter. Others see themselves as a law maker "as does a legislative body." A third type sees a judge as adjudicator who "substitutes the principle of accommodation and mediation for personal views concerning each case." Finally, it was hypothesized that another group of judges perceive the role of judge to be administrator "akin to that of an executive." It was further hypothesized that three basic types of indicators represent judges' perceptions of their roles. These include: (1) their characterization of their jobs, (2) the focus or goals they pursue, and (3) the major criteria they use in making decisions.

A literature review of articles written by federal and lower court judges was undertaken to produce statements about the way judges view their roles. A total of 500 statements resulted. From these, 48 were selected so that four items represented each of the four role types according to each of the three role expectations.

These statements were typed on cards and sent with a set of instruction to 109 Ohio state judges (38 appellate and 71 lower court). The instructions requested that the judge read each statement and rate the extent to which he or she agreed or disagreed on an 11-point scale. They placed the cards on which the statements were written in a stack ranging from +5, "most agree" through 0, "neutral" to −5, "most disagree." The judges were also asked to place only four statements in each of the categories except 1, 0, and −1. In these stacks, they were requested to place 5, 6, and 5 cards respectively.

Fifty judges responded (20 appellate and 30 lower court) by returning the statements in the sorted order. These data were then factor analyzed using a Q methodology in which correlations are calculated between subjects rather than between responses to each statement. The factor loads that resulted indicated the type to which each judge had the most similarity.

Principal component factor analysis indicated five factors resulting from the 50 judges. These factors were rotated to simple structure using a varimax criterion. When the responses of the judges to the Q sort were compared for each factor, only three of the original four role types were evident. The law interpreter, adjudicator, and administrator role types were clearly indicated by the factor analysis. The two new factors were labeled "trial judge" and "peacekeeper." The "trial judge" combines qualitites possessed by the other roles, but shows a combination that is a unique perception of the judicial role. The "peacekeeper" was characterized by only five judges and was therefore too small to provide a solid basis for assessment. However, "this type of judge perceives the role of the court not only with reference to the results of particular cases, but also in terms of an activist in maintaining harmonious social relations" (Ungs & Baas, 1972, p. 360).

Response Mode

The respondent is asked to rate each statement along an 11-point continuum ranging from "most disagree" (−5) to "most agree" (+5).

Scoring

Since the Q methodology was used, the only way to categorize the role type of judges is to compare their responses to those typical responses of the judges who formed the five factors.

TABLE 19. A Comparison of Mean Factor Loadings for Trial and Appellate Judges

	I Interpreter	II[a] Adjudicator	III Administrator	IV[b] Trial judge	V Peace- keepers
Appellate court	.41	.43	.21	.10	.10
Lower court	.39	.28	.16	.19	.14

[a] $p < .01$.
[b] $10 > p > .05$.

Norms

Table 19 compares the average factor load on each of the five factors for the 20 appellate judges and 30 lower court judges. Note that only factors two and four differentiated between the two samples of judges.

Reliability

No formal reliability information was presented. However, one type of interjudge reliability might be inferred from the Q factor analysis. The factors that resulted indicated relative agreement between the judges within each of the factors.

Validity

An attempt to validate the typology resulted in a revised classification system that has not yet been cross-validated. The first three factors, however, law interpreter, adjudicator, and administrator are role types that were both hypothesized and observed.

Comments

This effort is not a scale, but a methodology. It helps to fill a need for information on orientation of judges. While not a formal scale, the method and data can serve as a good beginning for research and instrument development.

REFERENCES

Ungs, P. D., & Baas, L. R. Judicial role perceptions: A Q-technique study of Ohio judges. *Law and Society Review,* 1972, *6,* 343–366.

JUDICIAL ROLE PERCEPTION SCALE

Instructions: Rate each of the following statements on an 11 point continuum ranging from most disagree (-5) to most agree (+5) by placing the number of your choice beside each item.

-5   -4   -3   -2   -1   0   +1   +2   +3   +4   +5
Most   Most
Disagree   Agree

Factor I: Law Interpreter

No interpretation of the law which fails to take due account of the separation of powers can be considered constitutionally sound. (+5)

The judicial judgment must move within the limits of accepted notions of justice and is not to be based upon the idiosyncracies of a merely personal judgment. (+5)

Our judgment cannot be rested on the hypotheses of tomorrow, but must take the facts as they are presented today. (+4)

When the social needs demand one settlement rather than another, there are times when we must bend symmetry, ignore history, and sacrifice custom in the pursuit of other and larger ends. (-4)

Courts are not the only agency of government that must be assumed to have the capacity to govern, for the removal of unwise laws appeal lies not to the courts, but to the ballot and the processes of democratic government. (+4)

The ultimate function of the judge is nothing less than the arbitration between fundamental and ever present rival forces or trends in our organized society. (-4)

We interpret the law. That's our function. We're not authorized to write the law. We can only act in one way. That is to be solely interpreters of the law. (+3)

Adherence to precedent then must be the rule rather than the exception if litigants are to have faith in the evenhanded administration of justice in the courts. (+4)

Stare decisis is at least the everyday working rule of the law. (+2)

Judges always made law and always will. In interpretation you're trying to give answers to problems that were not considered by the legislature, and you try to guess what the legislature would have done. (-5)

The law is what we say the law is to be. (-5)

Factor II: The Adjudicator

Not only should a judge be expert in statutory construction and profoundly versed in tenets of the common law and principles of equity jurispruduence, but he should be endowed with fervor for substantial justice and possessed of a warm heart controlled by a cool brain. (+5)

The law is not an end in itself, nor does it provide ends. It is preeminently a means to serve what we think is right. (+4)

The fundamental purpose is to bring order and fair play into society; to define and to assure to each his rights; to invest business with a measure of decency; to interpose barriers against deceit, and at the same time to guard against arbitrary conduct on the part of government officials. (+ 5)

Justice can be achieved by judges who consider a law suit not a game, the object of which is to award a prize to the more skillful of the two contestants, but as society's method of achieving social peace and justice under law. (+ 5)

It is the spirit and not the form of law that keeps justice alive. (+ 5)

The function of the judge is primarily adjudication. This not a mechanical craft, but the exercise of a creative art, whether we call it legislative or not, which requires great ability and objectivity. (+ 4)

The inescapable judicial task is to balance contending principles. This task requires judgment. (+ 3)

Our task is great. Its performance brings into play those qualities of knowledge, social idealism, courage, and integrity which have always been considered the attributes of a good judge. (+ 3)

Adherence to precedent then must be the rule rather than the exception if litigants are to have faith in the evenhanded administration of justice in the courts. (-3)

We interpret the law. That's our function. We're not authorized to write the law. We can only act in one way. That is to be solely interpreters of the law. (-4)

Stare decisis is at least the everyday working rule of the law. (+ 1)

Judicial power, as contradistinguished from the power of the law, has no existence. Courts are the mere instruments of the law and can will nothing. (-4)

It is important that judges keep in continuous fruitful contact with the changing social background out of which controversies arise. (+ 2)

The judicial function is to pursue justice in every case. (+ 5)

The chief function of our judicial machinery is to ascertain the truth. (+ 4)

The ultimate function of the judge is nothing less than the arbitration between fundamental and ever present rival forces or trends in our organized society. (-3)

When the social needs demand one settlement rather than another, there are times when we must bend symmetry, ignore history, and sacrifice custom in the pursuit of other and larger ends. (-4)

Factor III: The Administrator

Judging is administration. (-4)

While justice is a natural virtue, it is also a social virtue. In the administration of justice, therefore, lawyers and judges must believe in, subscribe to, understand, and sustain the institutions of government and must oppose any persons or ideals inconsistent with those principles. (+ 1)

The Anglo-American judge requires distinctive skill to work competently with the complex nature of the law. These skills may be said to be far more important to the judge than legal scholarship. (+ 5)

Justice can be achieved by judges who consider a law suit not a crime, the object of which is to award a prize to the more skillful of the two contestants, but as society's method of achieving social peace and justice under law. (+ 5)

If there were no rules, we would be governed by men, not laws. Order is not only Heaven's first law, but order is the essence and the end of all jurisprudence. (+5)

Judges administer justice judiciously, not according to some abstract right and justice, but according to the rules laid down by society in its code of laws to which it gives its sanctions. (+2)

It is our responsibility, new judges and old, to clean up the accumulations of pending cases and to maintain current dockets in every court so that equal justice for all will be insured by prompt justice to all. (+4)

The crucial question is not whether the court has kept up with its calendar, but whether it has kept up with justice. (-1)

The judicial function is to pursue justice in every case. (-2)

Stare decisis is usually the wise policy, because in most matters it is more important that the applicable rule of law be settled than that it be settled right. (+3)

Factor IV: The Trial Judge

Stare decisis is at least the everyday working rule of the law. (+5)

Adherence to precedent then must be the rule rather than the exception if litigants are to have faith in the evenhanded administration of justice in the courts. (+5)

Stare decisis is usually the wise policy, because in most matters it is more important that the applicable rule of law be settled than it be settled right. (+2)

The judicial judgment must move within the limits of accepted notions of jurisprudence and is not to be based on the idiosyncracies of a merely personal judgment. (+4)

Laws are designed to establish justice. Thus the protection of these laws should be the aim of the judicial task. (+3)

If there were no rules, we would be governed by men, not laws, order is not only Heaven's first law, but order is the essence and end of all jurisprudence. (+5)

The judicial function is to pursue justice in every case. (+5)

The chief function of our judicial machinery is to ascertain the truth. (+4)

Our judgment cannot be rested on the hypotheses of tomorrow, but must take the facts as they are presented today. (+1)

Judging is administration. (+4)

It is our responsibility, new judges and old, to clean up the accumulation of pending cases and to maintain current dockets in every court so that equal justice for all will be insured by prompt justice for all. (+3)

Factor V: The Peacekeeper

Courts governed by the rule of law may not achieve spectacular results in particular cases, but they satisfy more effectively the need of modern society for peace in the relations between the individuals composing it and between them and the state. (+5)

It is for us to meet the administration of justice in a spirit ripened by the experience of the past — with eyes fastened on the future, and the aim to achieve a better ordered life. (+4)

COURTS AND THE LAW

Justice can be achieved by judges who consider a law suit not a game, the object of which is to award a prize to the more skillful of the two contestants, but as society's method of achieving social peace and justice under law. (+5)

The fundamental purpose is to bring order and fair play into society; to define and to assure to each his rights; to invest business with a measure of decency; to interpose barriers against deceit, and at the same time to guard against arbitrary conduct on the part of government officials. (+5)

Courts as an institution are too deeply imbedded in our society to take a back seat. (+1)

Courts are not the only agency of government that must be assumed to have the capacity to govern, for the removal of unwise laws appeal lies not to the courts, but to the ballot and to the processes of democratic government. (-4)

Inevitably a judge makes law as does a legislative body; no matter how you decide a case, you're making law. (-5)

I take judge-made law as one of the existing realities of life. (-5)

Judges, when construing statutes, necessarily engage in a species of lawmaking, the legislature often does no more than provide a general standard. (-3)

We interpret the law. That's our function. We're not authorized to write the law. We can only act in one way. That is to be solely interpreters of the law. (+4)

Judicial power as contradistinguished from the power of the law has no existence, courts are the mere instruments of the law and can will nothing. (+1)

Our task is great. Its performance brings into play those qualities of knowledge, social idealism, courage, and integrity which have always been considered the attributes of a good judge. (+4)

The inescapable judicial task is to balance contending principles. This task requires judgment. (+3)

Stare decisis is at least the everyday working rule of the law. (-3)

The judicial function is to pursue justice in every case. (+3)

The chief function of our judicial machinery is to ascertain the truth. (+5)

Probation Officer–Client Relationship Valence Scale

Development and Characteristics

The *Probation Officer–Client Relationship Valence Scale* (POCRVS) was designed to measure "the attraction of the client toward the probation officer–client relationship" (Deming, 1972). This attraction is believed to be important, because the scale developer feels that the officer–client relationship should constitute a primary group and that if the relationship is viewed positively by the probationer, "desirable resocialization will result."

Fifteen of the 30 items that make up the scale are revisions of items contained in the *Group Morale Scale* (Goldman, 1957). Fifteen other items evolved from a list of all the attitudes that the developer felt were indicative of the officer–client relationship. All items were written in Likert format in the final version of the scale.

Response Mode

A standard Likert response is requested. The respondent reads each statement and notes whether he or she: (1) "strongly agrees," (2) "agrees," (3) "is uncertain," (4) "disagrees," or (5) "strongly disagrees."

Scoring

A score for each item is obtained by assigning a value of 5 to the alternative that most strongly favors the relationship and 4, 3, 2, 1 in order of decreasing strength of response. The total score is a sum of the item scores.

Norms

A sample of 100 adjudicated delinquents who had been granted probation attained an average score of 120 for their relationships with five probation officers.

Reliability

Deming (1974) reports a coefficient of reliability of .94 (a score calculated from item intercorrelations).

Validity

Goldman (1957) found that his full 20-item scale differentiated between members of bookclubs, student campus groups, classroom groups, and labor unions. The revised Likert items, however, have not been tested independently or in conjunction with the additional items.

Comments

This scale seems reliable and straightforward and a normative sample is available; the question of validity is, however, generally unanswered, although the items do seem to have face validity.

REFERENCES

Deming, R. R. *Valence as a measurement of the effectiveness of probation officer–client relationship.* Unpublished manuscript, Northeastern University, 1972.
Deming, R. R. Valance as a measurement of the effectiveness of probation officer–client relationship. *Journal of Criminal Justice,* 1974, 2, 157–162.
Goldman, G. *A study of group morale.* Chicago: Psychometric affiliates, 1957.

PROBATION OFFICER-CLIENT RELATIONSHIP VALENCE SCALE

Below are a number of statements about probation and probation officers, with which some people agree and others disagree. Please give me your opinion of your probation and your probation officer.
Please circle your choice.

SA	Strongly agree
A	Agree
U	Uncertain
D	Disagree
SD	Strongly disagree

SA	A	U	D	SD	1.	I believe I could be honest with my probation officer.
*SA	A	U	D	SD	2.	My probation officer acted as if he was too busy to see me.
*SA	A	U	D	SD	3.	My probation officer was more interested in catching me "messing up" than in helping me.
*SA	A	U	D	SD	4.	My probation officer did not help me in any way.
SA	A	U	D	SD	5.	My probation officer helped me from "messing up."
SA	A	U	D	SD	6.	I will be able to use the advice my probation officer gave me for the rest of my life.
SA	A	U	D	SD	7.	My probation officer treats me like a man.
SA	A	U	D	SD	8.	I feel good after talking to my probation officer.
*SA	A	U	D	SD	9.	My probation officer is wishy-washy.
SA	A	U	D	SD	10.	My probation officer is firm but fair, a right guy.
SA	A	U	D	SD	11.	I was not able to see my probation officer as much as I wanted.
*SA	A	U	D	SD	12.	I always felt nervous when I was with my probation officer.

SA	A	U	D	SD	13. My probation officer was usually interested in listening to me.
*SA	A	U	D	SD	14. I never told my probation officer any of my personal problems.
*SA	A	U	D	SD	15. I believe that my probation officer has ideas that are unfair.
SA	A	U	D	SD	16. My probation officer would help me if I needed help.
*SA	A	U	D	SD	17. My probation officer is out for his own good; he didn't care about me.
SA	A	U	D	SD	18. My probation officer could always be counted on to do the right thing.
*SA	A	U	D	SD	19. I just would say what my probation officer wanted me to say.
*SA	A	U	D	SD	20. My probation officer was square and didn't think about important things.
*SA	A	U	D	SD	21. I would never want my probation officer as a friend.
SA	A	U	D	SD	22. My probation officer was out to help me as much as he could.
*SA	A	U	D	SD	23. I seldom paid attention to what my probation officer said; I believe in making my own decisions.
SA	A	U	D	SD	24. I feel that I have made a lasting friend in my probation officer.
SA	A	U	D	SD	25. I feel that I could have asked my probation officer for advice.
*SA	A	U	D	SD	26. My probation officer was stubborn, no amount of argument would change him.
*SA	A	U	D	SD	27. My probation officer got his job because he has connections, not because of his ability.
*SA	A	U	D	SD	28. Sometimes I liked coming here, but most of the time I hated it.
SA	A	U	D	SD	29. My probation officer would risk his own neck if it were necessary to save mine.
SA	A	U	D	SD	30. I believe that my probation officer would "stab me in the back" if it meant he could get ahead that way.

*Reversed items.

Problem Checklist

Development and Characteristics

The *Problem Checklist* (PC) was designed to predict success on probation (Simon, 1971). The original item pool was composed of 61 variables that probation officers had suggested might predict success on probation. Some items referred to factual information (i.e., childlessness, brothers and sisters, etc.) and others required the judgment of the probation officer (i.e., unstable behavior, callousness, etc.).

The entire set of 61 items was submitted to multiple regression analysis and predictive attribute analysis. Both techniques indicated that items 45 and 57 ("Has little conscience" and "Has delinquent tendencies," respectively) were most powerful. Correlations between these items and success, however, were so small that they were considered of little value as predictors.

Next a set of 10 items (from the original 61) was chosen to serve as a deviance scale. These items were chosen by the research team to represent problems of deviance. All 10 items refer to qualities of the parolee that are based on the evaluative judgments of a probation officer. This 10-item version appears to be the most promising and will be described as the PC.

Response Mode

No response is required of the probationer. The probation officer is asked to read each item and decide whether the probationer: (1) does not have the problem; (2) has the problem to a "mild" degree; (3) has the problem to a "moderate" degree; (4) has the problem to a "severe" degree; or (5) has the problem to a "very severe" degree.

Scoring

Each item score indicates the degree of severity of the item problem. Possible item scores are 0 (absence of problem), 1 (mild), 2 (moderate), 3 (severe), or 4 (very severe). The total score is the sum of the item scores. The PC has a range from 0 to 40 and is calculated so that the higher the score, the less likely an individual is believed to be successful during probation.

Norms

When the scores of a total of 682 individuals were compared to measures of probation success, a cutting score of 22 was found to be most predictive. Mean scores of 11.62 ($SD = 7.51$) and 10.10 ($SD = 7.29$) were obtained for samples of 303 and 379 probationers respectively.

Reliability

Reliability was assessed by test–retest stability over a three week period for a total of 142 probationers (age 17 and over, male and female). A reliability coefficient of .62 resulted.

Validity

Samples of 379 and 303 probationers were tested and their success or failure during probation was recorded. Probation was considered a success if the probationer was not rearrested within one year and a failure if he or she was arrested for any offense. The point–biserial correlations that resulted between the two measures were .32 ($p < .01$) and .24 ($p < .01$), respectively.

Comments

The PC may be a valuable set of items for assessing a probation officer's opinion of probationers. As an applied predictor of deviance or probation success, however, it accounts for less than 10% of the variance in the one predictive study.

REFERENCES

Simon, F. H. *Prediction methods in criminology*. London: Her Majesty's Stationery Office, 1971.

PROBLEM CHECKLIST

Instructions: Read each item and note whether the probationer (1) does not have the problem, (2) has the problem to a "mild" degree, (3) has the problem to a "moderate" degree, (4) has the problem to a "severe" degree, or (5) has the problem to a "very severe" degree.

1. Childishness
2. Anxiety
3. Apathy
*4. Irresponsibility
5. Conflicting feelings
6. Hostility
7. Self-centeredness
8. Parents with criminal record
9. Parents with delinquent values
10. Brothers and sisters with criminal record
11. Brothers and sisters with delinquent values
12. Demanding behavior

13. Apparent seeking for punishment
14. Aggressiveness
15. Dependence
16. Depression
17. Elation
18. Delinquent friends or associates
19. Member of delinquent gang (or peer group)
20. Tension
21. Low intelligence
22. Withdrawal
23. Delinquent street or neighborhood
24. Insecurity
*25. No loyalties
26. Unreasonable fears (phobias)
27. Unstable behavior
28. Physical illness, handicap or abnormality
*29. Callousness
30. Feelings of persecution
31. Personal matrimonial problems
32. Parents' matrimonial problems
33. Poor relationship with parents
34. Financial problems
35. Poor sibling relationships
36. Overcrowding, accommodation problem
37. Other family problem
38. Plausibility
*39. Anti-authority attitudes
*40. Anti-social attitudes
41. Lack of judgment
42. Attempts to manipulate people
*43. Dishonesty
*44. Untruthfulness
*45. Little conscience
46. Irrational thoughts
47. Impulsiveness

48. Ignorance of law (regarding his offense)
49. Easily led
50. Feelings of guilt
51. Temper outbursts
52. Showing off
*53. Drunkenness
54. Low tolerance of frustration
55. Lack of friends
56. Lack of self-control
*57. Delinquent tendencies
58. Emotional deprivation
59. Lack of parental control
60. Unemployment
61. Others

*Deviance score items.

COURTS AND THE LAW DESCRIPTION: LISTINGS

Goal Attainment Scale

Conter, K. K., Seidman, E., Rappaport, J., Kniskern, D., & Desaulniers, G. *A comparative evaluation of two college student volunteer programs by the volunteers themselves: The importance of commitment and supervision* (1976). Document #4 of the Community-Based Adolescent Diversion Project, Community Psychology Action Center, 51 East Gerty Drive, Champaign, IL 61820

This scale is a 26-item questionnaire, 24 items of which use a 7-point rating scale to evaluate a student volunteer working in a companionship role with youths on probation or in legal jeopardy. The items assess the program, personal impact, and efficacy of and reaction to training, supervision and peers.

Judicial Roles Questionnaire

Sheldon, C. H. Judicial roles: Backgrounds and norms. *California Western Law Review,* 1973, 9, 497–513.

This questionnaire was designed to measure judicial functioning and activities: The roles of adversary, law interpreter, adjudicator, and political roles are assessed for influence on judicial decisions. Fourteen judicial tasks are rated in order of importance, as are five lawyers' roles in terms of importance to the Bar.

Juvenile Court Role Expectations Questionnaire

Brennan, W. C., & Khinduka, S. K. Role expectations of social workers and lawyers in the juvenile court. *Crime and Delinquency,* 1971, *17,* 191–201.

The role expectation questionnaire was designed to ascertain the perceived functions of social workers and lawyers in 21 activities in juvenile court.

Perception of Stigma Interview Procedure

Foster, J. D., Dinitz, S., & Reckless, W. C. Perceptions of stigma following public intervention for delinquent behavior. *Social Problems,* 1972, *20,* 202–209.

This interview procedure is designed to measure the degree to which boys perceive having incurred any social liability as a consequence of their encounters with police or juvenile courts. Perceived liabilities are assessed in interpersonal relationships, parental attitudes, school difficulties, police encounters, and future employers' attitudes.

Probationer and Volunteer Evaluation Questionnaires

Beier, E. G., & Zautra, A. J. *The evaluation of the effectiveness of volunteers and probation officers in misdemeanant services.* Proceedings of the International Congress of Psychology, Argentina, 1972. (Also available in expanded form, E. G. Beier, Psychology Department, University of Utah, Salt Lake City, Utah 84112.)

The 19-item probation questionnaire and 20-item volunteer questionnaire are mixed format. They were designed to assess the perceptions of the probationer and volunteer worker regarding the nature, intensity, and success of the volunteers' efforts.

CHAPTER 8
Corrections

Within this chapter, *corrections* refers to individuals who are incarcerated in penal institutions and to the correctional institutions and processes themselves. Parole and parolees, parole officers, and correctional employees are included within the scope of this definition.

Customarily, corrections as a field is considered to be limited to the postconviction phase of punishment that results in imprisonment or other punitive action. However, since institutions per se have been identified here as part of corrections, scales that concern juvenile detention—even though the residents are in preadjudication status—have been included.

Within corrections, for the first time, our category of milieu ratings truly comes into play. Two milieu rating instruments, the *Correctional Institution Environment Scale* and the *Prison Profile Inventory*, are reviewed. In addition, seven others are listed and noted.

This chapter also presents scales assessing psychological and therapeutic treatment in correctional settings with correctional clientele. Thus the *Attitude to Psychiatry Scale*—which is not really about attitudes toward psychiatry, but rather attitudes toward psychiatric treatment within the prison—is listed, as is the *Attitudes Toward Enforced Therapy Scale*. Several scales that have emerged from the Differential Treatment work using the *I*-Level schema are also listed.

Two other chapters overlap with *Corrections* content. Chapter 12 on *General Scales* contains many scales that have been applied to correctional populations. However, the *object* of such personality or attitude scales is not corrections specific; only the respondents are corrections subjects, and thus the scales are not presented here. The second chapter to which the correctional researcher should refer is Chapter 10 on *Offenders*. In that chapter, offenders are defined more broadly than simply correctional institution residents. Nevertheless, there are scales in that chapter of related interest.

CORRECTIONS ATTITUDE SCALES: REVIEWS

Attitudes toward Juvenile Detention

Development and Characteristics

The *Attitudes toward Juvenile Detention Scale* (ATJDSG) was designed to measure the attitudes of criminal justice officials, especially probation and police officers, toward the detention of juveniles (Gottfredson, 1970). This scale applies specifically to the confinement of juveniles before adjudication. The assumptions underlying the scale development are that the differential rates of preadjudication detention are a function of characteristics of the children, those responsible for the decision, and the circumstances of the specific situation. In an effort to measure some aspects of characteristics of the decision makers, the second source of variation, 25 vignettes, were assembled into a questionnaire. These short-case examples give the details of the crime an individual is accused of, a brief social history, including information on his or her family, some direct quotes from the accused, and other relevant information.

The scale was administered by mail to an exploratory sample of 92 juvenile court jduges, probation officers, and field staff of the National Council on Crime and Delinquency. It was noted that there was a great deal of variability in the responses, so a factor analysis was undertaken. Four items were excluded because of their small degree of variability and lack of discriminating ability. Four factors were extracted, but since only two produced eigenvalues greater than 1, only these two factors were rotated.

Factor one seemed to represent those vignettes dealing with runaways, truants, or petty thieves. Usually the parent–child relationships were unhealthy and the parent seemed to add to the child's problems. Gottfredson (1970) felt that the tendency to detain this group was due to a "concern for the welfare of the child." Therefore, he labeled this factor "Protection of the Child."

The second factor seemed to be related to a tendency toward detention because the juvenile showed involvement in serious crimes or was continually in trouble. This factor was labeled "Protection of Society" to denote the reason for detention.

Response Mode

The respondent is asked to read each vignette carefully, then to note, on a 6-point scale, his or her feelings about detention of the individual portrayed in the story. On this scale, 1 represents "certainly not detain" and 6 represents "certainly detain." The numbers between are gradations of these two extremes.

Scoring

Two methods of scoring may be followed. First, since the vignettes offer much information, the detention decision is often complex and does not offer "pure" lines of decision making. Thus, one can note the responses to individual items and make inferences about attitudes. (A single total score would be of little value because, as the developer has noted, the items are not homogeneous.)

The second scoring procedure is more complex. It involves converting the raw scores to two factor scores and using this as the base of comparison. Since factor weights were not reported, the original weights must be replaced by those from new factor analyses.

A third possible scoring system, which was presented by the developer, involves summing the item scores for the vignettes that are used to define the two factors. These are Items 2, 3, 6, 14, 16, and 17 for Factor 1, and Items 1, 9, 11, 13, 18, 19, and 20 for Factor 2.

The lack of a standard scoring procedure is an indication that the scale is still very much in the exploratory stage. With this in mind, many different scoring methods and uses can be analyzed and tried.

Norms

As noted in the *Scoring* section, no standardized scoring system has been developed. This makes the presentation of norms inappropriate.

Reliability

No reliability measures other than internal consistency from the factor analysis were reported.

Validity

Validity was assessed in three ways. First, a second sample of 141 criminal justice workers were administered the scale. When factor analyzed, these data supported the original two-factor structure. Second, the developer hypothesized that police officers would score high on Factor 2 (Protection of Society), while probation officers would score high on detention for "Protection of the Child" (Factor 1) and vice versa. When these two groups were compared, however, only Factor 2 was able to discriminate between them in the predicted direction. Third, other evidence for validity was found when scale scores were compared to a ratio of juveniles detained to total number of juveniles apprehended. Again, only Factor 2 discriminated between officials in counties with high detention ratios and those with low ratios.

Comments

The ATJDSG holds much promise. The vignettes themselves are realistic and reflect the central issues relating to the detention decision. The scale developer has defined two factors, one of which shows validity between contrasted groups.

This scale, however, presents many unresolved problems. First is the question of scoring. Observing individual item scores could be useful, but limits the power of the instrument. The use of factor scores is too complex a procedure for routine use. Finally, the summing of two sets of items as factor-based subscales lowers the impact of the entire set of vignettes, but seems to be the preferred choice at present.

Another issue is validity. The relationships presented offer some indication that the scale measures relative strength of attitude toward detention. It does not, however, discriminate as predicted between the types of attitudes. In both comparisons, factor one, the better defined factor, was unable to differentiate between the criterion groups.

Finally, the developer suggests that part of the problem with this scale is the complexity of the vignettes. He offers such conflicting information that the decision of detention is most difficult. The "simplification" or "purification" (making the reports less conflicting) may make responding to the test less difficult, but this may also move the vignettes a few steps away from reality.

Moreover, although this scale clearly captures the richness of clinical factors influencing detention of juveniles, the scoring uncertainties are sufficiently severe that no standardized use is possible without further investigation.

REFERENCES

Gottfredson, D. *Measuring attitudes toward juvenile detention*. Davis, California: National Council on Crime and Delinquency Research Center, 1970.

ATTITUDES TOWARD JUVENILE DETENTION

Instructions: Twenty-five case situations or "vignettes" requiring detention decisions are presented in this questionnaire. The vignettes portray relatively complex family situations, but most persons whose work involves juvenile detention decisions will discover much that is familiar in the problems presented.

Please read each of the vignettes. In each case, six choices are open to you. Please check only one choice for each vignette.

CORRECTIONS

1. Ernie, age 17, is brought in by the police charged with assault with a deadly weapon. According to the officers, he and two friends crashed a party, disrupted the proceedings by bullying, and made insulting advances toward the girls. In the ensuing fight, Ernie used a broken coke bottle to seriously gash the host's arm.

   Contrary to witnesses' statements, Ernie insists that he was invited to the party and did nothing objectionable there. He justifies use of the weapon in that five or six of the boys "jumped" him because he was "making out" with the girls.

   A Central Records check reveals several police contacts, at least one year old, due to suspicious loitering and curfew violation. Eight months ago, he and the same two friends were placed on probation after they stole a car to drive to a party. Progress reports indicate very satisfactory improvement. He has avoided further difficulty, has re-enrolled in school, and has maintained passing grades while working part time in a gas station.

Certainly not detain	Probably not detain	Slightly against detention	Slightly for detention	Probably detain	Certainly detain

2. Sally, age 14, is brought in by her parents, who insist she be detained. They describe her as becoming increasingly defiant, disobedient, poor in her schoolwork, and truant. They say the trouble started when she met Tina, a 16-year-old dropout who "does as she pleases."

   Recently, Sally stayed out overnight on a weekend, without permission. Earlier in the day, she and Tina had been picked up as runaways after two days away from home, apparently heading for New York. The parents suspect the girls of sexual misbehavior and drug use.

   Sally admits trying to get away from her parents by going to live in New York with relatives. She denies the other allegations and describes her father's temper and parents' arguments as intolerable. She states also she probably will run away again if the parents' contemplated divorce becomes a reality.

Certainly not detain	Probably not detain	Slightly against detention	Slightly for detention	Probably detain	Certainly detain

3. Ronnie, age 13, is carried in by two policemen, kicking and screaming. They report that a variety shop owner and his wife had caught the boy who had, six times in the past month, dashed into the store and run off with small items. His description had been given to the police, and it corresponded with that which had been given by other petty theft victims in the area. The boy would not give his name; however, a customer at the shop identified him and accused him of minor acts of mischief in the neighborhood.

   The school vice-principal reveals that Ronnie was enrolled eight weeks ago, from out-of-state, and expelled four weeks later due to fights, defiance, and disobedience. He has not been back, and the family has not responded.

   A telephone call to the home elicits from the boy's aunt that his mother, who is at work, has not been told of his difficulties. The aunt states that she doesn't want to worry her. The mother was recently widowed and had to move to the city to support her children. The mother, by phone, verified the aunt's statements and said she would come to the office immediately.

Certainly not detain	Probably not detain	Slightly against detention	Slightly for detention	Probably detain	Certainly detain

4. Bill, a 17-year-old college freshman, is brought in by police when neighbors complained of a wild party. Police found six people, under age 21, in various stages of undress and obvious intoxication. Alcoholic beverages and marijuana cigarettes were found in the apartment. Bill is the youngest of the six.

From the information the police have put together, it is apparent that Bill has been living for several weeks with the 19-year-old coed to whom the apartment is rented. Particles of marijuana were found in his shirt pocket. He has no police record.

Bill states that he has never been in trouble, says he has been living with the girl, admits he was "a little high" from drinking, but claims he has never used marijuana. His claim that he carried marijuana cigarettes for his grilfriend is supported by her statement to the police. The father, on the phone, states, "Ship him back here, or do what you like. He insisted on going to school out there. He got himself into trouble, now he'll have to face it like a man."

Certainly not detain	Probably not detain	Slightly against detention	Slightly for detention	Probably detain	Certainly detain

5. Phillip, age 17, the son of a prominent doctor, is brought in, charged with vehicular hit and run, while driving well over the speed limit, according to witnesses. His car allegedly sideswiped another when he failed to stop at a red light. An estimated $300 damage was done to the other vehicle, and the driver suffered slight injuries.

It is established that Phillip, an only child, had his license revoked two weeks ago, for one year, due to repeated moving violations. He has had several police contacts in the past three years for illegal use of firearms, being intoxicated, participating in wild parties, reckless driving, and possession of alcohol. However, no court action was taken in any of these situations. His school record is above average, and he is known as a good boy, but wild. The parents are very cooperative with the authorities, but they are ineffectual in controlling Phillip's behavior.

Certainly not detain	Probably not detain	Slightly against detention	Slightly for detention	Probably detain	Certainly detain

6. Linda, age 17, a reported runaway, was found living with her 24-year-old fiance. She admits she has been with him two weeks and is two months pregnant. For the past four months, her parents have refused them permission to marry. When she discovered her pregnancy, she decided to leave home because she was afraid of her parents' reaction.

Linda has no police record, and she appears average in all respects. However, her parents insist that she be "locked up." They feel she would be a bad influence on the younger children and do not want her "contaminating the rest of the family with her filth."

School officials state Linda has average grades in her senior year. She could be reinstated; and if the lost work were made up, she could be graduated with her class in three months.

Certainly not detain	Probably not detain	Slightly against detention	Slightly for detention	Probably detain	Certainly detain

7. Robert, age 14, is brought in after a neighbor discovered him in an act of intercourse with her 10-year-old daughter. He ran, and the woman states she obtained

the following information from her daughter while the police were looking for him. Robert forced her the first time, then threatened to tell her father if she didn't keep doing it. Repeated sex acts have occurred in the past several months, with both the 10-year-old and her 11-year-old sister. The sister, under questioning, gave the same story and indicated that Robert had similarly coerced her 11-year-old girlfriend.

Robert's mother, when contacted by the police regarding his whereabouts, was moderately intoxicated, sexually provocative, and relatively unconcerned about her son. The father is a traveling salesman who is currently on the road.

Robert is sullen and uncommunicative, saying only that he didn't do anything wrong; he sees his parents doing it all the time. He has no police record. The school states that he is one and one-half years retarded academically; except for several unexcused absences, his school adjustment is described as satisfactory.

Certainly not detain	Probably not detain	Slightly against detention	Slightly for detention	Probably detain	Certainly detain

8. Danny, an hour ago, struck a male teacher with his fist, threatened to break a chair over his head, then walked out of the school. After this happened, three students reported that he repeatedly struck them and threatened them with beatings if they told on him. The high school vice principal requests that a petition be filed on Danny, and asks that he be detained due to his propensity for physical attacks on others.

A month ago he verbally threatened two teachers. During the resultant parent conference, the mother confided that she was afraid of him because he had struck her and his step-father on several occasions. She felt that the severe beatings the step-father had administered when Danny was younger had turned the boy into a bully. Though bright, he has been an underachiever academically. He has no police record.

Certainly not detain	Probably not detain	Slightly against detention	Slightly for detention	Probably detain	Certainly detain

9. Sam, age 14, stole a horse. His father had always promised him one, and a year ago he had been given one by his father's friend. However, the feed bill accumulated and the father did not want the expense. He sold the horse for a few dollars more than the bill. Several times Sam asked the farmer's permission to ride the horse, but he was refused. Yesterday morning he took the horse and rode 15 miles to a friend's ranch where he had stayed often for several days.

The farmer is pressing charges for grand theft. The father is furious at the boy's actions and wants him punished. Sam has no police record, but his school record is very poor. He has several failing grades, poor study habits, and has been absent any time he could manage it. His only interests are animals and ranching.

Certainly not detain	Probably not detain	Slightly against detention	Slightly for detention	Probably detain	Certainly detain

10. Joe, age 17, has been in trouble since age 11 for petty theft, grand theft (auto), truancy, intoxication, receiving and selling stolen goods, and neighborhood gang fights. He spent eleven months in a boys' rehabilitation center, where he made a very good adjustment; and he has been home four months. Reports indicate his progress since returning to the community is well above average. He has worked steadily as a mechanic's helper, has given part of his salary to his family, and his employer has only praise for him.

However, parents of a 15-year-old girl insist that he be locked up. They claim he raped their daughter by getting her drunk and taking advantage of her. Joe admits to the sexual intimacy, but he states that they love each other, want to get married, and "one thing led to another." He feels that her parents were against him from the beginning because of his record, and they are trying to get rid of him by having him put in jail.

Certainly not detain	Probably not detain	Slightly against detention	Slightly for detention	Probably detain	Certainly detain

11. Barbara, age 15, is due to be released from medical observation this afternoon. She attempted suicide, two days ago, by an overdose of barbiturates obtained outside the home. In an interview this morning she revealed that she has been on pills and pot for almost six months. A boy she has been dating has kept her supplied, and she recently "went all the way with him." She feels that her life is ruined, that she would be better off dead, and states "they should have left me alone."

Barbara's mother has noticed her daughter "acting strangely lately," but states her daughter would not confide in her. Barbara has been staying out late at night and had to be disciplined. School officials report that Barbara was an outstanding student, but they state her work has deteriorated this year.

Certainly not detain	Probably not detain	Slightly against detention	Slightly for detention	Probably detain	Certainly detain

12. Pete is brought in today by police, along with four companions, after they were discovered in a stolen car. Pete was not driving and claims ignorance that the car was "hot." Pete is 15.

A court hearing is pending on a petition alleging that he is guilty of grand theft (auto) and $1,000 property damage to the stolen vehicle (plus several parked cars) while trying to elude the police during a high-speed chase.

However, two of the boys confessed to the police that they stole the car. They state that when Pete was told about it, he said "Crazy man, these are the wheels we need for the party tonight."

The school authorities describe Pete as an indifferent student who associates with the "undesirable element." They say he is usually found wherever there is trouble. The parents both work; and though they seem to mean well, they do not take any definite action about Pete's behavior.

Certainly not detain	Probably not detain	Slightly against detention	Slightly for detention	Probably detain	Certainly detain

13. Ted, age 16, has been known to the Probation Department for the past five years. At first, it was petty theft and malicious mischief. Then it was bicycle and auto theft for the sale of parts. He has been to rehabilitation facilities twice, and he is still on probation.

Last night, he was picked up at his home after investigation revealed that he had several younger boys working for him stripping cars. He acted as a fence for the stolen goods, giving the boys a small percentage of the selling price. The police have statements from most of the boys, and they found a quantity of stolen goods in the garage at Ted's residence. He denies everything, says he's being "framed," and demands an attorney.

Ted's parents died when he was seven and he has lived with various relatives ever since. He currently lives with an uncle who appears unconcerned about the boy's actions. Ted is not in school, nor is he employed.

Certainly not detain	Probably not detain	Slightly against detention	Slightly for detention	Probably detain	Certainly detain

14. Martin, age 17, is vaguely aware of his surroundings. He was medically examined and found to be under the influence of marijuana. Five marijuana cigarettes were found on his person by the police when they arrived at his friend's house after being summoned by the latter's parents.

Martin returned to the community two days ago after seven months in a Youth Authority facility. The commitment was the result of his conviction for the possession and sale of narcotics. The boy's father is currently in prison on the same charge. The mother has no influence on her older children other than to engender guilt after they do something wrong.

Certainly not detain	Probably not detain	Slightly against detention	Slightly for detention	Probably detain	Certainly detain

15. Sharon, age 13, is charged with repeated shoplifting. The police request that she be detained. The store manager stated that this was the second time she had been caught in his store, and he gave the names of three other store managers who had similar experiences with her. A check of local merchants turned up nine known instances of shoplifting in seven stores. They have been previously unwilling to prosecute because she seemed like such a nice girl.

A school counselor reports that Sharon, an only child, is a quiet girl of average ability who has been no problem in school. The principal states that both parents have good jobs; they are described by teachers as "rather strange, aloof, uncommunicative people."

Sharon indicates that she knows she was wrong in what she did, but she "likes to have nice things like other girls," and her parents claim they are "too poor to waste money" on the things she asks for. These are the same statements Sharon made to each shopkeeper after being caught stealing.

Certainly not detain	Probably not detain	Slightly against detention	Slightly for detention	Probably detain	Certainly detain

16. John, age 14, has been increasingly truant during his last year in junior high school. When picked up at his home by the attendance officer, John insisted that he would not return to school.

Both parents work, but they have escorted him to school daily. As soon as they are out of sight, he returns home to watch television. They report that he behaves reasonably at home, but he only wants to watch TV, which he seems to be content to do for days at a time. They complain that they have tried everything, including harsh discipline, and now are at their wits' end.

John states that he hates school, sees no reason to go. "The teachers are stupid, and the subjects are more so." He claims to have no problem with the work, when he wants to do it. This is supported by the school report which indicates that he has a superior IQ, but is failing all subjects due to 30 days' absence out of the last 60.

Certainly not detain	Probably not detain	Slightly against detention	Slightly for detention	Probably detain	Certainly detain

17. Henry, age 12, has repeatedly been the subject of angry phone calls to the police due to damage he has allegedly done with stones and bricks. To date, he has been accused of breaking three school windows, a store window, and windows in two neighboring homes. He has also inflicted minor injuries upon other children. Today, police report he threw a stone through the windshield of a passing police car.

His statement is, "They make me mad, and I throw rocks;" and he childishly justifies his actions. A neighbor asserts also that the boy turned on a hose down his chimney after he wet him while putting out a fire the boy had set on the man's property.

The school describes Henry as a very poor student who has little ability and a very nasty temper. He comes from a transient family of marginal means. The father is suspected of alcoholism.

Certainly not detain	Probably not detain	Slightly against detention	Slightly for detention	Probably detain	Certainly detain

18. Teresa, age 15, on probation for petty theft, is the subject of a complaint filed by her aunt, who states "I went to see my sister, but just Teresa and three boys were in the house. She was having sex with all of them at one time, in different ways. From what I've been able to find out, she is sleeping with every boy in the neighborhood. Sometimes she gets money for it. From the way they act, I think she has had sex with her older brothers, too. My sister is an alcoholic and can't take care of the children. She made a very bad marriage after Teresa's father died. I want Teresa to live with me."

Teresa is silent, except for one angry outburst: "That bitch, what does she care what I do. Nobody did anything when my stepfather raped me. He likes me better than my mother."

The vice-principal describes her as a very indifferent student who is considered both crazy and "fast." Boys continually flock around her.

Certainly not detain	Probably not detain	Slightly against detention	Slightly for detention	Probably detain	Certainly detain

19. Audrey, a 13-year-old girl, was referred by the police for running away from home and being incorrigible. Audrey had left home and was staying at her maternal grandmother's house. Mr. Marens, her father, had reported her as a runaway because he didn't want her at the grandmother's. Since Audrey's natural mother had died there was a lot of hostility between Mr. Marens and the maternal grandmother. Mr. Marens stated that the grandmother was not able to properly supervise the child. Audrey's reason for moving to her grandmother's was that she just couldn't get along with her stepmother. She hated her since she had moved in soon after her mother died. Audrey stated that she was always wrong and her stepmother was always right. She refused to return to her father's home and insisted that she be granted permission to stay with her grandmother. The father has legal custody.

Certainly not detain	Probably not detain	Slightly against detention	Slightly for detention	Probably detain	Certainly detain

CORRECTIONS

20. Rudy is a 16-year-old boy referred by the police for auto theft. He was apprehended after the police chased a 1965 Ford which had been reported stolen. The youngster stopped the car and was walking away when the police caught up with him. He denied being the one driving the car and when brought into the juvenile office he stated he knew his rights and wanted an attorney. He strongly denied stealing the car and challenged the officers to prove it. He stated that he wasn't in the car when apprehended. Rudy insisted that nobody was going to railroad him into admitting it and that he had been that route before. He refused to answer any further questions.

Certainly not detain	Probably not detain	Slightly against detention	Slightly for detention	Probably detain	Certainly detain

21. Alvin, 15, was referred to the probation department by police. He was arrested at home on information supplied by two other young adults who implicated Alvin in burglary of seven rifles from Ace Gun Shop. The two young adults are free on bond of $1,000 each, and they turned over to police five rifles. They and Alvin are members of the "Last Chance" gang. Alvin is alleged to have the other two weapons.

Alvin seems marginally retarded but this has not been determined. He told investigating officers that he had no guns, had not pulled a job, and as far as he is concerned, "the cops can go to hell." His father and mother accompanied Alvin to the probation department, were very defensive of their son and stated that authorities "have nothing to go on" in making this arrest. They have no guns in their house according to them and both insist that Alvin is a "good boy." Throughout this time, Alvin sat with a sneer on his face and refused to talk with police except to say that "Maybe I'll get me a lawyer."

Certainly not detain	Probably not detain	Slightly against detention	Slightly for detention	Probably detain	Certainly detain

22. Richard is a 16-year-old boy who was referred by the police for theft over $50. The youngster was apprehended breaking into a 1967 Oldsmobile in a shopping center. Richard admitted that he and three of his friends has been breaking into cars for several months and stealing credit cards from the autos. The police determined that the boys had taken about 100 credit cards. The cards were being sold by them to youngsters at the high school for $2 each. Merchandise and gasoline were being charged against the credit cards in the amount of $4,500.

During the investigation, Richard's attitude was one of arrogance and defiance. He stated he had notified his father already and that his father and his attorney were on the way to pick him up. Mr. Smith is a well-known businessman here in the city. Richard said his father would make complete restitution, and he couldn't understand what all the fuss was about.

Mr. Smith and his attorney arrived, and they wanted the child released immediately. Mr. Smith stated he would make complete restitution to cover all losses.

Certainly not detain	Probably not detain	Slightly against detention	Slightly for detention	Probably detain	Certainly detain

23. Max is a 12-year-old youngster referred to the juvenile probation department by the police department for shoplifting a 59-cent belt from Ajax Department Store. His attitude regarding the referral is passive, and he states he has stolen better articles in

the past. He asked to be locked up at the detention home because some of his friends were there. He was told that "they eat good" there and he wants to go see for himself.

Certainly not detain	Probably not detain	Slightly against detention	Slightly for detention	Probably detain	Certainly detain

24. Jerry and Paul, brothers ages 10 and 11, were referred by the police for burglary and theft. Jerry and Paul were apprehended by the police while in a restaurant. They had broken into the place around midnight and were eating some food when arrested. They had also taken some milk, potato chips, and bread in a paper bag. They seemed frightened. They admitted to breaking into the cafe to get some food, as both were very hungry. When questioned regarding the food they were preparing to take with them, they stated they were going to take it home to their brother and sisters.

(Further investigation proved that there were nine children in the home. The father had been killed nine months previous to this incident and there was no food in the home.)

Certainly not detain	Probably not detain	Slightly against detention	Slightly for detention	Probably detain	Certainly detain

25. Tim, age 11, is accused by police of being one of three boys who broke into his school last weekend and turned it into a shambles. Supplies were scattered, ink and paints smeared on the walls, books torn, and teachers' desks broken open.

A stopwatch taken from one desk was found on Tim when he was taken into custody at his home. He admitted everything, and the father attempted to thrash him on the spot. Both parents insisted that the boy deserved to be severely punished "for the disgrace to our family."

Tim seems bewildered by his own actions. He says that they saw the open window, went in, got started, and couldn't stop. It was his idea to smear the paint and ink. There is no history of previous difficulty.

Certainly not detain	Probably not detain	Slightly against detention	Slightly for detention	Probably detain	Certainly detain

Institutional Life Questionnaire

Development and Characteristics

The *Institutional Life Questionnaire* (ILQ) was designed to measure various aspects of attitudes toward institutional life and procedures within the Grendon Underwood psychiatric prison (Marcus, 1969). This English hospital-prison offers a milieu therapy in which treatment is the purpose accepted by staff and inmates. It was hypothesized that if milieu therapy were in practice: (1) There would be little social distance between staff officers and inmates; (2) there would be little distance between staff officers and professional staff; and (3) staff officers would identify with the official values of the institution (Marcus, 1969, p. 276).

The questionnaire includes 50 items developed from contact with the uniformed staff. Marcus believes that these items tap important areas of anxiety or hostility, as well as staff feelings about the milieu therapy orientation of the institution.

Response Mode

The ILQ uses a 5-point, Likert-type response mode. Respondents are asked to read each item, then note whether they: "strongly agree," "agree," "are uncertain," "disagree," or "strongly disagree."

Scoring

No scoring procedures have been established. Items are interpreted separately, based on average responses to each item.

Norms

No relevant norms are available.

Reliability

No reliability estimates were obtained.

Validity

The central ILQ issue presented was how answers to the 50 items related to responses to the statement "It is a good thing for officers to take groups of inmates." (That is, officers should lead counseling session for inmates.) The developer believed that staff members who agreed that such talking in officer conducted group counseling was of value would be those individuals who agreed with the milieu type of treatment program. Items that show a significant relationship to this particular item were assumed to measure attitudes toward the treatment program in general. Using this rationale and χ^2 tests of significance, Items 3, 6, 8, 9, 10, 11, 17, 28, 29, 32, 33, 37, 40, 42, 44, 48, and 49 were found to be valid items. Each of these showed significant relationships with the key item ($P < .05$).

Comments

The ILQ items appear to have content validity. As a whole, however, the questionnaire seems to tap several dimensions rather than one view of the institution. For example, some items appear to measure attitudes toward other staff members, while some measure attitudes toward the institution, inmates, the practice of milieu therapy, group work, and even therapists, as opposed to other staff members. Thus, some test for heterogeneity within the ILQ would be very helpful.

In addition, some possible improvements might include the use of vocabulary that is less specific to a particular institution. Terms such as the centre office, the institution name, staff position titles and other such local and British references are limiting factors.

This instrument is in an early stage of development in an area that has received little systematic attention. It purports to measure the attitudes of staff members to the use of milieu therapy in a psychiatric prison. Although in its present form it is not useful as an attitude scale, the items may serve as a guide and stimulus for future work in the area.

REFERENCES

Marcus, D. Correlates of attitudes to group work. *British Journal of Criminology,* 1969, *9,* 272–281.

INSTITUTIONAL LIFE QUESTIONNAIRE

Following are some statements with which you may agree or disagree. Beside each number make the symbol which best represents your position, as follows:

SA Strongly Agree
A   Agree
U   Undecided
D   Disagree
SD Strongly Disagree

1. The Center Office does a good job of work.
2. Officers should use their initiative, without consulting the therapist, in talking to inmates about personal problems.
3. The senior staff are more interested in the inmates than in the officers.
4. The so-called therapeutic atmosphere at Grendon protects inmates who misbehave.
5. Therapists see inmates pretty promptly when they are asked.
6. Inmates are too familiar with officers.
7. The senior staff do not participate enough in the social life of the community.
8. Inmates spend too much time in groups.
9. Inmates have too easy a time here.

10. Wing meetings serve no useful purpose.
11. Work should play a larger part in the inmates' day.
12. Lack of opportunity for overtime is the main reason for officers asking for transfers from Grendon.
13. It is easier to speak frankly at meetings or groups where the Medical Superintendent is not present.
14. Communications here are, on the whole, poor.
15. There should be more frequent wing meetings (on adult wings).
16. Arrangements for time off are satisfactory.
17. Therapists act as if they were on the side of the inmate against the officer.
18. Staff morale used to be much higher than it is now.
19. Officers who ask for transfers mostly do so because they are dissatisfied with working conditions in the prison.
20. The Chiefs are rather remote.
21. The P.O.s do not communicate enough information to their staffs.
22. It is difficult to speak frankly at meetings of the whole staff.
23. Not enough attention is paid to acquainting officers of important decisions and information.
24. Therapists do not pay enough attention to what officers say and write about inmates.
25. Wing P.O.s are easy to approach.
26. An officer should put an inmate on report for all cases of insubordinate behavior.
27. Therapists get on well with wing staff.
28. Working Grendon makes an officer less suitable for working at other establishments.
29. The professional staff do not do enough to support officers in the difficult position they find themselves in at this prison.
30. Therapists should come into the prison at weekends.
31. Inmates should not be addressed as "Mr."
32. Wing staff meetings are useful.
33. It would be a good thing if officers had lectures on psychiatric and psychological subjects.
34. Young offenders quickly get disillusioned when they come here.
35. It is a good thing for officers to take groups of inmates.
36. Apart from the fact that the Principal Psychologist does therapy, nobody knows much about what the Psychological Department does.
37. Therapists tend to behave like a race apart.
38. The Medical Superintendent makes his policy clear to all grades of staff.

39. It is easier to talk to therapists than to chief officers.
40. Small weekly groups of officers, taken by a therapist, are useful.
41. An officer who speaks freely on staff meetings is bound to suffer in the long run.
42. Officers cannot do much to improve the state of affairs at Grendon.
43. Not enough use is made of officers' skills in handling men.
44. It would be a good thing if everyone, from the Medical Superintendent downwards, addressed each other by Christian names.
45. The large staff meetings serve no useful function.
46. The Deputy Governor is easy to speak to frankly.
47. The welfare department in effect aids and abets inmates who try to manipulate the staff.
48. Officers are encouraged to make their views known to therapists.
49. The welfare staff do their best to communicate with other members of the staff.
50. The Medical Superintendent is always willing to talk to individual officers.

Rehabilitation in Correctional Settings Attitude Scale

Development and Characteristics

The *Rehabilitation in Correctional Settings Attitude Scale* (RICS) was designed to assess "the attitudes of inmates and workers in jail settings" (Rice, 1970). A total of 144 items (from a pool of 285) was found to load heavily on six factors when the responses of 298 inmates and 85 correctional workers in local jails and state prisons were factor analyzed. These dimensions are labeled: (1) Attitude toward Image of Self-Competence (IMSC); (2) Attitude toward Inmates (IN); (3) Attitude toward Treatment of Inmate (TIN); (4) Attitude toward Society (SOC); (5) Attitude toward the Legal System and Figures of Authority (LSFA); and (6) Attitude toward the Law (LAW).

Two forms of the scale have been constructed, with 72 items in each form, representing 12 items for each of the 6 factors.

Response Mode

This is a standard Likert-type scale in which the respondent reads a statement and notes whether he or she: (1) "strongly disagrees," (2) "disagrees," (3) "is neutral," (4) "agrees," or (5) "strongly agrees."

Scoring

Each item is scored using a 5-point scale in which higher scores are assigned in the direction of the attribute labeled in the subscales. Subscale totals are then calculated.

Norms

Normative data are available for 166 prison inmates, 130 county jail inmates, 65 correctional officers, 20 deputy sheriffs, 21 civic organization members, and 12 drag-race club members (Rice, 1973). The inmates were most positive in attitudes toward treatment of inmates, while the correctional officers were most favorable in attitudes toward law and image of self-competence.

Reliability

Rice (1973) reported parallel form reliabilities ranging from .75 to .89 among the six subscales, test–retest reliabilities (after one week) hovering about .80, and full length internal reliabilities (all items) ranging from .69 to .88.

Validity

Factoral validity is present due to the method of construction. When the six normative samples were compared using Multiple Discriminate Analysis (Rice, 1973), the scale correctly discriminated inmates' ratings 88% of the time and noninmates' ratings 86% of the time.

Comments

This scale has adequate reliability, support for validity, and offers potential for many research uses. In addition, this preliminary work indicates it may have usefulness as a diagnostic tool.

REFERENCES

Rice, R. G. *A scale for measuring attitude changes among inmates of local jails and among correctional workers.* Unpublished doctoral dissertation, University of Florida, 1970.

Rice. R. G. Intentions and the structures of attitudes among inmates and noninmates. *Journal of Research in Crime and Delinquency,* 1973, *10,* 203–207.

REHABILITATION IN CORRECTIONAL SETTINGS ATTITUDE SCALE

FORM A

Below are some sentences with which you may agree or disagree. There are no right or wrong answers, so do your best to answer each sentence the way you feel. The meaning of the letters to the left of each sentence is as follows:

- SA   Strongly Agree
- A   Agree
- U   Undecided
- D   Disagree
- SD   Strongly Disagree

As the letters indicate, you may choose to strongly agree to strongly disagree with each sentence. Circle one for each sentence to indicate the extent to which you agree or disagree with the sentence. While there is no time limit, do not spend too much time on any one sentence.

1. SA A U D SD   Society makes the world a "dog-eat-dog" place to live.
2. SA A U D SD   Laws make a community safer.
3. SA A U D SD   Breaking the law is OK; the sin is getting caught.
4. SA A U D SD   It is all right to break the law to help your family.
5. SA A U D SD   Laws were only made for the poor man.
6. SA A U D SD   Inmates should be allowed more visitors.
7. SA A U D SD   Laws are a man's best friend.
8. SA A U D SD   I wish I could be someone else.
9. SA A U D SD   Inmates who work should be paid for it.
10. SA A U D SD   Inmates care how others feel.
11. SA A U D SD   Inmates try hard to con everyone.
12. SA A U D SD   The law officer is out to frame you.
13. SA A U D SD   Society gives the poor man a raw deal.
14. SA A U D SD   The only way to get ahead is to break the law.
15. SA A U D SD   Laws are OK but the courts are crooked.
16. SA A U D SD   Inmates should be worked hard so they can learn to like honest work.
17. SA A U D SD   One can be proud of our courts.
18. SA A U D SD   Jail workers are only in it for the money.
19. SA A U D SD   Jail workers want to help the inmate.

20.	SA	A	U	D	SD	Inmates are about like everyone else.
21.	SA	A	U	D	SD	Inmates should have a choice of food at meals.
22.	SA	A	U	D	SD	Society only cares for you if you have a lot of influence.
23.	SA	A	U	D	SD	Inmates have no morals.
24.	SA	A	U	D	SD	Society looks out for jail inmates.
25.	SA	A	U	D	SD	Society allows the newspapers to mark a man who has a record.
26.	SA	A	U	D	SD	After being arrested, inmates should lose their civil rights.
27.	SA	A	U	D	SD	Inmates are not loafers if you give them work.
28.	SA	A	U	D	SD	Most laws are fair.
29.	SA	A	U	D	SD	Judges treat everyone about the same.
30.	SA	A	U	D	SD	If an inmate likes you, he is trying to con you.
31.	SA	A	U	D	SD	Girls' groups should come into the jail and give parties for inmates.
32.	SA	A	U	D	SD	Society should provide for and protect a man's wife while he is an inmate.
33.	SA	A	U	D	SD	Inmates work hard to become rehabilitated.
34.	SA	A	U	D	SD	I rarely get my bills all paid.
35.	SA	A	U	D	SD	Society will never understand the inmate.
36.	SA	A	U	D	SD	The courts should let inmates out sooner than they do.
37.	SA	A	U	D	SD	I am proud of most things I have done.
38.	SA	A	U	D	SD	When I believe in something, I do it.
39.	SA	A	U	D	SD	New programs are needed to rehabilitate inmates.
40.	SA	A	U	D	SD	Jail workers envy smart inmates.
41.	SA	A	U	D	SD	I wish I could like myself better sometimes.
42.	SA	A	U	D	SD	Being friendly with inmates does not pay.
43.	SA	A	U	D	SD	Inmates act nice to throw you off guard.
44.	SA	A	U	D	SD	I can look up to myself.
45.	SA	A	U	D	SD	Society wants to help inmates be rehabilitated.
46.	SA	A	U	D	SD	Society should let a man do what is natural for him to do.
47.	SA	A	U	D	SD	Inmates should be allowed to run loose in the jail during the days.
48.	SA	A	U	D	SD	The law protects our civil liberties.
49.	SA	A	U	D	SD	It is easy for me to take a stand on things I believe.
50.	SA	A	U	D	SD	A man with a record still gets a fair trial.
51.	SA	A	U	D	SD	Getting things to working right is a problem for me.

52.	SA	A U D	SD	Inmates do what they can get away with.
53.	SA	A U D	SD	Inmates need to suffer to cure them.
54.	SA	A U D	SD	Laws are good, even if you don't have money.
55.	SA	A U D	SD	I would let a former inmate date my daughter.
56.	SA	A U D	SD	I seem to keep my bills paid better than most.
57.	SA	A U D	SD	The law makes us more free to live happily.
58.	SA	A U D	SD	I put on a front around other people.
59.	SA	A U D	SD	Society is set up to help the poor man better himself.
60.	SA	A U D	SD	If society were just, everybody would be in jail.
61.	SA	A U D	SD	I think highly of myself.
62.	SA	A U D	SD	Unjust laws have put most people in jail.
63.	SA	A U D	SD	Inmates do not have a voice in society.
64.	SA	A U D	SD	Good laws do no good because the courts are unfair.
65.	SA	A U D	SD	The law officer is on your side.
66.	SA	A U D	SD	My wife (or girlfriend) and I don't get along very well.
67.	SA	A U D	SD	Being mean is the way to rehabilitate inmates.
68.	SA	A U D	SD	The laws work well most of the time.
69.	SA	A U D	SD	For good behavior, inmates should be allowed to go home on special days.
70.	SA	A U D	SD	What society needs is more law officers to enforce the laws.
71.	SA	A U D	SD	Inmates generally have pleasant personalities.
72.	SA	A U D	SD	Inmates should not be allowed to speak to any women.

REHABILITATION IN CORRECTIONAL SETTINGS ATTITUDE SCALE

FORM B

Below are some sentences with which you may agree or disagree. There are not right or wrong answers, so do your best to answer each sentence the way you feel. The meaning of the letters to the left of each sentence is as follows:

SA   Strongly Agree
A   Agree

	U	Undecided
	D	Disagree
	SD	Strongly Disagree

As the letters indicate, you may strongly agree to strongly disagree with each sentence. Circle one for each sentence to indicate the extent to which you agree or disagree with each sentence. While there is no limit, do not spend too much time on any one sentence.

1. SA A U D SD   You have to break the law in order to get ahead.
2. SA A U D SD   Most laws are lousy.
3. SA A U D SD   Inmates should be allowed to talk with jail workers or anyone they want to.
4. SA A U D SD   I like "me" just as I am.
5. SA A U D SD   It is a mistake to let inmates become too close to anyone.
6. SA A U D SD   A man gets justice under the laws we have today.
7. SA A U D SD   The law only protects the rich man.
8. SA A U D SD   Inmates should be treated the same as anyone else.
9. SA A U D SD   Laws promote a healthy society.
10. SA A U D SD   Inmates are good enough to eat with law officers and jail workers.
11. SA A U D SD   I do not approve of the way I am.
12. SA A U D SD   I would let a former inmate marry into my family.
13. SA A U D SD   Society gives you nothing but taxes anyway.
14. SA A U D SD   Inmates can become skilled at almost any job they are placed on.
15. SA A U D SD   Inmates do not cooperate in plans for rehabilitating them.
16. SA A U D SD   Laws are wonderful.
17. SA A U D SD   I am pretty well satisfied the way I am.
18. SA A U D SD   I can usually work my problem out.
19. SA A U D SD   Law officers want to keep inmates out of jail.
20. SA A U D SD   I would like to be different.
21. SA A U D SD   Laws are no good without a clever lawyer.
22. SA A U D SD   I find myself doing things I do not believe in sometimes.
23. SA A U D SD   The law is unfair to most inmates.
24. SA A U D SD   Being kind to inmates only helps them trick you.
25. SA A U D SD   Respect is what inmates need.
26. SA A U D SD   Laws are good rules to live by.

27.	SA	A U D SD	Locking an inmate up alone is a poor penal method.
28.	SA	A U D SD	Society is to blame for inmates' problems.
29.	SA	A U D SD	Society holds a whip hand over a man with a record.
30.	SA	A U D SD	The legal system does not care about the inmate, they only care about his money.
31.	SA	A U D SD	Education classes can help rehabilitate inmates.
32.	SA	A U D SD	Law officers are in it for the money.
33.	SA	A U D SD	It is all right to break the law if you do not get caught.
34.	SA	A U D SD	I get along well with my family.
35.	SA	A U D SD	Managing money is one of my problems.
36.	SA	A U D SD	Inmates are fed poor food.
37.	SA	A U D SD	Society can disrupt a man's family while he is an inmate.
38.	SA	A U D SD	Jail workers are to be admired for the fine work they do.
39.	SA	A U D SD	Society envys the things inmates know how to get.
40.	SA	A U D SD	Inmates will run the first chance they get.
41.	SA	A U D SD	Work-release lets inmates off too easy.
42.	SA	A U D SD	People should not know when a person has a past record.
43.	SA	A U D SD	Inmates really want you to like them as a friend.
44.	SA	A U D SD	Ask an inmate to do a little something and he gets upset.
45.	SA	A U D SD	The only way to win in court is with lots of money.
46.	SA	A U D SD	Law officers and judges listen to the inmate's side of a story.
47.	SA	A U D SD	If society were just, most inmates would be turned loose.
48.	SA	A U D SD	The law protects everyone about the same.
49.	SA	A U D SD	Inmates have poor ways.
50.	SA	A U D SD	Jail workers want you to trust them so they can convict you.
51.	SA	A U D SD	Inmates are fairly honest with you.
52.	SA	A U D SD	Law officers do not try to look big and made you look little.
53.	SA	A U D SD	People bug me so I bug them.
54.	SA	A U D SD	People are never bigger then the law; it must be obeyed.
55.	SA	A U D SD	The courts put the right people in jail.
56.	SA	A U D SD	The way to win in court is to have pull with the judge or jury.
57.	SA	A U D SD	Inmates are nice most of the time.
58.	SA	A U D SD	All society wants to do is help inmates.
59.	SA	A U D SD	I can't seem to make ends meet.
60.	SA	A U D SD	Inmates should be allowed visits from only close relatives.

61.	SA	A	U	D	SD	Inmates gripe too much.
62.	SA	A	U	D	SD	Inmates' wives ought to be allowed to stay with them sometimes.
63.	SA	A	U	D	SD	Society allows the businessman and loan people to cheat the poor.
64.	SA	A	U	D	SD	I don't let my friends lead me into bad situations.
65.	SA	A	U	D	SD	Courts are one big joke.
66.	SA	A	U	D	SD	Often I start a project and never find time to finish it.
67.	SA	A	U	D	SD	Society owes an inmate another job when he gets out.
68.	SA	A	U	D	SD	Society does not care how the inmate feels.
69.	SA	A	U	D	SD	Society should ask inmates which laws are bad.
70.	SA	A	U	D	SD	The law is against a man once he is arrested.
71.	SA	A	U	D	SD	Hard work is the answer to rehabilitating inmates.
72.	SA	A	U	D	SD	Society wants to help inmates help themselves.

CORRECTIONS ATTITUDE SCALES: LISTINGS

Attitude toward the Death Penalty

Thomas, C. W., Petersen, D. M., & Nelson, C. C. *Methodological issues in attitude scale construction.* Paper presented at the Southern Sociological Society Convention, Washington, D.C., April 1975.

This is a 6-item, yes-no scale designed to illustrate techniques for construction of attitude scales. It is believed to measure an individual's attitude toward the death penalty.

Attitudes toward Enforced Group Psychotherapy

Sadoff, R. L., Roether, H. A., & Peters, J. J. Clinical measure of enforced psychotherapy. *The American Journal of Psychiatry,* 1971, *128,* 116–119.

This 7-item, multiple-choice scale was designed to assess offenders' evaluation judgments about enforced group therapy.

Attitude to Psychiatry Scale

Gunn, J., Robertson, G., Dell, S., & Way, C. *Psychiatric aspects of imprisonment.* London: Academic Press, 1978.

The *Attitude to Psychiatry Scale* is a 7-item, Likert-type instrument that was designed to measure prisoners' attitudes toward treatment as well as a desire for psychiatric help. Supporting reliability and validity information and norms are available.

Attitude toward Punishment of Criminals

Shaw, M. E., & Wright, J. M. *Scales for the measurement of attitudes.* New York: McGraw-Hill, 1967.

This 34-item Thurstone scale has forms for college and high school students. The items consist of judgmental statements about punitive treatment of criminals.

Parole Officer Punishment and Reintegrative Orientation Questionnaire

Dembo, R. Orientation and activities of the parole officer. *Criminology,* 1972, *10,* 193–215.

This 18-item rating scale assesses "orientation postures" with regard to punishment and reintegration of parole officers.

Rehabilitative Value Perception Scale

Shihadeh, E. S. The perceptions of parolees and parole officers. *The Journal of Psychology,* 1973, *84,* 335–343.

Shihadeh, E. S., & Nedd, A. N. B. The perceptions of penitentiary inmates and staff. *Journal of Social Psychology,* 1974, *92,* 217–224.

This 14-item, Likert-type scale was designed to measure parole officers' and parolees' perceptions of the utility of investigating an offender's institutional adjustments and attitude changes. An 11-item version of the questionnaire was designed to measure perception of the rehabilitative value of inmate membership on the residential committee.

CORRECTIONS BEHAVIOR RATINGS: REVIEWS

The Prison Adjustment Index

Development and Characteristics

The *Prison Adjustment Index* (PAI) was designed to measure inmates' behavioral adjustment to prison (Wolfgang, 1961), using empirical criteria based in part on prison administrators' views of the adjustment of inmates. After an examination of the files at a state penitentiary, Wolfgang suggested that there were three major indices that could be used to form a behavioral image of inmates. "These devices include: (1) the number of jobs and the length of time a job was held by each inmate in prison, (2) the number of times an inmate was discharged from his or her job because of misconduct, and (3) the number of bad statements recorded by cell block guards" (Wolfgang, 1961, p. 611).

There are many reasons for an inmate to change jobs during imprisonment, such as improper classification, services required elsewhere at a later date, job change because of displeasure with associates, or the job itself. A high frequency of changes, however, over a relatively short period of time was said to indicate an instability and possibly an inability to adjust to the prison environment. The second major index, job dismissals for reason of misconduct, although related to frequency of job changes, was not subsumed under it. This index was indicative of more severe adjustment problems than those that might be associated with job transfer for other reasons. The third aspect of the PAI, block reports, deals with the number of negative statements about an inmate's conduct made by the cell block officers in their reports.

Response Mode

Information for the PAI is obtained from prison records and therefore requires no subject responses.

Scoring

Since each of the three categories can be influenced by the number of years spent in prison, standardization is achieved by calculating a mean number of months per score. Thus, the mean number of months per job is compared to the mean number of months per job for a total group of inmates. Using one-quarter standard deviation to indicate one unit of departure from the mean, a scale ranging from approximately -3 through 0 to $+3$ can be obtained. In this case, a score of -3 would mean that an inmate had scored three-quarters of a standard deviation below the mean number of months spent on a prison job. Likewise the score of $+3$ would indicate the inmate had scored above three-quarters of a standard deviation below the mean number of months spent per job.

Similarly, a quarter deviation score is obtained for the number of job dismissals due to misconduct and the number of bad statements entered in an inmate's block report. Since a large number of dismissals for misconduct indicates poor adjustment, the larger number would receive minus quarter deviation scores as would larger numbers of "bad statements" in block reports.

A total score is obtained by summing the quarter deviation scores from each of the three items. A total score higher than 0 indicates some degree of adjustment and a total score less than 0 indicates poor adjustment.

TABLE 20. Prison Adjustment Index for
Convicted Murderers ($N = 44$)

Item	Mean	SD
Duration of jobs	29.09	14.49
Dismissals for misconduct	19.00	13.20
Block reports	2.29	2.22

Norms

Wolfgang (1961) presented, in Table 20, means and standard deviations for 44 convicted murderers (9 white and 35 nonwhite) who had been incarcerated for an average of 8.65 years.

Reliability

No measures of reliability were reported.

Validity

Wolfgang (1961) has reported several relationships between the PAI and other variables, using data obtained from the 44 convicted murders. By dichotomizing murders into adjusted and maladjusted groups, he found that there was a significant association between positive prison adjustment and inmates 35 years of age or older, who had been married, whose murder was other than a felony murder, and who had prior imprisonment (Wolfgang, 1961, p. 617). In addition, there was no relationship between adjustment and race, length of incarceration, intelligence, achievement, or personality (as measured by the *Woodward Personality Inventory*).

Comments

The PAI has provided evidence for validity by demonstrating predicted relationships from theoretical positions. Further, these measures seem to be good behavior indicators for prison adjustment. There are issues, however, concerning the PAI that have not been resolved. For example, in determining the mean and standard deviations for scoring each of the three items, should researchers use Wolfgang's average and standard deviations or should they estimate their own from the sample under study. Nevertheless, this index is a relatively straightforward and valid instrument that lends itself to use by both researchers and practitioners.

REFERENCES

Wolfgang, M. E. Quantitative analysis of adjustment to the prison community. *Criminal Law, Criminology, and Police Science*, 1961, *51*, 607–618.

Recidivism Outcome Index

Development and Characteristics

The *Recidivism Outcome Index* (ROI) was designed "to evaluate the relative degrees of success and failure on parole" (Moberg & Ericson, 1972). This rating system is based upon the amount and type of contact with law enforcement that one encounters subsequent to parole. The classification categories were based on the laws of Minnesota, but the developers suggest that the scale can be easily adapted to fit other states or jurisdictions.

The ROI items were constructed after an extensive review of the literature and consultation from judges, members of the Minnesota paroling commissions, institutional officials, parole agent supervisors, deputy commissioners in the Minnesota Department of Corrections, members of the advisory committee of the project, and other professionals. The result was a set of 11 mutually exclusive categories that serves as an 11-point rating continuum. The score is an indication of the relative success or failure of a parolee to avoid official processing in subsequent crimes. The scale uses known offenses only; therefore one would receive a score representing success if he or she has not been apprehended for crimes committed while on parole. Although this omission may be a major limitation, the developers suggest the patterns of subsequent criminal activity will be detected by the scale. The developers report that "the scale in general reflects a progression of degrees of seriousness of offense patterns, and thus, of degrees of failure or success on parole" (Moberg & Ericson, 1972, p. 54).

Response Mode

The ROI is a rating system based on information from an individual's police record. Therefore, no response to the index itself is required on the part of the subject.

Scoring

This scale consists of all categories that are ranked according to seriousness of the law or parole rule violation during the period of time under consideration. A score of 0 indicates the most undesirable police report, e.g., reimprisonment as a result of conviction of a felony. A score of 10 represents the most desirable outcome of parole, e.g., no official record of illegal activities whatsoever. Positions between these two scores indicate the degree of success or failure demonstrated by a parolee.

Norms

Normative data on frequency of particular scores are not useful. However, the ROI developers indicate that scores of seven or less should be interpreted as recidivism.

Reliability

The two developers independently rated 164 parolees. When the results are compared, the ratings were almost identical. In those few discrepancies, the differences were easily resolved when the raters compared notes.

Validity

The results of the ROI for 164 parolees were compared to their scores on the *California Index on Severity of Offenses* (adapted on the basis of appropriate assumptions to fit Minnesota laws). This comparison showed that 82.5 % of those offenders classified by the ROI as nonrecidivists (a score of 8–10) received low severity scores on the *California Index* (0, 1, or 2), and 91.1% of those labeled as recidivists by the ROI (scores 0–7) scored 3 or higher on the California Index (indicating its more severe scores).

An attempt was made to compare ROI scores to the *Sellin-Wolfgang Index on Delinquency,* but lack of information prevented complete comparisons. The developers, however, suggested that from the data available, there was a strong relationship between the two instruments and there is evidence for support of ROI validity.

Comments

The ROI was designed for and received support as a measure of relative degrees of success or failure on parole. In addition, the authors suggest that it might be useful for other purposes when modified appropriately. For example, by changing categories 0–4 to be imprisoned instead of reimprisoned, 5–7 to be wanted instead of absconder, and ignoring the first part of category seven, the index could be adapted to measure "the criminality of probationers or other offenders who have not been imprisoned" (Moberg & Ericson, 1972, p 56). With little more difficulty, the ROI could be used as an indicator of "the relative severity of delinquency by alleged and adjudicated juveniles."

This instrument has some support for reliability and validity and appears to be useful for comparative purposes. The ROI would appear to be valuable when researchers need a finer measure of recidivism than the customary dichotomous judgment of success-failure.

REFERENCES

Moberg, D. O., & Ericson, R. C. A new recidivism outcome index. *Federal Probation,* 1972, *36,* 50–57.

RECIDIVISM OUTCOME INDEX

Scoring Code	Disposition and Description of Conduct
0	Reimprisoned: Convicted of felony.
1	Reimprisoned: Felony admitted, confessed, or agent-alleged, but no prosecution or no conviction for the offense. (This includes parolees reimprisoned for other reasons who have felonies on the record other than the one leading to Commission action, and "killed while attempting armed robbery.")
2	Reimprisoned: Convicted of misdemeanor.
3	Reimprisoned: (1) Misdemeanor admitted, confessed, or agent-alleged, but no prosecution or no conviction for the offense; (2) technical violation with evidence or suspicion of misdemeanor or felony but no confession or admission to having committed it; (3) technical violation with prior and separate misdemeanor for which sentence has already been imposed and/or served on an earlier occasion during current parole; (4) technical violation with absconding on the record, whether part of the current charge or not.
4	Reimprisoned: Technical violation without any evidence, allegation, or suspicion of other offenses.
5	Absconder: Also wanted for or charged with an alleged felony, or has been convicted of or confessed to a felony on the same or a separate charge; or arrested and arraigned for an alleged felony and awaiting disposition.
6	Absconder: Also wanted for or charged with an alleged misdemeanor, or has been convicted of or confessed to a misdemeanor on the same or a separate charge; or arrested and arraigned for an alleged misdemeanor and awaiting disposition.
7	Absconder: Has no record of any other convictions nor of any alleged offenses during the current parole; or offenders convicted of one or more offenses for which a sentence of more than 90 days in a jail or workhouse or a fine of over $100 has been imposed.

8	Offenders convicted of a law violation for which a jail or workhouse sentence of 90 days or less or a fine over $25 and up to $100 has been imposed; or technical violators of parole rules whose violations have been officially reported to the paroling authorities but have not had their parole revoked as a result.
9	Offenders arrested and temporarily jailed without charges supported by arraignment or other substantial evidence; or offenders convicted of one or more law violations for which there has been no jail sentence and no fine of more than $25; or technical violators of parole rules, including any illegal activities reported in quarterly illegal activities reports, progress reports, or chronological case records of the parole officers but for which no revocation of parole was recommended to the paroling authorities.
10	No illegal activities or any available official records; or parolees returned to a correctional institution for placement only without any other offense record; or parolees reimprisoned or otherwise prosecuted for offenses that occurred prior to the current parole period who have not committed any other technical violations or illegal activities of any kind recorded in official records.

Multiple offenses are classified according to the most serious (lowest score) disposition category.

In cases of doubtful classification which would involve significant movement, including 8 to 9 or 4 to 5 and vice versa, additional evidence should be secured from the parole officer or other official sources.

The index scores may be grouped into broader categories as follows:

0-4	Failure	Recidivism
5-7	Marginal failure	Recidivism
8	Marginal success	Nonrecidivism
9	Qualified success	Nonrecidivism
10	Success	Nonrecidivism

CORRECTIONS BEHAVIOR RATINGS: LISTINGS

Probation Program Ratings

Jesness, C. F., Allison, T. S., McCormick, P. M., Wedge, R. F., & Young, M. L. *The cooperative behavior demonstration project.* Sacramento: California Youth Authority, 1975.

A series of behavior ratings for probationers and probation programs were developed. These include a relationship questionnaire, a behavior checklist, an objective rating scheme for case review outlines, and a self-administered background rating.

Work–Release Staff Role Questionnaire

Scott, R. J. *Role conflict resolution and job related attitudes and job performance of community based correctional workers.* Unpublished doctoral dissertation, Southern Illinois University, 1974.

The *Work–Release Staff Role Scale* was designed to assess how staff members handled an array of problems they encountered while working in a work–release program. Five detailed situations are presented with several options for action, and an objective coding system for responses is employed.

CORRECTIONS PERSONALITY ASSESSMENT: REVIEWS

Prison Projective Test

Development and Characteristics

The *Prison Projective Test* (PPT) was developed by Driscoll (1949) as part of a master's thesis. Designed "to uncover basic underlying attitudes actuating inmate behavior," the PPT materials consist of 10 photographs of artist drawings portraying inmates in social and institutional situations. These 5" × 7" cards are not commercially distributed, but are available from the Regents of the University of Wisconsin. The rationale for development and use of this test was that inmates would identify with the photographs and thus expose prison-related attitudes readily and freely. The cards themselves consist of the following situations:

1. Two inmates are playing checkers while a third inmate stands and looks out a barred window.
2. Three inmates, two of whom are very close to each other, are standing in a prison yard.
3. Two inmates are talking alone at a dining table. One is looking down and the other is looking at him.
4. An inmate is working at a machine table with a hammer and other tools on it. A guard is standing behind him.
5. A solitary inmate is digging at a high pile of earth near a trench in the prison yard.
6. An inmate is lying on top of a bunk looking straight up.
7. Two inmates are walking single file near a guard who is facing and looking at them. Three other inmates are in line in the distance in the prison yard.
8. An inmate with only his backview in sight is sitting across a table from a woman. A man in suit is standing behind and to the side of the woman, and a guard is standing nearby with arms crossed.

9. An inmate is sitting on his bunk, alone in a cell. He has paper on a writing board and a pencil in his hand.
10. An inmate is sitting across a desk from a man in a jacket, white shirt, and tie. The man has his finger on a piece of paper on the desk.

Response Mode

The instructions are patterned after the *Thematic Apperception Test*. The subjects are told that they are being tested for creative imagination and should tell a story (What is happening; What the persons are thinking, saying, and feeling.) after viewing a picture. In group administrations, the subjects write their responses with pencils on lined paper. Individual administrations allow the option of either written or verbal responding.

Scoring

Protocols are scored on a 6-point "attitudinal" rating scale that ranges from positive and dominant responsibility to negative and dominant responsibility. A total responsibility score is drawn from the sum of these ratings. The 10 factors that are rated are: parents and relations; home, wife, and children; other people, friends, and co-workers; present duties and work; property; vocational advancement; self-development; self-evaluation; agreement with legal authority; and adjustment to prison life and administration. Suggestions for qualitative scoring procedures in the manual (Driscoll, 1952) follow standard *Thematic Apperception Test* instructions.

Norms

No normative data are available.

Reliability

Independent ratings by two judges of 60 prisoners' protocols yielded a product–moment correlation of +.87. The reliability of ratings over a 14-day interval by one judge with the same 60 subjects was +.93 and the retest reliability for 49 of these inmates was +.75 after 60 days.

Validity

Of the original 60 subjects, Driscoll (1949) failed to discriminate between the high and low 15 PPT scores on the basis of the MMPI scales, age, marital status, and incidence of bad conduct reports. When a median split of PPT scores was used, however, there were significantly more bad conduct reports among low responsibility inmates ($p = .02$). In clinical use, it has been reported by Driscoll that the PPT produces indications of adjustment to the prison milieu and attitudes toward oneself as a prisoner.

Comments

This is a test with interesting stimuli related to prison life. The PPT cards are somewhat amateurishly drawn, but still capture the essence of many institutional situations. Reliability of the PPT is high, but the modest validity data that is available gives little support for applied use of the test. The PPT may be considered to have been neglected, since it has not been used or studied other than in the development report—nevertheless the PPT is a direct and interesting adaptation of the *Thematic Apperception Test* to prison assessments and as such merits further attention.

REFERENCES

Driscoll, P. J. *Comparison of three measures of adjustment in a prison population.* Unpublished master's thesis, University of Wisconsin, 1949.

Driscoll, P. J. *Manual: The prison projective test.* Madison: Regents of the University of Wisconsin, 1952.

CORRECTIONS PERSONALITY ASSESSMENT: LISTINGS

Alienation Measure

Seeman, M. Alienation and social learning in a reformatory. *American Journal of Sociology,* 1963, *69,* 270–284.

The *Alienation Measure* is a 40-item forced-choice scale designed to assess an inmate's sense of powerlessness.

Prisoner–Therapist Q-Sort

Unpublished material available from:
Arthur L. Mattocks,
Supervisor of Research,
California Medical Facility,
Vacaville, California 95688.

Three Q-sorts of 50 items each were developed for the descriptions by inmates of self, ideal self, and therapist. These Q-sorts are designed to predict treatment outcomes and are prisoner related modifications of the Butler–Haigh Q-sorts.

CORRECTIONS MILIEU RATINGS: REVIEWS

Correctional Institutions Environment Scale

Development and Characteristics

The *Correctional Institutions Environment Scale* (CIES) was designed to aid in conceptualizing and measuring environmental characteristics of correctional institutions (Wenk & Moos, 1972). It is built on the premise that the individual, the environment, and individual–environment interaction all contribute significantly to behavior variance (Moos, 1968). Guided by Murray's concept of environmental press, or characteristic demands perceived by those who live in the particular environment, the CIES was developed in the hope that systematic assessment of correctional environments might detect institutional tensions before a crisis level is reached.

The items in the initial form of the CIES were adapted from the *Ward Atmosphere Scale* (Moss & Houts, 1968) by residents and staff who were familiar with correctional institutions. The items came from careful observations of ward differences, books describing prison life, and interviews with prison staff and residents. Items were included to detect strong positive or negative "halo" perceptions of an environment. The resulting 194 items were administered to a total of 384 residents and 92 staff members in 16 correctional units. There were seven units from a training school for boys, aged 16–20; four from a training school for men, aged 18–30; a male and female unit from a juvenile hall; and three boys' camps with extensive vocational programs.

The 120 item form (Form B) of the CIES were selected by three criteria: (1) The item should discriminate significantly between units; (2) the overall item split between positive and negative "halo" items should be as close to 50–50 as possible; (3) and the items should not correlate highly with the *Marlow-Crowne Social Desirability Scale,* which was also administered to the residents and staff of the 16 units. In addition, positive and negative "halo" scales were constructed from extreme items by three criteria: (1) The item should not discriminate significantly between units; (2) the item should be answered in the scored direction by less than 15% of the total resident sample; (3) and each scale should have 10 items, 5 scored "true" and 5 scored "false." There is also an "ideal unit" form, Form I, of the CIES consisting of reworded and rearranged items from Form B.

Further modifications of Form B were made to produce Form C. The changes included: (1) The subscales involvement and affiliation were combined to form a new *Involvement Scale* and items with low item–subscale correlations were eliminated; (2) the *Variety Scale* was eliminated due to low item–subscale correlations; (3) the *Aggression Scale* was eliminated; (4) both *Halo Response Scales*

TABLE 21. Correctional Institutions Environment Scale Form R—Description of Subscales

1. *Involvement:* Measures how active and energetic inmates are in the day-to-day functioning of the program—i.e., interacting socially with other inmates, doing things on their own initiative, and developing pride and group spirit in the program.
2. *Support:* Measures the extent to which inmates are encouraged to be helpful and supportive toward other inmates and how supportive the staff is toward inmates.
3. *Expressiveness:* Measures the extent to which the program encourages the open expression of feelings (including anger) by inmates and staff.
4. *Autonomy:* Measures the extent to which inmates are encouraged to take initiative in planning activities and take leadership in the unit.
5. *Practical orientation:* Measures the extent to which inmates' environments orients them toward preparing for release from the program. Such things as training for new kinds of jobs, looking to the future, and setting and working toward goals are considered.
6. *Personal problem orientation:* Measures the extent to which inmates are encouraged to be concerned with their personal problems and feelings and to seek to understand them.
7. *Order and organization:* Measures how important order and organization are in the program, in terms of inmates (how they look), staff (what they do to encourage order), and the facility itself (how well it is maintained).
8. *Clarity:* Measures the extent to which the inmate knows what to expect in the day-to-day routine of other programs and how explicit the program rules and procedures are.
9. *Staff control:* Measures the extent to which the staff uses measures to keep inmates under necessary controls—i.e., in the formulation of rules, the scheduling of activities, and in the relationships between inmates and staff.

were excluded; and (5) new scoring keys were designed to account for these changes and items were eliminated until the item set yielded acceptable item–item and item–subscale correlations and reasonable item splits. A final version, Form R, resulted from the rearrangement of the items and the inclusion of four "filler" items.

These changes resulted in a 90-item scale with nine subscales and three central dimensions pertaining to correctional institutions. Table 21 describes the nine subscales of Form R. Scales 1, 2, and 3 are "people-to-people" relationship scales. They measure the type and intensity of interpersonal relationships in the unit. Scales 4, 5, and 6 pertain to institutional programs and tap feelings relevant to the type of program and how well it meets needs of the inmates. Scales 7, 8, and 9 deal with institutional functioning and assess perception of the institutional organization.

Response Mode

Each of the 90 items of CIES, Form R is answered true or false by the respondent.

Scoring

One point is added to the relevant subscale when an item is answered in the appropriate direction. This results in a single numerical score for each of the nine subscales. A high score indicates a greater emphasis or degree of the relevant dimension for the subscales.

Norms

For Form R, national norms were calculated from samples of inmates from 41 institutional units and staff members from 15 units. This is the same sample which was used to build Form C. There are no norms available for Form I.

Reliability

No direct measures of the temporal stability of Form C, R, or I have been reported. Internal consistency for subscales is evidenced by the method of construction. Items that were poorly correlated with their subscale were eliminated.

Validity

Evidence for content validity comes from the method of construction and refinement. Further, a systematic review of the items indicates adequate coverage of relevant concepts.

Form B has been shown: (1) To significantly differentiate between inmate responses from 16 different institutional units; (2) to show low correlations between inmates' ages, lengths of stay at the unit, and scores on the *Marlow-Crowne Social Desirability Scale,* and (3) to be appropriately related to number of residents at the unit, resident–staff ratios, aggressive and rebellious behavior, and the degree of "adult status" accorded residents at the unit.

Form C has successfully differentiated between a community treatment center (which was much higher than normative values on all scales except staff control) and an isolated correctional work camp (which approximated national resident norms). The community treatment center revealed significantly more agreement between staff and residents than the work camp in which staff members rated the unit higher on eight of the nine scales (Wenk & Moos, 1972). Changes in treatment programs within units also were reflected by the CIES. Improved conditions produced high resident scores after the first of the new programs. There was a reversal noted in a third testing, but this result was believed to be due to intergroup conflicts at the time of testing. The CIES has also been used to gauge social climate changes for behavior modification treatment projects (Jesness, De Risi, McCormick, & Wedge, 1972) and pay incentive programs (Wenk & Frank, 1973).

No further information is available for Form R or I.

Comments

In general, reliability and validity evidence is adequate. Temporal stability estimates would be helpful, as would further work with validity of individual subscales. Further, subscale–subscale and subscale-to-general dimension correlations would indicate the degree of heterogeneity within the three principle dimensions (people–people relationships, institutional programs, and institutional functioning) and interrelationships across dimensions. External validity indicates that the CIES Forms C and R may serve as a useful measure of resident and staff perceptions for research purposes and as one source for information about the social climate of a correctional unit.

Moreover, the CIES is as important for its focus of attention as it is for its sociometric qualities. Most research and measurement scales in criminal justice assess qualities of individuals or groups of individuals. In contrast, the CIES attends to characteristics of institutions and thus yields alternative perspectives in understanding correctional processes.

REFERENCES

Jesness, C. J., DeRisi, W., McCormick, P., & Wedge, R. *Program impact on social climate* (The Youth Center Research Project). Sacramento, California: American Justice Institute, 1972.

Moos, R. H. The assessment of the social climates of correctional institutions. *Journal of Research in Crime and Delinquency,* 1968, *5,* 174–188.

Moos, R. H. Differential effects of the social climates of correctional institutions. *Journal of Research in Crime and Delinquency,* 1970, *7,* 71–82.

Moos, R. H., & Houts, P. S. The assessment of the social atmospheres of psychiatric wards. *Journal of Abnormal Psychology,* 1968, *73,* 595–604.

Wenk, E. A., & Frank, C. Some progress in the coalition of institutional programs. *Federal Probation,* 1973, *37,* 30–37.

Wenk, E. A., & Moos, R. H. Social climates in prison: An attempt to conceptualize and measure environmental factors in total institutions. *Journal of Research in Crime and Delinquency,* 1972, *9,* 134–148.

CORRECTIONAL INSTITUTIONS ENVIRONMENTAL SCALE

This scale is commercially distributed by Consulting Psychologists Press, Inc., 577 College Avenue, Palo Alto, California 94306. The following are sample items from Form R.

Residents rarely talk about their personal problems with other residents.

People say what they really think around here.

The staff very rarely punish residents by restricting them.

The staff discourage talking about sex.

On this unit staff thinks it is a healthy thing to argue.

The staff do not tolerate sexual behavior by residents.

Prison Profile Inventory

Development and Characteristics

The *Prison Profile Inventory* (PPI) was designed to serve as a quantified multidimensional portrait of the prison environment as experienced by the inmate (Toch, 1975). After intensive interviews with inmates, the developer outlined eight dimensions that represent the concerns of inmates about the prison environment. These are: privacy, safety, structure, support, feedback, social stimulation, activity, and freedom. Each of the dimensions is represented by a number of items. The final form of the questionnaire pairs items from each dimension twice with items from the other dimension and requests that the most desirable of the two be noted. This procedure yields a total of 56 pairs.

When this version of the PPI was administered to 632 inmates, 39 items discriminated between comparison groups.

Response Mode

The respondent is asked to read each item-pair and choose the alternative that he or she believes is the more desirable of the two.

Scoring

An item from each dimensions is paired twice with each other dimension. The pairing yields a total of 14 opportunities to choose one dimension over the others. The number of times a dimension is chosen serves as the score for that dimension.

TABLE 22. Average PPI Dimension Scores

Dimension	Sample or population					
	NY $N = 299$	CT $N = 201$	PA $N = 314$	CA $N = 327$	Federal $N = 512$	Combined samples $N = 1,653$
Privacy	5.8	5.4	4.7	5.5	5.5	5.4
Safety	7.4	6.0	7.3	7.6	7.5	7.3
Structure	6.1	6.1	6.4	5.4	6.9	6.3
Support	10.2	9.9	10.2	10.1	9.3	9.9
Feedback	7.8	8.8	8.4	7.9	8.7	8.3
Social stimulation	6.5	6.7	7.3	7.0	6.6	6.8
Activity	8.7	7.4	8.6	8.1	6.7	7.8
Freedom	3.7	5.9	3.3	4.5	5.0	4.5

Norms

Table 22 presents the mean scores for the PPI dimensions that were obtained from one federal and four state prisons.

Reliability

Table 23 shows the average reliability estimates (parallel forms and split half) obtained from a sample of 1,326 inmates from one federal and four state prisons.

TABLE 23. The Reliability of the PPI Dimensions

Dimension	Average r	
	Parallel test	KR 20
Privacy	.69	.65
Safety	.70	.64
Structure	.54	.50
Support	.48	.46
Emotional feedback	.68	.62
Social stimulation	.53	.46
Activity	.52	.51
Freedom	.72	.67
$\bar{X}$	.61	.56

Half the dimensions (structure, support, social stimulation, and activity) show average reliabilities around .50 while the others (privacy, safety, emotional feedback, and freedom) average .60 or greater.

Validity

The choice of the dimensions indicates coverage of the concerns of inmates, and the systematic pairing of items from each dimension with items from each other dimension allows comparison for relative strength.

Toch (1975) reports that sets of individual item-pairs are able to discriminate between: (1) Adult and youth inmates; (2) male and female inmates; (3) normal and "weak company" inmates (those who are known to worry about staff authority, power, and discipline); and (4) "invalids" and adult inmates.

Comments

Reliability estimates indicate borderline acceptability. Yet, support is available for item validity and there is some evidence that dimension scores can appropriately differentiate between comparison groups. There is a need to measure the strength of the differentiating ability of the dimensions. Further validation of the dimensions would also be a desirable step in developing the construct validity of the PPI.

This is an ipsative scale, in which high scores must be balanced by low scores on other dimensions. Thus, all scores are relative to the other ratings. Such a scale limits the interpretation of results for different groups and settings.

REFERENCES

Toch, H. *Prison environments and psychological survival.* Unpublished manuscript, School of Criminal Justice, State University of New York, Albany, N.Y., 1975.

Toch, H. *Living in prisons: The ecology of prison survival.* New York: Free Press, 1977.

PRISON PROFILE INVENTORY

NO ONE LIKES DOING TIME. But there are some things that can make life in prison EASIER, and some that make it HARDER.

We'd like to know some of the things you LIKE MOST about prisons. First, we'll give you a list of things you can choose from, and we'd like to know which of them you PREFER.

Here is an example:
I'd prefer   A PAROLE DATE   CHICKEN NEXT SUNDAY

We'd like you to CIRCLE the one you prefer. If you are like most people, you'll want the parole date. If you do, please circle it: your answer will look like this:

I'd prefer   (A PAROLE DATE)   CHICKEN NEXT SUNDAY

Some of the choices will be tougher than this one, but please try your best. Even if you have a hard time deciding, or you have only a SLIGHT preference, let us know which way you lean.

Remember to CIRCLE the one you LIKE BEST, and DON'T SKIP ANY.

1.	I'd prefer	GUARDS WHO ARE CONSISTENT	HOUSING THAT KEEPS OUT NOISE
2.	I'd prefer	HOUSING IN WHICH NO ONE CAN HARM ME	STAYING AWAY FROM GUARDS
3.	I'd prefer	INMATES WHO KNOW THEIR RIGHTS	INMATES WHO MAKE NO NOISE
4.	I'd prefer	HOUSING WHERE PEOPLE RAP	A FRIEND WHO SHARES MY PROBLEMS
5.	I'd prefer	KNOWING MY PEOPLE STILL LOVE ME	A GUARD WHO OVERLOOKS INFRACTIONS
6.	I'd prefer	EDUCATIONAL ADVANCEMENT	PROTECTION FROM DANGER
7.	I'd prefer	STAFF WHO STICK TO THEIR RULES	STAFF WHO CARE HOW I FEEL
8.	I'd prefer	STAFF WHO LET ME RUN MY LIFE	STAFF WHO ARE HONEST
9.	I'd prefer	STAFF WHO HELP A MAN WHO'S DEPRESSED	A SHOP WHERE THEY TEACH YOU SKILLS
10.	I'd prefer	BEING BY MYSELF	LEARNING SOMETHING
11.	I'd prefer	INMATES I KNOW WELL FROM THE STREETS	GUARDS WHO ACT THE SAME EVERY DAY
12.	I'd prefer	GETTING A GOOD JOB IN PRISON	BEING SAFE IN PRISON
13.	I'd prefer	KNOWING THAT I'M LOVED	GETTING PEACE AND QUIET
14.	I'd prefer	STAYING IN MY CELL	FEELING SAFE
15.	I'd prefer	HAVING NO GUARDS AROUND	HAVING LOTS OF FRIENDS
16.	I'd prefer	A PLACE WITH NO CROWDS	A PLACE WHERE YOU ARE SAFE

17.	I'd prefer	KEEPING ACTIVE	LOVING SOMEONE
18.	I'd prefer	A JOB WHERE I HAVE FRIENDS	A JOB WHERE I WORK ALONE
19.	I'd prefer	STAFF WHO PROTECTS MY INTERESTS	NOT HAVING A BOSS
20.	I'd prefer	HAVING A GOOD TIME	BEING CLOSE TO SOMEONE
21.	I'd prefer	HAVING CONSISTENT RULES	BEING BUSY ALL DAY
22.	I'd prefer	TEACHERS FROM WHOM I LEARN	GUARDS WHO PROTECT ME
23.	I'd prefer	HOUSING WHERE I KNOW EVERYBODY	HOUSING IN WHICH I KEEP BUSY
24.	I'd prefer	RULES THAT TELL ME WHAT TO EXPECT	AS FEW RULES AS POSSIBLE
25.	I'd prefer	A PLACE WITH FRIENDS	A QUIET PLACE
26.	I'd prefer	A VERY BUSY DAY	A MESSAGE OF LOVE
27.	I'd prefer	A FRIENDLY GAME	NO SUPERVISION
28.	I'd prefer	AN ACTIVE PROGRAM	TIME BY MYSELF
29.	I'd prefer	NO ONE TO DISTURB ME	NO ONE TO FORGET ME
30.	I'd prefer	NO ONE CHECKING UP ON ME	NO TIME TO BE BORED

We'll ask you about some things now you probably DON'T like. What we want to know is which of two things you like LEAST.

For instance, if you were forced to live with

AN INMATE WHO SNORES ALL NIGHT
or AN INMATE WHO READS ALL DAY

Which would bother you more? If you sleep nights and you have good ears, you'd probably say, "an inmate who snores all night." Your answer would be:

I'd be more bothered by  AN INMATE WHO SNORES ALL NIGHT   AN INMATE WHO READS ALL DAY

Here are some other pairs like this. In each case, please CIRCLE the one you LIKE LEAST.

31.	I'd be more bothered by	TOO MUCH TIME TO THINK	TOO MUCH TALK AND NOISE
32.	I'd be more bothered by	HOUSING WHERE PEOPLE COULD TRAP ME	HOUSING WHERE NO ONE KNOWS ME
33.	I'd be more bothered by	SITTING AROUND	GETTING NOWHERE
34.	I'd be more bothered by	INMATES WHO ARE ALWAYS NOISY	STAFF WHO ARE ON MY BACK

35.	I'd be more bothered by	HAVING NO FRIENDS	HAVING ENEMIES
36.	I'd be more bothered by	FEELING UNSAFE	FEELING UNLOVED
37.	I'd be more bothered by	HAVING NOTHING TO DO	LEARNING NOTHING NEW
38.	I'd be more bothered by	HAVING NEW FRIENDS	HAVING NO MONEY
39.	I'd be more bothered by	A PRISON WITH NO PROTECTION	A PRISON WITH NO RULES
40.	I'd be more bothered by	NOT KNOWING THE RULES	NOT FEELING SAFE
41.	I'd be more bothered by	BEING DEPRESSED	BEING CONFUSED
42.	I'd be more bothered by	INMATES WHO ARE DANGEROUS	INMATES WHO ARE RATS
43.	I'd be more bothered by	GUARDS GIVING PETTY ORDERS	FAMILY WHO FORGET YOU
44.	I'd be more bothered by	PEOPLE WHO TALK LOUD	PEOPLE WHO USE ME
45.	I'd be more bothered by	INMATES WHO PICK FIGHTS	INMATES WHO ARE SQUARES
46.	I'd be more bothered by	NOT KNOWING ANYONE	THINKING TOO MUCH
47.	I'd be more bothered by	NO VISITS FROM HOME	TENSION IN PRISON
48.	I'd be more bothered by	LOTS OF DANGEROUS PEOPLE	LOTS OF IDLE TIME
49.	I'd be more bothered by	BEING USED	BEING TOLD WHAT TO DO
50.	I'd be more bothered by	BEING BORED	HAVING RULES CHANGED
51.	I'd be more bothered by	AN UNCERTAIN ASSIGNMENT	PROGRAMS THAT DON'T HELP ME ENOUGH
52.	I'd be more bothered by	NOISY TIERS	NO RULES AT ALL
53.	I'd be more bothered by	A LOT OF RULES	A LOT OF BOREDOM
54.	I'd be more bothered by	A PRISON WITH CHANGING RULES	A PRISON WITH NO FRIENDS
55.	I'd be more bothered by	PROGRAMS THAT DON'T HELP ME MAKE PAROLE	STAFF WHO KEEP CHANGING RULES
56.	I'd be more bothered by	STAFF WHO DON'T TEACH YOU SKILLS	STAFF WHO DON'T CARE HOW YOU FEEL

Prison Profile Inventory — Key

1	STRU	PRI	29	PRI	FEED
2	SAF	FREE	30	FREE	ACT
3	FREE	PRI	31	ACT	PRI
4	SOC	FEED	32	SAF	SOC
5	FEED	FREE	33	ACT	SUP
6	SUP	SAF	34	PRI	FREE
7	STRU	FEED	35	SOC	SAF
8	FREE	STRU	36	SAF	FEED
9	FEED	SUP	37	ACT	SUP
10	PRI	SUP	38	SOC	SUP
11	SOC	STRU	39	SAF	STRU
12.	ACT	SAF	40	STRU	SAF
13	FEED	PRI	41	FEED	STRU
14	PRI	SAF	42	SAF	FREE
15	FREE	SOC	43	FREE	FEED
16	PRI	SAF	44	PRI	SUP
17	ACT	FEED	45	SUP	SOC
18	SOC	PRI	46	SOC	ACT
19	SUP	FREE	47	FEED	SAF
20	SOC	FEED	48	SAF	ACT
21	STRU	ACT	49	SUP	FREE
22	SUP	SAF	50	ACT	STRU
23	SOC	ACT	51	STRU	SUP
24	STRU	FREE	52	PRI	STRU
25	SOC	PRI	53	FREE	ACT
26	ACT	FEED	54	STRU	SOC
27	SOC	FREE	55	SUP	STRU
28	ACT	PRI	56	SUP	FEED

CORRECTIONS MILIEU RATINGS: LISTINGS

Child Care Work Questionnaire

Unpublished report available from:
 D. W. Roush,
 Calhoun County Juvenile Home,
 14555 18½ Mile Road,
 Marshall, Michigan 49068.

This 11-item scale was designed to gauge the perceptions of the child-care staff at a juvenile correctional institution about their working conditions, professionalization and career opportunities.

Classification for Placement in Training Schools

Birkenmayer, A. C., & Lambert, L. R. *An assessment of the classification system for placement of wards in training schools: I. The determination of outcomes.* Planning and Research Branch of the Ministry of Correctional Services, Ontario, Canada, 1972.

The correctional classification system was designed to classify juvenile offenders into correctional institutions using the following three dimensions: 1. Current status of community/or institutional involvement: five categories; 2. criminal activity subsequent to inmate's release: five categories; and 3. history of work and/or school involvement since first placement: eight categories.

Group Evaluation Criteria Card Sort

Sternbach, J., & Pincus, A. Differences in perception of the group by cottage parents and social workers. *Child Welfare*, 1970, *49*, 327–335.

The group evaluation criterion card sort is a set of 10 cards containing criteria for evaluating or assessing a cottage group. The results of the card sort indicate perceptions of the social structure of the cottage.

Index of Perspectives on Institution and Staff

Street, D. The inmate group in custodial and treatment settings. *American Sociological Review*, 1965, *30*, 40–55.

This 7-item scale is designed to measure inmate perceived helpfulness of custodial and treatment settings. This index has been used in conjunction with a series of additional indices of inmate and staff assessments of correctional milieu.

Institutional Living and Inmate Code Scales

Tittle, C. R. Institutional living and self-esteem. *Social Problems,* 1972, *20,* 65–77.

These brief scales were designed to measure aspects of institutional problems for inmates in a narcotics hospital. The 3-item *Institutional Living Scale* queries about contact with clinical staff members and felt deprivation of autonomy. The 5-item Guttman-type *Inmate Code Scale* deals with rule violations and interactions with security staff.

Response to Incarceration Questionnaire

Hindman, R. L. Inmate interaction as a determinant of response to incarceration. *British Journal of Criminology,* 1971, *11,* 382–390.

This 5-item questionnaire consists of one item designed to measure inmates' perceptions of justness of treatment, one item on the effect of this incarceration after release, and three "interaction" items dealing with inmate friendships, guard contact, and contact with outside friends and relatives.

Training in Differential Treatment Assessment Instruments

Tolhurst, D. E. *Center for training in differential treatment: Final report of phase one, part two. Major assessment instruments used in project.* The Institute for the Study of Crime and Delinquency, in cooperation with the California Youth Authority. (NIMH Project MH 10893 Report, undated.)

This series of questionnaires and rating scales was designed to assess agency treatment climate and operation, and training functioning and knowledge prior to, during and following *I*-level training.

CORRECTIONS PREDICTION: REVIEWS

Hunch Parolability Scale

Development and Characteristics

The *Hunch Parolability Scale* (HPS) was designed to measure "the unit characters which combine to form the concept of parolability" (Laune, 1936, p. 19). *Parolability,* here, refers to an inmates readiness to take a responsible role in society and is ultimately defined by his or her ability to avoid arrest and conviction in the future. The developer believes that one's opinion of another, along any dimension, is expressed as hunches that can be traced to definite criteria.

These criteria surface during discussion of the question of parole. To test this assumption, a pair of experienced investigators (whose judgments of inmates had been shown to represent all the elements considered by a wide range of observers) were asked to discuss at great length each of 150 applicants for parole.

Careful stenographic records indicated that 42 characteristics were mentioned during discussions. Some of these characteristics are viewed as positive (indicative of parole success), others are viewed as negative (indicative of parole failure). For example, an inmate who has a previous work record has one positive (+) attribute. An inmate who is a recidivist has a negative (−) attribute.

Since this form of the scale does not allow each person to be rated on every item, comparison of potential parolees was inappropriate. To solve this problem, the scale was modified by constructing two items for every factor that could be + or − and by rewording negative items to form positive (+) stems. The result was a scale of 54 items worded in the direction of "desirable" characteristics. When scores on this new version were compared to corresponding scores on the original scale, correlation coefficients ranged from .56 to .84.

Response Mode

The rater of a potential parolee is asked to read each attribute or factor and note whether it is characteristic of the individual under consideration. If a factor is characteristic of the ratee, he or she receives a plus (+); if not, a minus (−).

Scoring

A total score is obtained by summing a number of pluses and subtracting the number of minus ratings.

Norms

No relevant norms are available.

Reliability

Interrater reliability coefficients range from .69 to .78 for 150 subjects.

Validity

Content validity is established by the method of scale construction. The systematic review of discussions of respondents produced 27 attributes after only six cases were discussed. The entire 42 were found by the 102nd case. No more were mentioned in the remaining 48 cases discussed. The developer suggests that this is evidence for the completeness of the criteria list. Also, it is suggested that these criteria are subjective only to the degree that verbal symbolism forces subjectivity. The discussions were allowed to flow naturally, thereby permitting the respondents free expression.

Comments

The HPS represents an interesting approach to item construction. Recording the spontaneous verbal rationale for opinions is a logical first step to understanding how decisions are made. There are, however, some shortcomings that should be considered. The developers deal with each item as an independent factor, then sum the number of plus (+) responses to obtain a single total score. If each attribute is independent, this would be supported by a test of heterogeneity. Inspection of the items, however, shows contamination. For example, intelligence is related to "absence of stupidity." This interrelationship weights each multi-item dimension more heavily than single-item factors.

Another area of concern is generalizability of these particular factors. First, cross-validation of the raters' criteria should be attempted. This would provide information on the universality of the item-attributes. Next, there is some question whether the particular items that were drawn from the transcripts would be chosen by another researcher as key phrases.

In general, this scale offers a logical approach and acceptable reliability estimates. There is support for validity of the HPS as a predictor of parolability, but more research and scale modifications are needed. This version represents a stage of development that allows parolability estimates to be made by someone familiar with the individual under consideration. In addition, a set of questions, known as the *Parolability Questionnaire,* which allows the inmate to provide this information to decision makers on parole boards is also provided.

REFERENCES

Laune, F. F. *Predicting criminality: Forecasting behavior on parole*. Chicago: Northwestern University Press, 1936.

HUNCH PAROLABILITY SCALE

Instructions: Read each of the following factors and indicate whether it is a characteristic of the individual under consideration. Place a (+) beside those items which are attributes of the individual being rated and a (-) beside those which are not.

I. Psychological and Physical Factors

1. Intelligence
2. Absence of stupidity
3. Timidity
4. Absence of foolhardiness
5. Strength of character
6. Absence of weakness of character
7. Pleasing personality
8. Phlegmaticness
9. Absence of emotional instability
10. Shrewdness
11. Critical qualities
12. Absence of lack of discrimination
13. Selfishness
14. Absence of altruism
15. Lack of conceit
16. Absence of argumentativeness
17. Absence of love of comfort
18. Religiosity
19. Long view of future
20. Absence of short view of future
21. Absence of tendency to be an agitator
22. Learned Lesson
23. Absence of failure to learn lesson
24. Absence of sharp practices
25. Absence of positive Wasserman reaction
26. Absence of physical defects

II. Factors Connected with Industry

27. Industry
28. Absence of laziness
29. Previous work record
30. Trade
31. Working ability
32. Absence or lack of working ability

III. Factors Connected with High Life

33. Absence of inordinate desire for clothes
34. Absence of sex craving
35. Absence of desire for white lights
36. Absence of wanderlust

IV. Factors Connected with Family

37. Absence of broken family
38. Absence of lack of love for relatives
39. Family ties

40. Rural type
41. Happily married
42. Good outside environment
43. Absence of bad outside environment
44. Absence of criminality in family

V. Factors Connected with Criminal Record

45. Absence of previous hoodlum activities
46. Absence of recidivism
47. Absence of good job in prison
48. Absence of gangster status
49. Absence of minor racketeering
50. Favorable age relation
51. Absence of unfavorable age relation
52. Break in criminal record
53. Long time to serve on Maximum X
54. Absence of short time to serve

Parolability Questionnaire

Development and Characteristics

The *Parolability Questionnaire* (PQ) was designed to objectively measure the degree to which an inmate meets the criteria for a good parole risk (Laune, 1936). These criteria were developed through the procedure described in the HPS. The parolability factors derived from the HPS were carefully studied and questions answerable by "yes" or "no" were formulated for each factor. The 54 factors produced a total of 1,691 questions. To these, 10 "index" questions were added as a check on truthfulness of response. Each of these questions is worded so that the response that is most likely true presents a less than perfect view of the respondent. For example, one question is "Have you ever broken a prison rule?". If an inmate responds no, he or she is likely to be lying, since few people could exist without breaking at least one prison rule. A "no" response, then would indicate that he or she was trying to present a socially desirable picture; thus, the questionnaire answers would become suspect.

These 1,701 items were presented to 57 inmates who agreed to be totally honest with their responses. Another group of 228 inmates were administered parts of the entire item pool so that 57 additional completed questionnaires and a total of 114 questionnaires resulted.

In an attempt to reduce the number of items and include only the best predictors, the developer utilized various techniques of factor analysis. These were felt to be ineffective in uncovering true factors, however, and it was decided that items would be retained only if (1) their variance with "Hunch" responses was low, or (2) an inmate's responses to the PQ items was consistent with other inmates' hunch predictions about him or her. The resultant total was 161 items.

Response Mode

The respondent is asked to read each question and to circle the appropriate alternative, "Yes" or "No."

Scoring

Each item is keyed in the direction of favorability of response to successful parole. Therefore, a total parolability score is obtained by summing the number of responses in the direction of parolability.

Norms

No relevant norms were available.

Reliability

No reliability estimates were reported.

Validity

Content validity is indicated by the method of scale construction. The use of inmate hunches about other inmates as a set of basic factors uses peer rating information that is normally unavailable in parole decision. Further, a systematic review of the items shows a consistent pattern of relevant questions.

The PQ, the HPS, and the *Burgess Inmate Information Scale* were administered to 57 volunteers at the Illinois State Penitentiary at Joliet. Using Pearson correlation coefficients, Hunch scores correlated with the PQ $+.48$, the questionnaire correlated with the Burgess Scale $+.49$ and the Hunch Scale correlated with the Burgess Scale $+.29$. This indicates that the PQ is correlated with the HPS and is measuring in part a related construct. The PQ is valid to the degree that inmate hunches about other inmates' likelihood of successful parole are valid.

Comments

The basis for the information of the PQ is interesting and shows potential that has not been realized through subsequent research. The most appropriate test of validity of a predictive scale is how well it predicts. Although work of this nature was reported in 1936 to be in progress (by the developer), a literature search revealed no subsequent work with the instrument.

Modification in the PQ might include a check for the number of questions on the final version that relate to each factor. An unequal distribution of items would tend to weight the total scale score accordingly. Consideration should also be given to a factor analysis of the entire 1,701 item questionnaire to determine what constructs are being measured. Many more than 57 respondents would be needed for such a large item pool.

In general, the PQ has received some empirical support but has not been sufficiently tested. It is worthy of further work because of its innovative basis for development—peer evaluation.

REFERENCES

Laune, F. F. *Predicting criminality: Forecasting behavior on parole*. Chicago: Northwestern University Press, 1936.

PAROLABILITY QUESTIONNAIRE

Instructions: Answer the following questions by drawing a circle around the correct answer to each. For example,

Are you in prison now?.	Yes	No
Are all prisoners honest?.	Yes	No

Be sure to answer every question whether it applies to you or not. If you are not married and are asked "Do you love your wife?" you will have to answer "No," because if you have no wife, you cannot love her. To some questions it will be hard to answer either "Yes" or "No," but mark the answer you think is more nearly true. BE SURE TO ANSWER EVERY QUESTION. Also be sure to fill in your number and name in the spaces at the top of this page.

1. Have you worked longer than a year at any trade in prison?....... Yes No
2. Did you ever spend as much as $25 for an evening's entertainment in a cabaret? .... Yes No
3. Do you intend to have the same friends after your release as before your arrest?.. Yes No
4. Do your brothers or sisters visit you or write to you? .... Yes No
5. When you are in company with others, do you make the decision as to how the evening will be spent more frequently than they do? Yes No
6. Do you make inquiries about a man's reputation before becoming friendly with him?.. Yes No

7.	Could you hold a clerical position?......................................	Yes	No
8.	Do you generally plan far into the future?...........................	Yes	No
9.	Are your parents the finest people in the world?.................	Yes	No
10.	Are you considered strong-minded by others?..................	Yes	No
11.	Are you going back to your wife when you are released?.........	Yes	No
12.	Do you like to go stepping out every night?.....................	Yes	No
13.	Do you think it is a waste of time to spend years learning some profession when you might be out working?...................	Yes	No
14.	Are you a better man now than when you were received in prison?	Yes	No
15.	Do you generally get quite enthusiastic over hearing some bit of good news?..	Yes	No
16.	Do you know what methods most lawyers use to beat "raps"?....	Yes	No
17.	Did you go out with girls as often as five times a week?..........	Yes	No
18.	Were you ever in any other penal institution?...................	Yes	No
19.	Has your wife been loyal to you in your trouble?................	Yes	No
20.	Would you like to take it easy for the rest of your life?...........	Yes	No
21.	Has prison taught you to fear punishment?....................	Yes	No
22.	Do you spend much time working out complicated plans in advance?..	Yes	No
23.	Did you buy only what clothes were absolutely necessary?.......	Yes	No
24.	Do most people like you?...................................	Yes	No
25.	Have you ever promoted a quarrel between two people?.........	Yes	No
26.	Have you been in more than ten states of the Union?............	Yes	No
27.	Were you the only one in your group engaged in criminal activities?..	Yes	No
28.	Do you consider yourself very bright?........................	Yes	No
29.	Are you very particular about the people with whom you associate?..	Yes	No
30.	If you were working with a group who were slacking, would you slack?...	Yes	No
31.	Do you feel at home in the city?.............................	Yes	No
32.	Are you something of a leader in prison?.....................	Yes	No
33.	Would you be better satisfied working for only half a day than for a whole day?..	Yes	No
34.	Have you many friends?....................................	Yes	No
35.	Have you a good job in prison?..............................	Yes	No
36.	Have your brothers and sisters done more for you than you have done for them?...	Yes	No

37.	If your cell partner brought an electric stove into your cell, would you be very frightened that you might be punished?		Yes	No
38.	Would you be happy just taking it easy?		Yes	No
39.	Has prison experience had a good moral effect on you?		Yes	No
40.	Do you pray regularly?		Yes	No
41.	Have you ever done work of a specialized nature?		Yes	No
42.	Have your parents stuck with you through thick and thin?		Yes	No
43.	Are you highly impressionable?		Yes	No
44.	Have you ever dreamed about the future and worked with the idea of realizing that dream?		Yes	No
45.	Are you now an expert at any occupation you have learned in prison?		Yes	No
46.	Are your parents separated?		Yes	No
47.	Do you ever lie down and have a good cry?		Yes	No
48.	If a close pal of yours were in some jail charged with some crime and he had plenty of money, would you know how to go about putting in a fix for him?		Yes	No
49.	Were you considered a ladies' man?		Yes	No
50.	Have you been in more than one jail?		Yes	No
51.	If a man made a statement in your hearing about a matter of fact and you knew he was wrong, would you call him on it?		Yes	No
52.	Is it proper to put crooked dice in a game if the fellows playing are fools enough to permit it?		Yes	No
53.	If you were earning $25, would you spend more than $6 a week on clothes?		Yes	No
54.	Have you any moral scruples against stealing?		Yes	No
55.	Have any of your brothers or sisters ever broken the law?		Yes	No
56.	Did you ever tell a man someone else was making a sucker out of him?		Yes	No
57.	Did you ever get a job on the strength of your personality?		Yes	No
58.	Have you ever broken a prison rule?		Yes	No
59.	Have you ever hopped freights around the country?		Yes	No
60.	Were you considered a hoodlum before you were fifteen?		Yes	No
61.	Did you have to go out and earn your own living as soon as you could get a job?		Yes	No
62.	Would you sacrifice others to your own advancement?		Yes	No
63.	Is it easy to become friendly with you?		Yes	No
64.	Do you have any hobbies?		Yes	No
65.	Did you ever indulge in minor thievery of any description?		Yes	No

66.	Have you ever pitched hay?	Yes	No
67.	Do girls run after you?	Yes	No
68.	Did you have your own special chair in which you always sat on the outside?	Yes	No
69.	Were there frequent intervals between your jobs?	Yes	No
70.	Have you been more fortunately placed in prison than the average?	Yes	No
71.	Have your brothers and sisters been loyal to you?	Yes	No
72.	If you had a chance to escape, would the fear of the punishment if you were caught stop you?	Yes	No
73.	Are you worse off morally now than when you came to prison?	Yes	No
74.	Do you consider it beneath your dignity to accept work other than in your own chosen line?	Yes	No
75.	Are you easily picked on?	Yes	No
76.	Do you spend much time studying things now for which you have no immediate use but which you think may come in handy in the future?	Yes	No
77.	Are you known as a good tipper?	Yes	No
78.	Does it generally take really important things to upset you?	Yes	No
79.	Did you ever know of a case, yourself, where a member of the jury was bought?	Yes	No
80.	Did you ever live in a house of ill-fame?	Yes	No
81.	Did your wife try to "keep you straight"?	Yes	No
82.	Do you think a man is justified in winning the confidence of others in order to "clip" them?	Yes	No
83.	Did your gang have certain sections of the city where they could operate safely because the "fix" was in?	Yes	No
84.	Have you ever gone over to the deputy to try and get someone else out of the hole?	Yes	No
85.	Did your hoodlum activities start just before you were arrested?	Yes	No
86.	Do you make friends only with cultured people?	Yes	No
87.	Would you go crazy if you had nothing to do?	Yes	No
88.	Have you the reputation of being conceited?	Yes	No
89.	Were you ever fired from a job?	Yes	No
90.	Have most of your jobs been in the same line of work?	Yes	No
91.	Do your brothers and sisters send you money?	Yes	No
92.	Have you ever committed a crime?	Yes	No
93.	Are you afraid of the "hole"?	Yes	No
94.	Are you religious?	Yes	No

95.	Have you the ability to hold any job other than purely unskilled labor?...	Yes	No
96.	Has prison done you good mentally?........................	Yes	No
97.	Is your mother much sweeter than other mothers?	Yes	No
98.	Do you try to model your conduct on some plan you have thought out in advance?...	Yes	No
99.	Do you often give your favorite entertainer $5 to sing some particular song?...	Yes	No
100.	Have you stuck to one trade pretty much all your time in prison?..	Yes	No
101.	Do you ever plan business operations that extend more than a few months into the future?...................................	Yes	No
102.	Do you ever get "down in the dumps"?......................	Yes	No
103.	Do you think the intimidation of witnesses is a good way to beat the rap?..	Yes	No
104.	Do you consider your imprisonment as merely a temporary interruption of your life plans?.................................	Yes	No
105.	Were many of your activities indulged in for the purpose of making a hit with girls?.......................................	Yes	No
106.	Have you been in more than two penal institutions?	Yes	No
107.	Has your wife done everything she could to help you?...........	Yes	No
108.	Do you spend much time arguing?..........................	Yes	No
109.	Are you a pretty good schemer?	Yes	No
110.	Do you spend more on clothes than you do on any one other item?...	Yes	No
111.	Are you sometimes all pepped up?..........................	Yes	No
112.	Have your parents ever broken the law?......................	Yes	No
113.	Did you ever point out to a fellow that he was being taken advantage of?..	Yes	No
114.	Has your ability to persuade people ever helped you when you were in trouble?...	Yes	No
115.	Would you be uncomfortable if you had to remain in one town very long?...	Yes	No
116.	Were you less than 15 years old when you pulled off your first job?..	Yes	No
117.	Do you look out for your own welfare most of the time?..........	Yes	No
118.	Did your family own an automobile?.........................	Yes	No
119.	Do you "rap" to nearly everybody?..........................	Yes	No
120.	Would you have made a bigger success of life if you had been willing to work harder?..	Yes	No

121.	Do you know what "laying paper" is?	Yes	No
122.	Have you ever shucked corn?	Yes	No
123.	Are you entirely without influence with other prisoners?	Yes	No
124.	Would you be much distressed if you had to eat eggs without salt?	Yes	No
125.	Did you work regularly?	Yes	No
126.	Did you have as good shoes outside as you have here?	Yes	No
127.	Have your brothers and sisters done all they should for you?	Yes	No
128.	Are you considered reckless by others?	Yes	No
129.	Do you feel that imprisonment has debased you morally?	Yes	No
130.	Do you believe that it is hypocritical to be religious in prison?	Yes	No
131.	Are you too weak to do heavy work?	Yes	No
132.	Did your parents neglect your training when you were young?	Yes	No
133.	Are you always planning things for the future?	Yes	No
134.	Do you often get drunk?	Yes	No
135.	Do you feel that you are as well equipped in any line as the average outside worker?	Yes	No
136.	Do you think that the fact that your family is broken had anything to do with your being here?	Yes	No
137.	Is it hard to make you feel really blue?	Yes	No
138.	Do you think you could beat nearly any "rap" if you had enough money?	Yes	No
139.	Have you ever had a veneral disease?	Yes	No
140.	Have you been in more than four jails?	Yes	No
141.	Do you like to stay home with your wife?	Yes	No
142.	Do you frequently consult the almanac or the dictionary to prove an argument?	Yes	No
143.	Did you ever "outcon" a con man?	Yes	No
144.	Are you really interested in clothes themselves?	Yes	No
145.	If something that you could steal was very necessary to your complete happiness and there was an excellent chance that you would not get caught, would you steal it?	Yes	No
146.	Are you the only member of your family ever to be arrested?	Yes	No
147.	Have you ever helped get signatures to a petition?	Yes	No
148.	Does it get on your nerves to remain long in one town?	Yes	No
149.	Do you think you have a pleasant personality?	Yes	No
150.	Did you associate with any hoodlums a year before your arrest?	Yes	No

151.	Have any of your friends on the outside have police records?.....		Yes	No
152.	Are you often influenced by what others may think of your actions?..		Yes	No
153.	Are you afraid of snakes?.....................................		Yes	No
154.	Do you have to know all about a man before you will accept him as a friend?..		Yes	No
155.	Do you think work is a blessing?.............................		Yes	No
156.	Have you ever committed petit larceny?		Yes	No
157.	Are you a hoosier?		Yes	No
158.	Do you know anyone who you think has a better personality than you?...		Yes	No
159.	Would you be terribly upset if the hot water were turned off in your home for a day?...		Yes	No
160.	Have you often been without work?		Yes	No
161.	Would you do easier time if you had some other job in prison?....		Yes	No

CORRECTIONS PREDICTION: LISTINGS

Institutional Adjustment Inventory

Coe, R. N. Characteristics of well-adjusted and poorly-adjusted inmates. *Journal of Criminal Law, Criminology, and Police Science,* 1961, *52,* 178–184.

The *Institutional Adjustment Inventory* is a 41-item list of variables designed to predict prison adjustment. The variables fall into the categories of personal data, early social data, present data, and criminal data.

Parole Adjustment Scale

Weiner, R. I. *Probation case load classification study in the United States District Court for the District of Columbia.* Director, Community and Clinical Programs, Center for the Administration of Justice, American University, Washington, D.C. 20016.

This 12-item rating scale of base expectancy data was designed to predict parole adjustment.

Parole Prediction Procedure with Women Offenders

Pauze, B. K. *Parole prediction in Iowa.* Unpublished master's thesis, University of Iowa, 1972.

The *Parole Prediction Procedure* combined five variables to predict parole success with confined women. Nine "surviving" variables included time served, age at release, disciplinary reports, and age left home.

Parole Prediction Scale

Rogers, J. W., & Haymer, N. S. Perception, optimism and accuracy in decision-making. In R. L. Henshel & R. A. Silverman (Eds.), *Perception in criminology.* New York: Columbia University Press, 1975.

This 20-item list of prisoner case history and offense factors is designed to allow comparisons of judgments by different criminal justice personnel.

Parole Prediction through Variable Interactions

Duggan, T. J., & Dean, C. W. Statistical interaction and parole prediction. *Social Forces,* 1969, *48,* 45–49.

This model for the introduction of attribute variables, so that their interaction predicts parole success, utilized three items within each of these categories: situation variables, identification with criminal/other variables, and value orientation variables.

Parole Success Attributes

Grygier, T., Blum, F., & Porebski, O. R. Decision and outcome: Studies in parole prediction. *Canadian Journal of Criminology and Corrections,* 1971, *13,* 133–146.

This instrument is a set of 31 attributes related to parole outcome. The attributes are divided into four categories according to parole board usage and success rates.

Postprison Success Prediction

Sampson, A. Post-prison success prediction: A preliminary Florida study. *Criminology,* 1974, *12,* 155–173.

This list of 33 variables was used to predict success for released prisoners. This procedure is a Florida prison population adaptation of the *Base Expectancy Scale,* using many ordinary rather than dichotomous variables.

Recidivism Base Expectancy Scale

Metzner, R., & Weil, G. Predicting recidivism: Base rates for Massachusetts Correctional Institution, Concord. *Journal of Criminal Law, Criminology, and Police Science,* 1963, *54,* 307–316.

Seven dichotomous base expectancy variables were coded to assess parole risk and success.

Recidivism Prediction Scale

Laulicht, J. Problems of statistical research: Recidivism and its correlates. *Journal of Criminal Law, Criminology, and Police Science,* 1963, *54,* 163–174.

This instrument provides a system of variables and scoring procedures that concern the likelihood that a prisoner would make a successful parolee. Seventeen variables from a master list of 84 variables successfully predicted recidivism in training school boys. These 17 items were all available from case files, and may be said to constitute a recidivism scale.

CORRECTIONS DESCRIPTION: REVIEWS

Index of Conformity to Staff Expectations

Development and Characteristics

The *Index of Conformity to Staff Expectations* (ICSE) was developed to identify the extent to which prisoners agree with staff role expectations (Wheeler, 1961). It seeks to measure "the acceptance or rejection of norms and role definitions applied to inmates by the prison staff." This questionnaire consists of five hypothetical situations, which evoked from 75 to 93% response agreement among 99 staff members and which produced considerable variability in responses of 214 inmates. The ICSE standardization samples were employed or confined at a close custody western penitentiary for young adults.

Each ICSE item describes an inmate in a situation that clearly taps approval of value systems from either staff or inmates. A sixth item, not included in ICSE scoring, indicated that noninstitutional law-abidingness yielded similar patterns to the Index's prison-centered items.

Response Mode

The first four items are answered on a four choice "approve" or "disapprove" dimension. Item 5 is answered by choosing between two alternatives of inmates actions.

Scoring

Items 1 and 3 are scored for "approve," Items 2 and 4 for "disapprove," and Item 5 for "should clear himself," to produce the numerical value of conformity to staff expectations. Subjects whose responses agree with staff in 4 or 5 situations are considered "high conformists;" subjects agreeing in 2 or 3 situations are "medium conformists;" and subjects agreeing in 0 or 1 situation are "low conformists." When compared to other variables, ICSE data are usually expressed in percentages of subjects in each conformity group.

Norms

The 214 prisoners studied by Wheeler consisted of 35% high conformists, 51% medium conformists, and 14% low conformists. Normative data that is available on segments of this sample have been studied by length of time served, quality and breadth of inmate contacts, and other variables.

Reliability

Although the developer collected no direct reliability data, the objective scoring procedure and the fact that conformity incidence stays fairly constant over time suggests that there may be very high interrater reliability.

Validity

The development procedures lack a cross-validation on another sample, but they do indeed indicate that the ICSE is an accurate measure of the largely custodial staff expectations at one institution, for five conflict areas. The small number of items raises the issue of how well they represent or sample the full range of inmate interactions with staff and other inmates.

The validation data are based on ICSE scores in contrasting groups. High conformists occur most frequently in a "protection" living unit for informers (83%), followed by residents of a reception unit (47%), an honor farm (44%), a medium custody living unit (34%), a close custody unit (21%), and a segregation unit (14%). High conformists to staff expectations were also found to be significantly ($p < .025$) associated with the following variables: length of times served for first offenders; high primary (inmate) group contacts; high group intensity; and institutional career phase first offenders.

The absolute value of the median gamma coefficient was .31 for the same data. Thus the scope of validity information is limited, but the results are positive and of moderate elevation.

Comments

This brief index has been developed to give a measure of consensual staff expectations of inmates in five hypothetical conflict situations. It has limited norms and little reliability information, but has moderate validity with respect to time and phase of confinement and relationship to fellow inmates.

REFERENCES

Wheeler, S. A study of prisonization. *American Sociological Review,* 1961, *26,* 699–712.

INDEX OF CONFORMITY TO STAFF EXPECTATIONS

Items one through four are answered on a four category approve-disapprove continuum. On item five, the subjects are asked "What should Smith do?" and they select either:

> He should clear himself by telling about the escape plans of Brown and Henry.
>
> He should keep quiet and take the punishment himself.

1. An inmate, Owens, is assigned to a work crew. Some other inmates criticize him because he does more work than anybody else on the crew. He works as hard as he can.

2. Inmate Martin goes before a committee that makes job assignments. He is given a choice between two jobs. One job would call for hard work, but it would give Martin training that might be useful to him on the outside. The other job would allow Martin to do easier time in the institution. But it provides no training for a job on the outside. Martin decides to take the easier job.

3. An inmate, without thinking, commits a minor rule infraction. He is given a "write-up" by a correctional officer who saw the violation. Later three other inmates are talking to each other about it. Two of them criticize the officer. The third inmate, Sykes, defends the officer, saying the officer was only doing his duty.

4. Inmates Smith and Long are very good friends. Smith has a five-dollar bill that was smuggled into the institution by a visitor. Smith tells Long he thinks the officers are suspicious, and asks Long to hide the money for him for a few days. Long takes the money and carefully hides it.

5. Inmates Brown and Henry are planning an escape. They threaten inmate Smith with a beating unless he steals a crowbar for them from the tool shop where he works. He thinks they mean business. While he is trying to smuggle the crowbar into the cell house, he is caught by an officer, and Smith is charged with planning to escape. If he doesn't describe the whole situation, he may lose up to a year of good time. He can avoid it by blaming Brown and Henry.

Organizational Structure and Prisonization Scale

Development and Characteristics

The *Organizational Structure and Prisonization Scale* (OSPS) (Thomas & Zingraff, 1974) is a composite of four scales designed to detect the influence of the organization and structure of a prison on its inmates. The four measures are: (1) A powerlessness scale; (2) a more specific measure of organizational powerlessness; (3) a scale to measure postprison expectations; and (4) a measure of prisonization, or assimilation into the inmate subculture.

The powerlessness scale is a revision of a scale designed by Neal and Rettig (1967), while the other measures were developed specifically for a study of the effect of organizational structure (Thomas & Zingraff, 1974). The composite scale was administered to 267 boys who were institutionalized at a school for juvenile delinquents. The original form of the powerlessness scale (Neal & Rettig, 1967) was used, but after an item analysis was performed, only those items which showed an item-to-total correlation of .35 or greater were retained (7 items).

Response Mode

All items are presented in a standard 5-point Likert format in which the respondent reads a statement then notes whether he/she: "strongly agrees," "agrees," feels "neutral," "disagrees," or "strongly disagrees."

Scoring

Each scale receives a separate score that is the sum of all item responses within the scale. Response alternatives are arranged so that: (1) The higher the powerlessness score, the greater the feeling of powerlessness; (2) the higher the organizational powerlessness score, the less control is felt over the institution by the individual; (3) the higher the postprison expectations score, the less one feels he or she has to look forward to after release from prison; and (4) the higher the prisonization score, the more one has become assimilated into the inmate counterculture.

Norms

The means and standard deviations (see Table 24) were reported (Thomas & Zingraff, 1974) for a sample of 267 institutionalized boys.

No comparison groups were presented.

TABLE 24. OSPS Means and Standard Deviations among Confined Male Delinquents

Subscale	Mean	SD
General powerlessness	21.35	4.23
Organizational powerlessness	13.47	4.03
Postprison expectations	22.51	7.41
Prisonization	27.06	5.65

Reliability

Item-to-total subscale correlations were calculated and presented with the scale items. These ranged from .36 to .67. No measures of temporal stability were reported.

Validity

The major support for validity comes from the consistency of the data with predictions made from the theoretical concepts. For example, one would predict that internalized socialization prior to incarceration would hinder adoption of the inmate subculture. Significant inverse relationships between SES of origin and the prisonization scale, SES of attainment and the prisonization scale, and age and the prisonization scale support this hypothesis. All scales were correlated in expected directions. In addition, a review of the items in the scale indicate support for content validity. Yet, the low item-to-total correlations suggest some degree of heterogeneity within the scales and suggest that the concepts might be multidimensional or that the scales should be further refined.

Comments

This scale is still in an early stage of development. Reliability is moderately acceptable and modest support for validity is available. Moreover, the concepts, as suggested by the developers, may be extremely important in dealing with management of total institutions.

REFERENCES

Neal, A. G., & Rettig, S. On the multidimensionality of alienation. *American Sociological Review,* 1967, *32,* 54–64.

Thomas, C. W. Prisonization or resocialization? A study of external factors associated with the impact of imprisonment. *Journal of Research in Crime and Delinquency,* 1973, *10,* 13–21.

Thomas, C. W., & Poole, E. D. The consequences of incompatible goal structures in correctional settings. *International Journal of Criminology and Penology,* 1975, *3,* 27–42.

Thomas, C. W., & Zingraff, M. T. *Organizational structure as a determinate of prisonization: An analysis of the consequences of alienation.* Unpublished work, College of William and Mary, Williamsburg, Va., Feb. 1974.

Thomas, C. W., & Zingraff, M. T. Organizational structure as a determinant of prisonization. An analysis of the consequences of alienation. *Pacific Sociological Review,* 1976, *19,* 98–116.

ORGANIZATIONAL STRUCTURE AND PRISONIZATION SCALE

Instructions. Following are some statements with which you may agree or disagree. Beside each statement write the symbol which best represents your position on that statement.

Symbol	Feeling
SA	Strongly Agree
A	Agree
N	Neutral
D	Disagree
SD	Strongly Disagree

General Powerlessness

*1. People can do almost anything in this country if they work hard enough.

*2. The average citizen has a good deal of influence on the things that happen to him.

3. The world is run by a few people in power and there's not much people like me can do about it.

4. Whether you like it or not, chance plays an awfully large part in what happens to all of us.

5. You can't help feeling helpless when you see what's going on in the world today.

*6. An average citizen can have an influence in things like government decisions if he makes himself heard.

7. It is only wishful thinking to believe that a person like me can have an influence in the world today.

Organizational Powerlessness

*1. We're allowed to make a lot of decisions for ourselves here.

2. You can't help feeling like a caged animal in a place like this.

3. None of us have any influence on how we're treated here.
4. There's really not much I can do about what happens to me here.

Postprison Expectations

1. Nobody at home cares whether I live or die anymore.
2. So many bad things have happened to me that the future doesn't look good for me when I go home.
*3. I'm confident that things will be better for me when I leave here.
4. My family and friends have just about given up on me.
*5. The people I knew before I came here will still respect me when I go home.
*6. I don't think that having been here will hurt my chances for getting a good job after I get out.
*7. I think people will give me a fair chance when I leave as long as I stay out of trouble.
8. People on the outside believe that anyone who has been here is bound to get into trouble again.
9. Being sent here has ruined my whole life.
10. I'm afraid to face the people I knew on the street when I get out.
11. Most people on the outside don't give someone who has been here a fair chance.

Prisonization

1. The other boys are right when they say, "Don't do anything more than you have to."
2. It's better to tell the staff what they want to hear than to tell them the truth if you want to get out soon.
3. It's a good idea to keep to yourself here as much as you can.
*4. I probably spend more of my free time talking with people on the staff than most of the other boys do.
5. Anyone who talks about his personal problems with people on the staff is weak.
6. I try to stay out of trouble but nobody is going to push me around and get away with it.
*7. I have more in common with people on the staff than I do with most of the boys.
8. When a boy deals with staff, he should stick up for his own beliefs and not let the staff tell him what's good and what's not.

*Indicates reversed item scoring.

Public Offender Counseling Inventory

Development and Characteristics

The *Public Offender Counseling Inventory* (POCI) is a multidimensional scale designed to "assess the effectiveness of counseling or changing attitudes of participating inmates" (Page & Myrick, 1978). An original pool of 40 items was used to tap the "types of attitudes prison inmates might be expected to have toward themselves, the development of interpersonal relationships, authority, and counselors" (Page & Myrick, 1978, p. 142).

These items were presented in a standard 5-point, Likert-type format to 106 inmates of a Southeastern correctional institution. This sample included blacks (62%) and whites (38%), males (49%) and females (51%), and inmates imprisoned for a variety of offenses (murder, grand larceny, sales of drugs, etc.). The responses of these individuals to the items were then factor analyzed resulting in three factors that were clearly defined by the item pool. Using a criterion factor load of .40 as a cutting point representing whether an item contributes to a factor, a total of eight items defined the first factor, nine defined the second factor, and six defined the third factor. Based on item content analysis, the factors were labeled Confidence in Interpersonal Involvement (CIPI), Counseling Readiness (CR), and Self-Reliance (SR), respectively.

Response Mode

The respondents are requested to read each statement and note whether they (1) "strongly agree," (2) "agree," (3) are "undecided," (4) "disagree," or (5) "strongly disagree."

Scoring

Scores for each of the three subscales are obtained by adding the scores for each of the items which comprise each scale. The range of possible scores is 8–40 for the CIPI, 9–45 for the CR, and 6–30 for the SR. For each of these scales, a high score indicates increased personal involvement, increased readiness for counseling, and increased self assurance, respectively.

Norms

No norms are available.

Reliability

Page and Myrick (1978) performed a test–retest reliability check after a one week interval for 26 inmates (13 males and 13 females) of a Southeastern prison.

The Pearson product–moment correlation for the 40 item scale was .90. Correlations for the CIPI, R, and SR were .86, .84, and .82, respectively.

Validity

In addition to factorial validity, the POCI has been used to assess the impact of marathon group therapy on female drug users (Page, 1976). In this study, the responses of 24 randomly selected control subjects were matched to those of 24 individuals (from the same population) who had undergone marathon group therapy. The comparison revealed a statistically significant difference ($p < .05$) between the two groups on the CIPI scale, with the therapy group scoring higher. Although no significant differences occurred on the CR and SR subscales, the marathon sample scored consistently higher on both.

Comments

The POCI has adequate reliability and has received support for validity through factor analysis. The developers, however, suggest that the instrument is not sufficiently well established to merit wide applicability. Although factors have been defined, a more systematic review of the items within the subscales in the form of a content analysis should be undertaken. More representative names for the subscales components may result. For example, "Self-Reliance" may not represent items such as 3, 16, 37, and 40 as well as some other construct might.

REFERENCES

Page, R. C. Marathon group counseling with imprisoned female drug users (Doctoral dissertation, University of Florida, 1976). *Dissertation Abstracts International,* 1976, *37,* 1682A.

Page, R. C., & Myrick, R. The public offender counseling inventory: An instrument for assessing counseling outcomes in prisons. *Criminal Justice and Behavior,* 1978, *5,* 141–150.

PUBLIC OFFENDER COUNSELING INVENTORY

For each statement below, decide which of the responses best applies for you. Place the number of the response in the space at the left of each statement. Respond as honestly as possible.

1. Strongly Agree
2. Agree
3. Undecided

4. Disagree
5. Strongly Disagree

	_____	1.	I feel awkward when others discuss their problems with me.
	_____	2.	Others misunderstand me.
SR *	_____	3.	I care about others.
CR *	_____	4.	I can benefit from counseling.
CR *	_____	5.	I am able to confront others in ways they can accept.
	_____	6.	I can influence people like me.
CIPI	_____	7.	I don't think people like me.
CR *	_____	8.	I respect the staff of this institution.
CIPI	_____	9.	Others provoke me into saying things I don't mean to say.
CIPI	_____	10.	I have difficulty understanding other people's feelings.
CIPI	_____	11.	I have difficulty controlling my anger when others misinterpret my actions or feelings.
	_____	12.	People treat me fairly.
CIPI	_____	13.	I don't have much to offer in conversations with people.
CR *	_____	14.	I respect police officers.
CIPI	_____	15.	I shut out people when they criticize me.
SR	_____	16.	I am suspicious when others try to help me.
CR *	_____	17.	I plan to seek out counseling in the future.
	_____	18.	I can put into words what others feel.
	_____	19.	I avoid my problems until circumstances make me take action.
	_____	20.	Others are interested in what I say.
	_____	21.	The establishment is out to get me.
	_____	22.	Other people use me.
	_____	23.	I trust people who are close to me.
CR *	_____	24.	I listen carefully to others when they speak.
CR *	_____	25.	Counseling can help people help themselves.
	_____	26.	It is easy for me to make decisions.
	_____	27.	I actively seek others' opinions of me.
	_____	28.	This institution has had a positive influence on my life.
CIPI	_____	29.	I keep my feelings to myself.

		30.	I often feel as if fate were against me.
		31.	I am a lovable person.
CIPI		32.	I don't know what to do when I get mad.
SR *		33.	My goals in life are clear.
		34.	I avoid becoming personally involved with others.
SR *		35.	If I work hard, I can made a success of life.
		36.	I find it difficult to talk with staff.
SR		37.	I dislike myself.
CR *		38.	I feel at ease in groups.
CR *		39.	I feel counselors can be trusted with confidential information.
SR		40.	I have not met many people I like.

*Scoring is reversed for these items.

CORRECTIONS DESCRIPTION: LISTINGS

Alternatives to Incarceration Client Questionnaire

Mathews, M., Steinburn, T., & Bennett, C. *Assessment of alternatives to incarceration.* Seattle, Washington: Battelle Memorial Institute. (Final report, LEAA Grant NI 71-087-G, May, 1973.)

This 5-part questionnaire uses a varied response format to measure offenders' feelings about their experiences in a community corrections program.

Assessment of *I*-Level Knowledge

Tolhurst, G. E. Center for Training in Differential Treatment: Final Report of Phase One, Part Two. Major assessment instruments used in project. The Institute for the Study of Crime and Delinquency, and The National Institute of Mental Health (MH 10893) in cooperation with the California Youth Authority.

This 5-part test was designed to assess objectively pretraining *I*-Level knowledge for comparison with posttraining knowledge. Five definitions and 59 multiple choice items are used.

CJC Questionnaire

Griffiths, K. S., Seckel, J. P., & Raab, B. J. *Assessment of junior college programs for youthful offenders in a institution.* Sacramento: California Youth Authority, Research Report No. 65, June, 1973.

This 30-item, multiple choice instrument was designed to tap youthful offenders' reactions to their experiences at Columbia Junior College (CJC).

Correctional Officers' Interest Blank

Wenk, E. A. Assessment of the prison community: A collaborative research project. Davis, Calif. National Council on Crime and Delinquency research center, July, 1970, p. 36.

This 50-item questionnaire is a short, simple test designed to assess correctional personnel's opinions of their work and roles.

Critical Incident Test

Tolhurst, G. E. Center for Training in Differential Treatment: Final Report of Phase One, Part Two. Major assessment instruments used in project. The Institute for the Study of Crime and Delinquency, and The National Institute of Mental Health (MH 10893) in cooperation with the California Youth Authority.

This test was designed to assess a trainee's understanding of the characteristics of different *I*-Level subtypes and the trainee's integration of the implications of client characteristics for appropriate treatment approaches. Five actual incidents are presented, along with *I*-Level ratings of other involved youths; in addition, the trainee is asked what happened, why, and what the appropriate response should be.

Differential Treatment Pretraining Questionnaires—Trainees' Supervisor

Tolhurst, G. E. Center for Training Differential Treatment: Final Report of Phase One, Part Two. Major assessment instruments used in project. The institute for the Study of Crime and Delinquency, and The National Institute of Mental Health (MN 10893) in cooperation with the California Youth Authority.

This series of questionnaires was designed to evaluate the impact of the Center's training programs on trainees and their agencies, using predominantly seven-point rating scales, supervisors rate unit treatment philosophy and practices

(17 items), the program (37 items), the trainee (30 items), the probable receptivity to *I*-Level (40 items), and the trainee and Agency *I*-Level receptivity (5 open-ended questions).

Inmate Questionnaire

Kassebaum, G., Ward, D., & Wilner, D. *Prison treatment and parole survival: An empirical assessment.* New York: Wiley, 1971.

This 37-item,true-false questionnaire was designed to assess acceptance of the inmate code, isolation and alientation in the prison, opinions of group counseling, and personal values.

Inmates' Recreation Activities Checklist

Orton, D. J. *An investigation of the past, present, and future leisure-time activities of adult inmates in Iowa's correctional institutions.* Unpublished master's thesis, University of Iowa, 1975.

The *Inmates' Recreation Activities Checklist* is a 9-part checklist of 146 hobbies, games, sports, and outdoor, musical, and other recreational activities. This checklist was designed to assess the past, present, and desired future leisure time activities of adult male and female prisoners.

Inmate Social Role Adaptation Scale

Thomas, C. W., & Foster, S. C. The importation model perspective on inmates social roles, an empirical test. *Sociological Quarterly,* 1973, *14,* 226–234.
Thomas, C. W., & Foster, S. C. *On the measurement of social role adaptation in the prison community: A research note.* Williamsburg, Va.: Metropolitan Criminal Justice Center, College of William and Mary, February, 1974.

This 23-item, true-false instrument was designed to provide five operational measures of the following social role adaptations within the informal inmate organization: Square John, Ding, Politician, Right Guy, Outlaw.

Institutional Impact Questionnaires

Sandhu, H. S. The impact of short term institutionalization on prison inmates. *British Journal of Criminology,* 1964, *4,* 461–474.

Six scales were constructed to measure the impact of institutionalization on prisoners in Punjab, India. A value questionnaire (40 items) was designed to measure wrongfulness of listed behaviors. Two hostility schedules measured open hostility and muffled hostility (10 items each). A 15-item scale was designed to measure rationalization of the offense. Two final scales tested convicts self-concept in relation to prison impact and post-release attitudes.

Interview Rating Questionnaire

Tolhurst, G. E. Center for Training in Differential Treatment: Final Report of Phase One, Part Two. Major assessment instruments used in project. The Institute for the Study of Crime and Delinquency and The National Institute of Mental Health (MH 10893) in cooperation with the California Youth Authority.

This 12-item, 4-point questionnaire was designed to assess progress in a trainee's ability to make accurate diagnoses both as interviewer and as a second rater within a range of *I*-Level subtypes.

Long-Term Prisoners Interview Schedule

Gunn, J., Nicol, R., Gristwood, J., & Foggitt, R. Long-term prisoners. *British Journal of Criminology,* 1973, *13,* 331–340.

This 35-item interview schedule was designed in conjunction with official records to measure a number of social and criminological facts about a long-term prison population.

Parole Decision Instruments

Hoffman, P. B., & Goldstein, H. M. *Do experience tables matter? Parole decision-making: Supplemental Report Four.* Prepared for the National Institute of Law Enforcement and Criminal Justice, Law Enforcement Assistance Administration, U.S. Department of Justice: NCCD Research Center, Davis, California, June, 1973.

This 6-item rating scale was designed to assess relative contributions of prisoner case studies and base expectancy scores in parole decision making.

Parole Decision Making Scale

Hoffman, P. B., & DeGostin, L. K. Parole decision-making: Structuring discretion. *Federal Probation,* 1974, *38,* 7–15.

This scale was designed to provide a more rational and consistent method for parole selection decisions. Parole guidelines are drawn from a matrix of six categories of offense severity by four categories of parole prognosis.

Parole Officer Evaluation of Vocational Rehabilitation Services

VanBoskirk, C. Vocational rehabilitation services in a maximum security setting. New York State Education Department and New York Department of Correctional Services, December, 1974, pp. 44–48.

This 3-part, 15-item questionnaire assesses parole officers' knowledge and evaluative judgements of vocational rehabilitation services for parolees.

Prerelease Furlough Questionnaire

Holt, N. California's pre release furlough program for state prisoners: An evaluation. Research Division Department of Corrections, State of California, December, 1969.

This instrument consists of six open-ended questions designed to tap what inmates did on furloughs and their reactions to their first prerelease furloughs.

Pretraining Questionnaire—Trainee

Tolhurst, G. E. Center for Training in Differential Treatment: Final Report of Phase One, Part Two. Major assessment instruments used in project. The Institute for the Study of Crime and Delinquency, and The National Institute of Mental Health (MH 10893) in cooperation with the California Youth Authority.

This set of questionnaires was designed as a self-evaluation instrument for the trainee in a differential treatment center. It includes sections to measure: (1) background interests and self-assessment (29 items—mixed-response format); (2) comparisons of the trainee to the "typical" parole or institutional worker (21 items—7-point scale); (3) self-ratings of the trainee's ability as a treater (4 items—7-point scale); and (4) ratings of the trainee's personal abilities (23 items—7-point scale).

Prison Guard Job Perceptions Questionnaire

Sandhu, H. S., & Allen, D. E. The prison guard: Job perceptions and inservice training in India. *The Indian Journal of Social Work*, 1971, *32*, 115–120.

This 14-item questionnaire was designed to measure prison guards' judgments of themselves as custodial officers, in terms of suitability, acceptance, effects, and functions. All responses are made on a 3-point scale. Although developed for use with Indian prison guards, the items are simply written and would be readily understood by English-speaking officers in general.

Treatment–Custody Conflict Questionnaire

Scott, R. J. *Role conflict resolution and job realted attitudes and job performance of community based correctional workers.* Unpublished doctoral dissertation, Southern Illinois University, 1974.

This 5-item questionnaire consists of three open-ended and two 11-point questions designed to identify intensity and causes of treatment–custody conflicts in work–release settings.

Values and Sociometric Choices Questionnaire

Hautaluoma, J. E., & Scott, W. A. Values and sociometric choices of incarcerated juveniles. *Social Psychology,* 1973, *91,* 229–237.

This questionnaire was designed to measure value orientations and sociometric choices of confined young male prisoners. The questionnaire contains 77 value items and 17 sociometric questions that are combined into 10 value scales and 3 sociometric indices.

CHAPTER 9
Delinquency

The scales in this chapter are concerned with delinquency and delinquents. This topic includes the social process by which youths become delinquents, the extent and severity of their delinquent acts, and the societal reaction to those acts. Thus, one scale is included that evaluates the juvenile probation officer's punitive reaction to a youthful probationer's law violation.

Originally, we had planned to include a separate chapter devoted exclusively to scales used in school settings or with schools as the objects of study. Only three such scales were found, however, and thus they are included within this chapter. The category of *Milieu Rating* was applied to those scales that describe schools, as well as the family, and juvenile homes.

We offer additional advice on where to look for what. Since this chapter's scales are purported to measure delinquency, when some other concept, such as self-esteem in general (as opposed to self-esteem specific to delinquency) was assessed in delinquents, the scale listing was placed in the later chapter titled *General Scales*. In addition, there are many different kinds of scales assessing values. When the developer presented a scale concerned primarily with adjustment or personal dynamics, it has been listed under personality assessment. On the other hand, when the scale is more descriptive or general, it has been placed in the *Description* grouping.

Behavior Ratings as a category is prominent in delinquency research. Twenty rating scales, checklists, and self-report inventories are reviewed or listed. Similarly, *Personality Assessment* measures are in abundance, with nine such instruments reviewed in this chapter and an additional 14 listed.

DELINQUENCY ATTITUDE SCALES: REVIEWS
Attitudes toward Juvenile Delinquency

Development and Characteristics

The *Attitudes toward Juvenile Delinquency Scale* (ATJDS) was designed to "measure the attitudes of the general public toward juvenile delinquency"

(Reuterman, 1975, p. 1). Primarily, the ATJDS emphasizes whether individuals favor a punishment or a rehabilitative approach.

The original form of the test contained 23 "short paragraphs which describe, in as much detail as possible, situations which involve the commission of a delinquent act" (Reuterman, 1975, p. 2). These paragraphs present a situation and two possible endings. Respondents are asked to choose which of the endings most accurately reflects their feelings for the situation. One of the alternative statements represents a prorehabilitation approach while the other represents a propunishment view.

The test developer indicates three principle reasons for his use of a forced-choice format. First, he suggests that these issues may not be the type encountered often by the average individual, and thus the respondent may not hold a firmly crystallized opinion. If this is true, the form used for this attitude measurement allows the respondent to organize his or her feelings. Second, presenting situations in this form allows an individual to focus on the two alternative dispositions and thus decide more accurately which one is the more appropriate. Finally, requesting that the subject check one alternative reduces the bias of positive or negative wording; each choice is stated in the affirmative. In addition, the sequencing of the options is randomized so that one does not habituate in choosing the same alternative on each item.

The 23 items were tested on a sample of 50 college students enrolled in the University of Colorado at Denver. Interitem and item-to-total correlations were calculated. The results indicated that two items were negatively correlated with a number of the other items. Therefore, they were discarded. One other item was discarded because of its low discriminatory power. This left a final version containing 20 items.

Response Mode

As noted in the previous section, respondents are to read each of the situations and then choose which alternative most accurately represents their probable actions, feelings, or thoughts. A blank space is provided at the end of each of the two statements where a check mark may be made.

Scoring

A value of 1 is assigned to the prorehabilitation responses and 0 to the propunishment response. The total score is a sum of the numerical values for the items. Therefore, the higher an individual's score, the more prorehabilitative the attitude.

Norms

The norms for this test were established on 34 students in an introductory sociology course at the Denver Extension Center of the University of Colorado and 16 full-time students from a psychology class at the Boulder campus. The Denver Extension is a community-based college and is believed to attract a wider range of students than the main campus. The sample included ages 18 to 66 years, racial and ethnic minority groups such as Negro, Italian, Jewish, and a broad cross-section of social classes. The means and standard deviations for the two groups were as follows: Extension Center, $\overline{X} = 15.32$, $sd = 5.56$; Boulder Campus, $\overline{X} = 15.12$, $sd = 5.71$.

Reliability

A test–retest correlation coefficient of .95 was obtained using the product–moment correlation formula on a sample of 44 students. The second test was administered one week after the first. Because product–moment correlation coefficients have been criticized as an inappropriate measure of test stability, an intraclass correlation coefficient also was computed. The resultant correlation of .95 offered further evidence of reliability.

Since there is a strong possibility that individuals might remember their answers from the first testing, a Cronbach's Alpha was calculated. This is a generalized version of the Kuder-Richardson formula 20 for split-half reliability. It was found to be .89.

A Homogeneity Ratio of .29 indicated "a relatively high homogeneity or average intercorrelation among all pairs of the items in the test" (Reuterman, 1975, p. 7).

Validity

The first attempt to validate the scale was through theoretical comparison using three other scales. These were: (1) a scale measuring attitudes toward capital punishment (Bologh & Mueller, 1960); (2) one test measuring the value placed on the trait of studiousness; and (3) a 24-item form of the Buss (1961) *Aggression Scale*. It was believed that there should be a strong relationship between attitudes toward capital punishment and juvenile delinquency, on the assumption that the two tests were measuring the same attribute. It was also expected that individuals who held an aggressive outlook toward life would favor punishment over a rehabilitive approach. Finally, it was believed that a studious person would be likely to favor a treatment approach.

The results of the comparisons showed: (1) A moderate correlation between attitudes toward capital punishment and preference for rehabilitation of juvenile delinquents, .50 ($p < .005$); (2) a moderate weak relationship between the aggression scale and attitudes toward juvenile delinquency, .31 ($p < .025$); and (3) a weak, unreliable relationship ($p > .05$) between attitudes toward delinquency and studiousness.

The second attempt to establish the validity of the juvenile delinquency scale was through the use of a criterion group. The scale was administered to 98 sociology students in a course on juvenile delinquency. During the semester these students had been exposed to the protreatment approach to the handling of juvenile delinquency. For this reason, it was believed that they would score higher on the scale than would beginning students. This prediction was accurate. The means between the two groups were found to be significantly different beyond the .001 level. The means were 17.16 for the juvenile delinquency students and 13.73 for the others.

The third validation procedure used an experimental approach that attempted to produce attitude change and measure this change with the scale. Students were divided into three groups. One group was exposed to both a rational-factual lecture and a lecture that attempted to influence them through an appeal to authority or through citing a prestigious individual. Both of these emphasized the rehabilitative approach. The second group was exposed to similar types of lectures that, however, favored a punishment approach. The third group received no lectures. Then the scale was administered.

Inspection of the data showed that the mean of the punishment group was lower than that of the treatment group ($p < .005$). There was no statistically significant difference between the treatment group and the control group.

Since this attempt at validation was inconclusive, another experimental approach was attempted. A class of introductory psychology students was used as its own control. The students were given the test without prior discussion. After two weeks, the students were given the protreatment talk followed by a second administration of the test. Means of 13.81 and 17.12 respectively indicate that, according to the scale, there was a change in attitude ($p < .005$).

Comments

This scale has the advantage of presenting individuals the opportunity to encounter situations and develop attitudes for circumstances that they may never have experienced previously. Because of this, it may serve to tap "real" attitudes or it may serve to contaminate to the degree that it influences the molding of attitudes.

Reliability is well established and attempts at validation seem to offer some support that the scale measures attitudes toward delinquency with respect to a rehabilitation–punishment continuum. A major concern is with the sample on which the scale was tested. Although students, part-time and regular, may be a representative sample for this type of testing, there is a need for cross-validation. Other problems that should be attended to include the fact that it takes a long time to complete the scales, the syntax is occasionally cumbersome, and some items (e.g. Item 9) seem to strain the rehabilitation–punishment choice.

REFERENCES

Bologh, J. K., & Mueller, M. A. A scaling technique for measuring social attitudes towards capital punishment. *Sociological Social Research,* 1960, 45, 24–26.

Buss, A. H. *The psychology of aggression.* New York: Wiley, 1961.

Reuterman, N. A. *A measure of attitudes toward juvenile delinquency.* Unpublished manuscript, Delinquency Study Center, Southern Illinois University, Edwardsville, Illinois, 1975.

ATTTUDES TOWARD JUVENILE DELINQUENCY

Instructions: We are interested in how people make decisions when they have incomplete information on which to base their decisions. The following pages contain a number of descriptions of situations. For each situation, we would like you to indicate how you believe you would act, feel, or think. Two choices are supplied for each situation. Please check the one which comes closest to describing how you believe you would feel or act in the situation. If neither of the choices describe how you believe you would feel or act, check the one that comes closest. Please check only one answer for each situation. Be sure to answer every item.

1. One night a group of teenage vandals badly damage your neighbor's car. Later when you are talking to your neighbor about the incident, he tells you that the boys have been apprehended and that all of them have long police records for vandalism. Your neighbor says that this reminds him of an article he read describing research efforts to determine what causes delinquency. He says that this incident suggests to him that trying to find the causes of delinquency may take a long time and that one sure way to stop it is to lock up the offenders for a good long time.

    Would you: (1) agree with your neighbor that a sure way to stop vandalism etc. is to lock up the offenders ___, or (2) disagree with him and maintain that efforts to find the cause of delinquency should be continued or increased ___.

2. There is a series of serious beatings and robberies in your home town over the course of the last few months. Several of your good friends have been victims and one is confined to the hospital because of the injuries he received. Recently the police captured a group of teenagers who have been committing these crimes. It turns out that the gang was doing these things just for the fun of it. A good friend of yours expresses the opinion that what is needed is a much more harsh mode of punishment to make young hoods like these think a little before they act. An editorial in a local newspaper says that these incidents seem to point to the need for more and improved recreational, guidance and counseling facilities for teenagers.

    Would you: (1) agree with your good friend that more strict punishment is needed ___, or (2) agree with the newspaper that recreation and guidance facilities are needed ___.

3. A 17-year-old boy is arrested for attempting to sell addicting drugs in the local high school. Your younger brother was one of the students to which he tried to sell the

drugs. Several days later you are talking to some of your neighbors about the incident. One of them says that anyone who would do something like this should be locked up and the key thrown away. Another one says that what the boy needs is a re-education in the values of society.

Which of your neighbors would you support in this discussion: (1) the one who favors re-education ____, or (2) the one who favors locking the boy up ____.

4. While coming home late one night you are driving through a section of town that has a reputation for being a rough neighborhood. Suddenly another car pulls out from a side street. You stop to avoid an accident. A group of teenagers get out of the other car and drag you out of your car, saying that they are going to teach you a lesson for driving recklessly. You are saved from any sort of injury by the appearance of several police officers. With the policemen is another individual who identifies himself as a social worker from a nearby agency. The policemen urges you to press charges against the boys because this is not their first offense and they need to be taught a lesson. The social worker urges you not to press charges but to let him continue to work with the boys.

Whose advice would you follow: (1) that of the social worker ____, or (2) that of the police____.

5. A 16-year-old boy is caught beating a younger child. After some questioning by school authorities he admits to beating several other young children, including your younger brother. The school authorities are faced with either turning the boy over to the police or sending him to the guidance counselor in the school.

Which decision would you prefer: (1) notify the police ____, or (2) send him to the guidance counselor ____.

6. The police are chasing what they believe to be a stolen car. During the course of the chase the stolen car hits and permanently injures a pedestrian who happens to be a close friend of yours. Upon apprehending the car the police find that the driver is a 17-year-old boy who has a long string of arrests for various offenses. Because of the serious injury to your friend and the boy's bad record there is some disagreement as to whether he should be tried in the adult criminal court or in the juvenile court.

Which course of action would you favor: (1) try him in the adult court ____, or (2) try him in the juvenile court ____.

7. A ring of teenage shoplifters is apprehended by the police. Upon questioning it is found that this gang has taken several hundred dollars worth of articles in the last several months. Since most of those arrested are already on probation for other offenses, the judge must sentence them to an institution if the merchants involved press formal charges. If no formal charges are pressed, he can refer them to a newly established guidance clinic.

If your father were one of the merchants involved, would you: (1) encourage him not to press charges ____, or (2) encourage him to press charges ____.

8. One night several hubcaps disappear from your car. Several days later a group of teenagers are apprehended by the police, and it is found that they are guilty of stealing your hubcaps as well as numerous other ones. When they are brought up for trial, the judge is faced with deciding whether to commit them to a juvenile institution for three months or to release them on probation and assign a social worker to try to help them.

Which decision would you be most pleased with: (1) commit them to the institution ____, or (2) put them on probation and assign a social worker to them ____.

9. Late one night two of your friends are returning home. Suddenly they are stopped and threatened by a group of teenage boys. A fight starts and one of your friends is beaten and the other is stabbed. The next day your friend who was stabbed dies

from his injuries. Several days later the gang of boys are caught and one of them confesses to the stabbing. One day while visiting your other friend he tells you that the police have told him that the boy who did the stabbing has a long record of arrests for various crimes, but he has always been released on probation because of his willingness to attend a guidance clinic on a regular basis. Your friend tells you that this time the police are determined to get the boy locked up and that he is going to do everything he can to help them. He says that it is obvious to him that any sort of help the boy may have been getting at the clinic has not done him any good, since he is capable of killing.

Would you: (1) agree with your friend that the clinic is not any help and that he should do everything he can to get the boy locked up ____, or (2) disagree with your friend, saying that the boy probably needs more help than the clinic can give ____.

10. After reading an account of the work a local social work agency does with teenagers who are apprehended for various minor offenses, an older friend of yours comments that when he was a teenager and got into any kind of trouble, a trip "in back of the wood shed" with his father quickly cured him of any future inclinations toward that particular kind of trouble. Your friend says that instead of treating troublemakers like somebody special, they should be handled the same as he was and if their fathers cannot do this, then the police or somebody else should.

If your friend asked you for your opinion you should: (1) disagree with him and say that teenage troublemakers need help rather than punishment ____, or (2) agree with him that teenage troublemakers are treated too well these days ____.

11. Two 17-year-old boys rob a small grocery store located a short distance from your home. In making their escape their car hits a 4-year-old girl who later dies from her injuries. The girl is the daughter of one of your neighbors. A few hours later the two boys are apprehended. Shortly before the day set for the boys' hearing a petition is circulated in your neighborhood. The purpose of the petition is to get the boys tried in an adult criminal court rather than in a juvenile court.

On the basis of the above information would you sign the petition: yes ____, no ____.

12. A good friend of yours works in a local business establishment. One evening a group of teenagers enter the establishment and attempt to walk out with several articles of merchandise. Your friend sees them, tries to stop them and a fight starts. In the course of the fight one of the boys stabs your friend and he is very seriously injured. The next day an editorial in the newspaper says that anyone capable of committing a crime like this should be prepared to take the consequences. The newspaper favors treating the boy just as an adult who committed the same crime would be treated. It is against sending him to any kind of juvenile institution, saying that he is obviously a common criminal and should be treated as such.

Do you: (1) agree that the boy should be treated like any adult criminal ____, or (2) think he should be given special consideration because of his age ____.

13. During the night a group of teenage vandals break several windows in your car and spill paint on it. Since this is not their first offense they can be sentenced to a juvenile institution for half a year and then released or they can be put in an instituion for three months and then released to the custody of a social worker for another six months.

Which sentence would you rather see them get: (1) commit them to the instituion for three months and then release them in the custody of a social worker for six months ____, or (2) commit them to the institution for a half a year ____.

14.* A 17-year-old boy is sent to a juvenile correction institution for a series of robberies. This is the first time he has ever been put in an institution although he has been put on probation for other offenses. He proves to be very difficult to handle in the institution; on two occasions he rather badly injures other boys in fights. Also he seems very concerned with escaping from the institution, having made five attempts in three months. Shortly after his last escape attempt the institution staff has a meeting to decide what should be done with this boy. It turns out that some members of the staff favor sending him to a maximum security prison while others favor sending him to a psychiatric clinic for a complete examination.

If you were a member of the staff which course of action would you favor: (1) send him to a maximum security prison ____, or (2) send him to the psychiatric clinic ____.

15. One night several homes in your neighborhood are badly damaged by teenage vandals. A large picture window and several smaller windows are broken in your own home (or that of your parents). While talking to your neighbors later in the day, one of them says that he thinks that kids who would do something like this should be locked up for a long time until they learn to respect the property of others. Another neighbor disagrees with this and says that they need help and understanding.

Which view would you support in the argument: (1) they need help and understanding ____, or (2) they should be locked up until they respect the property of others ____.

16. Shortly after stealing your car a 16-year-old boy has a wreck, doing considerable damage to the car. The police notify you and tell you that you can either press formal charges against the boy in which case he will be held in the city jail for several days until arrangements can be made for a hearing, or you can agree not to press formal charges in which case the boy will be sent to the juvenile detention home and the juvenile division of the police force will handle the case and the boy will simply be released to the custody of a social worker.

Which course of action would you be most likely to follow: (1) press formal charges against the boy ____, or (2) do not press formal charges against the boy ____.

17. A group of teenage boys badly beat a good friend of yours and threaten you. The police intervene and this probably saves you from a beating also. Since this particular gang of boys are known as troublemakers, there is some discussion among the police officers about whether they should be confined in the city jail or sent to the juvenile detention home.

You would let the police know that you would prefer that the boys: (1) be taken to the detention home ____, or (2) be taken to the city jail ____.

18. A 17-year-old boy is picked up by the police after he is seen seriously mistreating a dog. Upon questioning the police find that this same boy is responsible for cruelly killing or harming quite a few other pets over the past several months. Since one of the dogs harmed belonged to you the police contact you and give you the choice of either pressing charges against the boy — in which case he will go to court — or of agreeing to sending him to a local guidance center.

Which course of action would you follow: (1) press charges ____, or (2) agree to let him go to the guidance center ____.

19. A candidate for mayor of your city favors, as part of his platform, the idea that many teenagers get in trouble with the police because law enforcement is not strict enough and this causes the teenagers to have little respect for the laws. He says that much teenage crime results from the fact that punishment of juveniles is not harsh enough and that teenagers know this and thus are not worried if they get into trouble. It is his intention, if he is elected, to make punishment for teenage crime more in line with punishment for similar crimes committed by adults.

On the basis of this information would you vote for this candidate: no ___, yes ___.

20.* Your younger brother is hit and badly injured by a car. Shortly thereafter the police stop the car for running a red light. They find that it is occupied by five teenage boys who have been drinking heavily. Later you are talking about the incident with several of your friends. The question of what will happen to the boys arises. One of your friends says that what should happen is that the boys should be locked up and really taught a lesson. However, he says that what will happen is that probably blame will be put on the boys' parents or their living conditions or something like that and they will be released. Another friend says that maybe it is not the boys' fault and that they do not know any better.

Which of these views would you support: (1) the boys are responsible for what happened and should be taught a lesson ___, or (2) it was not the boys' fault and they do not really know any better ___.

21.+ One night a group of teenage boys do considerable damage to a new hospital that is under construction in your neighborhood. This hospital is very badly needed and will enable much more adequate medical care for the people living near it. The damage done by the teenage vandals delays construction for several months. When the boys are apprehended it is found that several of them are minors and their names are withheld from the public. An editorial in the local newspaper condemns the practice of withholding the names of what it calls "young criminals," saying the public has a right to know who commits acts against public welfare.

Would you agree with the editorial that the names of the boys should be made public: no ___, yes ___.

22. Two teenage boys attempt to rob a store in your neighborhood. The owner, who is a good friend of yours, attempts to stop the boys; one of them shoots him, and he later dies from the wound. The boys are caught and sentenced to a juvenile correctional institution. The local newspaper expresses the opinion that this is an adult crime and thus the boys should be treated as adults and sentenced to an adult prison. Several of your neighbors agree with this view, while others say the boys need to be educated to appreciate the rules of society rather than punished as adults.

Which position would you favor: (1) the boys need re-education and help ___, or (2) the boys should be treated as adult criminals because their crime was certainly of an adult nature ___.

23. Recently there has been a wave of teenage crime in your home town. This had included vandalism, robberies, beatings, and car theft. Several letters from local citizens are published in the newspaper. One of these says that what is needed is a return to old-fashioned ways of punishment because teenage crime was much less years ago than it is now. Another letter says that what is needed is expanded guidance facilities and increased understanding of teenagers who get into trouble.

Which of these views would you favor: (1) return to old-fashioned methods of punishment because teenage crime was less years ago ___, or (2) increased guidance facilities and understanding of teenagers ___.

---

*   This item was dropped from the final form of the scale because of its low discriminatory power and because of a relatively low item-by-total correlation.

\+   These items were dropped from the final form of the scale because of a relatively high number of negative correlations with other items and because of a relatively low item-by-total correlation.

DELINQUENCY ATTITUDE SCALES: LISTINGS

Juvenile Delinquency Attitude Scale

Alberts, W. E. Personality and attitudes toward juvenile delinquency: A study of Protestant ministers. *Journal of Social Psychology,* 1963, *60,* 71–83.

Shaw, M. E. & Wright, J. M *Scales for the measurement of attitudes.* New York: McGraw-Hill, 1967.

This 23-item scale was designed to assess ministers' attitudes towards juvenile delinquency. Using a 6-point response mode, this scale measures moralistic versus understanding orientations toward delinquents.

DELINQUENCY BEHAVIOR RATINGS: REVIEWS

Delinquency Checklist

Development and Characteristics

The *Delinquency Checklist* (DCL) was designed to measure the extent of antisocial or delinquent behaviors in boys of high school age (Kulik, Stein, & Sarbin, 1968). The original item pool consisted of 52 descriptions of delinquent behaviors which ranged in severity from "mild misbehaviors" such as parental disobedience to "severely antisocial acts" such as armed robbery, or use or sale of drugs.

The original items were submitted to three different factor analyses, each of which was performed on a separate sample. The first sample consisted of a group of 200 high school age boys. One hundred of these boys were enrolled in public high school, the other 100 boys were institutionalized as delinquents. The second sample for factor analysis consisted of 100 other incarcerated delinquents. Finally, the responses of 105 nondelinquent high school boys were factor analyzed. The results from all three factor analyses indicated that four oblique factors were inherent in the 52-item DCL. These factors were carefully examined and labelled: (1) delinquent role, (2) drug usage, (3) parental defiance, and (4) assaultiveness. The factors included 10, 4, 5, and 5 items respectively.

Response Mode

The respondent is requested to read each question and note whether he has "never" engaged in the activity, or committed it "once or twice," "several times," "often," or "very often."

Scoring

Each item received a score ranging from 0 to 4 indicating the degree of frequency with which an individual has engaged in the act. Scores for each of the scales are obtained by adding individual item scores for items included in each scale. Further, a total delinquency score may be obtained by adding item scores for all of the 24 items. For each scale, a high score indicates participation in those types of activities.

Norms

Table 25 presents the means and standard deviations on each of the four scales of the DCL for a group of 100 high school students between the ages of 14 and 18, and a group of 100 delinquent boys (ages 14 to 18) institutionalized as delinquents.

Scores for drug usage and assaultiveness are low for both groups (nondelinquents and delinquents). Delinquents, however, score significantly higher. The Parental Defiance factor shows the least amount of difference between delinquents and nondelinquents. The difference does, however, reach the .001 level of significance.

Reliability

Kulik *et al.* (1968) report coefficient alphas of .95 for delinquent role, .92 for drug usage, .78 for parental defiance, and .88 for assaultiveness. The estimated coefficient alpha for the total DCL score is .96. These estimates are based on a

TABLE 25. Means, Standard Deviations, and *t* Values of Raw Cluster Scores Comparing 100 Nondelinquents and 100 Delinquents

Cluster	Nondelinquent		Delinquent		
	M	SD	M	SD	t
Delinquent role	5.54	5.36	20.00	9.73	13.01[a]
Drug usage	0.04	0.20	3.20	4.79	6.59[a]
Parental defiance	4.82	3.19	6.59	3.92	3.50[a]
Assaultiveness	0.23	0.60	3.18	3.79	7.69[a]

[a] $p < .001$.

sample of 200 male adolescents, 100 of whom were selected from public high schools and another 100 who were institutionalized as delinquents.

Validity

As indicated in the norms sections, each of the four DCL scales appropriately discriminates between delinquent and nondelinquent boys.

Further refinement of the DCL's ability to discriminate was accomplished through cluster analysis in which the profiles of delinquent boys were grouped into common types. Kulik *et al.* (1968) found seven basic protocol types in their group of 391 delinquents. Further, when they compared protocol types along the variables, race, socio-economic status, slang word usage, IQ, and anxiety measures, they received further support for the seven delinquent protocol structures.

Comments

The DCL and the four delinquency scales that constitute the set have acceptable reliability and appear to be valid measures of delinquency. Further, there is evidence that these scales may be used to differentiate several different types of delinquent boys. The scale construction techniques, the research efforts, and the reliability and validity investigations have been well designed and executed.

REFERENCES

Kulik, J. A., Stein, K. B., & Sarbin, T. R. Dimensions and patterns of adolescent, antisocial behavior. *Journal of Consulting and Clinical Psychology,* 1968, *32,* 375–382.

DELINQUENCY CHECKLIST

Instructions: Read each of the following questions and indicate how often you have been involved in a similar circumstance by writing, "never," "once or twice," "several times," "often," or "very often" beside each question.

Delinquent Role

1. Obtained liquor by having older friends buy it for you?
2. Skipped school without a legitimate excuse?
3. Drunk so much that you could not remember afterward some of the things you had done?
4. Used alcohol excessively?

5. Gone for a ride in a car someone had stolen?
6. Taken part in a "gang fight?"
7. Carried a switchblade or other weapon?
8. Bought or drank beer, wine, or liquor? (Including drinking at home.)
9. Had sexual intercourse with a person of the opposite sex?
10. Come to school late in the morning?

Drug Usage

1. Used narcotic drugs, other than marijuana?
2. Smoked marijuana?
3. Sold marijuana to someone?
4. Sniffed "glue" or taken "bennies" for kicks?

Parental Defiance

1. Defied your parents' authority (to their face)?
2. Shouted at your mother or father?
3. Cursed at your mother or father?
4. Gone against your parents' wishes?
5. Struck your mother or father?

Assaultiveness

1. Taken part in a robbery involving the use of physical force?
2. Taken part in a robbery involving the use of a weapon?
3. Taken part in any robbery?
4. Resisted arrest, or fought with an officer trying to arrest you?
5. Hit a teacher?

Delinquency Questionnaire

Development and Characteristics

The *Past and Future Delinquency Questionnaires* (PFDQ) were designed to serve as "unofficial measures of delinquency of adolescents over time" (Erickson, 1972). Both scales were constructed using the Guttman scalogram procedure. An original pool of items of an undisclosed number was presented to a group of 282 boys who were sophomores and juniors in a public high school. This group comprised approximately 90% of the entire sophomore and junior classes. The remaining 34 boys from these classes were dropped from the research because of nonresponse to one or more parts of the questionnaire. The entire set of items was presented to the respondents in two different ways. Items relating to the past delinquent behavior of an individual began with the wording "I have . . ." Items referring to future delinquent behavior began with the words "I might . . ." The *Past Delinquency Questionnaire* results indicated that 8 items were scalable. Analysis of the *Future Delinquency Questionnaire* revealed 12 scalable items.

Response Mode

Both scales are comprised of standard Guttman items, which require that the respondent read each statement and note whether the statement is true for him or her.

TABLE 26. Delinquent and Nondelinquent Scale Types Based on Reported Past Violations of the Law

Scale type[a]	Offense[b]							
	1	2	3	4	5	6	7	8
0	0[c]	0	0	0	0	0	0	0
1	x	0	0	0	0	0	0	0
2	x	x	0	0	0	0	0	0
3	x	x	x	0	0	0	0	0
4	x	x	x	x	0	0	0	0
5	x	x	x	x	x	0	0	0
6	x	x	x	x	x	x	0	0
7	x	x	x	x	x	x	x	0
8	x	x	x	x	x	x	x	x

[a] The coefficient of reproducibility of the original scale was .9025.
[b] Offenses are as follows:
  1. Using tobacco regularly.
  2. Drinking beer, wine or other liquor.
  3. Skipping school without excuse.
  4. Taking things worth $2 to $50.
  5. Buying tobacco.
  6. Purposely damaging or destroying public property.
  7. Buying beer, wine or other liquor.
  8. Defying teachers' authority to their faces.
[c] In all cases, "0" means that boys assigned that scale type indicated that they thought they wouldn't commit that offense. The "x" indicates that the boys in that scale type indicated that they thought they would or might commit that offense in the future.

TABLE 27. Delinquent and Nondelinquent Scale Types Based on Estimates of Future Law Violations[a]

Scale type	Offense[b]											
	1	2	3	4	5	6	7	8	9	10	11	12
0	0[c]	0	0	0	0	0	0	0	0	0	0	0
1	x	0	0	0	0	0	0	0	0	0	0	0
2	x	x	0	0	0	0	0	0	0	0	0	0
3	x	x	x	0	0	0	0	0	0	0	0	0
4	x	x	x	x	0	0	0	0	0	0	0	0
5	x	x	x	x	x	0	0	0	0	0	0	0
6	x	x	x	x	x	x	0	0	0	0	0	0
7	x	x	x	x	x	x	x	0	0	0	0	0
8	x	x	x	x	x	x	x	x	0	0	0	0
9	x	x	x	x	x	x	x	x	x	0	0	0
10	x	x	x	x	x	x	x	x	x	x	0	0
11	x	x	x	x	x	x	x	x	x	x	x	0

[a] The coefficient of reproducibility of the original scale was .93.
[b] Offenses are as follows:
  1. Skipping school without legitimate excuse.
  2. Taking things worth more than $50 other than a car.
  3. Breaking into a place illegally (i.e, store, home, etc.).
  4. Purposely damaging or destroying private property.
  5. Purposely damaging public property.
  6. Taking things worth $2 to $50.
  7. Buying beer, wine or other liquor.
  8. Buying tobacco.
  9. Using tobacco.
  10. Drinking beer, wine or other liquor.
  11. Gambling (playing poker, betting race horses, etc.).
  12. Getting in a fight with someone.
[c] In all cases, "0" means that boys assigned that scale type indicated that they thought they would not commit that offense. The "x" indicates that the boys in that scale type indicated that they thought they would or might commit that offense in the future.

Scoring

Since both the PFDQ were found to be "scalable," a score for each is determined by matching the responses of an individual to one of the "pure" scale types provided by the items. Tables 26 and 27 present the scale types for the PFDQ. For example, an individual who stated that he or she (1) used tobacco regularly and (2) drank beer, wine, or other liquor, would receive xs for Items 1 and 2. This matches Scale Type 2 so a score of 2 would be given to this set of responses.

As can be seen from the tables, most respondents are classified according to the number of delinquent acts in which they have engaged in the past or believed they might engage in in the future.

Norms

No normative information is available.

Reliability

Erickson (1972) reports coefficients of reproducibility of .90 and .93 for the *Past Delinquency Questionnaire* and the *Future Delinquency Questionnaire*, respectively.

Validity

Erickson (1972) calculated gamma coefficients between official court records and the PFDQ. These coefficients may be interpreted as the "proportion reduction of error in predictions or the amount of predictive knowledge which is added to the understanding of the variability in a variable by the introduction of the second variable" (p. 393). The results indicate that when the number of contacts with each of the 282 boys was correlated with PFDQ, coefficients of .72 and .62, respectively, were obtained.

After approximately two years, 259 boys from the original sample lived within the same jurisdiction and their official court contacts were examined. Gamma coefficients representing their relationship between PFDQ and official court appearances during the preceding two years were .66 and .70, respectively.

Comments

Both of these delinquency questionnaires have been well constructed and appear to have good reliability and validity. The high relationships between questionnaire scores and official court records make the instruments especially impressive as measures of delinquency.

REFERENCES

Erickson, M. L. The changing relationship between official and self-reported measures of delinquency: An exploratory predictive study. *Journal of Criminal Law, Criminology, and Police Science*, 1972, *63*, 388–395.

Delinquency Questionnaire

Instructions: For each of the following statements place a check (✓) if it is true for you and a cross (X) if it is false for you.

Past Delinquency Questionnaire

1. I have used tobacco regularly.
2. I have drunk beer, wine or other liquor.
3. I have skipped school without a legitimate excuse.
4. I have stolen things worth $2 to $50.
5. I have bought tobacco.
6. I have purposely damaged or destroyed public property.
7. I have bought beer, wine or other liquor.
8. I have defied teachers' authority to their faces.

Future Delinquency Questionnaire

1. I might skip school without a legitimate excuse.
2. I might take things worth more than $50 other than a car.
3. I might break into a place illegally (i.e., store, home, etc.).
4. I might purposely damage or destroy private property.
5. I might purposely damage public property.
6. I might take things worth $2 to $50.
7. I might buy beer, wine or other liquor.
8. I might buy tobacco.
9. I might use tobacco.
10. I might drink beer, wine or other liquor.
11. I might gamble (play poker, bet on horses, etc.).
12. I might get in a fight with someone.

Self-Reported Delinquency Scales (Arnold)

Development and Characteristics

The *Self-Reported Delinquency Scales* (SRDSA) were designed to measure the frequency of offenses relating to attacks against persons, vandalism, and theft (Arnold, 1965; Dentler & Monroe, 1961). The *Attacks Against Persons Scale* (AAPS) was developed from a pool of 13 items relating to antisocial behavior concerning other people. The *Vandalism Scale* began with 13 items believed to relate to acts of aggression against property. Finally, the item pool for the *Theft Scale* consisted of six items describing instances of theft. Five of these items were contained in the *Theft Scale* developed by Dentler and Monroe (1961).

All three item pools were subjected to a pretest that resulted in the rewording of five items for clarity. Next, the scales were analyzed according to the Cornell technique of scaleogram analysis. This analysis was performed on the responses of 200 high school sophomores who had been randomly selected from six urban high schools. Scalability was determined by "the tabulating procedure for determining scalability for more than six questions" (Ford, 1954). Responses to the AAPS showed that 2 of the 13 items received too few positive responses to be included in the scale. Three other items produced much error and failed to prove reproducibility when submitted to image analysis. The remaining eight items showed acceptable levels of margin and scale reproducibility.

Responses to the *Vandalism Scale* indicated that 10 items produced the highest overall reproducibility coefficient (8.35%). When these items were subjected to image analysis, one item did not fit into either image and one other item failed to contribute to the reproducibility of the scale. Therefore, a total of eight items was left for the *Vandalism Scale*.

Responses from both males and females indicated that the original five items from the Dentler and Monroe (1961) *Theft Scale* were appropriate. The sixth item, which related to check fraud, was eliminated because it produced a small number of positive responses.

Response Mode

All three scales are composed of Guttman-type items in which each item is a description of a particular activity. The respondents are requested to read the statement and indicate the number of times they have performed the act described: 1 or 2 times, 3 or 4 times, 5 to 10 times, and more than 10 times.

Scoring

A standard Guttman-type scoring procedure is used for all three scales. Each item can receive a score of 0 or 1 based on the alternative chosen. The score that each alternative received is designated below the item in the scale presentation section.

Since all three scales have received acceptable scalability ratings, a total of eight scale types are possible for the AAPS, eight are possible for the *Vandalism Scale* and five are possible for the *Theft Scale*. A high score on the AAPS indicates a high frequency of aggression against authority. A high score on the *Vandalism Scale* indicates increased activities involving damage to property and a high score on the *Theft Scale* indicates a high frequency of theft.

Norms

No standard norms are presently available. Arnold (1965) reports that 35% of his sample (200 randomly-selected high school sophomores) were located in Scale Types 2 through 5 on the *Theft Scale*, 4 through 8 on the *Vandalism Scale* and 5 through 8 on the AAPS. On the other hand, Liska (1974) reports that 63% of his respondents (133 college students between the ages of 17 and 19) were located in Scale 2 through 5 on the *Theft Scale*. Sixty-two percent of his respondents were located in Types 4 through 8 on the *Vandalism Scale* and 84% of his sample were placed in Scale Types 5 through 8 on the AAPS.

Reliability

Indications of internal consistency using coefficients of reproducibility are the only types of reliability information available. Arnold (1965) reports coefficients of reproducibility of .89, .91, and .94 for the AAPS, the *Vandalism Scale* and the *Theft Scale*, respectively. Liska (1974) reports reproducibility coefficients of .94 for the AAPS, .92 for the *Vandalism Scale*, and .93 for the *Theft Scale*.

Validity

All three scales appear to have partial construct validity based upon the use of the scalogram construction technique (as discussed in *Development and Characteristics*). This procedure tends to build in unidimensionality. Yet, when Arnold (1965) attempted to show that individuals within the lower socioeconomic status would score higher on the three self-reported delinquency scales than individuals in middle and upper socioeconomic levels, the results failed to support his position. Liska (1967) examined the responses of 133 college students between the ages of 17 and 19, comparing their scores on the three self-reported delinquency scales with a measure indicating the delinquent peer associations, delinquent involvement, and delinquent attitudes. The results showed that the AAPS was significantly related to delinquent attitudes ($r = .32$), the *Vandalism Scale* was related to delinquent involvement, ($r = .22$), and the *Theft Scale* was related to delinquent peer associations ($r = .20$).

Comments

These three scales present an interesting method for achieving self-reported delinquency information. They have the benefits of delinquency checklists in that specific examples of delinquent behavior are presented as stimuli for responses. They also have an advantage of being quickly scored and easily interpreted. All three scales seem to be well constructed, reliable, and easily adaptable to a variety of research settings.

The *Theft* and *Vandalism Scales* seem to be acceptable measures of the degree to which an individual reports his or her participation in theft and vandalism. The AAPS, however, appears to measure "antisocial behavior which is less serious than the crimes normally called attack against persons" (Arnold, 1965, p. 64), and that caveat should be considered in its use.

REFERENCES

Arnold, W. R. Continuities in research: Scaling delinquent behavior. *Social Problems,* 1965, *13,* 59–66.

Dentler, R. A., & Monroe, L. J. Social correlates of early adolescent theft. *The American Sociological Review,* 1961, *26,* 743.

Ford, R. N. A rapid scoring procedure for scaling attitude questions. In N. W. Riley, J. W. Riley, & J. Tobey (Eds.), *Sociological studies in scale analysis.* New Brunswick, N.J.: Rutgers University Press, 1954.

Liska, A. E. Causal structures underlying the relationship between delinquent involvement and delinquent peers. *Sociology and Social Research,* 1974, *59,* 23–26.

SELF-REPORTED DELINQUENCY SCALES

Instructions: For each of the following activities indicate whether you have participated in it "none," "one or two times," "three or four times," "five to ten times," or "more than ten times."

Vandalism Scale

1. Walked on some grass, yards, or fields where you weren't supposed to: none 0; one or two times 1; three or four times 1; five to ten times 1; more than ten times 1.

2. Marked with a pen, pencil, knife, or chalk on walls, sidewalks, or desks: none 0; one or two times 1; three or four times 1; five to ten times 1; more than ten times 1.

3. Thrown eggs, tomatoes, garbage, or anything else like this at any person, house, or building: none 0; one or two times 1; three or four times 1; five to ten times 1; more than ten times 1.

4. Broken out any windows: none 0; one or two times 1; three or four times 1; five to ten times 1; more than ten times 1.

5. Broken down anything such as fences, a flower bed, or a clothes line: none 0; one or two times 1; three or four times 1; five to ten times 1; more than ten times 1.

6. Put paint on anything you weren't supposed to be painting: none 0; one or two times 1; three or four times 1; five to ten times 1; more than ten times 1.

7. Broken out any light bulbs on the street or elsewhere: none 0; one or two times 1; three or four times 1; five to ten times 1; more than ten times 1.

8. Let the air out of somebody's tires: none 0; one or two times 1; three or four times 1; five to ten times 1; more than ten times 1.

Attacks against Persons Scale

1. Disobeyed your parents: none 0; one or two times 0; three or four times 0; five to ten times 0; more than ten times 1.

2. Purposely said mean things to someone to get back for something they had done to you: none 0; one or two times 0; three or four times 1; five to ten times 1; more than ten times 1.

3. Had a fight with one other person in which you hit each other or wrestled: none 0; one or two times 0; three or four times 1; five to ten times 1; more than ten times 1.

4. Disobeyed teachers, school officials, or others who told you what to do: none 0; one or two times 1; three or four times 1; five to ten times 1; more than ten times 1.

5. Defied your parents' authority to their face: none 0; one or two times 0; three or four times 1; five to ten times 1; more than ten times 1.

6. Made anonymous phone calls just to annoy the people you called: none 0; one or two times 0; three or four times 1; five to ten times 1; more than ten times 1.

7. "Beat up" anybody in a fight: none 0; one or two times 1; three or four times 1; five to ten times 1; more than ten times 1.

8. Signed somebody's name other than your own name to an excuse for absence from school: none 0; one or two times 1; three or four times 1; five to ten times 1; more than ten times 1.

Theft Scale

1. Taken little things (worth less than $2) that you were not supposed to take: none 0; one or two times 1; three or four times 1; five to ten times 1; more than ten times 1.

2. Taken things from someone else's desk or locker at school that the person would not want you to take: none 0; one or two times 1; three or four times 1; five to ten times 1; more than ten times 1.

3. Taken things of value (between $2 and $50) that you were not supposed to take: none 0; one or two times 1; three or four times 1; five to ten times 1; more than ten times 1.

4. Taken a car for a ride without the owner's permission: none 0; one or two times 1; three or four times 1; five to ten times 1; more than ten times 1.

5. Taken things of large value (over $50): none 0; one or two times 1; three or four times 1; five to ten times 1; more than ten times 1.

Self-Reported Delinquency Scale (Gibson)

Development and Characteristics

The *Self-Reported Delinquency Scale* (SRDSG) was designed to indicate the types of delinquent behavior exhibited by juvenile boys (Gibson, 1971). The SRDSG began as an interview technique that became structured into a questionnaire. The final checklist version was developed by Gibson in 1971.

Response Mode

A variety of response modes are possible; for example, each of the 31 activities might be typed on a separate card and presented to the respondents. They can then be requested to sort the cards into two separate stacks. One stack indicates that they have never participated in such an act, the other, that they have participated.

A second type of presentation and response mode might take the form of a checklist in which the 31 activities are listed on a sheet of paper. The respondents could then be requested to place a check mark beside each activity in which they have participated.

A third type of presentation is verbal. In this procedure, each of the activities is read to the respondents and they are asked to state whether they have participated in the act.

Scoring

Total scores are obtained by adding the number of activities in which a respondent has participated.

Norms

Farrington (1973) has reported mean scores on the 31-item scale for four groups of 14 and 15 year old boys. The groups consisted of 307 nondelinquents, 51 boys who had become delinquent in the last four years (late delinquents), 47 boys who had been labelled delinquent before their 10th birthday (early delinquents) and 38 boys who had not been labelled delinquent in their lives (not early delinquents). For the total of 405 boys, a mean score of 9.6 was obtained. Scores of 8.3, 12.1, 8.9 and 15.5 were obtained for nondelinquents, late delinquents, not early delinquents, and early delinquents, respectively.

Reliability

An internal consistency coefficient of .89 was reported for a group of 405 delinquent and nondelinquent boys between the ages of 14 and 15 (Farrington,

1973). Farrington (1973) retested a group of adolescent boys after a two-year period to measure the temporal stability of the scale. However, he has cautioned that tests of this sort should not show temporal stability for two reasons. First, as time passes there is an increased likelihood of the commission of more acts. Secondly, he has noted that there is a tendency for respondents to deny at later ages some activities which they admitted to committing at earlier ages.

Validity

Gibson (1971) submitted a 39-item version of the SRDSG to a total of 402 boys, ages 14 and 15. He concluded that three factors were involved in the responses to the scale. The first he labelled "general" factor of delinquency. The second and third, less important factors, were labelled active theft versus cheating and pilfering and maturity versus immaturity, respectively.

Farrington (1973) has reported that neither of the subscales was more predictively valid than the full scale score. Further, when he tested a total of 405 delinquent and nondelinquent youths, he found that the total scale score discriminated between nondelinquent, late delinquents, and early delinquents with the scores being in the appropriate direction. That is, nondelinquents scored lowest (8.3), late delinquents scored next highest (12.1) and early delinquents (boys who had been defined as delinquent early in age) had the highest mean scores (15.5).

Comments

The SRDSG appears to have content validity. This is especially important for, as Christie (1968) has commented, "the major problem has not to do with getting the informants to give honest answers, but to know what to ask them to be honest about. Basically it is a problem of sampling of acts" (pp. 8–9).

This scale has received attention in the research literature and appears to be reliable and valid. However, as Farrington (1973) pointed out "predictive efficiency is not sufficient for practical purposes" (p. 108). It does seem to be useful as a research tool and further refinement may make its applicability to other uses possible.

REFERENCES

Christie, N. *Hidden delinquency: Some Scandanavian experiences*. Paper presented at the National Conference on Research and Training in Criminology. Cambridge University: Institute of Criminology, 1968.

Gibson, H. B. Factorial structure of juvenile delinquency: A study of self-reported acts. *British Journal of Clinical and Social Psychology,* 1971, *10,* 1–9.

Farrington, D. P. Self-reports of deviant behavior: Predictive and stable? *Journal of Criminal Law and Criminology,* 1973, *64,* 99–110.

SELF-REPORTED DELINQUENCY SCALE

Instructions: For each of the following activities place a check (✓) if you have participated in such an act or a cross (X) if you have not.

1. Riding a bicycle without lights (or with no rear light) after dark.
2. Driving a car, motor bike, or motor scooter under the age of 16.
3. Belonging to a group (of ten or more people) who go around together, making a row, and sometimes get into fights or cause a disturbance.
4. Playing truant from school.
5. Deliberately traveling without a ticket or paying the wrong fare.
6. Setting off fireworks in the street.
7. Taking money from home — with no intention of returning it.
8. Taking an unknown person's car or motor bike for joyriding (with no intention of keeping it for good).
9. Smashing, slashing or damaging things in public places — in streets, cinemas, dance halls, railway carriages, buses.
10. Annoying, insulting, or fighting other people (strangers) in the street.
11. Breaking into a big store, garage, warehouse, pavilion, etc.
12. Breaking into a small shop (private tradesman), whether or not anything was stolen.
13. Stealing things out of cars.
14. Carrying some kind of weapon (knife or cosh) in case it is needed in a fight.
15. Attacking an enemy or someone in a rival gang (without using any sort of weapon) in a public place.
16. Breaking the windows of empty houses.
17. Using any kind of weapon in a fight — knife, cosh, razor, broken bottle, etc.
18. Drinking alcoholic drinks in pubs under the age of 18.
19. Going into pub bars under the age of 16.
20. Stealing things from big stores, supermarkets, multiple shops (while shop is open).
21. Stealing things from small shops or private tradesmen (shop open).
22. Deliberately littering the streets or pavement by smashing bottles, tipping dustbins, etc.
23. Buying cheap, or accepting as a present, anything known or suspected of being stolen.

24. Planning well in advance to get into a house, flat, etc., and steal valuables (and carrying the plan through).
25. Getting into a house, flat, etc., and stealing things (don't count cases where stealing results from planning well in advance).
26. Taking a pedal cycle belonging to an unknown person and keeping it.
27. Struggling or fighting to get away from a policeman.
28. Attacking or fighting a policeman who is trying to arrest someone else.
29. Stealing school property worth more than about 5p.
30. Stealing tools, materials or any other goods worth more than 50p. from employers (all in one go in working hours — don't count breaking-in here).
31. Trespassing (e.g., railway lines, goods yards, private gardens, empty houses).
32. Going to "X" films under age.
33. Often spending £1 or more a week on gambling under the age of 16.
34. Regularly smoking cigarettes under the age of 15.
35. Stealing goods or money from slot machines, jukeboxes, telephones, etc.
36. Stealing from people's clothes hanging up anywhere.

Self-Reported Delinquency Scales (Nye and Short)

Development and Characteristics

The *Self-Reported Delinquency Scales* (SRDS) were designed to measure delinquency at an interval rather than dichotomously (Nye & Short, 1957). Both scales follow the Guttman scalogram method of construction and both were designed using items from the original Nye and Short *Self-Reported Delinquency Questionnaire*.

Responses from a total of 3,186 delinquent and nondelinquent boys and girls were gathered from a set of items which included the original 23 questionnaire items and items designed to detect an overconformer. These responses were submitted to Guttman scalogram analysis. A total of 11 items were found to be "scalable." This list of items became the *Severe Delinquency Scale*.

When the 11 items were examined closely, it was discovered that the last four represented activities in which only certain types of delinquents would become involved. For this reason, these four were dropped and a 7-point *Low Severity Delinquency Scale* was created.

Response Mode

The respondent is requested to read each question and indicate whether he or she had participated in the activity described.

TABLE 28. Distribution of Delinquency Scale Types for 3,186 Boys, Ages 16 and 17

Scale type	Scalable items										
	1	2	3	4	5	6	7	8	9	10	11
00	0	0	0	0	0	0	0	0	0	0	0
01	1	0	0	0	0	0	0	0	0	0	0
02	1	1	0	0	0	0	0	0	0	0	0
03	1	1	1	0	0	0	0	0	0	0	0
04	1	1	1	1	0	0	0	0	0	0	0
05	2	1	1	1	0	0	0	0	0	0	0
06	2	1	1	1	1	0	0	0	0	0	0
07	2	1	1	1	1	1	0	0	0	0	0
08	2	1	2	1	1	1	0	0	0	0	0
09	2	1	2	2	1	1	0	0	0	0	0
10	2	1	2	2	1	1	1	0	0	0	0
11	2	1	2	2	1	1	1	1	0	0	0
12	2	2	2	2	1	1	1	1	0	0	0
13	2	2	2	2	1	1	1	1	1	0	0
14	2	2	2	2	1	1	2	1	1	0	0
15	2	2	2	2	2	1	2	1	1	0	0
16	2	2	2	2	2	2	2	1	1	0	0
17	2	2	2	2	2	2	2	1	1	1	1
18	2	2	2	2	2	2	2	1	2	1	1

Scoring

Both scales follow the standard Guttman scoring procedure. Each item is given a score of 1 if the respondent answers yes to the question, 2 if he or she participated in the act more than once or twice, and 0 if he or she never committed the offense under consideration. A score is then obtained by comparing an individual response pattern with one of the pre-established scale types. Table 28 represents the scale types presented by Nye and Short (1957).

The possible scale types for the 7-item delinquency scale end at scale type Number 9; however, a total of 18 scale types are possible for the 11-item version.

Norms

Nye and Short (1957) report that a cut-off point at Scale Type 9 on the 11 item scale maximized the difference between 570 nondelinquents and 125 delinquent boys. This criterion correctly identified 89.5% of the public school boys (nondelinquent) and 67.1% of the training school boys (delinquent).

The 7-point scale maximally discriminated between delinquents and nondelinquents when a cutoff point was made between Scale Types 7 and 8. This criterion correctly identified 71% of the 125 delinquent boys and 85% of the 570 nondelinquent boys.

Reliability

Internal consistency as measured by the coefficient of reproducibility was found to be .78 for the *Severe Delinquency Scale*. This coefficient was improved to .97 when the Israel Gammage Image was performed. The coefficient of reproducibility for the seven-item *Low Severity Scale* ranged between .97 and .99 for three separate samples of boys between the ages of 14 and 16.

Validity

Since the items were originally drawn from official lists of delinquent behavior, they have content validity. Further the process of scalogram analysis and the acceptable coefficient of reproducibility indicate that each of these delinquency scales is unidimensional.

Further support for validity for these two scales comes from the ability of each to discriminate with relative accuracy between individuals who have been officially defined as delinquent or nondelinquent based on police records. In addition, when responses from boys in public school in two different states (Western and Midwestern) were compared, no significant differences were found. This finding indicates that both scales may be generalized to more than one part of the country.

Comments

Both scales have adequate reliability and have received support for their validity from studies of comparison groups. Despite the favorable evidence, the developers suggest that these scales should be used for research only and not replace the collection of official data from police or other formal records. Further, the items in the SRDS are similar to those from other delinquency scales. This overlap may diminish the usefulness of the SRDS.

REFERENCES

Nye, F. I., & Short, J. F., Jr. Scaling delinquent behavior. *American Sociological Review*, 1957, 22, 326–331.

SELF-REPORTED DELINQUENCY SCALES

Instructions: For each of the following activities place a check (✓) if you have participated in such an act and a cross (X) if you have not.

The Low-Severity Delinquency Scale

1. Driven a car without a driver's license or permit? (Do not include driver training courses.)
2. Taken little things (worth less than $2) that did not belong to you?
3. Bought or drank beer, wine, or liquor? (Include drinking at home.)
4. Purposely damaged or destroyed public or private property that did not belong to you?
5. Skipped school without a legitimate excuse?
6. Had sex relations with a person of the opposite sex?
7. Defied your parents' authority (to their face)?

SELF-REPORTED DELINQUENCY SCALES

Instructions: For each of the following activities place a check (✓) if you have participated in such an act and a cross (X) if you have not.

Serious Delinquency Scale

1. Driven a car without a driver's license or permit? (Do not include driver training courses.)
2. Taken little things (worth less than $2) that did not belong to you?
3. Bought or drank beer, wine, or liquor? (Include drinking at home).
4. Purposely damaged or destroyed public or private property that did not belong to you?
5. Skipped school without a legitimate excuse?
6. Had sex relations with a person of the opposite sex?
7. Defied your parents' authority (to their faces)?
8. "Run away" from home?
9. Taken things of medium value (between $2 and $50)?
10. Taken things of large value (worth more than $50)?
11. Used or sold narcotic drugs?

Traits Indicating Attitude Scale

Development and Characteristics

The *Traits Indicating Attitude Scale* (TIAS) (Russen, 1969) was designed to measure the degree to which an individual holds delinquent attitudes. The scale is based on the assumption that delinquent acts occur for two reasons: (1) The individual acts without regard for the effects of his/or her actions on other people, or (2) the individual acts with regard for the effects of one's actions, but was unaware of the harm the action would bring to others. Since only the former reason involves a willingness to offend others, the developer feels that it is this attitude and the underlying motivation that should be of prime importance in determining whether an individual is delinquent. It follows, then, that a "delinquent is characterized by a readiness to cross a line between being unwilling to hurt others and being willing to hurt others, whether or not his behavior is considered to be within the law" (Russon, 1969, p. 39).

If a willingness to hurt others is reflected in an individual's behavior, then an observer should be able to infer from one's actions which basic attitudes are guiding his or her behavior. To accomplish this in a systematic manner, the developer designed the delinquency differential. This is a set of five pairs of generalized inferences about an individual whose behavior has been observed. It allows for a determination of predominance of delinquent or nondelinquent attitudes and consequently some classification. Table 29 lists the set of criteria that were used to classify institutionalized juveniles.

TABLE 29. Differentiating Characteristics of Nondelinquent and Delinquent Personalities (Delinquency Differential)

	Nondelinquent	Delinquent
1.	Governing of behavior by regard for legality	Absence of due regard for legality
2.	Ability to adapt with legal alternative to delinquency in problem situation	Tendency to single response without alternative adaptation
3.	Regard for the value of service to others. Willing to accommodate others even though for own ends.	Essentially self-centered, without regard for others
4.	Awareness of nonmaterial value systems	Tendency to translate everything into material and physical values
5.	Ability to tolerate anxiety and to inhibit its expression through offensive behavior	Reduced tolerance for anxiety; manifest behavioral equivalents of anxiety

These issues are usually discussed by a team of staff members, each of whom has had opportunities to observe the individual being studied. They discuss the alternative that most accurately describes the juvenile's behavior.

This technique was revised to form the TIAS by bringing the concepts from the abstract to slightly more concrete levels and dividing the behavior types into three sections (1) nondelinquent, (2) delinquent-antisocial, and (3) delinquent-asocial. This process extended the behavior list to 35 items and offered more detailed descriptions.

Response Mode

The respondent is identified as a person who has had an opportunity to observe the subject. He/she is requested to read each of the 35 descriptions and note which are true for the subject.

Scoring

A score is obtained by counting the number of descriptions within each category that apply to the subject. This is not an absolute value, however. A ratio (or percentage) is tabulated for the relative number of delinquent versus nondelinquent descriptions.

Norms

No norms were reported.

Reliability

No measures of reliability were reported.

Validity

The developer does not report evidence for validity. However, the scale does seem to have content validity. The descriptions relate directly to judgements of attitudes that are directly related to social interaction and determine whether the person is likely to be a delinquent. The emphasis is on regard for others and ways of dealing with others.

Comments

The perspective involved in the construction of this scale is refreshing and potentially insightful. It places importance on the intent and motivation of behavior, rather than on the behavior alone. Because of this, the effect of circumstance is lessened in importance.

The technique of behavior rating is helpful and the use of a group rating adds to the stability of the measure. Unfortunately there is a lack of reliability and validity tests. In addition, some standard set of explanations of each item would be helpful, since it is possible that a variety of definitions and inferences could be obtained from each item.

REFERENCES

Russon, G. Basic attitude in delinquency. *Corrective Psychiatry and Journal of Social Therapy*, 1969, *15*, 38–48.

TRAITS INDICATING ATTITUDE

Instructions to Rater: Put a check (✓) beside each statement which is true and a cross (X) beside each statement which is false for the individual being rated.

Non-Delinquent (Relevant to General Attitude)

1. Shows ability to govern actions by consideration of feelings, rights, and property of others.
2. Usually leads a law (or rule) -abiding life.
3. Has awareness of the value of service to others and to the self.
4. Willing to go out of way to be of service to others.
5. Tries to avoid hurting others physically and/or psychologically.
6. Usually able to tolerate frustration without "taking it out" on others.
7. Adheres to high standard of conduct.
8. Acts according to a personal code of ethics.
9. Concerned about the suffering of others.
10. Has genuine deep feelings for humanity.
11. Sincerely tries to put feelings for humanity into action.
12. Afraid to break the law. (Afraid of being caught.)
13. Regards breaking the law as stupid or foolish.
14. Will not offend because he knows vaguely that offending is "wrong."
15. Acknowledges own actions.

Delinquent, Anti-Social (Relevant Only to Offending Behavior)

1. Offending is deliberate rather than due to error in judgment.
2. Shows willful, i.e., intentional, disregard for the feelings, rights, or property of others.
3. Is aware of the full implications of hurting or endangering others.
4. Holds grudges and attempts retaliation.
5. Obtains satisfaction from hurting or causing misfortune to others.
6. The realization that others find his actions offensive does not stop him. No response to group pressure to control him. May have an "I don't care" attitude.
7. Openly resentful, with resentment readily expressed through behavior.
8. Does not hesitate to hurt others physically or psychologically. Is aware of the choice between hurting and not hurting.
9. Offenses are planned and deliberate, as offenses.
10. Outwardly appears pleasant and courteous but actually is spiteful or vicious.

Delinquent, Asocial (Relevant Only to Offending Behavior)

1. Selfish — thinks primarily in terms of benefit to self at time of offending.
2. Offending is due more to thoughtlessness than to hostility.
3. Impulsive — rarely considers alternatives of action.
4. Indifferent to the welfare of others.
5. Assumes rights and privileges of the self which do not actually exist.
6. Offending is due mainly to irresponsibility or lack of exercise of self-control.
7. Is insensitive to fact that others find his behavior offensive.
8. Tends to be unduly arrogant and superior in attitude — "Knows it all."
9. Often is an unwitting accomplice in offending others.
10. Ignores or is oblivious to the taking of responsibility for own actions, and appears to believe that others will assume the responsibility he neglects.

Violence Scale

Development and Characteristics

The *Violence Scale* (VS) was designed to "evaluate the extent and degree of violent crime within a . . . population, making it possible to chart trends over time, and to identify results of differential treatment methods or placements" (Andrew, 1974, p. 124). The scale consists of 65 descriptions of acts that may be considered delinquent. These are ranked in ascending order of severity and denote past behaviors.

The items represent the crimes listed in the records of 172 delinquents who were referred for psychological evaluation during a 27-month period. These acts were, then, rank ordered for severity by two psychologists who worked with delinquents and by two probation officers. When the order was numbered and nine additional acts were included, the relative scoring weights of each item were established as the numerical average of the item's rank order.

Response Mode

The VS is a rating scale compiled from the record of a juvenile; therefore the rater checks the applicable categories of law violation.

Scoring

The VS score is obtained by adding the rank value of all infractions committed by the individual and then dividing by the sum of the number of infractions.

Norms

Table 30 presents the scores of 172 delinquents and provides a basis of comparison.

Reliability

No reliability estimates were reported.

Validity

No validity measures were reported.

TABLE 30. Violence Scale Scores

	Mean				
	Anglo	Mexican	Negro	Other	Total
Males					
Study I	30.96	35.04	40.32	21.75	36.67
Study II	41.42	39.61	49.84	22.50	42.38
Females					
Study I	16.32	22.00	22.20	18.50	19.13
Study II	37.71	14.50	32.55	—	32.55

Comments

The VS is in an early stage of construction. The method for item selection and ranking is commendable, but there is some question about the numerical weights that represent the severity of each item. Also, the wording and criteria for each item should be more clearly defined. For example, is one given credit for smoking as a delinquent act only if it is officially reported, or if it is just noted by the rater? Must one be convicted of assault, or only accused, to be considered assaultive?

Finally, there is the question of the use of official records as criteria for behavior patterns. As with all such instruments, the VS is dependent on the sometimes questionable accuracy of official records.

REFERENCES

Andrew, J. M. Violent crime indices among community-retained delinquents. *Criminal Justice and Behavior*, 1974, 2, 123–130.

VIOLENCE SCALE

Instructions to Rater: Please check all infractions in which the subject has been involved.

1.	Smoking
2.	Curfew
3.	Sexual misbehavior by a girl
4.	Homosexuality (male)
5.	Trespassing
6.5	Runaway
6.5	Truancy
8.	Destroying own personal belongings
9.	Indecent exposure
10.	Beyond control
10.88a	Mail theft
11.	Verbal fights, verbally assaultive
12.	Bad checks (NSF)
13.	Drunk in public place
14.	Receiving stolen property (or possession of stolen property)

15.	Glue use
16.5	OD on drugs
16.5	Hospitalized on bad trip (LSD)
18.18[a]	Drunk on a bicycle
18.5	Suicide attempt
18.5	Temper
20.	Shoplifting
21.	Taking parent's car
22.5	Forgery
22.5	Drug use (unspecified or mj only) or poss. alc.
24.	Prowling
25.12[a]	Disturbing the peace
25.5	Stealing
25.5	Petty theft
27.	Seconal and barbiturate use, LSD
28.	Fight on school grounds
29.	Threats of violence
30.	Bizarre behavior such as cutting up clothes and hair
30.25[a]	Motorcycle theft or motorcycle joyriding
31.	Sales of marijuana
32.	Shooting an airgun
33.	Malicious mischief
34.	Grand theft
35.	Hits younger children
36.	Violent outbursts at school; physically aggressive
37.	Burglary
38.	Extorting
39.	Carrying a knife
40.5	Auto theft
40.5	Resisting arrest
42.	Sex play with children under 14
43.	Sales of drugs other than marijuana
43.42[a]	Displaying a weapon in a rude manner.
44.	Possession of a deadly weapon
45.00[a]	Inciting a riot

	45.5	Reckless driving
	45.5	Violence toward teacher (threw chair at teacher)
	47.	Drunk driving or drugged driving
	48.5	Battery of a police officer
	48.5	Assault
	48.55[a]	Drunk driving with accident
	49.75	Assault with a deadly weapon
	50.	Fire-setting
	51.	Wife-beating
	52.5	Battery
	52.5	Hit-and-run driving
	54.	Strong-armed robbery
	55.	Rape
	55.55[a]	Assault; intent to commit murder
	56.	Voluntary manslaughter

[a]Added later to the original 56-item list.

DELINQUENCY BEHAVIOR RATINGS: LISTINGS

Delinquent Behavior Interview Schedule

Gold, M. *Delinquent behavior in an American city*. Belmont, Calif.: Brooks & Cole, 1970.

This is a 17-item, Q-sort procedure by which adolescents categorize delinquent events in which they have participated.

Group Data Schedule

Hutcheson, B. R. *A prognostic classification for juvenile court first offenders based on a follow-up study: A method applicable to the field of mental illness. A report* (NIMH Special Grant No. 3M 9149 [C2]). South Shore Mental Health Center, Commonwealth of Massachusetts, Quincy, August 1963.

This 43-item rating schedule was designed to diagnostically measure delinquents' observable behavior interaction patterns with peers and leaders in a group, as well as other behavioral manifestations and psychological characteristics.

Inmate Management Scale

King, R. D., & Raynes, N. V. An operational measure of inmate management in residential institutions. *Social Science and Medicine,* 1968, *2,* 41–53.

This 16-item, forced-choice scale was designed to measure practices adopted in the management of youthful inmates of residential institutions.

Institutional Adjustment Index

Hand, J., & Lebo, D. Predicting the institutional adjustment of delinquent boys. *Journal of Criminal Law, Criminology, and Police Science,* 1955, *45,* 694–696.

The *Institutional Adjustment Index* is a rating procedure used to evaluate the rate and severity of offenses that delinquent boys committed while they were institutionalized. All institutional offenses are rated and an average "personal adjustment" score and an average "social adjustment" score are obtained.

Peer Rating Instrument

Gibson, H. B., & Hanson, R. Peer ratings as predictors of school behaviour and delinquency. *British Journal of Social and Clinical Psychology,* 1969, *8,* 313–322.

The *Peer Rating Instrument* is a behavior ratings scale that was designed to elicit a boy's rating of his peers with regard to seven attributes (I like as a friend, I want to be like him, gets into trouble most, honest, daring, clever, and like I am).

Self-Report Delinquency Questionnaire

Gold, M., & Mann, D. Delinquency as defense. *Journal of Orthopsychiatry,* 1973, *42,* 463–479.

This is a 16-item, self-report instrument designed to measure the types of delinquent acts in which boys have participated.

Self-Reported Delinquency Scale

Hindelang, M. J. The relationship of self-reported delinquency to scales in the CPI and MMPI. *Journal of Criminal Law, Criminology, and Police Science,* 1972, *63,* 75–81.

This is a 26-item, self-report instrument designed to measure the types of delinquent acts in which boys have participated.

Self-Reported Delinquent Behavior Questionnaire

Vaz, E. W. Delinquency and youth culture: Upper and middle class boys. *Journal of Criminal Law, Criminology, and Police Science*, 1968, *60*, 33–46.

This 17-item scale was designed as a self-report measure of level of delinquency involvement. Respondents are asked to indicate whether they have participated in each of the listed acts.

Youngster Behavior Inventory

Palmer, T., Pearson, J., & Haire, S. *Selected instruments used in the group home project.* California, Department of the Youth Authority, The Group Home Project (Differential Treatment Environments for Delinquents), Fall 1969.

This 85-item questionnaire was designed to provide a basis for behavioral assessment of the adjustment of youths placed in group homes. The behavior ratings are made by group-home parents on a 5-point scale.

DELINQUENCY PERSONALITY ASSESSMENT: REVIEWS

Beverly-Grant Opinion Schedule

Development and Characteristics

The *Beverly-Grant Opinion Schedule* (BGOS) was designed "to objectively measure levels of interpersonal maturity (I-levels) as postulated and described by Sullivan, Grant, and Grant (1957)" (Beverly, 1965, p. *i*). Since I-level represents a progression through a set of developmental stages, the measured level could help guide treatment for the delinquent.

A total of 600 statements were devised and administered to 264 inmates whose I-level had been determined in an interview by a clinical psychologist (Fowler, Ballard, & Fosen, 1961). Ninety-five items proved to be valuable at discriminating between individuals labeled "high maturity" and "low maturity." This finding was cross-validated on another sample of 84 inmates. The scale proved valuable at differentiating between the extremes (high versus low maturity), but could not make fine discriminations. When these items were examined more closely, 18 were found to form a useful scale (Beverly, 1965).

Response Mode

The BGOS is a group test with 18 statements that require a "true" or "false" response. The scale may be read by the respondent or, as the developer did, read aloud to the group as a whole to avoid reading problems.

Scoring

An individual's score is the sum of the statements answered in the direction of interpersonal maturity (as defined by the developer). The letters preceding the scale items indicate the correct answer for indicating maturity.

Norms

No relevant norms were presented.

Reliability

A split-half reliability coefficient of .686 was reported for 84 delinquent inmates (other characteristics of the inmates were not presented). When corrected by the Spearman-Brown prophesy formula, the reliability coefficient becomes .814.

Validity

Validity is difficult to establish for this scale if the criterion for inclusion is its ability to discriminate between the evaluated I-levels. Without the examination of a sample other than the one used to develop the instrument, little support for this type of validity can be presented. Evidence for concurrent validity indicates that the BGOS was found to correlate: (1) .78 with a similarly shortened version of the Jesness Inventory; (2) .368 (biserial correlation) with the California Test for Mental Maturity (CTMM); and (3) .206 with socio-economic status (SES).

Comments

Since only 18 items out of a pool of 600 successfully differentiate I-levels, a cross-validation is essential for supporting item selection and determining the usefulness of this scale.

REFERENCES

Beverly, R. F. The BGOS: An attempt at the objective measurement of levels of interpersonal maturity. California: Department of Youth Authority, 1965.

Fowler, R. D., Ballard, K. B., & Fosen, R. H. Classification study I—Summary status report. California Department of Corrections, Division of Research, April 1961.

THE BEVERLY-GRANT OPINION SCHEDULE

Put a check (✓) if the statement is true for you.
Put a cross (x) if the statement is false for you.

- F Where you end up in life is mostly a matter of luck.
- F It would be kind of dumb to vote for increasing your taxes.
- F It's not what you do, but whether or not you get caught that really counts.
- F People interfere with my thinking.
- F Honesty is usually a handicap in getting ahead in the world.
- F It's not what you know, but who you know that counts.
- F I always follow the rule that what people don't know won't hurt them.
- F All is fair in love and war.
- T When things go wrong I just try harder.
- F A person never knows when he will get in trouble.
- F Honestly looking at it, everyone is only interested in his own problems.
- F It's better to take each day as it comes than to plan about the future.
- F Policemen who bawl people out do so just to feel important.
- F A person who is different should try to be more like others.
- F Actually the most important single thing for a man to give his family is good support so that they will have all the things they want.
- T I can see many reasons why a person would vote to raise his own taxes.
- F Looking at it honestly, I think that all I have been doing here is putting in my time.
- F Some people just seem to have it in for me.

Correctional Staff Evaluation Scale

Development and Characteristics

The *Correctional Staff Evaluation Scale* (CSES) was designed to measure staff perceptions of institutionalized delinquent boys and, more specifically, the possibility of contradictions between administrative labels of an inmate and his status among his peers (Cheatwood, 1974). The label "R" is used in the Fairfield (Ohio) School for Boys to designate boys who are "restricted" because they may be dangerous to themselves and others, while "E" denotes a boy whose "emotional makeup" indicates a potential for "acting out," which may produce mental or emotional deterioration. Despite administrative labels, inmates rarely differentiate these individuals from other inmates. Since the staff members are "in the middle," the CSES was needed to reveal staff opinions of "R" and "E" boys and others.

A total of 17 items form the CSES. Each of these refers to the staff members' perception of a boy.

Response Mode

Each item is a statement which the respondent is asked to rate on a 10-point scale ranging from 0 (very true) to 9 (very false).

Scoring

Each item receives a score ranging from 0 to 9 representing the respondent's rating of an individual. No total score is calculated; however, one might be calculated for Items 1 through 15 on the assumption that these items fall along one dimension. (Items 5, 6, and 7 are reversed and should be converted for such a procedure.)

Norms

Table 31 shows the mean response of staff members at the Fairfield School for each item obtained from a sample that was labeled either "R" or "E" boys ($N = 25$) and a group of boys recently released ($N = 275$).

TABLE 31. Mean Scores

Item	"R" and "E"	Fairfield releases
1	4.44	4.78
2	4.60	4.68
3	4.68	4.52
4	4.24	4.44
5	4.08	3.63
6	3.56	3.79
7	4.08	4.30
8	5.60	5.21
9	4.44	4.76
10	5.56	5.33
11	4.56	4.75
12	4.68	4.58
13	4.24	4.51
14	4.00	4.06
15	5.04	5.11
16	4.20	6.48
17	5.04	6.42

Reliability

No measure of reliability is available.

Validity

The scale developer hypothesized that staff members, as intermediaries, would experience conflict and would: (1) perceive little difference between "R" and "E" boys and others (like the inmate subculture), yet (2) support the administrative label assigned to each boy. This is tested by comparing perceptions of staff of the "normal" and "R" and "E" boys. Items 1 through 15 refer to perceived attributes of boys. No significant differences were found between ratings of the boys on these items. However, Items 16 and 17, which indicate degree of agreement with administrative labels, were significant at the .05 level or better. Thus, support was found for the split identification of staff members and for the validity of the CSES.

Comments

This instrument was designed specifically to measure staff perceptions of delinquent boys. Items 1 through 15, however, may be useful for other purposes. As a scale, they could serve to quantify anyone's perception of delinquents. Either use, however, requires some tests of heterogeneity, reliability, and further tests of validity.

REFERENCES

Cheatwood, A. D. The staff in correctional settings: An empirical investigation of frying pans and fires. *Journal of Research in Crime and Delinquency,* 1974, *11,* 173–179.

CORRECTIONAL STAFF EVALUATION SCALE

Instructions: Using the following scale, rate the truthfulness of each statement by placing the appropriate number beside the statement number:

0	1	2	3	4	5	6	7	8	9
very true									very false

___ 1. He is honest in his relationships with others.
___ 2. His interpersonal approach to others is good.
___ 3. He is at ease with himself.
___ 4. He identifies with the staff.
___ 5. He thinks like a hood.
___ 6. He plays the inmate game.
___ 7. He rejects the institution.
___ 8. His attitudes seemed to have changed for the better.
___ 9. The other boys influenced him very little.
___10. The other boys picked on him very little.
___11. He thinks the institution has been very helpful to him.
___12. He feels that what happened to him here was very good.
___13. His self-concept is very good.
___14. He feels that being sent to the institution was very good.
___15. He defines himself as a good person.
___16. Regardless of this boy's actual status, he seems to have all the characteristics of an "R."
___17. Regardless of this boy's actual status, he seems to have all the characteristics of an "E."

Delinquency Scale (PN Version)

Development and Characteristics

The Psychopathic-Neurotic version of the *Delinquency Scale* (DS) (Peterson, Quay, & Tiffany, 1961) is an outgrowth of the scale developed by Quay and Peterson (1958). Like the earlier scale, the new version attempts to predict delinquency. It also, however, classifies the type of delinquent as either: (1) psychopathic— "tough, amoral, rebellious . . . impulsiveness, a conspicuous distrust of legal and other authority, and an apparent freedom from family ties" (Peterson, Quay, & Camerson, 1959, p. 397) or (2) neurotic— "impulsive but" with "intrapsychic concomitants and perhaps the dynamic bases, of remorse, tension, guilt, depression, discouragement—in short, neurotic responses— . . . with antisocial activity" (Peterson *et al.,* 1959, pp. 397–398). It was believed that knowledge of which type of delinquency pattern was operative would be useful for many purposes.

The PN version began with the 40 items of the DS to which the Gough and

Peterson's *Delinquency Scale* (1954) was added (Peterson *et al.,* 1959). This composite was factor analyzed and five factors proved to be effective in accounting for most of the variance in a group of 116 delinquents and 115 nondelinquents. These factors were labeled (1) psychopathy, (2) neuroticism, (3) family dissension, (4) inadequacy and (5) scholastic maladjustment. Since factors three and five were purely background variables, Factors 1, 2, and 4 were considered the main personality factors involved in delinquency (Peterson *et al.,* 1959).

Further research with adolescent boys (Peterson, Quay, & Tiffany, 1961) indicated that the third factor, inadequacy, was not valid for predicting an incompetence type of delinquency, but support was gained for the validity of the psychopathic and neurotic types of delinquency. The resultant scale, which is used to differentiate between *Psychopathic Delinquents* (Pd) and *Neurotic Delinquents* (Ne), contains the 52 true-false items, which loaded on these two factors.

Response Mode

This version, like that of Quay and Peterson (1958) is a paper-and-pencil test that requires an individual read each statement and indicate whether he or she feels it is true or false.

Scoring

Three scores may be obtained: (1) The overall DS score is calculated by summing the total number of responses labeled "delinquent." (These items and their direction were defined empirically by their predictive value, as noted in the section on *Development and Characteristics),* (2) the Pd score is obtained by summing the number of "psychopathic" responses, and (3) the Ne score is a sum of all the "neurotic" responses. Note that no interpretative cut-offs were reported, although norms are reported that may assist in interpretation.

Norms

Table 32 presents the means and standard deviations for a variety of offenders on each of the four scales.

Reliability

Persons (1970) reports the test–retest correlations on 194 first offenders and recidivists after a 20-week time lapse (Table 33). These coefficients, although acceptable, should be viewed cautiously. The concept of delinquency, in general, and as psychopathic or neurotically based is believed to be relatively stable. These correlations indicate that quite a bit of variation has occurred. This variation is

TABLE 32. Groups Means and Standard Deviations

Groups		Pd	Ne	DS	PN
133 First offenders, 1	M	8.51	12.12	20.68	−3.56
	SD	4.67	5.74	8.62	5.42
61 Recidivists, 1	M	8.25	12.08	20.33	−3.84
	SD	4.41	5.63	7.68	6.58
49 Disciplinary group	M	9.17	13.98	23.12	−4.84
	SD	5.09	5.76	9.15	5.87
141 Normative group	M	9.28	13.30	22.59	−4.24
	SD	4.80	5.91	9.35	5.17
133 First offenders, 2	M	8.73	11.72	20.50	−2.96
	SD	4.75	5.76	9.04	5.27
61 Recidivists, 2	M	9.69	12.33	22.02	−2.30
	SD	4.67	5.74	8.83	5.72
385 Long institutionalization	M	8.84	12.57	21.53	−3.81
	SD	4.47	5.74	8.51	5.91
48 Therapy group	M	6.17	8.23	14.46	−1.90
	SD	3.40	5.52	7.61	5.12

enough to question whether the test is reliable or whether some important changes have occurred to the subjects over the 20-week period.

Validity

Table 34 shows the relationships between the *Taylor Manifest Anxiety Scale* (MAS), the total *Delinquency Scale* score (DS), the Psychopathic Delinquency score (Pd), the *Neurotic Delinquency* score (Ne), and *Psychopathy minus Neuroticism* (PN) from the DS. The correlations indicate that the DS is appropriately related to MAS, Pd, and Ne. Further support is evidenced by the close relationship between Persons's (1970) and Becker's (1965) results. Support for the DS's ability to identify delinquents was reported for the 40 items DS.

Although evidence for the DS is strong as a predictor of delinquency and

TABLE 33. Test–Retest Correlations

	First offenders	Recidivists	M test–retest
DS	.67	.51	.59
Pd	.61	.39	.50
Ne	.63	.70	.67
PN	.48	.61	.55

TABLE 34. Correlation Matrix Reported in Persons (1970)[a]

	DS	Pd	Ne	PN
MAS	.68	.35	.74	−.48
DS		.80	.88	−.26
Pd			.43	.36
Ne				−.68

[a] All correlations $p < .01$.

even though the correlations between subscales and other instruments appear to be appropriate, the classification of delinquents as psychopathic or neurotic is tenuous. Becker (1965) suggests that since his results do not show the expected differences between anxiety levels (as measured by the MAS) for neurotic (anxious, remorseful, guilt-ridden) and psychopathic delinquents ("unsocialized aggression"), one must question the construct validity of these scoring subscales. The preceding table shows that there is, indeed, a stronger relationship between MAS and Ne than between MAS and Pd. Yet there should be essentially no relationship between MAS and Pd. However, since Ne and Pd are correlated .43, the Pd–MAS relationship could, conceivably, be due to the common variance of Ne and Pd.

Comments

Although this scale, on the surface, appears to be a strong, useful instrument, some serious concerns must be dealt with. First, the issue of construct validity of the Ne and Pd scores should be better resolved. The factor analysis is informative, but not conclusive. Second, since all but three items are worded so that a "delinquent" response is "true", there is a possibility that subjects will develop a "response set" in which they answer all questions with the same alternative. Next, neither Becker (1965) nor Persons (1970) makes clear the exact arrangement of the items as they were presented to the subjects. Most refer to a pattern of alternating between Pd, Ne, and inadequate statements, but the specific order of presentation is not reported. This could be an important factor in determining the overall results of the scale. Finally, one must question the relationship (.43) between Ne and Pd. The rationale for the two categories indicated that they represented two different types of delinquents. Perhaps they should be related to the degree that Ne and Pd are points on a continuum. This, however, needs clarification.

REFERENCES

Becker, P. W. Some correlates of delinquency and validity of questionnaire assessment methods. *Psychological Reports,* 1965, *16,* 271–277.

Gough, H. D., & Peterson, D. R. The identification and measurement of predispositional factors in crime and delinquency. *Journal of Consulting Psychology,* 1954, *16,* 207–212.

Persons, R. W., Psychometric evaluation of sociological factors in a boy's reformatory. *Psychological Reports,* 1970, *27,* 407–413.

Peterson, D. R., Quay, H. D., & Cameron, G. R. Personality and background factors in juvenile delinquency as inferred from questionnaire responses. *Journal of Consulting Psychology,* 1959, *23,* 395–399.

Peterson, D. R., Quay, H. C., & Tiffany, T. L., Personality factors related to juvenile delinquency. *Child Development,* 1961, *32,* 355–372.

Quay, H. C., & Peterson, D. R. A brief scale for juvenile delinquency. *Journal of Clinical Psychology,* 1958, *14,* 139–142.

DELINQUENCY SCALE (PN VERSION)

Instructions: For each of the following statements place a check (✓) if it is true for you or a cross (X) if it is false for you.

Psychopathy

The only way to settle anything is to lick the guy.

Winning a fight is more fun than anything.

The people that run things are usually against me.

Cops usually treat you dirty.

If you don't have enough to live on, it's OK to steal.

A lot of times it's fun to be in jail.

The only way to make big money is to steal it.

A person is better off if he doesn't trust anyone.

If the cops don't like you, they will get you for anything.

Life usually hands me a pretty raw deal.

Cops and judges will tell you one thing and do another.

A guy like me hits first and asks questions later.

It's dumb to trust older people.

I would do almost anything on a dare.

If somebody does something to me, I always get them back.

Most brothers and sisters are more trouble than they are worth.

I don't mind lying if I am in bad trouble.

I go out of my way to meet trouble rather than try to escape it.

I do what I want to do, whether anybody likes it or not.

I would rather be at home when things go wrong.

I got (or used to get) into a lot of fights in school.

I never cared much for school.

I have never done any heavy drinking.

I have run away from home because my folks treated me bad.

I'm really too tough a guy to get along with most kids.

Neuroticism

I often feel that I am not getting anywhere in life.

Sometimes I used to feel that I would like to leave home.

I seem to do things that I regret more often than other people do.

I have often gone against my parent's wishes.

My parents often disapproved of my friends.

I sometimes wanted to run away from home.

I often feel as though I have done something wrong or wicked.

I don't think I'm quite as happy as others seem to be.

People often talk about me behind my back.

With things going as they are, it's pretty hard to keep up hope of amounting to something.

I would rather go without something than ask for a favor.

I sometimes feel that I made the wrong choice in my occupation.

I have very strong likes and dislikes.

I often act on the spur of the moment without stopping to think.

I get nervous when I have to ask someone for a job.

Sometimes I feel (or used to feel) that if I could just get away from home, everything would be all right.

Cops and judges will tell you one thing and do another.

In school I was sometimes sent to the principal for cutting up.

My folks usually blame bad company for the trouble I get into.

Most of the time I feel happy.

I have more than my share of things to worry about.

It is hard for me to act natural when I am with new people.

It isn't their fault that most guys get into trouble.

My folks have sometimes been in trouble with the law.

When I was a little kid, I was always doing things my folks told me not to.

I used to steal sometimes when I was a youngster.

I have never been in trouble with the law.

Differential Behavioral Classification System

Development and Characteristics

The *Differential Behavioral Classification System* (DBCS) was designed to serve as a method for classifying individuals for placement into appropriate therapeutic groups or settings (Quay & Parsons, 1970). This procedure makes use of three different scales developed from factor analytic methods: (1) the *Behavior Problem Checklist* (BPC), (2) the *Personal Opinion Study* (POS), and (3) the *Checklist for Analysis of Life History Data* (CALHD). The BPC consists of 55 items to be completed by a correctional official who is in a position to make valid judgments about the offender's behavior. POS consists of 100 true-false items that are completed by the offender. The CALHD is based on the case history of the institutionalized offender and can be completed by anyone who has access to the case history data.

Response Mode

Quay makes use of these three inventories to gather data on four behavior categories (BC): (1) inadequate-immature (BC-1); (2) neurotic-disturbed (BC-2); (3) unsocialized-psychotic (BC-3); and (4) socialized-subcultural (BC-4). The POS is scored on BC-2, -3, and -4. The BPC is scored on BC-1, -2, and -3. The CALHD yields scores for all four behavioral categories. At the completion of the three inventories, each offender will have obtained 10 scores.

Scoring

A behavioral category data form is used to record the raw scores on each of the inventories. Each raw score is entered in a table and then the individual raw scores are transformed into T-scores by using the conversion procedures in Table 35. T-scores are then summed for each behavioral category and divided by the number of scores in that category.

This T-score average, or the initial composite T-score, is then standardized

TABLE 35. Conversion Table for Raw Scores to *T*-Scores

Raw scores	Test (POS)			Rating (BPC)			History (CALHD)			
	BC-2	BC-3	BC-4	BC-1	BC-2	BC-3	BC-1	BC-2	BC-3	BC-4
−2										27.5
−1							25.9	36.3	28.3	33.0
0	23.0	31.7	18.0	37.4	32.2	37.3	36.7	46.6	39.8	39.2
1	29.2	37.8	18.0	45.2	38.5	44.4	44.1	53.9	47.5	44.8
2	33.7	41.3	18.0	50.6	42.7	48.1	51.0	57.8	52.5	49.1
3	36.7	44.1	18.0	55.0	45.8	50.6	58.9	60.9	56.5	52.9
4	39.0	46.4	24.0	58.6	48.4	52.6	68.4	63.6	59.2	57.0
5	40.8	48.0	26.3	62.0	50.7	54.4		65.7	61.7	61.8
6	42.5	49.5	28.3	65.7	52.9	56.0		68.6	64.3	68.4
7	44.2	50.8	30.7	70.3	54.8	57.2		72.3	66.5	
8	45.8	51.9	33.4	77.0	56.5	58.5		76.0	68.7	
9	47.3	53.1	36.0		58.4	60.0		82.0	71.7	
10	48.7	54.3	38.1		60.7	61.5			76.0	
11	50.2	55.3	40.1		63.0	62.9				
12	51.5	56.1	42.6		65.8	64.3				
13	52.9	56.9	45.1		69.4	65.6				
14	54.2	57.9	47.6		74.1	67.4				
15	55.3	58.7	50.2			69.0				
16	56.6	59.4	52.9			70.5				
17	58.0	59.9	56.0			74.4				
18	59.5	60.7	59.1							
19	61.0	61.3	62.3							
20	62.4	62.1	66.2							
21	63.8	63.1	70.6							
22	65.5	63.8	76.0							
23	67.7	64.3	76.0							
24	69.6	64.9	76.0							
25	71.0	65.5								
26	72.3	66.1								
27	74.1	66.5								
28	78.0	67.1								
29	82.0	68.0								
30	84.0	68.6								
31		69.1								
32		69.8								
33		70.5								
34		71.4								
35		72.3								
36		73.4								
37		74.6								
38		75.1								
39		76.0								
40		77.0								
41		78.0								
42		82.0								
43		82.0								
44		82.0								
45		82.0								

by using a linear transformation to a mean of 50 and a standard deviation of 10. This linear transformation is accomplished by using the formula

$$F = \frac{X - M}{SD} (10 + 50)$$

where F = the final composite T-score; X = the initial composite T-score; M = the mean of the initial composite T-score; and SD = standard deviation of initial composite T-scores. The initial composite means and standard deviations are BC-1 ($\bar{X}$ = 49.63, SD = 6.54); BC-2 ($\bar{X}$ = 49.61, SD = 5.78); BC-3 ($\bar{X}$ = 49.63, SD = 6.18); and BC-4 ($\bar{X}$ = 49.42, SD = 7.54).

The final composite scores are rank ordered from largest to smallest. The offender's behavioral category is determined by the scale on which he or she obtains the highest composite final score. Thus, if the highest composite score is BC-3, this is the category to which this person is assigned.

Norms

Normative data on the three scales were obtained from 1,075 inmates at a number of federal youth correctional institutions across the country. The mean age of this sample was 19.3 years and the age range was 14.4–28.8. The 10 raw scores were transformed into normalized standard scores with means of 50 and standard deviations between 9 and 10.

Reliability

Internal reliability coefficients for the POS range from .62 to .92 depending upon the behavioral category being measured. The internal reliability coefficients for the BPC range from .68 to .89, and the coefficients for the CALHD range from .23 to .77. Four composite reliability coefficients for each of the behavioral areas were obtained from a linear combination of the KR-20 reliabilities of each scale into a single composite score. BC-1 had a composite reliability of .45, BC-2 was .82, BC-3 was .89 and BC-4 was .73. The interrater reliabilities for the BPC inventory on a sample of 126 kindergarten children were found to be .75 and .77 for two problem dimensions (Peterson, 1961). Other studies of interrater consistency have yielded variable results, ranging from .22 to .83 (Quay & Quay, 1965; Quay, Sprague, Shulman, & Miller, 1966; Quay & Parsons, 1970). No interrater or retest reliability coefficients were reported for the CALHD.

Test–retest reliability coefficients for each of the three categories measured on the POS were: BC-2 = .76, BC-3 = .75, and BC-4 = .61 (Quay & Parsons, 1970).

Validity

Factorial validity is presented as an integral part of the method of scale development. Quay reports that the scales and the obtained scores are reasonably empirically independent (Quay, 1964; Quay & Parsons, 1970). He notes that all four categories and all three instruments do differentiate between delinquents and nondelinquents. The BPC ratings have been found to differentiate high and low stimulation seekers (Skryzpek, 1969), those who have galvanic skin responses to auditory stimuli (Borkonec, 1970) and recidivist from non-recidivist delinquent males (Mack, 1969). Psychopathic delinquents identified on the POS test performed poorer than the other POS groups on an attention–concentration task (Orris, 1969).

The three scales have given evidence of being useful in combination. Confined youths identified as psychopathic were given a theoretically relevant treatment program and then compared to two quasi-control groups at the National Training School in Washington, D.C. (Ingram, Gerard, Quay, & Levinson, 1970). The group receiving the relevant program improved more in institutional adjustment.

Comments

The reliability of the DBCS appears to be well within the acceptable limits for an instrument of this kind. The validity is strengthened by the gathering of data from sources in addition to offender samples. The scoring procedure is not an overly complex one, considering that three instruments and four groupings are involved. The various behavior categories appear to be useful ones, and the instruments themselves seem to have generally adequate validity. While the weak link in this system is the present lack of reliability and validity research for the CALHD, overall the system has considerable research and applied promise for differentiation of confined delinquents in an empirically based manner related to treatment decisions.

REFERENCES

Borkonec, T. D. Autonomic reactivity to sensory stimulation in psychopathic, neurotic and normal delinquents. *Journal of Consulting and Clinical Psychology*, 1970, *35*, 217–222.

Ingram, G. L., Gerard, R. E., Quay, H. C., & Levinson, R. B. An experimental program for the psychopathic delinquent. *Journal of Research in Crime and Delinquency*, 1970, *7*, 24–30.

Mack, J. L. Behavior ratings of recidivist and nonrecidivist delinquent males. *Psychological Reports*, 1969, *25*, 260.

Orris, J. B. Visual monitoring performance in three subgroups of male delinquents. *Journal of Abnormal Psychology,* 1969, *74,* 227.

Peterson, D. R. Behavior problems of middle childhood. *Journal of Abnormal Psychology,* 1961, *25,* 205–209.

Quay, H. C. Personality dimensions in delinquent males as inferred from the factor analysis of behavior ratings. *Journal of Research in Crime and Delinquency,* 1964, *1,* 33–37.

Quay, H. C., & Quay, L. C. Behavior problems in early adolescence. *Child Development,* 1965, *36,* 215–220.

Quay, H. C., & Parsons, L. B. The Differential Behavioral Classification of the Juvenile Offenders. Morgantown, W. Va.: Robert F. Kennedy Youth Center, 1970.

Quay, H. C., Sprague, R. L., Shulman, H. S., & Miller, A. C. Some correlates of personality disorder and conduct disorder in a child guidance clinic sample. *Psychology in Schools,* 1966, *3,* 44–47.

Skryzpek, G. J. Effect of perceptual isolation and arousal on anxiety, complexity preference and novelty preference in psychopathic and neurotic delinquents. *Journal of Abnormal Psychology,* 1969, *74,* 321–329.

THE DIFFERENTIAL BEHAVIORAL CLASSIFICATION SYSTEM
Behavior Problem Checklist*†

Instructions: Please indicate which of the following constitute problems, as far as this child is concerned. If an item does not constitute a problem, encircle the zero; if an item constitutes a mild problem, encircle the one; if an item constitutes a severe problem, encircle the two. Please complete every item.

Scored on BC#		
	1.	Oddness, bizarre behavior.
3	2.	Restlessness, inability to sit still.
3	3.	Attention-seeking, "show-off" behavior.
4	4.	Stays out late at night.
2	5.	Doesn't know how to have fun; behaves like a little adult.
2	6.	Self-consciousness; easily embarrassed.
	7.	Fixed expression, lack of emotional reactivity.
3	8.	Disruptiveness; tendency to annoy and bother others.
2	9.	Feelings of inferiority.
4	10.	Steals in company with others.

3	11.	Boisterousness, rowdiness.
2	12.	Crying over minor annoyances and hurts.
1	13.	Preoccupation; "in a world of his own."
2	14.	Shyness, Bashfulness.
2	15.	Social withdrawal, preference for solitary activities.
3	16.	Dislike for school.
3	17.	Jealousy over attention paid other children.
4	18.	Belongs to a gang.
	19.	Repetitive speech.
1	20.	Short attention span.
2	21.	Lack of self-confidence.
	22.	Inattentiveness to what others say.
2	23.	Easily flustered and confused.
	24.	Incoherent speech.
3	25.	Fighting.
4	26.	Loyal to delinquent friends.
3	27.	Temper tantrums.
2	28.	Reticence, secretiveness.

Scored on BC#

4	29.	Truancy from school.
2	30.	Hypersensitivity; feelings easily hurt.
1	31.	Laziness in school and in performance of other tasks.
2	32.	Anxiety, chronic general fearfulness.
3	33.	Irresponsibility, undependability.
1	34.	Excessive daydreaming.
1	35.	Masturbation.
4	36.	Had bad companions.
2	37.	Tension, inability to relax.
3	38.	Disobedience, difficulty in disciplinary control.
2	39.	Depression, chronic sadness.
3	40.	Uncooperativeness in group situations.
2	41.	Aloofness, social reserve.

1	42.	Passivity, suggestibility; easily led by others.
	43.	Clumsiness, awkwardness, poor muscular coordination.
3	44.	Hyperactivity; "always on the go."
	45.	Distractibility.
3	46.	Destructiveness in regard to his own and/or other's property.
3	47.	Negativism, tendency to do the opposite of what is requested.
3	48.	Impertinence, sauciness.
1	49.	Sluggishness, lethargy.
1	50.	Drowsiness.
3	51.	Profane language, swearing, cursing.
	52.	Nervousness, jitteriness, jumpiness; easily startled.
3	53.	Irritability; hot-tempered, easily aroused to anger.
	54.	Enuresis, bed-wetting.
	55.	Often has physical complaints, e.g., headaches, stomach ache.

*Ten items on this inventory are not listed as belonging to a specific BC category.

†Although this inventory is scored on BC-1, BC-2, and BC-3 only, items 4, 10, 18, 26, and 36 have factor loadings above .48 on BC-4.

Behavior Checklist for the Analysis of Life History Data

Instructions: Place a check mark before each behavior trait which has been used in the history to describe the subject.

Scored on BC#

3	1.	Assaultive, attacks others with little or no provocation.
4	2.	Had bad companions.
4-2	3.	Seclusive, stays to himself.
3	4.	Initiates fights.
4	5.	Engages in gang activities.
4-2	6.	Shy.
3	7.	Cruel.
4	8.	Engages in cooperative stealing.
2	9.	Apathetic, emotionless.

Scored on BC#		
3	10.	Quarrelsome.
	11.	Loses interest quickly.
3	12.	Defies authority.
1	13.	Engages in furtive stealing.
2	14.	Worries.
	15.	Engages in malicious mischief.
	16.	Habitually truant from school.
2	17.	Sensitive.
1	18.	Unable to cope with a complex world.
2-3	19.	Timid.
	20.	Has inadequate guilt feelings.
1	21.	Habitually truant from home.
2	22.	Submissive.
4	23.	Stays out late at night.
3	24.	Irritable.
4	25.	Accepted by a delinquent subgroup.
2	26.	Lonesome.
3	27.	Verbally aggressive, impudent.
4	28.	Strong allegiance to selected peers.
1	29.	Incompetent, immature.
3	30.	Obscene, uses foul language.
3	31.	Feels persecuted, believes others unfair.
2	32.	Has anxiety over own behavior.
1	33.	Callous, little concern for others.
2-3	34.	Seems unable to profit by either praise or punishment.
	35.	Suspicious, trusts no one.
	36.	Has engaged in sex delinquency.

The Personal Opinion Study

Mark true or false.

Scored on BC#		
3-T	1.	The best teachers are the ones who are very easy.
4-T	2.	I would be a happier person if I could satisfy all of my parent's wishes.

Scored on BC#		
4-T	3.	Sometimes I wonder if I'll ever grow up.
4-T	4.	My folks usually blame bad company for the trouble I get into.
3-T	5.	In this world you're a fool if you trust other people.
4-T	6.	Before I do something, I try to consider how my friends will react to it.
4-T	7.	We ought to pay our elected officials better than we do.
4-T	8.	I never used to steal little things from the neighborhood stores.
3-T	9.	My teachers have given me lower grades than I deserve just because they think I am a troublemaker.
3-T	10.	I don't worry about the future; there's nothing much I can do about it anyway.
4-T	11.	I often say mean things to other people and then feel sorry for it afterwards.
3-T	12.	When I think I am right nobody can change my mind.
3-T	13.	I don't mind hurting people who get in my way.
3-T	14.	Most people are squares.
4-T	15.	I am always hurting the people I love the most.
2-T	16.	I am so touchy on some subjects that I can't talk about them.
3-T	17.	You have to get the other guy before he gets you.
4-T	18.	Most boys stay in school because the law says they have to.
3-F	19.	Policemen are friendly and try to help you.
3-T	20.	You have to admire somebody who has enough guts to talk back to a cop.
3-T	21.	One day I will get even with everybody who has done me dirty.
3-T	22.	I have never seen a policeman yet who cared about anyone but himself.
2-T	23.	I feel tired a good deal of the time.
2-T	24.	People seem to like me at first, but I have trouble keeping friends.
4-T	25.	When a group of boys get together they are bound to get into trouble sooner or later.
3-T	26.	You gotta fight to get what's coming to you.
2-F	27.	I never wish that I were dead.
3-T	28.	Only a fool would spend his life working a 40-hour week.
3-T	29.	I never worry about a thing.
2-T	30.	It seems as if people are always telling me what to do, or how to do things.
3-T	31.	I do what I want to do, whether anybody likes it or not.

Scored on BC#		
2-T	32.	At times I have a strong urge to do something harmful or shocking.
2-F	33.	I think people like me as much as they do other people.
2-T	34.	Even when things go right for a while I know it won't last.
3-T	35.	I can easily "shake it off" when I do something I know is wrong.
2-F	36.	I never have the habit of shaking my head, neck, or shoulder.
3-T	37.	A person is better off if he doesn't trust anyone.
3-T	38.	The best way to get ahead in the world is to be tough.
4-T	39.	It is very important to have enough friends and social life.
3-T	40.	All this talk about honesty and justice is a lot of nonsense.
4-T	41.	There is something wrong with a person who can't take orders without getting angry or resentful.
4-T	42.	I am doing as much or as well as my parents expect me to.
2-T	43.	When I see people laughing I often think they are laughing at me.
3-T	44.	The only way to settle anything is to lick the guy.
3-T	45.	It's dumb to trust older people.
2-T	46.	I just can't stop doing things that I am sorry for later.
4-T	47.	For all the things I have done I should have been punished more than I have.
2-T	48.	I usually feel well and strong.
2-T	49.	I sometimes feel that no one loves me.
4-T	50.	When I was going to school I played hooky quite often.
2-T	51.	My future looks bright.
4-T	52.	I find it hard to "drop" or "break with" a friend.
2-T	53.	Sometimes I think I won't live very long.
3-T	54.	It doesn't matter what you do as long as you get your kicks.
4-T	55.	I wish I had not been such a disappointment to my family.
3-T	56.	The most important thing is to win no matter how.
3-F	57.	Everyone should be required to finish high school.
3-T	58.	I owe my family nothing.
2-F	59.	My feelings are never hurt so badly that I cry.
3-T	60.	The only way to make big money is to steal it.
4-T	61.	In school I was sometimes sent to the principal for cutting up.
4-F	62.	I have never been in trouble with the law.
3-T	63.	The worst thing a person can do is to get caught.

Scored on BC#		
2-T	64.	I don't think I'm quite as happy as others seem to be.
2-T	65.	I sometimes wish I'd never been born.
3-T	66.	A guy's only protection is his friends.
3-T	67.	A person who steals from the rich isn't really a thief.
4-T	68.	I have had a real fight.
2-T	69.	My way of doing things is apt to be misunderstood by others.
3-T	70.	If you're clever enough, you can steal anything and get away with it.
4-T	71.	The average policeman is not strict enough about the law.
3-T	72.	The only way to get what you want is to take it.
2-T	73.	I must admit I find it very hard to work under strict rules and regutions.
3-T	74.	Success in this world is a matter of luck.
2-T	75.	I often get nervous; I have to get up and move around to calm myself down.
3-T	76.	Nobody has ever called me "chicken" and gotten by with it.
2-T	77.	I just don't seem to get the breaks other people do.
2-T	78.	I get so angry that I "see red."
2-T	79.	It's hard to get others to like me.
3-T	80.	I don't really care what happens to me.
4-T	81.	No matter how hard I try I always get caught.
2-T	82.	My eyes often pain me.
3-T	83.	Women are only good for what you can get out of them.
2-T	84.	My life is pretty boring and dull most of the time.
4-T	85.	I have been expelled from school or nearly expelled.
3-T	86.	The only way to make out is to be tough.
2-T	87.	It is hard for me to just sit still and relax.
3-T	88.	Once you've been in trouble, you haven't got a chance.
3-T	89.	Hitting someone sometimes makes me feel good inside.
3-T	90.	Being successful usually means having your name in the paper.
2-T	91.	Even when things go right I know it won't last.
2-T	92.	I'd like to start a new life somewhere else.
3-T	93.	If you don't have enough to live on, it's OK to steal.
3-F	94.	It is important to think about what you do.
3-T	95.	I can outwit almost anybody.

4-T	96.	On my report card I usually get some failure marks.
2-T	97.	I feel that I have often been punished without cause.
3-T	98.	Whenever I do something I shouldn't, it worries me.
3-T	99.	It's all right to steal from the rich because they don't need it.
4-T	100.	Sometimes I have stolen things I really didn't want.

Family Information Test

Development and Characteristics

The *Family Information Test* (FIT) was designed to serve as an "indicator of commitment to delinquency and of potential for treatment" (Venezia, 1968, p. 148). Venezia asserts that delinquent boys are "characterized by premature autonomy, attitudinal distance from the family, and lack of factual knowledge about family members" (p. 148). It is proposed that the rejection of the family and parental authority indicates a propensity to delinquency, and that the stronger the rejection of the family the less likely treatment will be successful.

Venezia (1968) suggests that rejection of family and parental authority might be measured by the amount of "family information" an individual is able to recall. For example, a person who rejected his or her family would be less likely to remember the ages of brothers and sisters than one who felt close family ties. Accordingly, the amount of factual information one recalls about one's family should indicate the degree of attachment one feels for the family, and acceptance of familial and parental authority. Thirty-two factual questions were developed to measure this level of family knowledge and constitute the basis for the FIT.

Response Mode

The scale can be disguised as part of the normal intake procedure and presented along with other information such as address and telephone number or the respondent may be asked to supply written or oral responses to the questions.

Scoring

A "don't know" or a guess response to a question is considered a failure and receives a score of 1, except for questions (13–17) for fathers and (25–29) for mothers who had been out of the home for one year or more, and a stepparent was not in the home. In these cases, those questions are scored one-fourth incorrect. Also, if a parent has been deceased for more than one year, the above mentioned questions are omitted and responses to all "don't know" and guess answers about the parent are scored one-fourth incorrect. (This eliminates the effects of forgetting information about an individual who is no longer a family member.) The final score is a total number of incorrect answers, rounded to the nearest whole number. Therefore, the higher the score, the less family information an individual possesses, the greater commitment to delinquency, and the less the likelihood for successful treatment.

Norms

Because the distribution of FIT raw scores was skewed and therefore inappropriate for parametric procedures, they were normalized by a modified square root transformation ($\sqrt{10(x + .5)}$). Table 36 shows the results of obtained score transformations.

The means of age, IQ, and FIT scores for a number of groups of subjects are presented in Table 37. These groups represent: (1) 312 delinquent boys between the ages of 13 and 16 who had been adjudicated and placed in a probationary program; (2) 16 of the above delinquent boys who had delinquent siblings; (3) 100 nondelinquent boys who had been selected as "good citizens of the academic community," but who were not achieving above average academ-

TABLE 36. Transformed Score Values for All Obtained FIT Scores

x	x_t	x	x_t
28	16.9	13	11.6
27	16.6	12	11.2
26	16.3	11	10.7
25	16.0	10	10.2
24	15.7	9	9.7
23	15.3	8	9.2
22	15.0	7	8.7
21	14.7	6	8.1
20	14.3	5	7.4
19	14.0	4	6.7
18	13.6	3	5.9
17	13.2	2	5.0
16	12.8	1	3.9
15	12.4	0	2.2
14	12.0		

TABLE 37. IQ, Age, and FIT Means of Experimental and Control Groups and Their Subgroups

	N	Mean		
		IQ	Age	FIT
All delinquent boys	312	86.0	14.5	10.30
Delinquent siblings	16	86.75	14.9	10.42
All nondelinquent boys	100	89.88	14.5	7.19
All nonsiblings	84	89.95	14.0	6.91
Nondelinquent siblings	16	90.31	14.1	9.33
Matched nondelinquent nonsiblings	16	87.63	14.1	6.81

ically. Other criteria for inclusion were a lack of prior police contacts and a distribution of age, ethnic group, and IQ characteristics within the group similar to that of the delinquent group, (4) 84 of the above nondelinquents who had no delinquent siblings; (5) 16 of the nondelinquent boys who had delinquent siblings; and (6) 16 nondelinquents who had been matched according to age and IQ with the delinquents who had delinquent siblings.

Note that FIT scores decrease as the respondents have less contact with delinquency.

Reliability

Reliability was determined using the split-half method. Since the test has sections that deal with different family members, two divisions were made, each using a random number table to order the questions. The odd-even coefficients for 312 delinquents and 101 delinquents (reordered) were both .59. When the Spearman-Brown prophesy formula was applied, a full scale estimate of .75 was obtained.

Validity

The FIT was administered to a group of 100 institutionalized delinquents and 120 nondelinquents in a pilot study. The results indicated that nondelinquents were able to answer four times as many items as delinquents.

Further evidence of validity can be noted from the table presented in the norms section. FIT scores (errors) increase as the group has more contact with delinquency. For example, delinquent boys score high (10.30), but delinquents with delinquent siblings score even higher (10.42). Nondelinquents score lower, and nondelinquents who have no delinquent siblings score even lower. Finally, nondelinquent boys who have delinquent siblings score much higher than matched nondelinquents who do not have delinquent siblings.

When FIT scores were correlated with staff member ratings of institutionalized delinquents, a correlation coefficient of .78 ($p < .001$) was obtained between FIT scores and "most delinquent versus least delinquent" ratings, .65 ($p < .001$) between FIT and "fair and poor versus excellent and good prognoses," and .53 ($p < .002$) between FIT and "formal gang versus peripheral and nonmembers."

Finally, when the FIT was used to predict outcomes of the institutionalization (i.e., graduated, A.W.O.L., removed, etc.), a predictive efficiency of 30% was obtained.

Comments

Although the FIT is developed from a theoretical position that might appear to be tenuous, its rationale, that tendency toward delinquency would pull one away from the family, is reasonable. In addition, there is support for reliability and validity and the hint that the scale may be "on target" as an indicator of delinquency commitment.

REFERENCES

Venezia, P. Delinquency as a function of intrafamily relationships. *Journal of Research in Crime and Delinquency,* 1968, 5, 148–173.

FAMILY INFORMATION TEST

Directions:

1. Before interviewing a boy, obtain a description of the family constellation from his case file. Indicate on the answer sheet the absence, and its duration, of any immediate family member from the home; for example: "Father dead 10 years — stepfather in home 7 years." When the parent substitute has been in the home more than one year, the questions about "father" should be applied to the stepfather. Indicate the whereabouts of any sibling who has been out of the home for more than a year. Any facts of this nature that are not made clear in the case file may be checked with the boy, after all questions have been asked.

2. Interview each boy privately, as part of an intake interview for face-sheet data. Do not prompt him to correct his answers. Ask each question in a neutral, nonprobing manner. However, establish some degree of rapport with the boy to insure his cooperation in trying to answer the questions correctly.

3. Make every effort to determine whether each answer given by a boy is a guess (an approximation) or a fact of which he is certain.

4. Use the following recording system: Fact — an answer given as a certainty; D.K. — an "I don't know" response to a question; Guess — an uncertain response (I think maybe . . . I'm not sure . . . About . . . Around . . . I guess). Indicate the response to each part of a multipart question. Verbatim answers may also be recorded if you wish; their content is often significant from a casework standpoint.

Siblings: Do not apply to siblings deceased or living out of the home more than one year.

1. What is the full name of each of your brothers and sisters? (The middle name is the item of importance here.)
2. How old is each of your brothers and sisters?
3. What is the birthday of each of your brothers and sisters?
4. What does each one like to do in his spare time?
5. What important sicknesses or accidents has each one had?
6. In what city did your parents meet each other?
7. How long have they been together?
8. When is their wedding anniversary? (Explain if necessary.)

Father: Apply the questions to stepfather, etc., if appropriate.

9. What is your father's first and middle name?
10. How old is he?
11. In what city was he born?
12. What is his birthday?
13. What kind of job does he do? (Get job description.)
14. Whom does he work for? (The name of the employer.)
15. On what street is his job located?
16. What does he do in his spare time?
17. What important sicknesses or accidents has he had?
18. In what city did he go to school?
19. What grade did he finish in school?

Mother: Use stepmother, etc., if appropriate.

20. What is your mother's first, middle and maiden name?
21. How old is she?
22. In what city was she born?
23. What is her birthday?
24. What kind of work does she do?
25. Whom does she work for? (The name of her employer.)

26. On what street is her job located?
27. What does she do in her spare time?
28. What important sicknesses or accidents has she had?
29. In what city did she go to school?
30. What grade did she finish in school?
31. If anyone in your home has died, what did he die of?
32. In what city (or town) were you born?

Future Events Test

Development and Characteristics

The *Future Events Test* (FET) was designed to measure the degree to which an individual has been socialized to schedule various goals and future events (Stein, Sarbin, & Kulik, 1968). It is assumed that delinquents have not been socialized adequately to have a realistic perspective on scheduling future events and thus would attempt to attain some goals prematurely and inappropriately.

Items for the FET were obtained from a group of delinquent and nondelinquent boys who were asked to list events they expected to occur in their lives. The resultant responses were written in the form of items and combined to form the 36 items of the FET.

Response Mode

The respondent is asked to read each of the 36 future events and decide, first, whether he ever expects to experience it. If not, he is requested to circle "never." If he feels this event will occur in the future, he is asked to estimate how old he will be when it happens.

Scoring

A single total score is obtained by averaging the ages estimated for the occurrence of future events. This eliminates the effects of events that are not applicable to an individual. It is assumed that the larger the score, the more the respondent is able to delay gratification. This delay is believed to represent more internalized socialization.

Norms

Stein *et al.* (1968) report (see Table 38) the means and standard deviations for 100 delinquents (boys with records of adjudication and institutionalization)

TABLE 38. Means and Standard Deviations of Mean Future Age Scores of Matched and Random Samples of Nondelinquent and Delinquent Boys[a]

Sample	Nondelinquent		Delinquent		t
	M	SD	M	SD	
Matched	29.77	3.955	27.49	4.146	3.950[b]
Random	29.88	4.256	27.04	4.321	4.127[b]

[a] $N = 100$ for both samples of nondelinquent and delinquent boys.
[b] $p < .01$.

and 100 nondelinquents who were matched according to age, race, vocabulary–intelligence scores, and social status. A second sample of 100 delinquents and 100 nondelinquents was selected at random for purposes of replication.

Reliability

No reliability estimates are available

Validity

As presented in the *Norms* section, the time estimates yielded a higher mean age for nondelinquents than delinquents, supporting the assertion that nondelinquents (with more internalized socialization) predict delays in the attainment of some goals. Further individual item analyses show more homogeneity of response for the more socialized group. This finding would be expected as a result of similar socialization processes.

Comments

The FET has support for validity, but lacks reliability information. In addition, uncertainty as to whether the difference in projected ages discriminates finely enough to be useful for individual applications or would be significant for a smaller sample remains. Another consideration that might affect the results is the possibility that nondelinquents might anticipate the occurrence of events that usually take place at a later age. That is, they might expect to go to college or become famous, etc., while delinquents only anticipate buying a car. This would inflate the age score for nondelinquents unless they were noncollege bound.

REFERENCES

Stein, K. B., Sarbin, T. R., & Kulik, J. A. Future time perspective: Its relation to the socialization process and the delinquent role. *Journal of Consulting and Clinical Psychology,* 1968, *32,* 257–264.

FUTURE EVENTS TEST

Listed below are a number of events that may happen sometime during the course of a person's life. Please read each one and decide whether you think each event will happen in your future. If you think it will not happen, circle "Never" in the first column. If you think it will happen, please make a guess as to how old you will be when the event will happen. Write this future age in the blank line. If the event has already occurred write the age at which you expect the event to happen again or circle "Never" if you don't expect it to happen again.

		IF YOU THINK IT WILL NOT HAPPEN, CIRCLE "NEVER"	IF YOU THINK IT WILL HAPPEN, GUESS AGE
1.	Finish college	Never	_____
2.	Visit a foreign country	Never	_____
3.	Have a new car	Never	_____
4.	Get a job you really want	Never	_____
5.	Get married	Never	_____
6.	Have an auto accident	Never	_____
7.	Die	Never	_____
8.	Buy a home	Never	_____
9.	Get a ticket for fast driving	Never	_____
10.	Move to another city	Never	_____
11.	Own a gun and rifle	Never	_____
12.	Get drunk	Never	_____
13.	Get rich	Never	_____
14.	Be a strong man	Never	_____
15.	Have first child	Never	_____
16.	Be hospitalized	Never	_____
17.	Fly an airplane	Never	_____
18.	Own a boat	Never	_____
19.	Graduate from high school	Never	_____
20.	Retire from job	Never	_____
21.	Long vacation	Never	_____
22.	Go to jail	Never	_____
23.	Become a grandfather	Never	_____
24.	Friend will die	Never	_____

25. Be satisfied with yourself	Never	_____
26. Win lots of money	Never	_____
27. Get a scholarship	Never	_____
28. Enjoy life your own way	Never	_____
29. Have sporty clothes	Never	_____
30. Be a hero	Never	_____
31. Your first child gets married	Never	_____
32. Be a big timer	Never	_____
33. Have flashy apartment	Never	_____
34. Become a great athlete	Never	_____
35. Be some kind of leader	Never	_____
36. Be famous	Never	_____

Jesness Inventory

Development and Characteristics

The *Jesness Inventory* (JIN) developed in the Fricot Ranch Project, a five-year research program on delinquency, was created to meet the need for an instrument that would reliably measure personality types while remaining sensitive to change over relatively short periods of time (Jesness, 1962). It was designed to distinguish disturbed or delinquent children from normals and to provide a basis for a meaningful child or adolescent personality typology.

An original pool of 250 items was reduced to 155 by eliminating items that did not discriminate between delinquent or disturbed and normal children or that were difficult for children to understand. A final modification in wording made the instrument suitable for use with a wider age range and with both sexes.

The JIN has 11 scales. Three of these (social maladjustment, value orientation, and immaturity) were derived from an item analysis of criterion groups. Seven of the scales were derived by cluster analysis. Both the item and cluster analyses were based on 970 delinquent and 1,075 nondelinquent males, ages 8 through 18. The majority of the delinquents came from reception centers of the California Youth Authority while the nondelinquents came from 10 California public schools, most of which were in "lower-class" socioeconomic areas. An effort was made to remove subjects with delinquent histories from the nondelinquent sample. A final scale, the *Asocial Index,* was based on a regression equation derived through use of a discriminate function analysis.

The 11 scales listed with the number of items and characteristics the scales are designed to measure are:

(1) *Social Maladjustment* (*SM*–63 items), attitudes common to persons unable to meet environmental demands in socially approved ways;
(2) *Value Orientation* (*VO*–39 items), attitudes and opinions characteristic of the lower socioeconomic classes;
(3) Immaturity (*Imm*–45 items), attitudes and perceptions of self and others which are inappropriate for the subject's age level;
(4) *Autism* (*Au*–28 items), tendency to distort reality in accordance with the individual's personal needs;
(5) *Alienation* (*Al*–26 items), degree of distrust and estrangement in attitudes towards others, especially authority figures;
(6) *Manifest Aggression* (*MA*–31 items), awareness of and discomfort concerning the control of unpleasant emotions, especially anger and frustration;
(7) *Withdrawal* (*Wd*–24 items), perceived lack of satisfaction with self and others, and a tendency toward isolation from others;
(8) *Social Anxiety* (*SA*–24 items), perceived emotional discomfort associated with interpersonal relationships;
(9) *Repression* (*Rep*–15 items), exclusion from conscious awareness of emotions and feelings or the individual's failure to label these emotions;
(10) *Denial* (*Den*–20 items), reluctance to acknowledge unpleasant events or aspects of reality; and
(11) *Asocial Index,* tendency to resolve social and personal adjustment problems in ways that show a disregard for social customs or rules.

Response Mode

Respondents are requested to read each item and indicate whether the statement is true for them.

Scoring

The 155 items of the JIN are answered "true" or "false" by the subject. Most of the items are scored on more than one scale, and several are scored on different scales in opposite directions.

The SM^x items are items of the *SM* scale that showed more than 20 percentage points separation between delinquents and nondelinquents at every age level. The SM^x score is used only in calculating the *Asocial Index,* which utilizes weighted raw scores obtained from conversion tables (Jesness, 1966) in the following formula: *(SM + SM^x) − (VO + Au + Al + MA + Wd + SA + Rep)* for males or *(SM + SM^x) − (VO + Au + Al + MA + Wd + SA + Den)* for females.

Norms

Jesness (1966) presented tables for converting raw scores to standard scores at each age level for both sexes. These standard scores were based on norms from a nondelinquent sample. Also given was the proportion of delinquent and nondelinquent subjects scoring at or above each *Asocial Index* score level. Actual raw score means and standard deviations for only the 15-year-old subjects, male and female, delinquent and nondelinquent, may be seen in Table 39.

Further raw score norms are available in Kelly and Baer (1969) and Fisher (1967). Kelly and Baer presented means and standard deviations for 60 male delinquents. Fisher gave means and standard deviations for 203 English Borstal boys, and for the 16, 17, and 18-year-old male delinquent and nondelinquent samples on which the JIN was developed.

TABLE 39. Means and Standard Deviations for 15-Year-Old Male and Female Delinquents and Nondelinquents on 10 Scales of the Jesness Inventory[a]

Scale	Group	Males[b] M	Males[b] SD	Females[c] M	Females[c] SD
SM	Delinquent	26.6	6.8	26.3	6.1
	Nondelinquent	18.7	6.1	17.7	6.3
VO	Delinquent	15.9	7.6	15.9	6.1
	Nondelinquent	13.7	7.1	12.4	7.3
Imm	Delinquent	13.2	4.5	12.4	3.5
	Nondelinquent	11.6	3.7	11.9	3.6
Au	Delinquent	7.7	4.1	7.6	3.3
	Nondelinquent	6.3	3.1	6.1	3.4
Al	Delinquent	8.4	5.3	7.9	4.6
	Nondelinquent	7.2	4.3	5.3	3.7
MA	Delinquent	15.4	6.9	15.2	5.4
	Nondelinquent	14.2	5.3	14.0	5.5
Wd	Delinquent	12.5	3.7	13.4	3.5
	Nondelinquent	11.3	2.8	12.3	3.2
SA	Delinquent	13.3	4.4	15.4	3.8
	Nondelinquent	13.7	3.5	15.4	3.6
Rep	Delinquent	3.7	2.6	3.4	2.1
	Nondelinquent	3.2	2.4	3.6	2.6
Den	Delinquent	12.2	3.7	10.2	3.4
	Nondelinquent	12.7	3.7	11.7	4.0
Asocial Index[d]	Delinquent	25.0	5.0	25.0	5.0
	Nondelinquent	15.0	5.0	15.0	5.0

[a] Modified from Jesness (1966).
[b] Delinquents: $N = 135$. Nondelinquents: $N = 123$.
[c] Delinquents: $N = 103$. Nondelinquents: $N = 105$.
[d] Estimated from data for combined age groups.

Reliability

Corrected odd-even reliability for 10 of the scales was calculated based on a sample of 1,862 boys, ages 10 to 18. With this sample of equal numbers of delinquents and nondelinquents, the reliability coefficients ranged from a low of .62 for *Wd* to a high of .88 for *VO*. The median reliability was .73.

Test–retest reliability was obtained on a sample of 131 delinquent males, ages 14 to 21. The testings occurred before and after the subjects had been in one of two state training schools for about eight months. The test–retest reliability coefficients ranged from a low of .40 on *Al* to a high of .79 on *SM* and *VO*. The median reliability was .66.

Validity

Validity data for the JIN come from a wide variety of sources. First, in the normative groups on which the inventory was developed, the delinquents scored significantly higher on the *SM, VO, Au, Al, MA, Wd,* and *Asocial Index* scales of the JIN. Of these, the *Asocial Index* yielded the largest difference between the groups. Delinquents also tended to score higher on the *Imm* and *Rep* scales, and lower on the *Den* scale.

Point–biserial correlation coefficients between scale scores and the delinquency–nondelinquency dichotomy ranged from $+.01$ on *SA* to $+.52$ on *SM* for males, and from $+.06$ on *SA* and *MA* to $+.55$ on *SM* for females. The highest correlation with delinquency, for both males and females, was $+.67$ for the *Asocial Index*.

Second, behavioral data were correlated with scores on the JIN scales for 210 delinquents, ages 10 to 14, in the Fricot Ranch Project (Jesness, 1962, 1966). The behavioral data came from a number of sources, including staff ratings, peer sociometric ratings, histories, school achievement, WISC IQs, achievement test scores, Rorschach responses, and semantic differential scale scores.

The behavioral data related to high scores on the scales are as follows:

SM: Poor social relationships with peers, aggressive behavior, poor school performance, and low WISC IQs.

VO: A tendency toward nonconforming, rule-violating behavior, lack of responsibility, and alienation in relations with adults.

Imm: Conforming, nonaggressive behavior, low social status, and low WISC IQs, below average achievement test scores, retardation in school, little insight, and poor social poise.

Au: Deviant Rorschach responses, fragmented, disjointed speech, lack of insight, social immaturity, lack of responsibility, a tendency toward hostile, aggressive behavior, being easily perturbed, and low social status.

Al: Nonconforming behavior, negative attitudes towards police, and history of group-related or gang-type delinquent activity.

MA: Showed the highest relationship of any scale with aggressive, assaultive behavior, and was also significantly related to a history of difficulty with peers.

Wd: Retarded, depressed behavior, and a history of isolation from others.

SA: Delinquent acts committed alone, problems with peers, ratings of retarded depression.

Rep: Low achievement test scores, low IQ, flat affect, lack of insight, and lack of social poise.

Den: Conforming social behavior and responsibility, high social status, and high achievement test scores.

The JIN also was administered to 60 male delinquents immediately before and after participation in a 27-day Outward Bound program. Significant changes occurred in the "healthy" or nondelinquent direction on 6 of 10 scales: *SM, VO, MA, Al, Au,* and *Rep* (Kelly & Baer, 1969).

In a study of 106 institutionalized delinquent boys, ages 12 to 18, Cowden, Peterson, and Pacht (1969) compared upper and lower thirds on the JIN distribution, using ratings of institutional adjustment made by counselors, social workers, and psychiatrists. These various ratings previously had been shown to be accurate indices of actual postrelease adjustment, as well as of institutional adjustment. High scores on the *SM, Al, VO, Imm* and *Asocial Index* scales of the JIN (ranked in order of their significance and consistency as predictors) were most clearly predictive of a poor prognosis and a poor institutional adjustment.

In a study of 161 male institutionalized delinquents, the lowest 14 and the highest 15 *Asocial Index* scorers were followed on postrelease adjustment for 4 to 7 months (Woychick, 1970). Significantly more of the high scorers were runaways or suffered parole revocation.

Jesness (1966) reports very high correlations between the JIN scales and *California Personality Inventory* (CPI) scales for a sample of 324 male and female delinquents, aged 10 to 20. The CPI scales with which each scale of the JIN correlated most highly are: *SM* ($-.76$), *VO* ($-.84$), and *Rep* ($+.59$) with CPI Achievement Via Conformity; *Au* ($-.69$) and *MA* ($-.88$) with CPI Socialization; *Wd* ($-.64$) and *SA* ($-.61$) with CPI Responsibility; *Den* ($+.72$) and *Al* ($-.71$) with CPI Intellectual Efficiency; *Imm* ($+.55$) with CPI Good Impression.

Finally, Jesness (1966) conducted a special study on the "fakeability" of the JIN. A group of 57 delinquent males was administered the scales on two successive days under different instructions. On the first or "honesty set" testing, the subjects were told the scores would be confidential and used for research purposes only. In the second or "fake good" testing, the subjects were told that their scores would be used by the institution's classification officer. Under these "fake good" conditions, three scales (*SM, VO,* and *Al*) changed significantly ($p < .05$) to the "healthier" direction.

Comments

The JIN was one of the first instruments of its kind to be developed specifically for use with delinquent subjects. Its merits are numerous—easy administration and objective scoring, a relatively large normative sample, adequate reliability, and a wide variety of data indicating better than average validity. It is useful in applied as well as research settings.

One deficiency is the lack of an interpretive principle that would allow a synthesis of the individual scale scores. Although the *Asocial Index* combines scores from eight of the scales, it would seem that much could be gained from a profile interpretation of the 11 scale scores.

REFERENCES

Cowden, J. E., Peterson, W. M., & Pacht, A. R. The MCI vs. the Jesness Inventory as a screening and classification instrument at a juvenile correctional institution. *Journal of Clinical Psychology,* 1969, 25, 57–60.

Fisher, R. M. Acquiescent response set, the Jesness Inventory, and implications for the use of "foreign" psychological tests. *British Journal of Social and Clinical Psychology,* 1967, 6, 1–10.

Jesness, C. G. *The Jesness Inventory: Development and validation.* California Youth Authority Research Report No. 29, March 1962.

Jesness, C. G. *The Jesness Inventory Manual.* Palo Alto, Cal.: Consulting Psychologists Press, 1966.

Kelly, F. J., & Baer, D. J. Jesness Inventory and self-concept measures for delinquents before and after participation in Outward Bound. *Psychological Reports,* 1969, 25, 719–724.

Woychick, T. Asociability Index scores' relationship to adjustment of youthful offenders. *Correctional Psychologist,* 1970, 4, 68–72.

JESNESS INVENTORY

This scale is commercially distributed by Consulting Psychologists Press, Inc., 577 College Avenue, Palo Alto, California 94306. The following are sample items.

When you're in trouble, it's best to keep quiet about it.

Sometimes I wish I could quit school.

It is easy for me to talk to strangers.

My father is too busy to worry much about me, or spend much time with me.

You can hardly believe what parents tell you.

Other people are happier than I am.

It is hard for me to talk to my parents about my troubles.

At home I am punished too much for things I don't do.

If you're not in with the gang, you may be in for some real trouble.

I feel alone even when there are other people around me.

Sometimes it seems like I'd rather get into trouble, instead of trying to stay away from it.

Miniature Situations Test

Characteristics and Development

The *Miniature Situations Test* (MST) was designed to assess ways an individual "responds to actual, physical stimuli of some potential significance to him rather than to conceptually or verbally defined stimuli" (Santostefano, 1960, p. 373). This instrument consists of 41 situations, pairs of acts, individually administered. The subjects are shown the two situations and asked to choose and perform one. Examples of the MST pairs are:

Examining with hand exterior of a box
Looking at a concealed picture

Driving in a spike
Pulling out a spike

Breaking a light bulb
Watering a plant

Reading a speech
Copying a speech

S handcuffing E
E handcuffing S

The MST is designed to allow individuals to cope with people and objects (rather than with paper and pencil) in ways that yield unequivocally identifiable behavioral acts.

Response Mode

The subjects are presented each pair in specified left-right order on a desk top in front of them. They are instructed to choose quickly one "game" and perform it, making use of the feelings they experience.

Scoring

The task preference is recorded.

Norms

Table 40 presents selected choice percentages for groups of "cell house" and "honor" incarcerated delinquent youth.

TABLE 40. Situations Discriminating between Honor and Cell House Delinquents (Percentage Choosing Each Act)

Situation	Honor delinquents	Cell house delinquents	χ^2
1. Knock flag down vs.	15	42	
raise flag	85	58	5.49[a]
2. Measure strength vs.	49	74	
honor Lincoln	51	26	4.05[a]
3. Tie E's wrist vs. help E	18	53	
put on gloves	82	47	8.70[b]
4. E reads to S vs. S reads	56	84	
to E	44	16	5.84[a]
5. Strike glass with hammer	18	45	
vs. refuse to strike glass	82	55	5.25[a]
6. Break large bulb vs.	44	71	
break small bulb	56	29	4.86[a]
7. Stick pin in cushion vs.	13	34	
place coin in Buddha			
doll	87	66	3.79[c]
8. Scribble on paper vs.	35	60	
erase line	65	40	3.74[c]
9. Play hard game vs. play	95	79	
easy game	5	21	3.02[c]

[a] Significance level .05.
[b] Significance level .01.
[c] Significance level .06.

Reliability

No information available.

Validity

A factor analysis of the performances of 150 randomly selected male high school students yielded five definable factors (Santostefano, 1960). The factors and the highest item loadings are displayed in Table 41.

A later validation contrasted the MST performances of 38 cell house delinquents (with poor behavioral controls) to 39 honor delinquents (responsible, with

TABLE 41. Items with Highest Factor Loads for 150 High School Students

1. Expressing (vs. inhibiting) overt forceful aggressions.	
Breaking a large light bulb	
Breaking a small light bulb	.80
Breaking a light bulb	
Watering a plant	.60
Driving in a spike	
Pulling out a spike	.55
2. Avoiding (vs. approaching) unknown stimuli interpreted as potentially injurious and difficult.	
Playing an easy unknown game	
Playing a hard unknown game	1.00^a
S shocking E	
E shocking S	.50
3. Displaying the self in conspicuous, solo behavior (vs. avoiding this display).	
S reading to E	
E reading to S	.66
Reciting a speech	
Copying a speech	.64
4. Expressing symbolic aggression (vs. expressing order and cleanliness).	
Scattering sawdust	
Sweeping sawdust	.63
Tearing paper	
Repairing paper	.51
5. Exercising control over others (vs. accepting control).	
S timing sorting cards	
S sorting cards for E	.47
S handcuffing E	
E handcuffing S	.43

^{a}This loading appears highly suspect.

good behavioral controls) (Santostefano & Wilson, 1968). Six situations distinguished between the groups significantly at the .05 level. Four of these situations dealt with authority. The two delinquent groups were surprisingly alike in several respects, suggesting needs for nurturance (preference of fur feeling to sandpaper), internalization of blame, immaturity, and staying with familiar tasks.

Comments

The MST is of interest because of the nature of its tasks and subjects' behavioral modes of responding. It represents an action alternative to paper and pencil testing and for that reason, holds promise for research uses with offender groups. Only limited norms, however, and no reliability data are available. The validity research produced five factors in one study and very modest evidence of the MST's ability to differentiate between contrasted groups. The key studies for validating the MST are yet to be performed: (1) Those studies contrasting paper-and-pencil tests with MST in populations that rationally would differ; and (2) studies relating MST results to more extensive, empirical manifestations of personality.

REFERENCES

Santostefano, S. An exploration of performance measures of personality. *Journal of Clinical Psychology*, 1960, *16*, 373–377.

Santostefano, S., & Wilson, G. Construct validity of the Miniature Situations Test. II. The performance of institutional delinquents and high school adolescents. *Journal of Clinical Psychology*, 1968, *24*, 355–358.

Way it Looks to Me—Self-Concept Inventory

Development and Characteristics

The *Way It Looks To Me* (WILTM) self-concept inventory was designed to measure and identify the self-concept reported by potentially delinquent children from the ages of 12 to 14 years (Dinitz & Reckless, 1962). An initial pool of self-concept items was administered to a group of sixth-grade boys. Sixteen items were found to discriminate between those who were rated as potentially delinquent and nondelinquent by teachers who had had at least eight months contact with the students. To these 16 items, another 16 "filler" items were added to give a total of 32. A short version of 14 items, 7 significant and 7 fillers, has also been devised.

The rationale for the WILTM is that self-concept and socialization patterns have developed by the age of 12, and that self-concept reflects socialization, which, in turn, is an indicator of whether adjustment to societal demands is favorable or unfavorable.

Response Mode

The developers suggest that the scale and instructions be read aloud to circumvent reading problems. Therefore, the respondent hears and reads along with each item that is in the form of a question. He or she is asked to mark whether his or her response to the question is "yes," "no," or "don't know" for all except the last five (in the long version), which ask for "often," "never," "sometimes," or other particular responses (see Items 28, 29, 30, 31, and 32).

Scoring

The even-numbered items are the significant ones and are the ones scored. Tables 42 and 43 show the scores for each item in a long and in a short form, respectively.

TABLE 42. Scoring Keys (Long Form)

Item	Scoring[a]		
2	Y = 3	N = 1	DK = 2
4	Y = 3	N = 1	DK = 2
6	Y = 3	N = 1	DK = 2
8	Y = 1	N = 3	DK = 2
10	Y = 1	N = 3	DK = 2
12	Y = 3	N = 1	DK = 2
14	Y = 3	N = 1	DK = 2
16	Y = 3	N = 1	DK = 2
18	Y = 3	N = 1	DK = 2
20	Y = 3	N = 1	DK = 2
22	Y = 1	N = 3	DK = 2
24	Y = 3	N = 1	DK = 2
26	Y = 3	N = 1	DK = 2
28	O = 1	N = 3	S = 2
30	O = 3	N = 3	S = 1
32	O = 1	A = 2	Ac. = 3

[a] The answers "often" and "never" were both equal in the unfavorable direction and this is the reason for giving "O" and "N" each a value of 3 and for giving "3" ("sometimes") a value of 1 (which is the most favorable answer for the question).

TABLE 43. Scoring Keys (Short Form)

Item	Scoring		
2	Y = 3	N = 1	DK = 2
4	Y = 1	N = 3	DK = 2
6	Y = 1	N = 2	DK = 2
8	Y = 3	N = 1	DK = 2
10	Y = 3	N = 1	DK = 2
12	Y = 3	N = 1	DK = 2
14	Y = 1	N = 3	DK = 2

The final score is a total of the item scores. Since these are in the direction of "low" self-concept, a high score is indicative of potential for delinquency.

Norms

No norms were presented.

Reliability

No reliability measures were available.

Validity

The WILTM was compared to the *Gough California Socialization Scale* using a group of young males and females. The results indicated that individuals who scored high on self-concept scored high on socialization and vice versa.

Comments

Reliability and validity have not been established and the theoretical position for the construction of this scale is debatable. For example, it seems possible that one might be delinquent and have a favorable self-concept. Interestingly, however, the "significant" items deal more with the respondents' relationship with authority than with self-concept. Often she or he is asked to guess how others evaluate her or him, not how she or he sees her or himself.

This procedure could prove useful, however, with a reconsideration of what is being measured. There seems to be a consistent theme within the significant items that shows promise as an indicator of feeling for the social structure.

REFERENCES

Dinitz, S., & Reckless, W. C. Self-concept measure of potential delinquency. *American Journal of Orthopsychiatry*, 1962, *32*, 159–168.

THE WAY IT LOOKS TO ME

Circle "Y" if your answer is Yes; circle "N" if your answer is No; and circle "DK" if your answer is Don't Know. For questions 28, 29, and 30, circle "O" for Often, "N" for Never, and "S" for Sometimes. For questions 31 and 32, put an "X" in the right space. There are no right or wrong answers. The right answer for you is the way you look at things.

Y N DK   1. Do you think that things are pretty well stacked against you?
Y N DK   2. Will you probably be taken to juvenile court sometime?
Y N DK   3. Did anyone ever tell you that you have a problem?
Y N DK   4. Will you probably have to go to jail sometime?
Y N DK   5. If you could start all over again, would you choose the same friends?
Y N DK   6. If you found that a friend was leading you into trouble, would you continue to run around with him or her?
Y N DK   7. Do you consider yourself to be a wise guy?
Y N DK   8. Do you plan to finish high school?
Y N DK   9. Do your parents punish you when you don't deserve it?
Y N DK 10. Do you think you'll stay out of trouble in the future?
Y N DK 11. Have you made up your mind that you won't get much out of school from now on?
Y N DK 12. Are grownups usually against you?
Y N DK 13. Do you expect people to give you an even break?
Y N DK 14. If you could get permission to work at 14, would you quit school?
Y N DK 15. Are you the kind of person that usually gets pushed around?
Y N DK 16. Are you a big shot with your pals?
Y N DK 17. Do your parents like it when you bring friends home?
Y N DK 18. Do you think your teacher thinks you will ever get into trouble with the law?
Y N DK 19. Are parents to blame if their children get into trouble?
Y N DK 20. Do you think that your mother thinks you will ever get into trouble with the law?

Y	N	DK	21. If you could start all over again, would you do the same things?
Y	N	DK	22. Do you think if you were to get into trouble with the law, it would be bad for you in the future?
Y	N	DK	23. Is it hard for you to have fun when you obey the law and your parents?
Y	N	DK	24. Have you ever been told that you were headed for trouble with the law?
Y	N	DK	25. Do you think your friends are good?
Y	N	DK	26. Have most of your friends been in trouble with the law?
Y	N	DK	27. Would you rather live somewhere else, than at your home?
O	S	N	28. Do you confide in your father? (Circle "O" for Often; "N" for Never; "S" for Sometimes.)
O	S	S	29. Do you think there is much fighting at home? (Circle "O" for Often; "N" for Never; "S" for Sometimes.)
O	S	N	30. Do your parents punish you? (Circle "O" for Often; "N" for Never; "S" for Sometimes.)
			31. If you were real honest about yourself, would you say that you feel you are better than most____ as good as most____ worse than most____? (Put an "X" in the right space.)
			32. Do you think you are quiet____ average____ active____? (Put an "X" in the right space.)

THE WAY IT LOOKS TO ME

Circle "Y" if your answer is Yes; circle "N" if your answer is No; and circle "DK" if your answer is Don't Know. There are no right or wrong answers. The right answer for you is the way you look at things.

Y	N	DK	1. If you could start all over again, would you choose the same friends?
Y	N	DK	2. If you found that a friend was leading you into trouble, would you continue to run around with him or her?
Y	N	DK	3. Do you consider yourself to be a wise guy?
Y	N	DK	4. Do you plan to finish high school?
Y	N	DK	5. Do your parents punish you when you don't deserve it?

Y N DK   6. Do you think you'll stay out of trouble in the future?
Y N DK   7. Have you made up your mind that you won't get much out of school from now on?
Y N DK   8. Are grownups usually against you?
Y N DK   9. Do you expect people to give you an even break?
Y N DK   10. If you could get permission to work at 14, would you quit school?
Y N DK   11. Are you the kind of person that usually gets pushed around?
Y N DK   12. Are you a big shot with your pals?
Y N DK   13. Do your parents like it when you bring friends home?
Y N DK   14. Do you think if you were to get into trouble with the law, it would be bad for you in the future?

What Teenagers Think

Development and Characteristics

The *What Teenagers Think* revised scale (WTAT-REV) was designed to measure personality characteristics that distinguish delinquents from nondelinquents (Stein, Sarbin, Chu, & Kulik, 1967). It is a revision of the *What Teenagers Think Scale* designed by Polk (1965). The first version was a modified form of the *Situational Appraisal Inventory* (Pittel, 1964), which was used as a measure of moral values for adults. The items were short descriptions of individuals' behavior in different situations. The respondent was asked to indicate, in his or her judgment, the degree of wrongness of the behavior (ranging from "not wrong" to "extremely wrong"). Polk (1965) rebuilt the test so that it might be appropriate for use with adolescents. When this scale was subjected to cluster analysis using self-reported delinquents and nondelinquents (Sarbin & Stein, 1965), five clusters emerged: (1) identity (or role) conflict, (2) displaced and indirect aggression, (3) informing or "snitching," (4) heterosexual inadequacy and the use of vicarious means of sexual gratification, and (5) verbal and fantasied aggression.

Because "informing" and "masculine inadequacy" had only a few items and because their reliabilities as separate scales were inadequate, these 40 items were combined with 40 of the original 50 items to form a new 80-item version. This revision enlarged on the informing and masculine inadequacy clusters.

This set of items was cluster analyzed using 100 matched pairs of delinquents (boys who had been adjudicated) and nondelinquents (boys with no legal record of delinquency). The results yielded four basic dimensions: (1) informing or "snitching"—15 items that deal with situations in which the central character informs on others; (2) masculine inadequacy—15 items dealing with heterosexual inadequacy and the use of vicarious means of gratification (i.e., girlie magazines or porno movies); (3) identity (or role) conflict—15 items referring to a variety of situations that show the central character (Larry) engaging in activities that show diffusion of role; and (4) aggression—15 items illustrating direct, person-specific aggression.

Response Mode

The test consists of 80 descriptive accounts of an individual's behavior in different situations, each followed by a 5-point scale for which "not wrong" receives a score of 1, "a little wrong"—2, "wrong"—3, "fairly wrong"—4, and "extremely wrong"—5. The respondent is asked to choose the alternative that most accurately reflects how he or she feels about what "Larry" did. (This may be done by filling out an answer sheet or by checking, underlining, or circling the appropriate choice.)

Scoring

Four scores (one for each of the subscales) are obtained. These scores are found by summing the scores for each item within a subscale. Therefore, the higher an individual's score, the more he or she feels the character (Larry) was wrong in his behavior concerning that category.

Norms

Stein *et al.* (1967) reported (see Tables 44 and 45) data for two samples of 200 boys each.

Note that there is little consistency between these two samples with reference to whether delinquents or nondelinquents score higher.

TABLE 44. Means, Sigmas and *T*-Ratios for Matched Samples of 100 Nondelinquent and 100 Delinquent Subjects

Cluster	N	Nondelinquent		Delinquent		*t*-ratios
		M	*SD*	*M*	*SD*	
1. Informing	15	42.78	14.16	47.71	17.37	−2.31[a]
2. Masculine inadequacy	15	38.63	11.85	41.60	13.34	1.45
3. Identity conflict	15	48.64	11.83	46.04	13.19	1.49
4. Aggression	15	57.91	12.22	60.71	10.78	−1.58

[a] $p < .05$

TABLE 45. Means, Standard Deviations and T-Ratios for Replicated Samples of 100 Nondelinquent and 100 Delinquent Subjects

Cluster	N	Nondelinquent		Delinquent		t-ratios
		M	SD	M	SD	
1. Informing	15	41.80	16.04	47.90	17.24	−2.59[a]
2. Masculine inadequacy	15	40.05	11.58	38.88	12.53	0.69
3. Identity conflict	15	48.40	11.86	43.02	13.47	2.99[a]
4. Aggression	15	60.31	10.69	58.85	12.38	0.89

[a] $p < .01$

Reliability

Stein *et al.* (1967) report good internal reliability within each subscale. Alpha coefficients are—informing (.95), masculine inadequacy (.93), identity conflict (.92), and aggression (.94).

Validity

Partial support for validity is found in the differentiation of four factors from the two samples of delinquents and nondelinquents. This is only partially detracted from by the fact that the factors aggression and identity conflicts are related ($r = .64$). All other intercorrelations between scales are .33 or less.

Attempts to form validity support by comparison of mean scores for delinquents and nondelinquents fall short (see Tables 44 and 45). Only the dimension "informing" consistently differentiates the groups. This is even questionable as a predictor because, as the designers point out, 95% of the delinquents were incarcerated at the time of testing. This alone could have a major influence because more peer control can be exercised under these conditions.

Comments

This set of subscales has undergone extensive developmental efforts and has evolved into an instrument with good evidence for content validity. It shows good internal consistency and uses a theoretical orientation which is appealing. Despite these favorable considerations, criterion-related validity is sparse. Further research on this potentially valuable scale is vigorously encouraged.

REFERENCES

Pittel, S. M. *Superego functions and the antecedents of guilt.* Unpublished doctoral dissertation, University of California, Berkeley, 1964.

Polk, F. F. *Toward a typology of the delinquent personality.* Unpublished doctoral thesis, University of California, Berkeley, 1965.

Sarbin, T. R., & Stein, K. B. *Self-role theory and antisocial conduct: A progress report* (Grant No. MN 08565, NIMH).Washington, D.C.: U.S. Govt. Printing Office, 1965.

Stein, D. B., Sarbin, T. R., Chu, C. L., & Kulik, J. A. Adolescent morality: Its differentiated structure and relation to delinquent conduct. *Multivariate Behavioral Research,* 1967, *2,* 199–210.

WHAT TEENAGERS THINK

This questionnaire is about a teenager named Larry and some of the things he does. Some people think that these things are OK, while other people might think they are not. We are interested in finding out what you think. If you think what Larry does is not wrong, circle number "1." If you think it is a little wrong, circle "2"; if wrong "3"; if fairly wrong, "4"; and if extremely wrong, "5." Mark what you think about each of the things Larry does. Remember: only put down what you think — not what others might think.

1. Larry's brother always gets Larry into trouble with his parents. Larry sometimes wishes his brother were dead.
   1. not wrong   2. a little wrong   3. wrong   4. fairly wrong   5. extremely wrong

2. Larry is so lacking in self-confidence that he never goes out on dates. Instead, he stays home and reads a lot of "dirty" paperback novels.
   1. not wrong   2. a little wrong   3. wrong   4. fairly wrong   5. extremely wrong

3. When Larry's parents go on vacation, he does many of the things he is not allowed to do when they are home, like staying up late and having wild parties.
   1. not wrong   2. a little wrong   3. wrong   4. fairly wrong   5. extremely wrong

4. When Larry learns that Jim and Sue are planning to get secretly married against their parents' wishes, he calls their parents and tells them what Jim and Sue are going to do.
   1. not wrong   2. a little wrong   3. wrong   4. fairly wrong   5. extremely wrong

5. One day Larry has an exam he hasn't studied for. He asks his mother to call the school and tell them that he is sick.
   1. not wrong   2. a little wrong   3. wrong   4. fairly wrong   5. extremely wrong

6. Larry was too shy to date very much in his old home town. But when his family moves to a new town, Larry tells all his friends that he was a great lover back where he used to live.
   1. not wrong   2. a little wrong   3. wrong   4. fairly wrong   5. extremely wrong

7. Larry is mad at the principal for suspending him from school. One day Larry is walking near the principal's house and sees his dog. Larry picks up a big stick and hits the dog with it.
   1. not wrong   2. a little wrong   3. wrong   4. fairly wrong   5. extremely wrong

8. Larry's mother refuses to give him money to take his girl to the movies. Larry tells his mother that he hates her.
   1. not wrong   2. a little wrong   3. wrong   4. fairly wrong   5. extremely wrong

9. Larry knows that Jim's parents strongly disapprove of drinking. When he sees Jim drinking one night at a party, he tells Jim's parents.
   1. not wrong   2. a little wrong   3. wrong   4. fairly wrong   5. extremely wrong

10. Larry is on the high school football team. In the big game of the year, he purposely tries to hurt the other team's quarterback so that his team will win.
    1. not wrong   2. a little wrong   3. wrong   4. fairly wrong   5. extremely wrong

11. Larry tried out for the basketball team but he gets cut from the squad. On his way home that afternoon he kicks some dirt at a little kid who is playing with a toy truck on the ground.
    1. not wrong   2. a little wrong   3. wrong   4. fairly wrong   5. extremely wrong

12. Larry gets invited to a marijuana-smoking party, but instead of going he tells the police when and where the party is to be held.
    1. not wrong   2. a little wrong   3. wrong   4. fairly wrong   5. extremely wrong

13. Larry's parents have a pet cat. One day when Larry is angry at his parents, he kicks the cat around.
    1. not wrong   2. a little wrong   3. wrong   4. fairly wrong   5. extremely wrong

14. Larry finds a wallet with a few dollars in it lying on the sidewalk. Since no one is around, he takes the money and leaves the wallet where he found it.
    1. not wrong   2. a little wrong   3. wrong   4. fairly wrong   5. extremely wrong

15. There are a lot of squirrels around Larry's house. He likes to throw rocks at them just to see if he can hit one.
    1. not wrong   2. a little wrong   3. wrong   4. fairly wrong   5. extremely wrong

16. Larry finds outs that his father was the driver of a hit-and-run car which badly hurt a young girl. He reports his father to the police.
    1. not wrong   2. a little wrong   3. wrong   4. fairly wrong   5. extremely wrong

17. Larry's English teacher is always criticizing him in front of the class. Larry dreams about the terrible things he would like to see happen to the teacher.
    1. not wrong
    2. a little wrong
    3. wrong
    4. fairly wrong
    5. extremely wrong

18. Larry has been watching some birds build a nest in a tree outside his window. One day when he is very annoyed with his mother, Larry gets out his BB gun and shoots at the nest.
    1. not wrong
    2. a little wrong
    3. wrong
    4. fairly wrong
    5. extremely wrong

19. Larry is so nervous around girls that he doesn't date. But he likes to hang around and watch when the boys on the weight-lifting team work out.
    1. not wrong
    2. a little wrong
    3. wrong
    4. fairly wrong
    5. extremely wrong

20. Larry hears that his friend Jim is planning to quit school and not tell his parents. Larry goes to Jim's parents and tells them of his plans.
    1. not wrong
    2. a little wrong
    3. wrong
    4. fairly wrong
    5. extremely wrong

21. Larry is a shy sort of guy when it comes to girls. He spends a lot of time reading muscle man magazines.
    1. not wrong
    2. a little wrong
    3. wrong
    4. fairly wrong
    5. extremely wrong

22. Every time Larry does the smallest thing wrong, his younger brother squeals to his parents. One day Larry turns his brother's pet turtle on its back and leaves it that way, hoping it will die.
    1. not wrong
    2. a little wrong
    3. wrong
    4. fairly wrong
    5. extremely wrong

23. One night Larry and Jim are setting off firecrackers. The police catch them and Larry tells the police that the firecrackers belong to Jim.
    1. not wrong
    2. a little wrong
    3. wrong
    4. fairly wrong
    5. extremely wrong

24. One of the guys who's not in Larry's crowd smokes against his parents wishes. Larry writes a letter to the boy's parents, telling them about it.
    1. not wrong
    2. a little wrong
    3. wrong
    4. fairly wrong
    5. extremely wrong

25. Larry is a pretty awkward guy when it comes to girls and rarely goes out on a date. Instead, he reads girlie magazines.
    1. not wrong
    2. a little wrong
    3. wrong
    4. fairly wrong
    5. extremely wrong

26. Larry knows that one of the liquor stores in town sells to the high school kids. He calls the police and tells them to watch the store more closely.
    1. not wrong
    2. a little wrong
    3. wrong
    4. fairly wrong
    5. extremely wrong

27. Jim challenges Larry to race their hot rods. Larry agrees to race because he doesn't want Jim to think he is afraid.
    1. not wrong
    2. a little wrong
    3. wrong
    4. fairly wrong
    5. extremely wrong

28. Larry is angry because his parents left him with his grandmother while they went on vacation. He doesn't answer their letters so they will worry about him.
   1. not wrong   2. a little wrong   3. wrong   4. fairly wrong   5. extremely wrong

29. Larry has a lot of homework to do, but when his friend urges him to come to the movies Larry agrees.
   1. not wrong   2. a little wrong   3. wrong   4. fairly wrong   5. extremely wrong

30. Larry learns that his friend Jim is secretly seeing a girl his parents forbid him to date. He feels he must inform Jim's parents, and does so.
   1. not wrong   2. a little wrong   3. wrong   4. fairly wrong   5. extremely wrong

31. Larry and his mother have a big argument at the airport just before she leaves for her vacation. As Larry watches her plane take off, he secretly hopes that it will crash.
   1. not wrong   2. a little wrong   3. wrong   4. fairly wrong   5. extremely wrong

32. Sometimes Larry's mother likes to have a few drinks. One night she tells Larry she is going to forbid him to see the girl he has been dating. Larry calls her a drunk.
   1. not wrong   2. a little wrong   3. wrong   4. fairly wrong   5. extremely wrong

33. When Larry's friends decide to go out one night to steal hubcaps, he agrees to go along because he doesn't want them to think he is chicken.
   1. not wrong   2. a little wrong   3. wrong   4. fairly wrong   5. extremely wrong

34. Years ago, Larry's mother was in a bad accident and had to have one of her legs amputated. One day when his mother denies Larry the use of the car, Larry calls her a dumb cripple.
   1. not wrong   2. a little wrong   3. wrong   4. fairly wrong   5. extremely wrong

35. When Larry catches wind of the illegal drag races some of the boys are holding outside of town, he tells the police about it.
   1. not wrong   2. a little wrong   3. wrong   4. fairly wrong   5. extremely wrong

36. Larry's mom and dad have told him he can't smoke until he is 18. He smokes anyway because most of his friends do.
   1. not wrong   2. a little wrong   3. wrong   4. fairly wrong   5. extremely wrong

37. Larry knows that the pastor of his church thinks drinking is sinful. When he sees the church's director of religious education coming out of a bar, he tells the pastor about it.
   1. not wrong   2. a little wrong   3. wrong   4. fairly wrong   5. extremely wrong

38. Every Sunday Larry tells his parents he is going to church but goes instead to see his girl friend.
   1. not wrong   2. a little wrong   3. wrong   4. fairly wrong   5. extremely wrong

39. Larry can never seem to get up the courage to ask a girl for a date. Instead, he spends a lot of time reading "marriage manuals."
    1. not wrong
    2. a little wrong
    3. wrong
    4. fairly wrong
    5. extremely wrong

40. Larry keeps a bottle of liquor hidden in the cellar and takes a drink every time things at home get to be too much for him.
    1. not wrong
    2. a little wrong
    3. wrong
    4. fairly wrong
    extremely wrong

41. Larry hears that Jim has been cutting school and using forged parental excuses. He reports Jim to the principal.
    1. not wrong
    2. a little wrong
    3. wrong
    4. fairly wrong
    5. extremely wrong

42. One night Larry accidentally burns a hole in the tablecloth with his cigarette. He covers the hole so no one will see it.
    1. not wrong
    2. a little wrong
    3. wrong
    4. fairly wrong
    5. extremely wrong

43. Because Larry feels bad about never going on dates, he tells his friends that he goes "out of town" to meet girls.
    1. not wrong
    2. a little wrong
    3. wrong
    4. fairly wrong
    5. extremely wrong

44. One day Larry goes into the men's room at school and sees several boys sharing a cigarette. Later in the day he reports the names of the boys to the principal.
    1. not wrong
    2. a little wrong
    3. wrong
    4. fairly wrong
    5. extremely wrong

45. Larry's mother has been in a mental institution several times and Larry knows that she is a sick woman. One day when she doesn't let him go out on a date, Larry calls her crazy.
    1. not wrong
    2. a little wrong
    3. wrong
    4. fairly wrong
    5. extremely wrong

46. Larry knows that his friend Jim is planning to run away from home and join the Air Force. He secretly tells Jim's parents.
    1. not wrong
    2. a little wrong
    3. wrong
    4. fairly wrong
    5. extremely wrong

47. Larry is a pretty bashful guy when it comes to girls, but when his friends are talking about their dating adventures he acts as if he's "been around" himself.
    1. not wrong
    2. a little wrong
    3. wrong
    4. fairly wrong
    5. extremely wrong

48. Larry and Jim share a locker at school, and they decide to hang pin-up pictures inside the door. One afternoon the principal is walking past when the door is open, and sees the pictures. Larry tells him the pictures are Jim's.
    1. not wrong
    2. a little wrong
    3. wrong
    4. fairly wrong
    5. extremely wrong

49. When Larry's friends ask him if he has been making out with the girl he is dating, Larry tells them he has. Actually, Larry is too shy to try to make out with her.
    1. not wrong
    2. a little wrong
    3. wrong
    4. fairly wrong
    5. extremely wrong

314   CHAPTER 9

50. Larry doesn't like one of his history teachers because she always picks on him in front of the class. One day Larry swears at her after being criticized.
    1. not wrong   2. a little wrong   53. wrong   4. fairly wrong   5. extremely wrong

51. Larry feels uneasy with girls and dates very little. Instead, he looks through art books and magazines for pictures of nudes.
    1. not wrong   2. a little wrong   3. wrong   4. fairly wrong   5. extremely wrong

52. One evening Larry sees his father going into a bar with a strange woman. He tells his mother what he saw.
    1. not wrong   2. a little wrong   3. wrong   4. fairly wrong   5. extremely wrong

53. The lady at the candy store is a grouch and always yells at Larry when he leafs through the magazines on the stand. Larry secretly wishes somebody would rob the store and beat her up.
    1. not wrong   2. a little wrong   3. wrong   4. fairly wrong   5. extremely wrong

54. One day Larry and his friend Jim are sharing Larry's cigarette in the school bathroom when the vice-principal walks in. Larry tells him that the cigarette belongs to Jim.
    1. not wrong   2. a little wrong   3. wrong   4. fairly wrong   5. extremely wrong

55. Larry learns that Jim is breaking into parking meters late at night. He informs the police of Jim's activities.
    1. not wrong   2. a little wrong   3. wrong   4. fairly wrong   5. extremely wrong

56. Although Larry has never really necked with a girl, he brags to his friends about how he always makes out so that they will think that he is a great lover.
    1. not wrong   2. a little wrong   3. wrong 3   4. fairly wrong   5. extremely wrong

57. Larry rarely goes out on dates because he is too afraid of girls. Very often he drives to the next town to see the girlie movies shown in the theatre there.
    1. not wrong   2. a little wrong   3. wrong   4. fairly wrong   5. extremely wrong

58. Through the grapevine Larry learns that Jim is a member of the gang which robbed the gas station. Larry reports Jim to the police.
    1. not wrong   2. a little wrong   3. wrong   4. fairly wrong   5. extremely wrong

59. When Larry is feeling low because of his nervousness with girls, he daydreams about what a great lover he'd be if he really had the chance.
    1. not wrong   2. a little wrong   3. wrong   4. fairly wrong   5. extremely wrong

60. Larry goes around hitting boys smaller than himself because he wants to feel like a big shot.
    1. not wrong   2. a little wrong   3. wrong   4. fairly wrong   5. extremely wrong

DELINQUENCY

61. Being around girls makes Larry feel uncomfortable, so he doesn't date much. He spends a lot of time reading men's adventure magazines.
    1. not wrong
    2. a little wrong
    3. wrong
    4. fairly wrong
    5. extremely wrong

62. One evening Jim drives Larry home from school, and brags that he doesn't have a license. The next day, Larry tells the police.
    1. not wrong
    2. a little wrong
    3. wrong
    4. fairly wrong
    5. extremely wrong

63. Because Larry isn't old enough to buy liquor, he gets a phony ID card and buys a bottle of whiskey to take to a party.
    1. not wrong
    2. a little wrong
    3. wrong
    4. fairly wrong
    5. extremely wrong

64. Larry's mother is constantly nagging him and trying to keep him from doing what he wants. When she becomes seriously ill and has to go to the hospital, Larry hopes she'll die.
    1. not wrong
    2. a little wrong
    3. wrong
    4. fairly wrong
    5. extremely wrong

65. Sue and Larry have been dating for some time, but one night she tells him she doesn't want to see him any more. When Larry gets home later, he takes it out on his little brother.
    1. not wrong
    2. a little wrong
    3. wrong
    4. fairly wrong
    5. extremely wrong

66. One of the boys is Larry's class has been setting fires in the fields near town, and the police are looking for him. Larry reports his name to the police.
    1. not wrong
    2. a little wrong
    3. wrong
    4. fairly wrong
    5. extremely wrong

67. Larry's sister has a bad case of pimples. One day they have a big fight and Larry asks her why she doesn't do something about her "ugly scarred-up face."
    1. not wrong
    2. a little wrong
    3. wrong
    4. fairly wrong
    5. extremely wrong

68. Larry has been told by his doctor that he should go on a diet because he is too heavy. He eats very little at home, but when no one is around he stuffs himself.
    1. not wrong
    2. a little wrong
    3. wrong
    4. fairly wrong
    5. extremely wrong

69. Although Larry is too unsure of himself to try to make out with a girl, he pretends to his friends that he has had a lot of "fun" on dates.
    1. not wrong
    2. a little wrong
    3. wrong
    4. fairly wrong
    5. extremely wrong

70. Larry discovers that one of the boys in his class is hooked on dope. He informs the police.
    1. not wrong
    2. a little wrong
    3. wrong
    4. fairly wrong
    5. extremely wrong

71. Larry's dad gives him permission to go to the movies but then he changes his mind. Larry goes anyway because he feels that parents should stick by what they say.
    1. not wrong
    2. a little wrong
    3. wrong
    4. fairly wrong
    5. extremely wrong

316   CHAPTER 9

72. When things are going bad for Larry, he often pushes little kids around because it makes him feel important.
    1. not wrong   2. a little wrong   3. wrong   4. fairly wrong   5. extremely wrong

73. Larry feels his unmarried aunt is always on his back about something. One days he tells her to lay off and calls her a shrivelled-up old maid.
    1. not wrong   2. a little wrong   3. wrong   4. fairly wrong   5. extremely wrong

74. A house is robbed in Larry's town, and some of the stolen items are described in the paper. Larry finds one of the items hidden in his father's workshop and calls the police.
    1. not wrong   2. a little wrong   3. wrong   4. fairly wrong   5. extremely wrong

75. Larry works as a stock boy and thinks he is underpaid for the amount of work he does. Whenever he gets the chance, he steals things from the store to make up for the low pay.
    1. not wrong   2. a little wrong   3. wrong   4. fairly wrong   5. extremely wrong

76. Larry finds out that he has flunked an important test in school. On his way home he hits a small boy and it makes him feel better.
    1. not wrong   2. a little wrong   3. wrong   4. fairly wrong   5. extremely wrong

77. Having his grandmother live with his family gives Larry a pain because she constantly argues with him and gives him lectures. Larry wishes the old lady would hurry up and die.
    1. not wrong   2. a little wrong   3. wrong   4. fairly wrong   5. extremely wrong

78. Larry likes to play cards with his friend Jim but he always loses. One evening when they are playing, Larry cheats because he thinks it is about time for him to win a game.
    1. not wrong   2. a little wrong   3. wrong   4. fairly wrong   5. extremely wrong

79. Late one night while driving home from a date, Larry scrapes the fender of a parked car. He takes off fast so that he won't have to pay for the damage.
    1. not wrong   2. a little wrong   3. wrong   4. fairly wrong   5. extremely wrong

80. Larry is too timid to date very much. He often goes to the library to look at the pictures of women in the anatomy books.
    1. not wrong   2. a little wrong   3. wrong   4. fairly wrong   5. extremely wrong

DELINQUENCY PERSONALITY ASSESSMENT: LISTINGS

Behavioral Syndromes

Field, E. *Types of delinquency and home background: A validation study of Hewitt and Jenkins' hypothesis.* London: Her Majesty's Stationery Office, 1967.

This modification of the *Delinquency Index* was designed to use child-rearing practices in the prediction of delinquency. Three behavioral syndromes that allow study of typical family upbringing and delinquency are identified as *unsocialized aggression* syndrome, *socialized delinquency* syndrome, and *overinhibited* syndrome. This extension of the Hewitt and Jenkins's work provides clarification of ambiguous items and ratings.

Delinquency Differential Classification System

Russon, G. W. A design for clinical classification of offenders. *Canadian Journal of Corrections,* 1962, *4,* 179–188.

This delinquency classification system is intended to provide for the identification of distinct delinquency clinical types, interpret dynamics of delinquent behavior, and develop therapeutic methods. The schema classifies delinquents on the main factors of *attitudes, maturity,* and *socialization* adequacy. The *attitude* factor leads to a "delinquency differential" between antisocial, asocial, and nondelinquent subdivisions. The *maturity* factor is drawn directly from the Sullivan, Grant, and Grant dimensions of interpersonal maturity. The *socialization index* identifies patterns of *submissive, power-oriented decompensating, power-oriented overcompensating,* and *co-operative* delinquents.

Delinquency Scale

Quay, H. C., & Peterson, D. R. A brief scale for juvenile delinquency. *Journal of Clinical Psychology,* 1958, *14,* 139–142.

This 40-item, true-false scale was designed to serve as a short objective scale for juvenile delinquency among males. In the present form, it has received little use; however, many of the items in this version were included in the later *Personal Opinion Study.*

Delinquency Self-Concept Scale

Donald, E. P., & Dinitz, S. Self-concept and delinquency proneness. In W. C. Reckless & C. L. Newman (Eds.), *Interdisciplinary problems of criminol-*

ogy, Columbus, Ohio: American Society of Criminology, Ohio State University Press, 1964.

This 56-item, yes-noresponse scale was designed to measure the self-concept of juvenile boys and predict any tendency in the direction of juvenile delinquency. In a validation study, 16 significant items were identified; these items may be considered a separate scale.

Delinquency Self-Concept Items

Jensen, G. F. Delinquency and adolescent self-conceptions: A study of the personal relevance of infraction. *Social Problems*, 1972, *20*, 84–103.

In order to measure adolescents' levels of self-esteem, the following two questionnaire items were used: (1) At times I think I am no good at all; (2) I certainly feel worthless at times. Six further items on the same questionnaire assessed self-reported delinquency on offenses of varying severity.

Foster Parent Preference Survey

Palmer, T., Pearson, J., & Haire, S. Selected instruments used in the Group Home Project. California, Department of the Youth Authority, The Group Home Project (Differential Treatment Environments for Delinquents), Fall 1969.

This 61-item, 4-point scale questionnaire is a modification of the *Jesness Staff Preference Survey*. It was designed to aid in matching institutional staff with youths in living units, based on *I*-level subtypes.

Group Home Parents Interview Schedules

Palmer, T., Pearson, J., & Haire, S. Selected instruments used in the Group Home Project. California, Department of the Youth Authority, The Group Home Project (Differential Treatment Environments for Delinquents), Fall, 1969.

This open-ended interview schedule was designed to obtain a comprehensive picture of the frame of reference, long term motivations, and major personality characteristics of group home parents. A 30-item schedule is used for potential group home parents and a 27-item schedule for follow-up interviews.

How the Future Looks to Me Scale

Landis, J. R., Dinitz, S., & Reckless, W. C. Differential perceptions of life chances: A research note. *Sociological Inquiry*, 1964, *34*, 60–66.

This 75-item scale was designed to measure differential perceptions of life chances of delinquent youths by assessing perceived likelihood of accomplishing or receiving desired attainments or desired objects.

Kohlberg Interview

Foder, E. M. Moral development and parent behavior: Antecedents in adolescent psychopaths. *Journal of Genetic Psychology,* 1973, *122,* 37–43.

Kohlberg, L. *The development of modes of moral thinking and moral choice in the years ten to sixteen.* Unpublished doctoral dissertation, University of Chicago, 1958.

The *Kohlberg Interview* presents nine hypothetical moral dilemmas to measure moral development in adolescents.

Parental Attitude Research Instrument

Palmer, T., Pearson, J.,& Haire, S. Selected instruments used in the Group Home Project. California, Department of the Youth Authority, The Group Home Project (Differential Treatment Environments for Delinquents), Fall, 1969.

This 60-item scale was designed to be administered to group-home parents in an attempt to measure three factors in parenting: (1) approval of maternal control of the child; (2) approval of expression of hostility; and (3) approval of positive attitudes toward child rearing.

Psychiatric Data Schedule

Hutcheson, B. R. *A prognostic classification for juvenile court first offenders based on a follow-up study: A method applicable to the field of mental illness. A Report* (NIMH Special Grant No. 3M 9149 [C2]). South Shore Mental Health Center, Commonwealth of Massachusetts, Quincy, August 1963.

The *Psychiatric Data Schedule* is a 63-item, 6- and 7-point rating form designed for therapists to explicate clinical judgments, explore circumstances leading up to delinquent acts and assess their dynamic meanings, and permit formulation of an overall psycho-social diagnosis.

Sentence Completion Test

Maher, B., & Stein, E. The delinquent's perception of the law and the community. In S. Wheeler (Ed.), *Controlling delinquents.* New York: John Wiley & Sons, 1968.

This 30-item sentence completion test was constructed to measure youthful prison inmates' feelings about experiences with the law and the institution. It has very short stems ranging from one to four words, including "This place," "When I get out," and "The law". A scoring manual has been constructed.

Treatment Personnel Inventory

Palmer, T., Pearson, J., & Haire, S. Selected instruments used in the Group Home Project. California, Department of the Youth Authority, The Group Home Project (Differential Treatment Environments for Delinquents), Fall 1969.

This 52-item rating form was designed to evaluate selected personality characteristics and professional orientations.

Value Consensus Scale

Jaffe, L. D. Delinquency proneness and family anomie. *Journal of Criminal Law, Criminology, and Police Science,* 1963, *54,* 146–154.

This 50-item scale was designed to measure value confusion by eliciting the delinquents' ratings of how they and their parents would handle specific critical situations.

DELINQUENCY MILIEU RATING: LISTINGS

Attitudes toward School Questionnaire

Roebuck, J., & Richardson, H. Attitudes of delinquents toward school. *California Youth Authority Quarterly,* 1963, *16,* 40–43.

This 29-item, yes-no scale was designed to assess the attitudes of delinquent boys toward three aspects of school, the curriculum, the social life, and general attitude.

Life Functioning Assessment

Deykin, E. Y. Life functioning in families of delinquent boys: An assessment method. *Social Service Review,* 1972, *46,* 90–102.

The *Life Functioning Assessment* uses behavioral anchor points of case history reports to quantify six major areas of family life functioning of delinquent boys.

Social Climate Questionnaire

Heal, K., Sinclair, I., & Troop, J. Development of a social climate questionnaire for use in approved schools and community homes. *British Journal of Sociology,* 1973, *24,* 222–231.

This 47-item questionnaire, a multidimensional scale, was designed to measure social climate of community homes in England. The seven dimensions being measured are staff support, strictness, clarity of expectations, satisfaction, inmate friendliness, behavior, and work.

DELINQUENCY PREDICTION: REVIEWS

Integrative Delinquency Scale

Characteristics and Development

The *Integrative Delinquency Scale* (IDS) is a 29-item scale, drawn from 465 items of the *Thorne Integration Level Test Series* (Thorne, 1965). The motivation for development of the IDS was the finding that the oneupsmanship and self-actualization subscales of the Thorne Series failed to distinguish meaningfully between youthful offenders and high school students. Thus Davis and Panton (1974) developed the IDS in order to predict delinquency "at the secondary school level of personality integration" (p. 186).

The development of the IDS was based on an item analysis of the Thorne Item Series, administered to 57 confined male youths and 61 male high school students. Both groups were equivalent in age, education level, I.Q., and socioeconomic characteristics. The 29 items that differentiated between the two samples by χ^2 tests at the .05 level became the IDS. The items were chosen exclusively by this empirical criterion, with no use of content-related selection.

Response Mode

The respondent is requested to read each item and note whether he or she agrees or disagrees with the statement.

Scoring

All except one item are first person opinion statements; all call for "true" or "false" responses and one point is given for each item answered in the same direction as the offender subjects. Sixteen items are scored only if answered false, and 13 items scored only if answered true.

TABLE 46. Scores on the Integrative Delinquency Scale

	Confined youthful offenders		Confined youthful misdemeanants	High school students	
	Sample 1	Sample 2		Sample 1	Sample 2
N	57	91	46	61	51
$\bar{X}$	16.2	15.6	15.2	9.5	9.1
SD	2.9	2.4	2.5	2.4	3.0

Norms

The norms are based on all male subjects (Table 46). A T-score conversion table is provided based on the 112 high school students' data.

Reliability

No information is available.

Validity

A cutting score of 13, chosen for its discriminatory effectiveness, accurately identified 87.8% of the offenders and 91.8% of the high school students in the standardization sample. The IDS was cross-validated on two additional samples of offenders and one more student sample, in which the same IDS cutting score correctly identified 87.9% and 84.1% of the offenders and 84.3% of the students (Davis & Panton, 1974).

There is some face validity to the items. Some items deal with personal failures or dissatisfaction and with authority problems. Not all items are scored in the face-validity direction ("I usually take the road of least resistance," when answered "false," is scored in the delinquency predictive direction).

Comments

This is a brief, easily administered true-false 29-item scale. While the IDS does differentiate between equivalent groups of confined youths and high school students, there is no information available about its ability to forecast delinquency. The IDS warrants further research.

REFERENCES

Davis, C., & Panton, J. H. A delinquency predictive scale for Thorne's integration level test studies. *Journal of Clinical Psychology*, 1974, *30*, 186–189.

Thorne, F. C. *The Integration Level Test series* (Research ed.). Brandon, Vt.: Clinical Psychology Publishing Co., 1965.

INTEGRATIVE DELINQUENCY SCALE

For each statement put a check (✓) if it is true for you or a cross (x) if it is false for you.

Item	Scored Response
Hard work is the best way to get ahead.	F
It is all right to take advantage of "suckers."	T
I usually take the road of least resistance.	F
I used to get punished more than other children.	T
I used to argue a lot with teachers.	T
I usually try to conform to the ruling powers.	F
I used to get away with a lot when I was a child.	T
I always try to follow the letter of the law.	F
I often let things go until the last minute.	F
I enjoy kidding or teasing other people.	F
I often feel the impulse to get away from everything.	F
I try to vote in all elections.	F
I am too shy to speak up in public meetings.	F
I would like to own a Cadillac or a Lincoln.	T
I always believe in telling people what I think at public meetings.	T
I have spent a lot of time drinking in bars and grills.	F
I never break the law if I can help it.	F
Up to now, I have not been too successful in life.	T
I have just about had it as far as experiencing any more troubles in life.	T
I never had any trouble getting along with the opposite sex.	T
I feel guilty because of the mistakes I have made in life.	T
I am more than "breaking even" in life.	F
Making mistakes bothers me too much.	T
I often wish that I were a child again.	T
All in all, I am satisfied with my life.	F
I consider myself a successful person.	F
Time passes too fast to suit me.	F
It wouldn't embarrass me to go on relief.	T
I have a lot of hobbies.	F

Delinquency Proneness Scale

Development and Characteristics

Marshall's Delinquency Proneness Scale (MDPS) (Marshall, 1973) is a modified version of Reckless and Dinitz's *Delinquency Proneness Scale* (Donald & Dinitz, 1964) which was designed in an attempt to revalidate the Reckless and Dinitz scale (which was administered in the U.S.) for a different country (Great Britain). However, new items of a similar kind were added in an effort to increase the power of the scale. Validation of this new scale began with a comparison of two groups of boys matched for school attendance and school attainment. The 81 boys labeled "delinquent" were 14-year old offenders, 36 of whom were minor offenders (e.g., firearms, minor damage, minor assaults). The control group consisted of 81 nondelinquents from the same school districts as the offenders.

A large item pool, which included Reckless and Dinitz's *Delinquency Proneness Scale,* was administered to the two samples. Item selection for the final version of this revised MDPS was based upon each item's ability to differentiate major delinquents from their controls, minor delinquents from their controls, and major delinquents from all others. In addition, items that offered extreme category positions were included, even when their predictive ability lacked statistical significance. The resultant scale consisted of 14 items, 6 of which were in the original Reckless/Dinitz scale.

Response Mode

The items that make up this scale require a variety of response types. Five items use yes/no alternatives. Three items require a choice between strongly agree, agree, neutral, disagree, and strongly disagree. Three items require a choice between several alternative descriptions. One item asks for relative frequency of disobedience, (seldom, sometimes, often). One item asks how much the respondent values doing well in school (Very, Quite, Not Very). Finally one item, the "sexual culture" scale, is a composite subscale score which is derived from the preceding items.

Scoring

The developer states that "the score for each category of answer was based on the ratio of delinquent to nondelinquent responses in that category" (Marshall, 1973, p. 229). These ratios, however, were not presented. An alternative to this scoring method might consist of noting the response category for each item that is most frequently used by delinquents (this information is available) and assigning a score of one to each item response that matches the delinquent response. This could yield a total of 14 points for a high delinquency proneness score, and a minimum of 0 for the lowest delinquency proneness score. Caution should be exercised because this scoring method has not been used.

Norms

No norms are available.

Reliability

The developer noted that when a split-half comparison or association was made using χ^2 contingency tables for the two halves of the scale against the criterion of police contact, the association was statistically significant at the .001 level. No measure of the strength of this relationship was reported.

Validity

The first validation attempt on this version of the MDPS was performed using a random sample of boys who were taken from 10 secondary schools in 3 towns. These boys were divided into groups according to whether they had police contact (court appearance or warning) or not. More boys were classified delinquent than nondelinquent. Since the random sample produced more nondelinquents than delinquents, *all* children who had a record of police contact were included in the delinquent group. This yielded a total sample of 225 nonoffenders and 208 offenders. When these boys were compared along a number of variables, the MDPS was found to be the most effective discriminant ($\chi^2 < .001$).

The predictive power of the MDPS was tested by administering the scale to 226 12-year-old boys and noting their later behavior with reference to police contact. Fifty-two of the boys under study subsequently had some encounter with the police. When these results were compared with MDPS predictions using a χ^2 test of significance, the chance probability was found to be less than .001.

When this procedure was used for a sample of 216 12-year-old girls, similar results were found. Twenty-six of the girls had contact with police officers subsequent to the administration of the MDPS. The χ^2 test indicated that the relationship between the MDPS and police contact was significant at the .001 level. In this case, however, the developer notes that because of the distribution of scores for girls, a lower cutoff point was necessary for the prediction of delinquency.

When an optimum cutoff point was established for the MDPS, it was found that scores below this point correctly predicted 81% of the nondelinquent cases, while scores above this point predicted delinquent status correctly in only 56% of the cases. This indicates that the scale may adequately describe nondelinquents, but fails to pick out less than half of the known delinquents. The developer suggests that two factors may be contributing to prediction errors. First, the delinquents as well as nondelinquents may be trying to present a picture of themselves as socially acceptable. Secondly, it is possible that the dependent variable, police contact, is not totally relevant for such a prediction.

Comments

MDPS has received support for validity and appears to be an adequate measuring instrument. Further work with the present version of the scale, possibly including additional items, might help to increase the predictive and discriminatory power of this scale.

One shortcoming that can be relatively easily overcome has to do with the information presented about the scale. No measure of strength of relationship between MDPS and police contact has been presented other than predictive rates. Some measure indicating the percent of variability explained by MDPS would be extremely helpful. Reliability information suggests internal consistency.

In general, the MDPS appears to be a brief and useful scale, developed empirically and supported by research. Its current applications are most appropriate in Great Britain, and it remains a research scale that is still too imprecise for accurate individual assessment and prediction.

REFERENCES

Donald, E. P., & Dinitz, S. Self-concept and delinquency and delinquency proneness. *Interdisciplinary problems in criminology: Papers of the American Society of Criminology,* 1964.

Marshall, T. F. An investigation of the delinquency self-concept theory of Reckless and Dinitz. *British Journal of Criminology,* 1973, *13,* 227–236.

DELINQUENCY PRONENESS SCALE

Instructions: Please respond to each of the following items as requested.

Do you think you will probably be taken to juvenile court sometime? Yes.

If you found that a friend was leading you into trouble, would you still go around with him, or her? Yes

Does your teacher think you will ever get into trouble with the police? Yes

Does your mother think you will ever get into trouble with the police? Yes

Which of the following best fits yourself:
   Most of my friends have been in trouble with the police;
   half of my friends have been in trouble with the police;
   hardly any, or none, of my friends have been in trouble with the police.
   FIRST TWO CHOICES.

Say whether you strongly agree, agree, disagree, or strongly disagree with the statement: There's always a chance you won't get caught for stealing little things, so you might as well try. S.A.

Which of the following best describes yourself:
   I am   seldom/sometimes/often disobedient? OFTEN.

How important do you think it is to do well at school?
   Very/Quite/Not Very. QUITE/NOT VERY.

Does your father think you will ever get into trouble with the police? Yes.

How important would the following be, if you wanted to be looked up to, or admired, by other people of your own age?
   (1) Good at games/athletics. NOT IMPORTANT.
   (2) Go out on lots of dates. IMPORTANT.
   (3) Daring. IMPORTANT.
   (4) Smoking. IMPORTANT.
   (5) Take part in lots of school activities. DEFINITELY NOT IMPORTANT.
   (6) Honest. NOT IMPORTANT.
   (7) A leader. DEFINITELY NOT IMPORTANT.

A "sexual culture" scale derived from questions similar to the above? VERY HIGH SCORES.

Say whether you strongly agree, agree, disagree, or strongly disagree with the statements:
   You should try to keep out of trouble at all costs. STRONGLY AGREE.
   Life does not have to be exciting to be worth living. DISAGREE/STRONGLY DISAGREE.

Which of the following best fits yourself:
   I am a quiet sort of person;
   I am no more quiet and no more energetic than most;
   I am a pretty active person? ACTIVE.

DELINQUENCY PREDICTION: LISTINGS

Individual Child Fact Sheet and Rating Form

Venezia, S. Youth-problem early warning and prevention system: A proposal. National Council on Crime and Delinquency Research Center, 1973. 609 Second Street, Suite D, Davis, Calif. 95616

This 21-item fact sheet and rating form uses a mixed response format based on teacher ratings of youths' behaviors and of family information.

KD Checklist

Kvaraceus, W. C. The KD Proneness Scale and Checklist. Western Psychological Services, 12031 Wilshire Blvd., Los Angeles, California 90025

The *KD Checklist* is a yes-no, 70-item rating list that is intended to tap variables that differentiate between delinquent and nondelinquent youths.

KD Proneness Scale

The KD Proneness Scale, Western Psychological Services, 12031 Wilshire Boulevard, Los Angeles, California 90025.
Balogh, J. K., & Rumage, C. J. Juvenile delinquency proneness: A study of the Kvaraceus scale. *Annals of American Sociology,* 1956, 1–35.
Feldhusen, J. F., Benning, J. J., & Thurston, J. R. Prediction of delinquency, adjustment, and academic achievement over a 5-year period with the Kvaraceus Delinquency Proneness Scale. *Journal of Educational Research,* 1972, 65, 375–381.

The *KD Proneness Scale* is a 75-item (60 of which are scored) multiple choice scale, in which the delinquent or potential delinquent respondents choose from one of four alternatives. This scale is designed to predict delinquency, a predictive goal not supported by the Balogh and Rumage, and Feldhusen, Benning, and Thurston research.

School Interest Inventory

Cottle, W. C. Indentifying potential delinquents in junior high school. *Measurement and Evaluation in Guidance,* 1972, 5, 271–276.

The *School Interest Inventory* was designed to identify potential school dropouts, male and female, in junior high school. The boys' form is a 61-item scale called the *Nonlinguistic Scale,* because it centers around nonlanguage activities and inanimate objects. The girls' form is an 85-item *Linguistic Scale,* centering on people and language-based activities. Both forms have been used to distinguish between delinquent and nondelinquent samples.

Student Opinion Survey and Parent Interview Schedule

Berleman, W. C., Seaberg, J. F., & Steinburn, T. W. The delinquency prevention experiment of the Seattle Atlantic Street Center: A final evaluation. *Social Service Review,* 1972, 46, 323–345.

The *Student Opinion Survey* was designed to identify high risk or delinquent prone youths. It is a 3-part, 100-item questionnaire that uses a varied response format. Its companion instrument, the *Parent Interview Schedule,* was used in the same delinquency prevention study. This interview schedule assesses parental perceptions of child, self, and social position, as related to several theories of delinquency causation.

DELINQUENCY DESCRIPTION: REVIEWS

Behavior Cards

Description and Characteristics

The *Behavior Cards* (BC) were designed to serve as "a low-pressure type of test-interview with delinquent children" (Stogdill, 1941, p. 1). The BC presents the child with a set of 150 cards containing questions about occurrences in his or her life. The child indicates whether he/she experienced each occurrence.

The test items were chosen from a pool of 400 items compiled after a review of delinquent case histories and books on delinquency. Items were excluded if they: (1) Did not differentiate between delinquents and nondelinquents; (2) showed little consistency with the other items; or (3) did not show satisfactory factorial validity.

Response Mode

The following instructions are read verbatim and describe how the subject is requested to respond.

> Here are some cards that ask you some questions about yourself. If a card *does* describe you, put it in the YES box. If it does *not* describe you, put it in the NO box. If there are any words you don't know lay the cards aside and I'll tell you what they mean (later). When you have sorted all the cards into the two boxes (tell me) or (bring them to me). Place the cards that *do* describe you in the YES box; those that *do not* describe you, in the NO box.

Scoring

The score is obtained by counting the number of cards that have been placed in the "yes" stack.

Norms

Table 47 shows the average scores for 200 delinquent boys who had been committed to the Bureau of Juvenile Research for study and observation, 50 delinquent girls, 50 public school boys, and 25 boy scouts.

TABLE 47. Norms for 150-Item Set

Subjects	N	Average score (150 cards)	SD (150 cards)
Delinquent boys	200	41.5	17.1
School boys	50	24.8	15.4
Boy scouts	25	20.6	10.6
Delinquent girls	50	28.2	15.3

Since many of the behaviors represent minor problems, norms for a set of 100 cards (Table 48) that indicate more serious offenses have been prepared.

Reliability

Stogdill (1941) reports odd-even reliability coefficients (when corrected by the Spearman-Brown formula) ranging from .83 for boy scouts to .92 for delinquent boys and .94 for school boys.

Validity

Three sources of information support the validity of the BC. First, the total scores differentiate between delinquents and nondelinquents (delinquents show a significantly higher score). Also when the percent of "yes" answers to each item is calculated, delinquents have a higher "yes" rate than nondelinquents.

Finally, when individual responses by delinquents to each item were checked against their social histories, validity coefficients range from .68 to .72.

Comments

In addition to the total score, this test can provide insight into specific problems that an individual might have, by noting which particular problems or experiences are placed in the "yes" box. The developer suggests that children are

TABLE 48. Norms for Abbreviated Scale of 100 Items (Items 1 to 50 and 76 to 125)

Subjects	N	Average score
Delinquent boys	200	37.1
Boy scouts	25	17.5
Delinquent girls	50	23.7

less inhibited to be honest by this "sorting" method than by a paper and pencil type test because it seems less permanent.

There is one reservation connected with the BC. The items and vocabulary may be outdated. This can be easily remedied, however, by substituting updated terminology.

Reliability and validity are acceptable, and except for the possible need for updating, this should be a useful instrument.

REFERENCES

Stogdill, R. M. *The Stogdill Behavior Cards: A test-interview for delinquent children.* Chicago: Stoelting Company, 1941.

BEHAVIOR CARDS

Instructions: Here are some cards that ask you some questions about yourself. If a card does describe you, put it in the YES box. If it does not describe you, put it in the NO box. If there are any words you don't know lay the cards aside and I'll tell you what they mean (later). When you have sorted all the cards into the two boxes (tell me) or (bring them to me). Place the cards that do describe you in the YES box; those that do not describe you, in the NO box.

1. Do some boys or girls tease you?
2. Do other children have trouble getting along with you?
3. Do people say you have a high temper?
4. Are you often late or tardy at school?
5. Do you get angry when the joke is on you?
6. Have you "hitch-hiked" to another town?
7. Did you ever hop a freight train?
8. Did you stay away from school a lot?
9. Do people accuse you of saying things that aren't true?
10. Do you tell lies?
11. Do you have trouble because of other boys or girls picking on you?
12. Do you like to play with boys or girls younger than you?
13. Do other boys or girls beat up on you?

14. Do you have quite a few fights?
15. Do you hate school?
16. Do you hate to play with girls?
17. Do you hate to play with boys?
18. Did you ever run away from home?
19. Did you ever stay out all night?
20. Did you run away from school sometimes?
21. Is your teacher always blaming you for things you didn't do?
22. Are there lots of people you would like to beat up on?
23. Do you swear at people when you are mad?
24. Do you have to stay in after school a lot?
25. Have you ever been accused of hurting an animal on purpose?
26. Have you been accused of hurting other children?
27. Did you ever play with some boys who had a meeting place or shack?
28. Did you play with boys or girls who got into lots of trouble?
29. Do your friends play hooky from school?
30. Did you ever go around with some bad boys?
31. Is someone always coaxing you to do things you should not do?
32. Have you ever sold papers on the streets at night?
33. Do you gather junk to sell for spending money?
34. Have you ever had dates?
35. Do you tell dirty stories?
36. Did you often take things that didn't belong to you?
37. Did you ever steal some money?
38. Did you ever steal things from stores?
39. Do you keep on doing something after you have been told to stop?
40. Do your parents get upset because you smoke?
41. Is your mother always afraid you will get sick?
42. Do you get on your mother's nerves?
43. Does your father beat you?
44. Do you get mad at your parents?
45. Did your mother ever go away and leave you?
46. Did your father ever go away and leave you?
47. Do you have bad dreams sometimes?
48. Do you have a bad habit that you think will ruin your health?

49. Are you afraid that you may go to hell?
50. Are you afraid that you may do something very bad sometime?
51. Is somebody trying to "get you" for something?
52. Are you angry about something most of the time?
53. Did you ever hit your teacher?
54. Did you ever have fits or fainting spells?
55. Do you wonder where babies come from?
56. Were you ever accused of doing something naughty to a little boy or girl?
57. Do you talk dirty around the girls?
58. Did you ever "do it" to a girl?
59. Do you "shoot craps" or gamble for money?
60. Did you ever take "dope"?
61. Did you ever set a building on fire?
62. Did a boy ever do dirty (naughty) things to you?
63. Did a man ever do dirty (naughty) things to you?
64. Are you afraid that one of your bad habits may make you lose your mind?
65. Did you ever help break into a house?
66. Did you ever help rob a store or filling station?
67. Did you ever hurt someone with a knife or gun?
68. Did you ever point a loaded gun at somebody?
69. Did you ever rob a man or woman?
70. Do your parents like your brother and sister better than you?
71. Did your parents ever make you leave home?
72. Do you always feel like beating up on someone?
73. Does your brother or sister pick on you a lot?
74. Have you been upset for a long time about things at home?
75. Do you worry about something that you can't tell anybody?
76. Do you have quite a few arguments?
77. Do you often sneak away from home?
78. Did you often stay out late at night?
79. Do you skip school a lot?
80. Do other children call you names?
81. Do other boys or girls talk you into doing things you shouldn't?
82. Do you break things to get even with somebody?
83. Do you get mad easily?

84. Does your teacher "bawl you out" in class?
85. Do your friends have nicer clothes than you have?
86. Do you pretend you don't hear what someone has said to you?
87. Do you go ahead and do things you were told not to do?
88. Did you hurt somebody when you got mad at him?
89. Do you sometimes feel like running away from home?
90. Have you had to be punished in school?
91. Do you skip school to go to the movies?
92. Do you want to quit school and go to work?
93. Do you say things that aren't true?
94. Do you usually tell a lie if you think it will get you out of trouble?
95. Do you usually play with older children?
96. Have most of your friends quit school?
97. Do you go with some boys who have been in court?
98. Did you ever belong to a gang?
99. Did you ever have a secret place that no one knew about?
100. Did you ever go around with some girls who got into lots of trouble?
101. Were you ever taken to a Detention Home or Juvenile Court?
102. Have you been in court more than once?
103. Do you have a brother or sister who has been in court?
104. Have you even stolen things?
105. Did you ever steal a bicycle?
106. Did you ever steal an automobile?
107. Did you ever break into a building and take something?
108. Do you go with some girls who have been in court?
109. Are you afraid of some bad boys?
110. Are you afraid of some bad men?
111. Did you ever wish you were dead?
112. Do your parents get angry with you often?
113. Is your mother always worrying about you?
114. Does your father try to catch you in doing wrong?
115. Are you afraid that the devil may take you away?
116. Do you use dirty talk sometimes?
117. Is your mother very much hurt by the things you do?
118. Do you go around with some boys or girls who drink a lot?

DELINQUENCY

119. Did you ever get drunk or sick from drinking too much?
120. Are people always telling things about you that aren't true?
121. Do you smoke cigarettes?
122. Do you feel upset when you can't get a smoke?
123. Do your parents get upset because you drink?
124. Do your parents try to keep you from having dates?
125. Is there something terrible that you worry about?
126. Is there someone who has double-crossed you?
127. Did someone ever try to put dope or poison in your food?
128. Do other children make fun of you at school?
129. Do you hate girls?
130. Do you hate boys?
131. Did you ever stay all night at a show?
132. Did you cuss and swear quite a lot?
133. Did you ever write dirty notes or letters?
134. Do you worry about babies?
135. Did you ever do something naughty with a girl?
136. Have you been accused of playing with yourself too much?
137. Did a boy ever "do it" to you?
138. Did a boy ever make you "do it" to him?
139. Did a man ever give you money to do something bad?
140. Did you ever cash a check that didn't belong to you and keep the money?
141. Did you ever carry a gun so you could "hold up" someone?
142. Did you ever write a note or letter to scare somebody?
143. Were you ever accused of burning down a house or barn?
144. Is it hard to get along with your brother or sister?
145. Are you afraid of your father?
146. Are you afraid of your mother?
147. Do your parents beat you?
148. Do you think you are not wanted at home?
149. Would like to live with someone else — not your parents?
150. Is there something you would like to tell but can't?

Comprehensive Miranda Rights Scale

Development and Characteristics

The *Comprehensive Miranda Rights Scale* (CMRS) was designed to serve as an empirically based guideline regarding the competence of juveniles to weigh Miranda rights (Grisso & Manoogian, 1977). It was developed to address the concerns whether arrested juveniles could validly and legally waive their rights.

The development of the CMRS has undergone several phases. First, a "large sample of adolescents in court detention centers" was asked to paraphrase the four Miranda rights. This set of responses was then grouped into common categories indicating the right to which the paraphrased response most likely referred. Next, a group of legal consultants (attorneys in juvenile law) were asked to review the responses and rate each one as an "adequate or inadequate" interpretation of the Miranda right to which it referred. During this stage of development, the developers decided that a third category was necessary. The legal consultants indicated that not all responses could be judged to be either totally adequate or totally inadequate. Some responses indicated a partial understanding of the right expressed in the Miranda warning.

Since the scoring system became a three point scale, clarification of criteria of each of the scores was necessary. Additionally, it became apparent that a set of "inquiry" questions should be included in situations where the raters were unable to judge clearly the degree of understanding expressed by the respondent being tested. These questions include such inquiries as: "What do you mean by" and other examples that are presented in the manual for administration and scoring.

This new scoring system was then presented to five other attorneys in juvenile law who were asked to judge whether the scoring system in general and the criteria in particular adequately measured an individual's understanding of the Miranda warnings. This procedure served as a cross-check against the criteria and provided the scale developers with information concerning the refinement of the scoring procedure.

Finally, a group of graduate student research assistants received training and experience in administration and scoring of the CMRS and estimates of interrater reliability were made. This final phase of development indicated that the scoring technique was clearly delineated and could be taught to individuals with no previous contact.

Response Mode

The respondents are given a set of cards upon which are written the statements of each of the four Miranda rights. They are then given the following instructions:

> I will be showing you some cards with some sentences on them. When I show you one I will read the sentence to you, then I want you to tell me what it is *in your own words*. Try

to tell me just what it says but in different words from those that appear in the sentence on the cards. Now, can you explain to me what it is I would like you to do?

If the respondents indicate that they do not understand the instructions, they are repeated and answers to specific questions are given. If respondents indicate that they do understand, they are asked to practice using a card which states "I have volunteered to be in this study." If they explain what is meant by the statement "I have volunteered to be in this study" adequately, the examination begins with the first of the Miranda rights and continues until all four rights have been explained by the respondents.

Scoring

Each of the four items (standard Miranda warnings) is scored on a 3-point scale in which 2 represents an adequate understanding of the warning, 1 represents questionable or partial understanding and 0 represents an inadequate understanding of the warning. A total score is obtained by adding each of the four item scores. Therefore, a range of 0–8 is possible, with a high score representing more understanding of the rights.

The scale developers have suggested that scoring should be performed only by individuals who have received training and feedback on the scoring procedure. Experience with 40 to 50 CMRS protocols is usually sufficient to produce reliable independent ratings.

Precise scoring, instructions, and examples are available in the manual for administration and scoring (Grisso & Manoogian, 1977).

TABLE 49. CMRS Means for Age and Race by IQ Classifications and Percentage with No Zeros on Any CMRS Items (in Parentheses)

Variable	IQ classification					Total
	70 or less	71–80	81–90	91–100	101+	
Age						
10/11	—[a]	2.00 (00)	3.50 (00)	4.66 (33)	—[a]	3.75 (12)
12	1.50 (00)	2.80 (20)	—[a]	5.33 (00)	5.75 (00)	4.66 (27)
13	3.40 (00)	5.00 (25)	5.58 (41)	6.57 (50)	6.15 (38)	5.64 (35)
14	2.92 (14)	5.39 (34)	6.00 (40)	6.41 (58)	7.10 (70)	5.84 (46)
15	4.38 (23)	5.56 (39)	6.10 (41)	6.51 (58)	6.69 (69)	6.04 (49)
16	4.30 (30)	5.67 (28)	6.17 (41)	6.29 (54)	7.45 (81)	6.11 (47)
Total	3.70 (19)	5.29 (31)	5.97 (42)	6.34 (53)	6.88 (65)	5.86 (45)
						$SD = 1.85$
Race						
white	4.86 (26)	5.65 (40)	6.10 (43)	6.36 (53)	6.92 (65)	6.26 (51)
black	3.15 (15)	4.75 (18)	5.62 (38)	6.25 (50)	6.20 (60)	4.74 (28)

[a] Insufficient number of subjects.

Norms

Table 49 presents CMRS means and standard deviations for different ages and IQ classifications, and the percentage of subjects in each group obtaining no credits on any Miranda warnings. The respondents include 431 juveniles (359 under court detention, 39 in a boys school, and 33 in a boys town).

Reliability

Grisso and Manoogian (1977) report an interscorer reliability estimate of .96 for the total CMRS for a group of graduate student research assistants who had been trained in the scoring technique. For that same group of scorers, interscorer reliability for the four individual item scores ranged from .89 to .97.

Validity

The CMRS has content validity and, through the systematic development of the scoring procedure, has support as a valid instrument. Other evidence in support of construct validity has been presented based on the responses of 431 juveniles (Grisso & Manoogian, 1977). This sample included 359 juveniles in St. Louis County Juvenile Court Detention, 39 juveniles at a boys school, and 33 juveniles at a boys town. The average age was 14.5 years (range 11 to 16), 55% were male, 26% were black, and 30% were of lower-middle and lower-socioeconomic status. These individuals represented approximately one-third of the detention admissions of a St. Louis County Juvenile Court Detention Center. No statistically significant differences were found between this group and the other two-thirds in the detention center along the variables age, socioeconomic class, or arresting offense.

When scores on the CMRS were compared to IQ, age, race, offense history, and socioeconomic status, the results indicated that: (1) IQ scores accounted for a moderate percentage of the variance in the CMRS scores ($r = .47, p < .001$); (2) age correlated .19 ($p < .001$) with CMRS scores; (3) race produced a biserial correlation with the CMRS scores of .42 (however, when race was included in a multiple correlation equation with IQ using CMRS as a dependent variable, the correlation between race and CMRS, with IQ partialled out, was only .20); (4) sex of the respondent was apparently unrelated to CMRS scores; (5) the offense history (i.e., number of court, felony, misdemeanor, status offense referrals, and number of detention admissions) showed no statistically significant relationships with the CMRS; and (6) socioeconomic status correlated $-.27$ with CMRS scores; however, when IQ was partialled out in a multiple R equation, the relationship between socioeconomic status and CMRS dropped to insignificance ($r = .04$).

The correlation between IQ and comprehension of Miranda rights was weaker than might be expected. The developers suggest that this might be due to the fact that adolescents reach a "plateau" of cognitive ability at about age 14. This does not mean that further learning ability stops, but merely that it slows for a period of time before continuing at a rapid rate.

Comments

The developers have stated two strong cautions concerning the use of the CMRS. First, they indicate that this scale represents only the cognitive aspects of understanding of the Miranda rights. They suggest that in addition to cognitive capacity, understanding involves the individual's expectancy regarding the consequences for her or himself, given the decision to waive or assert Miranda rights. Possible personality variables include aspects of oneself that might reduce competence to make a valid waiver of rights. The developers note the lack of cognitive capacity indicates that one may not make a valid waiver of rights, but that the presence of cognitive capacity does not necessarily indicate the potential for valid waiver of rights. Further, the developers caution against the use of the CMRS for decision making in clinical situations.

Grisso has also developed three related instruments. A *Comprehension of Miranda Vocabulary Test* assesses knowledge of the words used in the warning. A *Comprehension of Miranda Rights-II Scale* presents a series of true-false items about rights. Finally, the arrested youths are asked during interrogation about their comprehension of the function of their rights.

In general, the CMRS is well constructed and has presented evidence for content and construct validity. Reliability estimates are good between scorers after intensive training has been undertaken. This need for training may be a hindrance, however, the CMRS appears to be a useful instrument in an area which is in need of well constructed techniques.

REFERENCES

Grisso, J. T., & Manoogian, S. *Comprehension of Miranda rights: Manual for administration and scoring.* St. Louis University: Author, 1977.

COMPREHENSIVE MIRANDA RIGHTS SCALE (SCORING INSTRUCTIONS)

I. YOU DO NOT HAVE TO MAKE A STATEMENT AND HAVE THE RIGHT TO REMAIN SILENT.

2 Points

General: The idea that one does not have to say anything to the police, answer any questions, and/or make any formal or informal statements.

A. A paraphrase regarding one's choice or implied choice of whether or not to talk, without explanation.

Examples. You do not have to say a word to police or anyone (implied choice) — you do not have to say anything to anyone, but if you want to you can — you can tell them everything if you want, or just not say anything — you don't have to say anything.

B. Only the idea that one has a choice regarding whether or not to talk is essential. If a description or consequences associated with legal rights is given, it must be accurate.

Examples. You don't have to say anything, and if you don't, it will not be held against you in court — you don't have to say anything, and they can't make you if you don't want to — you don't have to answer any questions, because it can be used against you (might hurt your case, by incriminating, etc.).

1 Point

A. Choice or implied choice is present, but rationale for the right is erroneous, illogical, or inaccurate.

Examples. You don't have to talk if you don't want to, because you might not have done it (because the police might not want you to) (because your parents might get mad).

B. The idea that it is better not to say anything under any circumstances.

Examples. I think I should keep quiet — it means don't talk to the police — I would say it's best to say nothing — it means you better keep your mouth shut.

C. The idea that one can refuse not only to say anything, but also to do anything.

Examples. You don't have to do nothing you don't want to do — they can't make you do a thing — you can decide what you want to do.

0 Point

A. Stated lack of understanding.
Examples. I don't know — it doesn't mean anything at all to me.

B. The idea that you must remain silent and do not have the right or choice to talk if you want to.

Examples. You got to be quiet — it means you can't say anything — you must speak quietly.

C. The idea that you have to talk, stated generally or under certain circumstances; or that if you do not talk, it will go against you either with police or in court.

Examples. It means you don't have to talk unless you're guilty — you don't have to make statements but you have to tell them what they want to know — it means if you don't talk they lock you up.

II. ANYTHING YOU SAY CAN AND WILL BE USED AGAINST YOU IN A COURT OF LAW.

2 Points

General. The idea that confession or any other provision of information will be repeated in court and/or can be used as evidence to convict the suspect or others whom the information might incriminate. That is, <u>what you say</u> can be <u>incriminating and/or brought up in court.</u>

>**Examples.** Whatever you say can be used to try to convict you in court — if you say anything, it can hurt your case (be used as evidence) (will appear in court).

1 Point

A. The general idea that what you say may have negative consequences, but without an indication that subject understands that the consequences involve court hearing events.

>**Examples.** I could get in trouble if I talk — if I talk it might be bad for me — I think it means it's better not to talk — what you say can hurt you (be held against you).

B. A response which would qualify as a 2-pt. response, except that erroneous qualifiers have been added which spoil the response or indicate only partial understanding. Included here are responses referring to consequences in settings other than the court hearing.

>**Examples.** Since what you say can hurt you, they have told you to be silent — if you lie, that might go bad for you because they tell everything you said in court — they tell all you say in court, and you can't be found guilty if you don't confess — what you say could go badly for you in detention.

0 Point

Responses indicating lack of understanding, or responses which (whether true or not) do not focus upon potential self-incrimination. Some responses in this category emphasize the dangers produced by disobedience; others focus only on police as adversary.

>**Examples.** I can't figure out what it means — swearing at the cops will get you in trouble in court — it would hurt you to do or say anything you are not supposed to — it doesn't matter what you say, they are going to make it look like you did it and admitted it — you say you didn't do it and they say you did, it's your word against theirs — it just means you can't win.

III. YOU ARE ENTITLED TO CONSULT WITH AN ATTORNEY BEFORE INTERROGATION AND TO HAVE AN ATTORNEY PRESENT AT THE TIME OF THE INTERROGATION.

2 Points

General. The ideal that one has a right to consult an attorney before and during interrogation, or that one does not have to answer questions until a lawyer is present.

Examples. I can talk to a lawyer before anything else happens and during questioning — you can have your lawyer with you before and during talking to the cops — you can get a lawyer to come talk to you now and be with you at questioning — a lawyer can come and talk to you right now and be with you when cops talk to you — they can't question you without a lawyer if you want one — you can have your lawyer there while police talk to you.

1 Point

A. Responses in which the type of person with whom one may consult is left unclear; otherwise, the response is adequate.

    Examples. You can have someone working for you there when police talk to you — before and during questioning, you are allowed to talk to someone if you want — it's a procedure to help the defendant before or during any police questioning if you want.

B. (1) The time when legal counsel is available is not specified, even after inquiry; (2) Only before interrogation is specified.

    Examples. You can have a lawyer if you want — you can talk to your lawyer — everybody gets a lawyer if they want one — you can see your lawyer before being questioned — you can have a lawyer before interrogation, but I don't know what interrogation means.

0 Point

A. Responses indicating lack of understanding of the right to attorney.

    Examples. I don't understand that one — you can have someone question you about what you've done — you don't have to say anything if you don't want to — they are telling you that a lawyer is coming.

B. Responses in which legal counsel is referred to in conjunction with a legal or court procedure other than interrogation.

    Examples. You can have a lawyer when it comes time to go to court (when you have a hearing) — you can ask for a lawyer after you have been in detention a while — you can have a lawyer before court.

C. Responses in which who may be consulted is vague or incorrect, and no time is specified.

    Examples. You can have someone to be with you, I don't know who — a partner can see you through and give you advice.

D. Responses in which all elements may be correct, but someone other than attorney is specified.

>**Example.** You can talk to a social worker before the police ask you questions.

IV. IF YOU CANNOT AFFORD AN ATTORNEY, ONE WILL BE APPOINTED TO YOU.

2 Points

In all cases, it must be clear that an attorney, (lawyer, public defender, legal counsel) is being referred to. In addition, either of two conditions is sufficient to convey adequate understanding of the statement:

A. If the response includes a clear interpretation of "cannot afford" then any of a variety of substitute terms for "appoint" may be used.

>**Examples.** If you don't have money for a lawyer, the court will provide one for you — if you ain't got money to pay, a charity case lawyer will represent you instead — if you can't pay a lawyer, the court will get (give you) (have you represented by) (put you in touch with) (find you) a lawyer.

B. If the response does not include an interpretation of "cannot afford," then either the word "free" or an equivalent must appear in relation to acquiring legal counsel, or the word "give" must be used where "appoint" would be appropriate.

>**Examples.** The court will get you a lawyer free if you want a lawyer — they will give you a lawyer if you ask them to — the court will pay for a lawyer to represent you.

1 Point

A. Responses in which all above criteria are met except that an attorney is not specified — vague regarding who may be appointed.

>**Examples.** You can have them get you someone to talk to you for free — they will provide someone to help you if you don't have enough money to pay for help.

B. The idea that legal counsel is involved, but: (1) with neither a paraphrase of "cannot afford" nor the element of free counsel included in the response; or, (2) "cannot afford" is interpreted but "appoint" is not paraphrased correctly. Often these responses will mention court assistance in locating a lawyer.

>**Examples.** The court can get you a lawyer if you want — they will call a lawyer for you — they'll find a lawyer to take your case.

C. Legal counsel is mentioned, but reduced cost rather than free counsel is indicated.

>**Examples.** You can get a lawyer through the court at a minimum cost — if you are poor, they will find a lawyer for you at a reduced price.

0 Point

A. Responses indicating clear lack of understanding, and/or no sense of the financial benefit or court assistance extended by this right statement.

   Examples. I don't understand it — a lawyer will be coming to help me — you have an attorney with you — they don't do that well anyway — lawyers are hard to find — if you don't think you need an attorney, they'll get one anyway.

B. Response refers to someone other than an attorney.

   Examples. If you can't pay for a social worker, the court will get you one free.

Inmate Perception of Impact

Development and Characteristics

The *Inmate Perception of Impact Scale* (IPIS) was designed to measure the degree to which a juvenile is affected by the correctional facility into which he has been placed (Eynon, Allen, & Reckless, 1971). The instrument began as 320 5-point, Likert-type items that raise questions about experiences within the institution. When these were administered to 190 boys at the Training Institution of Central Ohio (TICO) and factored, it was found that six factors (represented by 60 items) accounted for the most variance within the test. These factors were labeled: (1) interpersonal approach—17 items; (2) inmate code for acting—8 items; (3) rejection of the institution—8 items; (4) inmate pressure—5 items; (5) rejection of positive impact—15 items; and (6) self-labelling—7 items. Each of these dimensions represents types of feelings for the institution and the processes that are inherent to it.

Response Mode

The respondent is asked to read the question or statement and choose the alternative that most accurately represents his feelings. The choices are based on a modified 5-point, Likert-type scale. Most response alternatives included: "strongly agree," "agree," "undecided," "disagree," and "strongly disagree." Because of the wording of other items, however, the alternatives were sometimes changed from "very good to very poor," "most of the time to some of the time," or other variations. An individual indicates his choice by circling the appropriate response.

Scoring

All items were designed so that the alternatives on the rightmost side of the page are indicative of an especially unfavorable impact, and those on the left side of the page show a favorable impact. A numerical value of one is given to the favorable response, and the value increases as the choice moves toward unfavorable so that, on a 5-point scale, the highest score for an item is 5. Items with only four alternatives yield a high score of 4.

Six scores are obtained, one for each factor. Since the factors contain different numbers of items, a ratio score (score within factor/number of items within factor) is used to allow for comparison between factors.

Norms

Table 50 presents the scores, on each of the six factors, obtained from a group of 443 adolescent boys (ages 15 to 18). All these boys had served some time at the TICO and were released between 1964 and 1966.

Sindwani and Reckless (1973) report similar results for 700 male prisoners in a maximum security institution.

Reliability

No stability measures were reported, but factor analysis lends support to the internal consistency of the factors.

Validity

The factor analytic technique by which the six clusters were extracted buttresses the scale's construct validity. Most of the validity findings for the impact scales are based on the normative sample. Intercorrelations of the inmates' scores on the 6 factors produced 4 of 15 intercorrelations that were nonsignificant and negative and 11 that were positive. Eynon et al. (1971) asserted that in "only six of the eleven positive correlations was there a high enough coefficient to suspect some concomitance of direction in perceptions of impact" (p. 98). These results

TABLE 50. Differential Impact of Institution as Measured by Scores of Perceptions on Six Factors (High Score in Unfavorable Direction)

Factor	Average score	Maximum score	Ratio
Interpersonal approach	34.80	82	.424
Inmate code	18.05	40	.451
Rejection of institution	24.66	38	.649
Inmate pressure	11.55	21	.550
Rejection of positive impact	31.72	74	.429
Self-labelling	15.55	35	.444

give added support to the independence of the six clusters derived by the original factor analysis. None of the actual correlations, however, were reported in the article itself.

Scores on the IPIS were correlated with staff members' ratings of each boy on a 15-item measure of observed impact of TICO (Eynon *et al.*, 1971). Most of the correlations were statistically insignificant, with even the few significant ones reported as being very low. Once again, no actual data were presented. Furthermore, there was no significant relationship between the boys' impact scales scores and the staff's predictions of post-release outcome.

Attempting to predict recidivism from impact scales scores of the normative sample, Miller and Dinitz (1973) found no significant association between scores on the scales and outcomes at the time of release from parole supervision, an average of eight months after institutional release. Interestingly, the trend was for boys with unfavorable attitudes concerning institutional impact to have *better* outcomes than those with positive attitudes towards TICO.

Comments

The items on the IPIS possess face validity regarding life at a state training institution. More importantly, the factor analytic method of development provides internal (construct) validity. Unfortunately, reliability data are absent and the concurrent and predictive validity information that exist are disappointing. There is a need for the scales to be cross-validated on other offender populations and in other correctional settings, since all of the preliminary results come from only one criterion group. Furthermore, as currently designed, the use of four- and five-point choices in the scoring system raised problems regarding consistency within the scaling.

The developers of the impact scales envision using them to assist in the improvement of correctional facilities. Until further studies of the measure are carried out, though, the utility of the impact scales appears to be questionable.

REFERENCES

Eynon, T. G., Allen, H. E., & Reckless, W. C. Measuring impact of a juvenile correctional institution by perceptions of inmate and staff. *Journal of Research in Crime and Delinquency,* 1971, *8,* 93–107.

Miller, S. J., & Dinitz, S. Measuring institution impact: A follow-up. *Criminology,* 1973, *11,* 417–426.

Sindwani, K. L., & Reckless, W. C. Prisoners' perceptions of the impact of institutional stay. *Criminology,* 1973, *11,* 461–471.

INMATE PERCEPTION OF IMPACT

The Way I Look At Things

This is not a test. There are no right or wrong answers. The right answer for you is the way you look at things. Make sure you answer each question the way you really think. CIRCLE the answer which best expresses how you look at things.

Factor No.

2   1. The best way to make it at TICO is to be slick.
       Strongly agree   Agree   Undecided   Disagree   Strongly disagree

6   2. At the present time, do you think of yourself as someone who had a raw deal?
       Strongly agree   Agree   Undecided   Disagree   Strongly disagree

1   3. Now that you are leaving TICO, do you feel ready to make a fresh start?
       Strongly agree   Agree   Undecided   Disagree   Strongly disagree

2   4. The best way to make it at TICO is to act tough.
       Strongly agree   Agree   Undecided   Disagree   Strongly disagree

4   5. Do the other boys make it hard or easy on a guy for following the rules at TICO?
       Very Hard   Hard   Not Sure   Easy   Very Easy

1   6. Regardless of what they say, the best way to get along here is to make friends with adults.
       Strongly agree   Agree   Undecided   Disagree   Strongly disagree

2   7. TICO seems to be a place where a guy waits around for others to tell him what to do.
       Strongly agree   Agree   Undecided   Disagree   Strongly disagree

6   8. Now that you are leaving TICO, do you see yourself as a person who has been a private at a military school?
       Strongly agree   Agree   Undecided   Disagree   Strongly disagree

4   9. Did any of the other boys pick on you while you were here?
       Strongly agree   Agree   Undecided   Disagree   Strongly disagree

2   10. Most of what you learn at TICO is learned from the other boys.
       Strongly agree   Agree   Undecided   Disagree   Strongly disagree

1	11.	At the present time do you think of yourself as someone who will straighten out? Strongly agree Agree Undecided Disagree Strongly disagree
5	12.	If I keep out of trouble on the outside, it will be because of what I have learned here at TICO. Strongly agree Agree Undecided Disagree Strongly disagree
5	13.	I think I am a better guy because I have been here. Strongly agree Agree Undecided Disagree Strongly disagree
1	14.	Now that you are leaving TICO, do you feel happy? Strongly agree Agree Undecided Disagree Strongly disagree
1	15.	Did some adult take an interest in you and help you while you were here? Helped me a lot Helped me some Helped me a little Didn't help me
3	16.	Have you ever broken rules here at TICO? Quite a few A few One or Two None
4	17.	Have you ever been "punched out?"* Lots of times Several times Once or twice Never
1	18.	Now that you are leaving TICO, do you see yourself as a guy who has paid his debt to society? Strongly agree Agree Undecided Disagree Strongly disagree
3	19.	At the present time, do you think of yourself as someone who won't let anybody push him around? Strongly agree Agree Undecided Disagree Strongly disagree
1	20.	Now that you are leaving TICO, do you feel hopeful for the future? Strongly agree Agree Undecided Disagree Strongly disagree
1	21.	Now that you are leaving TICO, do you feel untroubled? Strongly agree Agree Undecided Disagree Strongly disagree
1	22.	At the present time do you think of yourself as someone who has made a mistake? Strongly agree Agree Undecided Disagree Strongly disagree
4	23.	Did the other guys ever accuse you of "getting up on your pounds" because you wouldn't "mess up" with them?† Most of the time Some of the time Very little of the time None of the time
3	24.	I would agree to stay at TICO an extra month. Sure would Maybe Don't know Probably not Sure wouldn't

DELINQUENCY

3   25. TICO seems to be a place where a guy can lose his temper easily.
           Strongly   Strongly
           agree   Agree   Undecided   Disagree   disagree

1   26. At the present time, do you think of yourself as someone who wishes he hadn't done it?
           Strongly   Strongly
           agree   Agree   Undecided   Disagree   disagree

2   27. TICO seems to be a place where a guy will never get a break.
           Strongly   Strongly
           agree   Agree   Undecided   Disagree   disagree

1   28. Did you like the officers with whom you came in contact here at TICO?
           Most of   Some of   One or two   None of
           them   them   of them   them

1   29. Did watching your step help you while you were here?
           Helped me   Helped me   Helped me   Didn't help
           a lot   some   a little   me

6   30. Now that you are leaving TICO, do you see yourself as a person who had been a patient in a hospital?
           Strongly   Strongly
           agree   Agree   Undecided   Disagree   disagree

1   31. Regardless of what they say, the best way to get along here is to talk about yourself to some adult.
           Strongly   Strongly
           agree   Agree   Undecided   Disagree   disagree

5   32. Did the officers at TICO really try to help you?
           Strongly   Strongly
           agree   Agree   Undecided   Disagree   disagree

2   33. The best way to make it at TICO is not to rat.
           Strongly   Strongly
           agree   Agree   Undecided   Disagree   disagree

5   34. If a guy can get along here, he can get along on the outside.
           Strongly   Strongly
           agree   Agree   Undecided   Disagree   disagree

3   35. I learned more bad things during my time at TICO than I would have in the same time outside.
           Strongly   Strongly
           agree   Agree   Undecided   Disagree   disagree

5   36. I like myself better now than when I first came to TICO.
           Strongly   Strongly
           agree   Agree   Undecided   Disagree   disagree

1   37. Regardless of what they say, the best way to get along here is to run errands for the officers.
           Strongly   Strongly
           agree   Agree   Undecided   Disagree   disagree

5	38.	I am able to control my temper better than before I came here. Strongly agree Agree Undecided Disagree Strongly disagree
5	39.	If a friend of mine got into trouble, I would want him to be sent here. Strongly agree Agree Undecided Disagree Strongly disagree
3	40.	If I felt I were going to get into real trouble, I would ask to be sent back to TICO before it happened. Strongly agree Agree Undecided Disagree Strongly disagree
5	41.	While at TICO, the average guy learns how to get along better with other people. Strongly agree Agree Undecided Disagree Strongly disagree
5	42.	It really helps a guy to be at TICO. Strongly agree Agree Undecided Disagree Strongly disagree
5	43.	The average guy gets a chance to improve himself at TICO. Strongly agree Agree Undecided Disagree Strongly disagree
1	44.	Now that you are leaving TICO, do you feel friendly? Strongly agree Agree Undecided Disagree Strongly disagree
5	45.	If I felt I were going to get into real trouble, I would ask to be sent back to TICO before it happened. Strongly agree Agree Undecided Disagree Strongly disagree
6	46.	Now that you are leaving TICO, do you see yourself as a delinquent? Strongly agree Agree Undecided Disagree Strongly disagree
6	47.	Now that you are leaving TICO, do you see yourself as a person who has been a pupil at a boarding school? Strongly agree Agree Undecided Disagree Strongly disagree
5	48.	While he's here, the average guy finds out why he got into trouble. Strongly agree Agree Undecided Disagree Strongly disagree
6	49.	I got a bum rap by being sent to TICO. Strongly agree Agree Undecided Disagree Strongly disagree
1	50.	Regardless of what they say, the best way to get along here is to play it straight. Strongly agree Agree Undecided Disagree Strongly disagree

5	51.	The food at TICO is clean.

       Strongly agree   Agree   Undecided   Disagree   Strongly disagree

3   52. The program at TICO is:
       Very good   Good   50/50   Poor   Very poor

5   53. My stay at TICO has helped me.
       Strongly agree   Agree   Undecided   Disagree   Strongly disagree

3   54. If you were the superintendent at TICO, would you make any changes in the way this place is run?
       Quite a few   A few   One or two   None

2   55. The best way to make it at TICO is to outsmart the cottage leader.
       Strongly agree   Agree   Undecided   Disagree   Strongly disagree

2   56. TICO seems to be a place where a guy must obey a lot of phony rules.
       Strongly agree   Agree   Undecided   Disagree   Strongly disagree

1   57. Regardless of what they say, the best way to get along here is to try to figure yourself out.
       Strongly agree   Agree   Undecided   Disagree   Strongly disagree

5   58. Sending me to TICO was a good deal for me.
       Strongly agree   Agree   Undecided   Disagree   Strongly disagree

6   59. Now that you are leaving TICO, do you see yourself as a criminal?
       Strongly agree   Agree   Undecided   Disagree   Strongly disagree

4   60. Guys try to "put the 'nut' on you" at TICO.*
       Most of the time   Some of the time   Very little of the time   None of the time

       61. How many months have you been at TICO? _____

       62. Date of birth _____
                       (month)   (day)   (year)

*In the vernacular of the boys at TICO, "punched out" means hit with fists or slapped with hands by a staff member.

†In TICO inmate language, "getting up your pounds" signifies that a boy has found ways of getting in well with persons in authority, so as to receive small privileges.

**In TICO language "putting the nut on you" means that inmates put pressure on you to behave in accordance with their ideas and demands.

Seriousness of Delinquency Scale

Development and Characteristics

The *Seriousness of Delinquency Scale* (SDS) was designed to measure the perceived seriousness of illegal activities along two dimensions—(1) offensiveness; and (2) disruptiveness (Kelly & Winslow, 1970). The interest in separating these two considerations arose from the developers' concern over the implicit assumption (by other researchers) "that seriousness may be viewed as a 'global phenomenon' " (Kelly & Winslow, 1970, p. 127). The developers emphasize the possibility that the concept of seriousness may involve a combination of perceived moral "heinousness" (offensiveness) and structural disruptiveness.

The 60 items that constitute the SDS are brief descriptions of an individual's illegal activity. The selection of offense descriptions was based on the Federal Bureau of Investigations Uniform Crime Reports' 29 classification labels that have been refined through use in Sellin and Wolfgang's (1964, pp. 381–386) typology. For example, this index would break "forcible rape" into three variations.

> First, a person forcibly rapes a woman; her neck is broken and she dies. Second, a person forces a woman to submit to sexual intercourse; no physical injury is inflicted. Finally, a person drags a woman into an alley, tears her clothes, but flees before she is physically attacked. (Kelly & Winslow, 1970, pp. 128–129)

Response Mode

Each item is written in the form of a statement that describes an activity of a person. The respondent is asked to rank each offense, first according to "offensiveness" of the crime and next according to its "disruptiveness" to the general functioning of society (if it suddenly became widespread). This means that each item receives one rank between 1 and 60 for the two hypothesized dimensions.

Scoring

Two rank scores are obtained for each item, offensiveness and disruptiveness. Since these are ranks, no total is calculated.

Norms

No norms are available.

Reliability

No reliability measures are available.

Validity

The major difference between the SDS and the Sellin and Wolfgang (1964) scale is the use of offensiveness and disruptiveness as separate categories. Validity for this scale would be supported if items were ranked differently along offensiveness and disruptiveness.

When the responses of 150 male and female college students and 40 police-science students were analyzed, no statistically significant differences were found between dimensions. Further, when these results were compared to the rankings of Sellin and Wolfgang (1964), correlations were high (.72 to .91). This occurred despite the differences in descriptions between the two scales.

Comments

The SDS grew from the assumption that individuals' ratings of offenses are based on two dimensions. The data, however, do not support this position. In fact, the SDS gives results that are quite similar to the Sellin and Wolfgang *Seriousness Scale*.

Although the SDS is of little use as a two-dimensional measure, it may be valuable as an alternative to previously developed scales.

REFERENCES

Kelly, D. H., & Winslow, R. W. Seriousness of delinquent behavior: An alternative perspective. *British Journal of Criminology,* 1970, *10,* 124–135.

Sellin, T., & Wolfgang, M. W. *The measurement of delinquency.* New York: J. Wiley & Sons, 1964.

SERIOUSNESS OF DELINQUENCY SCALE

Please rank each of these items according to how "offensive" they are to you so that the least offensive item is ranked 1 and the most offensive item is ranked 60. Then rank each item according to its "disruptiveness" to society.

Sixty Acts Used for Questionnaire Construction*

1. A person knowingly passes a check that is worthless.
2. A person stabs an individual to death.
3. A person steals a book worth $5 from a public library.

+ 4. A person makes an obscene phone call.
†+*5. A person forcibly rapes a woman. Her neck is broken and she dies.
6. A juvenile runs away from home and thereby becomes an offender
7. A person is intoxicated in public.
8. A person robs a victim of $1,000 at gunpoint. The victim is shot to death.
+ 9. A person shows pornographic movies to a minor.
#10. A person fails to pay child support.
†+*11. A person runs a house of prostitution.
†+*12. An unmarried couple willingly have sexual intercourse.
13. A person embezzles $1,000 from his employer.
14. A person knowingly buys stolen property from the person who stole it.
15. A person sets fire to a garage.
16. A person breaks into a locked car, steals, damages, and abandons it.
#17. A juvenile is picked up for curfew violation.
+ 18. A person smokes marijuana.
+ 19. A person is engaged in a dice game in an alley.
20. A person beats a victim with his fists. The victim lives but requires hospitalization.
21. A person breaks into a residence, forces open a cash box, and takes $1,000.
†+*22. A person, married male, has sexual intercourse with a female not his wife.
+ 23. A person administers heroin to himself.
#24. A father beats his wife and children.
#25. A person burns his draft card.
26. A person has no residence and no visible means of support and thereby becomes an offender.
†+*27. A person forces a female to submit to sexual intercourse. No physical injury is inflicted.
28. A person stabs a victim with a knife. The victim does not require medical treatment.
29. A person steals a bicycle parked on the street.
30. A person operates a motor vehicle while under the influence of alcohol.
+ 31. A person runs a house where unlawful sale of liquor takes place.
32. A person embezzles $5 from his employer.
33. A person, using physical force, robs a victim of $1,000. No physical harm is inflicted.
#34. A person picks an individual's pocket of $100.
+*35. A person gets customers for a prostitute.

+ 36. A person sells heroin.

+ 37 A person runs a house where gambling occurs illegally.

38. A person defaces and breaks public statues causing $1,000 damage.

39. A person illegally possesses a knife.

† + *40. A person is a prostitute in a house of prostitution.

† + *41. Two males willingly engage in various homosexual practices.

#42. A person deserts his family.

43. A person disturbs the neighborhood with loud, noisy behavior.

44. A person signs someone else's name to a check and cashes it.

45. A person steals, damages, and abandons an unlocked car.

+ 46. A person is a customer in a house where gambling occurs illegally.

+ 47. A person sells marijuana.

† + *48. A person, over 16 years of age, has intercourse with a female under 16 who willingly participates.

49. A person throws rocks through windows.

50. A person robs a victim at gunpoint. The victim struggles and is shot to death.

† + *51. A person drags a woman into an alley, tears her clothes, but flees before she is physically harmed or sexually attacked.

#52. A person fires a gun at a victim who suffers a major wound requring extensive hospitalization.

† + *53. A person has sexual intercourse with his stepdaughter.

#54. A person engages in a racial protest march.

55. A person is found firing a rifle for which he has no permit.

+ 57. A person performs an illegal abortion.

+ 58. A person prowls in the backyard of a private residence.

59. A person, armed with a blunt instrument, robs a victim of $1,000. The victim is wounded and requires hospitalization.

60. A person breaks into a department store, forces open a cash register and steals $5.

---

*Represents position of acts on final questionnaire. Because of its neutral connotation, the phrase, "A person...," was used to preface statements; this is in lieu of Sellin and Wolfgang's phrase, "The offender..."

+ Moral offense.
†Sex offense.
#Act not included in Sellin and Wolfgang's listing or used in our comparisons.

Teenage Slang Test

Development and Characteristics

The *Teenage Slang Test* (TAST) was designed to serve as an index of delinquency (Kulik, Sarbin, & Stein, 1971). Three rationales are given for the use of language and word usage as a measure of delinquency. First, deviant subcultures apply different connotations to words than the culture at large. Slang words can be positioned in semantic space so that they communicate these connotations. Next, by using slang, a person identifies her or himself with a particular group. This can bias other people's responses toward him or her and establish a vicious cycle of a self-fulfilling prophesy (i.e., someone sounds delinquent, so you treat him or her as if he or she were delinquent. So, he or she responds in nonnormal or delinquent ways, etc.). Finally, the language an individual uses can give cues to his or her background and experiences.

The initial item pool was constructed after a review of (1) slang terms collected by Ephron and Piliavin (1961) during their work with street gangs; (2) slang dictionaries; (3) a slang thesaurus; and (4) popular magazines. The resultant pool contained 123 multiple-choice items. This number was reduced to 62 after an initial tryout on 60 psychology students and 12 members of a boys club. Of these 62 items, 48 were answered correctly more often by delinquents than nondelinquents.

A total of 996 high school boys (mean age, 16.18 years) were administered the scale. Of these, 605 were enrolled in school and 391 were institutionalized. Of the boys, 66% were white, 20% black, 3% Oriental, and 11% Hispanic. Their mean vocabulary intelligence score was at the 35th percentile and they had a mean of 10.21 grades completed in school.

An item analysis was performed on 100 matched pairs of delinquents and nondelinquents drawn from the overall sample. The boys were matched on age, SES, IQ, and race. The 62 item test showed that 30 terms differentiated between the two groups at the .01 level of significance. The delinquents did better on 28 of these items and the nondelinquents did better on two.

Response Mode

The TAST is a paper-and-pencil test that requires the respondent to read the item and choose the alternative he believes to be correct.

Scoring

Kulik *et al.* (1971) used three scoring procedures, all of which distinguish between delinquents and nondelinquents. The first is based on the total number of correct answers. The second is based on the number of correct responses for a set of 48 items that were more often answered correctly by the delinquent group.

TABLE 51. Comparison of Two Groups of 100 Matched Delinquents and Nondelinquents for Three Slang Scales

	Nondelinquents			Delinquents			
Item	M	SD	N	M	SD	N	t
First sample							
Slang/62 words	28.71	7.45	100	35.44	9.50	100	6.38[a]
Slang/48 words	21.57	6.38	100	29.28	8.48	100	7.27[a]
Slang/28 words	10.82	3.82	100	17.70	6.06	100	9.60[a]
Second sample							
Slang/62 words	30.76	6.91	100	33.32	10.36	100	2.02[a]
Slang/48 words	23.28	5.87	100	27.30	9.18	100	3.63[b]
Slang/28 words	11.83	3.91	100	16.88	6.25	100	6.75[b]

[a] $p < .05$.
[b] $p < .01$.

The third is the total correct on the 28 items on which high discrimination was possible and on which delinquents scored significantly higher. The specific items within each of these categories were not reported, therefore, only the score from the 62 item total is presently possible.

Norms

Table 51 presents the normative information available for the three scoring procedures.

Reliability

Kulik et al. (1971) report split-half reliability adjusted by the Spearman-Brown formula as .85 for the 62-item scale, .87 for the 48-item scale, and .88 for the 28-item scale.

Validity

The first support for the validity of the test as a measure of delinquency is presented in the *Norms* section. As the table indicates, all three scoring procedures were able to correctly distinguish between delinquents and nondelinquents at the .05 level of significance.

Another study that tended to support the validity of the scale divided subjects into five categories: (1) no police record; (2) police contact but no further action; (3) booked or adjusted; (4) institutionalized; and (5) recidivist. Table 52 gives the results of comparison of these groups.

The test makes distinctions between the extreme groups, but fails to discriminate between groups which are slightly different.

When the TAST was correlated with self-reported delinquent activities, a

TABLE 52. Comparison of Boys at Five Legal Levels

Level	M	SD	N	Comparison	t
1. No record	11.32	3.91	464		
				1 vs. 2	-2.67^a
2. Police contact	12.55	4.95	96		
				2 vs. 3	$-.64$
3. Booked or adjudicated	13.05	5.22	77		
				3 vs. 4	-6.06^a
4. Institutionalized	17.61	5.56	170		
				4 vs. 5	-1.39
5. Recidivist	18.51	5.86	140		

$^a p < .01$

two-item measure of delinquent self-image, self-report of legal and school disciplinary problems, and socialization scores from the *California Psychological Inventory* (CPI), the results were only partially supportive (see Table 53). The test seems to relate to actual activities, but not to the ways boys feel about themselves.

Comments

The TAST has received support for its validity; however a number of concerns should be expressed. First, and probably most important, is the issue of obsolescence. Because slang terms change so frequently, items comprising the TAST must be continually updated. Otherwise the items become meaningless. Similarly, scoring, reliability, and validity information must change as items are included and excluded.

A second concern is the lack of matching (of respondents) for religious characteristics. This variable might be of importance because religious orientation

TABLE 53. Relationship of Vocabulary and SES to Antisocial Behavior for 515 High School Boys

Item	Multiple R slang & verbal intelligence	Slang	Verbal intelligence	SES
Self-report of delinquent activities	$.36^a$	$.22^a$	$-.16^a$	$.09^b$
Delinquent self-image	$.31^a$	.07	$-.26^a$	.14
Self-report of legal and school disciplinary measures	$.33^a$	$.15^b$	$-.23^a$	$.13^a$
CPI socialization scale	$.30^a$	.00	$.28^a$	$-.11^b$

$^a p < .01$.
$^b p < .05$.

and/or the accompanying subcultural differences may affect one's exposure to slang but not to delinquent behavior.

The next issue to be considered is the manner in which the TAST is scored. Three approaches have been presented based on early research efforts. The scale would be more practical for future research if one standard procedure was endorsed. Based on the reliability estimates, the 28-item version might be the best.

The TAST is an interesting approach that seems reliable. The validity estimates and other problems, however, make it difficult for use by researchers.

REFERENCES

Ephron, L. R., & Piliavin, I. *A new approach to juvenile delinquency: A study of the Youth-for-Service Program in San Francisco.* Berkeley: Survey Research Center, 1961.

Kulik, J. A., Sarbin, T. R., & Stein, K. B. Language, socialization, and delinquency. *Developmental Psychology,* 1971, *4,* 434–439.

TEENAGE SLANG TEST

Mark on your answer sheet the answer that gives the meaning of each of the following slang expressions. Answer every item, even if you are not sure about some. There is no penalty for guessing.

1. To "split" means to
   1 arrive
   2 leave
   3 witness
   4 work
   5 bully

2. A "piece" is a
   1 car
   2 gun
   3 ten-dollar bill
   4 meeting place
   5 fight

3. A "spick" is a
   1 Negro
   2 Italian
   3 Jew
   4 Irishman
   5 Puerto Rican

4. "Horse" is
   1 heroin
   2 gasoline
   3 alcohol

  4 glue
  5 hair tonic

5. To "jap" is to
  1 throw quick jabs
  2 beat a retreat
  3 make a quick sneak attack
  4 squeal to the cops
  5 surrender

6. To "shoot up" is to take
  1 marijuana
  2 heroin
  3 benzedrine
  4 dexedrine
  5 peyote

7. A "roach" is a
  1 shot of whiskey
  2 a short marijuana butt
  3 hobo
  4 dealer in stolen goods
  5 hotel clerk

8. The "slammer" is
  1 home
  2 one's favorite hangout
  3 jail
  4 a bar
  5 a bookie joint

9. A "hype" is a
  1 heroin user
  2 musician
  3 loan shark
  4 squealer
  5 tough guy

10. "Half a year" is
  1 50¢
  2 $5
  3 $50
  4 $500
  5 $5,000

11. If it's "groovy," it's
  1 boring
  2 sad
  3 different
  4 ordinary
  5 very good

12. The term "fay" is used for
  1 Puerto Ricans
  2 Orientals
  3 Jews
  4 Caucasians
  5 Negroes

13. To "cop" is to
    1 smoke
    2 steal
    3 arrest
    4 rumble
    5 buy

14. If you got a "ranking," you were
    1 picked on
    2 promoted
    3 cheated
    4 praised
    5 greeted

15. How many persons actually fight in a "fair one"?
    1 none
    2 two
    3 four
    4 two gangs
    5 two syndicates

16. In making a "Molotov cocktail," one might use
    1 a tin can
    2 a cherry bomb
    3 a car inner tube
    4 a milk bottle
    5 hair tonic

17. A "button" is
    1 an attrative girl
    2 a capsule of heroin
    3 a police badge
    4 a one-dollar bill
    5 a switchblade

18. "Tea" is
    1 liquor
    2 cocaine
    3 cigarettes
    4 marijuana
    5 money

19. "The nabs" are
    1 prison guards
    2 cops
    3 handcuffs
    4 stolen goods
    5 guns

20. A "D.A." is a kind of
    1 trouser
    2 shoe

3 haircut
4 hat
5 suit

21. "The bulls" are
    1 the police
    2 the enemy gang
    3 cigarettes
    4 race horses
    5 the boys in the gang

22. If members of two gangs are "bopping," they are
    1 making peace
    2 fighting
    3 partying
    4 arguing
    5 playing on the same team

23. A "stomping" is a
    1 raid by the police
    2 big winning in craps
    3 large dance
    4 fight involving a few individuals
    5 dope party

24. A "crib" is one's
    1 car
    2 residence
    3 hangout
    4 place of work
    5 school

25. A "rod" is a
    1 tough cop
    2 car
    3 guy carrying a weapon
    4 ten-dollar bill
    5 tough guy

26. "T-bird" is
    1 marijuana
    2 a flashy dresser
    3 a card game
    4 a cheap wine
    5 a T-man

27. A "blood" is a
    1 Puerto Rican
    2 Italian
    3 Jew
    4 Caucasian
    5 Negro

DELINQUENCY

28. "Sides" are
    1. flashy clothes
    2. street gangs
    3. phonograph records
    4. neighborhoods
    5. hubcaps

29. "The heat" refers to
    1. the police
    2. guns
    3. drugs
    4. girls
    5. stolen goods

30. A likely target for "rat packing" would be
    1. an individual along in a park
    2. an opposing gang
    3. a friendly gang
    4. a motorcycle cop
    5. passengers in a subway car

31. To "turn over" a grocery store means to
    1. case it
    2. buy it
    3. use it as a front
    4. wreck it
    5. rob it

32. If a thing is "boss," it is probably
    1. cheap
    2. large
    3. high quality
    4. stolen
    5. too flashy

33. One who has been "busted" has been
    1. arrested
    2. sentenced
    3. released from prison
    4. found innocent by a jury
    5. convicted by a jury

34. "We're tight" means that we're
    1. friends
    2. enemies
    3. members of the same gang
    4. brothers
    5. engaged

35. To "cap" is to
    1 complain
    2 drink
    3 brag
    4 squeal
    5 rob

36. The one who is most likely to be called "big and bad" is
    1 a tough cop
    2 a good gang fighter
    3 an attractive girl
    4 a dope pusher
    5 a crooked gambler

37. A person who "has cool" is
    1 a possessor of stolen goods
    2 crazy
    3 able to handle himself
    4 unattractive
    5 dead

38. One "lights up"
    1 morphine
    2 cocaine
    3 heroin
    4 marijuana
    5 benzedrine

39. To "thump" is to
    1 dance
    2 laugh
    3 insult
    4 steal
    5 fight

40. "Short neck" refers to
    1 marijuana
    2 girls
    3 wine
    4 a souped-up car
    5 food

41. If "the dance turned out at midnight," that's when it
    1 started to swing
    2 became a fight
    3 became boring
    4 ended
    5 moved to another place

42. A "fink" is a
    1 cop
    2 squealer
    3 pickpocket

4 prison quard
5 confidence man

43. "P.O." stands for
    1 police officer
    2 political operation
    3 penal official
    4 presidential order
    5 probation officer

44. A person who wants to "hot wire" a car is planning to
    1 soup it up
    2 drag it
    3 steal it
    4 set it on fire
    5 buy it

45. A "kak" is
    1 an Italian
    2 a girl
    3 an old person
    4 a Jew
    5 a Puerto Rican

46. A "short" is a
    1 small guy
    2 car
    3 stick of dynamite
    4 one-dollar bill
    5 girl

47. The "black and white" are
    1 dice
    2 Negroes
    3 the police
    4 flashy clothes
    5 cards

48. If one is asked to "kneel down to a little game," he can expect a
    1 beating
    2 party
    3 game of craps
    4 frisking
    5 drink

49. "Juvey" refers to
    1 the juvenile squad of the police department
    2 a girl who is under age
    3 any young person
    4 a juvenile delinquent
    5 music

50. "Some sounds" refers to
    1 boring talk
    2 interesting conversation
    3 an argument
    4 a gang fight
    5 a sarcastic person

51. A "lemonhead" is
    1 an unintelligent girl
    2 a squealer
    3 an unintelligent person
    4 a blonde girl
    5 a sarcastic person

52. A "stud" is
    1 a loser
    2 an attractive girl
    3 a flashy diamond
    4 a deck of cards
    5 a tough guy

53. To be "shaken down" by the police is to be
    1 bullied by them
    2 searched by them
    3 arrested by them
    4 caught by them
    5 let go by them

54. If he "swings with" your gang, he
    1 belongs to an opposite gang
    2 belongs to your gang
    3 tags along
    4 is on the baseball team
    5 is the head of your gang

55. If a cop is "straight," he's
    1 a bully
    2 dishonest
    3 honest
    4 a plainclothesman
    5 a pushover

56. "Pot" refers to
    1 marijuana
    2 morphine
    3 cocaine
    4 heroin
    5 benzedrine

57. "Bread" is
    1 marijuana
    2 girls
    3 one's job

4 money
5 home

58. A "bone" is
 1 one dollar
 2 two dollars
 3 five dollars
 4 ten dollars
 5 one hundred dollars

59. "Skins" are
 1 Negroes
 2 Mexicans
 3 dollar bills
 4 drums
 5 flashy clothes

60. "Craps" on a pair of dice is
 1 3, 5, or 12
 2 2, 3, or 11
 3 4, 6, or 10
 4 2, 3, or 12
 5 3, 5, or 9

61. A "bindle stiff" is a
 1 man who has passed out from drinking
 2 detective assigned to the vice squad
 3 hobo
 4 safe-cracker
 5 crooked gambler who stacks the cards

62. "Half a rock" is
 1 50¢
 2 $5
 3 $50
 4 $500
 5 $5000

DELINQUENCY DESCRIPTION: LISTINGS

Approval of Illegal Behaviors Questionnaire

Hindelang, M. J. Moral evaluations of illegal behaviors. *Social Problems,* 1974, *21,* 370–385.

This instrument is a list of 19 illegal acts to which the respondents indicate personal approval or disapproval and best friend's approval or disapproval. The questionnaire was designed to measure the values delinquents and nondelinquents placed upon illegal involvements.

Characteristics of Youngsters Questionnaire

Palmer, T., Pearson, J., & Haire, S. Selected instruments used in The Group Home Project. California Department of the Youth Authority, The Group Home Project (Differential Treatment Environments for Delinquents), Fall, 1969.

This 28-item questionnaire was designed to measure the feelings of group home parent candidates concerning which types of youths they would prefer, enjoy, or would be able to help as friends.

Delinquency and Popularity Scale

Vaz, E. W. Explorations in the institutionalization of juvenile delinquency. *Journal of Criminal Law, Criminology, and Police Science,* 1971, *62,* 396–406.

This 12-item instrument draws its questions from a larger study of delinquent behavior. The *Delinquency and Popularity Scale* was designed to assess the rated popularity of youths refusing to participate in the listed acts. All items begin with the stem, "A boy who."

Differential Association Questionnaire

Jensen, G. F. Parents, peers, and delinquent action: A test of the differential association perspective. *American Journal of Sociology,* 1972, *8,* 562–575.

This questionnaire was designed to measure the type and strength of relationships associated with delinquent behavior. The respondents are asked about the presence of delinquent friends, perceptions of trouble in the neighborhood, and other items related to differential association theory.

Evaluation of Delinquency Preventative Measure

Seaberg, J. R. Case recording by code. *Social Work,* 1965, *10,* 92–98.

This article reports on a coding procedure for delinquent youths. It offers a consistent method for keeping account of professionals involved in a specific case and the circumstances surrounding contact between these people and delinquents.

Exposure to Deviance Index

Severy, L. J. Exposure to deviance committed by valued peer group and family members. *Journal of Research in Crime and Delinquency,* 1973, *10,* 35–46.

This two-part *Exposure to Deviance Index* was designed to evaluate three factors in exposure to family deviance and one factor in exposure to peer deviance. Two separate scores are obtained.

Family Background and Urban Delinquency Questionnaire

Walberg, H. J., Yeh, E. G., & Paton, S. M. Family background ethnicity and urban delinquency. *Journal of Research in Crime and Delinquency,* 1974, *11,* 80–87.

This 29-item, true-false questionnaire was designed to measure the family background and rate of delinquency among urban youths. Most of the items were taken from existing instruments. The item content included presence of school-relevant objects in the home, intellectually stimulating encounters in childhood, equality of education opportunity, and self-reported delinquent acts.

Family and Peer Group Valuation Scales

Severy, L. J. Exposure to deviance committed by valued peer group and family members. *Journal of Research in Crime and Delinquency,* 1973, *10,* 35–46.

These scales were designed to measure how highly youths value their families and friends. The *Family Valuation Scale* is an 11-item, true-false or yes-no response format scale. The *Peer Valuation Scale* is a 7-item, true-false scale.

Female Juvenile Recidivism Descriptive Checklist

Sepsi, V. J., Jr. Archival factors for predicting recidivism of female juvenile delinquents (Doctoral dissertation, Kent State University, 1971). *Dissertation Abstracts International,* 1971, *32,* 5368A. (University Microfilms No. 72-09281)

Sepsi, V. J., Jr. Girl recidivists. *Journal of Research in Crime and Delinquency,* 1974, *11,* 70–79.

A 104-item variable list described physical characteristics hypothesized to identify female juvenile recidivists. Six content areas were encompassed: physical characteristics; intellectual and educational characteristics; family variables; home before commitment; psychosocial history; and training school and parole factors. A 17-item descriptive checklist emerged which successfully differentiated recidivists from female juvenile nonrecidivists.

Goal Orientations Inventory

Clark, J. P., & Wenninger, E. P. Goal orientations and illegal behavior among juveniles. *Social Forces,* 1963, *42,* 49–59.

This 30-item, 3-point rating scale was designed to measure the degree to which delinquents value goals in their lives. Each goal is rated as having "great importance," "some importance," or "little or no importance."

Importance Questionnaire

Palmer, T., Pearson, J., & Haire, S. Selected instruments used in the Group Home Project. California Department of the Youth Authority, The Group Home Project (Differential Treatment Environments for Delinquents), Fall, 1969.

This 213-item inventory was designed to be administered to group home parents in an effort to determine their values. While eight content subsections have been identified, the questionnaire is scored by use of individual item comparisons between pre and post group home parent employment or experiences.

Interest and Activities Inventory

Hansell, N., Smith, W. G., & English, J. T. Community involvement, mental health and role performance: A study of college students, Peace Corps trainees, and delinquents. *Journal of Nervous and Mental Disease,* 1964, *138,* 268–276.

The *Interest and Activities Inventory* was designed to measure, among other things, the social behavior of delinquents. The inventory consists of 18 questions to which subjects respond with phrases, sentences, and short paragraphs. The questions are designed to elicit lists of social activity in terms of clubs, conversations, leisure activities, and important problems.

Juvenile Probation Administrative Action Scale

Cartwright, D. S., Kelling, G. W., Taylor, G. P., & Cameron, C. B. Measuring and predicting juvenile probation outcome: An exploratory study. *Criminology,* 1972, *9,* 143–160.

The *Administrative Action Scale* was designed to measure the degree to which a juvenile probationer penetrated the successive administrative boundaries between probation and commitment to an institution. It is a single-item, multiple-choice (seven alternatives), weighted measure of the severity of probation officers' decisions following a probationer's law violations.

Marion County Youth Study Questionnaires

Richmond, F. L., & Polk, K. The Marion County Youth Study, University of Oregon, 1859 East 15th Avenue, Eugene, Oregon 97403.

This 110-item questionnaire was designed to measure variables of transitions from adolescence to adulthood, which may be related to delinquency, among nonmetropolitan youths. Shifting commitments in education, work, family, and peers are included in the item content. Items are predominantly four-choice ratings from "agree strongly" to "disagree strongly."

Potential Cost Scales

Piliavin, I. M., Vadum, A. C., & Hardyck, J. A. Delinquency personnel costs and parental treatment: A test of a reward-cost model of juvenile criminality. *Journal of Criminal Law, Criminology, and Police Science*, 1969, *60*, 165–172.

The *Potential Cost Scales* are three parallel instruments constructed as measures of potential social costs for delinquency. They measure boys' concerns over fathers' respect and approval (six items), mothers' respect and approval (six items), and teachers' approval and interest in school performance (eight items).

Probation Counselors' Success Rating Scale

Cartwright, D. S., Kelling, G. W., Taylor, G. P., & Cameron, C. B. Measuring and predicting juvenile probation outcome: An exploratory study. *Criminology*, 1972, *10*, 143–160.

This rating is completed by the probation counselor based on the probationers' violations or good behaviors. A single rating is made from six choices ranging from "complete failure" to "very good," with examples presented to illustrate the meaning of each choice.

Sellin-Wolfgang Delinquency Index

Sellin, T., & Wolfgang, M. E. *Constructing an index of delinquency: A manual*. Philadelphia: Center of Criminological Research, 1963.

The *Sellin-Wolfgang Delinquency Index* was designed to yield a quantitative measure of type and seriousness of delinquent acts by multiplying number of acts or victims by a weighted score of offense.

Severity of Offense Scale

Palmer, T. B. *Community treatment project: An evaluation of community treatment for delinquents. Seventh Progress Report, Part 2: Recent Research findings and long-range developments at the Community Treatment Project*. California Youth Authority and the National Institute of Mental Health, October, 1968.

The *Severity of Offense Scale* is a 73-item list used to rank the severity of juvenile offenses on a scale from 1 to 10. Each item is also coded as violent or nonviolent and by type of violation (felony, optional felony, misdemeanor, technical violation, or other).

Social Data Schedule

Hutcheson, B. R. *A Prognostic Classification for Juvenile Court First Offenders Based on a Follow-Up Study: A Method Applicable to the Field of Mental Illness.* (A Report. NIMH Special Grant No. 3M 9149 [C1]). Quincy: South Shore Mental Health Center, Commonwealth of Massachusetts, August 1963.

This 78-item scale was designed to measure the interrelationships of delinquent youths emphasizing characteristics that may be considered causative of the delinquency and factual information that shows implications for future control.

Social Work Data Schedule

Hutcheson, B. R. *A Prognostic Classification for Juvenile Court First Offenders Based on a Follow-Up Study: A Method Applicable to the Field of Mental Illness.* (A Report. NIMH Special Grant No. 3M 9149 [C2]). Quincy: South Shore Mental Health Center, Commonwealth of Massachusetts, August 1963.

This 39-item instrument was designed to tap four major areas of data concerning each parent of a delinquent and one major area concerning both parents. It is a rating schedule that uses data obtained during a casework interview.

CHAPTER 10
Offenders

This chapter seeks to make available to the scientific public those research scales that were little used, but promising. We assumed that it was wasteful for researchers to begin afresh in development of scales when existing measures could be utilized. The pursuit of this objective becomes especially clear in the *personality assessment* section of this chapter on offenders. There four scales are reviewed: (1) the *Inmate Personality Inventory;* (2) the *Interpersonal Personality Inventory;* (3) the *Accessibility Scale;* and (4) the *Prison Fantasy Questionnaire.* All four scales show promise of validly assessing important aspects of offender functioning, and all four scales are not being used in contemporary research. The *Interpersonal Personality Inventory* (IPIC) is a good case study in nonutilization. It was developed in the early 1960s as part of an extensive investigation by a talented team of California investigators. The research project was completed, many members of the team soon drifted away, and the scale fell into a state of benign neglect.

While 20 behavior ratings appeared in the delinquency chapter, only 4 concern offenders, 2 of which are reviews and 2 of which are listings. Most of the delinquents' behavior ratings are of offenses. Two of the offenders' scales are offense rating schemes. The difference in number reflects the lesser emphasis the issue of defining offense severity and character has with adults as opposed to youths.

Scales concerned with the so-called "criminally insane" also are collected in this chapter. We recognize that the criminally insane are not legally offenders. Nevertheless they are also not members of the general public and the *Criminally Insane Attitude Scale* included here is the best fit among several possible classifications.

In the classification of scales, the categories of corrections prediction and offender prediction have yielded a very close pragmatic overlap. Theoretically, the corrections prediction category referred only to scales concerned with prediction in prison or parole settings. On the other hand, offender prediction scales were seen as being concerned with prediction of offenders' behaviors, regardless if the offenders were in or out of correctional confinement or on parole supervision.

For all practical purposes, the corrections prediction scales that are presented represent the total population. No "pure" offender prediction scales were found. Two scales attend to recidivism after release from prison by expiration of sentence. This offender population, however, was always studied *within* the prison or was mixed with parolees for research purposes. Thus, the scales were more properly considered corrections scales.

Finally, this chapter refers primarily to evaluation of people. Therefore, no reviews or listings of milieu measures are to be found.

OFFENDERS ATTITUDE SCALES: REVIEWS

Attitudes toward Offenders and Mental Patients

Development and Characteristics

The *Attitudes toward Offenders and Mental Patients Scale* (ATOMPS) was designed to assess the evaluative complex of ideas, beliefs, and attitudes toward people who have had mental illness or who have been in prison (Lamy, 1966). It was developed particularly to examine the public's diminution of social esteem concerning ex-mental patients. A control group that also possessed negative social attributes was necessary, and ex-convicts were chosen as a point of reference.

A set of 30 short vignettes were written that could refer to either an ex-mental patient or an ex-convict. These items were presented to 158 male and female undergraduate students in Oregon and Missouri. Of the 30 items, 16 yielded response patterns that were significantly different from chance in both samples. Therefore, the developers suggested that a general frame of reference existed regardless of geographical location.

The results also indicated that specific types of opinions were attributed to mental patients as opposed to ex-convicts. The ex-mental patient was viewed as more susceptible to breakdown and the ex-convict was seen as more reliable in an emergency.

Response Mode

The respondents are requested to read each statement and decide whether the statement is more appropriate for ex-convicts or ex-mental patients. The responses may be given verbally or in writing.

Scoring

Nelson, Thornton, and Pasewark (1973) suggest that a score might be obtained by awarding a 1 to each item that indicates a favorable response to ex-mental patients and a score of 0 to items that favor the ex-convict. Using this procedure, a score of 30 would indicate the most favorable response to mental patients and a score of 0 would indicate the most favorable response for ex-convicts.

Reliability

No estimates of reliability are available.

Validity

Nelson *et al.* (1972) used the ATOMPS to test whether members and caretakers of deviant groups would express more positive attitudes toward that group than another deviant group. They administered the ATOMPS to 32 residents and 30 staff members of an adolescent treatment unit in a state mental hospital, 28 residents and 18 staff members in a girls correctional school, and 87 residents and 39 staff members of a boys correctional school. Both staff members and residents of the correctional facilities expressed more favorable attitudes toward ex-convicts, while staff members and residents of mental institutions showed significantly more favorable attitudes toward former mental patients. Further, the initial validation study by Lamy (1966) supported the hypothesis that ex-patients and ex-convicts would elicit significantly different attitudes on the ATOMPS, and that highly specific differential patterns of attitudes are present toward the two groups.

Comments

The ATOMPS approach to measuring attitudes toward two groups indicates that aspects of the role of ex-mental patients are more undesirable than those of ex-convicts. The scale has support for validity as an attitude scale, but no evidence for temporal stability or internal consistency.

REFERENCES

Lamy, R. E. Social consequences of mental illness. *Journal of Consulting Psychology,* 1966, *30,* 450–455.

Nelson, M. B., Thornton, L. W., & Pasewark, R. A. Group membership and attitudes toward offenders and mental patients. *Journal of Community Psychology,* 1973, *1,* 425–426.

ATTITUDES TOWARD OFFENDERS AND MENTAL PATIENTS

Please read each statement and choose the alternative which you believe to be most appropriate.

1. A young lady about to be married would be more upset to learn that her fiance is an (a) ex-mental patient, (b) ex-convict.
2. A mother who is very solicitious of her children would be less willing to have them on go a weekend camping trip in the sole care of an (a) ex-mental patient, (b) ex-convict.
3. An employer seeking a man for a job involving minor responsibilities for the handling of large sums of money would be less likely to consider an (a) ex-mental patient, (b) ex-convict.
4. A wife can feel more confident of the family future if her husband is an (a) ex-mental patient, (b) ex-convict.
5. Most people feel that the man more responsible for his own trouble is an (a) ex-mental patient, (b) ex-convict.
6. The man who would feel more embarrassed about telling a potential employer of his stay in an institution is an (a) ex-mental patient, (b) ex-convict.
7. The man who is more likely to return to the institution is an (a) ex-mental patient, (b) ex-convict.
8. The mother who would be less worried about her children's having to spend time in the same institution as their father is the wife of an (a) ex-mental patient, (b) ex-convict.
9. An employer seeking a permanent member for his business who would be supervising many other people and handling a great deal of responsibility, would be less likely to hire an (a) ex-mental patient, (b) ex-convict.
10. Most people would feel more comfortable if assigned to share an office with an (a) ex-mental patient, (b) ex-convict.
11. If they had to choose, most men would rather be an (a) ex-mental patient, (b) ex-convict.
12. The man whom a woman, by her love, is more likely to feel she can keep from returning to the institution is an (a) ex-mental patient, (b) ex-convict.
13. Most people in the community feel that the parents more responsible for their son's trouble are the parents of an (a) ex-mental patient, (b) ex-convict.
14. The man who is more worried about his future is an (a) ex-mental patient, (b) ex-convict.
15. The man who would worry more about his children's having to go to the same institution as he did, is an (a) ex-mental patient, (b) ex-convict.
16. A lady having one single room for rent would less want to have for a roomer an (a) ex-mental patient, (b) ex-convict.
17. After he had had five years of good work on the job, an employer would be more inclined to give an important promotion to an (a) ex-mental patient, (b) ex-convict.

18. The man around whom his children would feel more relaxed is an (a) ex-mental patient, (b) ex-convict.
19. Kind, loving parents would have been of more help in preventing the problem of an (a) ex-mental patient, (b) ex-convict.
20. The man who could be more successful in seeing that his children did not have to go to an institution such as his, is an (a) ex-mental patient, (b) ex-convict.
21. The man about whom people could later say, "You'd never know he'd been in an institution," is more likely to be an (a) ex-mental patient, (b) ex-convict.
22. If we had a better economic system, we would have less people in the predicament of an (a) ex-mental patient, (b) ex-convict.
23. The man who will be less likely to give unselfish devotion to his wife and children is an (a) ex-mental patient, (b) ex-convict.
24. The man who would benefit more from trying to help others to keep out of the institution he was in is an (a) ex-mental patient, (b) ex-convict.
25. If he could find a good, steady job, the man more likely not to return to the institution is an (a) ex-mental patient, (b) ex-convict.
26. Should the same life situations appear again, the man less able to keep from going back into the same type of institution is an (a) ex-mental patient, (b) ex-convict.
27. The man who would be helped more by being trusted with responsibility on the job is an (a) ex-mental patient, (b) ex-convict.
28. The man whom most people would place more confidence in, in an emergency, is an (a) ex-mental patient, (b) ex-convict.
29. The man who would be helped more by joining the Army is an (a) ex-mental patient, (b) ex-convict.
30. If parents would pay more attention to disciplining their children, we would have less men in the predicament of an (a) ex-mental patient, (b) ex-convict.

Attitude toward Prisoners Scale

Development and Characteristics

The *Attitude toward Prisoners Scale* (ATPS) was designed to measure individuals' feelings about prisoners (Melvin, Koeblitz, & Gardner, 1978). It began with a pool of 70 statements about prisoners. These were placed in a standard Likert-type format. When the responses of 50 undergraduate psychology students and 43 residents of a medium sized community of about 80,000 people were factor analyzed, 36 items were shown to clearly define a single factor. Nineteen of the items are phrased to indicate a negative attitude toward prisoners. The remaining 17 indicate a positive attitude.

Response Mode

The respondents are asked to read each statement and indicate on a five-point scale the degree to which they agree or disagree. The response alternatives were: (1) strongly disagree, (2) disagree, (3) undecided, (4) agree, and (5) strongly agree.

Scoring

Each item receives a score from 1 to 5 indicating the degree of agreement with positive statements about prisoners and disagreement with negative statements about prisoners. Using this procedure, a high score indicates positive feelings for prisoners. A total score is obtained by adding the item scores and subtracting 36.

Norms

Table 54 shows the means and standard deviations for six groups of individuals who were tested. The groups were: (1) 90 students from introductory psychology classes, (2) 61 students from other undergraduate classes in psychology, (3) 35 students from a class in correctional psychology, (4) 23 law enforcement officers, (5) 5 professionals hired to classify prisoners, and (6) 14 "aftercare" counselors assigned to released prisoners.

Reliability

Melvin *et al.* (1978) report a test–retest reliability of .82 for 40 undergraduate students after a one week test–retest interval.

Odd–even split-half reliability estimates of .90 and .92 have been reported (Melvin *et al.*, 1978) for 66 undergraduate students and 23 law enforcement officers, respectively.

TABLE 54. Normative Means and Standard Deviations on the *Attitude toward Prisoners Scale*

Group	N	$\bar{X}$	SD
Introductory psychology students	90	90.2	15.86
Advanced psychology students	61	103.9	12.34
Correctional psychology students	35	100.0	11.99
Law enforcement officers	23	67.0	16.60
Prison classification personnel	5	113.2	16.92
"Aftercare" counselors	14	106.6	14.29

Validity

The ATPS possesses face validity and the results of the factor analysis support the unidimensionality of the scale.

Further evidence for the validity of the ATPS comes from its ability to differentiate between contrasting groups. As shown in the *Norms* section, law enforcement officers show a more negative attitude toward prisoners ($\bar{X} = 67.0$) than prison classification personnel ($\bar{X} = 113.2$) or aftercare counselors ($\bar{X} = 106.6$).

Comments

The ATPS, a systematic research effort, represents a move toward a valid prisoners' attitude instrument. It is well constructed, and has received support for reliability and validity. There is a small sample size in the prison classification personnel, but other evidence supports the usefulness of the ATPS.

REFERENCES

Melvin, K. B., Koeblitz, L., & Gardner, W. M. *A scale to measure attitudes toward prisoners*. Paper presented at the annual meeting of the Southeastern Psychological Association, Atlanta, March 1978.

ATTITUDE TOWARD PRISONERS SCALE

The statements listed below describe different attitudes toward prisoners in jails and prisons in the U.S.A. There are no right or wrong answers, only opinions. You are asked to express your feelings about each statement by indicating whether you (1) Disagree strongly, (2) Disagree, (3) are Undecided, (4) Agree, or (5) Agree strongly. Indicate your opinion by writing the number which best describes your personal attitude in the left-hand margin. Please answer every item.

Rating Scale

1	2	3	4	5
Disagree strongly	Disagree	Undecided	Agree	Agree strongly

*_____ 1. Prisoners are different from most people.

_____ 2. Only a few prisoners are really dangerous.

*_____	3.	Prisoners never change.
_____	4.	Most prisoners are victims of circumstance and deserve to be helped.
_____	5.	Prisoners have feelings like the rest of us.
*_____	6.	It is not wise to trust a prisoner too far.
_____	7.	I think I would like a lot of prisoners.
_____	8.	Bad prison conditions just make a prisoner more bitter.
*_____	9.	Give a prisoner an inch and he'll take a mile.
*_____	10.	Most prisoners are stupid.
_____	11.	Prisoners need affection and praise just like anybody else.
*_____	12.	You should not expect too much from a prisoner.
*_____	13.	Trying to rehabilitate prisoners is a waste of time and money.
*_____	14.	You never know when a prisoner is telling the truth.
_____	15.	Prisoners are no better or worse than other people.
_____	16.	You have to be constantly on your guard with prisoners.
*_____	17.	In general, prisoners think and act alike.
_____	18.	If you give a prisoner your respect, he'll give you the same.
*_____	19.	Prisoners only think about themselves.
_____	20.	There are some prisoners I would trust with my life.
_____	21.	Prisoners will listen to reason.
*_____	22.	Most prisoners are too lazy to earn an honest living.
_____	23.	I wouldn't mind living next door to an ex-prisoner.
*_____	24.	Prisoners are just plain mean at heart.
*_____	25.	Prisoners are always trying to get something out of somebody.
_____	26.	The values of most prisoners are about the same as the rest of us.
*_____	27.	I would never want one of my children dating an ex-prisoner.
_____	28.	Most prisoners have the capacity for love.
*_____	29.	Prisoners are just plain immoral.
*_____	30.	Prisoners should be under strict, harsh discipline.
*_____	31.	In general, prisoners are basically bad people.
_____	32.	Most prisoners can be rehabilitated.
_____	33.	Some prisoners are pretty nice people.
_____	34.	I would like associating with some prisoners.
*_____	35.	Prisoners respect only brute force.
_____	36.	If a person does well in prison, he should be let out on parole.

*Items reversed for scoring.

Criminally Insane Attitude Scale

Development and Characteristics

The *Criminally Insane Attitude Scale* (CIAS) was designed to "assess and compare attitudes of all the several disciplines who work with the criminally insane" (Khanna, Pratt, & Gardiner, 1962, p. 55). Items for this scale came from three sources. First, items that represented five major characteristics of attitudes toward criminally insane patients were constructed. These characteristics were: (1) attitudes regarding mental illness; (2) attitudes concerning criminally insane patients (these include attitudes that discriminate patients judged criminally insane, patients not judged criminally insane, general attitudes toward the criminally insane and attitudes reflecting differences due to the type of charge for which a criminally insane individual had been accused); (3) attitudes concerning treatment of criminally insane patients; (4) attitudes concerning discipline and punishment; and (5) attitudes concerning the role of patient caretakers.

A second set of items was obtained from staff clinical psychologists who were asked to give statements that they believed reflected attitudes toward the criminally insane. The third group of items consisted of a set of 15 statements (from the *Minnesota Multiphasic Personality Inventory*) that were believed to assess frankness or honesty. All items pooled together produced a 75-item questionnaire.

Finally, eight clinical psychologists rated each item as "psychiatrically favorable," or "psychiatrically unfavorable." The developers note that unanimity concerning the favorability or unfavorability of each item was obtained for all but 6 of the 75 items. For these six items, seven of the eight judges were in agreement.

Response Mode

The respondents are requested to read each of the statements and decide whether they "strongly agree," "mildly agree," "mildly disagree," or "strongly disagree." The response is indicated by drawing a circle around the appropriate alternative.

Scoring

The CIAS version of the standard Likert-type questionnaire offers only four alternatives, rather than five. Items that reflect favorable attitudes toward the criminally insane receive scores of 3, 2, 1, and 0 for strongly agree, mildly agree, mildly disagree, and strongly disagree, respectively. Items that reflect unfavorable attitudes toward the criminally insane receive scores of 3, 2, 1, and 0 for strongly disagree, mildly disagree, mildly agree, and strongly agree, respectively. Therefore, a high score represents a favorable attitude toward criminally insane patients.

Norms

No norms are available.

Reliability

Khanna *et al.* (1962) report a reliability coefficient of .87 for the CIAS, using Hoyt's technique. Information on sample size and characteristics of the group from which this result was obtained is not available.

Validity

Information is available for the concurrent validity of the CIAS as indicated by its relationship with intelligence (as measured by the Otis Employment Tests), length of employment, personality (as measured by the Cornell Index, Form N2, and the Harrower Multiple Choice Rorschach technique), social service orientation (as measured by the social service score from the Kuder Preference Record Vocational Form) age, education, and performance ratings (as measured by peers and supervisors). Table 55 shows the intercorrelation matrix between each of the variables. These responses represent the scores and ratings for 31 male aides who had been assigned to work with criminally insane patients. Their ages ranged from 22 to 74, with a mean of 45 years. Their education varied from eighth grade to three years in college; their average length of employment to date was 2.6 years with a range of 1 to 14 years.

Table 55 shows that the CIAS is positively related to intelligence (.64), social service orientation (.40), age (.44), and performance ratings (.41). The developers performed a factor analysis using CIAS scores and the other variables included in the intercorrelation matrix. The results supported the findings indicated by the intercorrelation matrix and show that the CIAS is appropriately correlated with the variables of intelligence, social service orientation, and performance ratings. No significant relationships existed between the CIAS and personality measures, or between the CIAS and education.

Comments

The CIAS seems to be a reliable instrument and has received support for its ability to measure attitudes toward the criminally insane. Concurrent validity measures have yielded positive results. There is, however, some question as to the unidimensionality of the scale. A factor analysis of the CIAS items alone

TABLE 55. Intercorrelations between "CI" Attitudes and Aide Characteristics

	Intelligence (IQ)	Length of employment	Cornell-Index	Rorschach (multiple-choice)	Social service orientation	Age	Education	Performance ratings
"CI" attitudes	.64[a]	.23	.19	.21	.40[a]	.44[a]	.25	.41[a]
Intelligence (IQ)		.21	.22	.03	.20	.12	.35[a]	.21
Length of employment			.08	.09	.20	.40[a]	.27	.09
Cornell-Index				.13	.08	.12	.28	.11
Rorschach (multiple-choice)					.09	.05	.23	.24
Social service orientation						.21	.20	.12
Age							.30	.49[a]
Education								.14

[a] Significant at .05 level.

could be informative. Finally, while the intent was to measure attitudes of the disciplines that work with the criminally insane, only data on aides have been reported.

REFERENCES

Khanna, J. L., Pratt, S., & Gardiner, G. Attitudes of psychiatric aides toward "criminally insane" patients. *Journal of Criminal Law, Criminology, and Police Science,* 1962, *53,* 55–60.

CRIMINALLY INSANE ATTITUDE SCALE

Read each of the statements below and then rate them as follows:

A	a	d	D
Strongly agree	Mildly agree	Mildly disagree	Strongly disagree

Indicate your opinion by drawing a circle around the "A" if you strongly agree, around the "a" if you mildly agree, around the "d" if you mildly disagree, and around the "D" if you strongly disagree.

Be sure to answer each question according to your own opinion. It is very important to the study that all questions be answered. Many of the statements will seem alike but all are necessary to show differences of opinion.

		Agree		Disagree	
1.	For the public protection all murderers should be hung.	A	a	d	D
2.	At times I feel like swearing.	A	a	d	D
3.	Only a few mental patients are dangerous.	A	a	d	D
4.	Mental disease appears suddenly without any warning.	A	a	d	D
5.	I do not read every editorial in the newspaper every day.	A	a	d	D
6.	It doesn't pay to give privileges because criminally insane patients (CI's) only take advantage of them.	A	a	d	D
7.	I do not like everyone I know.	A	a	d	D
8.	Thorazine will not cure most mental illnesses.	A	a	d	D
9.	Just talking to the patient, as in psychotherapy, is of little or no value.	A	a	d	D
10.	If you give a CI an inch he will want to take a mile.	A	a	d	D

11.	Some CI patients should be treated differently than other CI patients depending on their crimes.	A	a	d	D
12.	I would rather win than lose in a game.	A	a	d	D
13.	I like to know some important people because it makes me feel important.	A	a	d	D
14.	You can always pick out a "queer" (homosexual) from the rest of the patients.	A	a	d	D
15.	CI patients are no harder to handle than any other patients.	A	a	d	D
16.	Masturbation ("playing with oneself") can never cause insanity.	A	a	d	D
17.	Most criminals are mentally sick people and should be in a mental hospital rather than a prison.	A	a	d	D
18.	Anyone who has ever raped a child should die in the electric chair.	A	a	d	D
19.	For the good of the public all sex offenders should be castrated or sterilized.	A	a	d	D
20.	Most CI's are dangerous.	A	a	d	D
21.	Sometimes at elections I vote for men about whom I know very little.	A	a	d	D
22.	Through ward government by CI patients, they can become more responsible for themselves.	A	a	d	D
23.	I gossip a little at times.	A	a	d	D
24.	CI patients are generally stupid.	A	a	d	D
25.	Many patients who have killed someone long ago are now completely harmless.	A	a	d	D
26.	Mental illness is a disgrace.	A	a	d	D
27.	My table manners are not quite as good at home as when I am out in company.	A	a	d	D
28.	Some people can't keep from stealing even though they know it's bad.	A	a	d	D
29.	Murderers and sex offenders should always be separated on the ward.	A	a	d	D
30.	I would rather work on Dillon Building than anywhere else in the hospital.	A	a	d	D
31.	Mental illness is caused by bad blood.	A	a	d	D
32.	Most CI patients are sex crazed.	A	a	d	D
33.	Ward government by CI patients is dangerous.	A	a	d	D
34.	Other people at the hospital don't appreciate the job we aides do.	A	a	d	D

35.	For CI's, preventing escape is more important than the treatment for their mental illness.	A	a	d	D
36.	If mental patients had used will power they wouldn't be here in the first place.	A	a	d	D
37.	Given a chance most CI's will try to escape.	A	a	d	D
38.	If I could get into a movie without paying and be sure I was not seen I would probably do it.	A	a	d	D
39.	Once in a while I put off until tomorrow what I ought to do today.	A	a	d	D
40.	Physical punishment of CI's is occasionally necessary.	A	a	d	D
41.	Wet packs are not the best form of treatment.	A	a	d	D
42.	Most mental illness is really physical.	A	a	d	D
43.	Most aides are underpaid for the job they do.	A	a	d	D
44.	All CI patients who have committed a murder are still extremely dangerous.	A	a	d	D
45.	Most CI's should be in prison instead of the hospital.	A	a	d	D
46.	If a patient makes a lot of trouble, he should be given shock treatment to quiet him down.	A	a	d	D
47.	Patients who are here on bad check charges are not really mentally ill.	A	a	d	D
48.	Once in a while I think of things too bad to talk about.	A	a	d	D
49.	Most of the CI's sent from the pen are here for a soft touch.	A	a	d	D
50.	If you put a CI on an open ward you'll probably have trouble.	A	a	d	D
51.	All homosexuals ("queers") were born that way and can never change.	A	a	d	D
52.	CI patients are generally no different from other patients.	A	a	d	D
53.	Most aides would rather work anywhere in the hospital than on Dillon Building.	A	a	d	D
54.	Electric shock is a good punishment for CI patients.	A	a	d	D
55.	If you show that you are weak, CI patients will step all over you.	A	a	d	D
56.	CI's guilty of robbery should be in prison instead of the hospital.	A	a	d	D
57.	You can always tell a "queer" by the way he looks.	A	a	d	D
58.	CI patients should first of all be treated as criminals.	A	a	d	D
59.	If a "queer" makes a pass at somebody, they should beat him up.	A	a	d	D
60.	Sometimes when I am not feeling well I am cross.	A	a	d	D

61.	Since the aides know more about the patients they should have more to say about them.	A	a	d	D
62.	CI patients are generally as friendly as other patients.	A	a	d	D
63.	Electric shock treatment usually improves any patient's personality.	A	a	d	D
64.	Most mental disease starts in childhood.	A	a	d	D
65.	Most CI's need religion more than anything else.	A	a	d	D
66.	Electric shock treatment is bad for the patient's brains.	A	a	d	D
67.	If more discipline were handed out in childhood, there would be less patients in mental hospitals.	A	a	d	D
68.	Insanity runs in the family.	A	a	d	D
69.	I get angry sometimes.	A	a	d	D
70.	I do not always tell the truth.	A	a	d	D
71.	Once in a while I laugh at a dirty joke.	A	a	d	D
72.	Most CI's guilty of stealing did it because they needed the money.	A	a	d	D
73.	Most CI's are basically bad people.	A	a	d	D
74.	Sometimes for the patient's own good he has to be beaten up.	A	a	d	D
75.	CI patients are people who just had bad luck.	A	a	d	D

OFFENDER BEHAVIOR RATINGS: REVIEWS

Criminal Profile

Development and Characteristics

The *Criminal Profile* was designed (Gunn & Robertson, 1976) to "describe a man's criminal behavior in some meaningful way" (p. 156). It offers a rating of one's criminal contact with law enforcement along eight dimensions: theft, fraud, violence, motoring, drinking, drug taking, financial gain, relationship to drink. Each of these is rated on a 5-point scale, ranging from 0 (no conviction) to 4 (multiple convictions). The ratings indicate the relative involvement of offenders in these areas.

Response Mode

The ratings are made only after a man's criminal record has been read and the details of his offending behavior has been fully discussed with him.

Scoring

Scores are obtained by noting the number and severity of violations within each category. This number is the score for each category and contributes to the criminal profile.

Norms

No relevant norms are available.

Reliability

Table 56 lists correlations that were obtained for test–retest reliability over a two- to three-week period on 30 men in prison. (This correlation is also affected by the fact that two different raters were used in a switching process for the sample).

Validity

There is difficulty in validating a descriptive instrument. The question whether it is descriptive "enough" or "accurate" is determined by the needs of the user. Gunn and Robertson (1976) report "high agreement" between the *Criminal Profile* and a general description given by professionals within the system, as support for validity.

Comments

As mentioned earlier, evaluation of a descriptive instrument is based on its utility, which is in turn determined by the type of information one is seeking. If

TABLE 56. Test–Retest Correlations over a 2–3 Week Period for Men in Prison

Scale	r	N
Theft	0.92	20
Fraud	0.99	30
Sex	0.97	30
Violence	0.92	30
Motoring	1.00	30
Drink	0.87	30
Drugs	0.094	30

one is seeking a quick and reliable numerical rating that differentiates between types of property offenses, this method may be useful. The value of this scale is its ability to quantify the review of one's criminal record.

REFERENCES

Gunn, J., & Robertson, G. Drawing a criminal profile. *British Journal of Criminology,* 1976, *16,* 156–160.

CRIMINAL PROFILE SCALE

Theft

0   No convictions or reported behavior.
1   Self-confessed occasional theft in situations where a prosecution was a distinct possibility
    OR one or two convictions.
2   More than 2 convictions
    OR self-confessed frequent stealing.
3   Definite evidence of persistent criminal stealing, but no substantial profits made.
4   Substantial gains by persistent stealing.

Fraud

0   No convictions or reported behavior.
1   Self-confessed occasional fraud in situations where a prosecution was distinct possibility
    OR one or two convictions.
2   More than 2 convictions
    OR self-confessed frequent fraud.
3   Definite evidence of persistent criminal fraud, but no substantial profits made.
4   Substantial gains by persistent fraud.

Sex

0   No convictions for illegal sexual behavior.
1   One conviction for indecent exposure or other nonindictable offense.
2   Several nonindictable or one indictable offense.
3   Several indictable offenses.
4   Rape or sexual intercourse with children.

Violence

0 No convictions. Never gets into fights.

1 Evidence of minimal violence, i.e., occasional fights or damage to property. No convictions.

2 One or two convictions for violence, or repeated acts of violence to person or property, none of which has caused serious damage to life or health.

3 Three or more convictions for violence.

4 One or more severely violent episodes in which someone's life or health has been seriously endangered.

Motoring

0 No motoring convictions.

1 One to three offenses for speeding, traffic sign offenses, no insurance, no driving license, no license plates or careless driving.

2 Four or more offenses for speeding, traffic sign offenses, no insurance, no driving license, no license plates or careless driving.

3 Driving while disqualified
   OR one conviction for dangerous driving.

4 More than one conviction for dangerous driving
   OR causing death or serious injury by dangerous driving.

Drink

0 No drunkenness or drunken driving convictions.

1 One drunkenness or drunken driving conviction.

2 Two to four drunkenness or drunken driving convictions.

3 Five to twenty drunkenness or drunken driving convictions.

4 Twenty-one or more drunkenness or drunken driving convictions.

Drugs

0 No convictions or self-confessed illegality.

1 Self-confessed illegal drug activities on several occasions.

2 One conviction
   OR frequent self-confessed illegal drug activities.

3 Several drug convictions involving oral drugs.

4 Four or more drug convictions
   OR any intravenous use of illegal drugs.

Financial Gain

0 Any criminal activity which has ever involved financial gain.
1 Has made some profit from criminal activities but these have been very small and/or incidental.
2 Has made significant criminal profits but never been dependent upon crime for an income.
3 Largely financially dependent upon crime for significant periods. Activities may have been planned and regular but never large scale.
4 Professional crime. Large scale, well planned operations, usually involving several criminals.

Relationship to Drinking

0 Criminal activities have never been related to intake of alcohol.
1 Some evidence that some crimes have been committed under the influence of drink.
2 Evidence that a substantial part of criminal behavior is related to drink.
3 Evidence that majority, but not all, criminal activity is related to drink.
4 No criminal activity at all except in direct relationship to drinking.

Law Encounter Severity Scale

Development and Characteristics

The *Law Encounter Severity Scale* (LESS) was designed in an effort to precisely define the ex-offender's postrelease law-violating behavior (Witherspoon, de Valera, & Jenkins, 1973). Prior efforts with outcome criteria have frequently used recidivism, a dichotomous criterion that indicates nothing about the seriousness of the offense, or about the adjustment of the nonrecidivist. The LESS seeks to correct these deficits and to offer a vehicle for guiding treatment programs and indicating the cost of failure.

The LESS was developed as a result of two longitudinal follow-up studies, in 1969 and 1971, of adult male felons released into the community. The LESS consists of 38 items, which form a law encounter continuum (Witherspoon *et al.*, 1973, p. 4), ranging from "no law encounter" to "convicted of felony and sentenced to twenty years or more."

It was hypothesized that, in order to provide meaningful information about the ex-offender's behavior, a scale should be a continuum rather than a dichotomy, should generalize to all groups, should include "all offenses which can be verified by official records" (Witherspoon *et al.*, 1973, p. 3), and should group offenses by comparable cost (length of sentence).

The authors describe the data collection method as consisting of behavioral interviews, which lead to a five-point ranking of officially verified law encounters. Family members and parole officers, among others, often were interviewed as well as the client. Only the most severe law encounter in the 18.5 month average follow-up (range 11–26 months) was used to categorize the client.

Response Mode

The LESS is a measure of the individual offender's position on the violation continuum, which is more difficult than it initially appears. If one wishes to determine the subject's position by asking directly, he or she has first to be located. Then, one has to struggle with whether or not he or she is being truthful. Official records are not always reliable, and not always complete.

The developers indicate that the solution is to have "behavioral interviews" with the subject, and also to interview family and parole officers for leads. The conclusions should be verified by court record log books, since these are seen as more reliable than other official records.

Scoring

The LESS is divided into five groups of law encounter items.

Group I has only one item—"no law violations."

Group II has five items ranging in severity from "picked up and/or questioned or searched concerning a misdemeanor; not charged; released" to "arrested (charged) with felony(s); charges dropped; released."

Group III has 13 items ranging from "tried in court for misdeameanor(s), no conviction; released" to "convicted of misdemeanor; sentenced to 181 days or more or comparable fine."

Group IV has 15 items ranging from "felony warrant(s) issued; subject still not apprehended" to "convicted for felony(s); sentenced to less than one year."

Group V has four items ranging from "convicted for felony(s); sentenced to more than one but less than five years" to "convicted for felony(s); sentenced to twenty years or more."

Norms

The subjects on which the scale is standardized were described as adult male felons released into the community. Of these 142 men, 30% were in Group I, 15% in Group II, 18% in Group IV, 20% in Group V, and 4% in "Other."

Reliability

There was 95% agreement among three judges who ranked the items of the LESS in order of severity. No internal reliability, equivalent forms, or temporal reliability information was gathered. Furthermore, the authors reported that both other researchers and the scale developers may not always use the LESS in the exact form in which it is presented in this paper. This freedom to change the form is described as a flexibility that leads to greater scale applicability and generality.

Validity

The subjects falling into the five LESS groups were compared on the *Environmental Deprivation Scale* (EDS), which is an assessment of community support, and on the *Maladaptive Behavior Record* (MBR), which is an indicator of behavioral maladjustment. Generally, subjects falling below the mean on the EDS and the MBR, (that is, with successful adjustments) were found in LESS groups I and II. There also appears to be content validity in the sorting of the 38 items into their five groupings.

Comments

The LESS is intended to be a quantitative indicator of encounters with legal agencies. It is not a diagnosis of adjustment. It expands the dichotomous evaluation of recidivism and thus the LESS should allow justice programs to be more differentially evaluated. If widely used, it should make research results somewhat easier to compare.

The LESS relies heavily on the availability of court records and on the honesty of the offenders, and the offenders' relevant others, as well as depending on the patience and persistence of the user. Its use in large scale studies would be very time-consuming, since each offender must be interviewed and evaluated individually.

The reliability and validity estimates are limited. Yet overall this scale offers moderate promise. It expands a 2-point scale into a 5-point one, and permits more carefully defined descriptions of law encounters than are currently used.

REFERENCES

Witherspoon, A. D., de Valera, E. K., & Jenkins, W. O. The law encounter severity scale (LESS): A criterion for criminal behavior and recidivism. *Experimental Manpower Laboratory for Corrections,* Rehabilitation Research Foundation, Montgomery, Alabama, 1973.

LAW ENCOUNTER SEVERITY SCALE

Note: This information should be gathered through an interview and verified by court record log books.

Group I

1. No law encounters.

Group II

2. Picked up and/or questioned or searched concerning a misdemeanor(s); not charged; released.
3. Picked up and/or questioned or searched concerning felony(s); not charged; released.
4. Traffic violation(s); fined and/or sentenced (not including DWI).
5. Arrested (charged) with misdemeanor(s); charges dropped; released.
6. Arrested (charged) with felony(s); charges dropped; released.

Group III

7. Tried in court for misdemeanor(s); no conviction; released.
8. Tried in court for felony(s); no conviction; released.
9. Picked up for technical parole violation; had hearing; parole reinstated.
10. Picked up for technical parole violation; awaiting hearing.
11. Misdemeanor warrant(s) issued; subject still not apprehended.
12. Fugitive; bond(s) forfeited, subject still not apprehended (misdemeanor).
13. Arrested for misdemeanor(s); awaiting trial.
14. Arrested for misdemeanor(s); awaiting trial and a parole hearing.
15. Killed during the commission of a misdemeanor.
16. Convicted of misdemeanor; sentenced to 30 days or less or comparable fine.
17. Convicted of misdemeanor; sentenced to 31 days or more but less than 90 days or comparable fine.
18. Convicted of misdemeanor; sentenced to 91 days or more but less than 180 days or comparable fine.
19. Convicted of misdemeanor; sentenced to 181 days or more or comparable fine.

Group IV

20. Felony warrant(s) issued; subject still not apprehended.
21. Fugitive; bond forfeited on felony charge(s).
22. Absconded from parole; parole warrant issued.
23. Absconded from parole; parole warrant issued; and misdemeanor warrant(s) issued.

24. Absconded while on parole; parole warrant issued; and felony warrant(s) issued.
25. Absconded while on parole; charged and awaiting trial for misdemeanor(s).
26. Absconded while on parole; charged and awaiting trial for felony(s).
27. Arrested for felony(s); awaiting trial.
28. Arrested for felony(s); awaiting trial and parole hearing.
29. Picked up for technical parole violation; parole violated at hearing.
30. Parole violated at hearing; in prison awaiting trial for felony(s).
31. Parole violated for misdemeanor conviction; returned to prison.
32. Killed during the commission of felony.
33. Convicted for felony(s); placed on probation.
34. Convicted for felony(s); sentenced to less than one year.

Group V

35. Convicted for felony(s); sentenced to more than one but less than five years.
36. Convicted for felony(s); sentenced to more than five but less than ten years.
37. Convicted for felony(s); sentenced to more than ten but less than twenty years.
38. Convicted for felony(s); sentenced to twenty years or more.

Other Status Categories

Dead — deceased (natural or accidental).

OA — Subject moved out of study area (spent less than total of three months in follow-up study).

OFFENDERS BEHAVIOR RATINGS: LISTINGS

Index of Social Contacts

Arnold, W. R. A functional explanation of recidivism. *Journal of Criminal Law, Criminology, and Police Science*, 1965, 56, 210–220.

This 6-part index was designed to measure parolees' adjustment changes based upon their social contacts after release. A combination of data sources were combined in the index, including likely actions in hypothetical situations (presented in a questionnaire), interviews about changes in friendship patterns, and ratings by friends of the parolees.

Personal Characteristics Rating Report

VanBoskirk, C. *Vocational rehabilitation services in a maximum security setting.* (Final Report, Grant. No. RD-2473-G). Albany, N.Y.: Social Rehabilitation

Service, Department of Health, Education, and Welfare, Office of Vocational Rehabilitation, New York State Education Department, December 1974.

This 14-item, 5-point rating scale was designed to measure personal attributes of an inmate during vocational rehabilitation sessions as rated by a rehabilitation staff member.

OFFENDERS PERSONALITY ASSESSMENT: REVIEWS

Accessibility Scale

Development and Characteristics

The *Accessibility Scale* (AcS) was designed to aid the clinician working in the correctional setting in the early identification of "treatable" cases (Jacks, 1964). Since many of the treatment programs in correctional institutions today are continuing to use group therapy, it is important to be able to predict which individuals are appropriate for such an approach. With this in mind, the AcS was designed (Jacks, 1964) to measure the ability of an imprisoned individual to participate in group psychotherapy. To the degree that one carries into therapy a set of characteristics that indicate one's availability to treatment, one is accessible to therapy. Note that there is not necessarily a direct relationship between accessibility and whether an individual will benefit from the situation.

The instrument was constructed using a variation of the Thurstone equal appearing intervals method. The original pool of 189 items was obtained by reviewing the literature of group therapy and informally interviewing group therapists. The statements were worded so that some indicated an attribute favorable to the therapy and some showed an attribute unfavorable to therapy.

Six judges were asked to rank these items according to "relevance to group therapy accessibility," on a 5-point scale in which 1 was "most relevant" and 5 was "least relevant." When the rankings of the six judges were summed for each of the items, 83 had a score that indicated enough relevance to merit their inclusion in a final score.

The six judges were then asked to make a final rating of these items. Since the items could be agreed with or disagreed with, the statement was presented twice, once marked "I agree" and once marked "I do not agree." Therefore each of the judges was asked to rate 166 responses in a predetermined 9-point scale of accessibility. The rankings were as follows:

	Least Accessible							Most Accessible	
Rank	1	2	3	4	5	6	7	8	9
Frequency	8	12	20	26	34	26	20	23	8

When this was completed, an average of the six ratings for each of the 166 responses could be calculated and used as a weight in scoring.

The author suggests that inspection of the items shows the following factors in the scale to be of major importance: (1) awareness of emotional problems; (2) sensitivity to group opinion; (3) feelings of guilt and personal responsibility; (4) acceptance of need for treatment; and (5) identification with the family.

Response Mode

The respondent is instructed to respond "agree" or "disagree" to each of the statements.

Scoring

The scoring procedure requires that only the response to each item be weighted appropriately and these weights be summed. To simplify the scores, the obtained number is then divided by 10 and rounded to the nearest integer.

Norms

A sample of 68 inmates who were (1) English speaking, (2) nonpsychotic, and (3) nonhandicapped (physically), and who had also achieved an IQ score of 80 or higher on the Revised Beta examination, obtained a range of 269 to 417.5 and a mean of 334.7. This type of distribution would be expected, since the weights were formulated by a grouping-ranking procedure that forced a normal distribution of the weights.

Reliability

No reliability measurements were reported on this scale.

Validity

As a measure of predictive validity, scores on the scale were correlated with a criterion variable, group therapists' ratings of accessibility after 12 group sessions. The resultant correlation coefficient was .57 and is significant at the .01 level.

Other pretherapy ratings of accessibility included psychiatric interviews, projective psychological testing, and therapist interviews. These correlated .16, .32, and .35, respectively, with the criterion. Unfortunately, correlations between these and the scale were not presented.

Comments

This scale could be useful to the degree that one needs a measure of accessibility. If he or she is more interested in predicting those individuals who will benefit from therapy, he or she should look elsewhere.

With regard to the concept of accessibility, the AcS could be especially useful in corrections settings, because the wording of the items relates directly to the types of situations encountered by inmates of an institution. Caution should be exercised, however, in its clinical use. There are still questions of reliability and validity that need to be answered. Further research in these areas, and perhaps a test for heterogeneity, should be undertaken.

REFERENCES

Jacks, I. Accessibility to group psychotherapy of incarcerated adolescent offenders. *Journal of Criminal Law, Criminology, and Police Science*, 1964, *55*, 100–106.

ACCESSIBILITY SCALE

Put a check (✓) if you agree with the statement.
Put a cross (x) if you disagree with the statement

1. It is easier to "do a bit" in prison if you keep in touch with your family.
2. If I find something valuable lying in the street, my conscience would bother me if I didn't return it to its owner.
3. Whenever I go on a trip, I like to bring souvenirs home to my family.
4. Any man who commits a crime proves that he needs psychiatric treatment.
5. The advantage of psychiatric treatment is that it teaches a man how to go straight.
6. Every person alive has something wrong with him mentally, which could be helped by psychiatric treatment.
7. Most people feel a lot worse inside themselves than they ever show on the outside to other people.
8. I guess I am a pretty nervous person.
9. I missed some pretty good jobs because I felt too "shook up" to go for an interview.
10. I worry too much about small things.
11. I'm the kind of person who likes to stick to a problem until I've figured it out, even if it takes all night.

12. If any one stands around watching me work, even doing the easiest of things makes me go to pieces.
13. It never hurts to talk over one's troubles with the psychologist.
14. For a long time now, I've been trying to figure out what makes me get into trouble and wind up in these places.
15. I think it would do me good to talk over my problems with a psychologist.
16. Many times I have wanted to see the psychologist, but got cold feet at the last minute.
17. When I receive visits from my family in here, I feel ashamed to have them see me like this.
18. Although I know it's wrong to break the law, something in me makes me do it.
19. I'm glad I got caught, otherwise I might have gotten into a lot more serious trouble.
20. When I get out of here, I'm sure I'll be able to go straight.
21. When I make up my mind to do something, I usually get it done.
22. Talking before an audience is something I could never do without getting "all shook up."
23. If my home life had been better, I probably would not have gotten into trouble.
24. The hardest thing for me to do is to admit that I'm wrong in an argument.
25. I'm glad that I was picked to get psychological treatment.
26. Even though I doubt that there's anything seriously wrong with me, I guess I could be helped by receiving psychiatric treatment.
27. Whenever I feel tense or worried about something, my stomach gets upset.
28. I have diarrhea at least once a month.
29. If I had not had any brothers (or sisters), I would have gotten along better with my folks.
30. My brothers (or sisters) were treated better than me by my parents.
31. It's easier to discuss very personal problems if others with the same kind of problems are in the discussion also.
32. A man would be a fool to admit doing things that might get him into trouble.
33. I don't think that I would like the life that most people lead on the outside.
34. I wish I could be as normal as everybody else.
35. Sometimes my life seems so hopeless, I feel like crying inside.
36. Guys who get scared or cry make me feel disgusted with them.
37. Prisons nowadays do more to help the inmates then they used to.
38. When I was in school, I used to feel stupid and less capable than the other kids.
39. I can honestly say that I never hurt anyone on purpose.
40. I'd rather stay poor than get rich by cheating somebody else.
41. I've tried to help other people solve their problems by using psychology.

42. I've tried to psychoanalyze myself, and I believe I now understand myself better.
43. I read books on psychology whenever I can.
44. I'd be ashamed to have my buddies know that I was seeing a psychologist.
45. If I thought it would help me to stay out of trouble in the future, I'd be willing to finish up my time in here.
46. I'd rather talk to the psychologist privately about my problems, than discuss them in front of a group of other inmates.
47. I wish I understood why I do things that get me into trouble.
48. Most girls are true to their boyfriends, while the boys are in prison.
49. It's going to be hard to face the neighbors when I get out of here.
50. I wish I had more self-confidence.
51. Most of the time I feel depressed, down in the dumps.
52. If my parents had taken better care of me when I was younger, I probably would not be here now.
53. When a man makes up his mind to do something, he should first figure out if it will hurt anyone.
54. I enjoy sitting around with a group of guys and having a bull-session.
55. Whenever I get into a club or a crowd, I like to take charge of things.
56. It's easier for me to do a favor than to ask someone to do me a favor.
57. Most people have the same kind of problems as everyone else.
58. Whenever I start to worry about anything, I get an upset stomach.
59. It's easier for me to talk about personal matters in a group than to one person in private.
60. It's hard for me to act natural when I'm in a group.
61. I've been responsible for a lot of the trouble I've been in.
62. If I could get rid of the bad habits which I have acquired in my life, I would have a better life.
63. It's been a long time since I stopped and thought about my future life.
64. It takes me a long time to get going on a new task.
65. I try to get out of responsibilities because of a fear that I won't measure up.
66. I become tired more easily when I'm doing something that makes me anxious.
67. So much of my life consists of playing various parts, that the "real me" seems never to come out.
68. It's easier to promise to do things better than to actually do them better.

69. I criticize and resent the success of other people out of bitterness regarding my own lack of success.
70. Whenever I come into some new situation, I get panicky and worry about whether I will be able to do what's expected.
71. I frequently say things to people, especially important people, just to be agreeable, because of a fear of making them dislike me.
72. I prefer going on doing the same old things, because new things or new places frighten me.
73. I do my best work on jobs where someone else is likely to get the credit or blame for the outcome.
74. Whenever I get started on something that may do me some good, I seem to do something to spoil it.
75. I keep from getting too close to people, because I fear that getting close would result in their hurting me.
76. I feel more tense in some situations than in others.
77. I sometimes give reasons for my actions, which I know are not the real reasons.
78. Some of my ideas are so strange, that it would embarrass me to mention them to another person.
79. I'm afraid to admit even to myself some of the things I sometimes think about.
80. I feel disgusted everytime I "jerk off."
81. A man's friend usually understands him better than his family does.
82. How far a man goes in life depends pretty much on himself.
83. I enjoy discussions in which each person has a different idea or opinion on a subject.

Inmate Personality Survey

Development and Characteristics

The *Inmate Personality Survey* (IPS) was developed to assess the personality of incarcerated individuals (Carlson, 1972). Although many personality tests or inventories are available, the developer believes that few are appropriate for use within the prison setting.

This scale was begun with the idea that most personality tests were unsuitable for the prison population for three reasons. (1) Prisoners are often poorly educated and rarely read well enough to comprehend the language of the scale. (2) Prisoners find it difficult to dichotomize their responses into "true" or "false" feelings for a statement. (3) The stimulus items lack relevance to the criminal population. The IPS gives special consideration to these issues. It is written in simple language, using examples that are pertinent to incarcerated people, and offers a five-point Likert-type response set. There is also a space beside each statement for any additional comments the respondent might wish to make.

The survey construction began with a search through psychological, psychiatric, and social work reports of a correctional institution. From these descriptions of inmates, the scale developer was able to identify 10 content areas. They are: criminal attitudes, chemical abuse, background problems, thought disorder, emotional upset, hostility, assaultiveness, motivation for change, and self-depreciation.

After the format was decided on, a set of items was devised and underwent several revisions in which an item was discarded if it was difficult for respondents to understand, or if it showed a correlation of .2 or greater with any of the other subscales, or .5 or less with any of the items within its subscale. A statement was also discarded if it did not yield an even distribution of responses.

When the inventory was readministered and analyzed, internal consistency for each of the subscales was less than desirable so the test was revised again. This time it was felt that some of the subscales might actually be measuring the same dimension of personality. With this in mind, certain scales were consolidated and shortened. The inventory then included 50 items and the following five scales:

1. Validity: This scale reflects the degree to which the person maintains an acceptable test-taking attitude. The high scorer has failed to maintain the proper set, is answering carelessly or facetiously, or does not understand the questions.
2. Chemical Abuse: This dimension reflects the degree to which the person abuses drugs or alcohol and the relevance of these chemicals to his criminal behavior.
3. Psychotic tendencies: This dimension reflects disorganization of thinking, confusion, perceptual distortions and hallucinations, and feelings of unreality. These traits manifest themselves in unusual affect, particularly depression and anxiety. High scorers on this scale are indicating unusual problems in dealing with reality because they cannot organize themselves or the world around them. They are emotionally upset, and may be moody, hypochondriacal, miserable, despondent, and even suicidal.
4. Antisocial tendencies: This scale reflects a hostile animosity and socially defiant attitude in the person, as well as willingness to be assaultive or threatening. This assaultiveness may or may not culminate in actual physical aggression; it may be clearly demonstrated by malicious conversation and a mocking, unfriendly manner. High scorers are also likely to be cynical of other individuals, interpreting their behavior as unjust or always self-rewarding. Inherent in this scale is an acceptance of crim-

inal behavior. The person is not necessarily antiestablishment, but prefers the values and customs of those who commit criminal offenses. That is, he or she acts in an unethical and untrustworthy manner, but feels little or no guilt.
5. Self-depreciation: This dimension reflects the degree to which the person degrades himself and his actions. The high scorer generally does not value himself and refuses credit for any accomplishment.

Response Mode

One of the qualities the developer feels strongly about is the ease in responding to the statements. This feeling prompted the construction of a test booklet in which the responses may be recorded directly under the item rather than on a separate answer sheet. The subject reads the statement, decides which of the alternatives is closest to the way he or she feels, and puts an "x" beside his or her choice. If he or she wants to comment, a space alongside the item is provided.

Scoring

A scoring sheet is available that lists the number of each item within the respective subscales. The response alternatives for each item are prearranged so that they are weighted in the appropriate direction. This weight is added to the other response weights within each subscale and summed for a total subscale score. Then each of the scale scores are plotted on a profile sheet that is in the manual.

Norms

The norms for this inventory were presented as patterns of a total profile. The developer offers 15 types of profiles as a classification scheme. Each of these types is described according to the five subscales, and predictions are made as to how an individual with each type of profile will fare at other kinds of institutions or in civilian life.

Reliability

No test–retest measures were reported on the inventory. An inter-item correlation of .5 or greater within each subscale was used as a criterion for inclusion of any item in the final revision.

The test was administered to two samples of 206 inmates who were being held in an Ontario Correctional Centre for adult male first-incarcerates. They were serving a maximum sentence of two years (definite and indefinite) and a

TABLE 57. Reliability Statistics for Sample 1 ($N = 206$)

Scale name	Alpha reliability
Validity	0.18
Chemical abuse	0.73
Psychotic tendencies	0.80
Antisocial tendencies	0.82
Self-depreciation	0.67

minimum of 30 days. The mean age was 19.0 (SD was 3.3). Tables 57 and 58 show the Alpha Reliabilities obtained for each sample. Note that all scales (except validity) show good reliability.

Validity

As a first attempt at validation, the variables of age, sentence, IQ, misconduct reports, and return probability were studied with relation to each subscale of the IPS.

There was little relationship between IQ and the subscales and an inverse relationship between age and most of the scales. One unpredicted low correlation was between antisocial tendencies and misconduct reports. The developer suggests that the low coefficient indicates that another dimension, perhaps social control, determines whether an individual will "act out."

When the IPS was tested across the following types of offenses, it showed a probability of less than .001: (1) personal offenses, (2) property offenses, (3) offenses against morals and decency, (4) offenses against order and peace, and (5) armed robbery. Individual F tests for each of the subscales showed that only two of the dimensions (antisocial tendencies and self-depreciation) contributed to the discrimination to a statistically significant degree.

The third method used in validating the survey is cluster analysis. Two samples of 206 inmates support the use of 15 discrete profile types, which can be used in the discussion of these types.

TABLE 58. Reliability Statistics for Sample 2 ($N = 206$)

Scale name	Alpha reliability
Validity	0.16
Chemical abuse	0.70
Psychotic tendencies	0.80
Antisocial tendencies	0.81
Self-depreciation	0.72

Comments

This inventory was developed under the assumption that incarcerated individuals are different from civilians and that these differences should dictate the style of testing used within correctional institutions. Whether these differences exist or not, the attempts to make the test less noxious are valuable.

There is a major concern over the validity of the inventory. The correlations between misconduct reports or return probabilities and the subscale antisocial tendencies are low—less than .25. Also, the fact that only two of the scales, antisocial tendencies and self-depreciation, showed significant F ratios across the five offense categories is not encouraging (i.e., to the extent that one believes offense categories are meaningful criteria). The author suggests that other dimensions, such as self-control, may be the determining factor.

Overall, this instrument has been thoughtfully developed, has adequate reliability, and a presentation style that is simple and direct. It holds good potential for research in assessment of offenders.

REFERENCES

Carlson, K. A. *A handbook for the Inmate Personality Survey.* Kenneth Carlson, 1972, Department of Correctional Services, Ontario, Canada.

INMATE PERSONALITY SURVEY

Instructions. Put an X for the one correct answer to each question.

Comments

1. I drink alcohol:
   1. ____ never
   2. ____ once in a while
   3. ____ about once a week
   4. ____ more than once a week
   5. ____ all the time

2. My thinking is:
   1. ____ good, straight
   2. ____ good, but a little mixed up
   3. ____ mixed up, but I can do OK
   4. ____ mixed up
   5. ____ my head is all mixed up

3. I trust:
   1. ___ everyone
   2. ___ most people
   3. ___ some people but not others
   4. ___ only my best friends
   5. ___ no one

4. My life is:
   1. ___ very interesting
   2. ___ interesting
   3. ___ both interesting and dull
   4. ___ dull
   5. ___ really sad and depressed

5. I feel:
   1. ___ OK
   2. ___ a little down, but OK
   3. ___ sad some of the time
   4. ___ sad a lot of the time
   5. ___ really sad and depressed

6. I would use a weapon to rob someone:
   1. ___ never
   2. ___ almost never
   3. ___ maybe
   4. ___ would do it
   5. ___ have done it and would do it again

7. I have used drugs:
   1. ___ never
   2. ___ once or twice
   3. ___ some of the time
   4. ___ most of the time
   5. ___ all of the time

8. I see or hear things that are not there:
   1. ___ never
   2. ___ once or twice
   3. ___ more than once or twice
   4. ___ often
   5. ___ many times

9. I have told others off:
   1. ___ never
   2. ___ once or twice
   3. ___ more than once or twice
   4. ___ often
   5. ___ many times

10. I think my future will be:
    1. ___ very good
    2. ___ pretty good
    3. ___ not too bad

Comments

OFFENDERS

   4. ____ bad
   5. ____ nothing ever went right and nothing ever will

11. I speak English and:
    1. ____ no other languages
    2. ____ 1 or 2 other languages
    3. ____ 3 or 4 other languages
    4. ____ 5 or 6 other languages
    5. ____ 6 or more other languages

12. My nerves are:
    1. ____ pretty good
    2. ____ average
    3. ____ jumpy but OK
    4. ____ very poor
    5. ____ shot

13. In school, I have caused trouble:
    1. ____ never
    2. ____ once or twice
    3. ____ 3 or 4 times
    4. ____ 5 or 6 times
    5. ____ more than 7 times

14. When I got into trouble on my present charge, I had:
    1. ____ not been drinking or had drugs at all
    2. ____ only had a little
    3. ____ had a fair amount
    4. ____ had too much
    5. ____ had so much I did not know what I was doing

15. When I watch a TV show, I can understand what is going on:
    1. ____ always
    2. ____ almost all of the time
    3. ____ much of the time
    4. ____ some of the time
    5. ____ never

16. When I was younger, the police picked up:
    1. ____ none of my friends
    2. ____ one or two of my friends
    3. ____ some of my friends
    4. ____ most of my friends
    5. ____ all of my friends

17. People seem to think I do things:
    1. ____ very good
    2. ____ good
    3. ____ better than average
    4. ____ average
    5. ____ poor

18. When I get out, I will drink alcohol or take drugs: Comments
    1. ___ never
    2. ___ once in a while
    3. ___ once a week
    4. ___ 2 or 3 times a week
    5. ___ more than 3 times a week

19. Physically, my body and health are:
    1. ___ perfect
    2. ___ very good
    3. ___ pretty good
    4. ___ not too good
    5. ___ poor

20. I think most of the staff in this place are:
    1. ___ nice and helpful
    2. ___ helpful
    3. ___ OK
    4. ___ not too bad
    5. ___ stupid

21. Most people seem to think I am:
    1. ___ a very good person
    2. ___ a bit better than others
    3. ___ just like everyone else
    4. ___ a bit worse than others
    5. ___ a very bad person

22. I believe that drugs have made me think and do:
    1. ___ I do not use drugs
    2. ___ bad things
    3. ___ have no effect on me
    4. ___ better things than I usually do
    5. ___ very good things

23. I have trouble remembering the names of my friends:
    1. ___ never
    2. ___ once in a while
    3. ___ some of the time
    4. ___ most of the times
    5. ___ all of the time

24. I have been in gang fights:
    1. ___ never
    2. ___ never but wish I had
    3. ___ once
    4. ___ 2 or 3 times
    5. ___ more than 3 times

25. I think I do the best thing:
    1. ___ all the time
    2. ___ almost all the time
    3. ___ much of the time
    4. ___ some of the time
    5. ___ once in a while

OFFENDERS

26. I have lived in this country and:
    1. ___ no other country
    2. ___ 1 or 2 other countries
    3. ___ 3 or 4 other countries
    4. ___ 5 or 6 other countries
    5. ___ 7 or more other countries

27. I change from happy one minute to sad the next:
    1. ___ never
    2. ___ once in a while
    3. ___ some of the time
    4. ___ most of the time
    5. ___ all of the time

28. I enjoy fighting:
    1. ___ not at all
    2. ___ a little
    3. ___ some
    4. ___ much
    5. ___ very much

29. Most of my best friends drink alcohol:
    1. ___ never
    2. ___ once in a while
    3. ___ about once a week
    4. ___ more than once a week
    5. ___ all the time

30. People I know seem like strangers to me:
    1. ___ never
    2. ___ once in a while
    3. ___ some of the time
    4. ___ most of the time
    5. ___ all the time

31. When I think about my offense, I am:
    1. ___ very sorry
    2. ___ sorry
    3. ___ not sorry or never think about it
    4. ___ might do it again
    5. ___ will do it again

32. People seem to like it better when:
    1. ___ I talk a lot
    2. ___ I talk a little
    3. ___ I am there but do not bother them
    4. ___ I just listen
    5. ___ I am not there

33. When I think about my problems, I:
    1. ___ know they will work out
    2. ___ never think about them or have no problems
    3. ___ worry little

4. ___ worry a lot 5. ___ get so scared I feel sick	Comments

34. If someone tried to cheat me, I would:
    1. ___ forgive and forget
    2. ___ forgive but not forget
    3. ___ not forgive him
    4. ___ make him sorry
    5. ___ kill him

35. Most of the time I sleep:
    1. ___ every night
    2. ___ twice a week
    3. ___ once a week
    4. ___ almost never
    5. ___ never

36. Dreams have made me wake up in the middle of the night:
    1. ___ never
    2. ___ once or twice
    3. ___ 3 to 5 times
    4. ___ more than 5 times
    5. ___ I wake up every night

37. If someone hit me, I would:
    1. ___ I do not know what I would do
    2. ___ go away or ask him why he did it
    3. ___ hit him once
    4. ___ beat him up
    5. ___ kill him

38. Most of my friends use drugs:
    1. ___ never
    2. ___ once or twice
    3. ___ some of the time
    4. ___ most of the time
    5. ___ all the time

39. I forget what I was going to say:
    1. ___ never
    2. ___ once in a while
    3. ___ some of the time
    4. ___ most of the time
    5. ___ all the time

40. I think:
    1. ___ all laws are good
    2. ___ most laws are good
    3. ___ laws are good and bad
    4. ___ many laws are bad
    5. ___ all laws are bad

OFFENDERS

41. When I do things, I do them:
    1. ____ very good
    2. ____ good
    3. ____ better than average
    4. ____ average
    5. ____ poor

42. Little things worry me:
    1. ____ never
    2. ____ once in a while
    3. ____ some of the time
    4. ____ most of the time
    5. ____ all the time

43. If I hurt someone, I would feel:
    1. ____ very bad
    2. ____ bad
    3. ____ bad, but not too bad
    4. ____ depends on the person and how I would feel
    5. ____ would not care

44. When I am drunk or on drugs, I:
    1. ____ do not get drunk or take drugs
    2. ____ never get into trouble
    3. ____ try not to get into trouble
    4. ____ sometimes get into trouble
    5. ____ always get into trouble

45. I will be in trouble:
    1. ____ never again
    2. ____ do not want to be again
    3. ____ do not want to be again but probably will be again
    4. ____ once or twice more
    5. ____ for the rest of my life

46. The drug I have taken the MOST is:
    1. ____ no drugs
    2. ____ marijuana or hashish
    3. ____ LSD or drugs like LSD
    4. ____ speed or drugs like speed
    5. ____ heroin or drugs like heroin

47. I feel sick:
    1. ____ never
    2. ____ once in a while
    3. ____ some of the time
    4. ____ most of the time
    5. ____ all the time

48. I get a kick out of seeing someone put down:
    1. ____ never
    2. ____ once in a while

        3. ___ some of the time
        4. ___ most of the time
        5. ___ all the time

49. My life has been:
        1. ___ better than most people
        2. ___ as good as most people
        3. ___ average
        4. ___ as bad as most people
        5. ___ worse than most people

50. I have carried a weapon on me:
        1. ___ never
        2. ___ once or twice
        3. ___ some of the time
        4. ___ most of the time
        5. ___ all the time

Comments

Interpersonal Personality Inventory

Development and Characteristics

The *Interpersonal Personality Inventory* (IPIC) was designed (Ballard, Fosen, Neiswonger, Fowler, Belasco, & Tyler, 1966) to serve as a relatively simple and objective means of classifying inmates as "high" or "low" in levels of integration (I-levels) of interpersonal maturity within the theoretical framework of Sullivan, Grant, and Grant (1957). I-levels 2 and 3 were defined as low maturity; I-levels 4 and 5 as high maturity. The impetus for its development came from the results of the Camp Elliot study (Grant & Grant, 1959), in which interpersonal maturity of military retrainees, as assessed by a lengthy interview, was found to interact with type of success of treatment.

Forty-eight items were retained following an item analysis of an original pool of 600. The item pool came from scales developed in the Camp Elliot study, from the *California Psychological Inventory,* and the *Minnesota Multiphasic Personality Inventory,* and items that were hypothetically related to interpersonal maturity. Previously constructed "fake good" and "fake bad" scales added another 45 items to the final form of the inventory.

An hour-long individual interview classified 302 adult male prisoners into one of four levels of maturity. From an original subject pool of 628 men, these 302 subjects were assigned independently to agreed-upon maturity ratings by two out of three experts and typified the various maturity levels. They were randomly assigned to the construction and validation samples.

Response Mode

The respondents mark an answer sheet true or false, and are told to "Be sure to mark an answer for each of the statements, even if you are not too sure of some of them."

Scoring

The IPIC is composed of 93 true-false items, and yields a single raw score, which may be converted to a T score using a table in the manual. Subjects receiving a raw score of 27 or below are classified as low maturity, 30 or above as high maturity, with scores of 28 or 29 remaining unclassified. For the construction sample ($N = 161$), these cutoff points resulted in 8.1% unclassified and 13% misclassified. In the validation sample, 12.1% were unclassified and 18.4% misclassified.

Norms

The IPIC manual provides means, standard deviations, and frequency distributions for the 161 subjects in the construction sample, the 141 subjects in the validation sample, and for the two samples combined. Also included are means, standard deviations, standard scores and percentages for 1,029 consecutive male admissions to the Reception–Guidance Center during a one-year period. Table 59 shows the means and standard deviations of these four groups.

Reliability

The split-half reliability of the IPIC was $r = .73$ for the construction sample and .54 for the validation sample. Odd-even reliability coefficients were .78 and .86 for the construction and validation samples, respectively.

Validity

Scores on the IPIC were correlated with high and low maturity as assessed by independent interview judgments to study concurrent validity. The biserial correlation coefficient was .87 for the construction sample, .74 for the validation group and .84 for the combined construction and validation samples. Point biserial r's for the three groups were .69, .59, and .64, respectively. The IPIC means for the construction and validation samples were very similar for subjects classified

TABLE 59. IPIC Means and Standard Deviations for Four Samples

Group	M	SD
Construction sample ($N = 161$)	28.48	8.41
Validation sample ($N = 141$)	27.77	8.20
Combined ($N = 307$)	28.15	8.35
Male inmates ($N = 1,029$)	26.86	7.38

by interview as low maturity (23.3 and 24.2) and as high maturity (34.9 and 33.9). When the unclassified subjects are excluded, the combined samples yielded only 15.6% misclassification. Of the high maturity subjects, 18% were misclassified; of the low maturity subjects, 12.1% overall were misclassified. Thus substantial validity evidence is present.

Comments

The IPIC has been thoughtfully and empirically developed, has a sizeable normative population, adequate reliability, and good validity. It may be useful as a short, easily-scored method of dividing inmate populations into high and low maturity levels. When the construction and validation samples were divided into maturity levels by individual interview, 58.9% were classified as low maturity. The IPIC correctly classified 77.3% of the construction sample. Assuming that 58.9% is the base rate of occurrence of low-maturity subjects in the population, the IPIC provides an 18.4% improvement over classifying all subjects as low maturity. In view of the ease with which this improvement may be achieved, in comparison with individual interviews for all subjects, the IPIC appears to be a valuable aid for those investigating interpersonal maturity in male inmates and a most promising research instrument.

REFERENCES

Ballard, K. B., Jr., Fosen, R. H., Neiswonger, J., Fowler, R., Belasco, J., & Tyler, R. *Interpersonal Personality Inventory Manual.* Vacaville, California: Institute for the Study of Crime and Delinquency, California Medical Facility, September, 1966.

Grant, J. D., & Grant, M. Q. A group dynamics approach to the treatment of nonconformists in the Navy. *Annals of the American Academy of Political and Social Science,* 1959, *322,* 126–135.

Sullivan, C. E., Grant, J. D., & Grant, M. Q. The development of interpersonal maturity: Applications to delinquency. *Psychiatry,* 1957, *20,* 373–385.

INTERPERSONAL PERSONALITY INVENTORY

Directions: This is a test of your ability to understand yourself.

In this booklet there are a number of statements which are related to your opinions about the world in general and to your feelings about yourself.

Be sure to mark an answer for each of the statements, even if you are not too sure of some of them. Work straight through the statements; <u>DON'T</u> spend too much time on any one statement.

1. My parents wanted me to "make good" in the world.
2. If I were a millionaire, I am sure I could get anything I want.
3. I would never go out of my way to help another person if it meant giving up some personal pleasure.
4. I would rather have the respect of other people than be rich.
5. He who laughs last laughs loudest and longest.
6. Most people would be better off if they never went to school at all.
7. Actually I am not as sensitive as I think the average person is.
8. I get angry sometimes.
9. If I saw some children hurting another child, I am sure I would try to make them stop.
10. Voting is nothing but a nuisance.
11. It isn't too important to me whether other people like me or not.
12. Compromising with others with a different religion or ideals is the same as lowering your own standards.
13. The main satisfactions a man gets from the job usually are in terms of the kind of people he has to work with.
14. Everyone naturally loves his parents because they are his parents.
15. I get upset fairly often while locked up in a place like this.
16. I have very few quarrels with members of my family.
17. I do not read every editorial in the newspaper every day.
18. Man is powerless in the hands of fate.
19. I have learned that everyone really knows right from wrong so there is no need for argument.
20. I often think, "I wish I were a child again."
21. There are times when I have been discouraged.
22. There is a good type and a bad type that almost all people can be separated into.
23. I usually try to do what is expected of me, and to avoid criticism.
24. I would rather be a steady and dependable worker than a brilliant but unstable one.
25. I have often met people who were supposed to be experts who were no better than I.
26. Policemen "bawl out" people largely to satisfy their own sense of importance.
27. I feel about my parents the same now as I did when I was a child.
28. I don't really care much for reading newspaper stories about crime or criminals.
29. Most young people get too much education.
30. I hardly ever ask other people for advice.
31. In school most teachers treated me fairly and honestly.
32. I always follow the rule that what people don't know won't hurt them.

33. I like everyone I know.
34. Actually, the most important single thing for a man to give his family is good support so that they will have all the things they need.
35. I have enjoyed listening to symphony music.
36. Sometimes when I am not feeling well I am cross.
37. I could be perfectly happy without a single friend.
38. Sometimes I find myself admiring certain people a great deal.
39. I can see no reason why a person would ever vote to increase his own taxes.
40. It would be kind of dumb to vote for increasing your own taxes.
41. I have been angry at one or more people in my life.
42. It is by returning to our forgotten and glorious past that real social progress can be achieved.
43. I don't like poetry.
44. I have sometimes slacked off on my duties when I thought I could get away with it.
45. I admire anyone in authority.
46. I must admit that people sometimes disappoint me.
47. Women should stay out of politics.
48. To become really civilized, we should know about great stories and art.
49. When in a group of people I have trouble thinking of the right things to talk about.
50. I doubt if anyone is really happy.
51. All is fair in love and war.
52. In most groups I am in, I usually handle some of the leadership responsibility.
53. If a child is unusual in any way, his parents should get him to be more like other children.
54. I certainly feel useless at times.
55. I never seem to get hungry.
56. In most groups I am in, I usually accept some of the leadership responsibility.
57. Sometimes at elections I vote for men about whom I know very little.
58. I don't feel critical about my father and mother, and don't remember that I ever did.
59. People seem to ask my advice on decisions fairly often.
60. I would cheerfully do any job to which I was ordered regardless of how unsensible it seemed to me.
61. I never worry much about politics and war.
62. I always tell the truth.
63. Sometimes I forget things that I've been told.
64. I have always spoken the same way.
65. It is very important to me to find out what makes people "tick."

66. Some people exaggerate their troubles in order to get sympathy.
67. I almost never go to sleep.
68. I would rather win than lose in a game.
69. A person who won't take the responsibility of others will never grow up.
70. I would fight if someone tried to take my rights away.
71. I cannot do anything well.
72. People can be divided into two distinct classes: the weak and the strong.
73. Sometimes I've felt resentment when told to do something.
74. I gossip a little at times.
75. If I hadn't such bad luck I would be a lot better off today.
76. Offhand I can't think of anyone I really admire.
77. I never have any trouble breaking off with or dropping a friend.
78. People usually make friends because they know they may need friends later on to help.
79. Sometimes I feel like swearing.
80. Once in a while I put off until tomorrow what I ought to do today.
81. I do not like to loan my things to people who are careless in the way they take care of them.
82. It is impossible for an honest man to get ahead in the world.
83. I can't see that answering all these questions is going to be of any use to anybody.
84. Sometimes I've known authority to be wrong.
85. The Bible should be understood as meaning exactly what it says.
86. I don't think I have ever had the problem of thinking faster than I could speak.
87. There should be a fixed sentence decided on in advance and published for each offense.
88. Once in a while I laugh at a dirty joke.
89. It would make me feel terrible if I thought I had been mean to somebody.
90. Education is more important than most people think.
91. A person should not be expected to do anything for his community unless he is paid for it.
92. Standing up for the rights of others is everyone's duty.
93. Nowadays more and more people are prying into matters that should remain personal and private.

Prison Fantasy Questionnaire

Development and Characteristics

The *Prison Fantasy Questionnaire* (PFQ) was designed "to measure self-reported conscious fantasies in male prisoners" (Beit-Hallahmi, 1972, p. 553). It is based on the assumption that information can be gained about an individual from the frequency of occurrence of fantasy themes which are reported in his "waking stream of consciousness."

The original pool contained 136 items. Fifty of these were written by the developer in an "attempt to cover unique prison and criminal career experiences such as acquittal, trial, escape and early release" (Beit-Hallahmi, 1972, p. 552). The other 86 items (with minor modifications in language) were taken from questionnaires developed by Singer (1966) and Wagman (1965).

This set of items was administered to 44 male inmates of a state prison facility. An item analysis and intercorrelation matrix indicated that 54 items were uncorrelated with other items and item-groups. These were eliminated, leaving a total of 82 items in the revised form. Twelve items deal with "daydreaming," "nightdreaming," and "adjustment." The remaining 70 items that form 14 dream-content scales are sex, satisfaction, self-destruction, aggression, food, security, religion, unreal, bizarre, nurturance, sadism, escape, release, and achievement.

Response Mode

The PFQ is a self-administered scale that offers five response alternatives for each item. Each of these represents the relative degree of frequency of occurrence of an event or the degree of relative satisfaction with a situation.

Scoring

The 14 dream-content scales may be scored independently, or all items may be used to form a single total score. A scale score is obtained by adding the item scores for all items in the scale under consideration. A listing that indicates the items forming each scale is presented with the full scale.

Norms

No normative data are available.

Reliability

Beit-Hallahmi (1972) reports a split-half reliability correlation of .91 for 65 male inmates.

Validity

When the PFQ was administered to 65 male inmates (33 black and 32 white) of a state prison, no significant differences resulted between blacks and whites (except on the food and bizarre scales). No significant differences were related to IQ scores. As hypothesized, significant correlations existed between time in prison (in months) and the self-destruction scale (.38), the sadism scale (.32), and the escape scale (.31). This supports validity to the extent that self-destruction, sadism, and escape fantasies "can be seen as expressions of growing frustration as time in prison wears on" (Beit-Hallahmi, 1972, p. 553).

Comments

The PFQ appears to be well constructed and may prove to be useful along a variety of dimensions. The limiting factor will be the extent to which reported fantasies can be interpreted as indicators of basic needs or tendencies.

REFERENCES

Beit-Hallahmi, B. Developing the prison fantasy questionnaire (PFQ). *Journal of Clinical Psychology*, 1972, *28*, 551–554.

Singer, J. L. *Daydreaming: An introduction to the experimental study of inner experience*. New York: Random House, 1966.

Wagman, M. Daydreaming frequency and some personality measures. *Journal of Consulting Psychology*, 1965, *29*, 295.

PRISON FANTASY QUESTIONNAIRE

Each question has five possible answers. For each question, choose the answer which is most true or appropriate for you. Each answer corresponds to one of the numbers 1 through 5. Locate the number of each question on the answer sheet. Then fill in between the lines under the number that indicates your answer. PROCEED WITH THIS PART.

1. I daydream
   1. infrequently.
   2. once a week.
   3. once a day.
   4. a few times during the day.
   5. many different times during the day.

2. Daydreams or fantasies make up
   1. no part of my waking thoughts.
   2. less than 10% of my waking thoughts.
   3. at least 10% of my waking thoughts.
   4. at least 25% of my waking thoughts.
   5. at least 50% of my waking thoughts.
3. I have a night dream
   1. rarely or never.
   2. once a month.
   3. several times a month.
   4. several times a week.
   5. once a night.
4. I can recall a dream
   1. rarely or never.
   2. once a month.
   3. several times a month.
   4. several times a week.
   5. once a night.
5. I daydream at work
   1. infrequently.
   2. once a week.
   3. once a day.
   4. a few times during the day.
   5. many different times during the day.
6. I lose myself in daydreaming
   1. infrequently.
   2. once a week.
   3. once a day.
   4. a few times during the day.
   5. many different times during the day.
7. Whenever I have time on my hands I daydream
   1. never.
   2. rarely.
   3. sometimes.
   4. frequently.
   5. always.
8. I recall my dreams vividly
   1. rarely or never.
   2. once a month.
   3. several times a month.
   4. several times a week.
   5. once a night.
9. When I am at a meeting or show that is not very interesting, I daydream rather than pay attention
   1. never.
   2. rarely.
   3. sometimes.
   4. frequently.
   5. always.
10. How well adjusted to prison life do you consider yourself:
    1. poorly,
    2. less than average,

3. average,
4. better than average,
5. excellent.

11. Are you satisfied with your present job?
    1. Not at all.
    2. A little.
    3. OK.
    4. Really like it.
    5. Love it.

12. How is your supervisor satisfied with your performance on your present job?
    1. Not at all.
    2. A little.
    3. OK.
    4. Satisfied.
    5. Very satisfied.

Each item in this part describes a daydream or fantasy which may be similar, more or less, to one which you have had. Answer each item on the basis of how often you have had the fantasy — or one similar to it. Use the following key as an approximate guide to indicate how frequently you have had a given daydream.

Answer 1 on the answer sheet if you have never had the daydream.

Answer 2 if you remember having the daydream only once or twice in your lifetime.

Answer 3 if you remember having the fantasy several times in the past few years, but not in the past 6 months.

Answer 4 if you have had the daydream at least once in the past 6 months, but not as often as once a week.

Answer 5 on the answer sheet if you have the daydream frequently — as often as once a week.

When you have chosen your response to an item, locate on the IBM sheet the number which corresponds to the item. Then fill in between the lines under the appropriate number that indicates your response to the item, e.g., 1, 2, 3, 4, or 5.

CONTINUE ON THE SAME ANSWER SHEET

INSTRUCTIONS FOR THIS PART WILL BE REPEATED BEFORE EVERY PAGE OF ITEMS. THIS WILL MAKE YOUR WORK EASIER.

13. I imagine meeting a woman who will give me true happiness.
14. I imagine that people notice me as I enter a room and think I'm awfully good-looking.

15. I imagine having an exciting experience with an attractive woman who compliments me on my performance.
16. I anticipate the coming of another World War and picture the consequences of an atomic bombing of my hometown.
17. I picture myself eating foods in the finest restaurants.
18. I think of what Heaven or Life Eternal might actually be like.
19. I see myself getting revenge in a clever way on a teacher or supervisor who has criticized me.
20. I imagine being known as the best sexual performer in the world, admired by everyone for my potency.
21. I see myself in Heaven and see myself transformed.
22. I imagine the death of the judge that sentenced me to prison.
23. I see myself eating and drinking at a great banquet with unusual delicacies.
24. I imagine the death of the prosecutor that sent me to prison.
25. I picture my own funeral.
26. I think about how my digestive system is working.
27. I see myself married to a woman who is seriously ill and who needs constant loving attention from me.
28. I visualize sexual intercourse using a great variety of positions and forms of satisfaction.
29. I imagine myself having an inexhaustible supply of my favorite foods.
30. I imagine humiliating the woman with whom I am having sex relations.
31. I imagine being released due to a new law passed by Congress.
32. I imagine a miraculous escape from prison.
33. I imagine being pardoned by the governor.
34. As a child, I pictured myself as crippled or disfigured in some way.
35. I see myself as losing my mind and being placed in a mental hospital.
36. I imagine what would happen if a plane crashed on the prison.
37. I visualize the End of the World.
38. I see myself at the side of a dying loved one soothing and comforting him or her.
39. I imagine living in Ancient Rome and participating with complete abandon in a wild sex party.
40. I imagine reading in black headlines that New York has just been attacked by enemy missiles.
41. I imagine vacationing in a resort like Hawaii where I have a very lavish suite at the Royal Hawaiian Hotel.
42. I imagine that I have secretly had sexual relations with the spouses or sweethearts of all of my friends.
43. I imagine inventing fantastic forms of torture, to humiliate my sexual partner.

44. I imagine owning a considerable amount of clothing some of which is made to order for me in London and Paris.
45. I see myself as being seduced by an older woman of great wealth and influence who can protect me or further my career.
46. I picture the reaction of my friends as I commit suicide.
47. I imagine that I have enough money to insure security for myself and an inheritance for my children.
48. I imagine the death of the lawyer that defended me in my trial.
49. I see myself being judged for punishment in the afterlife.
50. I picture what it would be like to inherit one million dollars from a long-lost relative.
51. I imagine humiliating my sexual partner.
52. I imagine that a screen or TV producer sees me and asks me if I would be interested in a screen test.
53. I see myself committing the perfect crime: killing all my enemies on the outside without getting caught.
54. I imagine myself being acquitted by the Supreme Court of the United States.
55. I imagine different ways of making an initial advance to a woman.
56. I see myself committing the perfect crime: breaking into a bank and becoming a millionaire, then living in wealth for the rest of my life.
57. I imagine myself being able to fly over the walls of the prison.
58. I imagine torturing the woman with whom I am having sex relations.
59. I imagine a revolution and general release of all prisoners.
60. I imagine how life would be if I had had different parents.
61. I picture myself as a very different and more successful person than I am.
62. As a child, I imagined myself as a great saint of the Church or Biblical hero.
63. I sometimes imagine myself beating another person with my fists.
64. I imagine myself involved in sexual relations that are too embarrassing to admit to even on a questionnaire.
65. I imagine myself driving a high-powered race car.
66. I imagine beating up the woman with whom I have sexual relations.
67. I see myself having a relationship with a married woman.
68. I see myself "telling off" my parents.
69. I sometimes picture myself as having all my needs satisfied.
70. I like to imagine myself lying on a quiet beach in a warm afternoon sun.
71. I sometimes imagine myself having a sexual relationship with a teenage girl.
72. I daydream that someone I know dies.
73. I imagine myself undressing a woman.
74. I imagine a general prisoner rebellion in all prisons.

75. I imagine the second coming of Jesus.
76. I sometimes imagine myself lying on my back in a large field of grass and just gazing into the blue sky.
77. I see someone I know being injured or killed in an accident.
78. I picture myself taking my next important step in life.
79. I see my parents upset or crying because of something displeasing I have done.
80. I imagine myself living the life of a cow, gently eating grass in a quiet pasture.
81. I see myself in a daydream failing miserably to satisfy my sex partner.
82. I picture myself getting back at someone I dislike.

Fantasy Questionnaire (FQ) Scales

Scale	
Daydreaming	1, 2, 5, 6, 7, 9
Nightdreaming	3, 4, 8
Adjustment	10, 11, 12
Sex	15, 20, 28, 39, 42, 45, 55, 64, 67, 71, 73
Satisfaction	13, 14, 41, 44, 45, 47, 52, 61, 65, 69, 70, 76, 78
Self-destruction	25, 34, 35, 46, 49, 81
Aggression	16, 36, 37, 40, 59, 74, 19, 22, 24, 48, 53, 63, 68, 72, 77, 79, 82
Food	17, 23, 26, 29, 80
Security	13, 18, 41, 45, 47, 69, 76, 80
Religion	18, 21, 37, 62, 75, 49
Unreal	50, 54, 56, 57, 60
Bizzare	26, 35, 80
Nurturance	27, 38
Sadism	30, 43, 51, 58, 66
Escape	32, 57, 59, 74
Release	31, 33, 54
Achievement	44, 47, 50, 52, 53, 56, 61
Total	13-82

OFFENDERS PERSONALITY ASSESSMENT: LISTINGS

Criminal Self-Conceptions Assessment

Earnest, M. R. Criminal self conceptions in the penal community of female offenders: An empirical study (Doctoral dissertation, University of Iowa, 1971). *Dissertation Abstracts International,* 1971, *32,* 1656A. (University Microfilms No. 71–22019)

This seven-part assessment of criminal self-conceptions evaluates the way offenders see criminals, the extent to which they see themselves as criminals, and the extent to which others see them as criminals. There is a mixed format drawing on yes/no responses and names of individuals who are perceived to be judging the target person as a criminal.

I-Level Classification

Warren, M. Q. Classification of offenders as an aid to efficient management and effective treatment. *Journal of Criminal Law, Criminology, and Police Science,* 1971, *62,* 239–258.
Sullivan, C. E., Grant, M. Q., & Grant, J. D. The development of interpersonal maturity: Applications to delinquency. *Psychiatry,* 1957, *20,* 373–385.

The *I*-Level Classification System is a typology and assessment procedure designed to place offenders into maturity categories related to differential treatment. The system was developed and used with youthful offenders in the California Community Treatment Project for over a decade.

Inmate Dependency Scale

Mattocks, A. L., & Spencer, D. A correlational study of the dependency proneness of prison inmates and membership in social clubs. *Journal of Clinical Psychology,* 1971, *27,* 48–50.

This 50-item scale was designed to appraise the dependency of prison inmates on other inmate members of prison clubs and social groups.

Multimethod Assessment System

Baker, R. A., Kaiser, S., & Stewart, G. *The status of Kentucky felons: A demographic, socioeconomic, and psychological review.* Unpublished manuscript, Kentucky Department of Corrections, Frankfurt, 1977.
Available from Baker, R. A., Department of Psychology, University of Kentucky, Lexington, Kentucky.

This assessment system for adult male and female offenders applied and synthesizes 24 predictor subscales for research in inmate planning and decision-making. Among other products are a classification summary yielding scores and norms in the following primary characteristics: potential for aggressive behavior, intellectual status, vocational skills and educational achievement and interests, criminal sophistication, level of socialization, physical health, and mental health.

Porteus Maze Test

Porteus, S. D. *Guide to Porteus Maze Test*. Vineland, N.J.: The Training School at Vineland, New Jersey, 1924.

Porteus, S. D. *Porteus Maze Tests: Fifty years' application*. Palo Alto, Calif.: Pacific Books, 1965.

The *Porteus Maze Test* requires the respondent to trace with a pencil, the pathway through line mazes of increasing difficulty. This commercially published test has consistently been able to differentiate psychopathic, delinquent, and offender groups from control subjects.

Powerless Scale
Postprison Expectation Scale

Thomas, C. W., Haen, I., & Swain, B. W. *An examination of nondeterminants of alienation in the prison community*. Williamsburg, Virginia: Metropolitan Criminal Justice Center, The College of William and Mary, 1974.

Two Likert-type scales were developed as part of research into prisoner alienation. The *Powerlessness Scale* (6 items) measures a general feeling of helplessness and subordination to power that is granted to others. The *Postprison Expectations Scale* (9 items) is a measure of the extent to which inmates anticipate their release from prison with apprehension and fear.

Stereoscopic Resolution Procedure

Berg, P. S. D., & Toch, H. H. Impulsive and neurotic inmates: A study in personality and perception. *Journal of Criminal Law, Criminology, and Police Science*, 1964, 55, 230–234.

This procedure employs a set of 12 slides shown in 6 stereograms, designed as stimuli for the measurement of impulsivity versus socialization. Each pair of slides contain comparable human figures with one slide showing blatant impulsivity and the other showing a more civilized or social expression. After positive reversal to control for eye dominance, the total number of "impulsive" and "so-

Stratton Identification with Criminal Others and Orientation to Criminal Means Scales

Dean, C. W. New directions for parole prediction research. *Journal of Criminal Law, Criminology, and Police Science,* 1968, 59, 214–218.

These two scales both contain five items presented in a 4-point, Likert-type format. They were designed to measure both inmate change and parole outcome as related to identification with criminal others and orientation to criminal means of problem solving.

OFFENDER DESCRIPTION: REVIEWS

Inmates' Perception of Significant Others

Development and Characteristics

The *Inmates' Perception of Significant Others Scale* is a semantic differential scale, which is designed to "compare inmates' evaluative perceptions of themselves to their evaluative perceptions of significant others" (Chang, Zastro, & Blazicek, 1975, p. 86). The semantic differential is an established technique that uses a set of bipolar adjectives to assess the connotative meaning of target concepts. For example, to make an evaluation of the occupation of computer programmer, one might use the two adjectives "complicated" and "simple" as extreme ends of the continuum. Judgments could then be made about what place computer programming is on the continuum. Most researchers use either a 5-point or a 7-point scale. This allows for a neutral midpoint and is less complicated than a larger number of points on the scale.

Osgood, Suci, and Tannenbaum (1957), found three important dimensions of evaluation of meaning. These are activity, potency, and evaluation. For purposes of attitude measurement, Osgood *et al.* suggested that evaluation is sufficient. For this reason, only evaluative adjectives were used for this instrument.

Thirteen groups of people were designated as targets to be rated on a 5-point scale by the inmates, using 20 bipolar adjectives. These groups were: (1) people (in general), (2) medical doctors, (3) police officers, (4) politicians, (5) scientists, (6) lawyers, (7) prison inmates, (8) college students, (9) priests and ministers, (10) prison security officers, (11) businessmen, (12) American women, and (13) "I am." The 20 sets of adjectives were chosen due to their established validity and reliability in measuring connotative evaluative meanings.

Response Mode

Respondents are asked to think of the target concept and make a check mark at the point on the continuum between each of the bipolar adjectives that best describes their feeling for the concept. Since each is asked to rate 13 concepts along 20 continua, the respondent must make a total of 260 judgements.

Scoring

All adjective pairs are arranged using a five-point scale that moves from 1, a strongly negative perception, to 5, a strongly positive perception. Therefore, the higher the score, the more positively that target concept is viewed. A final score for each target concept is obtained by averaging the responses of each of the 20 adjective pairs for that target. Using this procedure, each respondent has a total of 13 scores, 1 for each of the target concepts.

Norms

Table 60 presents the results of an administration of this instrument to 220 inmates who had been convicted of various crimes and had become incarcerated

TABLE 60. Rank Order and Summated Means of Significant Others Evaluated by Inmates with the Semantic Differential Scale

Rank order	Categories	M
	Positive range	
1	Priests and ministers	3.936
2	Medical doctors	3.745
3	Scientists	3.578
4	"I am"	3.522
	Middle range	
5	Businessmen	3.440
6	Lawyers	3.376
7	American women	3.334
8	College students	3.334
9	Politicians	3.282
	Negative range	
10	People	3.126
11	Police officers	2.869
12	Prison security officers	2.693
13	Prison inmates	2.598

in a state penitentiary. (The crime or crimes for which the subjects had been convicted were not noted or included in the analysis.)

Reliability

The semantic differential has been tested under many different situations and has been found to be reliable (Osgood *et al.*, 1957). For this particular testing, however, no reliability measures were reported.

Validity

As in the case of reliability, the semantic differential has been suggested to have strong validity at measuring connotative meaning of concepts in a number of settings. The differential scores obtained for the target groups lends support for validity through contrasted groups, and the selection of target words offers content validity.

Comments

The semantic differential is a well-established technique that has proven useful in the search for meanings that individuals place on a variety of concepts. The evaluative dimension has been shown to be particularly effective in the search for attitudes towards such concepts (Osgood *et al.*, 1957). This procedure has the advantage of revealing individuals' feelings toward the target without threatening to disclose "undesirable" traits. They may be less inhibited in checking some point along a continuum than they would be under other conditions such as answering direct questions about their feelings.

There is a strong need for reliability and validity data for this particular type of administration and under these particular conditions. It is possible that respondents may react differently than those in the original reliability and validity test. The semantic differential, in general, and this application of the technique, in particular, seem to be quite useful in the criminal justice setting.

REFERENCES

Chang, D. H., Zastro, C. H., & Blazicek, D. L. Inmates' perception of significant others and the implications for the rehabilitation process. *International Journal of Criminology and Penology,* 1975, *3,* 85–96.

Osgood, C. E., Suci, G. H., & Tannenbaum, P. H. *The measurement of meaning.* Urbana: University of Illinois Press, 1957.

INMATES' PERCEPTION OF SIGNIFICANT OTHERS

Instructions: The following is a list of different (target) groups of people followed by pairs of descriptive words. Rate each of the target groups by placing a check (✓) at the point on each continuum which best represents your feelings for that group. For example, if you were rating priests and ministers along the complicated-simple continuum and you thought they were slightly simple, you should check the space just to the right of the center space.

Priests and Ministers

Complicated	___:___:___:___:___	Simple
Insane	___:___:___:___:___	Sane
Tense	___:___:___:___:___	Relaxed
Careless	___:___:___:___:___	Careful
Weak	___:___:___:___:___	Strong
Lazy	___:___:___:___:___	Hardworking
Unpredictable	___:___:___:___:___	Predictable
Dirty	___:___:___:___:___	Clean
Uneducated	___:___:___:___:___	Educated
Untrustworthy	___:___:___:___:___	Trustworthy
Dishonest	___:___:___:___:___	Honest
Foolish	___:___:___:___:___	Wise
Dangerous	___:___:___:___:___	Safe
Undependable	___:___:___:___:___	Dependable
Cold	___:___:___:___:___	Warm
Insincere	___:___:___:___:___	Sincere
Law-violating	___:___:___:___:___	Law-abiding
Sick	___:___:___:___:___	Healthy
Violent	___:___:___:___:___	Non-Violent
Sneaky	___:___:___:___:___	Frank

Medical Doctors

Complicated	___:___:___:___:___	Simple
Insane	___:___:___:___:___	Sane
Tense	___:___:___:___:___	Relaxed
Careless	___:___:___:___:___	Careful
Weak	___:___:___:___:___	Strong
Lazy	___:___:___:___:___	Hardworking
Unpredictable	___:___:___:___:___	Predictable
Dirty	___:___:___:___:___	Clean
Uneducated	___:___:___:___:___	Educated
Untrustworthy	___:___:___:___:___	Trustworthy
Dishonest	___:___:___:___:___	Honest
Foolish	___:___:___:___:___	Wise
Dangerous	___:___:___:___:___	Safe
Undependable	___:___:___:___:___	Dependable
Cold	___:___:___:___:___	Warm
Insincere	___:___:___:___:___	Sincere
Law-violating	___:___:___:___:___	Law-abiding

OFFENDERS 431

Sick ___:___:___:___:___ Healthy
Violent ___:___:___:___:___ Non-violent
Sneaky ___:___:___:___:___ Frank

Scientists

Complicated ___:___:___:___:___ Simple
Insane ___:___:___:___:___ Sane
Tense ___:___:___:___:___ Relaxed
Careless ___:___:___:___:___ Careful
Weak ___:___:___:___:___ Strong
Lazy ___:___:___:___:___ Hardworking
Unpredictable ___:___:___:___:___ Predictable
Dirty ___:___:___:___:___ Clean
Uneducated ___:___:___:___:___ Educated
Untrustworthy ___:___:___:___:___ Trustworthy
Dishonest ___:___:___:___:___ Honest
Foolish ___:___:___:___:___ Wise
Dangerous ___:___:___:___:___ Safe
Undependable ___:___:___:___:___ Dependable
Cold ___:___:___:___:___ Warm
Insincere ___:___:___:___:___ Sincere
Law-violating ___:___:___:___:___ Law-abiding
Sick ___:___:___:___:___ Healthy
Violent ___:___:___:___:___ Non-violent
Sneaky ___:___:___:___:___ Frank

"I am"

Complicated ___:___:___:___:___ Simple
Insane ___:___:___:___:___ Sane
Tense ___:___:___:___:___ Relaxed
Careless ___:___:___:___:___ Careful
Weak ___:___:___:___:___ Strong
Lazy ___:___:___:___:___ Hardworking
Unpredictable ___:___:___:___:___ Predictable
Dirty ___:___:___:___:___ Clean
Uneducated ___:___:___:___:___ Educated
Untrustworthy ___:___:___:___:___ Trustworthy
Dishonest ___:___:___:___:___ Honest
Foolish ___:___:___:___:___ Wise
Dangerous ___:___:___:___:___ Safe
Undependable ___:___:___:___:___ Dependable
Cold ___:___:___:___:___ Warm
Insincere ___:___:___:___:___ Sincere
Law-violating ___:___:___:___:___ Law-abiding
Sick ___:___:___:___:___ Healthy
Violent ___:___:___:___:___ Non-violent
Sneaky ___:___:___:___:___ Frank

Businessmen

Complicated ___:___:___:___:___ Simple
Insane ___:___:___:___:___ Sane
Tense ___:___:___:___:___ Relaxed
Careless ___:___:___:___:___ Careful

Weak	__:__:__:__:__	Strong
Lazy	__:__:__:__:__	Hardworking
Unpredictable	__:__:__:__:__	Predictable
Dirty	__:__:__:__:__	Clean
Uneducated	__:__:__:__:__	Educated
Untrustworthy	__:__:__:__:__	Trustworthy
Dishonest	__:__:__:__:__	Honest
Foolish	__:__:__:__:__	Wise
Dangerous	__:__:__:__:__	Safe
Undependable	__:__:__:__:__	Dependable
Cold	__:__:__:__:__	Warm
Insincere	__:__:__:__:__	Sincere
Law-violating	__:__:__:__:__	Law-abiding
Sick	__:__:__:__:__	Healthy
Violent	__:__:__:__:__	Non-violent
Sneaky	__:__:__:__:__	Frank

Lawyers

Complicated	__:__:__:__:__	Simple
Insane	__:__:__:__:__	Sane
Tense	__:__:__:__:__	Relaxed
Careless	__:__:__:__:__	Careful
Weak	__:__:__:__:__	Strong
Lazy	__:__:__:__:__	Hardworking
Unpredictable	__:__:__:__:__	Predictable
Dirty	__:__:__:__:__	Clean
Uneducated	__:__:__:__:__	Educated
Untrustworthy	__:__:__:__:__	Trustworthy
Dishonest	__:__:__:__:__	Honest
Foolish	__:__:__:__:__	Wise
Dangerous	__:__:__:__:__	Safe
Undependable	__:__:__:__:__	Dependable
Cold	__:__:__:__:__	Warm
Insincere	__:__:__:__:__	Sincere
Law-violating	__:__:__:__:__	Law-abiding
Sick	__:__:__:__:__	Healthy
Violent	__:__:__:__:__	Non-violent
Sneaky	__:__:__:__:__	Frank

American Women

Complicated	__:__:__:__:__	Simple
Insane	__:__:__:__:__	Sane
Tense	__:__:__:__:__	Relaxed
Careless	__:__:__:__:__	Careful
Weak	__:__:__:__:__	Strong
Lazy	__:__:__:__:__	Hardworking
Unpredictable	__:__:__:__:__	Predictable
Dirty	__:__:__:__:__	Clean
Uneducated	__:__:__:__:__	Educated
Untrustworthy	__:__:__:__:__	Trustworthy
Dishonest	__:__:__:__:__	Honest
Foolish	__:__:__:__:__	Wise
Dangerous	__:__:__:__:__	Safe

OFFENDERS

Undependable	___:___:___:___:___ Dependable
Cold	___:___:___:___:___ Warm
Insincere	___:___:___:___:___ Sincere
Law-violating	___:___:___:___:___ Law-abiding
Sick	___:___:___:___:___ Healthy
Violent	___:___:___:___:___ Non-violent
Sneaky	___:___:___:___:___ Frank

College Students

Complicated	___:___:___:___:___ Simple
Insane	___:___:___:___:___ Sane
Tense	___:___:___:___:___ Relaxed
Careless	___:___:___:___:___ Careful
Weak	___:___:___:___:___ Strong
Lazy	___:___:___:___:___ Hardworking
Unpredictable	___:___:___:___:___ Predictable
Dirty	___:___:___:___:___ Clean
Uneducated	___:___:___:___:___ Educated
Untrustworthy	___:___:___:___:___ Trustworthy
Dishonest	___:___:___:___:___ Honest
Foolish	___:___:___:___:___ Wise
Dangerous	___:___:___:___:___ Safe
Undependable	___:___:___:___:___ Dependable
Cold	___:___:___:___:___ Warm
Insincere	___:___:___:___:___ Sincere
Law-violating	___:___:___:___:___ Law-abiding
Sick	___:___:___:___:___ Healthy
Violent	___:___:___:___:___ Non-violent
Sneaky	___:___:___:___:___ Frank

Politicians

Complicated	___:___:___:___:___ Simple
Insane	___:___:___:___:___ Sane
Tense	___:___:___:___:___ Relaxed
Careless	___:___:___:___:___ Careful
Weak	___:___:___:___:___ Strong
Lazy	___:___:___:___:___ Hardworking
Unpredictable	___:___:___:___:___ Predictable
Dirty	___:___:___:___:___ Clean
Uneducated	___:___:___:___:___ Educated
Untrustworthy	___:___:___:___:___ Trustworthy
Dishonest	___:___:___:___:___ Honest
Foolish	___:___:___:___:___ Wise
Dangerous	___:___:___:___:___ Safe
Undependable	___:___:___:___:___ Dependable
Cold	___:___:___:___:___ Warm
Insincere	___:___:___:___:___ Sincere
Law-violating	___:___:___:___:___ Law-abiding
Sick	___:___:___:___:___ Healthy
Violent	___:___:___:___:___ Non-violent
Sneaky	___:___:___:___:___ Frank

People

Complicated	___:___:___:___:___	Simple
Insane	___:___:___:___:___	Sane
Tense	___:___:___:___:___	Relaxed
Careless	___:___:___:___:___	Careful
Weak	___:___:___:___:___	Strong
Lazy	___:___:___:___:___	Hardworking
Unpredictable	___:___:___:___:___	Predictable
Dirty	___:___:___:___:___	Clean
Uneducated	___:___:___:___:___	Educated
Untrustworthy	___:___:___:___:___	Trustworthy
Dishonest	___:___:___:___:___	Honest
Foolish	___:___:___:___:___	Wise
Dangerous	___:___:___:___:___	Safe
Undependable	___:___:___:___:___	Dependable
Cold	___:___:___:___:___	Warm
Insincere	___:___:___:___:___	Sincere
Law-violating	___:___:___:___:___	Law-abiding
Sick	___:___:___:___:___	Healthy
Violent	___:___:___:___:___	Non-violent
Sneaky	___:___:___:___:___	Frank

Police Officers

Complicated	___:___:___:___:___	Simple
Insane	___:___:___:___:___	Sane
Tense	___:___:___:___:___	Relaxed
Careless	___:___:___:___:___	Careful
Weak	___:___:___:___:___	Strong
Lazy	___:___:___:___:___	Hardworking
Unpredictable	___:___:___:___:___	Predictable
Dirty	___:___:___:___:___	Clean
Uneducated	___:___:___:___:___	Educated
Untrustworthy	___:___:___:___:___	Trustworthy
Dishonest	___:___:___:___:___	Honest
Foolish	___:___:___:___:___	Wise
Dangerous	___:___:___:___:___	Safe
Undependable	___:___:___:___:___	Dependable
Cold	___:___:___:___:___	Warm
Insincere	___:___:___:___:___	Sincere
Law-violating	___:___:___:___:___	Law-abiding
Sick	___:___:___:___:___	Healthy
Violent	___:___:___:___:___	Non-violent
Sneaky	___:___:___:___:___	Frank

Prison Inmates

Complicated	___:___:___:___:___	Simple
Insane	___:___:___:___:___	Sane
Tense	___:___:___:___:___	Relaxed
Careless	___:___:___:___:___	Careful
Weak	___:___:___:___:___	Strong
Lazy	___:___:___:___:___	Hardworking
Unpredictable	___:___:___:___:___	Predictable

OFFENDERS

Dirty	___:___:___:___:___	Clean
Uneducated	___:___:___:___:___	Educated
Untrustworthy	___:___:___:___:___	Trustworthy
Dishonest	___:___:___:___:___	Honest
Foolish	___:___:___:___:___	Wise
Dangerous	___:___:___:___:___	Safe
Undependable	___:___:___:___:___	Dependable
Cold	___:___:___:___:___	Warm
Insincere	___:___:___:___:___	Sincere
Law-violating	___:___:___:___:___	Law-abiding
Sick	___:___:___:___:___	Healthy
Violent	___:___:___:___:___	Non-violent
Sneaky	___:___:___:___:___	Frank

Prison Security Officers

Complicated	___:___:___:___:___	Simple
Insane	___:___:___:___:___	Sane
Tense	___:___:___:___:___	Relaxed
Careless	___:___:___:___:___	Careful
Weak	___:___:___:___:___	Strong
Lazy	___:___:___:___:___	Hardworking
Unpredictable	___:___:___:___:___	Predictable
Dirty	___:___:___:___:___	Clean
Uneducated	___:___:___:___:___	Educated
Untrustworthy	___:___:___:___:___	Trustworthy
Dishonest	___:___:___:___:___	Honest
Foolish	___:___:___:___:___	Wise
Dangerous	___:___:___:___:___	Safe
Undependable	___:___:___:___:___	Dependable
Cold	___:___:___:___:___	Warm
Insincere	___:___:___:___:___	Sincere
Law-violating	___:___:___:___:___	Law-abiding
Sick	___:___:___:___:___	Healthy
Violent	___:___:___:___:___	Non-violent
Sneaky	___:___:___:___:___	Frank

Ohio Penal Classification Test

Development and Characteristics

The *Ohio Penal Classification Test* (OPCT) was developed (Sell, 1952) to serve as a "group test of mental ability that would prove especially adaptable to penal populations" (p. 1). The designer suggests that the need for the test is a result of the "extremity of individual differences and the heterogeneity of educational achievement" as well as temporal and economic considerations within the prison population.

The test is comprised of four subtests: (1) a pictorial block-counting test; (2) a symbol–digit matching test, in which respondents are asked to judge whether numbers and symbols are matched appropriately; (3) a series–expansion test, in which the respondent is asked to discover the relationship of a set of numbers and then to deduce the two following numbers; and (4) a memory-span-for-objects test that asks the respondent to recite the names of ten objects, having just been shown drawings of each object.

Response Mode

Each subtest uses a different mode of response. For Test 1, the respondent enters on the answer sheet the number of blocks in each picture; for Test 2, he or she makes a checkmark under any symbol–number pairs that are matched differently than the stimulus set; for Test 3, he or she writes the next two numbers of the sequence; and for Test 4, he or she writes the names of the objects he or she remembers.

Scoring

Raw scores are obtained by summing the number of correct responses for each subtest except for Test 2, in which the raw score is equal to the number of right answers, minus the number of wrong answers. These scores are converted to standard scores through the use of a conversion table which is provided in the manual. The manual also contains a table that shows comparable IQ scores for the standard scores.

Norms

A standardization population of 550 inmates and 107 ninth-grade boys produced the conversion factor that established a total standard score of 100 as the "average" performance and a standard deviation of 29.85. The inmate group contained 385 whites and 165 blacks from the Ohio State Reformatory. The age range was 17 to 30 (mean = 23). The ninth-grade boys attended a junior high school in Mansfield, Ohio (mean age = 15).

Reliability

Sell (1952) reports a test–retest reliability coefficient of .87 (the time between administrations was not presented) for 138 randomly chosen subjects from the standardization population.

Validity

The designer suggests that the major criterion for a test of an abstract concept such as intelligence is "expert judgment" or "expert agreement." If this is true, the OPCT has support for its validity as a mental abilities test, because the items included on the test have all been widely accepted and used in other ability tests.

Further support for the validity of the test is presented in Table 61 showing high correlations between OPCT and other mental abilities tests.

Comments

The OPCT is one of only a few tests designed specifically to measure mental ability within the prison population. This is a difficult task because of the wide range of subcultural backgrounds within penal institutions. The OPCT seems to do an adequate job of measuring the full range of levels for the areas being tested. Further work is needed in the area of reliability and scoring standardization, as well as some consideration for adding a verbal component to the test. In general, however, this is an intelligent combination of established tests that should be useful within the criminal justice system.

TABLE 61. Correlations of OPCT with Other Measures of Intelligence

Test	Subjects	N	r	r^a	PEr	rho	PErh
Wechsler-Bellevue (full) scale	Penal inmates	155	.79	.90	.02	—	—
Revised Beta examination	Penal inmates	90	.73	.83	.03	—	—
Wechsler-Bellevue (full) scale	Penal inmates	10	—	—	—	.93	.03

^{a} Corrected for attenuation.

REFERENCES

Sell, D. E. *Manual of instructions for the Ohio Penal Classification Test.* Chicago: Psychometrics Affiliates, 1952.

OFFENDERS DESCRIPTION: LISTINGS

Community Follow-up Interview

Steadman, H. J. Mental Health Research Unit, New York State Department of Mental Hygiene, 44 Holland Avenue, Albany, New York 12208.

The *Community Follow-Up Interview* contains 51 fill-in and multiple-choice queries designed to measure the community adjustment of former patients of institutions for the criminally insane.

Criminality Scales

Glaser, D. *The effectiveness of a prison and parole system.* Indianapolis: Bobbs-Merrill, 1961.

Hazelrigg, L. E. An examination of the accuracy and relevance of staff perceptions of the inmate in the correctional institution. *Journal of Criminal Law, Criminology, and Police Science,* 1967, *58,* 204–210.

The *Criminality Scales* consist of three separate scales. The *Inmate Loyalty Scale* is a 4-item, Guttman-type scale designed to measure inmates' normative solidarity with their membership groups. The *Criminality Scale* is a 4-item, Likert-type scale assessing adherence to criminal value orientations. The *Criminal Identification Scale* is 3-item, Likert-type scale that measures positive identification and perceived similarity with criminals.

Criminal Attitudes and Values Scales

Andrews, D. A., Young, J. G., Wormith, J. S., Searle, C. A., & Kouri, M. The attitudinal effects of group discussion between young criminal offenders and community volunteers. *Journal of Community Psychology,* 1974, *1,* 417–422.

Six scales were developed by the Research Branch of the Ontario Ministry of Correctional Services; these are identification with criminal others, tolerance for violations of the law, awareness of limited opportunity, the law and judicial process, value of education, and value of employment. All items use a 5-point, Likert-type response format.

Involvement Questionnaire

Perino, A. R. *The uninvolved prisoner* (Project Report 5-67). Fort Leavenworth, Kansas: Council for Research, Evaluation, and Staff Development, the United States Disciplinary Barracks, 1967.

The *Involvement Questionnaire* is a 14-item scale, with 10 true-false and 4 open-ended items. It was designed to obtain information regarding uninvolvement as a long term characteristic of prisoners by assessing friendships, isolation and reasons why uninvolved individuals did not participate in prison activities.

Images of Criminality Questionnaire

Reed, J. P., & Reed, R. S. Status, images and consequence: Once a criminal, always a criminal. *Sociology and Social Research,* 1973, *57,* 460–472.

This interview procedure with the general public was designed to determine whether individuals had a general image of the criminal, the consequences of this image for the selection of sanctions, and the kinds of facilities, activities, and relationships that individuals would be willing to share with criminals.

Perception of Addicts and Addiction Scale

Coates, R. B., & Miller, A. D. Patrolmen and addicts: A study of police perception and police citizen interaction. *Journal of Police Science and Administration,* 1974, *2,* 308–321.

This 8-item, true-false scale is part of a larger questionnaire used to study patrol officer's perceptions of and interactions with addicts. This scale assesses agreement with statements frequently used to describe heroin addicts, such as "Once a heroin addict, always a heroin addict."

Prisoner Attribute Typology

Sinclair, I., & Chapman, B. A typological and dimensional study of a sample of prisoners. *British Journal of Criminology,* 1973, *13,* 341–353.

A list of 45 dichotomous variables was utilized to produce a 7-category typology by which men in prison could be described.

Recidivism Seriousness Classification

Mandel, N. G., Collins, B. S., Moran, M. R., Barron, A. J., Gelbmann, F. J., Gadbois, C. B., & Kaminstein, P. Recidivism studied and defined. *Journal of Criminal Law, Criminology, and Police Science,* 1965, *56,* 59–66.

This rating was designed to serve as a method for differentiating types of recidivism. A 9-category classification scheme is provided.

Social Organization of Burglary Questionnaire

Shover, N. The social organization of burglary. *Social Problems,* 1973, *20,* 499–514.

This questionnaire attempts to explicate some external and internal characteristics of the social relationships that enable burglary offenders to carry on their activities.

CHAPTER 11
Crime and Criminality

Crime and Criminality scales encompass two very different kinds of research instruments. The first types of scales are the criminality instruments. These scales measure the degree to which people see certain acts as criminal, either in terms of their values and beliefs, or in terms of their actual behaviors. The *Criminal Attitude Scale* falls within this definition and was developed to measure peoples' degrees of criminality. These scales also attend to criminality as a phenomenon, as reflected in the *Attitude toward the Prevalence of Stealing Scale*.

We note that some scales that are called criminality measures are included in the *Offenders* chapter, while others of similar titles are reviewed here. The distinction between them is made on the basis of the actual object of study. If the object was people involved in criminal acts, the scale was put in the *Offenders* chapter. If the object was criminality as a phenomenon or construct, then the scale was placed in this chapter. One scale, the *Maladaptive Behavior Record,* overlaps the categories of people and constructs, and appears here.

Criminality seriousness instruments all seek to evaluate the severity of a variety of adult offenses. (Some juvenile severity measures have been discussed in the *Delinquency* chapter.) Seriousness measures have assumed increasing importance as researchers look toward sophisticated and multifaceted criteria for crime prevention programs. Seriousness assessment, however, has become an extensive, often complex, body of knowledge that is well outside the scope of the present handbook. A few seriousness measures are listed in this chapter so that references are available for the interested reader.

The second category of scales deals with aggression and hostility. These concepts apply to members of the general public, to persons who are successful, law-abiding citizens, and to normal interchanges between human beings. Yet the theoretical constructs of aggression, hostility, and violence have special relevance to criminal assaults and law violations. For this reason they are included here.

CRIME AND CRIMINALITY ATTITUDE SCALES: REVIEWS

Aggression-Altruism Scale

Development and Characteristics

The *Aggression-Altruism Scale* (AAS) was constructed to measure "hurting-helping" attitudes (Larsen, 1971). It assumes that attitudes of aggression and altruism form a continuum, and that such attitudes predispose individuals to behave in a certain manner. Therefore, a measure of one's position on this continuum should predict whether he or she is likely to behave aggressively or altruistically.

This scale was not specifically developed for use in criminal justice. Aggression toward people, however, is a major reason for incarceration and since the possibility of further aggressive acts is a major factor in parole decision making, the ability to predict such actions is relevant.

The Thurstone equal-appearing intervals method of scale construction was followed. Items for the original pool were selected by searching other scales for statements with aggressive content. These items and 33 items written by the author reflecting intensity of preference to hurt or help the attitudinal object completed a pool of 160 statements.

Fourteen senior and graduate students taking a seminar in attitude methodology judged each item as to the "direction and intensity with which it expressed intent of hurting or helping" (Larsen, 1971, p. 275). Thirty-seven of the items showed variability small enough (expressed as a Q value) to merit use in the final scale. Form A consisted of 20 of these items, and Form B was assigned the remaining 17 items.

Response Mode

The respondent is asked to read the items and note whether he or she agrees or disagrees with each statement.

Scoring

As with most scales constructed in this manner, each statement is weighted according to its ranked position of intensity of the attitude under consideration. In this case, only the weight for an affirmative response is given. Therefore, a total score is, apparently, obtained by summing the weights of those items checked "I agree."

Norms

No norms were reported.

Reliability

A test–retest correlation coefficient of .60 was obtained from a sample of 26 undergraduate students who, after being told that their first papers had been lost, were asked to retake the test two weeks after the initial administration.

An equivalent form correlation coefficient of .42 was found between Forms A and B on a sample of 48 undergraduate college students.

Validity

The AAS has been found to correlate $-.22$ ($p \leq .025$) with the *World-Mindedness Scale* (Sampson & Smith, 1957), .04 ($p > .10$) with the *Buss Hostility Scale*, and $-.20$ ($p \leq .01$) with the *Machiavellianism IV Scale*.

The AAS has also been shown to correlate $-.52$ ($p \leq .001$) with males' perception of their fathers as indicated by the *Parent Aggressiveness Training Scale*. There were no significant relationships between these two scales concerning females' views of their fathers and mothers or males' views of their mothers.

Comments

This scale has not been shown to possess the level of predictive capabilities necessary for individual decision making—but it was not designed for that task. The correlation of .04 with the *Buss Hostility Scale* indicates that the AAS may be measuring something other than a propensity toward hurting others. The AAS is unique among attitude scales in its developer's conceptualization of aggression and altruism as opposite points on a single continuum. Its major strength is its empirical scale development from a large item pool. The major weaknesses include modest reliability, lack of validation information, and the limitations of the racial and religious item content.

REFERENCES

Larsen, K. S. Aggression-altruism: A scale and some data on its reliability and validity. *Journal of Personality Assessment,* 1971, *35,* 275–281.

Sampson, D. L., & Smith, H. P. A scale to measure worldminded attitudes. *Journal of Social Psychology,* 1957, *45,* 99–106.

AGGRESSION-ALTRUISM SCALE

The following is a study of what the public thinks about a number of important social issues. You may find yourself agreeing with some of the statements and disagreeing with other statements. Put a check mark (✓) beside those statements with which you agree; put a cross (X) beside those with which you disagree.

Form A

		Scale Value	Q Value
1.	Capital punishment is hardly necessary	8.11	.72
2.	I can stand a "nigger" in his place but I cannot stand him as the equal of the white man	2.16	1.31
3.	Man can and should eradicate suffering from the face of the earth	10.77	.89
4.	Contact sports are an acceptable outlet for pent-up frustration	6.40	1.50
5.	One important reason Negroes are discriminated against in housing is that they are poor	5.91	1.22
6.	Spanking your child is necessary to teach him right from wrong	4.10	1.90
7.	You should take an obviously hurt, stray animal to the veterinarian	9.21	1.08
8.	A standing army of 2,000,000 men or over is necessary for our defense at all times	3.33	1.81
9.	Our country today is probably no better than many others	6.32	1.17
10.	One reason why social prejudice still exists today is the fact that Negroes are not white	5.81	.98
11.	Certain religious sects who refuse to salute the flag have their own beliefs and should be allowed to follow their own religion	7.42	1.35
12.	The fact that I love my country doesn't make me feel less kindly toward other countries	8.00	1.60
13.	A major fault of the Jews is their conceit, over-bearing, pride and their idea that they are a chosen race	3.05	.80
14.	Every criminal should be executed	1.04	.54
15.	People of underdeveloped countries are by nature incapable of self-government	4.21	.89
16.	Financial sacrifices should be made by American citizens to aid Hindu victims of famine in India	10.10	1.54
17.	It's good for the ego to inflict pain upon someone else	2.00	2.09
18.	Murder should be avoided at any cost	9.37	1.53

19. No punishment is too severe for the Negro guilty of the sex killing of a white child	1.15	.65
20. You should loan your umbrella to a friend	7.31	1.81

Form B

1. Poor people are the responsibility of society	8.30	1.50
2. War brings out both good and bad qualities in men	5.70	1.20
3. The Jews have helped build this country	7.33	1.66
4. Idealists must be brought back to reality, even though it may upset them	4.40	1.20
5. A child should be forced to obey if he does not do so immediately	3.09	1.21
6. School teachers need more freedom to discipline students as they feel necessary	4.19	.98
7. More people would favor communism if they only knew something about it	6.23	1.36
8. The white race must be kept pure at all costs, even if other races have to be killed off	1.04	.54
9. If Germany had been wiped out by the war, the world would be better off now	1.57	1.22
10. Children will usually see how far they can go	5.41	1.22
11. I am my brother's keeper	9.50	2.80
12. A child who steals money from his parents should be given understanding help and forgiveness	9.61	1.44
13. We should guarantee food for hungry people	10.60	.90
14. America surpasses other countries only in prosperity	6.50	1.26
15. The practice of executing murderers is just and necessary	2.75	1.68
16. The best way to eliminate the Communist menace in this country is to control the Jewish element which guides it	2.29	1.81
17. Execution of criminals is absolutely never justified	9.28	1.45

Attitude toward the Prevalence of Stealing

Development and Characteristics

This scale, the *Attitudes toward the Prevalence of Stealing Scale* (APSS), was developed in an attempt to provide a measurement of attitudinal difference between delinquents and nondelinquents in the single content area of stealing

(Ball, 1957). It was constructed using the Guttman method of scale formulation. The original item pool, requiring judgments about the proportion of people who steal in different situations or settings, consisted of 12 items. Two proved to be nonscale questions (according to scalogram criteria) and were discarded. Of the remaining 10 items, 5 items showed marginal frequencies within acceptable limits (20–80%). For this reason only five questions are used in scoring the scale. The other items serve as filler questions.

Response Mode

The subjects are presented with a copy of the scale questions, each of which is followed by five alternative answers. They are instructed to circle the answer that is closest to the way that they feel.

Scoring

For purposes of scale construction, the author dichotomized the responses into positive (+) attitude toward stealing and negative (−) attitude toward stealing. The first, second, and third answers to each question are considered positive and the fourth and fifth alternatives negative. Using this procedure for the 5-item scale allows six "scale types": (0) no positive attitudes (− − − − −), (1) one positive response (− − − − +), (2) two positive responses (− − − + +), (3) three positive responses (− − + + +), (4) four positive responses (− + + + +), or (5) five positive responses (+ + + + +).

ScaleTypes 0 and 1 are considered to have negative attitudes toward stealing whileTypes 2, 3, 4, and 5 have positive attitudes toward stealing.

TABLE 62. Distribution of Scale Types for Delinquent, Nondelinquent Male, Nondelinquent Female, and College Populations in Attitudes Toward the Prevalence of Stealing

Stealing scale type	Delinquent		Nondelinquent male		Nondelinquent female		College	
	N	%	N	%	N	%	N	%
0	14	13.1	32	33.0	45	53.6	23	28.0
1	17	15.9	28	28.9	17	20.2	34	41.4
2	15	14.0	13	13.4	4	4.8	9	11.0
3	15	14.0	4	4.1	6	7.1	3	3.7
4	15	14.0	10	10.3	2	2.4	10	12.2
5	31	29.0	10	10.3	10	11.9	3	3.7
Total	107	100.0	97	100.0	84	100.0	82	100.0

Norms

See Table 62.

Reliability

Ball (1957) reported a coefficient of reproducibility of .94 when all groups of subjects were combined and a reproducibility coefficient of .93 or more for each group taken separately.

Validity

Ball (1957) reported that delinquents held more positive attitudes toward stealing than nondelinquents. Further, he indicated that

> among the delinquents, those from rural places of residence, from broken homes, and from families of lower socioeconomic status had more positive attitudes toward stealing than those with converse attributes. Within the nondelinquent control group, those boys who were from rural areas as well as those who were retarded in grade placement held more positive attitudes toward stealing than non-retarded and urban boys. Little or no association between the attitude variable and age of subject, intelligence, or number of children in subject's family of orientation was reported with respect to either of the two populations. (p. 274)

These findings are presented by Ball as consistent with an extension of Sutherland's and Cressey's (1955) theory of differential association. Ball reports that the scale shows the relationships that are predicted by this widely held theoretical framework, yielding evidence for construct validity.

Comments

Green (1954) has suggested, among other things, that a good Guttman Scale should contain at least 10 items when the items are dichotomous. Ball (1957) (who is apparently aware of this) stated that his 10-item scale, which included all scalable items, was no better at discriminating between delinquents and nondelinquents than the current 5-item test.

This scale appears to be valid and reliable. There is, however, a need for more substantial reliability data. Although the coefficient of reproducibility is often used as a measure of reliability, its value is directly related to the number of subjects in the largest category. Therefore, the large samples inflate the reproducibility value (Shaw & Wright, 1967).

REFERENCES

Ball, J. Delinquent and nondelinquent attitudes toward the prevalences of stealing. *Journal of Criminal Law and Criminology,* 1957, 48, 262–264.

Green, B. F. Attitude measurement. In G. Lindsey (Ed.), *Handbook of social psychology*. Cambridge, Mass.: Addison-Wesley, 1954.

Shaw, M. E., & Wright, J. M. *Scales for the measurement of attitudes.* New York: McGraw-Hill Inc., 1967.

Sutherland, E. H., & Cressey, D. R. *Principles of criminology* (5th ed.). New York: J. B. Lippincott Co., 1955.

ATTITUDE TOWARD THE PREVALENCE OF STEALING

1. Do you think many people are honest?

    1. Almost all of them
    2. Most of them
    3. Some of them
    4. Only a few of them
    5. None of them (Circle one answer)

*2. How many people would steal something if they had a good chance?

    1. All of them
    2. Most of them
    3. About half of them
    4. Few of them
    5. None of them (Circle one answer)

*3. Do you think many people have taken things at some time?

    1. All of them
    2. Most of them
    3. About half of them
    4. Few of them
    5. None of them (Circle one answer)

4. Do you think many people would steal money if they had a good chance?

    1. All or almost all of them
    2. Most of them
    3. Some of them
    4. Only a few of them
    5. None of them (Circle one answer)

5. Do you think many people would steal from their parents?

    1. All of them
    2. Most of them
    3. About half of them
    4. Few of them
    5. None of them (Circle one answer)

*6. Do you think many people would steal from their friends?

   1. All of them
   2. Most of them
   3. About half of them
   4. Only a few of them
   5. None of them   (Circle one answer)

7. Do you think many people would steal from their *best* friend?

   1. Almost all of them
   2. Most of them
   3. About half of them
   4. Only a few of them
   5. None of them   (Circle one answer)

*8. How many people would steal from a store if they had a good chance?

   1. All of them
   2. Most of them
   3. About half of them
   4. Few of them
   5. None of them   (Circle one answer)

*9. How many people would steal from a school if they had a good chance?

   1. All of them
   2. Most of them
   3. About half of them
   4. Few of them
   5. None of them   (Circle one answer)

10. Do you think many people would steal from the place where they work?

    1. All of them
    2. Most of them
    3. About half of them
    4. Few of them
    5. None of them   (Circle one answer)

11. Do you think many people would steal money from a hospital if they had a good chance?

    1. Almost all of them
    2. Most of them
    3. Some of them
    4. Only a few of them
    5. None of them   (Circle one answer)

12. Do you think many people would steal money from a church?

    1. Almost all of them
    2. Most of them
    3. Some of them
    4. Only a few of them
    5. None of them   (Circle one answer)

*Items with asterisks were the five used in the main analysis.

Criminal Attitude Scale

Development and Characteristics

The *Criminal Attitude Scale* (CAS) was initially developed by Taylor in a study of group psychotherapy with borstal girls in New Zealand (Taylor, 1967a). The items were derived from statements of criminals whom Taylor had interviewed over a 15-year period; the items are intended to assess the subject's "degree of criminality" and to reflect "changes of attitude as a result of treatment or contamination" (Taylor, 1968, p. 37).

After the initial development with 33 borstal girls, the CAS was administered to three other groups of New Zealand females differing in presumed degree of criminality: 18 prisoners, 50 probationers, and 40 noncriminal controls (total female $N = 141$). The CAS was also administered to six groups of New Zealand males differing in presumed degree of criminality: 21 persistent criminals, 50 senior and 37 new borstal trainees, 34 probationers, 46 noncriminal controls and 42 first admissions to prison (total male $N = 230$). Item analysis eliminated two items from the scoring of the scale that did not discriminate between groups. The resultant scale contains 13 true-false items. The CAS is used with offender and nonoffender groups respectively, by selecting the appropriate alternative phrases or terms in each statement.

Response Mode

Respondents are requested to read each item and note whether it is true or false for them.

Scoring

For all subjects, Items 1, 3, 5, 9, and 12 are scored 1 point if answered false, and Items 4, 6, 7, 10, and 11 are scored 1 point if answered true. For females only, Items 2 and 13 are scored 1 point if answered true and item 8 is scored if answered false. Items 2, 8, and 13 are not scored for males.

Norms

Taylor (1968) presents norms based on the four female and six male standardization groups described above. The means and standard errors of the mean for these groups are presented in Table 63.

TABLE 63. CAS Means and Standard Errors of the Means for the Standardization Groups

	Groups	M	SE M
Females	Prisoners	5.44	.43
	Borstal trainees	5.09	.36
	Probationers	4.24	.26
	Noncriminal controls	3.12	.29
Males	Persistent criminals	5.29	.39
	Senior borstal trainees	4.02	.25
	Probationers	3.21	.31
	Noncriminal controls	2.91	.26
	First admissions to prison	2.62	.27
	New borstal trainees	2.49	.28

Reliability

Test–retest reliability for the CAS after a four-day interval for two groups of college students in a sociology class was .86 for males ($N = 26$) and .65 for females ($N = 31$).

Validity

The validity of the CAS was studied by contrasting the responses of three groups of delinquent females and a group of nondelinquent females in New Zealand (Taylor, 1968). Thus, for the female subjects, the CAS means formed a continuum (from highest to lowest) that corresponded to the presumed criminality represented by the groups. The noncriminal control group had significantly lower criminal attitude scores than all three of the criminal groups ($p < .01$). In addition, the prisoner group differed significantly from the probationers ($p < .05$). The results for the male subjects were not quite as well ordered; the first admissions to prison and the new borstal trainees scored lower than the noncriminal controls. The persistent criminal group scored significantly higher than all the other groups ($p < .01$), and the senior borstal trainees scored significantly lower than the persistent criminals ($p < .01$) and significantly higher than all other groups ($p < .05$).

In an earlier study with the group of 33 borstal girls (Taylor, 1967b), CAS scores failed to differentiate between 10 girls who were reconvicted within six months of release and the remaining 23 girls who were not reconvicted within the same period. When the girls were divided into three treatment groups—group psychotherapy, group counseling, and untreated control—the CAS scores improved significantly for the group psychotherapy and untreated control subjects from the pre- to post-treatment administrations. The group counseling CAS mean did not change (Taylor, 1967a). It is important to note that these results were obtained with the initial form of the CAS, and may not apply to the revised form.

Comments

The validity data for the CAS are modest. There is a lack of cross-validation on prison populations other than those with whom the scale was developed. A related problem is the need for normative data from countries other than New Zealand. Finally, there is no evidence that the two CAS forms are comparable.

The basic concept of the CAS is an attempt to measure criminal attitudes as indicators of the probability of criminal behaviors. The validity evidence is largely through comparison of criterion groups.

REFERENCES

Taylor, A. J. W. An evaluation of group psychotherapy in a girls' borstal. *International Journal of Group Psychotherapy,* 1967, *17,* 168–177. (a)

Taylor, A. J. W. Prediction for parole: A pilot study with delinquent girls. *British Journal of Criminology,* 1967, *7,* 418–424. (b)

Taylor, A. J. W. A brief criminal attitude scale. *Journal of Criminal Law, Criminology, and Police Science,* 1968, *51,* 37–40.

THE CRIMINAL ATTITUDE SCALE

Indicate your agreement or disagreement with each of the statements by answering true or false.

1. I deserved my sentence/criminals deserve their sentence.
2. I did not want the police to catch me/criminals do not want the police to catch them.
3. The judge or magistrate sentences you/criminals, not the probation officer.
4. The police hound you if you have a criminal record.
5. The authorities/officers are interested in you/criminals, and try to help you/them.
6. A fixed sentence is better than indeterminate sentence.
7. People get sentenced on their records, not on what they have done.
8. There is some point in planning for the future and not living from day to day.
9. I was able/criminals are able to get some peace when I was/they are caught.
10. Punishment begins on the day you are released from the court/institution.

11. Once a criminal/in trouble, always a criminal/in trouble.
12. It is the probationers/trainees/prisoners who cause the trouble for themselves, not other people.
13. Everybody knows me here: I have nothing to hide/criminals are at home in prison.

Criminality Level Index

Development and Characteristics

The *Criminality Level Index* (CLI) was designed "to measure the internalized amount of potential for involvement in crime as an adult. The assumption is that the accumulated residues of social experience create the potential" (Reckless, 1966, p. 73). The composition of the crime potential is a set of attitudes and perceptions relevant to such involvement.

As a starting point, 196 items used by Mylonnas (1963) to measure attitudes toward the law, legal institutions, and law enforcement officials were item analyzed for internal consistency; 89 items were judged to be homogeneous.

These items were then tested for discrimination ability by comparing the responses of 200 white male prisoners to 200 white labor union members. The 24 items that differentiated at the .001 level formed the final index. Fourteen of the 24 items reflected attitudes toward the police.

Response Mode

The CLI uses a standard 5-point, Likert-type response mode in which a respondent reads a statement and notes whether he or she: SA (Strongly Agrees), A (Agrees), U (is Undecided), D (Disagrees), or SD (Strongly Disagrees).

Scoring

Each item receives a score between 1 and 5. Response alternatives are arranged so that a score of 1 represents the most favorable attitude toward the law and 5 indicates the most unfavorable attitude. The sum of item scores yields a total score, which represents the degree of unfavorability of an individual's attitude toward the law.

Norms

The mean scores, listed in Table 64, were obtained from 335 men admitted to the Ohio Penitentiary (Maximum security), 324 young adult male prisoners at

TABLE 64. Average Scores on the CLI

Sample group affiliation	CLI items (24)[a]	N
Ohio penitentiary	70.42	335
Lebanon reformatory	67.89	324
Dayton probation	58.52	344
Labor union	53.61	195
Mormons	51.37	369

[a] The higher scores indicate the more unfavorable direction; the lower scores, the more favorable direction.

the Lebanon Reformatory (receiving the less hostile cases from Ohio's Mansfield Reformatory), 344 male probationers, 195 labor union members who were enrolled in a labor education extension course, and 369 small-town Mormons from a western state.

Reliability

The developer reports reliability coefficients of .86 (labor), .91 (reformatory), .91 (probation), .91 (penitentiary), and .93 (Mormon) when calculated using the Kuder-Richardson formula.

Validity

Since the CLI is believed to tap attitudes toward the law, the developer reasoned that residues of favorability of attitude toward the law would range from favorable for conservative citizens to very unfavorable for incarcerated criminals. Support for this position is evident from the table presented. As predicted, the Mormons showed the most favorable attitude (lowest score), followed by labor union members, probationers, reformatory prisoners, and, finally, the maximum security inmates, who showed the most unfavorable attitude.

As a test for concurrent validity, the CLI scores were compared to the *Socialization Scale (So)* of the *California Personality Inventory* (CPI) (which measures direction of socialization according to a favorable-unfavorable dimension) and 20 items from the *Crissman Moral Judgment Scale* (which measures moral perceptions or attitudes). The results indicated that mean scores on the *Socialization Scale* were inversely related to the CLI. The higher scores on the CLI, indicating greater unfavorability, was associated with lower CPI socialization scores, also indicating less favorable attitudes. Similarly, the moral judgment items were inversely related to the CLI.

Comments

This instrument was constructed using appropriate procedures, which yielded information supportive of reliability and validity. Visual comparison of mean scores on the various scales indicates that scores are in the appropriate direction. Still, tests of significance and some measure of the strength of relationship between these instruments would be helpful.

It is impossible to establish that an instrument is an index of potential criminality without showing its predictive value. Although the CLI has received positive validation support, there is no evidence to indicate that it achieves its predictive goal of measuring crime involvement potential.

REFERENCES

Mylonas, A. D., & Reckless, W. C. Prisoners' attitudes toward law and legal institutions. *Journal of Criminal Law, Criminology, and Police Science,* 1963, *54,* 479–484.

Reckless, W. C. The development of a criminality level index. *Criminology,* 1966, *4,* 71–82.

CRIMINALITY LEVEL INDEX

Following are some statements with which you may agree or disagree. Circle the symbol which best represents your position on each statement, as follows:

SA Strongly Agree
A   Agree
U   Undecided
D   Disagree
SD Strongly Disagree

SA	A	U	D	SD	It is more wrong to get caught than it is to steal.
SA	A	U	D	SD	Law is the enemy of freedom.
SA	A	U	D	SD	The law enslaves the majority of people for the benefit of a few.
SA	A	U	D	SD	Almost anything can be fixed in courts if you have money.
SA	A	U	D	SD	You can't get justice in court.
SA	A	U	D	SD	Juries seldom understand a case well enough to make really just decisions.
SA	A	U	D	SD	Most juries are fixed.
SA	A	U	D	SD	Prosecutors are nothing but politicians.

SA	A	U	D	SD	No decent lawyer would ever be a prosecutor.
SA	A	U	D	SD	Cops often carry a grudge against men who get in trouble with the law and treat them cruelly.
SA	A	U	D	SD	Police put on a show by arresting people.
SA	A	U	D	SD	A policeman usually judges you as guilty.
SA	A	U	D	SD	Police hound ex-convicts.
SA	A	U	D	SD	Police work rests mainly upon information given by stool pigeons.
SA	A	U	D	SD	The policeman's standing in his Department depends upon the number of arrests he makes.
SA	A	U	D	SD	Police often use the third degree to secure confessions.
SA	A	U	D	SD	Influential or rich suspects are not given the third degree; it is restricted to petty or non-influential cases.
SA	A	U	D	SD	Police rarely get their man in difficult cases.
SA	A	U	D	SD*	Police are careful not to arrest innocent persons.
SA	A	U	D	SD	Police disregard constitutional rights in the interest of efficiency.
SA	A	U	D	SD	Policemen are just as crooked as the people they arrest.
SA	A	U	D	SD	People rarely try to help people.
SA	A	U	D	SD*	Policemen should be paid more for their work.
SA	A	U	D	SD*	Police almost always respect constitutional rights of suspected criminals.

*Reversed, Strongly Agree = 1, Strongly Disagree = 5.

CRIME AND CRIMINALITY ATTITUDE SCALES: LISTINGS

Attitudes toward Violence Scales

Blumenthal, M. D. Predicting attitudes toward violence. *Science,* 1972, *76,* 1296–1303.

These two scales are both 5-item, 4-response interview schedules designed to measure attitudes justifying violence. All 10 items begin with the stem "The police should." The first scale measures attitudes justifying violence for social control, by asking five questions about how police should handle ghetto riots. The second scale measures attitudes justifying violence for social change by asking the same five questions about how police should handle student disturbances.

Public Attitudes toward Crime and Corrections Survey

Joint Commission on Correctional Manpower and Training. *The Public Looks at Crime and Corrections*, 1968. The Joint Commission on Correctional Manpower and Training, 1522 K Street, N.W., Washington, D.C. 20005.

This 43-item Louis Harris survey was designed to measure a wide range of the public's feelings concerning crime rates, law enforcement, corrections, the courts, community based correctional programs, financial support for corrections as a career, and other corrections-related topics.

Public Opinion about Crime Questionnaire

Gibbons, D. C., Jones, J. F., & Garabedian, P. G. Gauging public opinion about the crime problem. *Crime and Delinquency*, 1972, *18*, 134–146.

This multiple-choice and dichotomous response questionnaire was designed to measure public opinion concerning the crime problem (five items), personal safety (three items), due process for adults (eight items), due process for juveniles (five items), and punitive measures (five items). Additional questions concerning crime were also asked.

CRIME AND CRIMINALITY BEHAVIOR RATINGS: REVIEWS

Aggression in Youth

Development and Characteristics

The *Aggression in Youth Scale* (AYS) was designed to serve as a conceptually and empirically meaningful set of behavior items for lower class youngsters in England (Dembo, 1973). Previous measures were felt to be culturally biased because they had been developed for United States populations.

The items for the scale are the result of interviews with a group (the specific number was not noted) of male youth club members from a suburb of England. The interview was purported to be an effort to discover how the boys spent their leisure time. During the hour and a half interview, however, the researcher also "sought to elicit descriptions of what would constitute an aggressive lad in their own (the boys') terms of reference." (Dembo, 1973, p. 246).

After this group interview, individual interviews were conducted with boys who had been nominated as an example of the aggressive type. This interview was aimed at discovering self-image, values, and behavior. A distinction quickly developed between "hard guys" and "nonhard guys" which closely paralleled the

TABLE 65. Traits Describing "Hard" and "NonHard" Guys

Dimension	Hard guy	Nonhard guy
Relationships to teachers	1. Tends to be cheeky (or answer back) 2. Tends to act against (or break) school rules	Tends to accept school discipline and rules
Relations with classmates (both in and out of school)	3. Starts (or stirs up) fights with others to keep his name (reputation) 4. Uses his fists to get his own way	His membership in peer groups is of a different order, without reliance on forceful means of self-assertion and status defence

concept of aggressive and nonaggressive boys, respectively. The developer believed that the two dimensions "relationships to teachers" and "relationships with classmates" could be used to describe the "hard guys." Table 65 lists the descriptions that were used as the basic traits.

In its final form, the scale consisted of these four "hard guy" characteristics, each followed by a 5-point rating scale including "not at all," "sometimes," "half the time," "usually," "all the time."

Response Mode

The respondents are tested individually and the instructions are read to each subject. He is asked to rate a number of boys he knows using the four items. This is done by checking the appropriate position on the 5-point continuum.

Scoring

Although it was not explicitly stated, it is implied that the total score is the sum of the item scores. Each item score is a number from 1 to 5, representing the frequency with which the individual being rated exhibits the characteristic. Therefore, the higher the total score on an individual, the more aggressive he is perceived to be.

Since this scale would be used most often in cases where a group of boys are rating individuals within the group, an average score is usually the representative score. This would be the mean rating of an individual by all the other boys.

Norms

No norms are available.

Reliability

Dembo (1973) reports a mean interitem reliability coefficient of .81 for 13 groups of boys.

Validity

Evidence for validity comes from several directions. First, the average rating of an individual by his peers was compared to the ratings given him by a tutor who knew the boys. Of the correlations, 81% computed on these comparisons were statistically significant (level of significance was not reported). This, while reported as evidence of validity, may also be considered evidence of interrater reliability.

Factor analysis was begun, but when the intercorrelation matrix was completed, the correlations were so large between the items that it was obvious only one dimension was being tapped.

Support for validity also came from in-depth interviews with individual boys. The boys were tested and divided into "aggressive" and "nonaggressive" categories based on whether they scored above or below the mean for their group. In the interviews, they were asked questions dealing with self-image, character types they identified with, and values placed on varied subjects. It was found that "aggressive" boys know they were considered aggressive and identified with their peer-assessed actions. They agreed, more often than the others, with the statement, "You've got to be rough to get ahead in life" ($p < .01$). They identified with character descriptions of boys who were sportsmen, school rejectors, lovers, and "hard guys." Also, these boys placed a higher emphasis on success in sports and with girls.

Finally, the rating results were compared with self-reported acts ranging from drinking beer without parental permission to hurting someone badly enough to require a doctor's intervention. The results showed significant correlations between the AYS and factor scores from the self-report scale. AYS "aggressors" scored higher than nonaggressors on interpersonal aggression and on property damage–theft items, as well as items relating to problems at home.

Comments

The developer emphasizes the fact that this scale was designed to indicate aggression in working class or lower class British boys. This objective is evidenced slightly by the vocabulary of item one. The word "cheeky" is rarely used in the United States.

The scale purports to measure aggression rather than delinquency. One who is aggressive is not necessarily delinquent, but there is often a strong correlation. The results of the AYS research are consistent with these propositions.

Even though the test consists of only four items, it has received support for its validity and interjudge reliability. The use of peer ratings seems a good indicator of behavior patterns and these items appear to facilitate the rating system. There is a need to test the scale in other cultures, especially in the United States. Also, results should be examined to determine whether the aggression being measured is specific to lower socioeconomic subcultures.

REFERENCES

Dembo, R. A measure of aggression among working-class youths. *British Journal of Criminology,* 1973, *13,* 245–252.

Maladaptive Behavior Record

Development and Characteristics

The *Maladaptive Behavior Record* (MBR) is a behavior checklist which was designed to "systematically classify and measure the maladaptive behaviors that lead to criminal acts" (Witherspoon, Jenkins, deValera, & Sanford, 1975, p. 1). It is believed that, if aspects of the environmental stimulation are known, the behavioral responses to this stimulation should give indications of the level of adaptation of ex-offenders.

Items for the MBR were developed from the outcome of interviews with approximately 300 released offenders. The results of the interviews indicated that several classes of behaviors seemed to be associated with the type of maladjustment directly related to recidivism. Nineteen specific behavioral groups were defined as important considerations in determining adjustment of ex offenders to civilian life. These 19 behavior categories were used to build a first version of the MBR. When these categories were analyzed and refined, the number was reduced to 16 representing the more recent version of the instrument.

Response Mode

The MBR uses an interview format. Within the 16 behavior categories, the respondents are asked direct questions about specific aspects of their day to day activities that can be used to establish behavior patterns in response to environmental conditions.

Scoring

Scoring for each MBR item is dichotomous. Respondents receive a 0 if there is no evidence of maladaptive behavior, or a 1 if there is evidence of maladaptive behavior. Specific examples and criteria for scoring are presented with the scale. Since a total score is calculated by adding individual item scores, the possible range of the MBR is 0–16, with a high score indicating a large amount of maladaptive behavior and a low score indicating little maladaptive behavior.

Norms

The developers suggest that a score of 0 indicates an acceptable level of adjustment and functioning. Relatively low scores (1-3) represent a small degree of maladaptive behavior, but a generally socially acceptable behavior record. Scores of 4-7 indicate more serious behavioral problems and are predictive of minor law violations. Finally, scores of 8–16 represent extremely maladaptive behavior and correlate highly with major law violations and recidivism.

Reliability

Witherspoon *et al.* (1975) present several estimates of reliability of the MBR. In one study of test–retest reliability, 96 prison releasees were interviewed at 3–6 months and again at 12–15 months after release. Of the subjects, 90% scored within the same relative position on the first and second administration. The reliability coefficient obtained was .95. Similar results were obtained from a sample of 36 releasees on a monthly basis for 15 to 18 months. The developers add that MBR scores encountered change most at lower and upper ends, while the middle ranges remained relatively constant.

Interrater reliability estimates have been obtained from two sources. In one study, 25 subjects were interviewed by different interviewers; the reliability coefficient between these interviewers was .84. In the second study, MBR interviews were videotaped and shown to 15 observers who were requested to score each interview. Exact agreement from all 15 observers was obtained in 86% of the cases. Agreement within one point was received on an additional 13% of the respondents and agreement within two points of the MBR was obtained for the remaining 1%.

Validity

Witherspoon *et al.* (1975) report a comparison of 15 to 20 college students and business personnel, who had no major problems in social functioning, with a group of 119 criminal recidivists. Scores on the MBR for the college students and business personnel ranged from 0–5, while scores from the prison releasees ranged from 2–14. Further, when the releasees were divided into recidivists and those with no further law encounters, the recidivists produced an average MBR score of 8.5 while the nonrecidivist releasees averaged 3.0.

By substituting the word "school" for "job" in the MBR and rewording items 5 and 11, the scale was made appropriate for juveniles. When the responses of 29 juveniles who had had no law encounters were compared to the responses of 34 adjudicated juveniles, the MBR was shown to discriminate between the two groups. The no-law-encounters group averaged 2.2, while the adjudicated juveniles averaged 8.1. Further, as the severity of law encounters increased, the average MBR score also increased.

Finally, when a group of 165 recent prison releasees were tested using the MBR, the data indicated that the MBR was highly predictive of the severity of law encounters.

Comments

The MBR offers an interesting alternative as an instrument measuring the level of adjustment of recent prison releasees. It has adequate reliability as measured by interrater consistency and test–retest estimates; support for validity is good for both adults and juveniles. In general it appears to be a good research instrument.

REFERENCES

Witherspoon, A. D., Jenkins, W. O., deValera, E. K., & Sanford, W. L. *A manual for the use of maladaptive behavior record in corrections.* Montgomery, Ala.: Rehabilitation Research Foundation, 1975.

MALADAPTIVE BEHAVIOR RECORD

To the Interviewer: The Maladaptive Behavior Record (MBR) manual should be carefully studied before interviewing the client and using this scale. Several interview tryouts should be performed and critiqued in the light of the instructions in the manual before further interviewing of clients. The MBR interview is to be used to assess the client's behavior output in the community environment, either currently or immediately prior to being incarcerated in a institution. You should obtain sufficient behavioral information from the client to score each item. The client's opinions or judgments should not be allowed to confuse or interfere with the obtaining of behavioral information and the rating of the items on the basis of actual behavior.

Some items of the MBR require only the specification of the client's behavior. Other items require, in addition to specific behavior, the specification of features of the environment in order to pinpoint the client's behavior in response to certain conditions.

The MBR is forced choice. If the client has a maladaptive behavior problem, the interviewer enters a "1" by the corresponding item. If there is no maladaptive behavior a "0" is entered by the corresponding item. In either case, the interviewer specifies under each item the environmental condition(s) and the client's response(s) which served as the basis for rating the item. Enter the total score on the top of the first page of the MBR.

Score

Employment

_____ 1. Behavior Response to Income. Rate "1" if client's employment income, pay schedule, or commission arrangement fails to meet his basic needs and client is not responding to this problem appropriately by actively seeking other employment or a solution through his employer.

Specify:_____

_____ 2. Behavioral Response to Working Conditions. Rate "1" if client's working conditions, such as heating, cooling, schedule, breaks and safety, are associated with significant anxiety, discomfort, or inconvenience and the client is not actively seeking a solution to this problem.

Specify:_____

_____ 3. Interaction with Co-workers. Rate "1" if client has significant or continuing problems in his interactions with co-workers either by virtue of his behavior or by his failure to respond appropriately to problems generated by their behavior.

Specify:_____

_____ 4. Interactions with Employer. Rate "1" if client has significant or continuing problems in his interaction with his employer either by virtue of his behavior or by his failure to respond appropriately to problems generated by his employer's behavior.

Specify:_____

_____ 5. Work Attendance. Rate "1" if client has been late or absent without following procedures acceptable to his employer.

Addiction

_____ 6. Alcohol Use. Rate "1" if client uses alcohol to the extent that it interferes with his interpersonal relationships or employment or results in financial difficulty for him or his family.

Specify: _____

_____ 7. Drug Use. Rate "1" if client uses drugs to the extent that it interferes with his interpersonal relationships or employment or results in financial difficulty for him or his family.

Specify: _____

_____ 8. Gambling. Rate "1" if client loses money excessively, i.e., to the extent that it interferes with his interpersonal relationships or results in financial difficulty for him or his family.

Specify: _____

Interpersonal

_____ 9. Fighting. Rate "1" if client engages in (physical) fighting precipitated either by his inappropriate behavior or by his failure to respond to the behavior of others in such a manner as to avoid fights.

Specify: _____

_____ 10. Verbal Abusiveness. Rate "1" if client's verbal behavior toward others is abusive, or if client is the recipient of verbal abuse, or if there is reciprocal verbal abuse, between client and others, such as intense arguments.

Specify: _____

_____ 11. Maladaptive Associates: Rate "1" if client spends time with persons who exhibit maladaptive behavior in such areas as crime, drugs, alcohol, sex, money management, and employment.

Specify: _____

Economics

_____ 12. Management of Money. Rate "1" if client has difficulty in managing his money, i.e., spending for nonessentials, overextended installment purchasing to the extent that client is unable to purchase sufficient essentials, meet financial obligations, etc.

Specify: _____

Adjustment

____ 13. Responses to Physical Condition. Rate "1" if client has physical problems to which his responses are maladaptive, such as failing to secure and follow treatment or by failure to arrange his activities in accordance with his physical condition.

Specify: _____

____ 14. Psychological Adjustment

(a) Rate "1" if client's verbal accounts of his behavior indicate unrealistic or excessive responses of withdrawal, avoidance, dependency on others, self-criticism, overcompensatory behavior, denial of behavioral problems, etc.

(b) Rate "1" if client's verbal behavior indicates that fear, anxiety, or behavioral deficits significantly interfere with meeting people or with instituting and maintaining supportive interpersonal relationships.

(c) Rate "1" if client's behavior during the interview indicates marked fear, anxiety, or inadequacy as characterized by lack of eye contact, difficulty in speaking, trembling, excessive perspiring, etc., or if the client's behavior is excessively aggressive.

Specify: _____

Legal

____ 15. Behavioral Responses to Legal Processes. Rate "1" if client's behavior has resulted in minor legal problems or processes not involving arrest, such as ignoring reprimands for minor technical parole violations, repeated involvement with legal authorities, legal proceedings against him by virtue of his failure to abide by contractual agreements, etc. Also rate "1" if client is responding inappropriately to legal processes such as divorce or child custody litigation by avoiding subpoena, failing to appear in court, etc.

Specify: _____

____ 16. Other Behavioral Problems. Rate "1" if client has behavioral problems which are not covered in the preceding items. This item may include less frequently reported instances, such as sexual deviance (e.g., homosexuality, relations with prepubertal females, etc.) and a wide range of other behaviors such as maladaptive dress, hygiene, or residence maintenance, etc.

Specify: _____

CRIME AND CRIMINALITY PERSONALITY ASSESSMENT: REVIEWS

Giannell Index of Criminality

Development and Characteristics

The *Giannell Index of Criminality* (GIC) is the operational form of a theory of crime causation. Giannell (1966a, 1966b) has described a "criminosynthesis theory" in which six essential crime-conducive factors exist and may be evaluated to predict criminality. The theory suggests that the factors are important crime determinants to the degree they are psychosynthesized, or hold combined conscious, semiconscious, or unconscious significance for the experiencing individual.

The greatest probability of crime occurs with the following combination of the six factors: high need frustration, low internal inhibitions, low external inhibitions, low contact with reality, high situational crime potential, and high potential satisfaction. Any criminal act may be analyzed and reconstructed on these dimensions and each factor is described as important only in dynamic combination with the other factors. The GIC is determined usually by interviewer and subject together assessing the subject's position on a high-low dichotomization of each factor.

Response Mode

Giannell (1967a) has reported using the GIC in an interviewing schedule with inmates. When a schematic form of the index was used clinically with offenders being classified at New York's Clinton State Prison, the inmates talked freely, assessed themselves accurately, and some expressed a genuine interest in becoming noncriminal. The inmates made a verbal "high" or "low" self-assessment on each of the six index factors. A 5-point,Likert-type scale for felt strength of inhibitions has been administered, eliciting responses to five questions about 15 criminal situations (Giannell, 1970).

Scoring

Scoring for general interviewing procedures is drawn from the high-low summed ratings for each factor. The 5-point,Likert-type scale for internal inhibition was scored by "weighing the responses so that theoretically a score of 100% would be given if all five answers to all the five questions were 'Definitely Yes,' a score of 75% for 'Yes,' a score of 50% for 'Undecided,' a score of 25% for 'No,' and no score for 'Definitely Not' " (Giannell, 1970, p. 34). Then a mean percentage score was calculated across all 15 situations. No such procedure has been developed for the five factors other than internal inhibition.

TABLE 66. Descriptive Statistics and Ratios of Nonoffender and Offender Samples on Internal Inhibition Measure

Parameter	Nonoffender		Offender				
	Male	Female	Adult male Ohio	Adult male Federal	Adult female Ohio	Juvenile female Ohio	Juvenile female Michigan
N	144	288	104	61	102	101	32
Age							
M	18.29	18.61	34.58	32.36	29.37	16.51	15.97
SD	.99	2.60	9.78	9.10	8.78	4.50	1.02
Race							
White	144	288	58	38	60	68	17
Black	—	—	43	21	42	33	14
Other	—	—	3	2	—	—	1
Internal inhibition							
M	63.58	73.89	53.67	50.48	61.33	57.00	43.05
SD	16.95	12.54	17.72	22.70	20.74	19.39	21.51

Norms

Table 66 indicates norms on the internal inhibition factor for five offender groups and two nonoffender groups.

Reliability

Reliability estimates are not available.

Validity

Content validity is present; the factors seem to represent frequent themes that appear in the psychological literature on criminality.

Need frustration was specifically studied in 130 adult male offenders, 134 female adult offenders, 115 juvenile male offenders, and 104 female juvenile offenders, using the *Edwards Personal Preference Schedule* (EPPS) (Giannell, 1966a). Significant differences were found between these groups and the normal samples in most EPPS scales, supporting in this rather broad sense that need frustration differences were present.

In another study, Giannell (1966b) interviewed and tested with the EPPS 103 female homosexuals who were in midwest gay bars. Interviewing results indicated to him that these subjects were crime prone on all six factors. On the EPPS, the subjects differed significantly from the normative samples, but not from each other when divided into "Butch," "Femme," and "Neutral" subgroups.

No control group was used and the assumption was made that female homosexuality is a form of criminality.

Finally, Giannell (1970) compared 432 college students with 400 adult and juvenile, male and female prisoners on responses to the five questions (e.g., "Would your conscience stop you from doing it?) about 15 criminal behavior situations. Internal inhibitions from guilt, self-respect, kind-of-person, conscience, and religion, were found to be lower in the offender groups, as predicted.

Comments

This index and its antecedent theory are derived from some often-expressed observations of offender behavior, and potentially may have utility as a device to aid in interviewing prisoners and promoting some self-examination in them. However, four of the factors have not been operationally defined, only one research study genuinely relevant to the index has been carried out (Giannell, 1970), and strained extrapolations (Giannell, 1969) and sweeping claims made. Thus, the utility of the index would seem to be limited to experimental and exploratory work.

REFERENCES

Giannell, A. S. Psychological needs characteristic of four criminal offender groups. *Journal of Social Psychology,* 1966, *69,* 55–72. (a)

Giannell, A. S. Giannell's criminosynthesis theory applied to female homosexuality. *Journal of Psychology,* 1966, *64,* 213–222. (b)

Giannell, A. S. Giannell's criminosynthesis theory as an interviewing schedule for the assessment of criminality. *Corrective Psychiatry and Journal of Social Therapy,* 1967, *13,* 42–50. (a)

Giannell, A. S. Criminosintesi. *Quaderni di Criminologia Clinica,* 1967, *9,* 154–163. (b)

Giannell, A. S. A theoretical basis for police firmness in riot control. *Police Times,* 1969, *6,* 4.

Giannell, A. S. The role of internal inhibition in crime causation. *Journal of Social Psychology,* 1970, *81,* 31–36.

GIANNELL INDEX OF CRIMINALITY

1. *Need Frustration* " . . . before committing a crime a person is likely to feel unhappy, unsatisfied, resentful, or angry."

2. *Internal Inhibition.* " . . . internal forces which may prevent a person from committing a crime." Conscience, self-respect, a particular conception of self, guilt, and remorse are included.

3. *External Inhibition.* These are external forces, such as punishment, disgrace, possible prison sentence, and possible arrest, that may prevent a person from committing a crime.
4. *Contact with Reality.* This is the ability to accurately learn from mistakes and experience, assess situations accurately, and foresee consequences of actions. "... to produce the highest possible efficiency and happiness."
5. *Situational Crime Potential.* This factor is "... the actual and concrete possibility to commit the crime, provided by a given situation, environment, person, or circumstance."
6. *Potential Satisfaction.* This is "... the balance of what the individual has to gain and lose (of a psychological nature) when he commits a crime."

Intentionality in Criminal Situations Scale

Development and Characteristics

The *Intentionality in Criminal Situations Scale* (ICSS) was designed to measure the degree to which children use the concept "intent" in evaluating criminal behavior (Keasey & Sales, 1977). It was developed in response to Piaget's (1932) assertion that cognitive intentionality must be learned as an evaluative component. That is, children learn to use the concept of intent when evaluating the goodness or badness of one's behavior. Most adults judge others' behavior (to some degree) according to what they believe the other person's motives or intentions are. If this attribution of intent occurs at different ages, juvenile authorities should become aware of and make an effort to rate its existence or lack of existence in the cognitive set of minors.

To measure the degree to which intentionality affects judgments of children, four story themes were written which dealt with the crimes of arson, battery, homicide, and larceny. Each was written in four versions, which match high and low damage with good and bad intentions. Since the four themes can be presented in four different versions, a total of 16 stories are possible. These can then be paired, and children (whose verbal ability may be at a minimum) can choose the story that describes the "naughtiest" person in each pair.

Response Mode

Because children in the age range (5–8) for whom this test was originally constructed do not read well, the stories are read individually to the respondents. The children are then asked to: (1) Choose which of each story pair described the naughtiest person; (2) give the reasons for their choice; and (3) rate each story as "not naughty at all," "a little naughty," "naughty," "very naughty," or "very, very, naughty."

Scoring

Three intentionality scores (the degree to which intentionality influences evaluative judgments) can be calculated. First, one can count the number of times a respondent chooses "bad intention" as the naughtiest description. A second score is obtained by calculating the percent of references to intentionality (or lack of intentionality) when explaining why a story was chosen as the naughtiest. Finally, the Likert-type responses can be numbered in the appropriate direction and summed.

Norms

No relevant norms are available.

Reliability

No reliability estimates have been reported.

Validity

Content validity is supported by the systematic presentation of "good" and "bad" intentions under varying circumstances. The stories are simple and should be easily understood by children.

Support for construct validity comes from the results of testing with 5-, 6-, and 7-year-old children. Consistent with Piaget's theoretical position, younger children were less likely to consider intentionality and vice versa. Further, no significant differences were noted due to the type of crime committed.

Comments

The ICSS represents an interesting approach to understanding children's cognitive structure pertaining to crime. The developers suggest that it would serve well as a diagnostic and therapeutic guide for problem children. The type of treatment used could be directed by an indicator of cognitive set. A similar approach might be useful for older persons as well.

In general, there is support for validity, but reliability estimates are needed. The ICSS arises directly from theoretical positions and seems to offer profitable avenues for further research.

REFERENCES

Keasey, C. B., & Sales, B. D. An empirical investigation of young children's awareness and usage of intentionality in criminal situations. *Law and Human Behavior,* 1977, *1,* 45–61.

Piaget, J. *The moral judgment of the child.* New York: Harcourt, Brace, & World, 1932.

INTENTIONALITY IN CRIMINAL SITUATIONS SCALE

Instructions to Interviewer: Read each story pair to the child and ask him/her to (1) choose which of each story pair described the naughtiest person, (2) give the reasons for the choice, and (3) rate each story as "Not naughty at all," "A little naughty," "Naughty," "Very naughty," or "Very, very naughty."

Story-Pair 1: Arson: Classic Contrast (BL/HG)*

(BL) Chuck was mad at his parents because they would not buy him a new bike that he wanted. So he decided to burn down their house. Chuck could only get a small fire started, so only part of the kitchen floor and a chair were burned by the time firemen put out the fire.

(HG) Billy's mother was late getting home, so Billy decided to help her by lighting the oven so that dinner would cook. But Billy dropped the lighted match and suddenly things began to catch on fire. Most of the house burned down before the firemen could put out the fire.

Story-Pair 2: Battery: High Damage (BH/GH)

(BH) Johnny was the pitcher for his little league baseball team. Before the championship game, Johnny told the pitcher of the other team that he would hit him in the head if he was pitching too good. When the pitcher for the other team came to bat, Johnny threw the ball right at the other pitcher's head. The ball hit him in the head and knocked him out. He had to be taken to the hospital for an operation.

(GH) Henry was the pitcher for his little league baseball team. Before the championship game, Henry was telling everyone how excited he was. When the pitcher for the other team came to bat, one of Henry's pitches went wild. The ball hit the other pitcher in the head and knocked him out. He had to be taken to the hospital for an operation.

Story-Pair 3: Larceny: Low Damage (GL/BL)

(GL) One day at the store Frank was looking at a new comic book. Frank really wanted it but he didn't have enough money to buy it. Just then the store owner walked past Frank and bumped into the rack of new comic books. Suddenly all the comics began to fall out of the rack on to the floor. Frank grabbed the rack and kept all the comics from falling on the floor. When Frank got home he discovered that one of the comic books had fallen into his grocery sack.

(BL) One day at the store George was looking at a new comic book. George really wanted it but didn't want to spend his own money for it. So when the store owner wasn't looking, George grabbed the comic book and hid it in his grocery sack. A few minutes later George sneaked out of the store with the comic book hidden in his grocery sack.

Story-Pair 4: Homicide: Classic Contrast (GH/BL)

(GH) One day David decided to help his father by cleaning up his father's closet. While he was cleaning, David found his father's gun on the floor. When David tried to put

*GH—High Damage/Good Intent; BH—High Damage/Bad Intent; GL—Low Damage/Good Intent ; BL—Low Damage/Bad Intent .

the gun back up on the shelf where it belonged the gun went off. The bullet hit and killed an older boy who was playing nearby.

(BL) For several weeks some older boys had been teasing Eddie after school and chased him home. One day Eddie decided to get even and do something to the older boys. After they had chased Eddie home, he went into the house and got his father's gun. Eddie went back out the front door shooting at the other boys. Nobody was hurt but one bullet broke a window.

CRIME AND CRIMINALITY PERSONALITY ASSESSMENT: LISTINGS

Hostility and Direction of Hostility Questionnaire

Caine, T. M., Foulds, G. A., & Hope, K. *Manual of the Hostility and Direction of Hostility Questionnaire (HDHQ).* London: University of London, 1967.

Phillip, A. E. Development and use of the Hostility and Direction of Hostility Questionnaire. *Journal of Psychosomatic Research,* 1969, *13,* 283–287.

The *Hostility and Direction of Hostility Questionnaire* was designed to measure a wide range of possible manifestations of aggression, hostility, or punitiveness. All items were drawn from the MMPI and the following five scales were developed: *Acting-Out Hostility, Criticism of Others, Delusional Hostility, Self-Criticism,* and *Delusional Guilt.*

Scrambled Sentence Test

Costin, F. The Scrambled Sentence Test: A group measure of hostility. *Educational and Psychological Measurement,* 1969, *29,* 461–468.

The *Scrambled Sentence Test* was designed to serve as a disguised measure of hostility. It consists of 70 sets of scrambled words. Respondents are requested to read the words and make sentences. Of the sentences 50 are scored as hostile or nonhostile responses and the remaining 20 are unscored buffer items.

Stereoscopic Perception of Violence

Shelley, E. L. D., & Toch, H. H. The perception of violence as an indicator of adjustment in institutionalized offenders. *Journal of Criminal Law, Criminology, and Police Science,* 1962, *53,* 463–469.

This instrument consists of a set of nine stereograms, each of which shows one violent and one nonviolent activity. The perception of violence is determined by the frequency the violent pictures were seen as opposed to the nonviolent pictures.

CRIME AND CRIMINALITY PREDICTION: REVIEWS

Anger Disposition Scale

Development and Characteristics

The *Anger Disposition Scale* (ADS) was designed as a projective measure of "an individual's potentiality for aggression" (Loy & Turnbull, 1964, p. 314). The projective type of test was used because the authors felt that this method was less likely to show falsified responses than direct measures. Although other projective techniques such as the *Thematic Appreciation Test* (Lesser, 1958), Rosenzweig's *Picture Frustration Study* (1945), and the incomplete story technique (Allinsmith, 1954) had been used for the measurement of aggression, they were felt to be insufficiently structured in scoring and interpretation.

The ADS consists of a set of 54 hypothetical situations in which a boy, Johnny, experiences frustration. The situations are systematically varied according to three dimensions: (1) Response class (the type of need that is being frustrated)—autonomy, dependency, and achievement; (2) Stimulus objects (the person who is the source of the frustration)—parent, other adult, and peer, (3) Frustration levels (the intensity of the frustration)—high, medium, and low.

It is assumed that "in judging the intensity of an imaginary boy's anger reaction to a given frustration, subjects would have to imagine themselves in such a situation, or recall comparable experiences of their own, and how they felt at the time" (Loy & Turnbull, 1964, p. 316).

Response Mode

The subject is presented with the question booklet and a separate answer sheet. The test booklet contains the 54 situations from which the subject is asked to judge how angry he thinks Johnny is. He is asked to rate the anger on a 6-point scale which ranges from "1—not at all angry" to "6—very angry."

Scoring

Scoring is a matter of summing the item scores of "anger expressed by the subject." Since the test is systematically varied across three dimensions, scores can be calculated for each treatment within each of these dimensions or a single total score may be computed.

Norms

The data in Table 67 were collected on 24 10th-grade boys at the Lookout Mountain School for Boys, Golden, Colorado, an institution for juvenile of-

TABLE 67. Nondelinquent and Delinquent Group Comparisons on ADS Frustration Levels

Groups	Frustration levels						t values	
	High M	Items SD	Medium M	Items SD	Low M	Items SD	High vs. medium t	Medium vs. low t
Nondelinquents	89.53	13.44	77.47	13.57	65.94	14.51	3.52[a]	3.23[a]
Delinquent	94.58	9.16	85.67	12.65	78.33	14.00	2.73[a]	1.87[b]

[a] .005 level of significance.
[b] .05 level of significance.

fenders, and 32 10th-grade boys in a physical education class from Golden High School, Golden, Colorado.

Reliability

No reliability estimates were reported.

Validity

The scale has content validity as reflected in systematic specification and variation of item content. A further validity indication is the ability of the test to differentiate between groups, as noted in the previous table.

Comments

Additional validation of the scale in general is needed, as well as support for the notion that it measures three different dimensions. Reliability must also be established.

There is a strong case for the relationship between anger and aggression. It is more difficult, however, to assess whether an individual can accurately predict the amount of anger he or she might experience in some hypothetical situation. The developers suggest that the instrument measures anger "dispositions," a cautious and reasonable position.

The scale offers an unusual technique for assessing anger reactions to frustrating situations. The extensiveness of the situations presented is of special interest. Furthermore, the scale is well seated within the frameworks of frustration–aggression and need–press theories.

REFERENCES

Allinsmith, B. B. *Parental discipline and children's aggression in two social classes.* Unpublished doctoral dissertation, University of Michigan, 1954.

Rosenweig, S. The picture–association method and its application in a study of reactions to frustration. *Journal of Personality,* 1945, *14,* 3–23.

Koy, D. L., & Turnbull, J. W. Indirect assessment of anger dispositions. *Journal of Projective Techniques and Personality Assessment,* 1964, *28,* 314–321.

Lesser, G. S. Conflict analysis and fantasy aggression. *Journal of Personality,* 1958, *26,* 29–41.

ANGER DISPOSITION SCALE

Instructions: Read each of the following stories and rate how angry you would become in this situation. Decide whether you would be:

       1. Not Angry at All
       2. Almost No Anger
       3. Barely Angry
       4. Angry
       5. Very Angry

Autonomy

Hi Parent M[*]

1. Every time Johnny tries to leave home and live by himself since he started earning his own money, his dad has said no and made Johnny give him most of his paycheck. On the next payday, Johnny's dad again demands Johnny's paycheck. Johnny says, "No, I'm going to live on my own." Johnny's dad hits him and tells him to give him his paycheck, get in his room, and stay there.

Hi Parent F

2. Johnny wants to get married and leave his mother whom he has lived with and cared for now almost two years. She says he can't and has said she will shoot Johnny's girl. He asks her one more time and promises to help pay for her support. His mother picks up a gun and runs for the door.

Med Parent M

3. Johnny has asked his dad several times to let him meet his friends who are expecting him since tonight is the final game of the season for a basketball team they have organized. Dad keeps saying, "No, you didn't shovel the walk like I asked." Finally Johnny says, "I'm going anyway." Dad says, "I'll knock you back into your room if you try it."

Med Parent F

4. Several of Johnny's friends are planning on spending the weekend at the mountain cabin. They're really looking forward to a good time. As the time gets nearer for them all to leave, Johnny keeps begging his mother to let him go. She keeps saying she won't allow it. When it is time to go, Johnny starts toward the door. Mother rushes to the door and stands in the doorway. She says, "You'll have to get past me to go."

Lo Parent M

5. Johnny wants to watch a show on TV tonight instead of studying his homework. He walks over and starts to turn on the TV. His dad says, "Get back to your room and start studying."

Lo Parent F

6. Johnny's mother makes him go to bed at 9:30 on weekdays. Johnny says that he is old enough now to go to bed later than 9:30. Tonight I'm staying up 'til 10:30. Mother says, "You're going to bed now!"

Hi Other Adult M

7. A man who lives next door insists that Johnny broke his window, but he didn't. The man wants Johnny to pay him for the window and keeps trying to grab him and make him pay when he walks by the house. One day the man catches Johnny and tries to drag him into the house.

Hi Other Adult F

8. Mrs. Brown, in charge of the Sunday School class, has insisted that Johnny be in the Christmas program. Every time he tries to get out, she grabs him and makes him stay. Finally Johnny tells her that he's had enough and is quitting. He starts out the door. Mrs. Brown grabs him and says, "You're not going anywhere."

Med Other Adult M

9. Johnny's uncle has made Johnny come over on a Saturday and work for him. Johnny wants to go to the show with his friends. Johnny tells his uncle he's leaving. His uncle says, "If you go now, I'll fix you good!"

Med Other Adult F

10. Johnny has been made to stay after school by Miss Green. Johnny wants to go to a party. Johnny gets up and says he's leaving. The teacher says, "If you do, I'll fail you."

Lo Other Adult F

11. Johnny had a summer job. He's hot and thirsty and asks the boss if he can get a drink. The boss says, "No!"

Lo Other Adult F

12. Johnny wants to go into the garage and work on the old car he was just able to buy. His sister who is older and was told to see that Johnny works, says, "You can't until you help me finish cleaning the house!"

Hi Peer M

13. Johnny's friend, Pete, has been forcing Johnny to help him steal gas from cars. Everytime Johnny tries to get away, Pete hits him and makes him help again. This time Johnny makes up his mind to get away. Johnny steps out of the car and says, "I've had enough." Pete says, "No, you haven't," and swings at him.

Hi Peer F

14. Mary, a girl Johnny's age, asks Johnny to go for a ride with her in her new car. After they drive out of town she tells him she stole the car in order to run away from home. She won't let him out of the car and tells him when she ditches the car, she will say he stole the car and kidnapped her. She stops the car to check a tire and threatens him with a gun.

Med Peer M

15. It's getting late and Johnny has promised to be home early. His friend, Mike, keeps insisting that they stay at the dance a while longer. Johnny says he's going home. Mike follows him out the front door and says he'll beat Johnny up if he leaves.

Med Peer F

16. Johnny wants to go to basketball practice, but Jane wants him to finish helping her. Johnny says that he has had enough and is leaving. She tells him he'd better stay or else. Finally Johnny starts to walk out the door and Jane says, "If you go out that door I'll kick you," and she stands in the middle of the doorway.

Lo Peer M

17. Johnny wants to study and his friend, Jim, is at the house. Johnny says he wants to study and Jim says, "I'll bother you so much you won't be able to study."

Lo Peer F

18. Johnny has been dancing with Jane all evening and Johnny doesn't like to dance. Johnny says that he wants to go home and Jane says, "No, we're going to dance a while longer."

Succorance

Hi Parent M

19. Johnny has been blamed for something he didn't do by the police. He will be sent to jail unless dad offers to watch out for him from now on. Dad has said he won't help. In court he says he has too many other things to worry about to look out for Johnny.

Hi Parent F

20. Mother isn't married to dad any more. Johnny has had to live in an orphanage and every time he writes to mother to take care of him she says no. Finally she visits Jimmy at the orphanage and he asks her again to take him with her. She says she is too busy.

Med Parent M

21. Three boys have beaten up Johnny before and when Johnny asked his dad for help, he said he wouldn't. The boys warn Johnny they're going to do it again. Johnny asks his dad for help again and dad says, "You're old enough to take care of yourself."

478   CHAPTER 11

Med Parent F

22. Johnny lost his best friend and he is real unhappy. He thinks if his mother calls his friend's mother and explains things, his friend will like him again. He asked her once and she said no. In tears he begs her again and she says "Handle it yourself."

Lo Parent M

23. Johnny wants to go to the show tonight. He's short just 5¢ of having enough money. Johnny asks his dad for the nickel and dad says, "No, do you think I'm made of money!"

Lo Parent F

24. Johnny accidentally cut himself. He goes to mother for help in putting a band-aid on. She tells him to do it himself.

Med Other Adult M

25. Last semester Johnny failed math. A man who really knows math lives next door. Several times before Johnny has asked him to help with his math. He has always refused. Johnny has a final math test tomorrow. Johnny begs him to help again. The man next door tells him to get out and quit bothering him.

Hi Other Adult F

26. Johnny has been accused of taking things from other kids' coats. He couldn't have done it because he was in Miss Johnson's room when it happened, helping her clean up. He sees her in the hall and asks her to tell the principal that he was with her when it happened. She says she has to hurry and doesn't have time, now or ever.

Hi Other Adult M

27. An uncle of Johnny's has always given Johnny's cousins money whenever they asked for it, but never Johnny. Johnny needs 50¢ to pay for a vase he broke in a department store or they will turn him over to the police. Just then his uncle comes along and Johnny asks him for the 50¢. His uncle says, "Get out and earn it."

Med Other Adult F

28. Johnny lives in the country and doesn't have a phone. A neighbor lady one mile down the road has a phone. She has not let him use the phone before, but this time if she won't let him use the phone, he won't get a ride into town. He needs the ride to see his dad who will be gone for six months. After he walks the mile to her house, the lady tells Johnny she won't let him use the phone.

Lo Other Adult M

29. Johnny asks his teacher, Mr. Smith, to help him with the model car he is building, since Mr. Smith is the shop teacher. Mr. Smith says he is too busy for such things.

Lo Other Adult F

30. Johnny is telling a neighbor lady about the time he was picked on by five kids on the way home from school. She says, "Knowing you, it's good enough for you!"

Hi Peer M

31. Johnny will be sent to jail if his friend, Jim, doesn't tell the police that Johnny was with him in the movie the night a store was robbed. Jim has said he doesn't want to get involved. Johnny meets Jim on the street and asks him to tell the police what he knows; Jim says, "Stay away from me, I hope they send you to jail!"

Hi Peer F

32. Johnny lost his girlfriend, Mary. Mary thinks that Johnny went out with Ann. Johnny didn't go out with Ann and time after time has asked Ann to tell Mary, but with little success. Johnny asks Ann once more to tell Mary that it isn't true. Ann says, "It's what you both deserve; I won't do it!"

Med Peer M

33. Bill is the best basketball player in school. Coach says Johnny can make the team if he improves his passing. Bill has helped several others on the team so Johnny asks Bill to help him. Bill keeps saying he doesn't care enough. Coach gives Johnny one more week to improve his passing before he selects the team. Johnny asks Bill once more and he says, "I couldn't care less!"

Med Peer F

34. Johnny spent the night at Jim's house. He told his sister, Jane, to tell his parents, but she didn't. Jim has left on a two-week vacation with his parents and Johnny's parents are very angry because they think Johnny spent the night with Jack whom they will not let Johnny see. Johnny keeps asking Jane to tell his folks where he was. She keeps saying she won't and after they tell Johnny he will have to stay in the house the next two weeks, Jane says, "That's good enough for you!"

Lo Peer M

35. Johnny needs a dollar for gas for his car in order to make his date tonight which is very important to him. He asks his friend, Jim, to loan him the dollar until he gets his paycheck tomorrow. Jim says, "I won't, I've got to save every cent I can!"

Lo Peer F

36. Johnny has just lost an important chance to spend a weekend at a fishing camp. He meets his friend, Mary, and tells her about it. She says, "Too bad, what am I supposed to do about it!"

Achievement

Hi Parent M

37. Johnny has become a star high school basketball player. Several colleges have offered him scholarships, but everytime a college scout comes to visit him at home,

his dad appears, drunk, and tells the scout to get out of the house. After this, they don't come back. There is only one college scout left to visit him. The same thing happens. Dad comes in drunk, and tells the basketball coach at State University to get out of the house, which he does.

Hi Parent F

38. Johnny's rich uncle has offered to put Johnny through college and take him into the business. He hints that someday he intends to have Johnny take over the company. Johnny's mother doesn't like the uncle. She says, "You're not going anywhere to college. You'll get a job like your dad and help support this family." Every time uncle phones to ask Johnny if he'll accept the deal, Johnny's mother makes Johnny hang up. Finally the uncle comes to the house to ask and Johnny's mother tells him to get out and stay out.

Med Parent M

39. Johnny's gets a job after school to earn money to buy a scooter. Twice he almost has enough money but his dad takes the money away from him and buys furniture for the house. Once again, Johnny is only $5 away from having enough money. His dad takes the money and says, "It's too dangerous for you to drive a scooter. Besides it's about time you pay your own way."

Med Parent F

40. Johnny wants to be part of the most important club in school. When he goes to their parties, his mother says he has to come home an hour before the party is over. The club members say they'll throw him out of the club if he doesn't stay later. Johnny tells his mother this on the day of another party. She says, "I'm not going to let you go at all tonight."

Lo Parent M

41. Johnny wants to enter a model car he is building in a contest. He has only one more evening to work on it. As he heads for his room to finish it, his dad says, "Son, you're going to help me clean the attic tonight."

Lo Parent F

42. Johnny has been told by the music teacher that he is very good on the trumpet. The teacher said that he would like to have Johnny enter the music contest next year if he keeps on improving. Johnny goes home and starts to practice. His mother says, "That settles it, I'm going to sell that noisy thing. Give it here!"

Hi Other Adult M

43. Johnny wants to amount to something in life. He's a good student and popular with the others. There's a teacher, Mr. Black, who really seems to have it in for Johnny. One time when Johnny tried to get into the leader's club, Mr. Black stood up and said that Johnny wasn't good enough to be a member. When Johnny was nominated for class president, Mr. Black said that he wouldn't think much of a group that elected Johnny president. Johnny is coming up for membership in the sports letter club and Mr. Black meets Johnny in the school hall and tells him that he's going to vote against him and make a speech to the members about why Johnny shouldn't belong.

Hi Other Adult F

44. Johnny has been trying to save enough money by working after school, on weekends, and in the summer to go to college. His aunt doesn't think hs should go to college, but should work in the family grocery store to help pay for the cost of bringing him up, as she puts it. Twice before, Johnny has had jobs and then his aunt comes in and tells the boss that Johnny is a criminal who steals and should be fired, which the boss does. Johnny has found another job as a carryout boy in a supermarket. His aunt comes into the store one night and loudly tells the manager in front of everyone that Johnny is a thief and should be fired.

Med Other Adult M

45. Johnny has been trying to make the football team. A neighbor, Mr. Green, who is interested in the team, laughs loudly and makes comments everytime Johnny doesn't look very good. After practice on the way home, Johnny meets Mr. Green who tells Johnny that he has been telling the coach he hopes Johnny doesn't make the team.

Med Other Adult F

46. Johnny is pretty good on the violin. He thinks he's good enough to enter the local music contest. For the past two years his teacher has called in her friend, Mrs. Smith, a neighbor of Johnny's, to help decide if Johnny is good enough to enter the contest. She keeps saying, "no." This year Johnny knows he is good enough. When his teacher calls in Mrs. Smith, she says, "He'll never be good enough."

Lo Other Adult M

47. In a woodworking class project everyone has been told to make something original. Johnny made an end table. When they are due, the teacher, Mr. Jones, looks at all of them and tells Johnny, "This is the worst I have ever seen."

Lo Other Adult F

48. Mrs. Thomas has promised Johnny five dollars if he does a good job cleaning up her basement. Johnny does the best he can and asks for his money. Mrs. Thomas says he didn't do well enough so she isn't going to give him anything.

Hi Peer M

49. A classmate of Johnny's named Joe doesn't like Johnny. Once Johnny went out for football and Joe got all of his friends to gang up on Johnny on every play. Johnny looked so bad he didn't make the team. Another time Johnny was supposed to make a speech in the school auditorium. Joe got all of his friends to laugh so hard that Johnny had to stop in the middle of the speech and leave the stage. Everyone who wants a scholarship to college has to take a test on a certain day. If they don't take the test, they don't get the scholarship. Joe gets his friends to take Johnny for a ride on the day of the test and Johnny misses the test. Joe meets Johnny the next day alone in the hall and says, "I really fixed you this time."

Hi Peer F

50. For some reason Jane doesn't like Johnny. She knows that once Johnny was in a little trouble with the law, but Johnny hasn't been in any trouble for a long time. Once Johnny tried to get into a club in school and Jane told the members they

didn't want a jailbird. Another time Johnny had a chance for a good job and Jane told the boss about his scrapes with the police and the boss wouldn't hire him. Johnny is good in basketball and a college scout offers him a scholarship to State University. Jane meets Johnny on the street and tells him that she wrote State University a letter telling them all about Johnny. She says, "I'll fix you as long as you try to be somebody."

Med Peer M

51. For the first time Johnny gets a chance to decorate the windows in the store he's been working at. Johnny knows that if he does well the boss will offer Johnny a job after he gets out of school, as a salesman. Jim, a boy who lives down the block, has gotten Johnny into trouble before and goes into the store where Johnny is working after hours and talks to Johnny. Johnny has just finished. They leave the store. The next day the boss calls school and tells Johnny he's fired. He says Johnny put up a sign with dirty words on it in the window. Johnny meets Jim after school and Jim says, "That was a pretty funny trick I played on you last night wasn't it, putting up that sign."

Med Peer F

52. Jane has made real trouble for Johnny several times. Johnny won't graduate from high school unless he hands in an essay or original paper for English. The papers are due on Friday. Johnny just gets it done on time and hands it in. The teacher calls him in the next week and tells Johnny he can't graduate. She says he turned in ten blank pages of paper. Jane meets Johnny on the street and tells him she sneaked into the teacher's room and exchanged the blanks for his paper. She laughs and says, "Too bad about your not graduating."

Lo Peer M

53. Johnny has been trying to do his math homework. It's a long, important assignment that's going to count pretty heavily in the final grade. Johnny has just finished it and is on his way home. He meets Frank and Frank grabs his paper and tears it up.

Lo Peer F

54. Johnny wants to get into the class play. He doesn't get the part and Mary tells him she argued the teacher out of giving him the part.

*None of the labels shown here are included on the actual test sheet.

Delinquency Potential Scale

Development and Characteristics

The *Delinquency Potential Scale* (DPS) was developed (Gunderson & Ballard, 1958) in an effort to "devise a paper-and-pencil attitude inventory which could aid in discriminating potential disciplinary offenders as part of Naval recruit screening" (p. 1).

The first form of the test consisted of 474 true-false items selected from the *California Psychological Inventory* and the *Minnesota Multiphasic Personality Inventory*. These items were administered to samples of imprisoned and nonimprisoned naval personnel. By discarding those items that did not discriminate at the .05 level and those items shown to be poor discriminators through item analysis, 119 items remained for the next step in the scale development.

The DPS was administered to approximately 20,000 men, and a three-year follow-up was performed to note the incidence of discipline problems. Those servicemen whose records had shown evidence of disciplinary action (including psychiatric discharges) were compared to a control group of randomly selected individuals whose records showed no disciplinary action. A total of 1,319 offenders or "disciplined" individuals were located and grouped according to seriousness of offense. The groupings included bad conduct discharges ($N = 91$), prison population—confined in brigs or retraining commands ($N = 620$), prison commitments—previously confined to a brig or retraining command ($N = 117$), deserters ($N = 52$), unsuitable discharges for psychiatric or neurological reasons ($N = 307$), unsuitable discharges for other good and sufficient reasons—primarily for ineptitude in training ($N = 116$), undesirable discharges—repeated minor offenses or an offense involving moral turpitude ($N = 129$), medical discharges for psychiatric reasons ($N = 134$), court-martial offenders—courts-martial without confinement or punitive discharge ($N = 56$), minor offenders—disciplinary actions that resulted in nonjudicial punishment ($N = 161$), and absentees—committed an absence offense, but later became successful servicemen with no further record of disciplinary action ($N = 94$).

As part of the DPS development, the first six (most serious) categories were combined to form the "combined offender sample." When the combined offenders were compared to nonoffenders, it was found that the test discriminated moderately well (60% of the combined offenders scored 40 or above compared with 36% of the nonoffenders). When all offenders were compared to the control group, it was found that combined offenders scores were significantly different from the control group and from the group of "minor offenders" (those whose offence fell into the last four categories). Furthermore, minor offenders' scores differed significantly from the control group. An item analysis was performed and a final version of the test resulted in 64 items that were accurate discriminators.

Response Mode

The respondent is given a copy of the 64 statements and is instructed to check the statement (true) if he or she agrees with it and make a cross (false) if he or she disagrees.

TABLE 68. Comparison of Nonoffenders and
Combined Offenders Groups on DPS Scores

	Cumulative percentages	
DPS scores	Nonoffenders	Combined offenders
10 or more	82	95
15 or more	59	83
17 or more	50	78
19 or more	40	68
21 or more	33	60
23 or more	25	51
25 or more	18	42
30 or more	9	23
	$N = 396$	$N = 343$

Scoring

Scoring is accomplished by comparing the response on each item to the "diagnostic answer." These are structured so that agreement between the subject's response and the diagnostic answer indicates one point in favor of delinquency. Therefore, a total of 64 points is the maximum achievable.

Norms

The norms in Table 68 were obtained from a sample of 739 respondents. The scores represent the responses to the 64 items chosen for the final version. The subjects were tested, however, using the 119 item scale.

Reliability

Odd-even and split-half reliabilities indicated a median correlation of .90 for the original 474 item scale. No reliability was reported on either the 119 or the 64 item version, but, based on the Spearman-Brown formula on effects of item number reduction, the extrapolated reliabilities would be .69 and .54 respectively.

Validity

The ability to differentiate between confined and nonconfined naval personnel speaks for the validity of the scale. Also, discriminating between seriousness of offence and control groups is supportive. There is a problem, however, in that these checks were performed during the process of development and revision of the test. Other validation attempts on the final version were not reported.

Comments

Although this scale was constructed for screening with military personnel, it could prove to be useful with civilian populations because the items appear to be applicable to the general population and the method of item selection is appropriate for the general philosophical perspective. The major source of concern with the scale is the lack of cross-validation. A large pool of items would be expected to show several items that discriminated well between many groups. Even the measures of reliability are not directly applicable to the final version of the test.

This scale has shown promise in the earliest stages of development. Its lack of cross-validation and current reliability limits its use in research and rules out its application to selection and decision making.

REFERENCES

Gunderson, E. K., & Ballard, K. B. *Prediction of delinquency in Naval recruits* (Ninth Technical Report, Revised). ONR Contract Nonr 1535 (00)), 1958.

DELINQUENCY POTENTIAL SCALE

Instructions: Read each statement and place a check (✓) beside those statements which are true for you and a cross (x) beside those statements which are false.

Diagnostic Answer	
False	I enjoy social gatherings just to be with people.
True	I often feel that I have made a wrong choice in my occupation.
False	A person who doesn't vote is not a good citizen.
True	I have had very peculiar and strange experiences.
True	Most people would tell a lie if they could gain by it.
True	I never cared much for school.
True	Life usually hands me a pretty raw deal.
True	A person is better off if he doesn't trust anyone.
True	Any job is all right with me, so long as it pays well.

True	My parents never really understood me.
True	I don't blame anyone for trying to get all he can grab in this world.
True	I never worry about my looks.
True	I have the wonderlust and am never happy unless I am roaming or traveling about.
False	I seldom act on the spur of the moment without stopping to think.
True	I always tried to make the best school grades I could.
True	I have had more than my share of things to worry about.
False	In school my marks in deportment (conduct) were quite regularly good.
True	When I am cornered I tell that portion of the truth which is not likely to hurt me.
True	It is all right to get around the law, if you don't actually break it.
True	I must admit I find it hard to work under strict rules and regulations.
True	We ought to let Europe get out of its own mess; it made its bed, let it lie in it.
False	I have never done any heavy drinking.
True	I think most people would lie to get ahead.
True	A person does not need to worry about other people if only he looks out after himself.
False	When I was going to school I practically never played hooky.
True	I often feel as if I had done something wrong or wicked.
True	It's no use worrying my head about public affairs; I can't do anything about them anyhow.
True	I used to steal sometimes when I was a youngster.
False	I really care whether people like or dislike me.
True	We ought to worry about our own country and let the rest of the world take care of itself.
True	My way of doing things is apt to be misunderstood by others.
False	I have lived the right kind of life.
True	At times I have had the strong urge to do something harmful or shocking.
True	I would have been more successful if people had given me a fair chance.
False	I often think about how I look and what impression I am making on others.
True	No one seems to understand me.
True	Sometimes I used to feel that I would like to leave home.
False	As a youngster in school I seldom gave the teachers any trouble.
True	Only a fool would vote to increase his own taxes.
True	It makes me angry when I hear of someone who has been wrongfully prevented from voting.

True	If people had not had it in for me I would have been much more successful.
True	If you are nice to people, they step all over you.
False	National elections have a lot to do with how I get along.
True	There are only two kinds of women — the good and the bad.
False	When people dislike me, I figure it's worthwhile to try to change their opinion.
True	A guy who doesn't look out for himself first is a sucker.
True	The bad effects of marijuana and other drugs have been overemphasized.
False	When I feel blue, drinking won't cheer me up.
True	Women are always trying to get some man to take care of them.
True	"Easy come — easy go" that's my motto.
False	I would just as soon have a lot of friends than be rich.
True	I get angry when a buddy tries to tell me what to do.
True	When someone does me a wrong I feel I should pay him back if I can, just for the principle of the thing.
True	My parents often disapproved of my friends.
True	With things going as they are it's pretty hard to keep up hope of amounting to something.
True	Most laws don't recognize people's needs.
True	Sometimes my conscience makes me do things that get me into trouble.
True	It is hard for me to sit still and relax.
False	Most of the time I feel happy.
True	When a man is with a woman he is usually thinking about things related to her sex.
True	When prices are high you can't blame a person for getting all he can while the getting is good.
True	Sometimes I rather enjoy going against the rules and doing things I'm not supposed to do.
True	I feel that I have been punished without cause.
True	Maybe some minority groups do get rough treatment, but it's no business of mine.

Hostility Scale–Aggression Scale

Development and Characteristics

The *Hostility Scale* (HOS) and the *Aggression Scale* (AS) were designed to measure feelings of anger and to predict the likelihood of aggressive behavior (Blackburn, 1974). They are based upon the assumption that hostility and aggression are meaningful dimensions of individual differences that can be assessed by self-report scales. Items for the HOS and AS were taken from personality scales of the MMPI, the *Buss-Durkee Hostility Inventory,* and the *Psychopathic Delinquency Scale.*

The original item pool was administered to 184 male patients admitted to Broadmoor Hospital in England. This group constituted approximately 75% of a two-year intake for that institution. Individuals were excluded only when they were unable to complete the questionnaire. In addition to this group of respondents, 38 third-year student nurses who were enrolled in a course of general psychology were asked to respond to the items (this was done to insure a wide range of item endorsement). Responses from the sample of 222 individuals were recorded and analyzed. Items that received marginal frequencies of endorsement of less than 10% or more than 90% were dropped. This left a total of 96 items to be factor analyzed. A principle axis analysis followed by a varimax rotation revealed that two components produced the most appropriate definition of the total items. These two factors appeared to be measuring the constructs hostility and aggression. When a criterion loading of .35 or greater was applied to permit inclusion of an item on a scale, 30 items were appropriately assigned to the HOS and 31 were assigned to the AS.

Response Mode

During the development of the HOS and AS, items were in the form of statements and respondents were requested to indicate whether the statement was true or false. Further refinement, however, produced a set of items that took the form of questions. The respondent could then answer yes or no to each question. The developer suggests that this format allows more efficient testing of individuals with restricted verbal ability. Further, he suggests that it also facilitates oral administration of the two scales.

Scoring

All 30 of the HOS items are worded so that a yes answer indicates hostility. Therefore, a yes response is given an item score of 1 and a no response is given an item score of 0. The total HOS score is the sum of the item score. The higher the HOS score, the more hostile an individual is believed to be.

The AS uses the same scoring procedure as the HOS. Items 1, 3, 6, 14, 15, and 23, however, are reversed so that a response of no receives a score of 1 and a response of yes receives a score of 0. A high score on the AS indicates increased likelihood of aggressive feelings.

TABLE 69. Means, Standard Deviations, and F-Ratio Comparisons of Patient and Nonpatient Samples on HOS and AS

Samples	HOS	AS
Broadmoor patients	9.82	10.84
($N = 90$)	(6.71)	(6.40)
Rampton patients	15.03	13.64
($N = 102$)	(6.17)	(5.76)
Student nurses	5.81	13.83
($N = 57$)	(4.24)	(5.50)
F-ratios	45.84[a]	6.78[a]
($df = 2/246$)		

[a] $p < .001$.
Note: Numbers in parentheses are standard deviations.

Norms

Table 69 presents the means and standard deviations for three different groups of respondents. These include (1) 90 patients admitted to Broadmoor Hospital over a one-year period (this is a psychiatric hospital for criminal offenders); (2) 102 patients at Rampton Hospital (this is also a psychiatric hospital for criminal offenders. Inmates of this institution, however, tend to be younger and more "dangerous" than those sent to Broadmoor); and (3) 57 student nurses who were enrolled in an introductory psychology course.

Reliability

The internal consistency of the HOS and AS were calculated from the responses of 86 Broadmoor patients. The Kuder-Richardson formula 20 equation was applied and produced reliability coefficients of .88 for the HOS and .88 for the AS.

Validity

The table presented in the *Norms* section indicates that the HOS and the AS differentiate between the three groups of individuals under study. As might be expected on the HOS, student nurses showed the lowest score, Broadmoor patients the next lowest and the Rampton patients the highest. On the AS, however, the student nurses produced the highest score. Rampton patients were second and Broadmoor patients had the lowest AS scores. Although this would appear to cast doubt on the validity of the AS, the developer suggests that these results may be due to the heterogeneity of the samples. Patients at the hospitals represent individuals who have exhibited many forms of antisocial behavior. This includes people who have been classified as "over controlled" personality. Such diversity within the patient population could tend to cancel the effects of averaged scores.

Blackburn (1974) reports that no significant correlation resulted between age and the HOS and AS or between intelligence, as measured by the *Wechsler Adult Intelligence Scale,* and either the HOS or the AS.

Both the HOS and AS have been compared to personality tests which include theEysenck-Withers *Personality Inventory* (Eysenck, 1967), the *Sixteen PF* Form E (Cattell, 1970), the *Sensation Seeking Scales,* Form IV (Zuckerman, 1972), the *Porteus Maze Test* (Porteus, 1959), the *Gibson Spiral Maze Test* (Gibson, 1965) and other scales, including a life scale, a psychopathic deviance scale, an anxiety scale, an extroversion scale, a shyness scale, a depression scale, an attention scale and an impulsivity scale. In general, the HOS and AS correlate significantly with scales indicating emotional disturbance. The HOS is not significantly related to either of the sensation seeking scales. Neither the HOS nor the AS is significantly related to subscales of the *Porteus Maze Test* and the *Gibson Spiral Maze Test.*

The case notes of 80 Broadmoor patients were read and scored on a five-point scale indicating degree of assaultiveness reported while in the institution. On this scale 0 indicates no injury of assault, 1 equals one episode of assault, 2 equals two episodes of assault, 3 equals three episodes of assault, and 4 indicates more than three episodes of assault reported. When the results of this rating were compared to the HOS and AS, the HOS correlation coefficient was not significant, but the AS correlation coefficient of .374 proved to be statistically significant at the .001 level. Further, when the HOS and AS were compared to nurse ratings of aggressiveness for 42 long-stay abnormal offenders at Rampton Hospital, correlations of .311 and .306 ($p < .05$) were reported for the HOS and AS respectively.

Comments

The HOS and AS are the result of empirical evaluation of established items taken from several scales. High estimates of reliability and significant correlations of the two scales with several personality instruments indicate that the two scales are tapping psychometrically meaningful dimensions of human behavior. There is some question, however, whether the definitions of these two scales are appropriate. For example, is the HOS a measure of hostility or paranoid beliefs and is the AS a measure of aggression or assertiveness? These are empirical questions that can be answered by further research into these promising instruments.

REFERENCES

Blackburn, R. *The development and validation of scales to measure hostility and aggression* (Special Hospital Research Reports). London: Special Hospitals Research Unit, 1974.

Cattell, R. B. *Provisional manual for the 16PF, Form E.* NFER, 1970.

Eysenck, S. B. G. *Manual of the Eysenck-Withers Inventory for subnormal subjects.* London: University of London Press, 1967.

Gibson, H. B. *Manual of the Gibson Spiral Maze.* London: University of London Press, 1965.

Porteus, S. D. *The Maze Test and clinical psychology.* Palo Alto, Calif.: Pacific Books, 1959.

Zuckerman, M. *Manual and research report for the Sensation Seeking Scale.* Department of Psychology: University of Delaware, 1972.

HOSTILITY SCALE

Instructions: For each of the following questions place a check (✓) if it is true for you and a cross (X) if it is false for you.

1. Do you feel that you get a raw deal from life?
2. Would you have been more successful if people had not had it in for you?
3. Do you feel that winning a fight is more fun than anything?
4. Do you think that the police treat people badly?
5. Do you do many things that you later regret?
6. Are the people who run things usually against you?
7. If people could see the way you feel, do you think you'd be thought a hard person to get along with?
8. Do you think if the police don't like you they'll get you for anything?
9. Has anyone got it in for you?
10. Do you ever get the feeling that you are being plotted against?
11. Do you ever get the feeling that you are being followed?
12. Do you often wonder what hidden reason a person may have for doing something nice for you?
13. Do you think that police and magistrates will tell you one thing and then do another?
14. Would you do almost anything for a dare?
15. Do you feel that most brothers and sisters are more trouble than they are worth?

16. Do you feel that someone has been trying to rob you?
17. Are people inclined to misunderstand your way of doing things?
18. Do you think that most people make friends because friends are likely to be useful to them?
19. Do you feel it is safer to trust nobody?
20. Do you feel that most people inwardly dislike going out of their way to help others?
21. Have you enemies who wish to harm you?
22. Have you sometimes stayed away from another person because you feared doing or saying something you might regret afterwards?
23. When you are feeling very happy and active, does someone who is miserable spoil it all?
24. Do people often disappoint you?
25. Have you ever felt badly over being misunderstood, when you were trying to stop someone making a mistake?
26. Have people often misunderstood your intentions when you were trying to put them right and be helpful?
27. Have you often met people who were supposed to be experts who were no better than you?
28. Have you often found people jealous of your good ideas just because they didn't think of them first?
29. Have you frequently worked under people who seem to take all the credit for good work, but pass off mistakes onto those under them?
30. Do you believe that a large number of people are guilty of bad sexual behavior?

AGGRESSION SCALE

Instructions: For each of the following questions place a check (✓) if it is true for you and a cross (X) if it is false for you.

*1. Are you a person who rarely strikes back, even if someone hits you first?
2. Do you sometimes feel like smashing things?
*3. Is it rare for you to quarrel with members of your family?
4. Do you sometimes have a strong urge to do something harmful or shocking?
5. Do people sometimes bother you by just being around?
*6. Do you feel that there's never a good reason for hitting anyone?
7. Do you often find it hard to understand why you've been so bad tempered?
8. Do you sometimes feel like picking a fist fight with someone?

9. When you are angry, do you sometimes sulk?
10. Are you irritated a great deal more than people realize?
11. Do you feel that the only way to settle anything is to beat the other fellow?
12. Do you lose your temper quickly and then get over it soon?
13. If someone hits you first, do you let him have it?
*14. Do you feel that you are always patient with others?
*15. Do you tend to avoid strong language, even when your anger is aroused?
16. Do you easily get impatient with people?
17. When you lose your temper, are you capable of slapping someone?
18. Do you often feel like a powder keg ready to explode?
19. When you get angry do you say nasty things?
20. Are you often said to be hotheaded?
21. Do you get into fights about as often as the next person?
22. Do you sometimes have a chip on your shoulder?
*23. Would you say that you are not easily angered?
24. Have you sometimes felt it necessary to be rough with people who were rude or annoying?
25. Would you resort to violence to defend your rights?
26. Are you inclined to go out of your way to win a point against someone who has opposed you?
27. Have you known people who pushed you so far you came to blows?
28. Do you think it is all right to lie if you are in serious trouble?
29. Do you find yourself being a bit rude to people you dislike?
30. If someone doesn't treat you right, does it annoy you?
31. Do you often find yourself disagreeing with people?

*Scored "NO."

Legal Dangerousness Scale

Development and Characteristics

The *Legal Dangerousness Scale* (LDS) was designed to predict "dangerous behavior" of individuals released from institutions after treatment (Cocozza & Steadman, 1974). The Guttman scalogram technique was used to discover four "scalable" items predictive of dangerousness for a sample of men who were subsequently released from a state mental hospital for convicted criminals. When age was included as a variable, prediction of those individuals who would not be dangerous was increased. Therefore, the four Guttman-type items (juvenile record, prior incarceration, violent crime convictions, and current offense) are used in conjunction with the age variable.

Response Mode

No response is required of the client. All information for the LDS comes from an individual's official record.

Scoring

Each item is dichotomous and is weighted according to importance in the prediction of dangerousness. A "nondangerous" response to item one receives a 0 and a dangerous response is scored 8. The remaining items, 2, 3, and 4 receive scores of 0 or 4, 0 or 2, and 0 or 1, respectively. A total score is obtained by summing item scores. This can range from 0–15 with a high score representing dangerousness and a low score a low likelihood of dangerous behavior.

Norms

The developer established dual points. A score of 5 or higher on the LDS and an age less than 50 was found to be predictive of dangerous behavior in 98 Baxstrom patients released to the community.

Reliability

Steadman and Cocozza (1974) report a coefficient of reproducibility of .906 for a sample of inmates who had received treatment at an institution for the criminally insane.

Validity

Cocozza and Steadman (1974) scored the LDS for 98 civilly committed individuals who had been released from a state mental hospital. They found that using the cut-off points given in the *Norms* section, they were able to predict all except 3 of the 20 patients who were subsequently arrested. Many of the offenses for which these men were arrested, however, were not violent. Further, some of the subjects under study participated in dangerous acts, but were returned to the hospital instead of being arrested. Since the rearrest indicator of "dangerous" seemed inappropriate, the data were reanalyzed using "only behavior involving violence against persons." Fourteen releasees met this criterion. Eleven of these were predicted by the LDS and age.

In an attempt to cross-validate the LDS, Koppin (1977) applied the items to 119 criminally insane patients released between July 1, 1972 and June 30, 1974. She reported a "correct" decision to release occurred 70% of the time. The number of false positive judgments was unknown because these subjects were still incarcerated.

Comments

The developers suggest that caution should be exercised in the use of this instrument. One reason is the high number of false positive predictions based on the LDS. There are approximately 35 (of the 98) cases who were predicted to be dangerous, while only 11 were actually harmful.

Some attention should be given to potential problems with the LDS itself. The coefficient of reproducibility is barely acceptable. This is important because of the small number of items that constitute the scale and thereby, directly influence the results. Despite these problems, the LDS is a carefully developed, promising instrument that appears to have some predictive value.

REFERENCES

Cocozza, J. J., & Steadman, H. J. Some refinements in the measurement and prediction of dangerous behavior. *American Journal of Psychiatry,* 1974, *131,* 1012–1014.

Koppin, M. K. *A validation of the Legal Dangerousness Scale with released criminally insane offenders.* Paper presented at American Psychology-Law Society Third National Conference, Snowmass, Colorado, June 1977.

Steadman, H. J., & Cocozza, J. J. The criminally insane patient: Who gets out? *Social Psychiatry,* 1973, *8,* 230–238.

LEGAL DANGEROUSNESS SCALE

Scoring

Variable		Score
Juvenile Record:	Yes	+8
	No	0
Number of Previous Incarcerations:	2 or more	+4
	0 or 1	0

Violent Crime
    Convictions: Any   + 2
                            None   0

Current Offense
    (charge or conviction): 1 thru 6 on attached code   + 1
                            7, 8, 9 on attached code   0

                  Legal Dangerousness Scale Score = TOTAL

Current Offense (Offense to which Baxstrom decision applies)

1. Offenses against the person involving injury, restraint, and intimidation (assault, homicide, robbery, extortion, menacing, kidnapping, coercion, murder, manslaughter, reckless endangerment, promoting a suicide attempt, criminally negligent homicide, arson 1st degree).

2. Offenses potentially against the persons (burglary 1st and 2nd degree).

3. Offenses involving sexual conduct (rape, sodomy, sexual abuse, sexual misconduct, carnal abuse).

4. Offenses involving damage to and intrusion upon property (burglary 3rd degree, criminal trespass, unlawful entry, criminal mischief, arson 2nd and 3rd degree).

5. Offenses involving theft (larceny, criminal possession of stolen property, jostling, fortune telling, unlawful use of a motor vehicle).

6. Offenses involving fraud (forgery, false written statements, unlawfully using slugs, issuing a bad check, criminal usury, criminal impersonation).

7. Offenses against public health and morals (dangerous drug offenses, i.e. possession of and/or selling dangerous drugs, gambling, prostitution, obscenity, impairing the morals of a minor).

8. Offenses against marriage, the family, and the welfare of children and incompetents (incest, bigamy, adultery).

9. Other (loitering, intoxication, noncriminal trespass, disorderly conduct, vagrancy, tramp, offensive exhibition, public lewdness, harassment, exposure of or promoting the exposure of a female, indecent exposure, truancy, violation of immigration laws, weapons possession, possession of burglary tools).

CRIME AND CRIMINALITY DESCRIPTION: REVIEWS

Ethics Inventory

Development and Characteristics

The *Ethics Inventory* (EI) was developed to measure the "self-represented ethical, antisocial, and aversive value systems in process and reactive schizophrenics, penitentiary inmates, and normals" (Watson, 1972, p. 479). Watson's working assumption was that pathological behavior in schizophrenics might be an attempt to manipulate the staff. He set out to discover the degree to which patients' behaviors were governed by ethical considerations by presenting a set of descriptions of hypothetical situations that required moral decisions. The alternatives consisted of three types of behaviors: (1) those considered *moral;* (2) those with an *antisocial* tone; and (3) those which reflect an *aversive* outlook.

Since several authors have found that schizophrenics respond differently to stress than normals, 10 descriptions were written to correspond to nonstressful situations and 10 were written to parallel these, except that stress was a factor. From these 20 situations (10 pairs of parallel content high-stress and low-stress items) the author derived nine scores: moral-stress, moral-nonstress, moral-total, antisocial-stress, antisocial-nonstress, antisocial-total, aversive-stress, aversive-nonstress, and aversive-total.

Although the inventory was constructed to test the degrees of ethical concern in schizophrenics, the EI may be useful in the study of ethical concerns and criminal justice.

Response Mode

The subject is presented with a typed copy of the test booklet and instructions. This booklet contains 20 descriptions, each of which are followed by three specific responses. The respondent is required to place a check mark beside the alternative that indicates how he/she would proably act.

Scoring

Scoring consists of counting the number of responses that are moral, antisocial, and aversive, a straightforward procedure taking about 10 minutes per completed inventory. The author further uses the nine categories mentioned earlier, but the EI allows variations on the scores used. For example, one may use only moral, antisocial, and aversive totals or the totals of each of these under stress and nonstress situations.

Norms

The norms in Table 70 represent "99 randomly chosen diagnosed schizophrenics under 60 at the St. Cloud (Minnesota) Veterans Hospital who volunteered to participate in the project, 44 inmates of the Stillwater (Minnesota) State Prison, and 55 normals (volunteering employees of the Veterans Administration Hospital)" (Watson, 1972, p. 480).

Table 70 indicates that prisoners score significantly less moral, more anti-

TABLE 70. EI Normative Means and F Tests for Differences between EI Means

Scale	Group				F's for all four groups (df = 3,171)
	Normals (N = 44)	Process schizophrenics (N = 55)	Reactive schizophrenics (N = 44)	Prisoners (N = 32)	
Moral-stress	6.45	6.65	6.86	3.62	12.12[a]
Moral-nonstress	6.82	7.80	7.57	4.69	13.80[a]
Moral-total	13.27	14.45	14.43	8.31	14.82[a]
Antisocial-stress	1.64	1.05	1.39	3.31	16.49[a]
Antisocial-nonstress	1.34	.53	1.14	2.69	19.35[a]
Antisocial-total	2.98	1.58	2.52	6.00	21.22[a]
Aversive-stress	1.86	2.29	1.75	3.03	3.50[b]
Aversive-nonstress	1.75	1.64	1.36	2.47	2.93[b]
Aversive-total	3.61	3.93	3.11	5.47	4.01[c]

[a] Significant at .001.
[b] Significant at .05.
[c] Significant at .01.

social, and more aversive than normals and schizophrenics under stress and nonstress conditions. Interestingly, the schizophrenics differed significantly from normals only on the nonstress antisocial and total antisocial scores.

Reliability

Test–retest correlations over a period of one week were calculated on 25 normals, 30 prisoners, 24 process, and 27 reactive schizophrenics and are represented in Table 71.

The prisoners' responses were most reliable with most of the coefficients at or above .90. The reliability coefficients for normals were quite acceptable. The schizophrenics showed least reliability for this scale, particularly process schizophrenics.

Validity

The situations presented in the scale offer a variety of ethical encounters and appear to tap basic values. As a test of the validity on the subscales, a clinical

TABLE 71. EI Test–Retest Correlations

Scale	Group			
	Normals ($N = 25$)	Process schizophrenics ($N = 24$)	Reactive schizophrenics ($N = 27$)	Prisoners ($N = 30$)
Moral-stress	.64	.53	.50	.92
Moral-nonstress	.81	.29	.81	.96
Moral-total	.77	.45	.73	.96
Antisocial-stress	.62	.22	.66	.91
Antisocial-nonstress	.72	.00	.51	.96
Antisocial-total	.77	.06	.70	.96
Aversive-stress	.77	.57	.17	.84
Aversive-nonstress	.83	.60	.78	.84
Aversive-total	.84	.67	.57	.90

psychologist was asked to judge whether each of the responses to each item was moral, antisocial, or aversive. In each case, his response agreed with the designation of the test developer.

Another indication of validity is the ability of the scale to discriminate between normals and prisoners. On all scales the comparisons of means yielded results in the predicted direction.

Comments

Although this scale does not discriminate well between schizophrenics and normals, it does differentiate well between prisoners and normals. It is difficult to determine whether the differences occurred before incarceration or as a result of such an environment. Nevertheless, this scale may accurately reflect basic ethical values of prisoners. It could, possibly, be used as an indication of points in time when the socialization process failed or rewarded unethical behaviors. It could even be used clinically as a therapeutic aid. There is potential for a strong social desirability set. The EI seems to work well for groups, and more research may show it to be an indicator of law-abidingness.

REFERENCES

Watson, C. G. A comparison of the ethical self-presentations of schizophrenics, prisoners and normals. *Journal of Clinical Psychology,* 1972, *28,* 479–483.

ETHICS INVENTORY

How far did you go in school? _____ Age:_____

We are interested in learning how people tend to react in various types of difficult situations. Please read each question and put a check in front of the answer that tells what you would probably have done if caught in the situation described.

This is not a test, and there are no "right" or "wrong" answers. Actually, an answer is only "right" if it tells how you really feel you would probably act.

Do NOT put your name on this form. YOUR ANSWERS ARE TO BE KEPT SECRET. PLEASE BE SURE YOU ANSWER EACH ITEM HONESTLY. Since your identify is being kept secret, your future will not be affected in any way by your answers.

Be sure to answer each question and record your age and education at the top of the page.

Your filling out this form will be very helpful to us in our study. Our thanks in advance for your cooperation.

1. You go to your car one morning to find that one of your hubcaps is missing. Because they were expensive hubcaps and because you know you don't have the money to buy a replacement, you are very, very disappointed. However, you know where you could steal a hubcap to replace the lost one. You would:

    _____ a. Not steal it, since it would be the wrong thing to do.
    _____ b. Steal it. After all the loss would probably be covered by the owner's liability insurance and someone else has already stolen yours.
    _____ c. Not steal it because you might be caught.

2. You are a college student in danger of failing a mathematics course. It is now the night before the exam and you realize that you cannot possibly learn enough before the test to pass the couse. You would:

    _____ a. Study all night and take the test even though it is already clear that you will fail.
    _____ b. Take advantage of the fact that your roommate has stolen a copy of the examination and has the answers. You should cheat just enough to pass the course and save having to sadden your parents with the news of your failure.
    _____ c. Drop the course to avoid getting a bad grade.

3. You are pulling into a parking space when you inadvertently scrape the side of the car next to yours with your bumper. The damage is very, very slight. You will:

    _____ a. Find the owner and tell him what has happened.
    _____ b. Drive to another parking space before the owner comes back, so you won't be caught.
    _____ c. Leave the car where it is and try very hard to forget about the whole thing.

4. You have a bad fight with your wife. It is mainly her fault and you know it. You will:

    _____ a. Apologize for your part in the fight.
    _____ b. Go downtown for a few beers so you can forget about it.
    _____ c. Continue the fight and tell her off.

5. You are a little boy and accidently break a vase. You will:

    _____ a. Blame it on your younger brother.
    _____ b. Clean it up and hope she won't notice that it's gone.
    _____ c. Tell your mother and take your punishment.

6. You are in a terrific hurry and are driving 60 miles an hour in a 50-mile-an-hour zone when you see a police car driving two blocks behind you. You will:

    _____ a. Speed up so as to get far ahead of the police car.
    _____ b. Slow down because you should not be driving over the legal speed limit anyway.
    _____ c. Slow down since it would be bad to be caught going too fast.

7. You are a teenager and spot a new car on a deserted street at night with the keys in the ignition. You would like nothing better than to get a chance to drive the car. You will:

    _____ a. Take the car but return it in a few minutes.
    _____ b. Not take the car because it is not the right thing to do.
    _____ c. Not take the car because it would be dangerous.

8. You are a football player and have been getting elbowed illegally by one of your opponents throughout the game. Late in the fourth quarter you have a chance to knock your opponent down illegally without being seen by the referee. You will:

    _____ a. Avoid knocking over the other player because it would be bad sportsmanship.
    _____ b. Avoid hitting your opponent since it is possible that the referee might turn around and see you.
    _____ c. Get even with your opponent by knocking him over hard.

9. You would like to buy your mother a new purse for Christmas, but you do not have the money. You will:

    _____ a. Shoplift the purse from a large department store where the loss would probably not be noticed by the store's owner.
    _____ b. Buy something cheaper because you might get caught if you tried to steal something.
    _____ c. Buy something cheaper because it would be wrong to steal.

10. You have been loaned your boss's Cadillac and come out to the car after work to find one of the hubcaps has been stolen. Because it was expensive and because you know you don't have the money to replace it you are very upset, because the boss might fire you. However, you know where you could steal a hubcap to replace the one stolen from the boss's car. You will:

___ a. Not steal it, since it would be the wrong thing to do, and "face the music" when you return the car to your boss.
___ b. Not steal it because you might be caught.
___ c. Steal it. After all the loss would probably be covered by the owner's liability insurance.

11. You are driving on a residential street when you glance at the speedometer and are surprised to find that you are going ten miles over the speed limit. There are no other cars around. You will probably:

___ a. Continue at the same rate of speed.
___ b. Slow down so as to stop breaking the law.
___ c. Slow down because of the possibility you might be seen going too fast.

12. You are a college student and have a term paper due tomorrow. You can work on the paper tonight and get it finished in time, but you would rather go see a special movie downtown. A friend of yours offers to write the paper for you. You will:

___ a. Stay home and write the paper yourself, since you will probably learn something from the experience.
___ b. Stay home and write the paper yourself, because if you let your friend do it, it is always possible that he might tell someone you are a cheater.
___ c. Let him write the paper since you would like to see the movie and he enjoys writing anyway.

13. While you were backing into a parking space you accidentally nicked the car next to you. Your father, who is a very conscientious dictatorial man, is with you and notices you have hit the other car. You will:

___ a. Try to find the driver of the other car, since your father will give you a lot of trouble if you don't.
___ b. Try to find the driver of the other car and tell him what has happened because that would be the "good" thing to do.
___ c. Drive to another parking space so that the driver of the car will not know who put the dent in his automobile.

14. One night you get into a high-stakes poker game with some real card sharks. You find yourself dealing in a hand where the **pot has reached several thousand** dollars, including several hundred dollars of your own. You realize that your cards are not good enough to win but that if you would deal yourself the bottom card on the deck, you would complete a royal flush and avoid losing your money. You would probably:

___ a. Not deal yourself the card for fear of getting caught.
___ b. Deal yourself the card, although only to avoid losing a great deal of money.
___ c. Not deal yourself the card because it wouldn't be fair.

15. As you are waiting in line at a drugstore, the man ahead of you accidentally drops a 20-dollar bill on the floor. Suppose that you have great financial need — that your car payment just came due, you have no savings, and you have just lost your job. You would probably:

___ a. Pick it up and keep it to relieve some of the financial pressures on you.
___ b. Pick it up and return it in order to be honest.
___ c. Pick it up and return it because you might get caught if you try to keep it.

16. As you are going into a crowded movie theater with a friend, the ticket taker doesn't notice you and fails to take your tickets. It occurs to you that, if he wouldn't take

them, you might be able to go to next week's movie on the tickets you bought for tonight's movie. You will probably:

    ____ a. Throw away the tickets because if you try to get in on it next week the management might notice that it is the ticket for the wrong show and catch you.
    ____ b. Keep the tickets and use them next week.
    ____ c. Throw away the tickets because you don't want to cheat the theater.

17. Suppose you had kept the tickets referred to in item 16 in your pocket but hadn't decided whether to use them or not. A week later you return to the same theater with a very wealthy girl who has just been elected homecoming queen at your school. You are very nervous because you are naturally shy and she is acting as if she wishes she hadn't gone out with you. Suddenly you realize that you forgot your wallet at home, though you could probably get in to see the movie on last week's tickets. You would:

    ____ a. Tell the girl you've decided not to take her to the movie and that you are going to take her somewhere else instead.
    ____ b. Use last week's tickets to avoid being badly embarrassed.
    ____ c. Tell the girl what has happened and not go to the movie because you are too honest to cheat the theater.

18. Suppose you are a 4-year-old child and you accidentally broke a cheap toy belonging to your younger brother. You would probably:

    ____ a. Blame it on your brother.
    ____ b. Tell your mother, who probably won't care to much, since it wasn't expensive.
    ____ c. Throw away the pieces so no one will notice.

19. You and the salesgirl at the dime store have a disagreement which is largely your fault. You will probably:

    ____ a. Apologize for the disagreement.
    ____ b. Leave the store to avoid getting into a big argument.
    ____ c. Tell her off.

20. Suppose you were a hold-up man. Pretend you are coming out of a grocery store after having stuck it up. You look down the street and see two policemen running toward you a block or two away. At the same time you spot an empty car with the motor running next to you. You would probably:

    ____ a. Not take the car, because it is the wrong thing to do.
    ____ b. Not take the car because if you get caught the resulting penalty will be worse.
    ____ c. Take the car to get away.

PLEASE CHECK TO SEE THAT YOU HAVE ANSWERED ALL THE QUESTIONS. THANK YOU.

Parental Punitiveness Scale

Development and Characteristics

The *Parental Punitiveness Scale* (PPS) was designed to "reliably measure children's perceptions of parental punitiveness toward aggression," (Epstein & Komorita, 1965, p. 130). As a first step in development, 85 elementary school children between the ages of 7 and 15 were asked to complete 12 semiprojective stories. In each story, a fictitious child displayed some form of aggression that elicited a parental response. The children being tested were then asked to describe how the parents in the story might respond to the child's aggression. The content of the responses was analyzed and yielded 31 frequently described discipline techniques.

Next, a group of 70 children of various socioeconomic levels was asked to rate the relative severity of these 31 discipline techniques by using three five-point semantic differential adjective pairs. Each technique was rated on the following three five-point continua,—fair-unfair, right-wrong, and good-bad. A single score and a mean for each discipline technique were obtained by weighing the three scales as described by Osgood, Suci, and Tannebaum and the 31 techniques were ranked from least to most severe.

Based on this information, four discipline techniques were selected to serve as response alternatives for each item in the scale. These four alternatives had been chosen because they represent the range of severity rating, they have the smallest variability (this minimizes disagreement among children regarding severity ratings), and the alternatives do not differ significantly in severity ratings across social class groups (this enables generalization of the scale across social class groups). For purposes of scoring, each of the alternatives was arbitrarily assigned an interval weight, ranging from 1, least severe, to 4, most severe. The alternatives are: (1) Have a long talk with me; (2) take away my television; (3) send me to bed without supper; and (4) whip me. A total of 45 items serve as descriptions of situations in which a child acts aggressively. These descriptions include a wide range of circumstances in which the child displays verbal, physical, or indirect aggression.

Response Mode

The respondent is asked to read each item, then note by making a check mark which of the four alternatives most closely matches what his/her father would do under the circumstances. Next, he/she checks the alternative which he/she feels best represents what his/her mother would do under similar circumstances. This procedure is followed for the entire 45 item test.

Scoring

The alternatives for each item are randomized to prevent bias. However, each of the four alternatives is scored so that a choice of "have a long talk with me" is rated 1, or least severe; "take away my television" is rated 2, or the second least severe; "send me to bed without supper" is rated 3, or next to the most severe; and "whip me" is rated 4, or the most severe. Using these weights, total severity scores for the mother and for the father are calculated. The higher the value of the score, the more severe the parent is believed to be in the punishment of aggression.

Norms

No norms were reported.

Reliability

Epstein and Komorita (1965) report split-half reliability coefficients of .93 and .92 for father and mother respectively (when calculated by the Kuder-Richardson formula 20). These results were obtained from a sample of 120 children between the ages of 7 and 13 years who were attending a private school in a suburb of Detroit. They were of above average intelligence and came from middle- to upper-class families.

Validity

The method of scale construction and a systematic review of the items are supportive of content validity for the scale. The items offer a wide range of aggressive acts for which the child might be punished. There is some question, however, as to whether lying to someone (Items 3, 6, and 20) or talking back to a sibling (Item 12) is an act of aggression.

The developers suggested that the more punishment the child perceived his or her parents gave for aggressive behavior, the more likely he/she was to "scapegoat" and direct his/her own aggression away from parents or in-group members onto what might be labeled as out-group members. This was tested by comparing the results of the PPS with the results of the *Bogardus Social Distance Scales*, for 120 children in a suburb of Detroit. It was believed that expressed social distance from a number of ethnic, religious, or minority groups would be indicative of ethnocentrism or a direction of aggressive feelings toward "out-groups." The results indicated that rather than a linear relationship between these two variables as predicted, a curvilinear relationship existed in which both high and low parental punitiveness was associated with low ethnocentrism, while moderate parental punitiveness was associated with high ethnocentrism. The developers suggest that this contradiction of their original hypothesis is explained by the power theory of identification. "According to this theory, children are least likely to identify with either highly permissive or highly punitive parents" (Epstein & Komorita, 1965, p. 135). Therefore, if there is little identification with the parents, there would be no direction of hostility toward out-group members, but rather to the parents themselves. Only the case of moderate discipline, which combines elements of reward and punishment, would be conducive to identification and ethnocentrism.

Another attempt to support the validity of the PPS compared the children's averaged scores to scores that were obtained by parents on a modified form of the PPS. A correlation coefficient of .26 ($p < .05$) indicated a statistically significant but weak relationship. When the responses were further analyzed by comparing the mothers' reports of their discipline to children's perceptions of the mothers' discipline, a correlation coefficient of .12 ($p > .05$) was found. However, when fathers' reports of their own discipline and children's perception of the fathers' discipline were compared, a correlation coefficient of .36 ($p < .05$) was obtained.

Comments

The reliability of the PPS is good and indicates interdimensionality. Also, content validity through careful development procedures and item selection is good. Other efforts to validate the scale, however, have been only partially successful, even though these discrepancies can be explained by the use of other theoretical positions.

REFERENCES

Epstein, R., & Komorita, S. S. The development of a scale of parental punitiveness toward aggression. *Child Development*, 1965, *36*, 129–142.

PARENTAL PUNITIVENESS SCALE

Instructions: When children do something wrong, their parents may react in different ways. We would like to know what you think would happen if you did something wrong.

Look at the following example:

CRIME AND CRIMINALITY

	If I hit another child,	
MY	a. whip me .... a.	MY
FATHER	b. send me to bed without supper .... b.	MOTHER
WOULD	c. have a long talk with me .... c.	WOULD
	d. take away my television .... d.	

Make believe that you hit another child. Your parents might react in different ways. Your father might react by: whipping you, sending you to bed without supper, having a long talk with you, or taking away television.

Show what you think your father would do by putting a <u>circle</u> around the letter a or b or c or d. Then, show what your mother might do by putting a <u>circle</u> around one of the letters on the other side. Circle one letter on the "Father" side and one letter on the "Mother" side.

Any questions?

1. If I put paint on someone's house,
MY	a. take away my television .... a.	MY
FATHER	b. have a long talk with me .... b.	MOTHER
WOULD	c. whip me .... c.	WOULD
	d. send me to bed without supper .... d.	

2. If I throw a rock at someone's car,
MY	a. send me to bed without supper .... a.	MY
FATHER	b. take away my television .... b.	MOTHER
WOULD	c. whip me .... c.	WOULD
	d. have a long talk with me .... d.	

3. If I lie to my brother (or sister),
MY	a. whip me .... a.	MY
FATHER	b. have a long talk with me .... b.	MOTHER
WOULD	c. take away my television .... c.	WOULD
	d. send me to bed without supper .... d.	

4. If I throw something at my brother (or sister),
MY	a. take away my television .... a.	MY
FATHER	b. send me to bed without supper .... b.	MOTHER
WOULD	c. whip me .... c.	WOULD
	d. have a long talk with me .... d.	

5. If I steal something that belongs to a teacher,
MY	a. send me to bed without supper .... a.	MY
FATHER	b. take away my television .... b.	MOTHER
WOULD	c. whip me .... c.	WOULD
	d. have a long talk with me .... d.	

6. If I lie to another child,
MY	a. take away my television .... a.	MY
FATHER	b. whip me .... b.	MOTHER
WOULD	c. have a long talk with me .... c.	WOULD
	d. send me to bed without supper .... d.	

7. If I scream at another child,
   MY FATHER WOULD
   a. send me to bed without supper....... a.
   b. take away my television............. b.
   c. have a long talk with me............ c.
   d. whip me........................... d.
   MY MOTHER WOULD

8. If I break something that belongs to another child,
   MY FATHER WOULD
   a. whip me........................... a.
   b. send me to bed without supper....... b.
   c. take away my television............. c.
   d. have a long talk with me............ d.
   MY MOTHER WOULD

9. If I talk back to another child,
   MY FATHER WOULD
   a. have a long talk with me............ a.
   b. whip me........................... b.
   c. take away my television............. c.
   d. send me to bed without supper....... d.
   MY MOTHER WOULD

10. If I start a fire on someone's lawn,
    MY FATHER WOULD
    a. send me to bed without supper....... a.
    b. take away my television............. b.
    c. whip me........................... c.
    d. have a long talk with me............ d.
    MY MOTHER WOULD

11. If I kick another child,
    MY FATHER WOULD
    a. have a long talk with me............ a.
    b. take away my television............. b.
    c. whip me........................... c.
    d. send me to bed without supper....... d.
    MY MOTHER WOULD

12. If I talk back to my brother (or sister),
    MY FATHER WOULD
    a. send me to bed without supper....... a.
    b. whip me........................... b.
    c. have a long talk with me............ c.
    d. take away my television............. d.
    MY MOTHER WOULD

13. If I hit my brother (or sister),
    MY FATHER WOULD
    a. take away my television............. a.
    b. send me to bed without supper....... b.
    c. have a long talk with me............ c.
    d. whip me........................... d.
    MY MOTHER WOULD

14. If I break a window,
    MY FATHER WOULD
    a. have a long talk with me............ a.
    b. send me to bed without supper....... b.
    c. whip me........................... c.
    d. take away my television............. d.
    MY MOTHER WOULD

15. If I scream at a teacher,
    MY FATHER WOULD
    a. take away my television............. a.
    b. send me to bed without supper....... d.
    c. whip me........................... c.
    d. have a long talk with me............ d.
    MY MOTHER WOULD

CRIME AND CRIMINALITY

16. If I put ink on someone's clothing,
    MY   a. have a long talk with me.............a.   MY
    FATHER   b. send me to bed without supper.......b.   MOTHER
    WOULD   c. whip me...........................c.   WOULD
                 d. take away my television............d.

17. If I hit a teacher,
    MY   a. whip me...........................a.   MY
    FATHER   b. take away my television............b.   MOTHER
    WOULD   c. send me to bed without supper.......c.   WOULD
                 d. have a long talk with me.............d.

18. If I steal something that belongs to my brother (or sister),
    MY   a. send me to bed without supper.......a.   MY
    FATHER   b. whip me...........................b.   MOTHER
    WOULD   c. have a long talk with me.............c.   WOULD
                 d. take away my television............d.

19. If I scream at my brother (or sister),
    MY   a. whip me...........................a.   MY
    FATHER   b. have a long talk with me.............b.   MOTHER
    WOULD   c. take away my television............c.   WOULD
                 d. send me to bed without supper.......d.

20. If I lie to a teacher,
    MY   a. take away my television.............a.   MY
    FATHER   b. whip me...........................b.   MOTHER
    WOULD   c. have a long talk with me.............c.   WOULD
                 d. send me to bed without supper.......d.

21. If I break something that belongs to my brother (or sister),
    MY   a. whip me...........................a.   MY
    FATHER   b. take away my television............b.   MOTHER
    WOULD   c. send me to bed without supper.......c.   WOULD
                 d. have a long talk with me.............d.

22. If I swear at my brother (or sister),
    MY   a. have a long talk with me.............a.   MY
    FATHER   b. send me to bed without supper.......b.   MOTHER
    WOULD   c. take away my television............c.   WOULD
                 d. whip me...........................d.

23. If I kick my brother (or sister),
    MY   a. send me to bed without supper.......a.   MY
    FATHER   b. have a long talk with me.............b.   MOTHER
    WOULD   c. whip me...........................c.   WOULD
                 d. take away my television............d.

24. If I put sand in someone's car,
    MY   a. have a long talk with me.............a.   MY
    FATHER   b. send me to bed without supper.......b.   MOTHER
    WOULD   c. take away my television............c.   WOULD
                 d. whip me...........................d.

25. If I swear at another child,
    MY   a. have a long talk with me .... a.   MY
    FATHER   b. whip me .... b.   MOTHER
    WOULD   c. send me to bed without supper .... c.   WOULD
                d. take away my television .... d.

26. If I pull up the flowers in someone's garden,
    MY   a. take away my television .... a.   MY
    FATHER   b. whip me .... b.   MOTHER
    WOULD   c. have a long talk with me .... c.   WOULD
                d. send me to bed without supper .... d.

27. If I swear at my parents,
    MY   a. have a long talk with me .... a.   MY
    FATHER   b. whip me .... b.   MOTHER
    WOULD   c. take away my television .... c.   WOULD
                d. send me to bed without supper .... d.

28. If I mess up someone's lawn,
    MY   a. whip me .... a.   MY
    FATHER   b. send me to bed without supper .... b.   MOTHER
    WOULD   c. have a long talk with me .... c.   WOULD
                d. take away my television .... d.

29. If I steal something that belongs to another child,
    MY   a. send me to bed without supper .... a.   MY
    FATHER   b. have a long talk with me .... b.   MOTHER
    WOULD   c. take away my television .... c.   WOULD
                d. whip me .... d.

30. If I throw something at my parents,
    MY   a. have a long talk with me .... a.   MY
    FATHER   b. send me to bed without supper .... b.   MOTHER
    WOULD   c. take away my television .... c.   WOULD
                d. whip me .... d.

31. If I hit another child,
    MY   a. whip me .... a.   MY
    FATHER   b. send me to bed without supper .... b.   MOTHER
    WOULD   c. take away my television .... c.   WOULD
                d. have a long talk with me .... d.

32. If I swear at a teacher,
    MY   a. whip me .... a.   MY
    FATHER   b. send me to bed without supper .... b.   MOTHER
    WOULD   c. take away my television .... c.   WOULD
                d. have a long talk with me .... d.

33. If I steal something that belongs to my parents,
    MY   a. take away my television .... a.   MY
    FATHER   b. send me to bed without supper .... b.   MOTHER
    WOULD   c. have a long talk with me .... c.   WOULD
                d. whip me .... d.

34. If I tear someone's book on purpose,
    MY   a. whip me .... a.   MY
    FATHER   b. have a long talk with me .... b.   MOTHER
    WOULD   c. take away my television .... c.   WOULD
                d. send me to bed without supper .... d.

CRIME AND CRIMINALITY

35. If I kick my parents,
    MY   a. send me to bed without supper.......a.   MY
    FATHER   b. whip me.........................b.   MOTHER
    WOULD   c. take away my television............c.   WOULD
                d. have a long talk with me............d.

36. If I throw something at a teacher,
    MY   a. take away my television............a.   MY
    FATHER   b. send me to bed without supper.......b.   MOTHER
    WOULD   c. have a long talk with me............c.   WOULD
                d. whip me.........................d.

37. If I break something that belongs to a teacher,
    MY   a. have a long talk with me............a.   MY
    FATHER   b. whip me.........................b.   MOTHER
    WOULD   c. send me to bed without supper.......c.   WOULD
                d. take away my television............d.

38. If I throw something at another child,
    MY   a. send me to bed without supper.......a.   MY
    FATHER   b. have a long talk with me............b.   MOTHER
    WOULD   c. take away my television............c.   WOULD
                d. whip me.........................d.

39. If I kick a teacher,
    MY   a. whip me.........................a.   MY
    FATHER   b. send me to bed without supper.......b.   MOTHER
    WOULD   c. have a long talk with me............c.   WOULD
                d. take away my television............d.

40. If I lie to my parents,
    MY   a. take away my television............a.   MY
    FATHER   b. send me to bed without supper.......b.   MOTHER
    WOULD   c. have a long talk with me............c.   WOULD
                d. whip me.........................d.

41. If I talk back to a teacher,
    MY   a. send me to bed without supper.......a.   MY
    FATHER   b. take away my television............b.   MOTHER
    WOULD   c. have a long talk with me............c.   WOULD
                d. whip me.........................d.

42. If I hit my parents,
    MY   a. whip me.........................a.   MY
    FATHER   b. send me to bed without supper.......b.   MOTHER
    WOULD   c. take away my television............c.   WOULD
                d. have a long talk with me............d.

43. If I scream at my parents,
    MY   a. send me to bed without supper.......a.   MY
    FATHER   b. whip me.........................b.   MOTHER
    WOULD   c. have a long talk with me............c.   WOULD
                d. take away my television............d.

44. If I talk back to my parents,
    MY   a. take away my television............a.   MY
    FATHER   b. whip me.........................b.   MOTHER
    WOULD   c. have a long talk with me............c.   WOULD
                d. send me to bed without supper.......d.

45. If I break something on purpose that belonged to my parents,
    MY   a. send me to bed without supper .... a.   MY
    FATHER   b. whip me .... b.   MOTHER
    WOULD   c. take away my television .... c.   WOULD
               d. have a long talk with me .... d.

Risk Perception Questionnaire

Development and Characteristics

The *Risk Perception Questionnaire* (RPQ) was designed to measure the degree of perceived risk (of being caught) involved in the commission of crimes (Claster, 1967). The questionnaire is divided into three parts. The first asks that the respondent make judgments as to the percentage of individuals who commit specific acts and are arrested. The second section asks that the respondent estimate relative frequencies of conviction for the crimes noted in section one.

The third part of the RPQ consists of questions that: (1) ask whether the respondent can conceive of himself or herself in the commission of a specific type of crime; (2) ask him or her what his or her chances are of avoiding arrest for that crime; and (3) ask what he or she believes are his or her chances of being found "not guilty" if caught and brought to trial. No response was expected for (2) if the respondent stated, in (1) that he or she could not commit the crime. Neither was a judgment requested for (3) if he or she did not believe he or she would be arrested.

The items and the form of the questionnaire were intuitively based on the author's experience in the area.

Response Mode

The respondent is asked to read each item and choose the alternative that is appropriate for him or her. This takes the form of making estimates of the perceived likelihood of a number of events.

Scoring

Sections 1 and 2 are scored by noting whether the response is consistent with present statistics for each crime. If the respondent makes a correct judgment, the item is scored 0. If he or she misses by 10 percentage points, the respondent receives a $+1$ for an overestimation and a -1 for an underestimation. A 20% error would receive a $+2$ (overestimation) or a -2 (underestimation), and so on. These scores are then added to represent a net over or underestimation.

Items for (1) of the third section are scored 3 for a response of "definitely could," 2 for "probably could," 1 for "probably could not," and 0 for "definitely could not." The sum of item scores then represents self-perceived absence of control.

Parts (2) and (3) of Section 3 are scored the same as (1) except the total scores for these are averaged rather than summed. This controls the effect of subjects who did not respond to all questions in these sections. These averages indicate the degree to which the respondent believes he or she is likely to be arrested and punished for crimes.

Norms

No norms are available.

Reliability

No reliability estimates are available.

Validity

The developer hypothesized that delinquents would underestimate the frequency of arrests and convictions. However, no significant differences were found between delinquents and nondelinquents in sections one and two.

Section 3 indicated that delinquents feel more likely to commit crimes. Further, they tend to think they are less likely to be arrested and convicted for the crimes. These results were in the hypothesized direction.

No significant correlations have been found between age or IQ and the RPQ.

Comments

The RPQ has received little support for validity and lacks reliability estimates. The technique for scoring and assumptions upon which they are based are, as yet, unsupported. The RPQ does, however, draw on related research on offenders' estimates of being caught, and offers a test of a key theoretical question in criminology and crime deterrence.

REFERENCES

Claster, D. S. Comparison of risk perception between delinquents and nondelinquents. *Journal of Criminal Law and Police Science*, 1967, 58, 80–86.

RISK PERCEPTION QUESTIONNAIRE

The following questions ask you to guess about how laws against certain crimes work in the United States. Everyone knows the the police usually catch those who commit some crimes, but there are other crimes that the police don't solve as often. For example, they are more likely to catch a murderer than a man who sometimes drives his car faster than the speed limit.

In each case here you are asked to guess the percent of crimes which end up with someone being arrested for them. As you know, percent means number out of every hundred. If half the people who commit a particular crime get arrested, the answer is 50 percent (50%), because 50 is half of 100.

The more people out of every hundred breaking a law who get arrested, the higher the percent. But it can never be more than 100%. The fewer people who get caught for a particular crime, the lower the percent.

I want you to do your best to guess the correct answers in this section. To see that you do, I will grade these questions, and after I have given them to a number of other boys and girls here, I will give a prize of two dollars to the person who has the most correct answers in this part and the next part of the test.

I want to be sure you know what each crime means, so there is an explanation of the crime just before each question about it.

Notice that these questions are not asking about the people arrested being found guilty or not guilty, only the percent of crimes which end up with someone being arrested.

Make an X in the box next to the answer which you think is correct for each question. Of course most people do not know the exact figures, so just make your best guess.

Here is an example of how the questions should be answered:

JUVENILE DELINQUENT — a law breaker under 18 years of age.

What percent of juvenile delinquents are girls?
- ☐ 5%
- ☐ 10%
- ☐ 15%
- ☒ 20%

An X has been placed in the 20% box because 20% of juvenile delinquents are girls.

Now finish the remaining questions. Remember, don't leave any out. Even though you don't know the right answer, make the best guess you can.

1. <u>Murder</u> — killing a person on purpose. For instance: A man plans to kill his wife. He buys a gun, takes it home, and shoots her. What percent of murders end up with someone being arrested for the crime?

    ☐ 62%
    ☐ 72%
    ☐ 82%
    ☐ 92%

2. <u>Negligent manslaughter</u> — killing a person without wanting to, but because of some carelessness. For instance: A man throws a can out the window without looking. Someone is passing on the street. The can hits him on the head and kills him. What percent of negligent manslaughters end up with someone being arrested for the crime?

    ☐ 63%
    ☐ 73%
    ☐ 83%
    ☐ 93%

3. <u>Aggravated assault</u> — trying to hurt another person badly. For instance: A man gets angry at another man who insulted him. He beats him up so badly that the other man is taken to a hospital. What percent of aggravated assaults end up with someone being arrested for the crime?

    ☐ 66%
    ☐ 76%
    ☐ 86%
    ☐ 96%

4. <u>Robbery</u> — taking something from another person by means of force. For instance: A man stops another man in an alley. He makes him hand over his wallet by telling him he'll get hurt if he doesn't hand it over. What percent of robberies end up with someone being arrested for the crime?

    ☐ 8%
    ☐ 18%
    ☐ 28%
    ☐ 38%

5. <u>Burglary</u> — breaking into a building to steal something. For instance: A man breaks into a house when the family is away to steal their silverware. What percent of burglaries end up with someone being arrested for the crime?

    ☐ 30%
    ☐ 40%
    ☐ 50%
    ☐ 60%

6. <u>Auto theft</u> — stealing another person's car. For instance: A man is walking along the street. He sees a car with the keys in it and decides to take a ride. He drives it a hundred miles away and leaves it in a field. What pecent of auto thefts end up with someone being arrested for the crime?
   - ☐ 6%
   - ☐ 16%
   - ☐ 26%
   - ☐ 36%

The first six questions asked about the percent of crimes for which arrests were made. The next questions are different. They ask <u>what percent of the people charged with different crimes are found guilty.</u> These questions are part of those I will grade to see who gets the most correct and gets the two-dollar prize.

The same crimes are listed below, along with explanations. Make an X in the box next to the percent which you think is the correct answer. Remember not to leave out any questions. Even though you do not know the exact answer, make the best guess you can.

7. <u>Murder</u> — killing a person on purpose. What percent of the people charged with murder are found guilty?
   - ☐ 60%
   - ☐ 70%
   - ☐ 80%
   - ☐ 90%

8. <u>Negligent manslaughter</u> — killing a person without wanting to, but because of some carelessness. What percent of the people charged with negligent manslaughter are found guilty?
   - ☐ 16%
   - ☐ 26%
   - ☐ 36%
   - ☐ 46%

9. <u>Aggravated assault</u> — trying to hurt another person badly. What percent of the people charged with aggravated assault are found guilty?
   - ☐ 33%
   - ☐ 43%
   - ☐ 53%
   - ☐ 63%

10. <u>Robbery</u> — taking something from another person by means of force. What percent of the people charged with robbery are found guilty?
    - ☐ 29%
    - ☐ 39%
    - ☐ 49%
    - ☐ 59%

11. Burglary — breaking into a building to steal something. What percent of the people charged with burglary are found guilty?

	☐ 57%
	☐ 67%
	☐ 77%
	☐ 87%

12. Auto theft — stealing another person's car. What percent of the people charged with auto theft are found guilty?

	☐ 64%
	☐ 74%
	☐ 84%
	☐ 94%

The next questions do not have any right or wrong answers. They simply ask for your ideas about your own behavior. Since there are no correct or incorrect answers, there is no prize for answering these questions.

Please answer these questions as carefully as you can. Here we want to know your ideas about laws and your own behavior.

And remember that your answers will not be used by anyone except in the scientific survey. Now go on and answer the rest of the questions.

13a. Do you think that you could ever become so angry with another person that you could kill him?

	☐ Definitely could
	☐ Probably could
	☐ Probably could not
	☐ Definitely could not

Answer parts b and c ONLY IF YOU THINK THAT YOU DEFINITELY COULD or PROBABLY COULD KILL ANOTHER PERSON IF YOU BECAME ANGRY WITH HIM.

13b. If you did kill someone in anger, do you think that you would have a better than even chance of being arrested for the crime, about a 50-50 chance, or a better than even chance of getting away without being arrested?

	☐ Better than even chance of being arrested
	☐ 50-50 chance of being arrested
	☐ Better than even chance of getting away without being arrested

13c. If you killed someone in anger and were arrested for the crime, do you think you would have a better than even chance of being found guilty, a 50-50 chance of being found guilty, or a better than even chance of being found not guilty?

	☐ Better than even chance of being found guilty
	☐ 50-50 chance of being found guilty
	☐ Better than even chance of being found not guilty

14a. Do you think that you could ever need money so badly that you would break into a house when you knew nobody was home to steal money that you knew was in the house?

☐ Definitely could
☐ Probably could
☐ Probably could not
☐ Definitely could not

ANSWER PARTS b AND c ONLY IF YOU <u>DEFINITELY COULD</u> OR <u>PROBABLY COULD</u> STEAL MONEY FROM A HOUSE WITH NOBODY HOME.

14b. If you did steal money from a house when nobody was home, do you think that you would have a better than even chance of <u>being arrested</u> for the crime, about a <u>50-50 chance</u>, or a better than even chance of <u>getting away</u> without being arrested.

☐ Better than even chance of <u>being arrested</u>
☐ <u>50-50 chance</u> of being arrested
☐ Better than even chance of <u>getting away</u> without being arrested.

14c. If you did steal money from a house when nobody was home and were arrested for the crime, do you think you would have a better than even chance of being found guilty, a 50-50 chance of being found guilty, or a better than even chance of being found <u>not guilty</u>?

☐ Better than even chance of being found <u>guilty</u>
☐ <u>50-50 chance</u> of being found guilty
☐ Better than even chance of being found <u>not guilty</u>

15a. Do you think that you could ever be so careless in driving a car that you would go through a red light and kill someone crossing the street?

☐ Definitely could
☐ Probably could
☐ Probably could not
☐ Definitely could not

ANSWER PARTS b AND c ONLY IF YOU THINK YOU <u>DEFINITELY COULD</u> OR PROBABLY COULD ACCIDENTALLY KILL SOMEBODY BY DRIVING THROUGH A RED LIGHT.

15b. If you did accidentally kill someone driving through a red light, do you think you would have a better than even chance of <u>being arrested</u> for the crime, about a <u>50-50 chance</u>, or a better than even chance of <u>getting away</u> without being arrested?

☐ Better than even chance of <u>being arrested</u>
☐ <u>50-50 chance</u> of being arrested
☐ Better than even chance of <u>getting away</u> without being arrested.

15c. If you did accidentally kill someone by driving through a red light and were arrested for the crime, do you think you would have a better than even chance of being found <u>guilty</u>, a <u>50-50 chance</u> of being found guilty, or a better than even chance of being found <u>not guilty</u>?

☐ Better than even chance of being found <u>guilty</u>
☐ 50-50 chance of being found guilty
☐ Better than even chance of being found <u>not guilty</u>.

CRIME AND CRIMINALITY DESCRIPTION: LISTINGS

African View of Crime Interview Schedule

Clifford, W. The African view of crime. *British Journal of Criminology*, 1964, *4*, 477–486.

This interview technique was designed to discover how African people view crime. The interview topics were traditional views of crime, attitudes toward the police, and treatment of offenders. This technique has been applied to interviewing urban Africans residing in Lusaka.

Attitudes toward Crime and Punishment

Gibbons, D. C. Crime and punishment: A study in social attitudes. *Social Forces*, 1969, *47*, 391–397.

The *Attitudes toward Crime and Punishment* questionnaire was designed to elicit dispositional preferences of citizens concerning various crimes in their "normal" forms. To do this, 20 different kinds of criminality were described in relatively brief paragraphs. The respondents were then asked to indicate which punishment they deemed most fitting for the crime. The sentences included execution, a prison term of over five years, prison sentence between one and five years, a six month jail term, a one month jail sentence, probation under supervision, a fine of $100 without jail or probation, and no penalty. In addition, the respondents were given an opportunity to note any other penalty that they thought was more suitable than the options listed for each of the 20 crime scenarios.

Crime Control Orientation Scale

Boggs, S. L. Formal and informal crime control: An exploratory study of urban, suburban, and rural orientations. *Sociological Quarterly*, 1971, *12*, 319–327.

This 11-item interview schedule was designed to determine how likely respondents think it is that certain crimes might happen in their neighborhood, how much they rely on neighbors and police for protection, and whether they consider their neighborhood safe.

Crime Seriousness Ratings

Rossi, P. H., Waite, E., Bose, C. E., & Berk, R. E. The seriousness of crimes: Normative structure and individual differences. *American Sociological Review*, 1974, *39*, 224–237.

This instrument was designed to measure the perceived seriousness of 140 crimes through a task of sorting IBM cards containing crime descriptions into nine seriousness levels. Ratings on this 9-point scale are available on the 140 offenses.

Criminal Justice Attitudes and Knowledge Scale

Harrell, B. *Analysis of data from a correctional psychology questionnaire.* Center for Correctional Psychology, Department of Psychology, The University of Alabama, University, Alabama 35486.

This questionnaire was designed to ascertain the knowledge and attitudes that residents of an area have about the criminal justice system. It contains 59 forced-choice questions.

Exposure to Family and Peer Deviance Indices

Severy, L. J. Exposure to deviance committed by valued peer group and family members. *Journal of Research in Crime and Delinquency,* 1973, *10,* 35–46.

These two scales were designed to measure the exposure to family members and peers who had engaged in deviant or delinquent activities. The *Exposure to Family Deviance Index* consists of family member offense rates, offense seriousness, and depth of legal involvement. The *Exposure to Peer Deviance Index* assesses percentage of peer group members committing serious delinquent offenses.

Fear of Crime and Fear of the Police Interviews

Block, R. L. Fear of crime and fear of the police. *Social Problems,* 1971, *19,* 91–101.

The *Fear of Crime and Fear of Police Interview* questions were designed to survey the feelings of crime victims and nonvictims concerning fear of crime, fear of police, support for police, and support for civil liberties.

Offense Perception Assessment

Sherman, R. C., & Dowdle, M. D. The perception of crime and punishment: A multidimensional scaling analysis. *Social Science Research,* 1974, *3,* 109–126.

This study uses an offense-ranking procedure that emphasizes the multidimensionality of decisions concerning crime characteristics. Similarity ratings, seriousness judgments, and crime knowledge are assessed for 34 familiar criminal offenses. A factor analysis yielded four dimensions associated with two subsets of crimes.

Perception of Crime Scale

Conklin, J. E. Dimensions of community response to the crime problem. *Social Problems,* 1971, *18,* 373–385.

The *Perception of Crime Scale* consists of three items designed to test relative perceptions of local crime rates among community residents.

Perception of Deviancy Schema

Lorch, B. D. The perception of deviancy by self and others. *Sociology and Social Research,* 1966, *50,* 223–229.

This procedure is a 5 × 5 classification schema that was designed for analyzing the perception of deviant behaviors by self and significant others.

Public Surveys of Crime and Criminal Justice

Hindelang, M. J. Public opinion regarding crime, criminal justice, and related topics. *Journal of Research in Crime and Delinquency,* 1974, *11,* 101–116.

This compilation of public survey items and responses identifies the patterns in research into fear of crime, perceptions of law enforcement agencies, perceptions of the courts, attitudes regarding legislative criminal sanctions, perceptions regarding drugs, and the use of drugs.

Treatment of Violent Patients Questionnaire

Tardiff, K. J. A survey of psychiatrists in Boston and their work with violent patients. *The American Journal of Psychiatry,* 1974, *131,* 1008–1011.

This 11-item questionnaire was designed to describe and quantify the involvement of psychiatrists in treatment of violent patients in urban settings.

CHAPTER 12
General Scales

In the search for crime-related scales, we uncovered hundreds of research studies conducted with scales developed for other purposes, then applied to offender or other justice populations. Our first inclination was to discard them; after all, they were not crime and delinquency specific. They had been used for studying neurotics, psychotics, slow learners, obese children, or other pathological subjects. Yet the frequency of their use suggested to us that they ought to be specifically called to the attention of crime and delinquency researchers. One further reason for including these measures was the simple time–investment issue. We had already gathered the listings and results of many such scales. For us, such an additional time investment was relatively short compared to the researcher who seeks out this information independently.

The material in this chapter, however, is not comprehensive. The reader interested in a further listing of general scales should seek out the other handbooks discussed in Chapter 1. The scales that are presented often represent personality assessments or personal descriptions, have been applied in some way pertinent to crime and delinquency, and seem to be of interest to crime researchers.

The scales chosen for inclusion can be subcategorized. One large group is that of complex scales with multiple subscales, one subscale of which is directed to justice and crime issues or populations. For example, the *Hand Test* yields an acting-out score, which is of considerable interest when working with potentially violent people.

A second category of scales is theoretically linked to offenders or justice processes. Thus the Eysenck *Personality Inventory* is scored on two dimensions related to the Eysenck theory of the nature of the criminal personality—high on both neuroticism and extraversion.

A third category of scales is pragmatically linked to crime research. Thus the Rokeach *Dogmatism Scale* has been applied in several interesting investigations with police, offenders and other justice subjects.

The last category of scales is directed to assessing qualities of the public at large from the perspective of some crime and justice related group. In these cases the object of the evaluative measure is a trait or group that falls within the people-in-general domain. However, the existing research with the judgments of offenders or criminal justice personnel makes these scales relevant here. An example of these instruments is the *Attitudes toward Government Workers Scale,* designed to evaluate inmate attitudes toward justice system and other government employees.

GENERAL ATTITUDE SCALES: REVIEWS

Attitude toward Any Institution

Development and Characteristics

The *Attitude toward Any Institution Scale* (ATAIS) was designed to measure one's attitude toward a specific target institution (Kelley, 1934). It was developed according to a standard Thurstone equal-appearing intervals procedure. This technique involves five major steps. First, a large number of items are formulated. Next, these items are sorted by judges into categories that the judges believe to be equally spaced in terms of the underlying attitudes. The piles of categories are then numbered (usually 11 categories are used) and the median score for each item is determined. Next, a measure of interjudge variability, typically interquartile range or Q values, is determined. Finally, a small number of items, those that have little interjudge variability (high agreement), are chosen to represent the scale. The ATAIS used a total of 402 respondents in the determination of items to be included; 100 of these were factory workers, 80 were students at Purdue University, and 222 were Seventh Day Adventists, Baptists, Methodists, and United Brethren. When all responses were analyzed, a total of 90 items appeared to be acceptable. These were individually analyzed and two 45-item equivalent forms were developed.

Response Mode

The respondent is asked to read each item and place a plus mark beside the items with which he or she agrees.

Scoring

Each item has a scale value obtained in the scale development. A total score is obtained by taking the median value from an ordinal listing of the scores of all items beside which the respondent has placed a plus mark. A high score indicates a positive attitude toward the institution.

Norms

No norms are available.

Reliability

Kelley (1934) reported the following equivalent form reliabilities when examining five different institutions: communism, .89, war, .77, Sunday observance, .98, marriage, .71, divorce, .81. Brodsky (1970) reported a test–retest correlation of .86 for 59 college students on attitude toward prisons using the ATAIS.

Validity

Kelley (1934) compared responses to the ATAIS with the responses to the *Attitude toward Communism Scale*, the *Attitude toward War Scale* and the *Attitude toward Sunday Service Scale*. One hundred factory workers produced a correlation of .82 between the two scales measuring communism. Eighty students at Purdue University produced a correlation coefficient of $-.15$ between the *Attitude toward War Scale* and the ATAIS. Finally, a sample of 222 church members produced a correlation of .78 between the ATAIS and *Attitude toward Sunday Service Scale*.

Brodsky (1970) administered this scale to 59 college students and 26 delinquent and predelinquent boys. These subjects were tested on their attitudes toward prisons, allowed to listen to a group of prisoners speak on crime and prisons, and tested again. The scores decreased in the posttest, indicating a less favorable attitude toward prisons.

Comments

The ATAIS appears to be reliable, and evidence for concurrent validity as well as criterion validity is adequate. Further, since the scale is phrased in a general manner and can be directed toward any particular institution, it appears to be useful for measuring a number of different attitudes within the criminal justice system. However, Shaw and Wright (1967) have cautioned against automatically accepting scale information and characteristics when applying the ATAIS to new target institutions.

REFERENCES

Brodsky, S. L. The prisoner as agent of attitude change: A study of prison profiles' effects. *British Journal of Criminology*, 1970, *10*, 280–285.

Kelley, I. V. Construction and validation of a scale to measure attitudes toward any institution. *Purdue University Studies in Higher Education*, 1934, *35*, 18–36.

Shaw, M. E., & Wright, J. N. *Scales for the measurement of attitudes.* New York: McGraw-Hill, 1967.

ATTITUDE TOWARD ANY INSTITUTION

Following is a list of statements about institutions. Place a plus sign (+) before each statement with which you agree about the institution or institutions listed at the left of the statements. The person in charge will tell you the institution or institutions to write in at the head of the columns to the left of the statements. Your score will in no way affect your grade in any course.

Form A

Scale Value

11.2	1.	It is perfect in every way.
11.1	2.	Is the most admirable of institutions.
11.1	3.	Is necessary to the very existence of civilization.
11.0	4.	Is the most beloved of institutions.
10.8	5.	Represents the best thought of modern life.
10.5	6.	Grew up in answer to a felt need and is serving that need perfectly.
10.3	7.	Exerts a strong influence for good government and right living.
10.2	8.	Has more pleasant things connected with it than any other institution.
10.2	9.	Is a strong influence for right living.
10.2	10.	Gives real help in meeting moral problems.
10.1	11.	Gives real help in meeting social problems.
9.8	12.	Is valuable in creating ideals.
9.8	13.	Is necessary to the very existence of society.
9.7	14.	Encourages social improvement.
9.5	15.	Serves society as a whole well.
9.3	16.	Aids the individual in wise use of leisure time.
9.1	17.	Is necessary to society as organized.
8.9	18.	Adjusts itself to changing conditions.

GENERAL SCALES

8.8	19.	Is improving with the years.
8.2	20.	Does more good than harm.
7.4	21.	Will not harm anybody.
6.4	22.	Inspires no definite likes or dislikes.
6.1	23.	Is necessary only until a better one can be found.
5.4	24.	Is too liberal in its policies.
5.3	25.	Is too conservative for a changing civilization.
4.9	26.	Does not consider individual differences.
4.8	27.	Is losing ground as education advances.
4.5	28.	Gives too little service.
4.4	29.	Represents outgrown beliefs.
4.2	30.	Gives no opportunity for self-expression.
3.5	31.	Promotes false beliefs and much wishful thinking.
3.3	32.	Is too selfish to benefit society.
3.1	33.	Does more harm than good.
3.0	34.	Is cordially hated by the majority for its smugness and snobbishness.
2.9	35.	Satisfies only the most stupid with its services.
2.8	36.	Is hopelessly out of date.
2.7	37.	No one any longer has faith in this institution.
2.3	38.	Is entirely unnecessary.
2.2	39.	Is detrimental to society and the individual.
2.1	40.	The world would be better off without this institution.
2.0	41.	Is in a hopeless condition.
1.9	42.	Will destroy civilization if it is not radically changed.
1.8	43.	Never was any good.
1.7	44.	Benefits no one.
1.6	45.	Has positively no value.

Form B

11.2	1.	The world could not exist without this institution.
11.1	2.	Is an ideal institution.
11.1	3.	Has done more for society than any other institution.
11.0	4.	Benefits everybody.
10.8	5.	Has more good points than any other institution.
10.7	6.	Appeals to man's highest nature.

10.4	7.	Develops good character.
10.2	8.	Furthers the most lasting satisfactions in life.
10.2	9.	Has a long useful life before it.
10.2	10.	Is a powerful agency for promoting individual and social efficiency.
10.1	11.	Is of real value to the civilized individual.
9.9	12.	Gives real help in meeting economic problems.
9.8	13.	Encourages moral improvement.
9.7	14.	Is fundamentally sound.
9.6	15.	Is retained in the civilized world because of its value to mankind.
9.4	16.	Offers opportunity for individual initiative.
9.2	17.	Is increasing in its value to society.
9.0	18.	Is necessary as a means of controlling society.
8.9	19.	Is improving in its service to mankind.
8.2	20.	Is in the process of changing and will come out a fit instrument.
7.5	21.	Is not sufficiently appreciated by the general public.
6.6	22.	Its good and bad points balance each other.
6.1	23.	Has not yet proved itself indispensable to society.
5.4	24.	Is too conservative.
5.3	25.	Is retained in the civilized world because of sentiment.
4.9	26.	Is decreasing in its value to society.
4.8	27.	Is too changeable in its policies.
4.6	28.	Regulates the individual's life too minutely.
4.4	29.	Grew up in frontier days and does not fit our industrial civilization.
4.2	30.	Is too radical in its views and actions.
3.6	31.	Is unfair to the individual.
3.3	32.	Is a tool of the mercenary.
3.1	33.	Is disgraced by its past.
3.0	34.	Is a tool of the unscrupulous.
2.9	35.	Is developing into a racket.
2.8	36.	Is fundamentally unsound.
2.7	37.	Is out of control of society and is running wild.
2.3	38.	Appeals to man's lowest nature.
2.2	39.	Is an enemy of truth.
2.1	40.	Has always cheated society.
1.9	41.	Thrives on the avarice, jealousy, hatred, and greed in man.

1.9	42.	Must be discarded immediately.
1.8	43.	Has more bad points than any other institution.
1.7	44.	Is the most despicable of institutions.
1.6	45.	Is the most hateful of institutions.

Attitudes toward Government Workers

Development and Characteristics

The *Attitude toward Government Workers Scale* (ATGW) was designed (Weston, 1965) to discover the relative attitudes of inmates toward government workers, especially those within the criminal justice system. Other government occupations are included to serve as a comparative base.

The main part of the test (Questions 1–10 and 13–22) asks the respondent to make Likert-type judgments as to how well members of specific occupations do their jobs and how honest they are. Questions 11 and 12 are filler questions.

Response Mode

The test is read aloud to a group of test takers who are asked to follow along. After each question, the respondent is asked to place a mark on a continuum at a point that represents the way he or she feels. Two continua are used. One is a 10-point Likert format ranging from "strong yes" to "strong no." The other is a 10-point scale in which the respondent is asked to rate the honesty of various government employees from 100% to 10%.

Scoring

Since the respondent chooses a number (in multiples of 10) between 10 and 100 to represent his or her feelings, a total score of 200 is the maximum possible for each of the 10 jobs (100 maximum for how well they perform their jobs plus 100 maximum for how honest they are). The total score for each job then is divided by two, and the final score is based on a maximum of 100. Thus, a measure of relative valence of the attitude is available for comparison between each category.

Norms

Table 72 shows the scores of 57 undergraduate students and 300 inmates drawn from an adult authority department of corrections, a youth authority department of corrections, and a county jail.

TABLE 72. Comparative Ranking—Inmate versus Control Group—All Occupations

Occupation	Inmate group		Control group	
	Percentage honest	Rank	Percentage honest	Rank
Postman	85	1	86	3
Fireman	85	2	87	1
Game warden	81	3	80	9
Clerk-typist	80	4	80	10
Teacher	78	5	84	6
Parole officer	70	6	85	5
Judge	68	7	86	2
District attorney	66	8	85	4
Public defender	65	9	84	7
Police officer	64	10	83	8

Note that, in general, inmates viewed these jobs less favorably than the students. Also, note that the inmates rated police officer, public defender, district attorney, judge, and parole officer much lower than did the students.

Reliability

Weston (1965) reports of test-retest reliability that "the greatest spread between the first and second test scores was 20" and "a variance of 10 one way or the other was average" (p. 91). No reliability coefficients were calculated.

Validity

Forty of the inmates were interviewed after they had taken the test in an effort to discover any discrepancies between their responses on the scale and their expressed feelings in the interview. Also, each inmate's criminal record was reviewed to discover any discrepancies. No unexplained differences were reported, supporting the construct validity of the scale.

Additional support for the validity of the instrument comes from its ability to differentiate the inmates from the control group, as illustrated in the *Norms* section.

Comments

Much work will be needed to make this an established, usable attitude scale. The evidence for reliability is sketchy, and only modest validity evidence is presented.

REFERENCES

Weston, P. B. The attitudes of offenders toward occupations in the administration of justice. *Criminology,* 1965, *6,* 83–96.

ATTITUDES TOWARD GOVERNMENT WORKERS

For items I through 12 read each question and circle the alternative which best represents your answer.

1. Do you think firemen do a good job?
   Strong yes   Neutral   Strong no
   100 90 80 70 60 50 40 30 20 10

2. Do you think game wardens do a good job?
   Strong yes   Neutral   Strong no
   100 90 80 70 60 50 40 30 20 10

3. Do you think teachers do a good job?
   Strong yes   Neutral   Strong no
   100 90 80 70 60 50 40 30 20 10

4. Do you think postmen do a good job?
   Strong yes   Neutral   Strong no
   100 90 80 70 60 50 40 30 20 10

5. Do you think clerk-typists do a good job?
   Strong yes   Neutral   Strong no
   100 90 80 70 60 50 40 30 20 10

6. Do you think judges do a good job?
   Strong yes   Neutral   Strong no
   100 90 80 70 60 50 40 30 20 10

7. Do you think parole officers do a good job?
   Strong yes   Neutral   Strong no
   100 90 80 70 60 50 40 30 20 10

8. Do you think public defenders do a good job?
   Strong yes   Neutral   Strong no
   100 90 80 70 60 50 40 30 20 10

9. Do you think district attorneys do a good job?
   Strong yes   Neutral   Strong no
   100 90 80 70 60 50 40 30 20 10

10. Do you think policemen do a good job?
    Strong yes   Neutral   Strong no
    100 90 80 70 60 50 40 30 20 10

*11. Do you think that there is a need for psychiatric tests for police?
    Strong yes   Neutral   Strong no
    100 90 80 70 60 50 40 30 20 10

*12. Which of the positions listed above might you be interested in?

Note: Questions 13 to 22 concern the "honesty" of persons in government occupations. Indicate the number you think are likely to be honest out of each hundred of the type of employee specified.

					Percentage					
13.	Firemen............	100	90	80	70	60	50	40	30	20	10
14.	Game Warden........	100	90	80	70	60	50	40	30	20	10
15.	Teacher.............	100	90	80	70	60	50	40	30	20	10
16.	Postmen............	100	90	80	70	60	50	40	30	20	10
17.	Clerk-typist..........	100	90	80	70	60	50	40	30	20	10
18.	Judge...............	100	90	80	70	60	50	40	30	20	10
19.	Parole officer........	100	90	80	70	60	50	40	30	20	10
20.	Public defender.......	100	90	80	70	60	50	40	30	20	10
21.	District attorney......	100	90	80	70	60	50	40	30	20	10
22.	Policemen...........	100	90	80	70	60	50	40	30	20	10

*Nonscored filler items.

Delinquent Attitudes and Self-Esteem Scale

Development and Characteristics

The *Delinquent Attitudes and Self-Esteem Scale* (DASES) is a semantic differential scale designed to test "the relationship between attitudes toward representatives of the social order and self-esteem among nondelinquents" and delinquents (Rathus & Siegel, 1973, p. 268). Osgood, Suci, and Tannenbaum (1957) suggest that the semantic differential technique measures the semantic space assigned to target concepts. This is done by acquiring a respondent's "feeling" for the target along continua bounded by bipolar adjectives.

The DASES was conceived in an effort to discover whether a subcultural theory or neutralization theory best explains the behavior of delinquents. In brief, the subcultural theory states that delinquents alienate themselves from the predominant social order. This alienation process attempts to raise their self-esteem by rejecting the values of the culture that has labeled them as "bad." The neutralization theory holds that delinquents have internalized and are committed to the norms and mores of the middle class, but tend to neutralize the sanctions against deviant behavior by attributing the cause of their actions to mitigating circumstances.

The DASES uses bipolar adjectives to measure the individual's perception of self, "policemen," "the law," "education," "work," "saving money," and "crime." By comparing an individual's response to "myself" with responses to middle-class values or institutions, one might infer whether these were internalized.

Response Mode

The DASES uses a 7-point continuum to represent intervals between adjective pairs. Values range from 0 to 6, with the lower numbers representing positive traits. The respondents place a mark at the point on the continuum between each adjective pair that best represents their feeling for the target concept.

Scoring

The seven "target concepts" are rated on various numbers of scales—4 adjective pairs are used to evaluate "myself," 2 for "policemen," "the law," "work," "saving money," and "crime," and 3 for "education." Since all evaluations are quantified in the same direction, raw scores can be analyzed and easily interpreted.

Norms

Table 73 presents the "myself" means and standard deviations for 63 male probationers (12–16 years of age), and 86 male high school students.

Reliability

No reliability measures were reported for this particular use, but Osgood et al. (1957) have presented evidence for the adequate reliability of the semantic differential.

TABLE 73. Comparison of the Self-Esteem of Nondelinquents and Delinquents[a]

Area of self-esteem	Nondelinquents ($N = 86$)		Delinquents ($N = 63$)		t
	M	SD	M	SD	
Niceness	1.84	1.13	2.11	1.30	1.39
Fairness	1.62	1.23	1.75	1.36	0.61
Smartness	2.03	1.31	2.44	1.03	2.13[b]
Strength	1.83	1.22	1.92	1.21	0.47

[a] Scores may range from 0 to 6, with 0 as the positive pole of each scale (e.g., "nice") and 0 as the negative pole (e.g., "awful").
[b] $p < .05$.

Validity

As shown in the table in the *Norms* section, only the smart-dumb scale for "myself" differentiated between delinquents and nondelinquents. This indicates that self-esteem (as measured by the DASES) is generally the same for delinquents and nondelinquents. When the self-esteem scores were correlated with the other scales, however, delinquents showed a significant number of negative correlations (as tested by χ^2) and nondelinquents showed a significant number of positive correlations. This indicates that, for delinquents, the higher one's self-esteem, the lower one's regard for the other targets, and vice versa. The opposite is true for nondelinquents. The higher one's regard for the other targets, the higher one's self-esteem. Only 8 of the 50 correlations were statistically significant at the .05 level, although a χ^2 test of significance indicated that the number of correlations in predicted directions (positive correlations for nondelinquents and negative for delinquents) was beyond chance. These significant results are consistent with the subcultural theory.

Comments

The DASES uses an established psychometric technique and a theoretical position to build a scale that will measure differences in self-concept between delinquents and nondelinquents. The research results, however, showed the scale to be of little use in discriminating between delinquents and nondelinquents, and of restricted value in assessing other targets.

REFERENCES

Osgood, C. E., Suci, G. J., & Tannenbaum, P. H. *The measurement of meaning.* Urbana: University of Illinois Press, 1957.

Rathus, A., & Siegel, J., Delinquent attitudes and self-esteem. *Adolescence,* 1973, *8,* 265–276.

DELINQUENT ATTITUDES AND SELF-ESTEEM SCALE

Instructions: The following list contains different (target) concepts followed by pairs of descriptive words. Rate each of the target concepts by placing a check (✔) at the point in each continuum which best represents your feeling for that concept.

Myself

Nice ___:___:___:___:___:___ Awful

GENERAL SCALES

	Myself	
Fair	___:___:___:___:___:___:___	Unfair
Smart	Myself ___:___:___:___:___:___:___	Dumb
Strong	Myself ___:___:___:___:___:___:___	Weak
Nice	Policeman ___:___:___:___:___:___:___	Awful
Fair	Policeman ___:___:___:___:___:___:___	Unfair
Valuable	The Law ___:___:___:___:___:___:___	Worthless
Fair	The Law ___:___:___:___:___:___:___	Unfair
Valuable	Education ___:___:___:___:___:___:___	Worthless
Pleasant	Education ___:___:___:___:___:___:___	Unpleasant
Strong	Education ___:___:___:___:___:___:___	Weak
Nice	Work ___:___:___:___:___:___:___	Awful
Strong	Work ___:___:___:___:___:___:___	Weak
Valuable	Saving Money ___:___:___:___:___:___:___	Worthless
Strong	Saving Money ___:___:___:___:___:___:___	Weak
Nice	Crime ___:___:___:___:___:___:___	Awful
Strong	Crime ___:___:___:___:___:___:___	Weak

GENERAL ATTITUDE SCALES: LISTINGS

Attitudes toward Deviant Behavior

Sieviking, N. A., Doctor, R. M., & Campbell, M. L. Possible community consequences of attitudes toward and models of deviant behavior. *Community Mental Health Journal,* 1972, *8,* 38–46.

This scale is a set of 16 social, behavioral, and physical problems, including criminality and juvenile delinquency, which are rated on 35 bipolar descriptions by community members to assess effects upon community policies. Responses to this set of items were factor analysed and five factors of attitudes toward problems were extracted. These factors are threatening undesirability, physical disease, accountability for mistakes, hopelessness, and strange inferiority.

Attitude toward Disabled Persons

Evans, J. H. Attitudes of adolescent delinquent boys. *Psychological Reports,* 1974, *34,* 1175–1178.

The *Attitude toward Disabled Persons* scale is a 20-item, Likert-type instrument designed to measure the degree to which individuals feel that disabled people are different from other people and the degree to which they feel that disabled people are in need of special treatment. This article reports the results of the administration of the *Attitude toward Disabled Persons Scale* on delinquent and nondelinquent junior high school boys.

Child–Parent Relationship Scale

Chwast, J. Perceived parental attitudes and predelinquency. *Journal of Criminal Law, Criminology, and Police Science,* 1958, *48,* 116–126.

This 63-item, forced-choice scale was designed to measure conscious attitudes regarding dominating, possessive, or ignoring behaviors of the mother, father, and parents in general. The scale has been applied to the study of predelinquent teenage boys.

Itkin Attitudes toward Parents and Children Scales

Shaw, M. E., & Wright, J. M. *Scales for the measurement of attitudes.* New York: McGraw-Hill, 1967.

The *Itkin Attitudes toward Parents and Children Scales* are a set of seven Likert-type scales designed to explore various aspects of parents' and children's attitudes. Two scales assess parents' opinions regarding child rearing and discipline. Five scales are completed by children, including an attitude toward discipline exercised by parents scale.

Policemen's View of Citizens' Support Scales

Kelly, R. M., & Farber, M. G. Identifying responsive intercity policemen. *Journal of Applied Psychology,* 1974, *59,* 259–263.

These Likert-type attitude scales were designed to elicit responses regarding police attitudes toward and relationship with citizens within their work area. They include a *Policemen's View of Citizens' Support Scale* (4 items), a *General Faith in People Scale* (4 items), *Police Fear of Citizens' Scale* (5 items), and *Police Stereotype of Poor People Scale* (4 items).

Stanford Parent Attitude Questionnaire

Winder, C. L., & Rau, L. Parental attitudes associated with social deviance in preadolescent boys. *Journal of Abnormal and Social Psychology,* 1962, *64,* 418–424.

Duncan, P. Parental attitudes and interactions in delinquency. *Child Development,* 1971, *42,* 1751–1765.

This 28-item, Likert-type scale was designed to measure parents' attitudes toward their children and their children's behavior. The original version was aimed at preadolescent boys, but Duncan (1971) has developed a version for girls.

GENERAL BEHAVIOR RATINGS: REVIEWS

Bristol Social Adjustment Guides

Development and Characteristics

The *Bristol Social Adjustment Guides* (BSAG) were developed in an attempt to "identify satisfactory units of disturbed behavior of children in school and then establish syndromes" (Stott, 1971, p. 232). The first effort was revised (Stott, 1971) to yield a version that included 150 indications of maladjustment, as noted by teachers. Of the indicators, 110 were found to discriminate between maladjusted and well-adjusted children completely enough to merit inclusion in a final revision.

The items fall into seven categories: (1) interaction with teacher, (2) social work, (3) games and play, (4) attitudes to other children, (5) personal ways, (6) physique, and (7) school achievement. These are subdivided into more specific categories that contain descriptions of the ways children might behave. The behavior descriptions are randomly ordered to reduce anticipatory choices of teachers.

Interpretation is not performed by the teacher. A transparency indicates the classes of underreaction maladjustment (UNRACT), overreaction maladjustment (OVRACT), and normal adjustment. This taxonomic device also includes "core syndromes" related to the above symptoms, such as unforthcomingness, withdrawal, depression, inconsequence, and hostility.

It is believed that by appropriately classifying the adjustment problems, inferences as to the causes and proper treatment can be drawn. In addition, the authors feel that identification of the problem will influence teachers to respond in ways more appropriate to the situation.

Response Mode

The child is rated according to his or her interaction patterns with the teacher and his or her peers.

Scoring

The procedure requires only that a scoring transparency be placed over the adjustment guide and the underlined descriptions be appropriately grouped and summed within each group to note the degree of symptomatology. This is, then, recorded on the diagnostic form.

Norms

Stott (1972) presents norms for 1,305 boys and 1,222 girls between the ages of 5 and 16 years. The manual presents distributions and percentages of children scoring at each level for overreacting and underreacting and for the five core syndromes.

Table 74 represents the scores used to gauge the degree of severity of UNRACT, OVRACT, and the five core syndromes.

Reliability

The BSAG manual reports reliability coefficients, using Winer's formula, for 10 separate scores and for a BSAG total score (see Table 75).

TABLE 74. Cut-off Scores for Gauging Degree of Severity (UNRACT, OVRACT, and the Five Core Syndromes)

	Cut-off scores	Boys N = 1,305		Girls N = 1,222	
		N	Percentage	N	Percentage
UNRACT					
Stability and near stability	0–2	782	59.92	763	62.44
Mild underreaction	3–5	258	19.77	238	19.48
Appreciable underreaction	6–8	135	10.34	107	8.75
Maladjusted underreaction	9–14	117	8.97	87	7.12
Severe maladjusted underreaction	15+	13	1.00	27	2.21
M		3.05		2.84	
SD		3.66		3.83	
OVRACT					
Stability and near stability	0–3	747	57.24	938	76.76
Mild overreaction	4–7	216	16.56	134	10.97
Appreciable overreaction	8–11	133	10.18	69	5.65
Maladjusted overreaction	12–24	185	14.18	74	6.06
Severe maladjusted overreaction	25+	24	1.84	7	0.56
M		5.11		2.11	
SD		6.60		4.80	
Unforthcomingness					
Nil or small	0–1	919	70.42	799	65.39
Mild	2–4	301	23.06	297	24.25
Moderate	5–7	73	5.59	91	7.46
Severe	8+	12	0.92	35	2.87
M		1.20		1.53	
SD		1.73		2.17	
Withdrawal					
Nil	0	926	70.96	1020	83.47
Mild	1	218	16.70	125	10.23
Moderate	2–3	127	9.73	58	4.75
Severe	4+	34	2.61	19	1.55
M		0.51		0.29	
SD		1.00		0.82	

(Continued)

TABLE 74. *(Continued)*

	Cut-off scores	Boys N = 1,305		Girls N = 1,222	
		N	Percentage	N	Percentage
Depression					
Nil or small	0	908	69.58	1007	82.41
Mild	1–2	278	21.30	163	13.34
Moderate	3–4	79	6.05	39	3.19
Severe	5+	40	3.06	13	1.06
M		0.66		0.36	
SD		1.32		1.00	
Hostility					
Nil or small	0–1	1026	78.62	1044	85.43
Mild	2–3	162	12.41	93	7.60
Moderate	4–7	85	6.51	71	5.81
Severe	8+	32	2.45	14	1.13
M		1.00		0.70	
SD		2.00		1.72	
Inconsequence					
None or small	0–3	944	72.34	1071	87.64
Mild	4–6	189	14.48	87	7.11
Moderate	7–10	123	9.42	52	4.25
Severe	11+	49	3.36	12	0.97
M		2.48		1.20	
SD		3.32		2.36	

TABLE 75. Reliability Estimates for the BSAG

Scales	Winer's formula reliability	Coefficient alpha internal reliability
BSAG total score	.80	—
UNRACT	.74	.83
OVRACT	.77	.91
Unforthcomingness	.67	.74
Withdrawal	.48	.59
Depression	.54	.66
Inconsequence	.71	.83
Hostility	.68	.80
Peer-maladaptiveness	.61	.76
Nonsyndromic OVRACT	.72	.67
Nonsyndromic UNRACT	.62	.57

Validity

Factor analysis reveals two dimensions that appear to coincide with UNRACT and OVRACT. Item to test correlations reveal that the items that were postulated to indicate maladjustment appear in association with other such items an average of 18.35 times more often than with "adjusted" items. Inherent in the logic of this validation check is the assumption that the test, as a whole, is an accurate predictor of maladjustment. The author argues that "since the descriptions had been compiled over many years by asking successive groups of teachers to describe the behavior of children who, acting against their own best interests, were not thriving emotionally or not coping with their environment, it is unlikely that this assumption is a false one" (Stott, 1971, p. 235).

As a measure of the validity of the syndrome groups, a scorer–nonscorer ratio was used to indicate "the probability that the behavior would occur in association with members of its own syndrome over that of its occurrence apart from them" (Stott, 1971, p. 236). Then a specificity ratio is obtained by dividing the scorer–nonscorer ratio of an item in its best syndrome by that in its next best. The results indicate that "all the items were highly valid as general indicators and those used as members of the core syndromes had adequate syndrome specificity" (Stott, 1971, p. 236).

The scale has also been accurate in discriminating between the scores on a sample of 133 juvenile delinquents and the scores of normal boys (Stott, 1972). In this case, the delinquents showed high overreaction.

Comments

This instrument seems to accurately predict maladjustment and to diagnose the source as due to overreaction or underreaction. If, as the author asserts, maladjustment is neurologically based, the guides provide information necessary for treatment of juveniles with problems of social adjustment. Even if maladjustment has a social basis, the scale may be useful as a taxonomic system.

The author's further contention that heterogeneous "core syndromes" make up the two factors, while appealing, does not receive strong support.

In general, the scale does a better job of identification and classification of social adjustment problems than most others used in this area.

REFERENCES

Stott, D. H. Classification of behavior disturbance among school-age students: Principles, epidemiology and syndromes. *Psychology in the Schools,* 1971, *3,* 232–239.

Stott, D. H. *EITS Manual: Bristol Social Adjustment Guides.* San Diego, California: Education and Industrial Testing Service, 1972.

Weekly Activity Record

Development and Characteristics

The *Weekly Activity Record* (WAR) was designed to analyze and predict criminal behavior and recidivism as a function of time spent performing various usual activities (Jenkins, Muller, DeVine, deValera, Witherspoon, & McKee, 1974). The basic concepts for the WAR were derived from feedback from behavioral interviews in a previous study (Jenkins, Barton, deValera, DeVine, Witherspoon, & Muller, 1972). A preliminary version of the WAR was administered to a group of released or paroled exoffenders and a group of college students. The results were reviewed and a revised form underwent further testing. This version was further modified and refined to yield the current WAR, which consists of 18 items. Each item represents a specific class of usual and basic activities that may be part of an individual's week. These include work, eating and drinking, cleaning and grooming, religious and other organizational behavior, shopping, physical activity and health, hobbies, intellectual activities, watching, reading and listening, family activities, social behavior, sexual behavior, antisocial behavior, daydreaming, maladaptive associates, travel, and waiting.

Response Mode

The WAR is presented in the form of a behavioral interview. The respondent is requested to answer questions and talk freely about himself or herself and his or her activities during the previous week.

Scoring

Three types of scoring procedures may be followed for the WAR. The most useful involves calculating the total number of hours reported for an individual and finding the average time spent in the 18 activity types. Next each item is scored according to whether it is "positive," "negative," or "neutral." Positive item responses that show above average time involvement receive a score of 0, indicating an adaptive response. Those below the average are assigned a value of 1, indicating a maladaptive response. For a negative item, the above average scores receive 1 and below average scores receive 0. The three neutral items showed slight trends and were scored such that items 2 and 15 were viewed as positive items and item 13 as negative. This procedure can yield a total numerical score with a potential range from 0–18, with a low score representing adaptive behavior and a high score representing maladaptive behavior.

Norms

Table 76 presents a comparison of the percentage of time on each of the WAR items spent by 114 prison releasees, 74 college students, and 50 business men. Only six items were not statistically different across the three groups. Three of these six items had been designated as neutral items and were not expected to show differences (Items 2, 13, and 15).

TABLE 76. Percentage of Time on WAR Items for Prison Releasees, College Students, and Businessmen

WAR items	Experimental groups			p
	Prison releasees ($N = 114$)	College students ($N = 74$)	Businessmen ($N = 50$)	
1. Work	14.3	19.9	21.4	.001
2. Sleep	25.7	26.4	25.2	.20
3. Eating and drinking	3.8	7.0	6.4	.001
4. Cleaning and grooming	2.7	5.5	5.6	.01
5. Religious and other organizational behavior	0.3	0.8	0.9	.01
6. Shopping	1.4	1.7	1.4	.20
7. Physical activity and health	0.9	2.7	1.2	.01
8. Hobbies	0.8	1.9	2.9	.001
9. Intellectual activities	0.7	3.9	2.7	.001
10. Watching, reading, and listening	8.5	5.7	7.3	.10
11. Family activities	4.7	3.9	13.6	.01
12. Social behavior	13.1	7.0	4.0	.001
13. Sexual behavior	2.1	3.5	1.9	.10
14. Antisocial behavior	4.9	1.1	1.1	.001
15. Daydreaming	3.3	3.1	2.1	.20
16. Maladaptive associates	5.7	0.7	0.1	.001
17. Travel	3.2	3.3	1.0	.20
18. Waiting	3.8	1.8	1.2	.001
Mean total hours	211.4	191.6	203.7	—

Reliability

Jenkins *et al.* (1974) report high test–retest reliability coefficients for a total of 114 prison releasees who were tested at 3–6 and 12–15 months. The correlation coefficient across all 114 respondents was .93.

Interrater reliability as measured by two independent examiners who interviewed the same 10 respondents within a 30-day period was estimated by the coefficient of concordance, which assesses judge agreement across all WAR items. The resultant coefficient was .96, indicating a high degree of interrater reliability.

Validity

The WAR was presented to 117 inmates in an Alabama state prison; they comprised 80% of the total prison population at the time of testing. Each subject was interviewed prior to release from prison and at postrelease intervals of 3–6 and 12–15 months. In addition, each subject's law encounters were recorded and dated. The average follow-up time was 18 months.

When the respondents were divided into groups based on the *Law Encounter Severity Scale,* the 18 items of the WAR showed significant differences between the groups. WAR scores of the prison releasees were then compared to the scores of 74 advanced undergraduate college students and 50 businessmen. Only 6 of the 18 WAR items did not show statistically significant differences between these three groups (Items 2, 6, 10, 13, 15, and 17). When scores for positive items, negative items, and neutral items were calculated across groups, positive and negative items showed significant differences at the .001 level, while neutral items were not significantly different across groups.

These results were based upon scoring systems which incorporated percentage of time spent on each activity. However, the 0–1 scoring scheme appears to give similar results.

Comments

The developers note that the major problem in supporting the WAR is the need for cross-validation. They suggest, however, that the information presented in the validation section represents cross-validation of the results that were presented in the development section.

The WAR appears to be a reliable instrument and it has received support for its validity as a predictor of recidivism as measured by the *Law Encounter Severity Scale*. Further, it appears to suggest types of activities that should promote healthy adjustment to civilian life for recent prison releasees.

REFERENCES

Jenkins, W. O., Muller, J. B., DeVine, M. D., deValera, E. K., Witherspoon, A. D., & McKee, J. M. The weekly activity record (WAR): A measure of time allocation in the analysis and prediction of criminal behavior and recidivism. *The Rehabilitation Research Foundation,* Grant No. 21-01-73-38, Manpower Administration, U.S. Department of Labor, 1974.

Jenkins, W. O., Barton, M. C., deValera, E. K., DeVine, M. D., Witherspoon, A. D., & Muller, J. B. The measurement and prediction of criminal behavior and recidivism. *Rehabilitation Research Foundation:* Montgomery, Alabama, 1972. (Contract No. 82-01-69-06, Manpower Administration, U.S. Department of Labor).

WEEKLY ACTIVITY RECORD

Enter in the space provided the <u>number of hours</u> in a typical week spent in each activity.

a	1.	JOB. Hours per week spent in occupational activities	_____
c	2.	SLEEP. Hours per week in day and night sleep	_____
a	3.	Hours spent at meals and snacks. Include time for meal planning and preparation	_____
a	4.	CLEANLINESS AND GROOMING. Hours spent at bathing, shaving, shampooing, hair combing, nail fixing, house cleaning, redecorating, clothes care, and other cleanliness behaviors	_____
a	5.	RELIGIOUS BEHAVIOR. Hours spent at church and Sunday school, in prayers, Bible reading, etc......................	_____
a	6.	SHOPPING. Food, drink, clothes, shoes, toilet articles, "looking," etc..	_____
a	7.	A. PHYSICAL ACTIVITY. Exercise, jogging, active sports. B. HEALTH. Visits to MD, Dentist, health aids, and acts	_____
a	8.	HOBBIES. Specify main one	_____
a	9.	INTELLECTUAL ACTIVITIES. Studying, reading for improvement, etc......................................	_____
b	10.	WATCHING, READING, AND LISTENING ACTIVITIES. TV, radio, news, records, music, sports, magazines, light fiction...	_____
a	11.	FAMILY ACTIVITES. Hours spent with parents, spouse, children, sibs, movies, dining out, outings, talks, phone calls, letters, visits, etc. (actually interacting)	_____
b	12.	SOCIAL BEHAVIOR. Parties, games, dates, talking with other than family..	_____

c	13.	SEXUAL BEHAVIOR. Engaging in and planning and preparation for all forms.................................. _____
b	14.	ANTISOCIAL BEHAVIOR. Fighting, verbal or physical, overuse of alcohol or drugs, other deviant behaviors, social withdrawal _____
c	15.	DAYDREAMING. Phantasizing, "doing nothing," "thinking about thinking," "sitting around" — solitary behavior. .... _____
b	16.	TIME SPENT WITH MALADAPTIVE ASSOCIATES INCLUDING EX-OFFENDERS .... _____
b	17.	TRAVEL. Commuting to and from work or to and from leisure activities.. _____
b	18.	WAITING. Waiting for action to start, driving around, etc. ..... _____
	19.	SCHOOL. Hours spent at school.......................... _____
	20.	ORGANIZATION. Hours spent in organizational activities, e.g., extracurricular clubs, church, social, athletic, etc. .... _____
		INTERVIEWER_____

a. positive items   b. negative items   c. neutral items

GENERAL BEHAVIOR RATINGS: LISTINGS

Behavioral Coding System

Cautela, J. R.,& Upper, D. *A behavioral coding system.* Unpublished manuscript, Boston College, 1973.

This coding system consists of 283 behaviors divided into 21 major behavioral categories. The system is designed to influence practitioners and institutions to focus on specific behavior patterns rather than global diagnostic labels.

GENERAL PERSONALITY ASSESSMENT: REVIEWS

Compulsive Masculinity Scale

Development and Characteristics

The *Compulsive Masculinity Scale* (CMS) was designed "to measure the boy's self-identification with tough behavior (e.g., weapon carrying, maintaining the reputation as a tough guy) and sexual athleticism" (Silverman & Dinitz, 1974, p. 505). The developers have suggested that the following characteristics are indicative of "compulsive masculinity": preoccupation with developing an athletic physique and with muscularity, weight lifting, tattooing, the extensive use of profanity, conceptualization of women as conquest objects, drinking, carrying of weapons, fighting, fearlessness and toughness, and the disregard for authority. Further, the developers suggest that these attributes polarize around two factors, toughness and sexual athleticism. With the help of several graduate students who had come from lower-class backgrounds, items were constructed to tap these basic issues in compulsive masculinity. Several boys from lower-class areas then discussed the items in an effort to make them clear and meaningful. The result was a total of 51 items that took the form of behavior descriptions.

When this form of the instrument was pretested on 74 boys at the Training School of Central Ohio (an institution for delinquent boys with serious behavior problems) 19 items were deleted because of lack of consistency with the other items and a lack of face validity. The remaining 32 items were retained and constitute the present form of the scale.

Response Mode

Each of the items in the CMS is a brief description of a particular behavior. The respondent is asked to read the statement and place a check mark in the appropriate position to indicate whether the statement is "like me" or "not like me."

Scoring

Each item in the scale is stated in the direction of "hypermasculinity." Therefore, any response of "like me" is indicative of that direction and is given a score of 1. The total score is then obtained by adding the number of "like me" responses.

Norms

The CMS was administered to 284 delinquent boys at the Fairfield School for Boys (a large Ohio Youth Commission facility for delinquent boys). Their

TABLE 77. Compulsive Masculinity Scores by Home Background

Home background	Mean rating
Natural parents	14.2
Parent & stepparent	16.0
Mother-based	14.4
Father-based	13.9
Surrogate	13.8

ages ranged from 14–19, with a median of 17, and institutional records indicated that 34.9% came from "mother-based homes" (homes where the mother assumed responsibility of the family), 24% came from natural parent family homes, and 28.9% came from homes which consisted of one biological parent and one stepparent. Table 77 shows the CMS mean scores by home background.

Reliability

No reliability estimates are available.

Validity

The concept of compulsive masculinity and delinquency has been related to family life in Parsons (1947). In conjunction with Parson's writings, the scale developers theorized that boys raised in "father absent homes" are forced to break their identification with the dominant mother and establish a male identity. This process results in overcompensation when a good role model is not easily available. Therefore, the developers believe that such youngsters become compulsively masculine and this leads to participation in delinquent activities. As presented in the *Norms* Chapter, mother-based homes did produce individuals with high compulsive masculinity scores. (No explanation was offered for the higher parent and stepparent mean score.) Further, it was found that white delinquents showed a lower mean score on CMS (14.1) than black delinquents (15.3), whose home life, the developers believe, is characterized by less availability of a masculine role model.

Although direct correlational measures were not reported, it was found that the CMS varied directly with the *Lykken Scale* which measures compulsiveness and proneness to activities that are high risk in nature and excitement oriented. The CMS varied inversely with the *Zuckerman Scale,* which measures field dependency or a tendency to be effected by environmental influences, such as peer pressures. Thus, individuals who scored high in compulsive masculinity were impulsive, excitement oriented and tended to be greatly influenced by environmental cues.

Comments

Evidence for validity appears to be adequate. However, there is some need for measures of strength of relationship. The developers report statistically significant differences between CMS scores and hypothesized directions. The sample size of 284, however, offers the hazard (or boon) of showing small differences to be statistically significant.

Another question that may be relevant to workers within the area of criminal justice involves the comparison of delinquent scores on the CMS to nondelinquents of approximately the same age and sex. If compulsive masculinity contributes to violent behavior and, hence, delinquency, delinquent boys should score higher on the scale than nondelinquents.

Silverman (1970) in an unpublished doctoral dissertation proposes that compulsive masculinity is polarized along two factors, toughness and sexual athleticism. If this is true, then some data presenting this heterogeneity would be helpful. Perhaps two scores instead of one would be even more predictive of delinquency and background characteristics.

Although these issues are important and should be pursued if the CMS is to be used further, the scale appears to be a good instrument for measuring compulsive masculinity and predicting possible delinquent behavior.

REFERENCES

Parsons, T. Certain primary sources and patterns of aggression in the social structure of the western world. *Psychiatry,* 1947, *10,* 167–181.

Silverman, I. J. *Compulsive masculinity and delinquency.* Unpublished doctoral dissertation, Ohio State University, 1970.

Silverman, I. J., & Dinitz, S. Compulsive masculinity and delinquency: An empirical investigation. *Criminology,* 1974, *11,* 498–515.

COMPULSIVE MASCULINITY SCALE

Directions: The following group of statements describes things that boys do. If you feel that a statement describes you, check "Like me." If a statement does not describe you, check "Not like me."

	Like me	Not like me
1. I am known in my neighborhood as a "mean dude."		
2. I can really signify a guy.		
3. I know how to steal a car.		
4. I am really hip to new dance steps.		
5. I would bust a guy who gets in my way.		
6. I know how to rob a store without getting caught.		
7. I like to go out drinking.		
8. I hang around with a group of guys that can fight well without blades and chains.		
9. I think women are only good for one purpose.		

		Like me	Not like me
10.	I can take a beating like a man.		
11.	Nobody tells me what to do.		
12.	I never let anyone tell me how late I can stay out.		
13.	I would never let a woman tell me what to do.		
14.	I would never back out of a fight.		
15.	I will stamp a guy who beats up my friends.		
16.	I am known in my neighborhood as a "hard" guy.		
17.	I know how to hold my booze.		
18.	I never let another guy get one up on me.		
19.	I would burn any guy who gets in my way.		
20.	I like to shoot the breeze (bull) with the guys.		
21.	I'm not afraid of nobody.		
22.	I always carry a blade in order to be ready for trouble.		
23.	I only go to school when I feel like it.		
24.	I never hang around with punks.		
25.	I would bust a guy who insulted my girl.		
26.	I know how to carry a weapon without anybody knowing that I have it.		
27.	I know how to get booze when I want it.		
28.	I often destroy things just for the hell of it.		
29.	I only hang around with tough guys.		
30.	I have the name of my girl tattooed some place on my body.		
31.	I take what I want from other people.		
32.	I really know how to smooth talk a girl.		

Hopelessness Scale

Development and Characteristics

The *Hopelessness Scale* (HS) was designed (Beck, Weissman, Lester, & Trexler, 1974) to quantify the experience of hopelessness. The 20-item test contains 9 items from a semantic differential type test (Heimberg, 1961) that measures attitudes about the future and 11 pessimistic statements made by psychiatric

GENERAL SCALES

patients whose cases were judged by clinicians as hopeless. After modifications in the wording of some items, a 20-item, true-false-type test resulted.

Response Mode

This is a true-false test. The respondent reads each statement, then decides whether he or she believes it to be correct or incorrect. He or she may write true or false or check the appropriate box on an answer sheet.

Scoring

Each item receives a score of 1 when it is answered in the direction of hopelessness and 0 when answered otherwise. The HS score is the sum of the item scores. Therefore, the higher an individual's score the more "hopeless" he or she is believed to feel.

Norms

No norms were presented.

TABLE 78. Reliability Estimates for the Hopelessness Scale

Item	r item-total
1	.69
2	.63
3	.49
4	.39
5	.50
6	.62
7	.72
8	.51
9	.64
10	.49
11	.76
12	.70
13	.66
14	.63
15	.74
16	.67
17	.72
18	.62
19	.70
20	.71

Reliability

Internal consistency, as measured by coefficient alpha (KR-20) for 294 hospitalized psychiatric patients, was .93. Table 78 lists item to total correlations for this sample.

Validity

Several attempts at validation have been undertaken. First, scores on HS were compared to independent ratings by clinicians for 23 outpatients in general medical practice and 62 hospitalized patients who had made recent suicidal attempts. The raters used an 8-point scale to estimate the degree to which the patient believed: (1) That he or she would never get well; (2) That he or she would not solve his or her problems; (3) That the future looked black; (4) That he or she had nothing to look forward to; and (5) That he or she would not achieve his or

TABLE 79. Varimax Rotated Factor Matrix of the Hopelessness Scale[a]

Item	Factor 1	Factor 2	Factor 3
1	.75	.25	.21
2	.49	.57	.02
3	.22	.50	.07
4	−.08	.11	.65
5	.45	.14	.25
6	.71	.24	.14
7	.39	.34	.54
8	.27	.07	.59
9	.16	.56	.41
10	.25	.16	.41
11	.40	.56	.39
12	.30	.50	.42
13	.74	.31	.07
14	.10	.49	.53
15	.64	.21	.47
16	.14	.80	.15
17	.45	.65	.18
18	.32	.18	.65
19	.50	.41	.37
20	.22	.74	.26
Percentage variance	41.7	6.2	5.6

[a] $N = 294$. Items with loadings greater than .50 were used to identify the meaning of each factor. All correlations were significant at .01 level.

her goals. Correlations of .74 ($p < .001$) and .62 ($p < .001$) were found between HS and clinical ratings for general practice patients and suicide attempters, respectively.

Next, the HS was compared to the *Stuart Future Test* (Stuart, 1962) for 59 depressed patients in a psychiatric unit of a general hospital. The resulting correlation coefficient, of .60, was significant at the .001 level. Also, when the HS scores for this sample were compared to their responses to the pessimism item on the Depression Inventory (DI), the correlation coefficient was .63 ($p < .001$).

Table 79 represents a factor analysis of the responses of 294 suicide attempters yielding three significant factors.

These factors seem to be measuring feelings about the future, loss of motivation, and future expectations.

Comments

This useful scale has been constructed in a thoughtful, systematic manner. Although no work to date has been reported for criminal justice uses of the scale, it seems to hold good promise for many applications. If hopelessness leads to alienation and aggression, it may serve as a predictor of illegal or destructive behavior. Further, rehabilitative efforts within criminal justice settings might be evaluated using this index. Finally, measuring adjustment to incarceration is a potential use of the HS.

REFERENCES

Beck, A. T., Weissman, A., Lester, D., & Trexler, L. The measurement of pessimism: The hopelessness scale. *Journal of Consulting Psychology*, 1974, 42, 861–865.

Stuart, J. L. *Intercorrelations of depressive tendencies, Time perspective, and cognitive style variables*. Unpublished doctoral dissertation, Vanderbilt University, 1962.

Heimberg, L. *Development and construct validation of an inventory for the measurement of future time perspective*. Unpublished master's thesis, Vanderbilt University, 1961.

HOPELESSNESS SCALE

For each statement put a check (✓) if it is true for you or a cross (X) if it is false for you.

Key	Item
True	2. I might as well give up because I can't make things better for myself.

	4.	I can't imagine what my life would be like in 10 years.
	7.	My future seems dark to me.
	9.	I just don't get the breaks, and there's no reason to believe I will in the future.
	11.	All I can see ahead of me is unpleasantness rather than pleasantness.
	12.	I don't expect to get what I really want.
	14.	Things just won't work out the way I want them to.
	16.	I never get what I want so it's foolish to want anything.
	17.	It is very unlikely that I will get any real satisfaction in the future.
	18.	The future seems vague and uncertain to me.
	20.	There's no use in really trying to get something I want because I probably won't get it.
False	1.	I look forward to the future with hope and enthusiasm.
	3.	When things are going badly, I am helped by knowing they can't stay that way forever.
	5.	I have enough time to accomplish the things I most want to do.
	6.	In the future, I expect to succeed in what concerns me most.
	8.	I expect to get more of the good things in life than the average person.
	10.	My past experiences have prepared me well for my future.
	15.	I have great faith in the future.
	19.	I can look forward to more good times than bad times.

Hostility and Aggression Scale

Development and Characteristics

The *Hostility and Aggression Scale* (HAS) was designed to measure cross-cultural differences in the ways individuals of different countries view and deal with hostility and aggression (Green & Santori, 1969). The scale began as a list of 60 items that were believed to reflect a wide range of values concerning social behavior. Emphasis was placed upon choosing items that related to hostile or aggressive activities.

An item analysis was performed on the responses obtained from 117 English subjects (74 male and 43 female) and 71 Italians (40 male and 31 female). The results indicated the existence of a set of items that could be combined to form a single homogeneous component. This was further confirmed when the results were factor analyzed.

More important than the factor analysis, however, is the fact that the factor structures between the two sets of responses (English and Italian) show many similarities. In only 12 items were the loadings for the Italians different from those of the English.

Response Mode

The respondent is requested to read each statement (in his or her native language) and note whether the statement is true for him or her.

Scoring

This scale is in an early stage of development and a standard scoring procedure has not been established. Only item responses are analyzed.

Norms

No scale norms are available.

Reliability

Although the items were factor analyzed, they were not clustered to form independent factors. This prohibits estimates of internal consistency. No estimates of temporal stability were reported.

Validity

The loadings of the items onto factors (or the principal components) could be used to form a single scale, but this has not been done. The items have been considered individually.

Support for the contention that Italians view hostility and aggression in much the same way as English people has been found. The similarity between the factor structure of the two samples is apparent. Only 12 items' factor loads were dissimilar enough to indicate a different response set.

In general, the items possess content validity. They should however, be subjected to a selection procedure that would eliminate items that have little to do with hostility and aggression (i.e., I hardly ever chew gum, I usually let escalators carry me without walking myself).

Comments

The field of criminal justice has an obvious dearth of scales indicating cross-cultural usage. For this reason, the HAS is a rarity. It provides a starting point for other researchers interested in cross-cultural considerations. There is little evidence of its reliability, and the support for validity comes strictly from item validity and the fact that the responses of Italians are similar to those of English people. The factor analysis and item analysis are good first steps, but they should be carried through to the item selection process. The elimination of useless items and the categorization of different factors could prove extremely useful in establishing construct validity.

In general, the HAS is still in an early stage of development, but represents an important effort in an area where little empirical research has yet been attempted.

REFERENCES

Green, R. T., & Santori, G. A cross-cultural study of hostility and aggression. *Peace Research,* 1969, *1,* 13–22.

HOSTILITY AND AGGRESSION SCALE

Instructions: For each of the following statements place a check (✓) if it is true for you and a cross (X) if it is false for you.

1. I hardly ever chew gum.
2. Most people are quite bright.
3. When someone goes to the front of a queue out of turn I do something about it.
4. Motor racing is a dull sport.
5. Power is important to most people.
6. I go to see horror films at the cinema.
7. If someone does me a bad turn I do feel obliged to pay him back.
8. Sometimes I will take a risk just for the fun of it.
9. I usually let escalators carry me, without walking myself.
10. It is best to forget about it when someone does you a bad turn.
11. I have strong feelings about the way sex is treated in our society.
12. Fighting back only provokes the other person still more.
13. If someone is continually talking in the cinema or theatre I complain.
14. I like to play practical jokes on my friends.
15. I avoid swearing as far as possible.
16. I believe that I sometimes grate my teeth when asleep.

GENERAL SCALES

17. If someone is rude to me I usually let it pass.
18. There is no need to hurt other people's feelings in order to get on in life.
19. As a child I quite enjoyed gnawing at a bone.
20. I have no strong feelings about Jews one way or the other.
21. Given the opportunity I would quite like to watch an execution.
22. Unless you fight for your rights no one will give them to you.
23. I have never wanted to kill anybody.
24. Most people try to get more out of life than they are willing to give in return.
25. I am satisfied with the way this country is run.
26. Justice does not depend a great deal on actual possession.
27. People are basically cruel.
28. I have no strong feelings one way or the other about the police.
29. Nearly every man has his price.
30. I feel strongly about the banning of certain books and films.
31. Boxing does not interest me at all.
32. I sometimes play at ducking people when bathing.
33. I lose my temper less often than most people.
34. I never bothered to write letters of complaint to a firm about poor service or shoddy goods.
35. I like to watch high waves breaking over a rocky shore.
36. Most people in authority are modest enough.
37. In any contest you must go all out to win, regardless of the rules.
38. There are times when I feel like picking a fight with someone.
39. I don't really mind people who throw their weight about.
40. It is a law of nature that the weakest should go to the wall.
41. Most people make friends just because they happen to meet someone they like.
42. I find it fairly easy to be patient, even with fools.
43. Most people preach one thing and do another.
44. I soon forgive people who let me down.
45. "Every man for himself" appeals strongly to many people.
46. If someone I did not like were laying down the law it would give me pleasure to take them down a peg or two.
47. As a child I did not mind doing as I was told.
48. I sometimes tell lies.
49. I never crack the joints of my fingers.
50. I enjoy a good argument.

52. I hardly ever crave excitement.
53. On occasion I have thought about committing suicide.
54. I like to shock conventional people.
55. There is a fair amount of justice in the world.
56. People should learn to stand on their own two feet.
57. I hold my views less strongly than most people.
58. I enjoy making decisions.
59. I am not in the least interested in the idea of firing a gun.
60. I would rather lose my sight than my hearing.

MEANS-ENDS PROBLEM-SOLVING PROCEDURE

Development and Characteristics

The *Means-Ends Problem-Solving Procedure* (MEPSP) is designed to assess both the qualitative and quantitative aspects of an individual's ability to address himself or herself to, and to conceptualize effective means of solving life problems. It has been used in a series of studies examining the role of effective problem-solving thinking in psychopathology.

The MEPSP began as a four-item set of imaginary stories that presented only a beginning and an end. The beginning tells about a situation in which a person is trying to achieve some goal, and the ending is the achievement of the goal. The respondent is asked to fill in the middle and tell how the ending was accomplished. The test developers (Platt, Spivack, & Bloom, 1971) feel that the way the stories are completed reveal the level at which individuals are solving their own life problems.

This procedure was tested using six items. The subjects' (normal adolescents) responses were ranked (by raters) based on the extent to which they reflected "means-ends thinking." Four items showed enough intercorrelation to be considered homogeneous items.

The scoring procedure was systematized, and the scale was administered to another group of normal adolescents and a group of "acting-out" adolescents at a residential treatment center for disturbed boys. The items were scored according to: "individual steps in problem solving (means), awareness of potential obstacles and awareness of the passage of time" (Platt *et al.*, 1971, p. 3). Six similar items also have been tested (by comparing normal and "acting-out" adolescents) and added to the previous four, yielding a 10-item scale.

Response Mode

Respondents are asked to read the beginning and end, then to "make up" the middle, describing how the goals were attained.

Scoring

Scoring may proceed along two lines, quantitative or qualitative. The first requires that the tester count the number of "relevant means" noted in the stories (those that directly facilitate the achievement of the goal) and divide this by the total number of responses described (relevant means plus any other story-directed response). This yields a "relevancy ratio."

Qualitative scoring is accomplished by noting the number of responses which fall into each of the following categories: (1) relevant means, (2) other story-directed responses, (3) enumerations of means (elaborations or additional explanations of steps involved in a mean), (4) obstacles and enumerations of obstacles (the notation of difficulties involved in the attainment of the goal), and (5) time (the mention of specific amounts of time passed during phases of the goal attainment). Content analyses of these dimensions are believed to offer insight into the level at which the respondent is operating.

Norms

Several sets of norms have been established. Tables 80 and 81 present norms on two measures of means-ends thinking that were selected for their relevance to the present discussion.

As the developers predicted, those individuals who have been institutionalized showed less effectiveness in providing the means to goal attainment. Note that those individuals being processed by the correctional system have scores that indicate more "means-ends thinking" than psychiatric patients, but less than other civilian groups.

Reliability

A test–retest Spearman *rho* of .585 was found for a group of 15 institutionalized adolescent girls ($\bar{X}$ age = 15.1) when retested after 2.5 weeks. Interrater reliabilities for number of means is .98 and for content areas is .84 (for two trained student raters).

Validity

The MEPSP has been able to discriminate between psychiatric patients and normals (Platt & Spivack, 1971). Additionally, when MEPSP was correlated with

TABLE 80. Relevancy Scores[a]

Sample (female)	Graduate students (N = 23)	State university upperclassmen (N = 31)	Student beauticians (N = 44)	Hospital employees (N = 45)	Acute psychiatric inpatients (N = 23)	Psychiatric outpatients (extended care) (N = 32)
Story	$\bar{X}$	$\bar{X}$	$\bar{X}$	$\bar{X}$	$\bar{X}$	$\bar{X}$
1	1.00	.96	.93	.91	.85	.40
2	1.00	.95	.92	.97	.68	.56
3	1.00	.97	.98	.80	.59	.69
4	1.00	.99	1.00	.91	.95	.68
5	1.00	.96	.97	.65	.53	.42
6	1.00	.99	.98	.96	.67	.65
7	1.00	.96	.89	.72	.88	.41
8	1.00	.93	.93	.89	.77	.64
9	1.00	.97	.85	.77	.27	.50
All stories	1.00	.96	.94	.84	.69	.55

[a] Ratio of relevant means/all story-directed responses, that is, means + irrelevant means (IM) + "no means" (NM).

GENERAL SCALES

TABLE 81. Number of Relevant Means Responses

Sample (male) Story	State university upperclassmen (N = 38)			Military college students (freshmen) (N = 28)			Hospital employees (N = 16)			Penitentiary inmates (N = 54)			Reformatory inmates (N = 36)		
	$\bar{X}$	SD	Range	$\bar{X}$	SD	Range	$\bar{X}$	SD	Range	$\bar{X}$	SD	Range	$\bar{X}$	SD	Range
1	2.00	1.17	0–4	1.78	1.16	0–5	1.50	.82	0–3	a	—	—	1.14	.83	0–3
2	2.79	1.47	0–6	1.96	1.24	0–4	1.81	—	0–3	1.26	.96	0–3	1.47	.93	0–3
3	2.10	1.16	0–5	1.37	.77	0–3	1.50	.52	0–2	.93	.64	0–2	1.06	.95	0–3
4	2.42	1.28	0–4	1.25	1.10	0–4	1.62	.81	0–3	1.04	.67	0–2	1.53	.84	0–3
5	1.62	1.01	0–4	1.47	1.29	0–5	.94	.85	0–2	a	—	—	a	—	—
6	3.66	1.67	0–6	2.25	1.56	0–5	2.06	1.23	0–4	1.52	1.00	0–3	1.72	1.06	0–4
7	2.05	1.43	0–6	1.91	1.61	0–7	.69	.66	0–2	.68	.65	0–2	1.06	.60	0–2
8	2.16	1.17	0–5	1.41	.91	0–3	1.33	.98	0–3	1.30	.92	0–2	1.27	.76	0–3
9	1.15	.76	0–3	1.00	.75	0–2	.75	.45	0–1	.81	.48	0–2	.86	.52	0–2
All stories	2.49			1.60			1.36			1.08			1.26		

[a] This story was not administered to this group.

social competence using 103 psychiatric patients as subjects, the results indicated that "subjects with higher social competence scores tended to have greater numbers of means as well as a greater proportion of relevant problem-solving responses" (Platt et al.,1971, p. 6).

Comments

This scale has been used predominately as an indicator of psychopathic thinking, but as the norms section shows, it discriminates prison inmates from others as well.

One might question whether there is a relationship between MEPSP and intelligence. When compared to the *Scholastic Aptitude Test* ($N = 19$ college males and 18 females), the *California Mental Maturity Test* ($N = 44$ female beauticians), the *Quick Test of Intelligence* ($N = 28$ male, military college freshmen), *Beta IQ* ($N = 52$ male prison inmates), and the *Preference for Complexity-Simplicity Test* ($N = 39$ male prison inmates), the correlations were within the "weak" to "no relationship" range.

Reliability is minimally acceptable, and support for validity is adequate, although the MEPSP has not been validated for applications in criminal justice. This approach, however, is reasonable and seems to hold promise in determining ways by which individuals deal with life problems.

REFERENCES

Platt, J., Spivack, G., & Bloom, M. *Means-ends problem-solving procedure: Manual and tentative norms*. Philadelphia: Department of Mental Health Sciences, Hahnemann Medical College and Hospital, 1971.

Platt, J. J., & Spivack, G. *The content of problem-solving thinking in psychiatric patients and controls*. Unpublished manuscript, Hahnemann Medical College and Hospital, 1971.

MEANS-END PROBLEM-SOLVING PROCEDURE*

Instructions:† In this procedure we are interested in your imagination. You are to make up some stories. For each story you will be given the beginning of the story and how the story ends. Your job is to make up a

---

* The male form is presented here. The female form is identical except for the sex of the protagonist.

† The MEPS can be either self- or E-administered. The educational background, motivational level, and general intellectual competence of the S should be taken into account in deciding which method to use. The MEPS has always been E-administered when given to psychiatric patients and educationally limited controls. Both self- and E-administered forms have been used with S's and no significant differences in mean story length or scores have been found as a result of the two methods of administration.

story that connects the beginning that is given you with the ending given you. In other words, you will make up the middle of the story. Write <u>at least</u> one paragraph for each story.

1. Mr. A. was listening to the people speak at a meeting about how to make things better in his neighborhood. He wanted to say something important and have a chance to be a leader too. The story ends with him being elected leader and presenting a speech. You begin the story at the meeting where he wanted to have a chance to be a leader.

2. H. loved his girlfriend very much, but they had many arguments. One day she left him. H. wanted things to be better. The story ends with everything fine between him and his girlfriend. You begin the story with his girlfriend leaving him after an argument.

3. Mr. P. came home after shopping and found that he had lost his new watch. He was very upset about it. The story ends with Mr. P. finding his watch and feeling good about it. You begin the story where Mr. P. found that he had lost his watch.

4. Mr. C. had just moved in that day and didn't know anyone. Mr. C. wanted to have friends in the neighborhood. The story ends with Mr. C. having many good friends and feeling at home in the neighborhood. You begin the story with Mr. C. in his room immediately after arriving in the neighborhood.

5. During the Nazi occupation a man's wife and children were viciously tortured and killed by an SS trooper, and the man swore revenge. The story begins one day after the war, when the man enters a restaurant and sees the ex-SS trooper. The story ends with the man killing the SS trooper. You begin when he sees the SS trooper.

6. One day Al saw a beautiful girl he had never seen before while eating in a restaurant. He was immediately attracted to her. The story ends when they get married. You begin when Al first notices the girl in the restaurant.

7. Bob needed money badly. The story begins one day when he notices a valuable diamond in a shop window. Bob decides to steal it. The story ends when he succeeds in stealing the diamond. You begin when he sees the diamond.

8. John noticed that his friends seemed to be avoiding him. John wanted to have friends and be liked. The story ends when John's friends like him again. You begin where he first notices his friends avoiding him.

9. One day George was standing around with some other people when one of them said something very nasty to George. George got very mad. George got so mad he decided to get even with the other person. The story ends with George happy because he got even. You begin the story when George decided to get even.

10. Joe is having trouble getting along with the foreman on his job. Joe is very unhappy about this. The story ends with Joe's foreman liking him. You begin the story where Joe isn't getting along with his foreman.

Reaction Inventory: ANGER

Development and Characteristics

The *Reaction Inventory-ANGER* (RIA) was designed to measure the degree to which stimulus situations may elicit anger (Evans & Stangeland, 1971). It is assumed that anger is stimulus specific and that aggression is merely a behavioral method used to reduce anger. If these assumptions are true, an instrument that can indicate ease of anger elicitation would be quite useful for both basic research and for diagnostic purposes.

The scale was constructed using a variation of the Likert-format in which each item sets up a situation that might make people angry. From a pool of 200 items, 76 were selected on an intuitive basis. The respondent is instructed to indicate how much he or she would be angered by the situation on a 5-point scale ranging from "not at all" to "very much."

A factor analysis using varimax rotation suggested 10 dimensions. These factors, the percentage of variance they account for, and those items that loaded 0.5 or greater on them are as follows:

(1) *Minor chance annoyances* (5.7%): 23. The telephone or doorbell ringing when you are busy at something, .62; 22. Running out of something you need at the moment, .59; 29. Missing an activity that you really wanted to attend, .59; 24. Not having enough money to buy something, .56; 25. Not having the right change for the telephone or parking meter, .55; 30. Finding out about something you would have liked to have seen after leaving a place, .50.

(2) *Destructive people* (5.5%): 34. People who litter public areas, .67; 32. Destructive people, .60; 27. Someone driving carelessly, .59; 28. Having to do something in a way which you know is inefficient, .55; 2. People being cruel to children, .51.

(3) *Unnecessary delays* (4.8%): 50. Being forced to repeat something several times, .65; 49. People who don't understand something you're trying to explain, .55; 38. Long waits for service in a restaurant, .54.

(4) *Inconsiderate people* (3.6%): 1. People pushing into line, .55.

(5) *Self-opinionated people* (7.5%): 69. People who think they are always right, .75; 55. People who think they know it all, .72; 70. Phony people, .71; 46. People who brag about things, .69; 68. People who speak on subjects they know nothing about, .58; 67. Ill-mannered people, .57.

(6) *Frustration in business* (6.0%): 43. Being cheated in a business transaction, .70; 74. Finding that someone has overcharged for services, .68; 71. Stores that fail to back their merchandise, .67; 64. Being underpaid in a job, .60; 61. Servicemen failing to repair things, .53.

(7) *Criticism* (5.2%): 76. Being teased about your faults, .67; 57. People trying to better you, .60; 53. Criticism, .59; 56. People being sarcastic toward you, .58.

(8) *Major chance annoyances* (6.1%): 4. Locking your keys in the car, .66; 9. Having things spilled on new clothes, .62; 8. Getting halfway to your destination and having forgot something, 61; 12. Running out of gas,

.61; 13. Being stuck in traffic when you're late, .54; 17. Losing money or valuables, .52.
(9) *People being personal* (2.6%): 10. People asking personal questions, .67; 16. People gossiping, .50.
(10) *Authority* (3.4%): 37. Having your movements restricted, .66; 44. Being forced to do something you don't want to do, .60; 54. Having to take orders, .52.

Response Mode

The respondent is asked to read each item and judge whether the situation would anger him or her "not at all," "a little," "a fair amount," "much," or "very much."

Scoring

The scale is scored on a separate answer sheet (which follows). Each item is scored from 1 ("not at all") to 5 ("very much"). Items are then summed to obtain a total score.

Norms

No norms are available.

Reliability

Internal consistency was measured in the form of item to test correlation coefficients. The mean of these was .46. Using this coefficient and the procedure outlined by Gaylord (1969), internal test reliability was estimated to be 0.95.

Validity

Since the author presumes a positive relationship between the frequency and strength of anger producing situations and the conventional conception of aggression, the correlations of .52 and .57 (two separate samples) with the *Buss-Durkee Inventory on Aggression* indicate concurrent validity.

Comments

This scale was constructed using appropriate techniques that tend to indicate that it can reliably do what it purports to do. It should be a useful instrument, although the theoretical basis for the connection between anger and aggression needs to be better developed.

REFERENCES

Evans, D. R., & Stangeland, M. Development of the reaction inventory to measure anger. *Psychological Reports,* 1971, *21,* 412–414.

Gaylord, R. H. Estimating test reliability from the item–test correlations. *Educational and Psychological Measurement,* 1969, *29,* 303–304.

THE REACTION INVENTORY: ANGER

Directions: The items in this questionnaire refer to things and experiences that may cause anger or other unpleasant feelings. On the separate answer sheet write the number of each item in the column that describes how much you get angered by it.

1. People pushing into line.
2. People being cruel to children.
3. People who destroy borrowed things.
4. Locking your keys in the car.
5. Waiting for someone who is late or doesn't show up.
6. People who are loud and obnoxious.
7. Injuring yourself.
8. Getting halfway to your destination and having forgot something.
9. Having things spilled on new clothes.
10. People asking personal questions.
11. Someone breaking something you value.
12. Running out of gas.
13. Being stuck in traffic when you're late.
14. People acting as though you are stupid.
15. Rude sales clerks.
16. People gossiping.
17. Losing money or valuables.
18. Waiting for a parking spot and having someone take it.
19. TV breaking down in the midst of a favorite program.

GENERAL SCALES

20. People making loud noises when you are trying to sleep.
21. Finding someone has lied to you.
22. Running out of something you need at the moment.
23. The telephone or doorbell ringing when you are busy at something.
24. Not having enough money to buy something.
25. Not having the right change for the telephone or parking meter.
26. Guests who arrive around meal time.
27. Someone driving carelessly.
28. Having to do something in a way which you know is inefficient.
29. Missing an activity that you really wanted to attend.
30. Finding out about something you would have liked to have seen after leaving a place.
31. People who don't control their children in public.
32. Destructive people.
33. Loud noises such as cars or motorcycles with no mufflers.
34. People who litter public areas.
35. People taking advantage of you.
36. Outdoor events being spoiled by bad weather.
37. Having your movements restricted.
38. Long waits for service in a restaurant.
39. Lazy people who won't do their share.
40. People complaining about things.
41. Windows that won't open.
42. Buying something, using it, and seeing it cheaper elsewhere.
43. Being cheated in a business transaction.
44. Being forced to do something you don't want to do.
45. Missing a bus, train, or plane.
46. People who brag about things.
47. Inaccurate newspaper articles.
48. Prejudiced people.
49. People who don't understand something you're trying to explain.
50. Being forced to repeat something several times.
51. Being interrupted.
52. Having to do something else when you're in a hurry.
53. Criticism.

54. Having to take orders.
55. Peole who think they know it all.
56. People being sarcastic toward you.
57. People trying to better you.
58. Unclean, smelly people.
59. People who can't follow your orders.
60. Breaking a tool in the midst of a job.
61. Servicemen failing to repair things.
62. People who are constantly fidgeting.
63. People who expect things done in their time, not yours.
64. Being underpaid on a job.
65. Seeing people's rights violated by authorities.
66. Having to re-do work.
67. Ill-mannered people.
68. People who speak on subjects they know nothing about.
69. People who think they are always right.
70. Phony people.
71. Stores that fail to back their merchandise.
72. Self-righteous people.
73. People who interfere in others' affairs.
74. Finding that someone has overcharged for services.
75. Being ignored by someone.
76. Being teased about your faults.

The Reaction Inventory Answer Sheet

	Not At All	A Little	A Fair Amount	Much	Very Much			Not At All	A Little	A Fair Amount	Much	Very Much
1.							39.					
2.							40.					
3.							41.					
4.							42.					
5.							43.					
6.							44.					

7.						45.					
8.						46.					
9.						47.					
10.						48.					
11.						49.					
12.						50.					
13.						51.					
14.						52.					
15.						53.					
16.						54.					
17.						55.					
18.						56.					
19.						57.					
20.						58.					
21.						59.					
22.						60.					
23.						61.					
24.						62.					
25.						63.					
26.						64.					
27.						65.					
28.						66.					
29.						67.					
30.						68.					
31.						69.					
32.						70.					
33.						71.					
34.						72.					
35.						73.					
36.						74.					
37.						75.					
38.						76.					

Self-Attitude Inventory

Development and Characteristics

The *Self-Attitude Inventory* (SAI), as designed by Bennett, Sorensen, and Forshay (1971), is a modified version of the self-esteem inventory developed by

Coopersmith (1967). The original version was prepared for adolescents, so changes were necessary when the scale was redesigned to measure the self-esteem of adults being processed by correctional institutions.

Coopersmith's (1967) scale contained a number of items that referred to childhood or adolescent activities. These were reworded for adults and yielded a test of 58 items. Eight of these were eliminated when an item analysis indicated a low item to total correlation for them. The result is a 50-item test that consists of statements about the respondent.

Response Mode

The scale is a paper-and-pencil test with statements about the respondent which he is asked to mark "like me" or "unlike me."

Scoring

The statements are worded so that, for 24 items, a "like me" response is indicative of high self-esteem and, for 26 items, "unlike me" indicates high self-esteem.

Norms

Bennett et al. (1971) report a modal score of 32 for 124 newly admitted inmates who had a mean age of 31.9 (SD = 10.65) and average educational level of 11.4 (SD = 1.14). Only those who showed a sixth-grade reading level or better were tested.

Reliability

The reliability estimates that were reported are presented in Table 82.

As can be seen, the reliabilities are quite adequate. There is some question about the reason for the sharp decline in reliability for the five-week interval.

TABLE 82. Reliability Estimates of the Self-Attitude Inventory

Reliability measure	N	r^a
Odd-even	95	.80
One-week interval	76	.77
Two-week interval	66	.80
Five-week interval	100	.60

[a] All r's significant beyond .01 level.

TABLE 83. Correlation between Self-Attitude Scores and Other Measures

Variable	N	r
Age	123	.09
Intelligence (AGCT)	60	.10
Tested grade placement (CAT)	113	.20[a]
Claimed grade placement	113	.26[b]

[a] Significant at the .05 level.
[b] Significant at the .01 level.

This decline may be due to the usual decrease in reliability over longer time periods, perhaps as a consequence of self-esteem decreases over time with incarcerations.

Validity

The items have content validity and Coopersmith (1967) reports high relationships between his version and ratings of high self-esteem.

In Table 83, Bennett et al. (1971) report the correlations between other variables and the SAI.

Even though the correlations between SAI and grade placement (tested and claimed) are statistically significant, the relationship is so weak that it is of little use as a predictor or as support for validity. However, grade placement would not be expected to correlate highly with self-esteem.

Comments

This instrument's predecessor has shown utility for children and adolescents. The SAI could be useful as an indicator of self-esteem for inmates, parolees, and probationers, but more evidence is needed for the validity of the scale on such individuals. The reliability is good and this version seems to be a promising mechanism for the area of criminal justice data gathering. Content validity appears satisfactory because of the SAI's developmental relationship with the Coopersmith (1967) inventory.

REFERENCES

Bennett, L.A., Sorensen, D.E., & Forshay, H. The application of self-esteem measures in a correctional setting: I. Reliability of the scale and relationship to other measures. *Journal of Research in Crime and Delinquency,* 1971, *8,* 1–9.

Coopersmith, S. *The antecedents of self-esteem.* San Francisco: W.H. Freeman & Company, 1967.

SELF ATTITUDE INVENTORY

Please mark each statement in the following way: If the statement describes how you usually feel, put a check (✔) in the column "Like me." If the statement does not describe how you usually feel, put a check (✔) in the column "Unlike me."

		Like me	Unlike me
1.	I spend a lot of time daydreaming.		x
2.	I'm pretty sure of myself.	x	
3.	I often wish I were someone else.		x
4.	I'm easy to like.	x	
5.	I never worry about anything.	x	
6.	My parents and I used to have a lot of fun together.	x	
7.	I wish I were younger.		x
8.	There are lots of things about myself I'd change if I could.		x
9.	I can make up my mind without too much trouble.	x	
10.	I'm a lot of fun to be with.	x	
11.	I get upset easily when dealing with others, especially with those close to me.		x
12.	I always do the right thing.	x	
13.	Someone always has to tell me what to do.		x
14.	It takes me a long time to get used to anything new.		x
15.	I'm often sorry for the things I do.		x
16.	I'm popular with people my own age.	x	
17.	I'm never unhappy.	x	
18.	I'm doing the best work that I can.	x	
19.	I give in easily.		x
20.	I can usually take care of myself.	x	
21.	I'm pretty happy.	x	
22.	I'm usually proud of what I am doing.	x	

GENERAL SCALES

		Like me	Unlike me
23.	My parents expect too much of me.		x
24.	I like everyone I know.	x	
25.	I understand myself.	x	
26.	It's pretty tough to be me.		x
27.	Things are all mixed up in my life.		x
28.	Younger fellows usually follow my ideas.	x	
29.	I never get scolded.	x	
30.	My parents understood me pretty well.	x	
31.	I can make up my mind and stick to it.	x	
32.	I really don't like being a male.		x
33.	I have a low opinion of myself.		x
34.	I don't like to be with other people.		x
35.	There are many times when I'd like to leave home.		x
36.	I'm never shy.	x	
37.	I often feel upset in school.		x
38.	I often feel ashamed of myself.		x
39.	I'm not as nice-looking as most people.		x
40.	If I have something to say, I usually say it.	x	
41.	The staff makes me feel I'm not good enough.		x
42.	I always tell the truth.	x	
43.	I don't care what happens to me.		x
44.	I'm a failure.		x
45.	Most people are better liked than I am.		x
46.	I usually felt as if my parents were pushing me.		x
47.	I always know what to say to people.	x	
48.	I get upset easily when I'm called down about something.		x
49.	Things usually don't bother me.	x	
50.	I can't be depended on.		x

x indicates an "Esteem" response.

GENERAL PERSONALITY ASSESSMENT: LISTINGS

The Adjective Checklist

Brown, B. S., Dupont, R. L., Kozel, N. J., & Spevacek, J. D. Staff conceptions of inmate characteristics: A comparison of treatment and custodial staffs at two differing institutions. *Criminology,* 1971, *9,* 316–329.

Gough, H. G., & Heilbrun, A. B. Adjective checklist manual. Palo Alto, Calif.: Consulting Psychologists' Press, 1965.

Hooke, J. F., & Krauss, H. H. Personality characteristics of successful police sergeant candidates. *The Journal of Criminal Law, Criminology, and Police Science,* 1971, *62,* 104–106.

The *Adjective Checklist* is a list of 300 adjectives designed to measure 15 separate personality traits. It has been used to assess ideal and average prison inmates and successful police position candidates, among other criminal justice applications.

Authoritarianism Scale (A Scale)

Newman, G. R., Articolo, D. J., & Trilling, C. Authoritarianism, religiosity and reactions to deviance. *Journal of Criminal Justice,* 1974, *2,* 249–259.

This 43-item, true-false scale was designed to measure authoritarianism while circumventing problems associated with the Eysenck and Adorno *Authoritarianism Scales.* Items that referred specifically to criminal and deviant acts were deleted in scale construction, to allow unbiased study of the relationship between authoritarianism and deviance control attitudes.

Balanced Dogmatism Scales

Ray, J. J. Balanced dogmatism scales. *Australian Journal of Psychiatry,* 1974, *26,* 9–14.

This scale is a 40-item, Likert-type instrument that was designed to measure dogmatism using equal numbers of items worded positively and negatively.

Barratt Impulsiveness Scale

Barratt, E. S. Factor analysis of some psychometric measures of impulsiveness and anxiety. *Psychological Reports,* 1965, *16,* 547–554.

This scale is an 85-item, forced-response instrument designed to measure the degree to which individuals make up their minds easily and act quickly on impulse.

Buss-Durkee Hostility Scale

Buss, A. H., & Durkee, A. An inventory for assessing different kinds of hostility. *Journal of Consulting Psychology,* 1957, *21,* 343–349.

This 75-item, true-false scale is designed to assess the following aspects of hostility: assault, indirect hostility, irritability, negativism, resentment, suspicion, verbal hostility, and guilt.

Cartoon Aggression Test

Patterson, G. A. A nonverbal technique for the assessment of aggression in children. *Child Development,* 1960, *31,* 643–653.

This is a nonverbal cartoon test designed to measure aggression in children. It consists of 12 cartoon stimulus cards used to elicit reactions from children concerning the actions they would take in the depicted situation.

Community Adaptation Schedule

Bartlett, F. E., Cook, P. E., & Price, A. C. The Community Adaptation Schedule: A validational study of federal prisoners and vocational students. *FCI Research Reports,* 1970, *2,* 1–7.

The *Community Adaptation Schedule* is a 217-item questionnaire intended to evaluate community mental health interventions, identify populations at risk, and assess effective clinical interventions. When administered to prisoners and technical school students, community adjustment was found to differ on a number of adaptation variables.

Edwards' Personal Preference Schedule

Edwards, A. L. *Edwards' Personal Preference Schedule.* New York: The Psychological Corporation, 1959.

This scale is a 225-item, forced-choice instrument designed to provide quick measures of relatively independent normal personality variables.

Eysenck Personality Inventory

Eysenck, S. B. G., & Eysenck, H. J. Crime and personality: Item analysis of questionnaire responses. *British Journal of Criminology,* 1971, *11,* 49–62.

This personality inventory is an 80-item, forced-choice scale designed to measure three factors reflecting the link between personality and criminal behavior. The factors are psychoticism, neuroticism, and extraversion.

F Scale and F Scale Revisions

Adorno, T. W., Frankel-Brunswik, E., Levinson, D. J., & Sanford, R. N. *The authoritarian personality.* New York: Norton, 1950.

Berkowitz, H. H., & Walkon, G. A forced choice form of the F Scale—Free of acquiescent response set. *Sociometry,* 1964, *27,* 57–65.

Christie, R., Havel, J., & Seidenberg, B. Is the F Scale irreversible? *Journal of Abnormal and Social Psychology,* 1958, *56,* 143–159.

Eysenck, H. J. *The psychology of politics.* London: Routledge & Kegan Paul, 1954.

This true-false scale was designed to measure authoritarianism, and such characteristics as cognitive rigidity and potential for aggression. It has had several revisions in response mode, item wording, and alternative definitions of authoritarianism.

Hand Test

Hoover, T. O. The Hand Test: Fifteen years later. *Journal of Personality Assessment,* 1978, *42,* 128–137.

Wagner, E. E. *The Hand Test: Manual for administration, scoring, and interpretation.* Springfield, Ill.: Charles C Thomas, 1962.

The *Hand Test* consists of nine stimulus cards, each with a drawing of a hand in an ambiguous position and a 10th blank card. It was designed to predict overt aggressive behavior. Sixteen scores are considered in various combinations to yield an "acting out score," a "withdrawal score," a "pathology score," and other measures.

Hogan Moral Conduct Scales

Hogan, R., & Dickstein, E. A measure of moral values. *Journal of Consulting and Clinical Psychology,* 1972, *39,* 210–214.

Hogan, R. Moral conduct and moral character: A psychological perspective. *Psychological Bulletin,* 1973, *79,* 217–232.

Hogan, R. Development of an empathy scale. *Journal of Consulting and Clinical Psychology,* 1969, *33,* 307–316.

As part of a theory of moral development, Hogan has developed an empathy scale, a survey of ethical attitudes, and a moral values measure. These instruments assess three of the five components in the moral conduct model.

Interpersonal Checklist

LaForge, R., & Suczek, R. F. The interpersonal dimension of personality: III. An interpersonal checklist. *Journal of Personality,* 1955, *24,* 94–112.

Leary, T. *Interpersonal diagnosis of personality.* New York: Ronald Press, 1957.

This scale is a 128-item list in which respondents record items descriptive of self, ideal self, mother, father, or other target persons. Data from the measures are drawn on dominant-submissive and love-hate dimensions, as defined by the interpersonal personality system.

Jourard Self-Disclosure Questionnaire

Brodsky, S. L., & Komaridis, G. V. Military prisonization. *Military Police Journal,* 1966, *15* (12), 8–9.
Jourard, S. M. *Self-disclosure: An experimental analysis of the transparent self.* New York: Wiley, 1971.
Parker, L. C., & Roth, M. C. The relationship between self-disclosure, personality, and a dimension of job performance of policemen. *Journal of Police Science and Administration,* 1973, *1,* 282–286.

Both 40- and 60-item, 4-response alternative, self-disclosure questionnaires are designed to assess degrees of personal revealing to mother, father, best same-sex friend, opposite-sex friend, and spouse. This instrument has been used as a measure of personal characteristics of police officers, prisoners, and other groups concerned with laws and justice.

Just World Scale

Rubin, A., & Peplaue, A. Belief in a just world and reactions to another's lot: A study of participants in the national draft lottery. *Journal of Social Issues,* 1973, *29,* 73–93.

The *Just World Scale* is a 16-item, agree-disagree instrument designed to measure the degree to which an individual believes that the occurrences in the world are fair and just.

Kahn Test of Symbol Arrangement

Kahn, T. C. Kahn Test of Symbol Arrangement: Clinical manual. *Perceptual and Motor Skills,* 1957, *7,* 97–168.
Kipper, D. A. Identifying habitual criminals by means of the Kahn Test of Symbol Arrangement. *Journal of Consulting and Clinical Psychology,* 1971, *37,* 151–154.

The *Kahn Test of Symbol Arrangement* (KTSA) calls for subjects arranging small symbol objects and then evaluating their reasons for the order and indicating what each object might symbolize. This test is intended to assess abstract thinking, and research indicates differences exist between criminal and noncriminal groups on the KTSA.

Maudsley Personality Inventory

Eysenck, H. J. *The Maudsley Personality Inventory: Manual.* San Diego, California: Educational and Industrial Testing Service, 1959.

Price, J. B. Some results on the Maudsley Personality Inventory from a sample of girls in Borstal. *British Journal of Criminology,* 1968, *8,* 383–401.

This 48-item scale follows the Eysenck theories of criminality and thus yields extraversion-intraversion and neuroticism scores. The more recent Eysenck, *Junior Maudsley,* and *New Maudsley Personality Inventory* are similar in goals and scores.

Miale-Holsopple Sentence Completion Test

Miale, F., & Holsopple, J. Q. *Sentence completion: A projective method for the study of personality.* Springfield, Ill.: Charles C Thomas, 1954.

Jenkins, R. L., & Blodgett, E. Prediction of success or failure of delinquent boys from sentence completion. *American Journal of Orthopsychiatry,* 1960, *30,* 741–756.

This 73-item sentence completion test has relatively long stems, compared to many other such tests. The median stem length is five words. There are six items that have direct relevance to offenders, including "When a criminal leaves the prison, he." Blind comparisons of Miale-Holsopple sentence completion results have been able to identify delinquent boys who were recidivists and those who were successes when returned to the community.

Mosher Incomplete Sentence Test (MIST)

Unpublished manuscript available from:
Donald L. Mosher,
Department of Psychology,
University of Connecticut,
Storrs, Connecticut 06268.

This 50-item, sentence-completion test draws heavily on stems related to aggression, sexuality, punishment and guilt. The stems include "If I felt like murdering someone" and "If I robbed a bank." The MIST is a widely used research tool, drawing on a structured scoring method and good evidence of reliability and validity. Its primary use has been for research with nonoffender populations, but some research has been done related to crime and delinquency issues and much of the content is justice related.

Offer Self-Image Questionnaire

Marohn, R. C., Offer, D., & Ostrov, E. Juvenile delinquents view their impulsivity. *American Journal of Psychiatry*, 1971, *128*, 50–55.

The *Offer Self-Image Questionnaire* is a 130-item self-administered personality inventory that yields 11 scales. It is used to measure the adjustment of teenage boys and girls between the ages of 14 and 18 and has been applied to delinquent populations.

Personal Orientation Inventory

Shostrom, E. L. *Manual for Personal Orientation Inventory*. San Diego: Educational & Testing Service, 1966.
Fisher, G. Felons' conception of societal self-actualization values. *Corrective Psychiatry*, 1973, *19*, 3–5.

The *Personal Orientation Inventory* (POI) is a 150-item scale designed to measure self-actualization within the theoretical framework of humanistic psychology. Research with the POI has indicated that offender males and delinquent males typically are below the normative means on most POI scales.

The Rokeach Dogmatism Scale

Guller, I. B. Higher education and policemen: Attitudinal differences between freshmen and senior police college students. *Journal of Criminal Law, Criminology, and Police Science*, 1972, *63*, 396–401.
Rokeach, M. *The open and closed mind*. New York: Basic Books, 1960.
Smith, A. B., Locke, B., & Walker, W. F. Authoritarianism in college and noncollege oriented police. *Journal of Criminal Law, Criminology, and Police Science*, 1967, *58*, 128–132.

Dogmatism or "closed-mindedness" refers to judging information on the basis of its source, and forming opinions from very limited information. The original *Rokeach Dogmatism Scale* is a 66-item, true-false questionnaire, and several revisions have been developed by various investigators. A major criminal justice application has been the study of dogmatism among police and offenders.

Rokeach Value Survey

Ball-Rokeach, S. Values and violence: A test of the subculture of violence thesis. *American Sociological Review*, 1973, *38*, 736–749.
Rokeach, M. *The nature of human values*. New York: Free Press, 1973.
Rokeach, M., Miller, M. G., & Snyder, J. A. The value gap between police and policed. *Journal of Social Issues*, 1971, *27*, 155–171.

The *Rokeach Value Survey* was designed to rank the "guiding principles of an individual's daily life." It consists of 18 instrumental values and 18 terminal values that are rank ordered by the respondents. This survey has been used in the study of values of young and adult offenders, and of criminal justice personnel.

Rotter I-E Scale

Rotter, J. B. Generalized expectancies for internal versus external control of reinforcement. *Psychological Monographs: General and Applied,* 1966, *80* (1 Whole No. 609).

This 29-item, forced-choice scale was designed to measure the degree to which an individual responded to internal versus external reinforcers. It has been applied frequently to offender populations.

Shapiro Adjective Checklist

Shapiro, J. L., & Gust, T. Counselor training for facilitative human relationships. *Counselor Education and Supervision,* 1974, *13,* 198–206.
Shapiro, J. L. *The Shapiro Adjective Checklist.* Unpublished manuscript, University of Hawaii at Manoa, undated.

This 39-item adjective checklist was designed to measure attributes of self, ideal self, or other specified targets; it has been used with criminal justice targets and sensitivity group participants. This instrument has been standardized on populations of incarcerated delinquent boys and girls.

Tennessee Self-Concept Scale (TSCS)

Fitts, W. H. *Manual for the Tennessee Self-Concept Scale.* Nashville: Counselor Recordings and Tests, 1965.
Hamner, W. T. *The self-concept of delinquents.* Nashville: Nashville Mental Health Center, 1968.
Joplin, G. H. Self-concept and the Highfields program. *Criminology,* 1972, *10,* 491–495.

This 100-item, true-false scale measures a general level of self-esteem, variability in self-judgments, uncertainty, conflict, and 24 other self-concept scores. The TSCS has been used frequently in research with delinquents.

Twenty Statements Test

Kuhn, M. H. &,McPartland, T. S. An empirical investigation of self-attitudes. *American Sociological Review,* 1954, *19,* 68–76.
Liu, W. T., & Fahey, F. Delinquency, self-esteem and social control: A retroductive analysis. *The American Catholic Sociological Review,* 1973, *24,* 3–12.

The *Twenty Statements Test* (TST) is intended as a direct measure of self-attitudes. Respondents are asked to give 20 answers to the question "Who am I?" The TST has been applied often to the study of delinquent populations.

Values Inventory for Children

Goldberg, L., & Guilford, J. S. Delinquent values: It's fun to break the rules. *Proceedings of the 80th Annual Convention of the American Psychological Association,* 1972, 237–238.

Guilford, J. S., & Gupta, W. Development of the Values Inventory for Children. *Proceedings of the 79th Annual Convention of the American Psychological Association,* 1971, 513–514.

The *Values Inventory for Children* is a 60-item pictorial-form instrument designed to elicit values that are meaningful to education and to the child. Factor analysis yielded eight factors, including "social conformity," "academic/health," "me first," and "masculinity". The inventory has been used to compare value orientations of delinquents with nondelinquents.

Zimmer Sentence Completion Test (ZSCT)

Zimmer, H. *Scoring manual for a sentence completion test of hostility, dependency, aggression anxiety, and projection of hostility* (2nd ed.). Athens: University of Georgia, 1964.

Kinzie, W., & Zimmer, H. On the measurement of hostility, aggression anxiety, projection and dependency. *Journal of Projective Techniques and Personality Assessment,* 1968, *32,* 388–391.

This 114-item sentence-completion test is directed particularly toward the measurement of hostility and aggression. Of the items 36 assess extrapunitive or intrapunitive hostility, while 15 more are intended to measure projection of hostility. The ZSCT correlates .71 with peer ratings of hostility. A scoring manual is available to allow objective scoring on the dimensions of hostility, aggression anxiety, projection of hostility, and dependency.

GENERAL SCALES—DESCRIPTION: REVIEWS

Awareness of Limited Opportunity Scale

Development and Characteristics

The *Awareness of Limited Opportunity Scale* (ALOS) was designed to measure the amount of perceived awareness of limited opportunity to advance within the middle class culture (Landis, Dinitz, & Reckless, 1963). It was developed along with the *Value Orientation Scale* in an effort to test the delinquency theory of Cloward and Ohlin (1960). Items for the ALOS were created to measure the degree of perceived blockage of life chances in fields such as education, occupation, power and influence, wealth, family, and neighborhood. A total of 126 items were developed. When the responses of 326 middle- and lower-class sixth- and ninth-grade boys and girls were compared, 14 items were found to differentiate between middle- and lower-class children.

Response Mode

The ALOS uses a standard 5-point Likert format in which the respondents are asked to decide whether they: (1) "strongly agree," (2) "agree," (3) are "neutral," (4) "disagree," or (5) "strongly disagree."

Scoring

All items are worded so that a high score indicates strong feelings about limited opportunity. For example, Item 2 is "a guy like me has a pretty good chance of going to college." Disagreement with this item indicates the awareness of limited opportunities, therefore, "strongly agree" would be given a score of 1, and "strongly disagree" a score of 5. The stem "Most people are better off than I" is phrased to indicate awareness of limited opportunity. Therefore, for this item a response of "strongly agree" would be given a score of 5, meaning high awareness of limited opportunity. A total ALOS score is then obtained by adding each of the individual item scores.

Norms

The average score of 492 public school boys was 30.85, while the average score for 515 incarcerated delinquent boys was 37.06. No measures of dispersion were reported.

Reliability

Landis *et al.* (1963) report a split half reliability coefficient of .84 for a sample of 1,030 adolescent boys and girls.

Validity

The ALOS appears to have adequate empirical validity. It has been shown (Landis & Scarpitti, 1965a,b) to differentiate between adolescents based on age, sex, and race, and to differentiate delinquent boys from nondelinquent boys.

When the ALOS was compared to the socialization scale of the *California*

Personality Inventory, they correlated $-.49$. That is, an increase in the awareness of limited opportunity produces a decrease in the socialization index. Also the ALOS was shown to correlate $-.31$ with the self concept scale of the *California Personality Inventory*.

Comments

The ALOS has acceptable reliability and evidence for its validity as a scale to measure individuals' perception of opportunity for a range of goals. The instrument has been carefully constructed and appears to be a useful research tool.

REFERENCES

Cloward, R. A., & Ohlin, L. E. *Delinquency and opportunity*. New York: The Free Press of Glencoe, 1960.

Landis, J. R., Dinitz, S., & Reckless, W. Implementing 2 theories of delinquency: Value orientation and awareness of limited opportunity. *Sociology and Social Research*, 1963, *47*, 408–416.

Landis, J. R., & Scarpitti, F. R. Perceptions regarding value orientation and legitimate opportunity: Delinquents and nondelinquents. *Social Forces*, 1965, *44*, 83–91. (a)

Landis, J. R., & Scarpitti, F. R. Delinquent and nondelinquent value orientation and opportunity awareness. *Criminologica*, 1965, *3*, 61–69. (b)

AWARENESS OF LIMITED OPPORTUNITY SCALE

Instructions: Following are some statements with which you may agree or disagree. Beside each statement write the symbol which best represents your position on that statement.

Symbol	Feeling
SA	Strongly Agree
A	Agree
N	Neutral
D	Disagree
SD	Strongly Disagree

1. I probably won't be able to do the kind of work that I want to do because I won't have enough education.
2. A guy like me has a pretty good chance of going to college.
3. Most people are better off than I am.

4. I'll never have as much opportunity to succeed as guys from other neighborhoods.
5. I am as well off as most people.
6. The world is usually good to guys like me.
7. Unless my family can afford to move out of our neighborhood, I won't get ahead very fast.
8. I won't be able to finish high school because my family will want me to get a job.
9. There is a good chance that some of my friends will have a lot of money.
10. My family can't give me the opportunities that most kids have.
11. I'll never have enough money to go to college.
12. There isn't much chance that a kid from my neighborhood will ever get ahead.
13. If a kid like me works hard he can get ahead.
14. Most successful men probably used illegal means to become successful.

Behavior Prediction Scale

Development and Characteristics

The *Behavior Prediction Scale* (BPS) was designed to measure the strength of the components involved in ethical decision making (Rettig, 1964). The scale is built around the "ethical risk" hypothesis, which postulates that unethical behavior varies predominately as a function of perceived risk (Rettig, 1964). Upon further consideration of the ethical decision making process, it was determined that considerations other than risk were also involved. The determinants are: (1) The expectancy that the offensive behavior will be instrumental in obtaining a gain *(Egn)*; (2) the magnitude of the gain *(RVgn)*; (3) the expectancy that the potential offender will be detected *(Ecs)*; (4) the severity of the censure that would follow detection *(RVcs)*; and (5) the severity of the offense. A sixth determinant, the reference group that would suffer the injurious consequences of the event, was also included initially, but was later dropped, since it proved to be of no significance in the previous studies (Rettig, 1964, p. 583).

A 32-item questionnaire was developed to measure these five determinants. Each question portrays a bank employee in conflict about taking money that does not belong to him from the bank. From the information given, the respondent predicts whether the employee would take the money. Each of the five determinants are present in either high or low levels in each item, and systematically varied throughout the scale. This factorial design of $2 \times 2 \times 2 \times 2 \times 2$ yielded a total of 32 items. Half were dropped, however, to exclude the dimension severity of offense, which was found to play a very little part in the decision to steal.

Sixteen final items remained. The following excerpt explains how each of the remaining four determinants were varied:

(1) The magnitude of gain *(RVgn)*: high—the money is needed for crucial operation; low—the money is needed to pay bills.
(2) The expectancy of gain *(Egn)*: high—the operation would definitely cure the illness, the money would pay all the bills; low—there was no guarantee that the operation would cure the illness, the money would pay only a small part of the debt.
(3) The severity of censure *(RVcs)*: high—the employee believed that if he or she were caught he or she would be publicly expelled from the bank and charged with criminal conduct; low—the employee thought he or she could settle the matter privately with the bank president.
(4) The expectancy of censure *(Ecs)*: high—the employee was sure his or her conduct would be detected; low—the employee was convinced his or her conduct would not be detected. (Rettig, 1964, pp. 584–585)

The questionnaire was administered to samples of 36 prisoners in a federal reformatory and 31 students from a nearby state university who were matched in age, sex, and socioeconomic status. The results indicated that the prisoners exercise much greater caution on each determinant than the students. Therefore, difference scores (e.g., the difference between the response to the high level of each determinant and the low level for that determinant) were used to compare the prisoner sample with the student sample.

Response Mode

The respondent is requested to read each question carefully and to make a prediction as to whether the bank employee would take the money, by circling a numerical score ranging from 0 (would definitely not take the money) to 6 (would definitely take the money). Each question includes the previously mentioned determinants *(Egn, RVgn, Ecs, RVcs)* presented in the same sequence, but varying the level of any one determinant from high to low (Rettig, 1964, p. 484).

Scoring

The responses to the eight items at the high and low levels are summed to produce a score on each determinant and the sum of the low items is subtracted from the sum of the high items. The possible range of scores is -48 to $+48$.

Norms

No normative information is available.

Reliability

Rettig (1964) reported reliability coefficients of .96 and .94 for prisoners and students, respectively, when corrected using the Kuder-Richardson formula. These values, however, were calculated for the original 32-item form of the scale. No reliability data are available for the 16-item version.

Validity

The design procedure of systematically varying each of the proposed determinants in the prediction model is evidence for content validity. Rettig (1964) found in general that prisoners, as compared to students, scored significantly lower for all variations of the determinants, thus appearing more defensive in their questionnaire responses. Difference scores or "sensitivity scores" for the severity of censure, were significantly greater ($p < .001$) than any of the other difference scores for prisoners. When compared with students, prisoners appeared relatively insensitive or inattentive to the expectancy and the magnitude of gain and to the expectancy of censure ($p < .05$). No significant differences, however, were obtained between students and prisoners on the severity of censure component.

Krauss, Coddington, and Smeltzer (1971) found that when first time offenders' (male youths confined for evaluation before disposition) responses were compared to inmates who had been returned because of some new behavior, the first offenders were more sensitive to expectancy of gain, while the other factors were not significantly different between the two groups. In general, these results are similar to those reported by Rettig (1964).

Krauss, Robinson, Janzen, and Cauthen (1972) compared the scores of 15 prisoners who had been defined as psychopathic on the basis of their *Minnesota Multiphasic Personality Inventory Profiles* with 15 nonpsychopathic prisoners of the same institution. Psychopathic prisoners indicated more risk taking than nonpsychopathic prisoners when expectancy of gain was high. Both groups of criminals were relatively insensitive to expectancy of censure.

These results are supportive of construct validity, especially when it is noted that normal subjects show sensitivity to all of the ethical risk components rather than only particular ones (Rettig & Rawson, 1963).

Comments

The BPS is a well constructed instrument that has been used by a number of researchers. There is considerable empirical evidence to support the construct validity of the BPS as a measure of sensitivity to determinants of ethical risk taking decision making. Content validity arises from the systematic variation of the measured determinants.

Internal consistency is good and lends support to the reliability of the test. This well-developed instrument has many research applications and lends itself to continued use in the study of risk taking and deterrence in crime.

REFERENCES

Krauss, H. H., Coddington, R. D., & Smeltzer, D. J. Ethical risk sensitivity of adolescents in legal difficulty: First contact and repeat contact groups. *Journal of Psychology,* 1971, *83,* 213–217.

Krauss, H. H., Robinson, I., Janzen, W., & Cauthen, N. Predictions of ethical risk taking by psychopathic and nonpsychopathic criminals. *Psychological Reports,* 1972, *30,* 83–88.

Rettig, S. Ethical risk sensitivity in male prisoners. *British Journal of Criminology,* 1964, *4,* 582–590.

Rettig, S., & Rawson, H. E. The risk hypothesis in predictive judgments of unethical behavior. *Journal of Abnormal and Social Psychology,* 1963, *66,* 243–248.

BEHAVIOR PREDICTION SCALE

This questionnaire presents 16 *different* situations, each situation portraying you in conflict about taking money which does not belong to you. You are to read each situation carefully and make a prediction as to whether or not you would take the money.

Each situation is followed by a set of numbers ranging from 0 to 6. Circle the *0* if you feel that you will *definitely not* take the money. Circle the *6* if you feel that you will *definitely yes* take the money. Circle the *3* if you feel that the chances are about equal that you will or will not take the money. Use the in-between numbers for the varying degree of certainty, *1* or *2* being more on the *no* side, *4* and *5* being more on the *yes* side.

Remember! Your choice of the numbers is to indicate whether or not you would take the money, *not* how wrong it would be to take the money. Although the 16 situations may appear to you very much alike at times, each situation *differs* in some respect from every other situation. Hence, DO NOT USE THE SAME NUMBER FOR EVERY QUESTION!

1. Assuming you are a bank employee who had to have some money in order to *lend it to other people* who needed it. You are thinking of *stealing* the money from the bank. The money you could get would be enough to help a *great number* of people. You are sure that your theft would go *unnoticed* by the bank. However, you knew that if you are caught, you would be *expelled* from the bank and charged with criminal conduct.

   definitely no   fifty-fifty   definitely yes
       0   1   2   3   4   5   6

2. Assuming you are a bank employee who had to have some money to pay for a crucial *medical operation* you needed. You are thinking of *stealing* the money from the bank. The operating surgeon *had guaranteed* you that the operation would cure your illness. You are sure that your theft would go *unnoticed* by the bank. However, you knew that if you are caught, you could be *expelled* from the bank and charged with criminal conduct.

   definitely no   fifty-fifty   definitely yes
       0   1   2   3   4   5   6

3. Assuming you are a bank employee who had to have some money in order to *lend it to other people* who needed it. You are thinking of *stealing* the money from the bank. The money you could get would be enough to help a *great number* of people. You are sure that your theft would go *unnoticed* by the bank. Furthermore, you are convinced that if you are caught, you could settle the matter *privately* with the bank president.

   definitely no   fifty-fifty   definitely yes
       0   1   2   3   4   5   6

4. Assuming you are a bank employee who had to have some money to pay for a crucial *medical operation* you needed. You are thinking of *stealing* the money from the bank. The operating surgeon *could not give you any guarantee* that the operation would cure your illness. You are sure that your theft *would be detected* sooner or later. However, you are convinced that if you are caught, you could settle the matter *privately* with the bank president.

   definitely no   fifty-fifty   definitely yes
       0   1   2   3   4   5   6

5. Assuming you are a bank employee who had to have some money to pay for a crucial *medical operation* you needed. You are thinking of *stealing* the money from the bank. The operating surgeon *could not give you any guarantee* that the operation would cure your illness. You are sure that your theft would go *unnoticed* by the bank. Furthermore, you are convinced that if you are caught, you could settle the matter *privately* with the bank president.

   definitely no   fifty-fifty   definitely yes
       0   1   2   3   4   5   6

6. Assuming you are a bank employee who had to have some money in order to *lend it to other people* who needed it. You are thinking of *stealing* the money from the bank. The money you could get would be enough to help a *great number* of people. However, you are sure that your theft *would be detected* sooner or later. However,

you are convinced that if you are caught, you could settle the matter *privately* with the bank president.

definitely no			fifty-fifty			definitely yes
0	1	2	3	4	5	6

7. Assuming you are a bank employee who had to have money to pay for a crucial *medical operation* you needed. You are thinking of *stealing* the money from the bank. The operating surgeon *could not give you any guarantee* that the operation would cure your illness. You are sure that your theft would go *unnoticed* by the bank. However, you knew that if you are caught, you would be *expelled* from the bank and charged with criminal conduct.

definitely no			fifty-fifty			definitely yes
0	1	2	3	4	5	6

8. Assuming you are a bank employee who had to have some money to pay for a crucial *medical operation* you needed. You are thinking of stealing the money from the bank. The operating surgeon *had guaranteed* you that the operation would cure your illness. However, you are sure that your theft *would be detected* sooner or later. Furthermore, you knew that if you are caught, you would be *expelled* from the bank and charged with criminal conduct.

definitely no			fifty-fifty			definitely yes
0	1	2	3	4	5	6

9. Assuming you are a bank employee who had to have some money in order to *lend it to other people* who needed it. You are thinking of *stealing* the money from the bank. The money you could get would only be enough to help a *very few* people. You are sure that your theft would go *unnoticed* by the bank. However, you knew that if you are caught, you would be *expelled* from the bank and charged with criminal conduct.

definitely no			fifty-fifty			definitely yes
0	1	2	3	4	5	6

10. Assuming you are a bank employee who had to have some money in order to *lend it to other people* who needed it. You are thinking of *stealing* the money from the bank. The money you could get would only be enough to help a *very few* people. However, you are convinced that your theft *would be detected* sooner or later. Furthermore, you knew that if you are caught, you would be *expelled* from the bank and charged with criminal conduct.

definitely no			fifty-fifty			definitely yes
0	1	2	3	4	5	6

11. Assuming you are a bank employee who had to have some money to pay for a crucial *medical operation* you needed. You are thinking of *stealing* the money from the bank. The operating surgeon *had guaranteed* you that the operation *would cure* your illness. You are sure that your theft *would be detected* sooner or later. However, you are convinced that if you are caught, you could settle the matter *privately* with the bank president.

definitely no			fifty-fifty			definitely yes
0	1	2	3	4	5	6

12. Assuming you are a bank employee who had to have some money to *lend it to other people* who needed it. You are thinking of *stealing* the money from the bank. The money you could get would only be enough to help a *very few* people. You are sure that your theft would go *unnoticed* by the bank. Furthermore, you are also certain that if you are caught, you could settle the matter *privately* with the bank president.

definitely no			fifty-fifty			definitely yes
0	1	2	3	4	5	6

13. Assuming you are a bank employee who had to have some money in order to *lend it to other people* who needed it. You are thinking of *stealing* the money from the bank. The money you could get would only be enough to help a *very* few people. You are sure that your theft *would be detected* by the bank sooner or later. However, you are convinced that if you are caught, you could settle the matter *privately* with the bank president.

definitely no			fifty-fifty			definitely yes
0	1	2	3	4	5	6

14. Assuming you are a bank employee who had to have some money to pay for a crucial *medical operation* you needed. You are thinking of *stealing* the money from the bank. The operating surgeon *could not give you any guarantee* that the operation *would cure* your illness. You are sure that your theft *would be detected* sooner or later. Furthermore, you knew that if you are caught, you would be *expelled* from the bank and charged with criminal conduct.

definitely no			fifty-fifty			definitely yes
0	1	2	3	4	5	6

15. Assuming you are a bank employee who had to have some money to pay for a crucial *medical operation* you needed. You are thinking of *stealing* the money from the bank. The operating surgeon *had guaranteed* you that the operation *would cure* your illness. You are sure that your theft would go *unnoticed* by the bank. Furthermore, you are convinced that if you are caught, you could settle the matter *privately* with the bank president.

definitely no			fifty-fifty			definitely yes
0	1	2	3	4	5	6

16. Assuming you are a bank employee who had to have some money in order to *lend it to other people* who needed it. You are thinking of *stealing* the money from the bank. The money you could get would be enough to help a *great number* of people. However, you are sure that your theft would be *detected* sooner or later. Furthermore, you knew that if you are caught, you would be *expelled* from the bank and charged with criminal conduct.

definitely no			fifty-fifty			definitely yes
0	1	2	3	4	5	6

Family-Change Scale

Development and Characteristics

The *Family-Change Scale* (FCS) was designed to measure "the various types of family change occurring within families" (Schneller, 1975a, p. 405). The developer suggests that incarceration of the "family head" can have severe effects on the social and psychological adjustment of the entire family.

The developer has defined three subscales within the FCS and constructed items for the measurement of each of these subscales. Of the 15-item scale 5 items are concerned with "social-acceptability-change," as indicated by number of friends gained or lost, quality of relationships with relatives, frequency of insults received because of the family head being incarcerated, amount of participation in social activities by family members, and the amount of embarrassment felt in public by family members as a result of having a prisoner in the family. Five items deal with "economic-change." These include changes in the family's income, housing, diet, wardrobe, and automobile. Finally, five items deal with "emotional-sexual-change." These pertain to needs for affection by family members, needs for companionship by family members, feeling of sexual satisfaction on the part of the wife as reflected in her desire for her husband, feeling of sexual satisfaction on the part of the wife as reflected in her interests in other men, and the amount of sexual satisfaction on the part of the wife as reflected in her desired frequency of conjugal visits with her husband (a hypothetical question) (Schneller, 1975b, pp. 30–31).

Response Mode

The FCS is conducted as an interview in which the 15 items are directed as questions toward the wife of an inmate. Some items require quantitative responses (e.g., number of friends gained or lost), while others seek qualitative, subjective judgements (e.g., sexual satisfaction of wife).

Scoring

The FCS is a Likert-type scale in which each item may receive a score from 1 to 5. Items are worded so that a low score (1 or 2) represents positive change after incarceration of the family head. A score of 3 represents no change. High scores (4 or 5) represent adverse changes due to incarceration of the head; that is, the higher the score for each item, the more adverse the changes which have occurred after incarceration of the family head. Since the FCS is an interview type scale, the rating of each item is done by the investigator who makes a decision as to the direction and severity of change.

Since all 15 items are scored in the same direction, that is, a higher score represents more adverse change, a total FCS score may be obtained by adding the 15 item scores. The social-acceptability-change score is represented by the total score of the five items within that scale (Items 1–5). The economic-change scale score is the total of Items 6–10 and the emotional-sexual-change score is represented by the total of Items 11–15.

Norms

Table 84 gives the mean score, the possible range of scores, and the observed range of scores for 93 wives of incarcerated men. The men were inmates of a medium security prison in the District of Columbia correctional system. All were black and had been incarcerated for five years or less at the time of the study.

Reliability

No measures of reliability were reported.

Validity

The FCS has been compared to 19 variables such as offense of husband, type of family income, and so forth. Of these 19, only two variables, type of marriage (common law versus civil) and marital adjustment before arrest (as measured by the *Locke-Short Marital Adjustment Scale*) showed statistically significant relationships. Type of marriage was statistically significantly related to the total family-change score and the sexual-emotional-change score. The *Marital Adjustment Scale* was related to the total-change score, economic-change score, and sexual-emotional-change score.

TABLE 84. Family Change Scores for 93 Wives of Prisoners

Scale	Scores		
	M	Possible range	Actual range
Family-Change Scale	52.9	15–75	29.5–68.5
Social-Acceptability Change Scale	15.7	5–25	8.5–21.5
Economic-Change Scale	17.0	5–25	7.0–25.0
Emotional-Sexual- Change Scale	20.2	5–25	9.0–25.0

Comments

The FCS has face validity as a measure of family changes related to social, economic, and sexual-emotional considerations. There has been, however, little support for the validity of the scale. Because only 2 of the 19 variables considered were significantly related to the FCS, results are only slightly better than chance. There is also concern over the limited generalizability of the norms and results from the sample. Only black inmates from the Washington, D.C. area were included in the sample. Further, there is some question as to the objectivity and interrater reliability of the scoring method.

REFERENCES

Schneller, D. P. Prisoners' families: A study of some social and psychological effects of incarceration on the families of Negro prisoners. *Criminology,* 1975, *12,* 402–412. (a)

Schneller, D. P. Some social and psychological effects of incarceration on families of Negro prisoners. *American Journal of Corrections,* 1975, 29–33. (b)

FAMILY-CHANGE SCALE

Note: No instructions were provided for this scale because the author obtained his data through an interview procedure. Any instructions which require the respondent to answer each question should suffice.

Social-Acceptability-Change

1. Number of friends (gained or lost because of family head).
2. Quality of relationships with relatives.
3. Number of insults received.
4. Amount of socializing in public.
5. Embarrassment.

Economic-Change

6. Amount of family income.
7. Housing.
8. Family diet (quality and quantity).
9. Family wardrobe.
10. Automobile.

Emotion-Sexual-Change

11. Affection.
12. Companionship.
13. Sexual satisfaction of wife (as reflected in desire for husband).
14. Sexual satisfaction of wife (as reflected in desire for other men).
15. Sexual satisfaction of wife (as reflected in desired frequency of conjugal visits — hypothetical question).

Value Orientation Scale

Development and Characteristics

The *Value Orientation Scale* (VOS) was designed to measure the degree of acceptance or rejection of middle-class values (Landis & Scarpitti, 1965a,b). It was first developed as a test of the theory that lower class boys reject middle class values and participate in street corner societies and gangs as a solution to their problems.

A pool of 250 value-orientation items was developed to measure the degree to which the individual has internalized such middle-class values as ambition, individual responsibility, rationality, motivation of manners and personality, control of physical aggression and violence, and respect for property (Landis & Scarpitti, 1965a). These items were then administered to 12- and 15-year-old middle- and lower-class boys and girls. Those items that differentiated most significantly between the middle- and lower-class samples were retained. Attempts were made to include items that fell within one of six general value dimensions. These were described as: (1) attitudes toward self-improvement, ambition and achievement, (2) attitudes toward the value of work and property, (3) attitudes toward aggression and physical violence, (4) attitudes toward responsibility and control of own destiny, (5) attitudes toward social and behavioral norms, such as manners, courtesy and social custom, and (6) attitudes toward social institutions, such as family, church, school and law.

A total of 13 value-orientation items were found to differentiate at a desired level. These items make up the final version of the VOS.

Response Mode

The VOS consists of a standard Likert-type format. A statement is made and the respondents are asked whether they "strongly agree," "agree," "are neutral," "disagree," or "strongly disagree."

Scoring

All the VOS items are worded so that a "strongly agree" response (1) indicates acceptance of middle class values, a "strongly disagree" response (5) indicates rejection of middle class values. Therefore, a total score is obtained by adding individual item scores. Higher total scores indicate greater rejection of middle class values.

Norms

The mean VOS score for 492 boys (sixth- through ninth-grade) was 33.7. The mean score for 515 boys incarcerated in the Fairfield School for delinquent boys was 38.8.

Reliability

Landis, Dinitz, and Reckless (1963) report a split half reliability coefficient of .84 for a sample of 1,030 boys and girls (white and black, middle- and lower-class ages,11–18).

Validity

The VOS showed significant differences between the scores of adolescent delinquent boys and adolescent boys from public schools (Landis & Scarpitti, 1965b). It was also able to differentiate between white and black boys and between 15-year-old and 16-year-old delinquent boys. Other differences reported include those due to age, sex, and socioeconomic status. In general, the results indicate a higher level of rejection of middle-class values from delinquents than from nondelinquents. When the VOS was correlated with the scores from the socialization scale of the *California Personality Inventory,* the results were in appropriate directions, but not statistically significant.

Comments

The VOS and the concepts underlying in it were originally designed to study the Cloward and Ohlin theory of delinquency. Content analysis and other validity evidence indicates that the VOS measures, to some degree, individuals' attitudes toward some middle-class values. Further, the reliability information is acceptable and the instrument seems to be a useful research scale.

REFERENCES

Landis, J. R., Dinitz, S., & Reckless, W. Implementing two theories of delinquency: Value orientation and awareness of limited opportunity. *Sociology and Social Research,* 1963, *47,* 408–416.

Landis, J. R., & Scarpitti, F. R. Perceptions regarding value orientation and legitimate opportunity: Delinquents and nondelinquents. *Social Forces,* 1965, *44,* 83–91. (a)

Landis, J. R., & Scarpitti, F. R. Delinquent and nondelinquent value orientation and opportunity awareness. *Criminologica,* 1965, *3,* 61–69. (b)

VALUE ORIENTATION SCALE

Instructions: Following are some statements with which you may agree or disagree. Beside each statement write the symbol which best represents your position on that statement.

Symbol	Feeling
SA	Strongly Agree
A	Agree
N	Neutral
D	Disagree
SD	Strongly Disagree

1. People should only keep promises when it is to their benefit.
2. Good manners are for sissies.
3. The law is always against the ordinary guy.
4. Only creeps go out for after-school activities.
5. It's mostly luck if one succeeds or fails.
6. Don't let anybody your size get by with anything.
7. Only squares take part in school clubs and school programs.
8. Money is meant to be spent.
9. It makes no difference whether you work or go on relief just so you get along.
10. Most police are crooked.
11. I should work hard only if I am paid enough for it.
12. The only thing I ought to be responsible for is myself.
13. It doesn't make much difference what a person tries to do; some folks are just lucky, others are not.

GENERAL SCALES—DESCRIPTION: LISTINGS

Deviance Control Scale

Newman, G. R., Articolo, D. J., & Trilling, C. Authoritarianism, religiosity and reactions to deviance. *Journal of Criminal Justice,* 1974, *2,* 249–259.

The *Deviance Control Scale* consists of descriptions of seven deviant acts; the respondents are asked to whom they would report the acts and how serious they are. This scale is designed to assess preferences for formal or informal deviance controls and judged seriousness of an act.

Role Behavior Test

Donnerwerth, G. V., Teichman, M., & Foa, V. G. Cognitive differentiation of self and parents in delinquent and nondelinquent girls. *British Journal of Social and Clinical Psychology,* 1973, *12,* 144–152.

Foa, U. G., & Foa, E. B. *Societal structures of the mind.* Springfield, Ill.: Charles C Thomas, 1975.

The *Role Behavior Test* was designed for recording interpersonal behavior in a given role pair, such as husband-wife, father-son, foreman-worker, pupil-teacher as perceived by a person in one of the two roles. Eight types of interpersonal behavior are assessed. Delinquent and nondelinquent youths have been compared with this test.

Semantic Differential Technique

Osgood, C. E., Suci, G. L., & Tannenbaum, P. H. *The measurement of meaning.* Urbana: University of Illinois Press, 1957.

Heskin, K. J., Bolton, N., & Smith, F. V. Measuring the attitudes of prisoners by the semantic differential. *British Journal of Social and Clinical Psychology,* 1973, *12,* 73–77.

Bhagat, M., & Fraser, W. I., Young offenders' image of self and surroundings: A semantic enquiry. *The British Journal of Psychiatry,* 1970, *117,* 381–387.

The *Semantic Differential Technique* provides the subject with a concept and a set of bipolar adjectives on which to assess that concept. This widely used research technique has been applied to offender populations in numerous studies.

Bibliography

Adams, D. K., & Horn, J. L. Nonoverlapping keys for the MMPI Scales. *Journal of Consulting Psychology,* 1965, *29,* 284.

Alker, H. A. Untitled review. In O.K. Buros (Ed.), *The eighth mental measurements yearbook: Volume 1.* Highland Park, N.J.: Gryphon, 1978.

Anastasi, A. *Psychological testing* (3rd ed.). New York: MacMillan, 1968.

American Correctional Association. The use of prisoners and detainees as subjects of human experimentation: Position statement officially adopted. *American Journal of Correction,* 1976, *38*(3), 14.

American Psychological Association. *Ethical principles in the conduct of research with human participants.* Washington, D.C.: Author, 1973.

American Psychological Association. *Standards for educational and psychological tests.* Washington, D.C.: Author, 1974.

Ballard, K. B., Fosen, R. H., Neiswonger, J., Fowler, R., Belasco, J., & Tyler, R. *Interpersonal Personality Inventory manual.* Vacaville, Calif.: Institute for the Study of Crime and Delinquency, California Medical Facility, 1963.

Beall, H. S., & Panton, J. H. *Development of a Prison Adjustment Scale (PAS) for the MMPI.* Unpublished paper, Central Prison, Raleigh, N.C., 1957.

Block, J. *The development of an MMPI-based scale to measure ego control.* Unpublished manuscript, Institute of Personality Assessment and Research, University of California, Berkeley, 1953.

Brodsky, S. L. Ethical issues for psychologists in corrections. In J. Monahan (Ed.), *Who is the client? The ethics of psychological intervention in the criminal justice system.* Washington, D. C.: American Psychological Association, 1980.

Buros, O. K. (Ed.). *The eighth mental measurements yearbook: Volume 1.* Highland Park, N.J.: Gryphon, 1978.

Butcher, J. N. (Ed.). *MMPI: Research developments and clinical applications.* New York: McGraw-Hill, 1969.

Caplan, N., & Nelson, S. D. On being useful: The nature and consequences of psychological research on social problems. *American Psychologist,* 1973, *28,* 199–211.

Clark, J. H. Application of the MMPI in differentiating AWOL recidivists from nonrecidivists. *Journal of Psychology,* 1948, *26,* 229–234.

Comrey, A. L., Baker, E., & Glaser, M. *A sourcebook for mental health measures.* Los Angeles: Human Interaction Research Institute, 1973.

Cook, W. W., & Medley, D. M. Proposed hostility and Pharisaic-virtue scales for the MMPI. *Journal of Applied Psychology,* 1954, *38,* 414–418.

Dahlstrom, W. G., Welsh, G. S., & Dahlstrom, L. E. *An MMPI handbook: Volume I, clinical interpretations.* Minneapolis: University of Minnesota Press, 1972.

Dahlstrom, W. G., Welsh, G. S., & Dahlstrom, L. E. *An MMPI handbook: Volume II, research applications.* Minneapolis: University of Minnesota Press, 1975.

Davis, K. R., & Sines, J. O. An antisocial behavior pattern associated with a specific MMPI profile. *Journal of Consulting and Clinical Psychology,* 1971, *36,* 229–234.

Eichman, W. J. Factored scales for the MMPI: A clinical and statistical manual. *Journal of Clinical Psychology,* 1962, *18,* 363–395.

Finney, J. C. Development of a new set of MMPI scales. *Psychological Reports,* 1965, *17,* 707–713.

Foulds, G. A., Caine, T. M., & Creasy, M. A. Aspects of extra and intrapunitive expression in mental illness. *Journal of Mental Science,* 1960, *106,* 599–610.

Fowler, R. D. *Development of a computerized MMPI reporting system for correctional use.* Unpublished manuscript, University of Alabama, 1974.

Goldman, B. A., & Saunders, J. L. *Directory of unpublished experimental mental measures, Volume I.* New York: Behavioral Publications, 1974.

Gottfredson, D. M. Research—who needs it? *Crime and Delinquency,* 1971, *17,* 11–22.

Gottfredson, D. M., & Ballard, K. B., Jr. *Social agency effectiveness study* (Report Number One). Vacaville, Calif.: Institute for the Study of Crime and Delinquency, California Medical Facility, September 1963.

Gough, H. D. *California Psychological Inventory Manual.* Palo Alto, Calif.: Consulting Psychologists Press, 1960.

Gough, H. G. *Manual for the California Psychological Inventory.* Palo Alto, Calif.: Consulting Psychologists Press, 1957.

Gough, H. G., McClosky, H., & Meehl, P. E. A personality scale for social responsibility. *Journal of Abnormal and Social Psychology,* 1952, *47,* 73–80.

Gough, H. G. *Reference handbook for the Gough Adjective Check List.* Berkeley, California: Personality Assessment and Research Center, 1955.

Gough, H. G. *California Psychological Inventory manual.* Palo Alto, Calif.: Consulting Psychologists Press, 1957.

Gough, H. G. *An assessment study of Air Force officers: Part IV, predictability of a composite criterion of officer effectiveness,* Technical Report no. 58-91 (IV), Dayton, 1958.

Gough, H. G. Theory and measurement of socialization. *Journal of Consulting Psychology,* 1960, *24,* 23–30.

Gough, H. G., McClosky, H., & Meehl, P. E. A personality scale for dominance. *Journal of Abnormal and Social Psychology,* 1951, *46,* 360–366.

Gough, H. G., & Peterson, D. R. The identification and measurement of predispositional factors in crime and delinquency. *Journal of Consulting Psychology,* 1952, *16,* 207–212.

Harris, R. E., & Lingoes, J. C. *Subscales for the MMPI: An aid to profile interpretation.* Unpublished manuscript, University of California, San Francisco, 1955. (Corrected version, 1968.)

Hathaway, S. R., & Monachesi, E. D. The personalities of predelinquent boys. *Journal of Criminal Law, Criminology, and Police Science,* 1957, *48,* 149–163.

Hathaway, S. R., & McKinley, J. C. A multiphasic personality schedule: I. Construction of the schedule. *Journal of Psychology,* 1940, *10,* 249–254.

Hirschi, T., & Selvin, C. *Delinquency research.* New York: The Free Press, 1967.

Johnson, J. H. A cross-validation of seventeen experimental MMPI scales related to antisocial behavior. *Journal of Clinical Psychology,* 1975, *31,* 564–565.

Johnson, O. G. *Tests and measurements in child development: Handbook II, volume I and II.* San Francisco: Jossey-Bass, 1976.

Kanun, C., & Monachesi, E. D. Delinquency and the validating scales of the MMPI. *Journal of Criminal Law and Criminology,* 1960, *50,* 525–534.

Kaplan, A. *The conduct of inquiry.* San Francisco: Chandler, 1964.

King, G. D. Untitled review. In O.K. Buros (Ed.), *The eighth mental measurements yearbook: Volume 1*. Highland Park, N.J.: Gryphon, 1978.

Kulik, J. A. *Interrelationships and sources of bias in several criteria of delinquency*. Unpublished doctoral dissertation, University of California, Berkeley, 1966.

Lake, D. G., Miles, B., & Earle, R. B., Jr. (Eds.). *Measuring human behavior*. New York: Columbia University Teachers College Press, 1973.

Lovegrove, S. A. The significance of three scales identifying a delinquent orientation among young Australian males. *Australian and New Zealand Journal of Criminology*, 1973, 6, 93–106.

Lyerly, S. B. *Handbook of Psychiatric Rating Scales* (2nd ed.). Washington, D.C.: U.S. Government Printing Office, 1973.

McKinley, J. C., & Hathaway, S. R. The MMPI: V, hysteria, hypomania and psychopathic deviate. *Journal of Applied Psychology*, 1944, 28, 153–174.

McLachlon, J. F. C. A hostility scale for Form R of the MMPI. *Journal of Clinical Psychology*, 1976, 32, 369–371.

Mahoney, M. J. *Scientist as subject: The psychological imperative*. Cambridge, Mass.: Ballinger, 1976.

Marks, P. A., Seeman, W., & Haller, D. L. *The actuarial use of the MMPI with adolescents and adults*. Baltimore: Williams & Wilkins, 1974.

Megargee, E. I. *The California Psychological Inventory handbook*. San Francisco: Jossey-Bass, 1972.

Megargee, E. I. (Ed.). A new classification system for criminal offenders. *Criminal Justice and Behavior*, 1977, 4, 107–216. (Special issue.)

Megargee, E. I., Cook, P. E., & Mendelsohn, G. A. Development and validation of an MMPI scale of assaultiveness in overcontrolled individuals. *Journal of Abnormal Psychology*, 1967, 72, 519–528.

Megargee, E. I., & Mendelsohn, G. A. A cross-validation of twelve MMPI indices of hostility and control. *Journal of Abnormal and Social Psychology*, 1962, 65, 431–438.

Miller, C. *Handbook of research design and social measurement*. New York: David McKay Co., Inc., 1970.

Mills, R. Personal communication, 1978.

Mitford, J. *Kind and usual punishment*. New York: Random House, 1973.

Monahan, J. (Ed.).*Who is the client? The ethics of psychological intervention in the criminal justice system*. Washington, D. C.: American Psychological Association, 1980.

National Advisory Commission on Criminal Justice Standards and Goals. *Program measurement and evaluation in criminal justice system*. Washington, D.C.: U.S. Government Printing Office, 1973.

Nehemkis, A., Macari, M. A., & Lettieri, D. V. (Eds.). *Drug abuse instrument handbook: Selected items for psychosocial drug research*. Washington, D.C.: U.S. Government Printing Office, 1976.

Office of the Secretary. HEW protection of human subjects: Proposed regulations in research involving prisoners. *Federal Register*, 1978, 43(3), 1050–1052.

O'Hagan, S. E. J. The validation of an MMPI scale of sociopathy. *FCI Research Reports*, 1972, 4(1), 1–26.

Palmer, L. I. Biomedical and behavioral research on prisoners: Public policy issues in human experimentation. In National Commission for the Protection of Human Subjects of Biomedical Research, *Research involving prisoners: Appendix to report and recommendations* (DHEW publication no. (05–76-132). Washington, D.C.: 1976.

Panton, J. H. *Manual for a Prison Classification Inventory (PCI) for the MMPI*. Raleigh: N.C. Department of Rehabilitation and Control, 1970.

Panton, J. H. Use of the MMPI as an index to successful parole. *Journal of Criminal Law, Criminology, and Police Science*, 1962, 53, 484–488.

Pirsig, R. *Zen and the art of motorcycle maintenance*. New York: Morrow, 1974.

Price, J. L. *Handbook of organizational measurement.* Lexington, Mass.: D. C. Heath & Co., 1972.
Robinson, J. P., & Shaver, R. *Measures of social psychological attitudes.* Ann Arbor: Institute for Social Research, University of Michigan, 1971.
Shaw, M. E., & Wright, M. *Scales for the measurement of attitudes.* New York: McGraw-Hill, 1967.
Siegel, S. M. The relationship of hostility to authoritarianism. *Journal of Abnormal and Social Psychology,* 1956, *52,* 368–372.
Simon, A., & Boyer, E. G. *Mirrors for behavior III: An anthology of observation instruments.* Wyncote, Pa.: Communication Materials Center, 1974.
Stein, K. B., Vadum, A. C., & Sarbin, T. R. Socialization and delinquency: A study of false negatives and false positives in prediction. *The Psychological Record,* 1970, *20,* 353–364.
Stein, K. B., Gough, H. G., & Sarbin, T. R. The dimensionality of the CPI Socialization Scale and an empirically derived typology among delinquent and nondelinquent boys. *Multivariate Behavioral Research,* 1966, *1,* 197–208.
Straus, M. A. *Family measurement techniques: Abstracts of published instruments, 1935–1965.* Minneapolis: University of Minnesota Press, 1969.
Sullivan, C. E., Grant, J. D., & Grant, M. Q. The development of interpersonal maturity: Applications to delinquency. *Psychiatry,* 1957, *20,* 373–385.
Tannenbaum, A. S., & Cooke, R. A. Research in prisons: A preliminary report. In National Commission for the Protection of Human Subjects in Biomedical and Behavioral Research, *Research involving prisoners: Appendix to report and recommendation* (DHEW publication no. (05–76-132). Washington, D.C.: 1976.
Toobert, S., Bartelme, K. F., & Jones, E. S. Some factors related to pedophilia. *International Journal of Social Psychiatry,* 1959, *4,* 272–279.
Tsubouchi, K., & Jenkins, R. L. Three types of delinquents: Their performance on MMPI and PCR. *Journal of Clinical Psychology,* 1969, *25,* 353–358.
Waldo, G. P., & Dinitz, S. Personality attributes of the criminal: An analysis of research studies, 1950–1965. *Journal of Research in Crime and Delinquency,* 1967, *4,* 185–202.
Welsh, G. S. An anxiety index and an internalization ratio for the MMPI. *Journal of Consulting Psychology,* 1952, *16,* 65–72. (Also reprinted in Welsh & Dahlstrom, *Basic readings.*)
Wiener, D. N., & Harmon, L. R. *Subtle and obvious keys for the MMPI: Their development* (Advisement Bulletin no. 16). Minneapolis: Regional Veterans Administration Office, 1946.

Index

Abbreviated Police Identification Scale, 95
Accessibility Scale (AcS), 373, 396–401
ADAPT Scale (Arrest Decisions As Precludes To), 95
Addiction and addicts. *See* Drug use
Adjective Checklist, 574
Adjustment to Prison Scale, 38
Adolescence
 delinquency, 370–371
 police and, 50–55, 60
 See also Children; Delinquency
African View of Crime Interview Schedule, 519
Age differences
 hostility/aggression, 490
 Miranda rights, 336–344
Aggression, 441, 442–445, 472, 576, 581
 anger and, 487–493, 564
 children, 575
 cross-cultural perspective on, 554–558
 parental punitiveness for, 504
 potential for, 473–482
 socioeconomic class and, 457–460
Aggression-Altruism Scale (AAS), 442–445
Aggression in Youth Scale (AYS), 457–460
Aggression Scale (AS), 487–493
Alcohol consumption, 387–391
 See also Drug use
Alienation Measure, 181
Alternative to Incarceration Client Questionnaire, 213
Altruism, 442
American Correctional Association, 26
American Psychological Association (APA), 14, 26
Anger, 487–498, 563–569
 See also Aggression; Hostility

Anger Dispositions Scale (ADS), 473–482
Anomic Authoritarianism Scale, 59, 62, 63
Antisocial tendencies, 402–403
Anxiety, 574
Approval of Illegal Behaviors Questionnaire, 367
Army Alpha Intelligence Test, 109
Arrest Decisions As Precludes To (ADAPT Scale), 95
Assaultiveness, 38, 237
Assaultive Sexual Offender Scale, 38
Assessment of I-Level Knowledge, 218
Attacks Against Persons Scale (AAPS), 241–242, 243, 244, 245
Attitude measurement, 22
Attitude scales (listings)
 corrections, 171–172
 courts and the law, 121–124
 crime and criminality, 456–457
 delinquency, 234
 general scales, 536–537
 law enforcement and the police, 69–71
Attitude scales (reviews)
 corrections, 150–171
 courts and the law, 97–121
 crime and criminality, 442–456
 delinquency, 225–234
 general scales, 524–535
 law enforcement and the police, 44–68
 offenders, 374–387
Attitudes toward Crime and Punishment, 519
Attitudes toward Deviant Behavior, 536
Attitudes toward Due Process and the Juvenile Court, 122
Attitudes toward Enforced Group Psychotherapy, 171

603

Attitudes toward Enforced Therapy Scale, 149
Attitudes toward Government Workers Scale, (ATGW), 524, 529–532
Attitudes toward Juvenile Delinquency Scale (ATJDS), 225–233
Attitudes toward Juvenile Detention Scale (ATJDSG), 150–160
Attitudes toward Law Enforcement, 69
Attitudes toward Legal Agencies, 122
Attitudes toward Offenders and Mental Patients (ATOMPS), 374–377
Attitudes toward Police (Diamond & Lobitz), 69
Attitudes toward Police (Larsen), 69
Attitudes toward Police Scale (ATPS) (Competence–Hostility), 44–46
Attitudes toward School Questionnaire, 320
Attitudes toward the Criminal Justice System, 69
Attitudes toward the Law (Thomas & Williams), 121–122
Attitudes toward the Legal System, 122
Attitudes toward the Police, 70
Attitudes toward Violence Scales, 456
Attitudes to Psychiatry Scale, 149, 171–172
Attitude toward Any Institution Scale (ATAIS), 524–529
Attitude toward Capital Punishment Scale (ATCPS), 97–99
Attitude toward Disabled Persons, 536
Attitude toward Law and Justice Scale (ATLJS), 107–111
Attitude toward Police Questionnaire, 50–55
Attitude toward Police Scale, 47–50
Attitude toward Prisoners Scale (ATPS), 377–380
Attitude toward Probation Officers, 123
Attitude toward Punishment of Criminals, 172
Attitude toward the Death Penalty, 171
Attitude toward the Law Scale (Katz), 104–107
Attitude toward the Law Scale (Martin & McConnell), 100–104
Attitude toward the Police, 70
Attitude toward the Prevalence of Stealing Scale (APSS), 441, 445–449
Authoritarianism, 117–121, 574, 576
Awareness of Limited Opportunity Scales (ALOS), 581–584

Balanced Dogmatism Scales, 574
Barratt Impulsiveness Scale, 574
Base Expectancy Scale, 207
Behavioral Coding System, 546
Behavior Cards (BC), 329–335
Behavior Prediction Scale (BPS), 584–590
Behavior ratings, 22
Behavior ratings (listings)
 correction, 178–179
 delinquency, 260–262
 law enforcement and police, 74–75
 offenders, 395–396
Behavior ratings (reviews)
 corrections, 172–178
 crime and criminality, 457–465
 delinquency, 234–260
 general scales, 537–546
 law enforcement and the police, 71–74
 offenders, 387–395
Behavioral Syndromes, 317
Beverly-Grant Opinion Schedule (BGOS), 262–264
Bimodal Personality Inventory, 12
Blacks, 100–104
Bogardus Social Distance Scales, 505
Bristol Social Adjustment Guides (BSAG), 537–542
Burgess Inmate Information Scale, 199
Burglary, 440
Buss-Durkee Hostility Inventory, 488
Buss-Durkee Hostility Scale, 575
Buss-Durkee Inventory on Aggression, 565
Buss Hostility Scale, 443

California F Scale, 112
California Index on Severity of Offenses, 176
California Psychological Inventory (CPI), 13, 31, 32–36, 37, 40, 358, 412, 483
Camp Elliot study, 412
Campus disturbances, 71
Capital punishment, 97–99, 111–114, 171, 227
Capital Punishment Attitude Questionnaire (CPAQ), 111–114
Cartoon Aggression Test, 575
Characteristics of Youngsters Questionnaire, 368
Child Care Work Questionnaire, 193
Child–Parent Relationship Scale, 536
Child-rearing practices, 317, 537

INDEX

Children
  aggression, 575
  behavior scales, 537–542
  criminal intent, 469–472
  parental punitiveness, 504–512
  police and, 83–86
  values, 581
  See also Adolescents; Delinquency; Group homes; Parents and family
Children's Perceptions of the Police Scale (CPPS), 83–86
Citizen Behavior Scale (CBS), 71, 72, 73
Citizens' Perception of Police Scale (CIPS), 86–89
CJC Questionnaire, 219
Classification, 193
  delinquency, 273–284, 317, 372
  offenders, 412–417
  recidivism, 440
Classification for Placement in Training Schools, 193
Client Telephone Questionnaire, 74
Clues Test, 81–83
Cluster analysis, 32
Cognition, 577
  See also Intelligence
Community Adaptation Schedule, 575
Community correction, 218
Community Follow-up Interview, 438
Community homes, 321
Competency Screening Test (CST), 124–128
Competency to Stand Trial Assessment Instrument (CTSTA), 128–132
Comprehensive Miranda Rights Scale (CMRS), 336–344
Compulsive Masculinity Scale (CMS), 546–550
Computer systems scales, 38
Confidentiality, 30
Conformity, 208–210
Cop Personality Questionnaire, 74
Cornell Index, 382
Correctional Institution Environment Scale (CIES), 149, 182–186
Correctional Officers' Interest Blank, 219
Correctional Staff Evaluation Scale (CSES), 264–267
Corrections, 149–223
  Attitudes toward Juvenile Detention (ATSDSG), 150–160
  behavior ratings listed, 178–179

Corrections *(cont.)*
  behavior ratings reviewed, 172–178
  Correctional Institutions Environment Scale (CIES), 182–186
  descriptions listed, 218–223
  descriptions reviewed, 208–218
  Hunch Parolability Scale (HPS), 194–198, 199
  Index of Conformity to Staff Expectations (ICSE), 208–210
  Institutional Life Questionnaire (ILQ), 160–164
  milieu ratings listed, 193–194
  milieu ratings reviewed, 182–192
  Organizational Structure and Prisonization Scale (OSPS), 211–214
  Parolability Questionnaire (PQ), 196, 198–206
  personality assessments listed, 181
  personality assessments reviewed, 179–181
  prediction scales listed, 206–208
  prediction scales reviewed, 194–206
  Prison Adjustment Index (PAI), 172–175
  Prison Profile Inventory (PPI), 186–192
  Prison Projective Test (PPT), 179–181
  Public Offender Counseling Inventory (POCI), 215–218
  Recidivism Outcome Index (ROI), 175–178
  Rehabilitation in Correctional Settings Attitude Scale (RICS), 164–171
  target institution, 22
Cottage group, 193
Counseling, 215–218
Courts and the law, 97–147
  Attitude toward Capital Punishment Scale (ATCPS), 97–99
  Attitude toward Law and Justice Scale (ATLJS), 107–111
  Attitude toward the Law Scale (ATLS) (Katz), 104–107
  Attitude toward the Law Scale (Martin & McConnell), 100–104
  Capital Punishment Attitude Questionnaire (CPAQ), 111–114
  Competency Screening Test (CST), 124–128
  Competency to Stand Trial Assessment Instrument (CTSTAI), 128–132
  descriptions listed, 146–147

Courts and the law (*cont.*)
  descriptions reviewed, 133–146
  Judicial Role Perception Scale (JRPS), 133–139
  Juvenile Court Volunteer Effectiveness Interview Scale (JCVEIS), 114–117
  Legal Attitudes Questionnaire (LAQ), 117–121
  milieu ratings listed, 133
  perceptions of, 521
  personality assessments reviewed, 124–132
  prediction measured listed, 133
  Probation Officer-Client Relationship Valence Scale (POCRVS), 139–142
  Problem Checklist (PC), 142–146
  target group, 22
Crime and criminality, 441–521
  Aggression in Youth Scale (AYS), 457–460
  Aggression Scale (AS), 487–493
  Anger Dispositions Scale (ADS), 473–482
  attitude scales listed, 456–457
  attitude scales reviewed, 442–456
  Attitude toward the Prevalence of Stealing (APSS), 445–449
  behavior ratings reviewed, 457–465
  causation theory, 466–469
  Criminal Attitude Scale (CAS), 450–453
  Criminality Level Index (CLI), 453–456
  Delinquency Potential Scale (DPS), 482–487
  description scales listed, 519–521
  description scales reviewed, 496–518
  Ethics Inventory (EI), 495–503
  Giannell Index of Criminality (GIC), 466–469
  Hostility Scale (HOS), 487–493
  Intentionality in Criminal Situations Scale (ICSS), 469–472
  Legal Dangerousness Scale (LDS), 493–496
  Maladaptive Behavior Record (MBRW), 460–465
  Parental Punitiveness Scale (PPS), 504–512
  personality assessments listed, 472
  personality assessments reviewed, 466–472
  prediction scales reviewed, 473–496
  Risk Perception Questionnaire (RPQ), 512–518
  target group, 22
Crime Control Orientation Scale, 519
Crime rates, 521
Crime Seriousness Ratings, 519–520
Criminal Attitude Scale (CAS), 441, 450–453
Criminal Attitudes and Values Scales, 438–439
Criminal Identification Scale, 438
Criminality Level Index (CLI) 453–456
Criminality Scales, 438
Criminal Justice Attitudes and Knowledge Scale, 520
Criminally insane. *See* Insanity
Criminally Insane Attitude Scale (CIAS), 373, 381–387
Criminal Profile, 387–391
Criminal Self-Conceptions Assessment, 425
Critical Incident Test, 219
Cross-cultural studies, 554–558
Cross validation, 31
Culture bias, 457
Cynicism, 75–80, 123, 124
Cynicism About the Law and Legal System Scale, 123, 124
Cynicism Questionnaire (CQ), 75–80

Death penalty. *See* Capital punishment
Debriefings, 29
Deceit, 28–29
Decision-making, 584–590
Delinquency, 122, 225–372, 579, 580–581
  Aggression in Youth (AYS), 457–460
  attitude scales listed, 234
  attitude scales reviewed, 225–233
  attitudinal differences, 445–446
  Behavior Cards (BC), 329–335
  behavior ratings listed, 260–262
  behavior ratings reviewed, 234–260
  behaviors, 462
  Beverly-Grant Opinion Schedule (BGOS), 262–264
  causation theory, 329, 372, 582
  Comprehensive Miranda Rights Scale (CMRS), 336–344
  Correctional Staff Evaluation Scale (CSES), 264–267
  descriptions listed, 367–372
  descriptions reviewed, 329–367
  Differential Behavioral Classification System (DBCS), 273–284
  family. *See* Parents and family

INDEX

Delinquency (cont.)
Family Information Test (FIT), 284–289
Future Events Test (FET), 289–292
Inmate Perception of Impact (IPIS), 344–351
Integrative Delinquency Scale (IDS), 321–323
Jesness Inventory (JIN), 292–298
Marshall's Delinquency Proneness Scale (MDPS), 324–327
masculinity and, 546–550
milieu ratings, 320–321
Miniature Situations Test (MST), 298–301
peer groups and, 260, 264–267, 368, 369, 520
personality assessment listings, 317–320
personality assessment reviews, 262–316
prediction, 482–487
prediction listings, 327–329
prediction reviews, 321–327
probation, 123, 370, 371
recidivism, 369, 578. See also Recidivism
Self-Reported Delinquency Scale (SRDSG) (Gibson), 246–249
Self-Reported Delinquency Scales (SRDSA) (Arnold), 241–245
Self-Reported Delinquency Scales (SRDS) (Nye & Short), 249–252 Seriousness of Delinquency Scale (SDS), 352–355
target group, 22
Teenage Slang Test (TAST), 356–367
Traits Indicating Attitude Scale (TIAS), 253–256
Violence Scale (VS), 256–260
Way It Looks to Me (WILTM), 301–306
What Teenagers Think (WTAT-REV), 306–316
Delinquency and Popularity Scale, 368
Delinquency Checklist (DCL), 234–237
Delinquency Differential Classification System, 317
Delinquency Index, 317
Delinquency Potential Scale (DPS), 482–487
Delinquency Proneness Scale (DPSL), 34 See also Marshall's Delinquency Proneness Scale
Delinquency Questionnaires (PFDQ), 237–241
Delinquency Scale (DS), 267–273
Delinquency Self-Concept Items, 318

Delinquency Self-Concept Scale, 317–318
Delinquent Attitudes and Self-Esteem Scale (DASES), 532–535
Delinquent Behavior Interview Schedule, 260
Description, 22
Description (listings)
corrections, 218–223
courts and the law, 146–147
crime and criminality, 519–521
delinquency, 367–372
general scales, 597
law enforcement and the police, 95–96
offenders, 438–440
Description (reviews)
corrections, 208–218
courts and the law, 133–146
crime and criminality, 496–518
delinquency, 329–367
general scales, 581–596
offenders, 427–438
Deviance Control Scale, 597
Deviancy
attitudes toward, 536
authoritarianism and, 574
control of, 597
parents and, 537
perceptions of, 521
Differential Association Questionnaire, 368
Differential Behavioral Classification System (DBCS), 273–284
Differential Treatment Pretraining Questionnaires—Trainees' Supervisor, 219–220
Disabled persons, 536
Dogmatism, 117–121, 523, 574, 579
Dogmatism Scale, 523
Dominace (Do) Scale, 35
Drug use
behavior, 463–464
delinquency, 237
offenders, 387–391, 402
perceptions of crime, 521
police interactions with, 439
Due process, 122

Edwards Personal Preference Schedule (EPPS), 467, 575
Embeddedness, 31
Employment, 382, 463
Error, 16

Ethical issues, 25–30
  decision-making, 584–590
  delinquency, 306
  See also Morality; Values
Ethics Inventory (EI), 496–503
Evaluation of Delinquency Preventative Measure, 368
Ex-convicts and ex-offenders
  behaviors, 460–465
  offenders, 374–377
  post-release behavior, 391–395
Exposure to Deviance Index, 368
Exposure to Family and Peer Deviance Indices, 520
Eysenck Personality Inventory, 575

Face validity, 17
Factor analyses, 16
Family. See Parents and family
Family and Peer Group Valuation Scales, 369
Family Background and Urban Delinquency Questionnaire, 369
Family Change Scale (FCS), 591–594
Family Information Test (FIT), 284–289
Fear of Crime and Fear of the Police Interviews, 520
Female Juvenile Recidivism Descriptive Checklist, 369
Financial gain, 387–391
Foot Patrolman Observation Test (FPOT), 43, 90–92
Foster Parent Preference Survey, 318
Fraternal Order of Police, 25
Fraud, 387–391
F Scale and F Scale Revisions, 576
Furloughs, 222
Future Delinquency Questionnaire, 237–241
Future Events Test (FET), 289–292

General scales, 523–597
  attitude scales listed, 536–537
  attitude scales reviewed, 524–535
  Attitudes toward Government Workers (ATGW), 529–532
  Attitude toward Any Institution Scale (ATAIS), 524–529
  Awareness of Limited Opportunity Scales (ALOS), 581–584
  Behavior Prediction Scale (PBS), 584–590

General scales (*cont.*)
  behavior ratings listed, 546
  behavior ratings reviewed, 537–546
  Bristol Social Adjustment Guides (BSAG), 537–542
  Compulsive Masculinity Scale (CMS), 546–550
  Delinquent Attitudes and Self-Esteem Scale (DASES), 532–535
  descriptive scales listed, 597
  descriptive scales reviewed, 581–596
  Family-Change Scale (FCS), 591–594
  Hopelessness Scale (HS), 550–554
  Hostility and Aggression Scale (HAS), 554–558
  Means-Ends Problem-Solving Procedure (MEPSP), 558–563
  personality assessments listed, 574–581
  personality assessments reviewed, 546–573
  Reaction Inventory: Anger (RIA), 563–569
  Self-Attitude Inventory (SAI), 569–573
  target group, 22
  Value Orientation Scale (VOS), 594–596
  Weekly Activity Record (WAR), 542–546
Geographical variation, 251
Giannell Index of Criminality (GIC), 466–469
Goal Attainment Scale, 146
Goal Orientation Inventory, 369
Good Impressions (Gi) scale, 35
Gough California Socialization Scale, 303
Government workers, 529–532
Group counseling, 220
  See also Group therapy
Group Data Schedule, 260
Group Evaluation Criteria Card Sort, 193
Group homes and parents, 262, 319, 368, 370
Group Morale Scale, 140
Group therapy, 220
  criminal attitudes, 450, 451
  enforced, 171
  screening for, 396–401
Guards, 222

Hand Test, 523, 576
Hogan Moral Conduct Scales, 576
Homicide, 97–99
Homosexuality, 467–468

Hopelessness Scale (HS), 550–554
Horrower's Multiple Choice Rorschach technique, 382
Hostility, 441, 443, 472, 575, 581
  cross-cultural perspective on, 554–558
  institutions, 220–221
  police attitudes, 44–46
Hostility and Aggression Scale (HAS), 554–558
Hostility and Direction of Hostility Questionnaire, 472
Hostility Scale (HOS), 487–493
How the Future Looks to Me Scale, 318–319
Hunch Parolability Scale (HPS), 194–198, 199

Ideological and Law-Abidingness Scales, 123
I-Level Classification, 425
Images of Criminality Questionnaire, 439
Importance Questionnaire, 370
Imprisonment. *See* Corrections; Incarceration
Impulsiveness, 426–427, 574
Incarceration, 107–111
  delinquency, 344–351
  family effects of, 591–594
  inmate loyalty, 438
  prediction, 373–374
  See also Corrections; Inmates
Index of Conformity to Staff Expectations (ICSE), 208–210
Index of Perspectives on Institution and Staff, 193
Index of Social Contacts, 395
Individual Child Fact Sheet and Rating Form, 327–328
Information Handling in Police Decision Making, 95
Informed consent, 28
Inmate Code Scale, 194
Inmate Dependency Scale, 425
Inmate Loyalty Scale, 438
Inmate Management Scale, 261
Inmate Perception of Impact (IPISI), 344–351
Inmate Personality Inventory, 373
Inmate Personality Survey (IPS), 401–402
Inmate Questionnaire, 220
Inmates
  delinquency, 320
  government workers and, 529

Inmates (*cont.*)
  problem solving, 562
  subcultures, 211, 220
  See also Corrections; Incarceration
Inmate Social Role Adaptation Scale, 220
Inmates Perception of Significant Others, 21, 427–435
Inmates Recreation Activities Checklist, 220
Insanity, 373, 381–387
  attitudes toward, 374–377
  community adjustment of, 438
  hopelessness scale, 550–554
Institutional Adjustment Index, 261
Institutional Adjustment Inventory, 206
Institutional Impact Questionnaires, 220–221
Institutional Life Questionnaire (ILQ), 160–164
Institutional Living and Inmate Code Scales, 194
Institutional Living Scale, 194
Institutions
  attitudes toward, 524–529
Instruments and scales. *See* Research instruments and scales
Integrative Delinquency Scale (IDS), 321–323
Intelligence
  hostility/aggression measurement, 490
  Miranda rights, 336–344
  offenders, 382, 383, 404, 436–438
  problem solving, 562
Intelligence testing, 18
Intentionality in Criminal Situations Scale (ICSS), 469–472
Interest and Activities Inventory, 370
Internal consistency, 16
Interpresonal Checklist, 576–577
Interpersonal Maturity Measurement (CPI-Z), 34–36
Interpersonal Personality Inventory (IPI), 34–36, 373, 412–417
Interrater reliability, 16
Interview Rating Questionnaire, 221
Involvement Questionnaire, 439
IQ. *See* Intelligence; Intelligence testing
Itkin Attitudes toward Parents and Children Scales, 536–537

Jesness Inventory (JIN), 292–298
Jesness-Staff Preference Survey, 318
Job Analysis and Interest Measurements, 95

Jourard Self-Disclosure Questionnaire, 577
Judges, 133–139, 146–147
Judgments, 30
Judicial Role Perception Scale (JRPS), 133–139
Judicial Roles Questionnaire, 146–147
Junior colleges, 219
Juries, 111–114
Just World Scale, 577
Juvenile Court Role Expectations Questionnaire, 147
Juvenile courts, 114–117, 122, 147
Juvenile Court Volunteer Effectiveness Interview Scale (JCVEIS), 114–117
Juvenile delinquency. See Delinquency
Juvenile Delinquency Attitude Scale, 234
Juvenile Justice—What Do You Think?, 123
Juvenile Probation Administrative Action Scale, 370

Kahn Test of Symbol Arrangement (KTSA), 577
KD Checklist, 328
KD Proneness Scale, 328
Knowledge of Student Rights Scale, 123, 124
Knowledge of the Law in General Scale, 123, 124
Kohlberg Interview, 319
Kuder Preference Record Vocation Form, 382

Labeling, 27–28, 29, 264–267, 356–367
Language, 356–367
Law. See Courts and the law
Law-Abidingness Scale, 123
Law and School Difficulty Scale (LS), 32, 36
Law Encounter Severity Scale (LESS), 391–395
Law enforcement and the police, 43–96
 attitude scales listed, 69–71
 attitude scales reviewed, 44–68
 Attitude toward Police Questionnaire, 50–55
 Attitude toward Police Scale (ATPS) (Competence–Hostility), 44–46
 Attitude toward Police Scale (Semantic Differential and Likert Formats), 47–50
 behavior ratings listed, 74–75
 behavior ratings reviewed, 71–74

Law enforcement and the police (*cont.*)
 Children's Perceptions of the Police (CPPS), 83–86
 Citizens' Perception of Police Scale (CIPS), 86–89
 Cynicism Questionnaire (CQ), 75–80
 descriptions listed, 95–96
 descriptions reviewed, 83–95
 Foot Patrolman Observation Test (FPOT), 90–92
 Law Enforcement Perception Questionnaire (LEPQ), 55–59
 milieu ratings listed, 81
 perceptions of, 521
 Perceptions of Police Scales, 59–65
 personality measures listed, 80
 personality measures reviewed, 75–80
 Police-Citizen Interaction Rating Scales (PCIRS), 71–74
 Police Task Preference Questionnaire (PTPQ), 92–95
 prediction scales listed, 83
 prediction scales reviewed, 81–83
 Prisoners' Attitude Scales (PAS), 65–68
 target group, 21
Law Enforcement Perception Questionnaire (LEPQ), 12, 55–59
Law Scale, 124
Learning theory, 469
Legal Attitudes Questionnaire (LAQ), 112, 113, 117–121
Legal Dangerousness Scale (LDS), 493–496
Life Functioning Assessment, 320
Linguistic Scale, 328
Long-Term Prisoners Interview Schedule, 221

Maladaptive Behavior Record (MBRW), 441, 460–465
Manifest Anxiety Scale (MAS), 269–270
Marion County Youth Study Questionnaire, 370–371
Marlow-Crowne Social Desirability Scale, 182, 184
Marshall's Delinquency Proneness Scale (MDPS), 324–327
Masculinity, 546–550
Maturity
 delinquency, 262–264, 273, 292–298, 317
 offenders, 412–417

INDEX

Maudsley Personality Inventory, 576
Means–Ends Problem-Solving Procedure
  (MEPSP), 558–563
Megargee classification system, 32, 37
Mental ability. *See* Intelligence
Mental hospitals, 26
Mental Measurement Yearbooks (MMY), 5, 8
Mental illness. *See* Insanity
Miale-Holsopple Sentence Completion Test,
  576
Milieu ratings, 22, 23
Milieu ratings (listed)
  corrections, 193–194
  courts and the law, 133
  law enforcement and the police, 81
Milieu ratings (reviews), corrections,
  182–192
Milieu therapy, 160–164
Minature Situations Test (MST), 298–301
Minnesota Multiphasic Personality Inventory
  (MMPI), 31–32, 36–40, 381, 412,
  483, 488
Miranda rights, 336–344
Morality
  delinquency, 306–316, 319
  development of, 576
  police, 59
  See also Ethical issues; Values
Mosher Incomplete Sentence Test (MIST),
  578
Multimethod Assessment System, 425–426
Murder, 97–99

National Commission for the Protection of
  Human Subjects in Biomedical and
  Behavioral Research, 26
Neurosis and neuroticism, 267–273, 523
Nonlingusitic Scale, 328
Norms, 16
Nursing home patients, 25

Offenders, 373–440
  Accessibility Scale (AcS), 396–401
  attitude scales reviewed, 374–387
  Attitudes toward Offenders and Mental
    Patients (ATOMPS), 374–377
  Attitude toward Prisoners Scale (ATPS),
    377–380
  behavior ratings listed, 395–396

Offenders (*cont.*)
  behavior ratings reviewed, 387–395
  Criminally Insane Attitude Scale (CIAS),
    381–387
  Criminal Profile, 387–391
  descriptions listed, 438–440
  descriptions reviewed, 427–438
  Inmate Personality Survey (IPS), 401–412
  Inmates' Perception of Significant Others,
    427–435
  Interpersonal Personality Inventory
    (IPIC), 412–417
  Law Encounter Severity Scale (LESS),
    391–395
  Ohio Penal Classification Test (OPCT),
    436–438
  personality assessments listed, 425–427
  personality assessments reviewed,
    396–424
  Prison Fantasy Questionnaire (PFQ),
    418–424
  target group, 22
Offense Perception Assessment, 520–521
Offer Self-Image Questionnaire, 579
Ohio Penal Classification Test (OPCT),
  436–438
Opportunity, 581–584
Organizational Structure and Prisonization
  Scale (OSPS), 211–214
Otis Employment Tests, 382
Overcontrolled Hostility (O-H) scale, 32, 40
Overstatement, 29–30

Parallel forms, 16
Parental Attitude Research Instrument, 319
Parental Punitiveness Scale (PPS), 504–512
Parent Interveiw Schedule, 329
Parents and family
  change in, 591–594
  child–parent relationship, 536–537
  delinquency, 114–117, 237, 284–289,
    320, 368, 369, 372, 520
  punitiveness, 504–512
  role behavior, 597
Parolability Questionnaire (PQ), 196, 198–206
Parole, 35, 38
  prediction, 194–198, 199, 206–207,
    373–374
  recidivism rates, 175–178
  violation of, 391–395

Parole Adjustment Scale, 206
Parole Decision Instruments, 221
Parole Decision Making Scale, 221
Parole Officer Evaluation of Vocational Rehabilitation Services, 222
Parole Officer Punishment and Reintegrative Orientation Questionnaire, 172
Parole Prediction Procedure with Women Offenders, 206–207
Parole Prediction Scale, 207
Parole Prediction Through Variable Interactions, 207
Parole Success Attributes, 207
Parole Violator Scale, 38
Past and Future Delinquency Questionnaires (PFDQ), 237–241
Peer groups
  delinquency, 260, 264–267, 368, 369, 520
  inmates, 438
Peer Rating Instrument, 261
Perception of Addicts and Addiction Scale, 439
Perception of Crime Scale, 521
Perception of Deviancy Schema, 521
Perception of Stigma Interview Procedure, 147
Perceptions of Justice Interview, 96
Perceptions of Police Scales, 59–65
Perceptions of Police Test, 59
Performance Rating Systems for Police, 75
Personal Characteristics Rating Report, 395–396
Personality, 575, 578
  delinquency, 292–298, 306–316, 320
Personality assessment, 22
Personality assessment (listings)
  corrections, 181
  crime and criminality, 472
  delinquency, 317–321
  general scales, 574–581
  law enforcement and the police, 80
  offenders, 425–427
Personality assessment (reviews)
  corrections, 179–181
  courts and the law, 124–132
  crime and criminality, 466–472
  delinquency, 262–316
  general scales, 546–573
  law enforcement and the police, 75–80
  offenders, 396–424

Personality Inventory, 523
Personal Orientation Inventory (POI), 579
Physical stimulation, 298–301
Piaget, J., 469
Picture Frustration Study, 473
Police
  attitude scales, 69–71
  attitudes toward, 453
  drug addict interactions with, 439
  fear of, 520
  juveniles, 150
  selection criteria for, 83
  See also Law enforcement and the police
Police Behavior Scale (PBS), 71, 72, 73
Police-Citizen Interaction Rating Scales (PCIRS), 71–74
Police Community-Relations Interview, 70
Police Flexibility Measurement Questionnaire, 80
Police Image Questionnaire, 96
Police Isolation Questionnaire, 96
Police Job Stress Interview, 80
Policemen's View of Citizen's Support Scales, 537
Police Opinion of Work Questionnaire, 70
Police Peer Evaluation Scale, 75
Police Personality Scale, 31
Police Perspectives and Behaviors in a Campus Disturbance, 71
Police Prediction of Public Attitudes Questionnaire, 96
Police Task Preference Questionnaire (PTPQ), 92–95
Police Task Performance Scale, 75
Police Task Preference Questionnaire, 43
Police Violence Scale, 59, 62
Policy decisions, 27
Popularity, 368
Porteus Maze Test, 426
Portune Attitude-toward-Police Scale, 71
Postprison Expectations Scale, 426
Postprison Success Prediction, 207
Potential Cost Scales, 371
Powerlessness Scale, 426
Pre-Call Observations Scale (PCOS), 71, 72, 74
Prediction, 22
  behavior, 453–456, 542
  delinquency, 247, 482–487
  offenders, 373–374

INDEX

Prediction (listings)
  corrections, 206–208
  courts and the law, 133
  delinquency, 327–329
Prediction (reviews)
  corrections, 194–206
  crime and criminality, 473–496
  delinquency, 321–327
Prerelease Furlough Questionnaire, 222
Pretraining Questionnaire—Trainee, 222
Pretrial Intervention Program Questionnaire, 133
Pretrial Release Decisions Scale, 133
Prison Adjustment Index (PAI), 172–175
Prisoner Attribute Typology, 439
Prisoners
  attitudes of, 65–68
  ethical issues, 25–26
  See also Corrections; Incarceration; Inmates
Prisoners' Attitude Scales (PAS), 65–68
Prisoner-Therapist Q-Sort, 181
Prison Fantasy Questionnaire (PFQ), 373, 418–424
Prison Guard Job Perceptions Questionnaire, 222
Prison Profile Inventory (PPI), 149, 186–192
Prison Projective Test (PPT), 179–181
Prisons. *See* Corrections
Probation, 34, 178
  delinquency, 114–117, 123, 370, 371
Probation Counselors' Success Rating Scale, 371
Probationer and Volunteer Evaluation Questionnaires, 147
Probation Officer-Client Relationship Valence Scale (POCRVS), 139–142
Probation officers, 123, 139–142, 150
Probation Program Ratings, 178
Problem Checklist (PC), 142–146
Problem solving, 558–563
Professionalization Assessment for Police Organizations, 81
Psychiatric Data Schedule, 319
Psychiatry, 171–172, 521
Psychopathic Delinquency Scale, 488
Psychopathic deviate scale (Pd), 32, 37
Psychosis, 267–273
  See also Insanity
Psychotherapy, 171
  See also Group therapy

Psychotic tendences, 402
Public Attitudes toward Crime and Corrections Survey, 457
Public Offender Counseling Inventory (POCI), 215–218
Public Opinion About Crime Questionnaire, 457
Public Personnel Association Test (PPA), 83
Public Surveys of Crime and Criminal Justice, 521
Punishment. *See* Corrections
Punitive Morality Scale, 59

Race
  ethical issues, 30
  police, 59
  Miranda rights, 336–344
Racial Discrimination Scale, 59, 62
Reaction Inventory: Anger (RIA), 563–569
Recidivism, 175–178, 578
  behaviors, 460–465
  classification of, 440
  delinquency, 369
  offenders, 374, 391
  prediction, 542
Recidivism Base Expectancy Scale, 208
Recidivism Outcome Index (ROI), 175–178
Recidivism Prediction Scale, 208
Recidivism Seriousness Classification, 440
Recreation, 220
Rehabilitation, 396–401
Rehabilitation in Correctional Settings Attitude Scale (RICS), 164–171
Rehabilitative Value Perception Scale, 172
Reliability, 16–17
Research instruments and scales
  acquisition of, 9, 10–12
  audiences and, 23
  categorization of, 21–23
  compilations of, 5–8
  criteria for, 3–4, 8
  criticisms of, 1–3, 4–5
  ethical issues in, 25–30
  identification of, 9–10
  limitations of, 18–19
  review of, 9, 14–18
  selection of, 9, 12–14
Response mode, 15–16
Response to Incarceration Questionnaire, 194
Responsibility (Re) scale, 32, 33, 35

Risk Perception Questionnaire (RPQ), 512–518
Rokeach Conservatism–Liberalism Scale, 112
Rokeach Dogmatism Scale, 579
Rokeach Value Survey, 579–580
Role. *See* Social role
Role Behavior Test, 597
Rotter I-E Scale, 580
Rotter Incomplete Sentences Blank Scale, 107

Scales and instruments. *See* Research scales and instruments
Schizophrenia, 496–497
School Interest Inventory, 328
Scoring, 15–16
Scrambled Sentence Test, 472
Self-actualization, 579
Self-Attitude Inventory (SAI), 569–573
Self-concept, 221
    delinquency, 301–306, 317–318
    offenders, 425
Self Control (Sc) scale, 32, 33, 35
Self-depreciation, 403
Self-esteem, 225, 318, 532–535, 571, 580
Self-fulfilling prophecies, 29
Self-image, 579, 580
Self-Report Delinquency Questionnaire, 261
Self-Reported Delinquency Scale (Arnold), 241–245
Self-Reported Delinquency Scale (Gibson), 246–249
Self-Reported Delinquency Scales (Nye & Short), 249–252
Self-Reported Delinquent Behavior Questionnaire, 262
Sellin-Wolfgang Index on Delinquency, 176, 371
Semantic Differential Scale, 59, 60, 62
Semantic Differential Technique, 597
Sentence Completion Test, 319–320
Separate scales (MMPI), 38, 39
Seriousness measures, 176, 352–355, 371–372, 441, 519–520
Seriousness of Delinquency Scale (SDS), 352–355
Severity of Offense Scale, 371–372
Shapiro Adjective Checklist, 580
Situational Appraisal Inventory, 306
Situations, 298–301
Social activities, 370

Social Agency Effectiveness Study, 34
Social Climate Questionnaire, 321
Social cost, 371
Social Data Schedule, 372
Social esteem, 374
Socialization, 289–292, 301–302, 317, 426–427
Socialization, Delinquency Proneness (CPI-Z) scale, 32
Socialization (So) scale, 32, 33, 34, 36, 40
Social Organization of Burglary Questionnaire, 440
Social role, 220
Social Work Data Schedule, 372
Socioeconomic class
    aggression, 457–460
    delinquency, 243
    masculinity, 547
    Miranda rights, 336–344
    values, 594–596
Sociopathy (Spy) scale, 32, 38, 40
Staff, 208–210, 219
    attitudes toward offenders, 375
    criminally insane and, 381–387
    delinquency perceived by, 264–267, 318
    work-release programs, 179
Standards for Educational and Psychological Tests, 14, 15, 16, 17, 18
Stanford Parent Attitude Questionnaire, 537
Stereoscopic Perception of Violence, 472
Stereoscopic Resolution Procedure, 426–427
Stigma, 147, 374
Stratton Identification with Criminal Others and Orientation to Criminal Means Scales, 427
Stuart Future Test, 553
Student Opinion Survey, 328–329
Subcultures
    burglary, 440
    delinquency, 273, 356–367
    inmates, 211, 220
Subscales, 32

Targets, 21–22
Taylor Manifest Anxiety Scale (MAS), 269–270
Temporal stability, 16
Tennessee Self-Concept Scale (TSCS), 580
Theft, 445–449
    delinquency, 241, 242, 243, 245
    offenders, 387–391

INDEX 615

Thematic Apperception Test, 180, 181, 473
Thorne Integration Level Test Series, 321
Thurstone Capital Punishment Attitude Scale, 112
Tolerance (To) scale, 35
Training, 218, 219, 220, 221, 222
Training in Differential Treatment Assessment Instruments, 194
Training schools, 193
Traits Indicating Attitude Scale (TIAS), 253–256
Treatment
 delinquency, 284–289
 maturity level and, 412–417
 screening for, 396–401
Treatment-Custody Conflict Questionnaire, 223
Treatment of Violent Patients Questionnaire, 521
Treatment Personnel Inventory, 320
Twenty Statements Test (TST), 580–581

Validity, 17
Value Consensus Scale, 320
Value Orientation Scale (VOS), 582, 594–596
Values, 579–580
 children, 581
 delinquency, 369
 ethics, 496–503
 group home parents, 370
 middle-class, 594–596
 See also Ethical issues; Morality

Values and Sociometric Choices Questionnaire, 223
Values Inventory for Children, 581
Vandalism, 241, 242, 243, 244–245
Victims, 520
Violence, 441, 472
 attitudes toward, 456
 delinquency and, 371–372
 offenders and, 387–391
Violence Scale (VS), 256–260
Vocational rehabilitation, 222, 396
Volunteer Evaluation and Probationer Questionnaire, 147

Ward Atmosphere Scale, 182
Way It Looks to Me (WILTM) self-concept inventory, 301–306
Weekly Activity Record (WAR), 542–546
What Teenagers Think (WTAT-REV), 306–316
Women, 206–207, 369
Work-release, 223
Work-Release Staff Role Scale, 179
World War II, 25

Youngster Behavior Inventory, 262
Youth. *See* Adolescents; Children; Delinquency
Youth Discrimination Scale, 59, 60, 62

Zimmer Sentence Completion Test (ZSCT), 581